The Philosophy of Religion

SCM CORE TEXT

The Philosophy of Religion

Gwen Griffith-Dickson

scm press

British Library Cataloguing in Publication data

A catalogue record for this book is available
from the British Library

0 334 02989 9

First published in 2005 by SCM Press
9–17 St Albans Place, London N1 0NX

www.scm-canterburypress.co.uk

SCM Press is a division of
SCM-Canterbury Press Ltd

Printed and bound in Great Britain by
William Clowes Ltd, Beccles, Suffolk

Contents

To my mother, Joan Doyle Griffith,
the first to teach me how to think about
religion analytically, and for many other things that
cannot be put into print.

Preface

The academic area of 'philosophy of religion' has traditionally worked almost exclusively with the philosophies and religions of Western civilization. There are of course other philosophies and other religions. Study of these in Western universities has often been housed in faculties or institutes labelled 'Oriental'; or arranged in faculties by culture or region. They may thereby enjoy close contact with people who study the languages, ancient and modern, the literatures and arts as well as histories of those other cultures. On the other hand, it means that the study of Japanese religion or Indian philosophy or Islamic or Buddhist approaches to logic have rarely had an impact on 'mainstream' study of philosophy in the West, or on the study of philosophical issues from within departments of 'theology'.

However, there has on occasion been serious engagement with the thought of other traditions' thinkers and ideas, particularly among scholars who have mined deep in the historical study of philosophy and philosophical theology. Those who have dealt closely with medieval philosophy have often found it natural to consider Islamic and Jewish arguments alongside Christian ones. Still, they have made little impact on the average undergraduate syllabus or reading list. Similarly, in more recent years some 'Readers' have included extracts from Eastern texts. Nevertheless, the world's philosophies of religion have not been integrated into the core issues of the discipline in the English-speaking world.

There are good reasons for this. It is difficult enough to acquire expertise in a single tradition, let alone several. More than mere competence in a few is not to be looked for. Moreover, there are fundamental questions about how easily or how accurately one can understand the thinking, ideas and beliefs of a very different culture, without long, arduous study and experience.

Nevertheless, I am convinced that it is time to integrate the thinking of different religious-philosophical cultures into the English-speaking world of 'philosophy of religion'. For a start, many people speaking English and studying the discipline are not Christians and are entitled to study their philosophical traditions and see them represented on the syllabus and the reading lists. Further, as the planet turned into a new century, changes around the globe – cultural, political and military – sparked an increasing awareness of religious diversity in Western consciousness. Reactions ran on a spectrum from seeing an inevitable 'clash of civilizations' to searching for ways to live together in peaceful understanding. Some regard different religions as a threat and danger, but others see a challenge to mutual understanding and an opportunity for joint progress. Among those who think and write about philosophy of religion, a few are beginning to see that this subject too should take some account of diversity. If the challenges to understanding can be negotiated, it can contribute to the richness of our reflection on religious issues and problems.

It appears to me that academic study needs to take this diversity far more seriously than heretofore. For one thing, as historians of philosophy know, each tradition has in fact been shaped and enhanced by the thinking of the other faiths in its environment. 'Multiculturalism' is an ancient phenomenon, and a multi-faith approach to considering religious issues and problems is not some new-fangled invention. So although some may think that the multi-faith treatment of issues in this book is somehow 'postmodern', 'New Age', or 'politically correct', I see myself as returning to an older tradition than 'philosophy of religion' in the post-1950s West.

This book therefore draws on the writings, ideas and arguments of a more diverse range of faiths and traditions than is common. Because it is not a textbook on 'world religions' per se and does not attempt to teach the content of each religion, these ideas are not carefully set in the context of the religion as a whole. It would be very desirable to approach the study of religions in this way, but that is for another course and another book! To compensate for the potentially disorientating experience of hopping from one tradition to another, there is a Glossary to situate thinkers, terms or schools.

This book of course is nevertheless the product of a culture – albeit, in my case, a multicultural culture, both from my birth in Hawaii and my long residence in London. The topics are governed and conditioned by a typical English-speaking syllabus. That means that although I would like to be as inclusive as possible, Buddhism, for example, suffers from under-representation, as do other religious traditions of India, China and Japan and elsewhere. Many of the typical topics, such as 'God', are not the central concerns of Buddhism, Jainism, Confucianism or Shinto. Meanwhile, many central Buddhist concerns such as ethics or views of the human person are not as yet on the average Philosophy of Religion topic list. I have tried to bring in Buddhist critiques of theistic issues, for example, but in the end I did not want to twist Buddhism and other traditions to fit Western notions of 'philosophy of religion' too much, and misrepresent them in the aims of presenting them at all. I do apologize.

One way to compensate for the lacks of this text is the supporting website that SCM-Canterbury Press has created: www.scmpress.co.uk/scmcoretextphilosophyofreligion. This will allow a greater exploration than was possible in the limits of a single text. In the first place, it will allow some complex issues to be explored in greater depth; for with an expansion of traditions represented comes an expansion in length, and great depth of analysis could not always be contained in the scope of the text. Further, it will allow longer extracts and readings to be placed there for you to read, which can be particularly useful for readers in countries where some of the texts or thinkers mentioned in this book are not available. Finally, it will allow us to go off the beaten track a little, and explore some of the issues that are less likely to appear on exam questions but which are very rewarding to think about. I look forward to meeting you there!

Acknowledgements

A number of people have been indispensable to the writing of this book, of unusually long gestation, in very different ways; but all exhibiting various degrees of heroism. My family members, who also happen to be competent in the field, gave tremendous support not only in the usual familial manner but also with expertise in theology, philosophy and editing, and my deepest aloha and mahalos to Joan Griffith, Andrew Dickson, Mary Weston and Richard Griffith. Colleagues and friends have read, commented and engaged in more hands-on ways to improve the text to the best of my, if not alas their, abilities. Heartfelt thanks go therefore to Vicky Mohammed, Arindam Chakrabarti, Mary Anne Perkins, Norman Ballantyne, Ali Kazimi, Michael Barnes and John Barton, as well as to Barbara Zollner and Victoria Harrison-Carter for concrete assistance. Wider collegial support from Sharon Hanson, Jacqueline Clarke, David-Hillel Ruben and Anna Colloms helped to make it practically and psychologically possible to write at all. Barbara Laing of SCM Press has been an extraordinarily supportive and astute editor and made it a pleasure to produce this text for SCM-Canterbury Press.

Birkbeck College has facilitated the work at helpful points by funding research assistance, and I would like to thank my Faculty and its Dean at that time, Tom Schuller.

Some of the material, as well as the overall approach, was forged in public lectures given at Gresham College. I would like to thank Gresham College, its Academic Board and the wider Council for its support at many points since 2001, in particular its Provosts Tim O'Shea and Lord Sutherland of Houndwood, as well as Barbara Anderson, its omnicompetent Registrar.

This book benefits more concretely than usual from the quotation of works of others. I would like to thank those authors and publishers for their generosity in allowing longer extracts to be published. Deborah Blake at Duckworth has been a sensitive and understanding editor in the past, and I would like to thank Duckworth for allowing previous work to develop into the present form. Other publishers and authors include Julius Guttman and Schocken Press; Tariq Ramadan and Oxford University Press; Raimundo Panikkar and Paulist Press; and William

Wainwright and Scholars Press as well as the late Murtaḍā Muṭahharī and Sayyid Muḥammad Ṭabāṭabā'ī, both published now by ICAS Press in London.

Glossary

ad hominem. A form of argument in which one attempts to disprove a person's views by attacking the person. Or arguing in a way that does not advance matters unless one holds a particular set of beliefs.

Advaita Vedānta. A tradition of Vedānta, sometimes said to have begun with Gauḍapāda. Its principle thinker was Śaṅkara (Śamkara) (8th cent.). Of the three 'ways' to salvation, it places greatest emphasis on the way of knowledge (see **Three Ways**). The purpose of philosophy is to lead to liberation from the bondage of our existence. This bondage arises from ignorance, and therefore liberation is achieved by its removal. True knowledge reveals that Brahman is ultimate reality, absolute and unchanging. All that seems to be other than Brahman, whether objects in the world or individual selves, is appearance.

ahimsā. The Jain doctrine of non-violence, non-hurting.

al-Ash'arī (873/4–935/6). Islamic theologian who reacted against the Hellenization of Islamic thought. Founder of the Ash'arite school, often uncompromising on questions relating to predetermination and God's powers.

al-Basrī, al-Hasan (d. 728) and Basrīan school. Ascetic and Islamic philosopher, an influence on the Mu'tazilite school. His circle was perhaps the first centre of discussions in Islamic philosophy and theology, initially in raising debates on free will and predestination. He believed in human free will in order to defend God's justice.

al-Bisṭamī, Abū Yazīd (d. 875). Sufi mystic whose sayings were collected by his contemporaries. He was an influential figure in the development of Sufi doctrine, although he wrote nothing himself.

al-Fārābī, Abū Naṣr (*c.*870–950). Islamic Aristotelian philosopher. He imported Aristole's logic into Islamic thought. He was also influenced by Neoplatonism, portraying creation as an emanation. See *The Virtuous City*.

al-Ghazālī, Abū Ḥāmid Muhammad (1059–1111). Islamic Ash'arite theologian who taught at Baghdad, he eventually abandoned theology for a life of contemplation. He was a notorious critic of the claims of Aristotelian philosophers; emphasizing intuition above reason. See his *The Incoherence of the Philosophers.*

al-Jaḥīẓ, Abu 'Uthman 'Amr ibn Bakr al-Basrī (766–868). Born in Basra to a working-class family, his mother recognized his academic potential and encouraged him to become a writer – successfully – for he wrote 200 works on a variety of subjects from science to philosophy, poetry, grammar and zoology. He was one of the first to write on such subjects accessibly for the non-specialist. He asserted the importance of evil as well as good in creation, particularly in stimulating our thought and inspiring trust in God. Everything in creation is ultimately beneficial and shows the signs of Allah.

al-Kindī, Yaqub ibn Isḥāq (d. after 866). An early Islamic philosopher who taught at Baghdad. He introduced Neoplatonic and Aristotelian thought into Islamic philosophy, himself translating the works of Aristotle and Plotinus. He tended to emphasize faith over reason.

al-Mu'tamir, Bishr ibn (d. 825). Muslim thinker who established the Baghdad school of **kalām.**

al-Naẓẓām, Ibrahim ibn Sayyar (d. 835 to 845). Basrian Mu'tazilite theologian, who advocated the use of sceptical method in philosophy to move beyond faith to true knowledge.

al-Sadiq, Ja'far (702–65). One of the twelve Imams of the early Shi'ite movement in **kalām.** He was among the masters of the members of the House of the Prophet; highly respected for his truthfulness, generosity, spirituality and wisdom.

Anselm (1033–1109). Christian medieval philosopher; born in Aosta, became archbishop of Canterbury from 1093 to 1109. Most famous for using the concept of God as 'that than which nothing greater can be conceived' in order to prove that this God must exist – the so-called 'Ontological Argument'. See *Monologion*, *Proslogion.*

Aquinas, Thomas (1225–74). Christian Dominican philosopher and theologian. He attempted a synthesis of Christian doctrine and the philosophy of Aristotle. He is famous for propounding Five Ways in which the existence of God can be demonstrated. He wrote the multi-volume works: *Summa contra Gentiles* and *Summa Theologica.*

Arama, Isaac ben Moses (*c.*1420–94). Spanish Jewish thinker. Author of the influential *Akedat Yizhak* (*Binding of Isaac*). He wrote on the relation between faith and reason, arguing that reason should not be the judge of faith. He was a critic of the rationalism of Maimonides.

Aristotle (384–322 BC). Greek philosopher. Pupil of Plato's and teacher of Alexander the Great. Invented the discipline of logic and pioneered ethics and physics. He stressed empiricism and natural science. Many traditional theological concepts derive from Aristotle – substance, for example.

atheologian. An atheistic theologian.

Ātman. The soul or self in Hinduism, Buddhism, Jainism.

Augustine of Hippo (354–430). Christian theologian. A convert from Manichaeism to Christianity. His most famous works are his autobiographical *Confessions*, and *The City of God.*

Aurobindo Ghose (1872–1950). Twentieth-century Indian philosopher, yogi, patriot. After a Cambridge education, rediscovered Hinduism; advocated a return to Vedāntism. Proposed Hinduism for the whole world, as the most advanced form of humanism.

Averroës, see **Ibn Rushd.**

Avicenna, see **Ibn Sīnā.**

Berkeley, George (1685–1753). Bishop in Ireland, of English descent. Principal philosophical work is *Principles of Human Knowledge.* One of the 'British empiricists', he is commonly viewed as an Idealist because of his doctrine that 'to be is to be perceived', leading some to suppose that he believes that all perceptions are really just ideas in the mind. However, because he believes that God perceives all and all is dependent on God, it seems more accurate to suppose him to be a realist who believes that things are independent of the *human* mind (though not God's).

Berkovits, Eliezer (1900–92). A Transylvanian Jew who lived in Germany and England before emigrating to Australia and then the United States. His work is an attempt to provide a theological response to the Holocaust. He developed the concept of Hester Panim (the hiding of the face) to explain how God can be conceived as gradually withdrawing from the world to make room for the fulfilment of human potential. See *Faith after the Holocaust* and *With God in Hell.*

Boethius, Anicius Manlius Torquatus Severinus (480–524). Christian philosopher. His most famous book, *The Consolation of Philosophy*, is an attempt to show how the soul can reach the vision of God through philosophy.

Brahman. Ultimate, unconditioned Reality; (variously) the divine being.

Buber, Martin (1878–1965). A Viennese Jew who grew up in Poland. He was a member of the Zionist movement and an advocate of Hebrew Humanism (working for reconciliation with the Arab people of Palestine). He is well known for his religious philosophy of dialogue, set out in *I and Thou*. He was also involved in fostering Jewish–Christian understanding.

Bultmann, Rudolf (1884–1976). German New Testament scholar. He was a pioneer of form criticism and an advocate of historical research. He used Heidegger's existentialist philosophy to interpret the Bible. He is most famous for his attempts to 'demythologize' the New Testament.

Calvin, John (1509–64). French Christian Reformer. His most influential book is the *Institutes of the Christian Religion*, which became a standard reading for Protestants. He is well known for his views on predestination.

Cārvāka (pronounced 'Charvaka'). An early materialist philosophy, atheistic, sceptical and hedonistic in nature. Said to be founded by the thinker Cārvāka, an Indian sage who was mentioned in the Mahābhārata, castigated in the *Bhagavad Gitā*. Matter alone is real. There is no God, soul, life after death; nor even good and evil, right and wrong, merit and demerit. Only perception yields knowledge; thus its epistemology is positivist in nature. What is imperceptible has no existence. See **Lokāyata Materialism.**

Cohen, Arthur (1928–86). Jewish theologian who is most famous for his work on post-Holocaust theology. See *Tremendum*. He proposed that human beings, rather than God, should be held responsible for the Holocaust.

Cohen, Hermann (1842–1918). German Jewish neo-Kantian philosopher. He developed a form of moral argument for the existence of God, conceived as an idea; the idea of God is the only ground for believing that moral obligations can be fulfilled. In *Religion of Reason out of the Sources of Judaism* he attempted to redefine the core features of the Jewish faith in accordance with reason.

Counterfactual. A conditional statement in which the 'if' part of the sentence is contrary to fact, e.g. 'If I had entered the race, I would have won.'

Crescas, Hasdai (1340–1412). Spanish Jewish theologian and statesman. As a statesman, he was concerned with combating Christian propaganda against the Jews. As a theologian, he was critical of Aristotelianism and the work of Maimonides.

Dharma. Fundamental concept in Indian philosophy. It refers to the order which makes life and the universe possible.

Daud, Abraham ben (1110–80). Jewish philosopher, physician, historian and astronomer. Born in Cordoba and lived in Spain until his death. His most important philosophical work is *Exalted Faith* (*Emunah Ramah*), which addresses the problems of determinism and free will.

Descartes, René (1596–1650). French philosopher and mathematician. One of the principal founders of modern philosophy. He advocated methodological doubt – abandoning all one's prior assumptions in order to reach certainty. With the proposition 'I think, therefore I am', Descartes believed he had found certainty. See *Discourse on Method* and *Meditations*.

de jure. A matter of right. Usually contrasted with *de facto* – a matter of fact.

Duns Scotus, John (*c.*1266–1308). Scottish Christian theologian. After becoming a Franciscan he taught in London and Paris. He was a prominent critic of the philosophy of Aquinas, arguing that faith cannot be rationally established and thus must be kept separate from philosophy. He wrote *Treatise on the First Principle.*

Ebner, Ferdinand (1882–1931). Austrian Catholic thinker, a schoolteacher, who wrote an early work, *The Word and the Spiritual Realities*, and a journal later published in several volumes. None of his work has been translated into English except in isolated passages. One of the personalists, or early thinkers in the 'dialogical philosophy', the heart of his thinking was the I–Thou relationship: not merely between human persons, but also between humanity and God. Language and dialogue play a central role. Influential on philosophers like Buber as well as theologians like Emil Brunner.

Epicurus (431–270 BC). Greek philosopher who proposed that the aim of philosophy is to enable us to live well.

Erasmus, Desiderius (*c.*1466/9–1536). Influential Catholic Dutch humanist. Scholar and statesman. He wrote *On the Freedom of the Will* against Luther, and *In Praise of Folly* against evils in the contemporary church and state.

eschatology. That part of theology which is to do with the 'end times' or 'last things'.

Fackenheim, Emil (b. 1917). German Jewish Reform rabbi. He is best known for his later theological work in which he explored the religious implications of the Holocaust. He attempted to explain the nature of God's presence in the death-camps; arguing that to give up Jewish belief as a response to the Holocaust would be to hand Hitler posthumous victories. See *To Mend the World.*

Gersonides (Levi ben Gershom) (1288–1344). Jewish philosopher, halakhist and scientist. Gersonides rejected the view of the Aristotelian philosophers that the existence of God, as Prime Mover, could be deduced from motions within the universe. Instead he proposes a form of the argument by design – a proof of the existence of God is based on the orderly processes that take place within the world. He argues that the regularity of certain processes implies that they are caused by an intelligence. His most famous book is *The Wars of the Lord.*

Halevi, Judah (*c.*1085–*c.*1141). Medieval Jewish poet and philosopher, whose poetic work is still revered today. Although engaged in philosophical work himself, he was sceptical about some philosophical approaches of metaphysics, as compared to revelation, religious experience and tradition.

Hamann, Johann Georg (1730–88). German Lutheran theologian and philosopher. He pioneered a holistic approach, attacking the dualism (for example, reason/passion) of many prominent Enlightenment philosophers.

Hegel, Georg Wilhelm Friedrich (1770–1831). One of the most influential of Western philosophers, although very difficult to understand. Principal themes include the importance of history, 'dialectic' and alienation. Came to believe that all reality is ultimately mental, hence espoused a form of idealism, which conceived of history as the process of Absolute Mind realizing itself in history.

Heidegger, Martin (1889–1976). Student of Husserl, therefore schooled in phenomenology, using philosophical method to analyse immediate experience; also influenced by Kierkegaard. Heidegger's work is one of the foundations of existentialism. His large early work, *Being and Time*, attempts to analyse human existence or being in the world (*Dasein*). Later work increasingly focused on the nature of language.

Hester Panim. Hebrew term meaning 'the hiding of the face'. See **Berkovits.**

Hume, David (1711–76). Scottish empiricist philosopher and historian. Notorious for his criticisms of Christian beliefs – for example, belief in miracles and in life after death. See *Essay Concerning Human Understanding* and *Dialogues Concerning Natural Religion.*

Ibn Rushd (Averroës) (1126–98). A highly influential Islamic Aristotelian philosopher. Most of his works were commentaries on Aristotle. His aim was to rescue Aristotle's work from the corruption of Platonic notions. He was a prominent critic of **Ibn Sīnā**. Against the rationalism of **al-Ghazālī**, he wrote *Incoherence of the Incoherence.*

Ibn Sīnā (Avicenna) (980–1037). Islamic Neoplatonist philosopher. Born in Bukhara, a wandering court scholar who died in Isfahan. He popularized a Neoplatonic version of Aristotelianism, which had a huge influence on thirteenth-century Christian scholasticism.

Irenaeus (*c*.115–90). Christian church father, born in Asia Minor. He wrote at length against Gnosticism. He is well known for his theory of recapitulation – people who lived prior to Christ could still be saved through Christ.

Kabbala (cabbala). Hebrew term meaning 'that which is handed down'. The term first referred to the books of the Jewish scriptures other than the Pentateuch; around 1200 its use was extended to cover the oral tradition of the Mishnah and Talmud. It combines angelology, cosmology, gnosticism and magic and has become an esoteric mystical tradition of interpreting the Jewish scriptures.

kalām. Arabic term for 'speech'. The term is used to refer to a variety of Muslim theological schools existing between the eighth and the eleventh centuries. These schools used philosophical proofs to justify religious doctrines. It has a similar role in Islam to the role of scholasticism in Christian theology. The practitioners of **kalām** were referred to as the *Mutakallimūn*. Mu'tazilite scholars emphasized that rational argument had a vital role to play in religious matters, and they attempted to employ Greek philosophy in the service of their faith.

Kant, Immanuel (1724–1804). German philosopher. In later life, wrote three 'Critiques' which have been extremely influential on Western philosophy: *Critique of Pure Reason* (1781), *Critique of Practical Reason* (1788), and *Critique of Judgement* (1790). The first Critique is concerned with knowledge, what can be known by pure reason and without experience. The second is concerned with action, especially moral action. The third is concerned with aesthetic and teleological judgements. He called his stance transcendental or critical idealism.

Kaplan, Mordecai (1881–1983). Jewish theologian. A Lithuanian Jew who emigrated to the United States as a child. Kaplan's work *Judaism as a Civilization* is the foundation of the Reconstructivist movement within Judaism. He proposed a naturalistic conception of religion, with Judaism being seen as an evolving religious civilization. Accusations of atheism and heresy led to his excommunication.

karma. Literally meaning action, then the effects of action, it refers more specifically to the doctrine in Hinduism, Buddhism and Jainism that the conditions of one's present existence are the effects of acts committed in previous existences.

Kierkegaard, Søren Aaby (1813–55). Danish Lutheran philosopher and theologian. Famous for the declaration that 'truth is subjectivity'; emphasizing that faith implies a decision, he is known as one of the most prominent modern exponents of fideism. See *Concluding Unscientific Postscript*.

Leibniz, Gottfried Wilhelm (1646–1716). German philosopher. Produced one of the great rationalist systems of the seventeenth century. Responsible for the notion that this is the best of all possible worlds. See his *Discourse on Metaphysics*, *Theodicy*, and *Monadology*.

Lokāyata Materialism. The earliest form of atheistic materialism in India. The earliest mentioned thinker is Brihaspati Lanka, who is mentioned in the Ṛgveda; he believed that matter was the ultimate reality, and did not believe in God, the immortality of the soul, or an afterlife. Other thinkers and important texts include Brigu, Parsvanatha (8th cent. BC), Kautsa, Purāna Kāsyapā, Makkhali Gosala, Ajita Kesa Kambalī. See also Cārvāka.

Luria, Isaac (1534–72). Jewish kabbalist. Grew up in Egypt, moving to Safed, Israel, where he lived until his death. He studied the early Jewish mystical tradition and developed this into a doctrine of his own. Luria conceived of creation as a negative act. The infinite had to bring into being an empty space by removing the divine light, so that there was a space for creation to take place in. This divine contraction was termed *Tsimtsum*, a form of divine exile.

Luther, Martin (1483–1546). German Christian. One of the principle Reformers. Famous for the doctrine of justification by faith; a doctrine which led him to deny the need for a priesthood and reject the idea that the Church was a mediator between people and God. His famous Ninety-Five Theses attacked current Catholic abuses, notably the practice of granting indulgences. He was tried in Augsburg in 1518, he finally broke with the Catholic Church and was excommunicated. His writings include *To the Christian Nobility of the German Nation* and *The Freedom of the Christian.*

Mādhva (13th cent.). Founder of a dualist form of Vedānta. God is one, but the world and individual selves are also ultimately real, and are dependent on God. He has a 'realist' epistemology: things can be known as they are, and sense-perception is valid. Against Śaṇkara, he believes that God is never free from attributes. God's attributes and actions are the same as God himself.

Mādhyamika (2nd cent. AD school of Buddhism). 'Middle School', also known as Śūnyavāda (śūnya = empty). No object of intellectual knowledge is real. Genuine insight into Being cannot be delivered by the intellect. Reality is completely non-accessible to reason. See also Aśvaghoṣa, **Nāgārjuna.** Other thinkers include Arya Deva (3rd cent. AD), Buddhapalita (5th cent. AD), Chadrakirti (7th cent. AD).

Mahābhārata. One of the two major epics of Indian scriptures, the other being the *Rāmāyana.*

Mahāvīr, Mahāvīra (*c.*599 BC–*c.*527 BC). Indian ascetic and wandering preacher. Regarded by Jains as the greatest teacher in their tradition.

Mahāyāna. One of the two major traditions of Buddhism, literally the 'greater vehicle'.

Maimonides, Moses (Moses ben Maimon) (1135–1204). Spanish Jewish philosophical theologian. He fled Spain during a period of persecution, settling in Fez and then Cairo, where he became head of the Jewish community. He attempted to reconcile Jewish thought with the philosophy of Aristotle. He was concerned with the relation between reason and faith, writing *Guide for the Perplexed* to show how they could be reconciled. His work influenced Aquinas.

Maṇḍana Miśra. Indian Advaita Vedānta philosopher probably of the eighth century; although not only the details but even the basic facts about his life and identity are uncertain. According to tradition, he was a pupil of Kumārila, and wrote several works in the Bhatta Mīmāṃsā tradition. Sent with his wife to debate with Śaṇkara, he ended up being converted by him to Śaṇkara's vision of Advaita Vedānta. He is the author of the *Brahmasiddhi*, a very important work in the Advaita Vedāntin tradition.

Malebranche, Nicolas (1638–1715). French philosopher. He attempted to reconcile the thought of Descartes with Catholic belief; this resulted in a highly innovative philosophical system. He propounded occasionalism – the view that matter cannot act on mind so things are known by us via an act of God. See his *Search for the Truth*.

māya. A term used in Indian philosophy referring to delusion or illusion.

Mendelssohn, Moses (1729–86). German Jewish Enlightenment philosopher. He was concerned to modernize Jewish life, and to this end he translated the Pentateuch into German. He wrote a number of philosophical works arguing for the existence of God, and defending the role of reason *vis-à-vis* faith.

Mīmāṃsā. Sometimes divided into Purva Mīmāṃsa and Uttara Mīmāṃsā. Arising about the fourth century BC, a non-theistic school of Vedānta. It was suggested by its first thinkers, Jaimini in *Mīmāṃsā Sūtra* and Kumārila Bhaṭṭa in *Ślokavārtikka*, that karma and the universal order need not presuppose the existence of a divine being. If karma is under the rule of God, it is a tautological category; if God is subordinate to the universal law of karma, God is not almighty and transcendent. Purva Mīmāṃsā heavily emphasized the rituals and practices of Vedic religion. Other thinkers include Prabhākāra, Parthasarathi. In their metaphysics, the empirical world is real, and not dependent on the knower. Their epistemology is realist; all knowledge is self-valid.

mokṣa, moksha. Liberation. Ultimate salvation in Indian religions, especially Hinduism.

Molina, Luis de (1535–1600). Spanish Christian theologian and Jesuit. His controversial *The Concord of Free Will with the Gift of Grace* was an attempt to defend, against Protestant doctrine, the view that we are free to resist or accept grace. This view became known as Molinism.

Mullā Sadr al-Dīn, Muhammad ibn Ibrāhīm Shīrāzi (Mullā Ṣadrā) (1571–1640). Shi'ite philosopher, born in Iran. He was concerned to reconcile Islam with Aristotelian philosophy and Gnostic systems. The controversial nature of his work forced him into frequent exile. See *The Four Journeys*.

Mutakallimūn. See **kalām.**

Mu'tazilite. See **kalām.**

Nāgārjuna. A philosopher of the second century AD of the Buddhist Mādhyamika school. Author of the *Mādhyamika Karika*. Ultimate reality cannot be known by the intellect. Reality is ultimate emptiness; both being and nothingness, neither being nor nothingness. The empirical world is unreal.

Nietzsche, Friedrich (1844–1900). German philosopher, controversial both on political grounds (scornful of democracy and egalitarianism, hostile to women) and on his philosophical importance (an influential philosopher or a mere aphorist and essayist?). His work can be interpreted in many ways, which has contributed to the diverse influence he has on twentieth-century philosophy, e.g. on existentialism and post-modernism. Raised critical and subversive questions about the possibility and nature of knowledge, morality, objectivity, rationality, 'facts' and truth; as well as the relationship between language and thought. Bitterly critical of religion and metaphysics.

nirvāna, nibbāna. Release from existence in the Buddhist tradition, the fruit of enlightenment.

Nyāya. 'Right reasoning'. An Indian philosophical school, the most concerned with epistemology and logic. Its metaphysics and epistemology are 'realist'; things and the world are real and independent of our mind or spirit. They are not all aspects of one reality; hence Nyāya philosophy is also 'pluralist'. Nature includes both nature, or matter, and spirit. Both are independent and real. Consciousness is partly a matter of spirit and not simply a function of the material body. God is one; omniscient, omnipotent, by which he guides the universe, directs souls inspiring them to act in accordance with their karma. Arguments were put forward to prove the existence of God.

Ockham, William (of) (*c.*1285–1349). English Christian theologian and philosopher. He was a Franciscan who had a strained relationship with the papacy due to his defence of the view that Jesus and the disciples owned no property. Ockham is famous as the leader of the nominalists, those who deny the reality of universals; he was a forerunner of British empiricist philosophy. His most important works are: *Four Books of the Sentences*, *The Summa of Logic*, and the *Quodlibeta septem*.

Origen (*c.*185–*c.*254). Greek Christian biblical scholar. Educated in Alexandria. He is famous for his ascetical lifestyle (going so far as to castrate himself). He was a prolific writer, although much of his work was destroyed when he was condemned by the Church for heresy. He wrote an apologetic work *Against Celsus*.

Paley, William (1743–1805). English scholar and archdeacon of Carlisle. He is renowned for his formulation of the argument from design. His form of the argument was based on a mechanistic view of creation which was compared to a watch on the seashore. Just as on finding the watch we must infer a watchmaker, so on finding the mechanistic universe we must infer a creator. See *Evidences of Christianity* and *Natural Theology*.

Patañjali. Principal exponent of Yoga, wrote *Yoga Sūtras*.

Philo (25 BC–AD 50). Alexandrian Jewish philosopher. Philo's writings are the fullest source of knowledge available about the philosophy of this crucial period. Philo himself combined Hellenistic philosophy and Alexandrian Judaism.

Plotinus (*c.* 205–70). Neoplatonist philosopher in Alexandria, later taught in Rome. His writings were later gathered into the *Enneads*. Ultimately all derives from The One, which is The Good. Mind emanates from The One, and Soul emanates from Mind; and thereafter the material world comes from Soul. Our ultimate goal should be to return to The One through contemplation.

Radhakrishnan, Sarvepalli. Twentieth-century philosopher and scholar of India.

Rāmānuja (11th cent.). Rāmānuja's Vedānta is a 'qualified non-dualism' as compared to Śaṇkara. Rāmānuja agrees with Śaṇkara that the absolute has the nature of consciousness, is foundation of all. Unlike Śaṇkara, he considers God to be personal. Religiosity can find no meaning in an absolute with no qualities and no feeling, thought, will. It doesn't meet our deepest needs, especially for fellowship and communion with an other. The Supreme Other must be a personality. His view is 'identity in and through and because of difference' (in Radhakrishnan's words). Individual existence is not illusory but real; liberation involves a gain of knowledge and bliss, not identification with God, and this comes about from continual remembrance of God.

Rāmāyana. One of the two major epics of Indian scriptures, the other being the *Mahābhārata*.

Rosenzweig, Franz (1886–1929). Jewish philosopher, like Ebner and Buber a 'personalist' or dialogical philosopher. Wrote *The Star of Redemption*, *Understanding the Sick and the Healthy* and *The New Thinking*. His work, critical of mainstream philosophy and its attitudes to thought, time and totality, proposes instead a dialogical or narrative philosophy, whose starting point is the triad God–World–Humanity.

Rubenstein, Richard (b. 1924). Jewish theologian and Conservative rabbi. His most important work is *After Auschwitz*. Rubenstein argues that it is impossible to hold a traditional view of God after Auschwitz. He proposes that a form of mystical Jewish paganism or nature worship would be the most appropriate expression of piety for today.

Saadia ben Joseph Gaon (882–942). The earliest great Jewish philosopher of the medieval period. Influenced by the Mu'tazilite kalām philosophers, he wrote treatises on a number of subjects. His most important philosophical work is *The Book of Beliefs and Opinions*. In an attempt to refute the claims of Christians, Muslims and Zoroastrians, he argued that there are four sources of knowledge: sense experience, intuition of self-evident truths, logical inference and reliable tradition.

saṃsāra. In Indian religions and philosophy, the cycle of birth, death, rebirth.

Śaṇkara, Śaṃkara (Śaṇkaracarya) (*c.*788–820). Indian religious philosopher. One of the most influential thinkers in the history of Indian religions. See **Advaita Vedānta.**

Sāṇkhya or Sāṃkhya. An Indian philosophical school, largely non-theistic. It emphasizes the reality of the empirical world. The world has no beginning or end; it has its origins in an uncaused cause, and it continues to unfold and develop. The whole of the physical universe has its origin in prakṛti, 'nature' or 'matter'. 'Spirit' or 'consciousness', puruṣa, is different; matter is not an aspect of it. The mental, the intellect, is identified with prakṛti not puruṣa. Puruṣa is formless, freedom, independent of qualities, pure consciousness, inactive, free from change, free from attachments. Puruṣa is plural: we are not all part of the same puruṣa. Each spirit is independent. Puruṣa is distinguished from the 'empirical self' (jīva). Jīva is temporal, changing, acting, whereas puruṣa is not. Jīva is the self as determined by the body. It experiences pain, pleasure, has other mental modes, unlike puruṣa. See **yoga.**

satori. Zen state of enlightenment.

Sautrānika. One of two main schools of Theravāda Buddhism, the other being Vaibhāṣika. It arose around the fourth century AD. It holds that the external world is real and perceptible, thus is realist. They still accept the momentariness of reality central to Buddhism, however.

Spinoza, Baruch (Benedict de Spinoza) (1632–77). A Dutch Jewish thinker, one of the earliest representatives of the Jewish Enlightenment. At the age of 23 he was excommunicated from the Jewish community for his heretical beliefs. Spinoza denied both creation and freedom, arguing that God is the totality of all bodies in the physical universe. He proposed that religion had to do with ethics, whereas philosophy had to do with truth.

Soloveitchik, Joseph (1903–93). Polish Jewish Talmudic expert and rabbi.

śūnya, śūnyatā. A particular concept of emptiness in Buddhism. See **Mādhyamika.**

Sureśvara. See also **Maṇḍana Miśra**; traditions say that the two are the same, Maṇḍana taking the name Sureśvara after his conversion to Śaṇkara's teaching, although some scholars doubt this. Indian Advaita Vedāntin philosopher. It is said that Śaṇkara gave him the task of commenting on two of his own works. Works attributed to him most reliably include commentaries on Śaṇkara's commentaries on several important Upaniṣads: the *Bṛhadāranyakopaniṣadbhāsyavārtikka* – long in content as well as in name – the *Taittirīyopanisadbhāsyavartikka*, *Naiskarmyasiddhi*; he is also credited with authorship of the *Dakṣinā-murtivartikka* (or *Mānasollāsa*) and the *Pañcīkaranavārtikka* (or *Pranavavārtikka*).

sūtra. A saying or aphorism, it also refers to the collection of sayings of Indian sages.

Svatantra-Vijñānavāda. See also **Vijñānavāda.** A school of Buddhist logic arising with the Vijñānavāda school of Mahāyāna Buddhism. Outstanding exponents were Diṇnāga (6th cent.), Dharmakīrti (7th cent.), Śāntarakṣīta and Kamalaśīla (8th cent.). In addition to the 'idealist' aspect of the Vijñānavāda school, it emphasizes the 'momentariness' of reality as taught by Buddhism: knowledge only reflects moments of existence; there is no permanence in anything that is an object of knowledge or consciousness. An object of knowledge is not the same from one moment to the next.

Tathāgata. An honorary name for the Buddha, Gautama Siddhārtha; it means 'thus gone'.

Tathāta. 'Thusness' or 'suchness'; used by Aśvaghosa to speak of 'non-self'.

Teilhard de Chardin, Pierre (1881–1955). French Catholic theologian and palaeontologist. His reputation is based on the book *The Phenomenon of Man*, where he argued that God is part of the evolutionary process. Christ is portrayed as the centre of the evolutionary process which is moving towards the Omega Point. His general attempt to unify science and theology has been more influential than the details of his theory.

Tertullian (*c.*160–225). From Carthage, converted to Christianity in his thirties. One of the church fathers of the Western (Latin) Church. Insisted on the sufficiency of the Bible, as opposed to secular philosophy for the knowledge of God.

theodicy. A term first used in its modern form by the philosopher Leibniz in 1710. The term goes back to a Greek word for 'justification of God'.

Theravāda. Literally 'The Teaching of the Elders'. One of two main traditions of Buddhism, also referred to as 'Hinayana' (the lesser vehicle). The other is Mahāyāna.

Three Ways. A Hindu tradition that there are three ways to salvation: of knowledge (jñana-marga), of devotion (bhakti-marga), and of action (karma-marga). These are not in opposition to each other, but are there for the sake of different types of people. Nyāya, Sāṇkhya, Yoga, Advaita Vedānta, Buddhist and Jain systems all favour the way of knowledge; bhakti is favoured by Rāmānuja, Mādhva, Nimbarka, Vallabha, Mahaprabhu Chaitanya, and Purva Mīmāṃsā; and other traditions of popular practice favour action and ritual.

Tillich, Paul Johannes (1886–1965). German Lutheran philosopher and theologian. He portrayed God as the ground of Being, who can be known through ultimate concern. See his three-volume *Systematic Theology*.

tochācha. A Jewish concept based on Lev. 26 and Deut. 28. Essentially it is the idea that humans not God cause evil. This concept was important in early medieval Jewish philosophical theology (particularly in the work of Saadiah ben Joseph Gaon), and has been used in more recent times with reference to the Holocaust.

Tsimtsum. Divine contraction. See **Luria.**

Wiesel, Elie (b. 1928). A Jewish writer, born in Romania and a survivor of Auschwitz. Famous for his autobiographical novel, *Night*, in which he portrays the development of his doubts about the existence and character of God as a response to the experience of the Nazi death-camps. His later works develop the theme of religious protest.

Upaniṣads. Literally, 'the final parts of the Vedas'. Sections of philosophical reflections added to the Vedas, the Hindu scriptures. See **Vedas.**

Vaibhāṣika. One of two main schools of Theravāda Buddhism, the other being the Sautrāntika school. It arose around the second century AD. Its outlook was one of straightforward realism. Objects are real, external to the mind, and lasting (cf. Svatantra-Vijñānavāda).

Vaiśeṣika. A school of Hinduism. It arose between the sixth and third centuries BC. It developed independently from Nyāya, but because of the similarities of views it is often assimilated to Nyāya and referred to as Nyāya-Vaiśeṣika. Its founder was Kaṇada. The Vaiśeṣika system is realist in its epistemology and metaphysics, and 'pluralist', in that objects and selves are independently real, not just appearance or illusion.

Vedas. The oldest Hindu religious texts. The Vedic period runs from approximately 1500 to 700 BC. The Ṛgveda was composed perhaps as early as 1500 BC; the other vedas are the Sāmaveda, Yajurveda, and Atharvaveda. The Upaniṣads are attached as conclusions to the Vedas, and are speculations and reflections of a philosophical nature, whereas much of the rest of the Vedas are hymns to the gods and instructions for ritual, sacrifice, etc. The Epic period runs from 800 BC to AD 200 . The two principal collections of epic literature are the *Mahābhārata*, which contains the *Bhagavad-Gitā*, and the *Rāmāyana*. The Sūtra period extended from 400 BC to AD 500. The Sūtras are aphorisms of the various Indian philosophical traditions (including Buddhism and Jainism). The Commentary period is from AD 400 to 1700, and contains the reflections and commentaries of the great thinkers on the vedas and Sūtras.

Vedānta. Literally, the last parts of the Vedas. A tradition of Indian philosophy, with important differences between schools, which based itself firmly on the Upaniṣads. In many ways, it is an attempt to reflect philosophically on certain passages which suggest an identity between Brahman and ātman, that underlying reality is one. This issue was handled differently by three main schools, the 'non-dualist', 'qualified non-dualist', and 'dualist' views. See also **Advaita Vedānta, Śaṇkara, Rāmānuja, Mādhva.**

veridical. Truthful. Veridical perceptions represent things as they genuinely are. Non-veridical or un-veridical perceptions are illusory.

Vijñānavāda. Also Yogācāra. A major school of Mahāyāna Buddhism, idealist in its epistemology and metaphysics. Everything inside and outside the mind has its origin in Universal Mind, or Cosmic Consciousness. The empirical world is not there; it arises from thought. Thus empirical knowledge can never be certain; true and ultimate knowledge is the point at which enlightenment breaks in. The founder of the school is said to be Maitreyanatha (4th cent.); followers include Asanga and his brother Vasubandhu (5th cent.), Diṇnāga (6th cent.), Dharmakīrti (7th cent.), Śāntarakṣīta and Kamalaśīla (8th cent.).

Wittgenstein, Ludwig (1889–1951). Wrote an early, massively influential work, *Tractatus Logico-Philosophicus* (1921), which deals with the possibilities and limits of language and how it represents and depicts the world. Later he turned against his own 'picture theory' of meaning as too simplistic, and decided that meaning is best discovered by examining the uses to which words are put. In *Philosophical Investigations* and later works (many published posthumously from notes) he views language as diverse, using the analogy of a 'tool' or as widely differing 'games' that can only be understood with reference to the life and community in which they are played. His later view saw philosophy as a therapeutic endeavour.

yoga. Not a mere system of exercise. It has the same fundamental metaphysics as Sāṇkhya, but is theistic. The world is real, and there is a real plurality of selves, they are not aspects of or modifications of God. God is the creator, but is coeternal with prakṛti and puruṣa. God directs evolution, in particular, in making the impact of merit and demerit, karma, be realized. God is conceived as personal, perfect, impassible. Ten qualities are ascribed to God: knowledge, detachment, lordship, austerity, veracity, forgiveness, patience, creative power, self-knowledge, superintendence. The foremost exponent of Yoga is Patañjali. See **Sāṇkhya.**

Yogācāra. See **Vijñānavāda.**

Zen. A tradition of Buddhism, principally identified with Japan, also practised in China and Korea.

Zeno (b. *c*.490 BC). Ancient Greek philosopher famous for his 'paradoxes' about motion. In one, he argues that an arrow in flight is in fact at rest. In another, he argues that since space is infinitely divisible, a runner in a stadium can never finish the course. Before he can reach the end, he must reach the half-way point; and before he can reach the quarter-way point, he must reach the eighth; and so on indefinitely. Since finite distances consist of an infinite series of points, and one can never complete an infinite series, one can never reach the end of the course.

Part 1

What Comes First

1

What Your Lecturer Doesn't Tell You About Religion

Philosophers are usually expected to begin by defining the key terms that they will use, but defining 'religion' is much more problematic than you may think. Dozens of different definitions have been proposed from within different academic disciplines, and none of them has been universally accepted. Recently when Britain needed a definition for the purposes of law, three contenders were put forward:

> Durkheim: '[A] unified system of beliefs and practices relative to sacred things, that is to say, things set apart and forbidden – beliefs and practices which unite into one single moral community called a Church all those who adhere to them';
>
> The *Oxford English Dictionary*: 'action or conduct indicating a belief in, reverence for, and desire to please a divine ruling power, the exercise or practice of rites or observances implying this . . . a particular system of faith worship';
>
> Lord Ahmad: 'a system of beliefs and practices centred around the worship of God which is derived in whole or in part from a book revealed by God to one of his messengers'.

How useful are these definitions for the study of philosophy of religion? One immediate problem is that each of them excludes a 'religion'. Buddhism, Jainism, Confucianism, Daoism and some traditions in Hinduism would not qualify to be 'religions' under Lord Ahmad's definition, because they are among a number of faith traditions that do not include a belief in one or more god(s). In order to fit the requirements of a definition, one must find features that are found in *all* of the systems that we deem to be religions, but do not also include other groups such as political parties or football clubs that also command strong adherence. Belief in a god, or an afterlife, or some activity like ritual sacrifice or prayer, may not be a part of *every* religion on the planet. For the legal definition a further requirement was that the definition must not only describe the religions that exist, but would in future determine whether emerging movements can be deemed a religion or not. It was not only describing existing groupings, but controlling into the future what religions must be or cannot be.

Since people use the word 'religion' all the time, and seem to know what is meant by it, why is it so hard to give a reliable definition of it? The word itself came into existence in the European languages, and therefore reflects that civilization's views of life. There is no word exactly equivalent to 'religion' in either Sanskrit or Hawaiian. It appears that some cultures don't divide faith in God from faith in one's political leaders, and don't have a word for 'religion' that doesn't include 'politics'. Perhaps in some cultures there isn't an overall term for part of life that includes praying and believing, but excludes eating or having sex; perhaps some do not have a word for 'religion' which excludes other 'good things to do' that Europeans consider non-religious.

The word 'religion', in European languages, evolved in a particular history and culture.

> *Although the word's precursor was in use even in Cicero's time, a narrative commonly given is that the modern use of the word and concept have their roots in the Enlightenment. Specifically, the origins would lie in the critique of Christianity and of Church power. Understood as a contrast word to Christianity, it sought to create a faith without Christian doctrines; and even in the twentieth century a theologian like Barth can oppose 'Christianity' and 'religion', to the latter's detriment. Understood in opposition to 'the secular', one Enlightenment project was to create, define and police a 'secular' social territory autonomous from the religious authorities, while another was to underwrite the claims of a 'secular' political power as a rival to Church power.*
>
> *So if the construction of a category called 'religion' is an Enlightenment project, it has never been separated from a particular agenda or ideology. Accordingly, the task of defining of the word and describing the category has been contested from the start. One fact sometimes overlooked is that there has never been agreement on the word and what it presupposes: first, that there can be an overarching theologically neutral category which successfully encompasses all the world's faiths; secondly, that the world is divided into two territories, and only in one of them does faith have any authority.*
>
> *So the word 'religion' is not a neutral term, even within American and European Christianity. Not least, its boundaries are disputed any time a question of policy, law or practice that has an ethical dimension arises within the 'secular' realms of science and medicine, or economics and governance. Moreover, the secular–sacred*

dichotomy within the genealogy of the word 'religion' is not culturally neutral. If this division is still contested within Western society, it is certainly not taken as self-evident in other cultures.[1]

At the same time, the European Enlightenment was not the first or the only time a dominant religion encountered other religions; and if we broaden our view beyond the West we can find historical examples of moments where a demographically dominant religion, such as Islam, also had to create a more 'neutral' concept of religion in order to engage with the people and the ideas of other faiths. (See the opening of Chapter 2 for an example.)

If a word and its use have evolved within one particular culture, then care needs to be taken before it is grafted onto another. Another civilization's beliefs and practices may not fit that model. The word 'religion' can be a dangerous starting point for understanding the faiths of the world. To the Western mind, 'religion' is a neutral term but this view is misleading, for it conceals religious assumptions we make, based on the familiar faiths of the West. When we use it to approach other faiths without considering their own framework, we are likely to try to squeeze them to fit inside our own Procrustean bed. Christians, for example, when they want to understand another religion, tend to look for doctrines they can list to understand that 'religion' by knowing its beliefs. But even with Christianity's ancestral relation, Judaism, this does not necessarily describe well what that faith is like from inside the community. Taoism, like many indigenous religions, may see itself more in ways of life, ritual practices or ethical beliefs than in formal dogmas.

Procrustes, a dwarf, had a dwarf-sized bed in his guest-room. This caused visitors some discomfort, but when they emerged, complaining, from their room, Procrustes would explain patiently that there was nothing at all the matter with his bed, as he followed them back into the room. When the disgruntled guest climbed into the bed to demonstrate its inadequacy – 'You see, my arm is hanging over the side . . . my feet are dangling off the end of the bed . . .' – Procrustes could demonstrate that this was not the case at all. He produced an axe and removed all the bits of the visitor that did not fit into his bed, to show how they did in fact fit perfectly within it.[2]

Similarly, Christians often look at religious patterns with a model of a 'core' religion, or mainstream; surrounded perhaps by deviant or 'fringe' spin-offs. The very name 'Hinduism' is a Western imposition of a single religious identity on a diversity of traditions in India. Such an approach also doesn't help to understand the relationships within African, Polynesian and Native American religions.

On the other hand, a Vaishnavite from India can incorporate Christian belief in Jesus into her spiritual outlook quite easily, while a Christian from Alabama is likely to find it very difficult to give the same houseroom to the Vaishnavite's beliefs. Where there are problems of understanding and epistemological acceptance, the difficulties are not always reciprocal and equal.

It endangers our attempts to understand other faiths if we assume in advance that we can tell what they are all about, because we know 'what religion is' and we know that this is a 'religion'.

At other times, when you contemplate another religious culture, the differences can be so striking that you can have the opposite reaction. What you see can look so alien that the possibilities for understanding it seem remote. Instead of bending it into a familiar frame, it sets off a different Euro-American tendency: the preoccupation with 'Self vs. Other'. This opposition has created a legacy of problems for Western philosophy; from the problem of 'other minds' to the suggestion that other cultures are so radically incommensurate that we cannot comprehend them at all. But why 'The Other' should be a philosophical problem at all, least of all an epistemic one, is not self-evident to philosophers in other regions. Nor do all other world views interpret 'difference' as 'division' or 'opposition'. Importing this kind of philosophical xenophobia into the business of understanding religion may prevent us from understanding faith traditions on their own terms, or in any meaningful way at all.

A thought-provoking view:

Timothy Fitzgerald questions our use of the word and concept of 'religion'. He suggests that it is not a genuine, cross-cultural category but something that we impose on different cultures. He argues that it arises from theology: 'liberal ecumenical theology', wishing to go beyond the study of Christianity and needing to define its object of study. The term 'religion' is meant to be neutral and apply to all cases, leaving out a faith commitment in the method of study. However, it still imports a host of assumptions that can distort the object of study; chief among them the assumption that 'religion' is about human responses to the divine. It imposes Western assumptions, values and frameworks on other societies; such as assumptions about the relationship between 'religion' and the 'secular', 'religion' and politics, religion and society or economics. Its categories, such as 'God', 'salvation' or 'the meaning of history', are derived from Judaeo-Christian monotheistic traditions. He thinks we should reconceive the field:

> *I propose that religious studies be rethought and rerepresented as cultural studies, understood as the study of the institutions and the*

institutionalized values of specific societies, and the relation between those institutionalized values and the legitimation of power.[3]

The phenomenon of religious diversity has grown in prominence in contemporary philosophy of religion. Initially the problem was not seen as one of mutual understanding, as I have outlined it above. Rather concern about diversity came from dealing with conflicting truth claims, an issue which arose at the birth of modern philosophy of religion in the atheist–theist debate characteristic of Anglo-American philosophers of the twentieth century. Difference was seen as a logical or epistemological problem. If you have two claims that 'conflict', they cannot both be true. 'How can "ultimate reality" be both a personal being and an impersonal principle, identical to our inmost self and forever "other", loving and utterly indifferent, good and amoral, knowable and unknowable, a plenitude and "emptiness"?'[4] Instead of adjudicating the claims, the atheist often argued that *both* are probably false. Hume claimed that in matters of religion, 'whatever is different is contrary'; as it is impossible that all the different religions are telling the truth, we should doubt that any of them is established on a solid foundation.

Partly driven by the need to defend against this atheist challenge, and partly as a way of being nice to all religions, there have been various attempts at creating some unity, some unified understanding of religion as a solution to the problem.

John Hick proposed an interpretation of religion which became the foundation stone for contemporary understandings of religious pluralism. He based his theory on a central idea from the philosopher Immanuel Kant: that there is a difference between 'things as we perceive them' and 'things as they are in themselves'. Hick suggested that we should make such a distinction when we consider Ultimate Reality; the many religions are 'different human responses to the one divine Reality', but Ultimate Reality as it is in itself we do not know. No-one has direct access to it or a privileged account of it and therefore each way of conceiving it is authentic, although different from all others.

This view proved to be popular and influential, but also controversial. Clearly it would be rejected by those who think they do have *the* right answer or *the* privileged account. Others stick resolutely to the idea that contradictory religious claims *cannot* both be true, no matter how polite we would like to be about differences.

Raimundo Panikkar's 'four attitudes'

Exclusivism

A believing member of a religion in one way or another considers his religion to be true. Now, the claim to truth has a certain built-in claim to exclusivity. If a given statement is true, its contradictory cannot also be true. And if a certain human tradition claims to offer a universal context for truth, anything contrary to that 'universal truth' will have to be false.

Inclusivism

In the present world one can hardly fail to discover positive and true values – even of the highest order – outside of one's own tradition. Traditional religions have to face this challenge. The most plausible condition for the claim to truth of one's own tradition is to affirm at the same time that it includes at different levels all that there is of truth wherever it exists. The inclusivistic attitude will tend to reinterpret things in such a way as to make them not only palatable but also assimilable.

Parallelism (often now called pluralism)

If your religion appears far from being perfect and yet it represents for you a symbol of the right path and a similar conviction seems to be the case for others, if you cannot dismiss the religious claim of the other nor assimilate it completely into your tradition, a plausible alternative is to assume that all are different creeds which, in spite of meanderings and crossings, actually run parallel to meet only in the ultimate, . . . at the very end of the human pilgrimage. Religions would then be parallel paths and our most urgent duty would be not to interfere with others, not to convert them or even to borrow from them, but to deepen our own respective traditions so that we may meet at the end, and in the depth of our own traditions.

Interpenetration

The more we come to know the religions of the world, the more we are sensitive to the religiousness of our neighbour, all the more we begin to surmise that in every one of us the other is somehow implied, and vice-versa, that the other is not so independent from us and is somehow touched by our own beliefs. We begin to realize that our neighbour's religion does not only challenge, but may even enrich, our own, and that ultimately, the very differences which separate us are somewhat potentially within the world of my religious convictions. We begin to accept that the other religion may complement mine and we may even entertain the idea that in some particular cases it may well supplement of my beliefs provided that my religiousness remains an undivided whole.[5]

Critique of Hick has also come from the more radical as well as from the more conservative. Such critics have queried: How does Hick know? If we cannot know the Ultimate Reality as-it-is-in-itself, how can we still know that all the different religions are authentic representations of it?

Hick's view also makes the various religions themselves, especially their more real-life aspects of practice and identity, relatively unimportant. But for many believers these concrete aspects of religious life are extremely precious and part of its identity. A comparatively abstract and flavourless describing of their faith as their particular approximation to the Ultimate Reality as-it-is-in-itself, does not adequately reflect its way of life and the fullness of belief. Taking this approach forces other religions into a framework which may distort them.

Hick's language and philosophical framework are not religiously and culturally neutral, but are still shaped by a particular set of Western assumptions (though we should note also that not every Western philosopher is a follower of Kant's line). So the claim to have bypassed Western or Christian bias turns out to be deceptive.

A challenge to Hick and his popularity

The modern myth of religion . . . is the conceptual framework upon which religious studies is based. It is the glue that holds together university departments of religion, school curricula, and publishing lists. There are a number of different components to the myth, and each time the story is retold it will appear in a slightly different form . . . Put simply, the myth is that there is one Ultimate Reality, God or The Transcendent, who is ontologically outside the world but who gives meaning and purpose to human relationships, to history and to suffering. This one unconditioned reality makes itself known to human individuals in special kinds of experiences, refracted through their different languages, symbols, and cultural institutions, implanting in them an awareness of moral codes and an underlying purpose of human life. These experiences lead them to strive for greater awareness of the unconditioned, to formulate doctrines and rituals and to form voluntary associations of the dissemination and celebration of this mystical knowledge. Sometimes this mystical awareness remains confined to limited sects and cults, and sometimes it permeates a culture, making it difficult for the analysts to decide where the truly religious elements should be demarcated from the non-religious ones. From time to time the transcendent being takes on limited human, animal, or demonic form and incarnates itself into the world as saviors, subordinate deities, enlightened masters, sons of God, prophets, bodhisattavas, gurus, and divine kings to show people the true way or to remind them of the path to deliverance. These paths are many since they are refracted through the different media or different cultures, but the goal is one.[6]

Can you, indeed, or *should* you, ask and answer the question on the level that Hick does: focusing on the wholesale justification of entire religions and their relations? We could start from different premises, like the following:

> We cannot give an abstract, theoretical account of how different religions interrelate. The relation between religious traditions is not a one-size-fits-all affair. How we understand 'Christianity vs. Judaism' cannot be given the same kind of answer as 'Buddhism vs. Islam'. The relations between various religions have to be addressed individually for historical, philosophical and theological accuracy.
>
> We can only give specific, scholarly accounts of how particular cultures or traditions have interacted in particular historical periods and places; not 'Christianity vs. Islam' as such.
>
> Similarly, we can only compare religious traditions and their accounts of themselves on the level of detail. We can compare and analyse different doctrines, philosophical arguments or religious ideas while not claiming to show a specific relation between the whole of these traditions.

Much of this book will undertake such an enquiry, as far as the philosophical ideas of different religions are concerned.

Finding a way to relate different traditions, moreover, must be addressed from *within* some particular community. How you express interfaith understanding as a Muslim will use different texts, beliefs and theologies from the Jew. A Hindu may have no trouble at all considering that a different religion's claims may be true, while an evangelical Christian may find it impossible.

A single account, whether philosophical or theological, of religious pluralism will not suffice. There can be no 'global' account of religious pluralism which will explain the existence of many faiths to the satisfaction of all. Such accounts are written for a specific audience (often a specific faith or indeed a specific denomination or sect within a broader grouping). Any account of religious pluralism is an important act of rhetoric: designed to persuade a particular audience to see this puzzling religious complexity in a particular way.

Interfaith accounts from within religious traditions

Tariq Ramadan: A Muslim argument for interfaith dialogue

So individuals, innocent and free, have to make their choices (either to accept or to reject the Revelation); there will necessarily be diversity among people, and so these three seemingly similar verses contain *teachings that augment and complete each other: 'Had God so willed, He would have united them [human beings] in guidance, so do not be among the ignorant'; (Qur'an 6:35) 'If your Lord had so willed, everyone on earth would have believed. Is it for you to compel people to be believers?'; (Qur'an 10:99) 'If God had willed, He would have made you one community but things are as they are to test you in what He has given you. So compete with each other in doing good.' (Qur'an 5:48) The first verse instructs us that diversity is willed by the Transcendent, the second makes clear that, in the name of that will, compulsion in matters of religion is forbidden,* and the Revelation teaches that the purpose of these differences is to test us in order to discover what we are going to do with what has been revealed to us: the last commandment is to use these differences to 'compete in doing good.' Diversity of religions, nations, and people is a test because it requires that we learn to manage difference, which is in itself essential: 'If God did not enable some men to keep back others, the world would be corrupt. But God is the One who gives grace to the words'; (Qur'an 2:251) 'If God did not enable some men to keep back others, hermitages, synagogues, chapels and mosques where the name of God is often called upon, would have been demolished.' (Qur'an 22:40) These two verses give complementary information that is of prime importance: if there were no differences between people, if power were in the hands of one group alone (one nation, one race, or one religion), the earth would be corrupt because human beings need others to limit their impulsive desire for expansion and domination. The last verse is more precise with regard to our present discussion; it refers to places of worship to indicate that if there is to be a diversity of religions, the purpose is to safeguard them all: the fact that the list of places begins with hermitages, synagogues, and chapels before referring to mosques shows recognition of all these places of worship and their inviolability and, of course, respect for those who pray there. So, just as diversity is the source of our test, the balance of power is a requirement for our destiny. Difference might naturally lead to conflict: therefore, the responsibility of humankind is to make use of difference by establishing a relationship based on excelling one another in doing good. It is vital that the balance of power is based not on tension born of rejection or mutual ignorance but fundamentally on knowledge: 'O people, we have created you from a male and a female, we have divided you into nations and tribes so that you might know one another.' (Qur'an 49:13) Knowing the other is a process that is unavoidable if fear of difference is to be overcome and mutual respect is to be attained. So human beings live a test that is necessary for their nature but that they can – and must – master by making the effort to know and recognise those who are not of their tribe, their country, their race, or their religion. Dialogue, particularly interreligious dialogue, is indispensible.*

**[Tariq Ramadan's footnote:]* *The Qur'an confirms this in a clear general rule: 'No compulsion in religion' (2:256).*[7]

Jonathan Sacks: A Jewish argument for interfaith dialogue

Judaism is a particularist monotheism. It believes in one God but not in one religion, one culture, one truth. The God of Abraham is the God of all mankind, but the faith of Abraham is not the faith of all mankind. . . . *God, the creator of humanity, having made a covenant with all humanity, then turns to one people and commands it to be different* in order to teach humanity the dignity of difference. *Biblical monotheism is not the idea that there is one God and therefore one truth, one faith, one way of life. On the contrary, it is the idea that unity creates diversity. . . . Judaism is about the miracle of unity that creates diversity. . . . God no more wants all faiths and cultures to be the same than a loving parent wants his or her children to be the same. That is the conceptual link between love, creation and diversity. We serve God, author of diversity, by respecting diversity.*[8]

Of course, we can fall into the lazy habit of speaking of these religions as if they are heterogeneous blocks which are in de facto competition and conflict with other blocks. But that is not so. The major world religions that we have today are complex because they have evolved over a long period of time. In that time, they have bumped into each other, and into different philosophical cultures, and in the process have absorbed and been influenced by the ideas and problems they encountered. Sometimes they have adopted each other's answers; at other times they have adopted each other's questions. Even when they have not done this explicitly, they have absorbed and diffused influences like spices in a mixture rubbing their aromas onto one another.

An example of this mutual infusing is the historical interaction of Christianity, Judaism and Islam, and the response of all three to ancient Greek philosophy. The religious framework or world view of these three monotheisms, with their emphasis on scriptural revelation, is quite different from the metaphysics of Plato or Aristotle. But paradoxically that meant that the philosophy did not necessarily contradict the tenets of their faith and could be adopted as a framework for articulating it. (However, this mix of different styles of reflection brewed up all sorts of new questions for the evolving faiths. We shall see examples of this in the chapters that follow.)

This 'infusing' does not mean that one of these traditions cannot remain truly itself without confusion or syncretism, even when it has taken on a whiff of something else. Soon, indeed, that flavour has become so much a part of it that it ceases to be foreign, as mind–body dualism, or a belief in an immortal soul, flavoured Christianity, ideas that had no clear biblical basis and were not part of its earliest form, yet are taken for granted by contemporary Christians. Religions do not necessarily compromise their identity in this process; they amplify it. They do not cease to be what they were; this is how they became what they are.

Christianity would not be what it currently is without Greek philosophy, which infused it in a manner quite different from its impact on Judaism or Islam. You can describe the absorption of Greek philosophy (and its rejection) into Islam or Judaism by naming specific individuals or movements. On Christianity, however, it was truly formative.

On other occasions we can more accurately picture it as the same or similar ingredients turning up all over; just as dairy products or noodles make their appearance in cuisines all round the world. The idea that God is infinite, though not a universal idea, is not a notion that had to be taught to one culture by another.

Sometimes related but not identical ingredients occur in traditions, which can form a kind of analogy to one another. The idea that God is beyond all attributes or characteristics appears in the Indian notion of *nirguna Brahman* and in the Christian *via negativa*, as well as mystical traditions in Judaism and Islam. The apodictic tradition in Christianity and *nirguna Brahman* are not merely 'the same idea', however.

And of course ingredients can be borrowed, ironically even in hostile exchanges, much as Western traders brought back spices from the East to flavour Western cuisines. Even when the three Western monotheisms were in conflict with one another, they tended to borrow arguments for the existence of God.

It is not always a gentle affair. We can see this in the sharp conflicts within Islamic thought, particularly characterized in al-Ghazālī's critique of 'philosophers' and the rebuttal of al-Ghazālī by Ibn Rushd. There is frequently a conflict between those who prize what they perceive as the purity of the tradition, and those who are excited by the new exotic possibilities on offer in the philosophical bazaar.

Similarities between religio-philosophical debates in different faiths are inescapable. Despite the enormous difference that a belief in Jesus and salvation makes for Christian theology, we still find that Islam and Christianity share a controversy: between free will and predestination in the question of who goes to heaven and why. Hindus and Buddhists were fierce in their debates, and Jains and Hindus profoundly different on the question of a deity; and yet they all share a belief in karma. These similarities can arise for different reasons. Some of these are:

Problems that can arise from similar doctrines: for example, transcendent monotheism in Judaism, Christianity and Islam, or the juxtaposition of a belief in rebirth and ethical thinking in the Indian religions. The problems may appear when you start to reflect within those boundaries. If you believe in a single all-powerful God, sooner or later you are going to wonder what that means in the context of human evil actions.

Certain problems seem almost to lie in the structure of situations; like when you combine belief in sacred texts that must be respected with free philosophical speculation, and give rise to a 'revelation vs. reason' problem. Similarly, when you attempt to reconcile religious demands of faith and logical constraints in any tradition you can create a 'faith vs. reason' conflict.

Sometimes different religions' philosophers all read the same books. Jews, Christians and Muslims all read Aristotle and encountered the same problem for divine knowledge after reading chapter 9 of *On Interpretation.*

And of course they read each other. Aquinas not only read Aristotle, he read 'Rabbi Moses' (Maimonides). The Muslim philosopher Ibn Rushd arguably had more influence on Christians than on Muslims.

The implications of this history of interaction are rather interesting.

At the moment, it seems there may be a new, emerging discipline of 'comparative philosophy' or a multi-faith approach to philosophy of religion. But the history I have sketched here shows that such a state of affairs is hardly some politically correct or fashionable new enterprise. Rather this is what philosophers have always done; they have always been 'promiscuous' in what they read and react to. So philosophers who currently attempt to engage with the thought of different religions, although *avant garde* in regard to recent practice in the West, are also deeply traditional.

Insofar as philosophers' contribution in shaping of their own tradition has been influenced by the thinking of other religions, it would seem that you cannot fully understand one religion without understanding the others who have been its nearest neighbours.

Finally, it also relativizes the modern 'emergence' of conflicting truth claims. This is not, after all, some postmodern problem raised to challenge religious faith for the first time in our lifetime. Religions have conflicted for millennia and their adherents have not only noticed this, but also taken account of this in their philosophical reflection. Does it, as Flew alleged, suggest that none of their claims can be true? That is a dangerous suggestion for a philosopher to make. For of course, philosophy itself is beset with conflicting claims. If the sheer fact of disagreement was enough to discredit a whole enterprise, philosophers would have to give up talking about truth, consciousness, the mind and the body, knowledge, induction and ethics and resign en masse from their university posts. What the history of both philosophy and philosophical theology shows, however, is that people who call themselves philosophers generally know how to resolve these issues: by following broadly agreed rules for fair play and the etiquette of how to keep the conversation going.

It is important to recognize, then, that religions are not monolithic, massive systems which are internally self-consistent and irrevocably in conflict with one another. Every religious tradition of any antiquity is made of strands of traditions, ideas, tendencies, stances. Some of these strands are internally in conflict with one another, such as the differences between Sunni and Shi'a Muslims on the use of *ijtihad*, or the conflicts between Lutheranism and Catholicism on the use of philosophy or reason. Meanwhile, some of those strands are in harmony or even total agreement with strands in other religious traditions. Islam had its conflicts on the merits of philosophy and independent reason, and its debates were remarkably similar to the Christians'. This means that some Muslims would agree with some Christians on the issue, and disagree with their fellow Muslims.

So when you disentangle a religion's philosophies, there are predictable and unpredictable areas of agreement and contradiction with other religions. Each of those strands is just about the right size for a single debate. Its assumptions, issues and problems can be examined in a single 'frame'. So this book does not 'compare Christianity and Islam'. We are not even talking about 'Christianity vs. Islam' on a single debate such as whether or not God can do what is logically impossible. We are talking about a debate in which the Christian and the Muslim who say God *can* do the logically impossible take issue with the Christian and the Muslim who say God *cannot*. This makes for a game in which all the religions for whom this is an issue can take part, pitching in their arguments, on a level playing field.

It seems that trying our best to begin a philosophical investigation in the proper manner, by defining our central term, has yielded some interesting results.

To start with, simply trying to define the term has led not to a tidy and abstract clarity, but rather to dispute. In the first place, there is disagreement over what should be counted as a 'religion' and what should be excluded. Next, some people challenge whether the term really refers to a valid phenomenon or not. Others, going further, suspect that the very creation and use of the term, if not quite sinister, at least falsifies reality and distorts the picture. If you find this annoying, I'm afraid you will have to become accustomed to it. Philosophy is often like this.

In the meantime, however, we did uncover something interesting: the concrete and colourful fact of religious diversity. The different paths that people follow, and the experience of being in the real world with many different faiths milling around, is surely part of what we should study.

This phenomenon alone – religious diversity – is a topic for philosophical discussion.

However, the investigation suggests that trying to understand 'religion' is going to be tricky, for there is not even agreement on what religion is or what counts as a religion. Moreover, the different bodies of thought and practice that form the basis of our study, formed as they were within different cultures, raise the question: how does one go about studying them wisely and well? That will be the focus of our next chapter.

Draw your own conclusions

Could we do without the category of 'religion' applied to different cultures? Do you think its usefulness outweighs any alleged problems?

Does any one of Panikkar's 'four attitudes' express your stance? What do you think are its strengths, and the shortcomings of the others?

'The tolerance you have is directly proportional to the myth you live and inversely proportional to the ideology you follow' (Panikkar).[9] How do you interpret this, and do you agree?

In the quotations in the textbox on pp. 10–12, do you think Ramadan and Sacks are saying the same thing, but to different audiences? Or do you think the points they are trying to make are quite different?

Further reading

Barnes, Michael (2002) *Theology and the Dialogue of Religions*, Cambridge, Cambridge University Press

Fitzgerald, T. (2000) *The Ideology of Religious Studies*, Oxford and New York, Oxford University Press

Hick, John (2004) *An Interpretation of Religion*, 2nd edn, Basingstoke, Macmillan

Panikkar, R. (1984) *The Intrareligious Dialogue*, New York, Paulist Press

Ramadan, T. (2004) *Western Muslims and the Future of Islam*, Oxford, Oxford University Press

Sacks, J. (2002) *The Dignity of Difference: How to Avoid the Clash of Civilizations*, London and New York, Continuum

Notes

1 See 'Religion: A Western Invention?', in H. Haring, J. M. Soskice and F. Wilfred (eds) (2003) *Learning from Other Faiths*, Concilium, London, SCM Press.

2 G. Griffith-Dickson (2000) *Human and Divine: An Introduction to the Philosophy of Religious Experience*, London, Duckworth.

3 T. Fitzgerald (2000) *The Ideology of Religious Studies*, Oxford and New York, Oxford University Press, p. 10.

4 C. F. Davis (1989) *The Evidential Force of Religious Experience*, Oxford, Clarendon Press, pp. 171f.

5 R. Panikkar (1984) *The Intrareligious Dialogue*, New York, Paulist Press.

6 Fitzgerald, *The Ideology of Religious Studies*, pp. 31–2.

7 T. Ramadan (2004) *Western Muslims and the Future of Islam*, Oxford, Oxford University Press, pp. 202–3.

8 J. Sacks (2002) *The Dignity of Difference: How to Avoid the Clash of Civilizations*, London and New York, Continuum, pp. 52–3, 54, 56.

9 R. Panikkar (1979) *Myth, Faith and Hermeneutics*, New York, Paulist Press, pp. 20f.

2

Ways of Thinking About Religion

Interfaith dialogue in the Middle Ages?

Julius (Yitzhak) Guttmann, writing an epic history of Jewish philosophy, records some of the seismic events of the early Middle Ages, when Judaism and young Islam occupied the same geographical territory and engaged with one another in both friendly and polemic ways. The debates encompassed Christianity, and with the spread of Islam to the East, the dualist system of the Parsees and the very different religious thinking of India. In particular this episode, in the tenth century, is rather eye-catching:

> The clash of the great religions and discord between the sects severely shook the naïve faith in religious authority. Within the ever-widening religious horizon, the rival religions were all seen on one level, and the opposing claims to exclusive truth seemed to cancel one another. Symptomatic of this mode of thought is the development in Islamic literature of the interest in comparative religion. Religion itself was made an object of theoretical inquiry, and the rich variety of its manifestations became a matter of scientific description and classification. This latent emancipation from naïve faith in authority appears quite explicitly, most impressively perhaps in the well-known report from the end of the tenth century on the friendly discussions concerning religion held in Baghdad between members of various religions. The participants agreed upon absolute tolerance toward one another; when their various faiths were being discussed, any dogmatic appeal to authority was ruled out. The only source upon which one could rely in the search for the true religion was the 'human intellect'. Reason, instead of authority, thus became the criterion for religious truth. We find the same mode of thought in a philosophic circle that flourished in Baghdad during this period and which was composed of adherents of different religions, including two Jews who, we are told, were very highly esteemed. In the discussions of this group, the question was raised whether philosophy could decide in favour of one of the com-

> peting faiths, or whether it permitted every individual philosopher to follow the faith in which he was nurtured. The answer has unfortunately not been preserved, but the very posing of the question is indicative of the spirit of the group.

(How frustrating that the answer has escaped us! But perhaps there wasn't one. Guttmann goes on:)

> This new rationalism was in many cases definitely antagonistic to religion. Participants in the above-mentioned philosophic discussion included 'materialists', and the polemics of Islamic and Jewish scholars mention the Dahriya, a sect which denied the existence of a divine Being, as taking part in the disputations. There were also religious rationalists who denied all positive revelation . . . Next to the radical denial of all revealed religion, we find the relativistic notion of the equal value of the various faiths. According to this view, every man should follow some one religion, for without religion no moral life is possible. The essence of religions is in their common ethical demands; this is attested both by the area of agreement between the positive religions and by rational evidence. Compared to the common rational core of the positive religions, their differences are relatively insignificant; the idea of their equal value was expressed by the disappearance of conversion from one religion to another, as well as by the rule of the Baghdad circle that every man should follow the religion given to him by God.[1]

It seems there is nothing new under the sun, especially in religion. What this little anecdote shows, in addition to the existence of something like twentieth-century theses of 'pluralism', is the reason why some in the West have chosen to uphold the demands of 'reason' over the demands of 'faith' in discussions of religion: it makes it possible (allegedly) to have a polite conversation and create an area of intellectual common ground, where creeds differ and may divide.

Note, however, that in this Baghdad circle the human intellect was not opposed to 'faith', but to religious authority. Notions of 'faith' are not identical in different religious or philosophical cultures. The notion that 'faith' is in sharp contrast (or even opposition) to 'knowledge' is a Western notion particularly sharpened by the Enlightenment; but it applies neither to concepts of faith nor of knowledge in Islam.

Wilfred Cantwell Smith offers an analysis of the meaning of the word īmān *(usually translated as 'faith') in Islam. In particular, it is often written that 'īmān' is 'taṣdīq'.* Taṣdīq *has often been understood as belief or believing, in particular since the Arabic logicians used it to denote making an intellectual judgement. But Smith argues that* taṣdīq *is better understood as 'recognize the truth of'. This has interesting implications for the concept of faith, if* īmān *is* taṣdīq.

> *To begin with, faith is then the* recognition *of divine truth at the personal level. Faith is the ability to recognize truth as true for oneself, and to trust it. Especially in the Islamic case, with its primarily moral orientation, this includes, or makes primary, the recognition of the authenticity and moral authority of the divine commands. Thus there is the recognition of the obligatoriness as applying to oneself, with the personal commitment then to carrying them out.*
>
> *Again: it is the personal making of what is cosmically true come true on earth: the* actualization *of truth. . . .*
>
> *More mystically, it is the discovery of the truth (the personal truth) of the Islamic injunctions: the process of personal verification of them, whereby, by living them out, one proves them and finds that they do indeed become true, both for oneself and for the society and the world in which one lives.*
>
> Taṣdīq *is the inner appropriation and outward implementation of truth: the process of making or finding true in actual human life, in one's own personal spirit and overt behavior, what God – or Reality – intends for man.*
>
> *And, with many a passage strongly insisting that faith is more than knowledge, that it is a question of how one responds to the truth, one may also render the proposition 'faith is* taṣdīq*' as 'Faith is the ability to trust, and to act in terms of, what one knows to be true.'*[2]

If this is a plausible understanding of the Islamic conceptions, it means that faith is in no way opposed to knowledge (or to reason). Faith is the personal response to knowledge. A simplistic 'faith vs. reason' opposition then would not apply in Islamic thought in the same way as has been suggested within Christianity.

'Faith' and 'reason' have often been used as labels for some perceived difference between whatever it is that philosophy is meant to be doing, and what it is not claiming to do. As a slogan for philosophical endeavour, however, it is at the mercy of the more fundamental question of what it is that philosophy is meant to be doing.

In this chapter we will explore the question of what philosophic discussion of religion might consist in.

Messy diversity?

> If someone were to collect all the 'isms' that have been called philosophy in Europe and America and list all their definitions, one would see that they have nothing in common except that they are not science.[3]

If Ayatullah Muṭahharī's perceptions of Western philosophy are accurate, then the prospects of having a clear answer to the question 'What is philosophy?' are not much more optimistic than they were for 'What is religion?'

On one (Western) version of the story, philosophy of religion and theology are dealing with the same subject matter, but using different methods. Philosophy of religion is doing something, such as talking about God, with one set of analytical tools and materials like logic, deduction; while theology uses another set of methods and materials: the Bible, church authority and tradition. In other words, one view is that philosophy of religion is doing something similar to theology, but doing it in a different way. Another view is that philosophy of religion is doing something different to theology. Thus, it might be using reason whereas religion or theology are matters of faith, or are dealing with 'revelation' or 'revealed truths', which philosophy is not. 'Revelation' and 'reason' are sometimes used to refer to different bodies of knowledge: one known by reason and accessible to anyone, and one known only by faith, accessible only by divine revelation.

One viewpoint is to say that philosophy of religion provides a rational ground for belief, or a foundation for belief or faith. One can see the task of philosophy as assessing claims, and the task of philosophy of religion is to assess religious claims. Anselm's famous description of his project, 'faith seeking understanding', is another formula that is often used. This implies that philosophy consists of a kind of 'unpacking' or clarifying what is held in faith. Quite another viewpoint might suggest that philosophy is not providing a foundation for theology which it shares unchanged with physics, for example, and archaeology, or a 'rational ground' for anything. Philosophy is a history of people who have thought about the same or similar problems and taken the trouble to leave us a record of their results; people whose mistakes and insights we can learn from when we confront the same questions.

One view on what philosophy is like, from Keith Yandell:

> *I take religious claims to be neither more nor less open to rational assessment than any other sorts of claims. Any difference there is concerns difficulty, not possibility. Nor do I see any reason to think that offering rational assessment of religious claims is in principle harder than, say, assessing attempts to offer a unified theory for all of physics, or to solve the problems of the foundations of modal logic. Contrary to the preferences of some philosophers, some Religious Studies professors, and even some religious thinkers themselves, religious traditions do make claims. They are anything remotely like what they claim to be only if what they say is true.*

Metaphysics, epistemology, and ethics are disciplines within philosophy. Metaphysics is the enterprise of constructing and assessing accounts of what there is. Epistemology is the enterprise of constructing and assessing accounts of what knowledge is and how it can be attained. Ethics is the enterprise of constructing and assessing accounts of what makes actions right or wrong, what makes persons good or evil, what possesses intrinsic worth, what sort of life is worth living, and how these matters are related. Philosophy of religion combines these enterprises in offering philosophically accessible accounts of religious traditions and assessing those traditions. Nothing very complex is involved in offering philosophically accessible accounts of religious traditions; the idea is simply to offer clear and literal expressions of key doctrines.[4]

So while there is a problem over defining 'religion', as we saw in the last chapter, there are also some issues about what 'philosophy' is or how it is to be practised. When philosophers deal with religion, therefore, the nature of their work will differ according to their conception of what philosophy is and what one is doing in 'doing philosophy'.

One dominant approach in the English-speaking world is usually called 'analytic philosophy', which sets itself over against what it describes as 'continental' philosophy (meaning Continental Europe, thinking only in the perspective of the Western world). While these two styles claim to be dealing with the same subject, such as language, the writing they produce is not merely different – they read each other with mutual incomprehension. Meanwhile, there is a feminist practice of philosophy, and also different regions in the world where something you might call philosophy is practised. Thinkers in India over the centuries have also dealt with philosophical problems around knowledge, language and the principles of logic. Their deliberations are different to Western logic, and both differ from traditional Arabic logic. There is Chinese and African philosophy. Within different religions there are those who have engaged in philosophical reflection on the problems that rise from looking at their own beliefs and, as the religions vary, we would expect this to produce substantial differences in their thinking.

There are also differences coming from past periods of history in which philosophy had been undertaken. You might not think this matters in the present, but some of those styles can still be found today, either because they had not entirely died out, or because they have been rediscovered and re-elaborated. Medieval scholastic philosophy, for example, has a *modus operandi* that has continued in use here and there in the Catholic tradition, and which interestingly has a certain affinity with analytic philosophers. Hume's style of deconstruction is still practised by British analytic philosophers, so much so that it has been said that until Russell, two hundred years of British philosophy consisted mainly of footnotes to Hume. Of course books on philosophy of religion also show differences in how much they engage with this history or how much they simply present arguments with their objections, counter-arguments, strengths and weaknesses, without the context of history and its cast of characters. If philosophy of religion consists only in assessing religious claims, do you need to know the history of those claims in order to assess them?

Another view on what philosophy is like

The American philosopher Richard Rorty has divided philosophers into two categories, the 'systematic' (he names Descartes, Kant, Russell, Husserl) and the 'edifying' (Kierkegaard, Nietzsche, later Wittgenstein and later Heidegger – I would add to this category Hamann, Feuerbach and Ebner):

> *Great systematic philosophers are constructive and offer arguments. Great edifying philosophers are reactive and offer satires, parodies, aphorisms. They know their work loses its point when the period they were reacting against is over. They are* intentionally *peripheral. Great systematic philosophers, like great scientists, build for eternity. Great edifying philosophers destroy for the sake of their own generation. Systematic philosophers want to put their subject on the secure path of a science. Edifying philosophers want to keep space open for the sense of wonder which poets can sometimes cause – wonder that there is something new under the sun, something which is* not *an accurate representation of what was already there, something which (at least for the moment) cannot be explained and can barely be described.*[5]

Even restricting consideration to English-speaking philosophy of religion as it is practised in the United States of America, there can be a distinct cultural difference between two American approaches to philosophy of religion. Some have perceived a division between two fundamentally different styles, and have tidied these down to a distinction between philosophers who belong to the American Philosophical Association (APA) and those who belong to the American Academy of Religion (AAR). This is seen to coincide with a difference between those who work in departments of philosophy vs. those who work in religious studies departments, between those whose approach is 'analytic' vs. those who take a 'hermeneutic' or 'continental' line. There is, in fact, a whole book devoted to laying out this division.

What American philosophers say about their 'styles'

Philosophers of religion whose primary affiliation is with the APA are more likely to identify themselves as analytic philosophers in the Anglo-American tradition, and those in the AAR as hermeneutic philosophers in the continental tradition, though that dichotomy has diminished in the past several decades. Members of each group often view the other as uncritical and naïve, but the content of that criticism differs in the two cases. APA philosophers view those in the AAR as insufficiently rigorous in logic and argumentation, while those in the AAR view their counterparts as insufficiently historical. . . . Philosophers in the APA are more likely to be interested in the problems of traditional theism, and those in the AAR in religion as a social and cultural phenomenon, as well as in problems of comparative religion.[6]

Analytic philosophers have been influenced by a tradition that in [the twentieth] century goes back to Moore and Russell; they prize such intellectual virtues as expository clarity and argumentative rigour; and they make use of techniques of philosophical analysis in their work. . . . [The] group includes Marilyn Adams, Robert Adams, William Alston, William Hasker, Peter van Inwagen, Norman Kretzmann, George Mavrodes, Alvin Plantinga, James Ross, Eleanor Stump, William Wainwright, Edward Wierenga, Nicholas Wolsterstorff and Linda Zagzebski, among others. These Christian philosophers are engaged in the traditional enterprise characterized as faith seeking understanding. Some of them would prefer describing what they do as philosophical theology to describing it as philosophy of religion.[7]

The revival of philosophical theology within analytic philosophy has been accompanied by some interesting developments in the ways in which analytic philosophers of religion respond to the history of philosophy. Analytic philosophers tend to view their predecessors as interlocutors rather than as museum pieces; they will tell one with a tone of pride that they are not mere historians of ideas. They find conversation partners among the medievals and modern philosophers before Kant. After all, such philosophers were, for the most part, theists of a traditional sort themselves; they valued clarity and rigor; and they employed many of the techniques of philosophical analysis in their work.[8]

*Practitioners of our field in departments of religious studies [i.e. 'AAR'] today tend, with some exceptions, to be nourished by the continental schools, by Kant and Hegel, Marx and Kierkegaard and Nietzsche, Hiedegger and Gadamer and Merleau-Ponty, and in some quarters even by the frivolous post-modernist French (*hélas!*). . . . The continental schools have had a broadly humanistic orientation, a*

> *tradition of cultural engagement, hermeneutic and criticism, well adapted to philosophical studies in the human practice of religion. Very technical, formal issues are certainly addressed in this tradition, but they bear fairly directly on existential concerns regarding conditions for the good life.*[9]

These two 'personality types' do not exhaust the possibilities, even in the English-speaking world – although they do dominate the syllabuses and the reading lists. You will also, if you are lucky or adventurous, come across books written with a careful attention to scholarly detail, and an extraordinary, encyclopaedic knowledge of thinkers, movements, ideas, eras. These are philosophers who verge on the discipline of 'history of ideas', because of their breadth of knowledge and reference. There is nothing 'mere' about such historical philosophers and they do have a profound critical grasp of the philosophical issues. Examples in the English-speaking world would be Harry Wolfson or Richard Sorabji. (They may not feature on the typical undergraduate reading list.) Meanwhile, some thinkers engaged with the familiar topics of philosophy of religion, like language or the nature of God, occupy a flank on the borders of philosophy and theology, and may sometimes designate themselves as philosophical theologians; examples would be David Burrell or Janet Soskice.

Before the present 'analytic' and 'continental' divide on philosophic styles, Europe had experienced two other divisions, the first in different ways of viewing religious truth and belief introduced by the Reformation. Then came the Enlightenment split between 'rationalist' and 'empiricist' tendencies, the first hoping to deduce all knowledge logically or 'rationally' and the second concerned entirely with what can be learned from experience.

Throughout the nineteenth century and into the twentieth, different streams flowed forward within philosophy in Europe: a speculative rationalism verging on idealism from Hegel and those who were pulled into his slipstream (and they were not only in Germany). Another was the development of the contrasting empiricism given new momentum by the advances in natural science. A third came from the new developments in logic based on the work first of Gottlob Frege and thereafter by Bertrand Russell in the twentieth century. A fourth was an increasing interest in the problems of interpretation and philosophy of language, partly developed by a new academic approach to biblical studies, as well as the contributions of thinkers like Johann Georg Hamann; this was taken forward by philosophers such as Friedrich Schleiermacher and Wilhelm Dilthey. These divergent streams have created the present delta in Euro-American philosophy, of which the APA–AAR difference is only one aspect.

Other religious traditions have their distinctions within the philosophical styles and movements. The twentieth-century Iranian Shi'a scholar Murtaḍā Muṭahharī formalizes a traditional classification of Islamic philosophers. Bear in mind that this is distinctively Shi'a; many traditions in Sunni Islam would be suspicious or even hostile to both 'deduction' and 'illumination', just as some Christian denominations can be hostile both to philosophy and 'reason', and to 'mysticism'.

Muṭahharī divides Islamic philosophers into the 'illuminationists' and the 'peripateticists'. The latter are in the lineage of Aristotle, and the former, supposedly of Plato; although Muṭahharī is rightly cautious about the validity of attributing many of the Islamic 'illuminationists' views backward to Plato; and the questions on which they chiefly differ have more to do with Islam than real differences between Plato and Aristotle.

What this immediately tells you is that Islamic philosophy was powerfully stamped by Greek pagan philosophy. Aristotle was one great influence, and the other was Neoplatonism, the post-Platonic scheme developed by Plotinus, Porphyry and Proclus, and which was a major framework of thought and belief at the time of Islam's birth and early intellectual development. One area of contrast between these views can be seen in the notion of God, or more specifically in God's relation to the world. Unlike the Qur'ānic and biblical picture of a freely creating transcendent God, Aristotle theorized an Unmoved First Mover, who acts to give form to pre-existing eternal matter. Meanwhile, the One of Neoplatonism gives rise to the world we see by a complex, staged sequence of emanations. (See Chapter 4 for more discussion of these issues.) These pictures of what is ultimate condition philosophers' views of reality (or metaphysics), knowledge (or epistemology) and so on. To combine the thought of Aristotle or of the Neoplatonists with Islamic revelation in the Qur'ān is an interesting challenge – a challenge faced in a similar way, for biblical revelation, by Christians and Jews in their Neoplatonic movements. Neoplatonic thinking is characterized by this rather dreamy (or rather alarming, depending on your views) taste for metaphysical speculation and uplifting prose; while Aristotle is characterized by a this-world focus and rigorous and clear argument. Somewhat confusingly, Neoplatonic thinking was taken up by Muslim thinkers under false disguise in their respect for Aristotle: a 'greatest hits' version of extracts of Plotinus' *Enneads* was known in the Arab world as *The Theology of Aristotle*.[10] Whether Aristotle would have been grossly offended or amused by the irony I cannot say.

Neoplatonism was to a certain extent 'outgrown' in Islam – viewed as decisively refuted by al-Ghazālī in his attack on 'the philosophers' (see below). The movement referred to by Muṭahharī therefore as 'illuminationist' is not necessarily out-and-out Neoplatonist, especially in its scheme of emanation, but nevertheless imbibes some of the spirit both of Plotinus and of Plato:

> The principal and essential difference between the two methods is that the illuminationists consider deduction and rational thought insufficient for study of philosophical questions, especially of divine wisdom, and the path of the heart, asceticism and purification of the soul as incumbent on anyone wishing to realize inner realities. Peripatetics rely solely on deduction.[11]

Illuminationists include Shihāb ad-Dīn Suhrawardī and Qutb ad-Dīn Shīrāzī. They use rational deduction and argument, but believe that one cannot understand the deepest realities by these means alone; purification of oneself is also necessary. The great French interpreter Henri Corbin chose to call the tradition of Suhrawardī and Mullā Ṣadrā 'theosophie' to reflect this slant. Historically, most Muslim philosophers however have been among the 'peripatetic' followers of Aristotle, such as al-Kindī, al-Fārābī, Ibn Sīnā, Ṭūsī, Ibn Rushd, and Ibn Baja.

Other schools of thought include *'irfān* (gnosis) and *kalām* (scholastic theology); and though they were opposed to both the illuminationists and the peripatetics, their debates helped to shape Islamic philosophy. *'Irfān*, the mystical or Sufi tradition, attains knowledge of God and truth by self-purification and the journey to God. 'The method of *'irfān* places no confidence at all in rational deduction. The *'urafā'** say that the deductionists stand on wooden legs. According to the method of *'irfān*, the goal is not just to uncover reality, but to reach it'[12] (**'urafā'* is 'those who know', as it were; practitioners of *'irfān*; singular *'arif*).

Kalām is further divided into schools or 'methods' as Muṭahharī considers them; the Mu'tazilites, the Ash'arites and the Shiites (see Glossary). While the *mutakallimūn* also use rational deduction, their object is the articulation and defence of Islam, whereas philosophers, according to Muṭahharī, are free and do not have 'the predetermined object of defending a particular belief'.[13]

Some Muslims, like some Christians with Christianity, find philosophy deeply inimical to Islam. Others, often in the Shi'a tradition, see the two in harmony:

> *A philosophical tradition is part and parcel of the intellectual universe of a civilization and shares its general features. The development of philosophical thought in the Islamic world occurred in the context of a religious tradition whose intellectual character was determined to a large extent by the contents of the Qur'ānic revelation and the prophetic teachings. However, philosophical thought is by nature independent of religious doctrine and differs from theology (*kalām*), which depends on revelation and tradition. A salient feature of the Islamic intellectual tradition has been the conviction that there can*

be no conflict between faith and reason, or, as they say, between Qur'ān, burhān *and* 'irfān, *that is, between revelation, reason, and mystical intuition. Philosophical thought in the Islamic world has never faced the kind of crisis that occurred in the Western world due to the contrary demands imposed by reason and faith. In the course of its development, philosophical thought in the Islamic world has been in deep harmony with religion while seeking to find a solid rational foundation for metaphysical solutions.*

*An overview of the development of theological thought (*kalām*), philosophy, and theoretical* 'irfān *reveals some interesting features. In the course of its effort to develop a sound conceptual foundation for its discourses and debates,* kalām *has become more and more philosophical. Theoretical* 'irfān *– since Ṣadr al-Dīn Qūnawī, and in the writings of his disciples – also became more philosophical in the effort of the great mystics to bring their teachings to a larger audience through expositions couched in a language familiar to philosophers and students of philosophy. Meanwhile, philosophy itself – perhaps as the result of the writings of the proponents of theoretical* 'irfān *– has taken long strides towards* 'irfān *in the thought of Sadr al-Muta'allihīn, who sought to establish the findings of* 'irfān *on sound rational foundations. As contemporary philosophy in Iran stands, the discourses of Muslim philosophers may be said to constitute a passage to the higher teachings of theoretical* 'irfān, *which may be regarded as a meta-philosophy.*[14]

Philosophy as practised by Jewish thinkers has taken place firmly and somewhat exclusively within the bounds of Jewish discourse, but Jewish thinkers have also been powerful contributors to what we are calling here 'Western' philosophy. The latter therefore should by no means be considered as purely Christian. Some thinkers who happened to be Jewish were not consciously working from within their tradition (particularly if, like Marx or Freud, they were atheists). Others, like Moses Mendelssohn or Hermann Cohen, saw their work as a specific engagement with the philosophy of the day, in order to create either a philosophy of Judaism or a sympathetic presentation of Judaism to a *goyische* philosophical audience. Jewish thinkers, in large part because of the particular situation Diaspora Jews have usually found themselves in, have tended more than Muslim thinkers to engage with the philosophy of their social or cultural context and either adopt, adapt or oppose it in relation to their texts, faith and way of life.

Julius Guttmann on the history of Jewish philosophy

The Jewish people did not begin to philosophize because of an irresistible urge to do so. They received philosophy from outside sources, and the history of Jewish philosophy is a history of successive absorptions of foreign ideas which were then transformed and adapted according to specific Jewish points of view.

Such a process first took place during the Hellenistic period. Judaeo-Hellenistic philosophy is so thoroughly imbued with Greek spirit, however, that it may be regarded, historically speaking, as merely a chapter in the development of Greek thought as a whole. It disappeared quickly without leaving behind any permanent impact upon Judaism.

Philosophy penetrated Jewish intellectual life a second time in the Middle Ages. It was Greek philosophy at second hand, for the philosophic revival took place within the orbit of Islamic culture and was heavily indebted to Islamic philosophy, which, in turn, derived from Greek systems of thought. This time, however, the vitality of Jewish philosophy proved stronger than during the Hellenistic period. It persisted from the ninth century to the end of the Middle Ages, and some traces of it are still discernable as late as the middle of the seventeenth century. Nonetheless, it is true to say that throughout this time, Jewish philosophy remained closely bound to the non-Jewish sources from which from which it originated.

After Judaism had entered the intellectual world of modern Europe, modern Jewish thought remained indebted to contemporary trends of European philosophy. This applies not only to the contribution of Jewish thinkers to the philosophic labors of the European nations, but also to those systems of thought specifically concerned with the interpretation and justification of the Jewish religion. The former has its place in the general history of modern philosophy; its dependence on contemporary thought is consequently a truism. But even Jewish philosophy in the specific and narrow sense of the term, like its Christian counterpart, operated within the framework, the methods, and the conceptual apparatus of modern European philosophy.

The peculiar character of a Jewish existence in the Diaspora prevented the emergence of a Jewish philosophy in the sense in which we can speak of Greek, Roman, French or German philosophy. Since the days of antiquity, Jewish philosophy was essentially a philosophy of Judaism. Even during the Middle Ages . . . philosophy rarely transcended its religious center. This religious orientation constitutes the distinctive character of Jewish philosophy, whether it was concerned with using philosophic ideas to establish or justify Jewish doctrines, or with reconciling the contradictions between religious truth and scientific truth. It is religious philosophy in a sense peculiar to the monotheistic revealed religions which, because of their claim to truth and by virtue of their spiritual depth, could confront philosophy as an autonomous spiritual power.

Armed with the authority of a supernatural revelation, religion lays claim to an unconditioned truth of its own, and thereby becomes a problem for philosophy. In order to determine the relationships between these two types of truth, philosophers have tried to clarify, from a methodological point of view, the distinctiveness of religion. This is a modern development; earlier periods did not attempt to differentiate between the methods of philosophy and religion, but sought to reconcile the contents of their teachings. Philosophy was thus made subservient to religion; and philosophical material borrowed from the outside was treated accordingly. In this respect the philosophy of Judaism, whatever the differences in content deriving from the specific doctrines and the concepts of authority of the religions concerned, is formally similar to that of Christianity and of Islam. Appearing for the first time in Jewish Hellenism, this type of philosophy, though not productive of original ideas, nevertheless proved of far-reaching significance and influence. From Jewish Hellenism it passed to Christianity, was transmitted to Islam, from whence it returned, in the Middle Ages, to Judaism.[15]

Philo is the great thinker of the Jewish Hellenism to which Guttmann refers. Living at approximately the time of Christ in Alexandria, Egypt, he absorbed the Greek philosophy of Plato and the Stoics. His work is a philosophical reflection on the Hebrew Scriptures. As Wolfson observes, Philo's works are 'on the one hand, an attempt to interpret the scriptural teachings in terms of Greek philosophy and, on the other, an attempt to revise Greek philosophy in the light of those scriptural traditions.'[16]

Philosophy in Judaism was quiescent after the Hellenistic period, with the centre of intellectual gravity in Talmudic Judaism. The next great flowering of philosophic endeavour arose again some 800 years after Philo, with the rise of Islamic philosophy; this continued until the end of the Middle Ages. Despite what you may assume about philosophy vs. spirituality, in this period of Jewish philosophy, it was widely influential even on aspects of spiritual life, as Guttmann claims:

> This central position of philosophy was not merely a theoretical program, but actually shaped the reality of spiritual life. All areas of religious literature were influenced by philosophy. Biblical exegesis searched for the deeper sense of the Bible in a philosophic spirit; religious poetry echoes the ideas of philosophy, and the philosophic preachers of the later Middle Ages sought to spread its ideas among the faithful.[17]

The womb of this development was Islamic philosophy, and kalām in particular.[18] The Jewish thinkers were much more closely engaged with their Islamic than with their Christian counterparts. The reasons for this were partly geographical – a shared home in the regions of the Middle

East – and partly linguistic, for Arabic was the mother tongue or lingua franca for many Middle Eastern Jews, while Latin, the scholarly language of Western Christians, was known by few. Thus it is that some scholars can refer to certain Jewish philosophers of the Middle Ages as part of 'Arabic philosophy' without batting an eye. Of course the philosophical framework which the Jews took on from the Muslims was Greek and pagan! Naturally, despite this intimacy of intellect, the motivations that drove both Islam and Judaism into philosophy in this period were often polemical, in seeking a common ground of philosophy in which to prove the other wrong.

Nearly 900 years after Philo, his fellow Egyptian Saadia ben Joseph Gaon was the next great name in Jewish philosophy, but in this entirely new religious context which contact with Islam and Christianity brought. He absorbed the influences of Plato and Aristotle as well as *kalām*, but in the service of a systematic philosophical treatment of Judaism. His desire to defend Judaism in his multi-faith milieu is shown in his refutations of Zoroastrian dualism, the Christian Trinity, and the Muslim view of biblical revelation, as well as rationalist attacks on religious revealed doctrines. A groundbreaker of Jewish philosophy, he engaged with many of the topics we shall investigate in this book, such as God's omniscience or the problem of evil and providence.

With Saadia, the influences of Greek philosophy were still firmly bedded into a theological context and a Jewish religious framework. The next milestone in Jewish philosophy comes with the thinkers who absorbed much more of the Neoplatonist framework, as opposed to borrowing Greek ideas, arguments and insights. Thus in a thinker such as Isaac Israeli, biblical doctrines of creation can be combined with a Neoplatonist scheme of emanation issuing from the One. (For more on this scheme, see Chapter 4.) Other thinkers moving in this orbit, if not all card-carrying Neoplatonists, are Solomon Ibn Gabirol, Baḥya ibn Pakuda and Joseph Ibn Saddiq. In his own category is Judah Halevi, who occurs at this juncture historically but whom we will look at later.

The other powerful dynamism in Jewish thought in the medieval period was Aristotelianism, which tended to replace Neoplatonism from the twelfth century onward. It is in this thought-world that we find Abraham ibn Daud, but also arguably the greatest of the Jewish medieval philosophers, Rabbi Moses ben Maimon or Maimonides, nicknamed the Rambam,[19] originally of Cordoba in Spain in the twelfth century. The Rambam's real greatness is shown in the fact that his thought not only dominated the Middle Ages among Jewish thinkers, but was also highly influential on the philosophies of other faiths, as the references to his work in Thomas Aquinas show. Like Aquinas, his greatness does not lie so much in originality but in a brilliance of analysis, and a genius for synthesis – in the Rambam's case, a blending of Aristotelianism, the Jewish and Muslim critiques of Aristotle, and biblical exegesis. Other thinkers of note following in his wake in this period are Levi ben Gerson or Gersonides and Hasdai Crescas. Crescas brings to a close the era of medieval Jewish philosophy.

Philosophy in Judaism is born again in the Western, largely Christian thought-world of the Enlightenment, with thinkers such as Baruch (Benedict) Spinoza in Holland and Moses Mendelssohn of Prussia. Both of these thinkers were thoroughly suffused with the dominant cultural philosophy of their time, and responded – even on questions about God – to the general philosophical problems of their time, rather than articulating a philosophical account of Judaism. They are truly European philosophers, whose contributions are part of a broader Western tradition. The same could be said for the Neo-Kantian philosophers such as Hermann Cohen. In some contrast, German-speaking thinkers such as Franz Rosenzweig and Martin Buber in the early twentieth century speak to two traditions: on the one hand, an emerging philosophy of person and dialogue that developed from Johan Georg Hamann and Friedrich Jacobi from the eighteenth century, and at the same time contributing to the development of distinctively Jewish thinking. In the same way, Emmanuel Levinas both drew from and contributed to powerful non-religious currents of twentieth-century French thought while remaining profoundly affected by, and affecting profoundly, Jewish experience and thinking.

While the philosophies we have been considering have roots in the same 'Abrahamic' traditions, further afield, India is rich in different schools of systematic thought. As Jose Pereira observes:

> Hindu, Buddhist and Jain thought is a theology concerned with clarifying, with maximum critical rigour, insights supersensibly guaranteed – either by a Revelation (personally or impersonally originant) or by the vision and authority of an enlightened sage. These insights originate in the Vedas – in the minds of those seers whom we may call the Fathers of Hindu Theology, indeed, the Fathers of Theology – and in the Tantras. Combinable indefinitely these insights disclose new meanings with every new combination, and thus constantly generate new systems. And Indic thought is remarkably fertile in theologies.[20]

In contrast to Christianity, Judaism, or Islam, in their differing ways, there is in Indian religion neither a single authority figure or a single text, nor a force for the unification of thought and teaching. This means that the Indian religions have generated, over the centuries, much more diverse, numerous, and fundamentally contrasting schools of thought, belief and practice.

The first fundamental distinction could be made between Vedic and non-Vedic systems; those that follow the Vedas, scriptures that we in the West call 'Hindu': these are the Ṛg, Sāma, Yajur and Atharva Veda. Tantric traditions follow the Tantras, and are mystical in character. Non-Vedic traditions include Jains and Buddhists.

Six orthodox schools of philosophy are commonly identified, not all of them theistic (believing in God). They are the earlier systems of 'Hindu' thought, predating some of the Vedāntic and Tantric systems. They provide much of the intellectual furnishing for later schools of thought and practice. Aspects of their philosophies will be unfolded in later chapters (consult the Glossary as well).

Sāṃkhya. Sāṃkhya does not believe in a god, but does believe in the reality of spirit, one of two fundamental realities – the other is matter. The world has no beginning or end; it has its origins in an uncaused cause, and it continues to unfold and develop. Knowledge is derived from experience, inference (from effect, cause and analogy) and testimony.

Yoga. The partner to Sāṃkhya, it uses the same philosophical system but is theistic. This God is not the creator of the universe but is co-eternal with matter and spirit. It involves mystical practice.

Mīmāṃsā. Another non-theistic branch of Hinduism, it evolved from the Vedic literature and emphasizes ritual practice. Knowledge derives from experience and testimony, and the truth of the scriptures is self-evident. Mīmāṃsā thinkers were sharp critics both of theistic strands of 'Hinduism' and of the Buddhists.

Nyāya. A strong logical school – one of its great thinkers, Vātsyayāna, advocated liberation through logic. It is strongly theistic, believing in a single God, the source of revelation. It uses arguments for the existence of God, and in this area engaged in sharp debates with Buddhism on this subject.

Vaiśeṣika. Closely related to the Nyāya school, the 'atomist' thinking of the Vaiśeṣikas sees reality as composed of eternal, unchanging particles that are not created but are rearranged by a Mind (God).

Vedānta is more complex. Here we must consider different streams. 'Hindu' traditions are often distinguished by an elemental metaphysical question, which gives rise to a distinction between three fundamental approaches.

A fundamental question in Indian metaphysics

Metaphysically, *it may be stated thus: Is reality one or many? We perceive a multitude of things, but, at the same time, our minds are incorrigibly given to conceiving them in unitary fashion, as, say, 'being,' 'reality' or 'existence.' Which of these are real and which unreal – our plural perception our unitary conception, or both? In other words, which is real and which unreal – Difference or Identity, or both?*

To this question three basic answers have traditionally been given, and from them our three basic types of theology have arisen:

Difference is real, Identity unreal: the theologies of Difference.
Identity is real, Difference unreal: the theologies of Identity
Both are real: the theologies of Difference-in-Identity.[21]

(The issue of difference and identity is discussed in Chapter 5. See the Glossary for lists of thinkers and schools for each of these categories.)

Vedānta thus divides into three schools along these lines: Non-dualist, Qualified non-dualist (or Difference-in-identity as Pereira calls it), and Dualist.

The Non-dualist school, or Advaita Vedānta, is best exemplified by the great thinker Śaṇkara. Its fundamental intuition is that all reality is one; this One is Brahman, pure consciousness, the Self (and the self of all of us). Its challenge is to explain the multiplicity and difference that we perceive, and the source of our apparent error in perceiving it.

Mādhva is a proponent of Dualist (Dvaita) Vedānta. In contrast to Advaita Vedānta, he maintains the difference is real, and we, individual selves and the world, are different from God. Things can be known as they are – his epistemology is realist in flavour in comparison with Śaṇkara's – and they can be reliably known by sense perception, inference and the scriptures.

The rather nuanced stance in between these two is taken by Rāmānuja. While he agrees with Śaṇkara that the absolute has the nature of consciousness, and is foundation of all, he begs to differ on the nature of Being: Rāmānuja considers it to be personal, unlike Śaṇkara. Our individual existence is not illusory but real; liberation involves a gain of knowledge and bliss. Brahman is not 'bare identity' but personal, for an absolute with no qualities and no feeling, thought or will, doesn't meet our deepest needs, especially for fellowship and communion with an Other.

To Rāmānuja, then, God is a person, and because he is a person, he is the unifying principle that brings all things together, not into a featureless but organic unity. In such a unity we have an ordered system of relations in which the relations are not all of the same type nor the relata all of the same kind. In Rāmānuja's view this is the highest kind of unity and belongs peculiarly to personality or spirit. It is in personality alone that unity comes to express itself in purpose, in works, cognition, enjoyment and freedom.[22]

Indian religion is not only a matter of logic, metaphysics, epistemology and argument. In addition to the way of knowledge, there are the followers of the way of devotion.

There are also the other schools of thought and belief that are not among the orthodox Hindu systems. These reject the authority of the Vedas, and are atheistic schools. Cārvāka or Lokāyata were materialist systems, believing only in what can be perceived by the senses. For them, spirit does not exist.

Jainism and Buddhism are two heterodox Indian systems that nevertheless might be described as 'religions', and therefore which developed philosophical thought on the topics that concern this book. Although we will not make a survey of their major themes, a few remarks will illustrate how a diversity of philosophical thinking arose with Buddhism as well.

Much of the Buddha's concern was to refute wrong views, which lead to discontent and suffering. In India, where Buddhism began and flourished from a few centuries before Christ until 1100, Buddhist philosophers constructed a holistic system of thought which integrated epistemology, metaphysics and ethics. With a central focus being the critique of Vedic ritual practices and the Vedas which enjoined them, early Buddhism emphasized the role of experience and reasoning over the authority of scriptures. This emphasis of course led Buddhist philosophers into detailed examination of logic and epistemology as key areas of Buddhist philosophical activity.

The early Buddhist scriptures written in the Pali language, the *Abhidhamma*, elaborate the doctrines of the original Buddhist texts, the *Sutta*. The dialogues of the *Sutta* are said to lead one to meditation; whereas the more philosophically technical discussions of the *Abhidhamma* lead to understanding and wisdom. This body of doctrine and thought became known as the Theravāda (the doctrine of the elders). Within a few centuries numerous schools had arisen; probably based on differences of doctrine or meditational practice. For our purposes, however, what is of note is the emergence of four greater schools of Buddhist thought: Sautrānika, Vaibhāṣika, Yogācāra and Mādhyamika schools. (See the Glossary for a brief note about these schools and the ones that follow.)

Mahāyāna Buddhism separated from Theravāda probably around 400 BC and then itself split into schools. (The reason for the split was religious, and to do with liberation: whether one strives to attain one's own liberation or labours towards nirvāṇa for all beings.) Philosophically, the

Theravādins believed in the impermanence of all things, whereas the Mahāyānists went further and believed that all things are ultimately void. Even truth is ultimately void, neither eternal nor non-eternal. Philosophically, Mahāyāna thinking developed in two directions: the Śūnyavāda or Mādhyamika school, and Vijñānavāda. The difference is largely one of method; 'while the Śūnyavādins were more busy in showing this indefinableness of all phenomena, the Vijñānavādins, tacitly accepting the truth preached by the Śūnyavādins, interested themselves in explaining the phenomena of consciousness by their theory of beginningless illusory root-ideas or instincts of the mind'.[23] Great thinkers associated with these schools were Aśvaghoṣa of the Vijñānavādins, and Nāgārjuna of the Śūnyavādins.

Surendranath Dasgupta identifies particular ontological questions on which the major schools of thought in India divided:

1. *The relation of cause and effect,*
2. *The relation of the whole and the part,*
3. *The relation of generality to the specific individuals,*
4. *The relation of attributes or qualities and the substance and the problem of the relation of inherence,*
5. *The relation of power to the power-possessor.*

Buddhism holds everything to be momentary, so neither cause nor effect can abide. One is called the effect because its momentary existence has been determined by the destruction of its momentary antecedent called the cause. There is no permanent reality which undergoes the change, but one change is determined by another and this determination is nothing more than 'that happening, this happened.' On the relation of parts to whole, Buddhism does not believe in the existence of wholes. According to it, it is the parts which illusorily appear as the whole, the individual atoms rise into being and die the next moment and thus there is no such thing as 'whole.' The Buddhists hold again that there are no universals, for it is the individuals alone which come and go. There are my five fingers as individuals but there is no such thing as fingerness as the abstract universal of the fingers. On the relation of attributes and substance we know that the Sautrānika Buddhists did not believe in the existence of any substance apart from its attributes; what we call a substance is but a unit capable of producing a unit of sensation. In the external world there are as many individual simple units (atoms) as there are points of sensations. Corresponding to each unit of sensation there is a separate simple unit in the objective world. Our perception of a thing is thus the perception of the assemblage of these sensations. In the objective world also there are no substances but atoms or reals, each representing a unit of sensation, force or attribute, rising into being and dying the next moment. Buddhism thus denies the existence of any such relation as that of inherence in which relation the attributes are said to exist in the substance, for since there are no separate substances there is no necessity for admitting the relation of inherence. Following the same logic Buddhism also does not believe in the existence of a power-possessor separate from the power.[24]

Buddhism travelled into China from missionaries from India and Central Asia, and began to interact with existing Chinese belief systems. After the first four centuries (roughly corresponding to the first four centuries AD) it was realized that much of the Buddhism that had taken root in China had mingled with Daoism and Confucianism, and a conscious attempt was made to refocus on the Indian scriptures. The development of schools parallel to the Indian schools took place until roughly the seventh century. But then the familiar pattern occurred: the generation of new schools as new challenges and new contexts came into being. Chinese Buddhism developed its own four schools – Tiantai, Huayan, Chan and Pure Land – and its own commentaries on the Buddhist scriptures. Even when there was communication from India, the developments in Indian Buddhist philosophy generally had little impact in China.

When Buddhism arrived in Japan along with other aspects of Chinese culture, it evolved yet again. Even more than the Chinese, Japanese Buddhists followed their own paths of reflection and development in relative independence from Indian Buddhism. Philosophical debate played a much less important role in Japanese Buddhism than in Indian Buddhism.

This necessarily brief and inadequate series of portraits of the diversity of philosophical reasoning in different cultures was not intended to give you a proper introduction the world's philosophies and their histories. Rather, it is meant only to serve as an illustration of the diversity of 'philosophy' that exists, even within a single religious tradition or civilization. 'Philosophy', even when engaged with religious issues, is not doing the same thing, with the same sources or methods, or dealing with the same issues. At the same time, there is considerable overlap between the religious traditions in the issues and questions they raise. If we begin to examine the idea that religious beliefs or claims are in some way in need of 'grounding', the different stances taken no longer correspond to religious differences. Rather, philosophers from different religions will line up together behind different banners.

One kind of 'grounding'

One view of what philosophy of religion does, as we saw at the beginning of the chapter, is that it sets out to ground religious beliefs and statements in rational argument. For example, Brian Davies explains:

> Philosophy can help us to see whether or not religious beliefs are worthy of acceptance . . . philosophers can single out particular religious beliefs and ask questions like 'Is this belief rationally defensible' or 'Can this belief be supported by argument or appeal to evidence?' Lying behind such questions is the assumption that religious beliefs are either true or false and that their truth or falsity can be settled or discussed at an intellectual level.[25]

In the West there has been a long history of philosophical desire and ambition: a desire for an absolute, reliable, certain and indubitable foundation for knowledge; and the ambition that philosophy will identify and provide it. One of the earliest philosophers – Plato – was concerned to distinguish real, hard-core knowledge from 'mere' belief. The search for the difference (if there is any) between 'knowledge' and 'justified true belief' is still with us today.

Descartes sought a single truth which could not be doubted, from which to deduce infallibly the rest of philosophy and the sciences, as if from a geometrical theorem. Famously, he found it in his own mental activity, after his doubting of every other proposition: 'I think, therefore I am.' The grounding and acquisition of the rest of human knowledge was relatively unproblematic after making that astounding discovery.

In a very different way, we can see the same anxiety in the later work of Immanuel Kant. He spent almost an entire career in being philosophically unremarkable until an encounter with the works of David Hume goaded him into becoming one of the greatest philosophers in Western history in his later life. (*The Critique of Pure Reason*, the first work which really conferred philosophical immortality on him, was published when he was 57.) For Kant, Hume's scepticism about the ability of reason to ground and provide even such scientifically indispensable notions as causality threatened to subvert all possibility of knowledge. This provoked Kant to produce his first Critique, whose aim was ostensibly to draw the limits to what could be known by 'pure' reason, that is, reason without the benefit of experience or experiment. This seemingly modest reflection on the limits to human mental capabilities might be seen as anything but humble, however, for his account of how we acquire knowledge has been taken as implicitly making the human mind the measure of all things, the foundation and source of all knowledge and truth.

Two contrasting efforts

At the beginning of the twentieth century the insistence that philosophy's task is to provide the foundations for knowledge, particularly for sciences, is dominant in such very different thinkers as the British philosopher Bertrand Russell and the German philosopher Edmund Husserl. Russell's emphasis on sensory experience is at least in part a reaction against what he saw as the licence and intellectual promiscuity of German philosophy and theology, which seemed to assert all manner of metaphysical and speculative nonsense with little concern for proof. *In contrast, in the Positivists at the beginning of the twentieth century, we see a desire to concern oneself only with hard facts, i.e. what is evident to the senses, self-evident, or capable of clear and certain proof. But critics claim that this lust for objectivity that leads one to take what seems most concrete and inarguable – one's immediate sense-data – as the ultimate building-bricks of knowledge, has a paradoxical or even perverse result: this 'objective' positivist approach in fact unrolls into its opposite: inescapable subjectivity. I can never swap my sensations with anyone else, nor can I ever be sure that another is perceiving and experiencing exactly what I am. Sensations can never be public, shared and therefore objective; rather they are the most private and inaccessible of philosophical data. An objective foundation for science and knowledge based on sensory experience, strictly speaking, can only be the foundation for* my *own personal knowledge, and it leaves me with nothing I could thus prove to you. Is this then 'objectivity' or the ultimate in subjectivism?*

Husserl, meanwhile, was busy founding a new philosophical school called 'phenomenology', which sought to restore primacy to human experience of the things of the world. Though anti-positivist, Husserl shared one of Russell's aims: to provide a certain foundation for knowledge and the sciences, as Descartes had earlier wanted. (One of his most famous works is called Cartesian Meditations.*) While rejecting some of Descartes's conclusions, Husserl attempts to repeat the same project: to strip himself of all assumptions and set aside all things which he thinks that he knows (Husserl calls this 'bracketing') in order to find a secure foundation which cannot be gainsaid. It is the same foundation for knowledge as Descartes', but with a Kantian twist: the 'transcendental ego'. This 'egology' is again to be the foundation for the knowledge and experience of the outside world. Although his fifth Meditation is an attempt to show that this does not amount to solipsism, because part of the ego's fundamental experience is the experience of other egos, this section is not entirely successful; and it is perhaps significant that the most famous 'phenomenologists' who followed him – Heidegger, Sartre, Merleau-Ponty – all rejected his 'transcendental idealism', this insistence on building the outside world onto the 'rock-solid' foundation of the human mind.*

Although attempts in Western philosophy at grounding knowledge have not been accorded universal success, a certain inferiority complex came over religious thinkers in the twentieth century when challenged to ground religious beliefs. Religious beliefs do seem to present special problems, being difficult to justify empirically.

One response in the latter half of the century has been to dispute the assumption that religious beliefs and statements either need or can have a rational ground. Some have rejected the view, now dubbed as 'evidentialism', the view that a belief is justified only insofar as it is in proportion to the evidence. Its classic exponent would be W. Clifford, who maintained that it was wrong to believe something without sufficient evidence.[26]

One attempt to do this has been described as 'Reformed Epistemology'; and another takes its inspiration from Wittgenstein. Some hold that a religious belief is itself already 'basic'. A 'basic' belief, in this context, means one such as 'I exist'; that is in itself is a rock-bottom tenet that does not need evidence to support it. It is seen, as Robert Pargetter describes it, as 'not justified, warranted by, or inferred from any other belief' but is 'nonetheless appropriately grounded or warranted'.[27] We all have beliefs that are 'basic' as based on our perceptions, or common sense. Unless I am a philosopher (and therefore peculiar in this respect), I just *believe* that I exist, without troubling myself over evidence to *prove* it. I believe that things do not spontaneously cease to exist for no reason, so if my keys are missing, they must be somewhere and it is worth looking for them. (A belief that you stole my missing keys would not be 'basic' but it would require evidence to support it.) If we had to justify everything we think, believe or assume by providing evidence for it, we should never rise from under the duvet in the morning. Philosophers of religion like Alvin Plantinga argue then that, far from needing evidence and 'grounds', belief in God is 'properly basic' in this sort of way.[28] As Nicholas Wolterstorff puts it,

> Deeply embedded in the Reformed tradition is the conviction that a person's belief that God exists may be a justified belief even though that person has not inferred that belief from others of his beliefs which provide good evidence for it. . . . And the Reformed tradition has insisted that the belief that God exists, that God is Creator, etc., may justifiably be found there in the foundation of our system of beliefs.[29]

Another way that one can reject the idea that religious beliefs need rational grounding is to argue precisely that belief in God is *groundless* – but also to claim that so too is most belief, even 'scientific' beliefs; this is an attempt to erode the class distinction between religion and science by denying objectivity and rational defensibility to *both*. The philosopher of science Paul Feyerabend,[30] who provocatively disputes the rationality of science, might be one starting-point (but rarely is, among philosophers of religion). Most modern exponents of this view tend to work from the later work of the philosopher Ludwig Wittgenstein. In his last work, *On Certainty*, Wittgenstein observed that much of our belief was groundless, or indeed, if one insists that belief needs grounds,

'Doesn't one need grounds for doubt?'[31] 'If you tried to doubt everything, you would not get as far as doubting anything. The game of doubting itself presupposes certainty.'[32]

Two philosophers of religion who deploy this line of thinking, sometimes known as 'Wittgensteinian Fideism', are D. Z. Phillips and Norman Malcolm. For Phillips, knowing that there is a God is not a matter of knowing a 'fact'. There is no *theoretical* knowledge of God; to treat religion as a theoretical affair is to distort it.[33] Belief in God or other fundamental religious beliefs are not facts just like all the others, which require evidence. Rather, they are the very framework of understanding and interpretation, which itself can never be justified by evidence. This is above all true because far from the evidence supporting the framework, it is only the existence of a framework which makes the evidence possible. A scrap of fabric on the ground is only a piece of rubbish – until a murder enquiry is established. Only then, in the framework of a murder and its investigation, are minute pieces of rubbish considered to be crucial evidence. In this way, one can reason that it is not evidence which leads to belief in God; it is only within the framework and context of believing in God that we find otherwise meaningless events to be of religious importance. Religion does not rely on external supports for its justification. 'In this sense religion is groundless; and so is chemistry', writes Malcolm.[34]

In these views and their opponents, we can see that the fundamental question for philosophy seems to be knowledge. Philosophy is all about knowledge, it seems, which means that the issues we confront are questions like: How do we know things? What is the difference between *knowing* something and 'merely' *believing* it? How can we acquire certainty? How can we justify or defend our claims to knowledge? Because religious 'knowledge' is highly controversial and the object of its 'knowledge' peculiar compared to empirical things, it has particular problems to be solved.

Texts and a community's tradition and the authority claimed for them carry no weight with conventional epistemologies; they are not enough to warrant a claim to 'knowledge'. Therefore their ground must be faith; and the contrasting style of reflection which is named reason has not merely the authority but even the obligation to adjudicate the other's territory. Alternatively the two are to be kept firmly apart.

The anti-grounding position disputes that religious beliefs need a grounding in some inferential move, whether from experience or from self-evident truth. However, the basic assumption that the issue is about knowledge and belief is still accepted.

Another kind of 'grounding'

A different stance on the essence of philosophy is to assert that the foundation of philosophy is metaphysics, or 'first philosophy', not epistemology. The fundamental question is not about knowledge. The fundamental question is how to understand Being. Only then can you understand knowledge, because it must be conceived in relation to the fundamentals of what exists to be known. As Ibn Sīnā says at the start of his *Metaphysics* – which Aquinas quotes at the opening of his work *On Being and Essence* – being and essence are what the intellect first conceives, and it is where one should start in order to avoid misunderstanding later on.[35] As Muṭahharī says: 'Being *qua* being is the subject of philosophy and all philosophical topics turn on it. Being – or existence – is to philosophy what the body is to medicine, number is to mathematics or quantity is to geometry.'[36] The designation 'being qua being' comes from Aristotle's *Metaphysics*.

What is metaphysics? A Shi'a philosopher's introduction

Metaphysics is a discipline that discusses being qua *(as) being. Its subject deals with the essential properties of being* qua *being. Its end is to achieve a general knowledge of existents and to distinguish them from that which is not really existent.*

To explain, when man considers himself, he finds his own self as possessing a reality. He also finds that there is a reality lying beyond his self that is within reach of his knowledge. Accordingly, when he seeks something, that is because it is what it is, and when he avoids something or runs away from something, that is because it is what it is. For instance, an infant groping for its mother's breast seeks real not imaginary milk. Similarly, a man running away from a lion runs away from what he considers to be a real wild beast, not something imaginary.

However, at times he may mistakenly regard something unreal as existing in eternal reality; for instance, luck and giants. Or, at times, he may consider something existing in eternal reality as unreal; for instance, the immaterial soul and the immaterial Intellect. Hence it is necessary, first of all, to recognize the characteristics of being qua *being in order to distinguish it from that which is not such. The science that discusses these matters is metaphysics.*[37]

What are the characteristics of being? What kind of beings are there? There is contingent or merely possible being – you, me, horses, furniture. There is also (some say) Necessary Being, that which necessarily exists. Since for most philosophers of this ilk the Necessary Being is God, this style of philosophical reflection moves smoothly from what it is supposed to do (think about being) to thinking about the problems of religion. So the topics of religion are not some unique, problematic case, as they can be seen to be in epistemology. The Ground of Being is God. The problem then is not how we can claim to know religious truths, but how the different kinds of being relate. How does the source of being, or necessary being, relate to all the individual beings of the world?

Quiddity refers to the 'whatness' of something rather than its 'thatness'. Here is my dog lying on the carpet. That he is there is his existence or being. What he is – a dog, rather than a horse lying in front of the fire – is his 'quiddity'. 'Quiddity' is what answers the question, what kind of thing is it?

With this complex history in Aristotle and Neoplatonism, and its inheritance by Christians, Jews and Muslims behind them, philosophers who work in this way tend to use language which can be strikingly similar. Here is Thomas Aquinas writing in 1252–6:

> First there is the one who is God, whose essence is his very existence. Indeed, because his essence is not different from his existence, some philosophers maintain that God has no quiddity or essence.[38]

And here is the Iranian Muslim philosopher Ṭabāṭabā'ī writing in the twentieth century:

> The essence of the Necessary Being is Its existence, in the sense that It has no quiddity besides Its particular existence; for were it to have a quiddity besides its particular existence, its existence would be accidental to Its essence. Since everything accidental is necessarily caused, Its existence too would be something caused, its cause being either Its quiddity or something else.[39]

So philosophers of this persuasion may seek to ground religious beliefs in something – but in their case, religious reflection is grounded in Being. This does not necessarily mean that the philosopher in question is 'otherworldly' or highly abstract. Thomas Aquinas, as an enthusiast for Aristotle, was insistent on the importance of empirical knowledge. 'Nothing is in the intellect that was not first in the senses,' Thomas tells us.

This fundamental impulse to think first about Being may be shared across different religious traditions – and what they think about Being may also be similar or identical, as the examples of Aquinas and Ṭabāṭabā'ī show. But this metaphysical impulse can also be seen in thinkers with very different ideas about Being, as we can see in Advaita Vedānta. Śaṇkara's starting-point, unlike the monotheist metaphysicians, is not to reflect on the different kinds of being there are. Śaṇkara's fundamental doctrine is non-difference; that there *are* no differences in being and reality, not even differences of identity that Aquinas or Ṭabāṭabā'ī would not question. Therefore when he comes to discuss knowledge, the work on epistemology that he must do is not to defend why what we perceive and believe is really true and reliable. On the contrary – his task is to explain how our common sense knowledge and perception can be so *wrong* as to perceive difference and opposition everywhere in the world.

> It is a natural course of worldly conduct resulting from false-ignorance, to superimpose the sense-objects and the subject of sense-objects which are absolutely different from each other, and their respective attributes, mutually on each other, through failure to discriminate or distinguish either of them from each other, and by coupling truth and untruth and to imagine thus – 'I am this,' 'This is mine.'
>
> (The opponent asks –) What indeed then, is this superimposition anyway? We reply – It is the unreal manifestation of some thing previously perceived and which is of the nature of remembrance, on some thing else. Some describe it as the superimposition of the attributes of one thing, on some other thing. (Some describe it) as the confusion based on the inability to discriminate between that which is superimposed on some thing else, and that some thing else on which it is superimposed. Others again describe it as the fictitious assumption in a thing, of attributes contrary to the attributes of that thing on which some thing else is superimposed. All the same, none of these definitions differ in any way as to the generally unreal assumption about the attributes of one thing as being the attributes of some other thing. Even so is our experience in the ordinary world. A mother-of-pearl appears as if it is silver. The moon, one as she is, appears as if she is two moons.[40]

The removal of error and acquisition of real knowledge needs to be grounded in the study of the scriptures. 'For the knowledge of Brahma is effected by the determination (brought about) by the consideration of the meaning of the Vedānta passages, and not by the other means of right knowledge such as inference etc.'[41] Not that Śaṇkara advocates what we would call 'fundamentalism' or a pure literalism, reading the answers straight out of the Holy Book. Scriptures itself, he tells us, accept the use of logic and human intelligence as an aid. The case differs for understanding of Brahman, and understanding proper religious practices. For the latter, the scriptures alone are authoritative. But for the right knowledge of Brahman, intuitional experience is also an aid.

Here Śaṇkara returns to ground that would be not only familiar, but congenial to Aquinas and Ṭabāṭabā'ī. The revelation of religious truths is in Scripture; it is simply a category mistake, as philosophers call it, to think that reasoning and logic alone can generate the ultimate religious truths. However, a profound understanding of these complex truths cannot simply be read off from the texts. Reasoning, intuition, logic and interpretation have their role to play. The role that they play, however, is *not* to 'ground' the religious beliefs in something more reliable. It is not the case, in their views, that logic or reason is more reliable than scriptural authority. Reasoning is a way of engaging with the text to explicate it. Reasoning and logic themselves need grounding; grounding in a true understanding of Being, which is ultimate.

Yet another kind of 'grounding'

Some philosophers seem to be anti-philosophers, particularly when it comes to religion. In a work called *The Incoherence of the Philosophers*, Abū Ḥāmid al-Ghazālī set out to destroy the influence of 'the philosophers' on his religion – Islam. The object of his attack was twenty theses he identified in the Aristotelian/Neoplatonist Muslim philosophers, chiefly al-Fārābī and above all Ibn Sīnā. In other words, his targets are not atheists or members of other religions, but co-religionists who have been seduced by philosophy into departing from the faith, mixing Qur'ānic belief in creation with Neoplatonist views of emanation and the like. Al-Ghazālī writes: 'The harm inflicted on religion by those who defend it in a way not proper to it is greater than the harm caused by those who attack it in the way proper to it. As it has been said: "A rational foe is better than an ignorant friend."'[42] As it happened, his exposition of their views was so clear, and the clash between himself and 'the philosophers' so fascinating, that he helped inadvertently to increase the awareness of 'the philosophers'' thinking in Islam. He was, at least, widely perceived by Muslims in the ensuing centuries to have won the argument.

But his method of destruction was not to quote scriptures in rebuttal, or to appeal to faith alone. He never simply quotes Ibn Sīnā, then quoting the Qur'ān, and pointing out the philosopher's deviation from revelation. Rather, he mounts a logical and detailed set of arguments, which function as a philosophical deconstruction of Neoplatonist Muslim ideas. He uses the same methods and style of philosophical argumentation as 'the philosophers', to expose the 'incoherence' of the philosophical argument. One of his basic strategies is to show the philosophers' inability to prove certain key beliefs. For example, he argues that the philosophers are unable to prove that God ('the First') does not have a body (Ninth Discussion). In effect, this could be seen as al-Ghazālī arguing that God *does* have a body; and of course al-Ghazālī does not believe that. He is demonstrating that some of the most important aspects of belief (and of philosophical coherence for that matter) cannot be demonstrated by the philosophers' arguments.

Such a thinker can not, therefore, simply be seen as taking the 'faith' side in a 'faith vs. reason' wrestling match. He relies equally on logic, the avoidance of contradiction and incoherence and clear thinking. Nevertheless, from the fact that he is 'reasoning' he cannot be seen superficially to take the side of 'reason' either. The idea that this issue can be reduced to an either/or of faith or reason crumbles in the face of such a complex and ironic figure as al-Ghazālī. For he is not simply engaged in the task of faith-sympathetic reasoning, as can be seen in Aquinas, Ṭabāṭabā'ī or Śaṇkara. Reasoning is not elucidating the Scriptures, or unpacking what revelation has brought in its portmanteau. More importantly, reason, logic or metaphysics do not have the power to disclose true knowledge of Being. Al-Ghazālī in fact became deeply disillusioned with ratiocination, gave it all up, and became a wandering mystic, writing powerful texts in a different key which are still appreciated today.

Judaism had a similar figure in the same era, the late eleventh to early twelfth century. Judah Halevi was a poet, and some of his creations are still revered by Jews. His philosophical work, nicknamed in Jewish circles the *Kuzari*, is *The Book of Argument and Proof in Defence of the Despised Faith*. It was in the literary form of a dialogue. Its setting was inspired by a story circulating at the time that the King of the Khazars, by the Caspian Sea, converted to Judaism after being unimpressed by the Christians and the Muslims. Halevi portrays the dialogue between the King and a Rabbi, and uses it as a vehicle to mount a stinging critique of philosophers and metaphysics. In some ways his points, as well as the nature of his argument, so closely mirror al-Ghazālī's, that it seems likely that he was fully conversant with al-Ghazālī's work of deconstruction.[43]

Halevi is critical of the aspiration of metaphysics to be on a footing with mathematics and logic, and like al-Ghazālī, he makes polemical use of the fact that there are no opposing schools of mathematics but numerous conflicting schools of metaphysics. Like al-Ghazālī, he also targets specific ideas, such as the idea of emanation of the world from the One, for mockery and deconstruction. And also in the manner of al-Ghazālī, even when he agrees with a belief put forward by the (chiefly Muslim) philosophers, he disputes the arguments and the assumption that rational and logical arguments *can* be given for religious tenets. Revelation, not logic, is the justification of beliefs.

Nevertheless he does not reject all ratiocination, debate and reasoned discussion. Once again, like al-Ghazālī, he believes that God's existence and God's uniqueness *are* rational truths, even if the ground for knowing them is not to be found in philosophy. But philosophy cannot provide true knowledge of the relationship between God and the world, nor of the ultimate ground of Being. Nor, contrary to the views of some of the Islamic philosophers, does intellectual argument and knowledge constitute a way to communion with the divine. The intimate relationship with God that all desire, in his view, is not granted by knowledge and argument. Reason cannot find its own way to God without revelation and without God's communication to us.

We can fast-forward now to a very different place and period: Germany in the eighteenth century. And yet the ideas may not feel totally unfamiliar.

Johann Georg Hamann of Prussia was a man in reaction to his time, the burgeoning Enlightenment of the eighteenth century. Although this period has stereotypically been known as 'the Age of Reason', more precisely there were particular controversies over the nature and the use of reason, even in 'secular' philosophy. At the very least, European philosophers were divided into two camps, depending on whether the secure foundations of knowledge were to be found in experience and the uses of the senses (empiricists) or whether the senses were inaccurate and deceptive and one should rely on infallible reasoning and logic (rationalists). Hamann tended to oppose both these points of view. Against the empiricists, who often tended towards materialism and thence to atheism, Hamann maintained the importance of what cannot be seen, touched or heard; and the necessity of faith, even to trust one's sense-experience! Against the rationalists he fought a more bitter struggle, often sarcastic in his exposure of reason's weaknesses, and opposed the near-deification of 'universal, healthy reason' of his times. (For example, he once characterized the reliance on reason as a 'screaming superstition'.)

He sought to create a more holistic picture of the human person and of knowledge than either party could deliver. His view was that the senses, experience, and reason – all fallible – should be employed in a harmonious way. 'Experience and revelation are one, and indispensable crutches or wings of our reason, if it is not to remain lame and crawling. The senses and history are the foundation and ground – the one may so deceive and the other be ever so simple: I give them precedence over all castles in the air.'[44] Much of his critique was directed against what he saw as misguided and overinflated valuations of the independence and infallibility of reason. But, particularly later in life when he needed to put the brakes on the emotive enthusiasm of some of his followers, he also stressed that emotion, faith or belief can just as easily lead us astray. As he writes to one friend, who was suggesting that there could be such a thing as a 'simple knowledge through emotion':

> Complex beings are not capable of simple emotion, still less simple knowledge. Feeling can as little be separated from reason in human nature as can reason from sensuousness. . . . Emotion must be delimited by rational grounds. Knowledge from belief is fundamentally identical

to: *Nil in intellectu*. [Thomas Aquinas's maxim quoted above – there is nothing in the intellect which was not previously in the senses][45]

Belief needs reason just as much as the latter needs the former. Philosophy is of idealism and realism: as our *nature* is composed of body and soul. . . . Only *scholastic reason* divides itself into idealism and realism. Correct and authentic reason knows nothing of this imagined difference, which is not grounded in the *nature of things*, and contradicts their *unity*, which lies at the foundation of all our concepts, or at least, *should* do so.[46]

Philosophy therefore must be an enterprise that unites these different capacities of the human person and which does not divide itself into idealism, based on reason and the world of ideas, vs. realism, based on the senses and the objects in the world.

Every philosophy consists of certain and uncertain knowledge, of idealism and realism, of sensuousness and deductions. Why should only the uncertain be called belief? What then are – *rational grounds*? Is knowledge without rational grounds possible, just as little as *sensus sine intellectu* . . .?[47] [Again, the maxim of Thomas: here he refers to 'senses without intellect'.]

For Hamann, the goal of philosophy as for art may be, as many Enlightenment figures suggested, the imitation or representation of nature; but if so it must be a shrewd and discerning one. Ultimately, for Hamann, to really understand the world we must realize that it has the nature of a text – a text with a divine Author, its creator:

God, nature and reason have as intimate a relation to one another as light, the eye, and all that the former reveals to the latter, or like the centre, radius and periphery of any given circle, or like author, book and reader. But where does the riddle of a book lie? In its language or its content? In the plan of its author or in the mind of the interpreter?[48]

Clearly such an assumption rests on faith. But so does the whole of philosophy, according to Hamann. He had made this provocative use from reading Hume, the sceptic about reason and the atheist: that even the conclusions of reason, like our conviction that one thing causes another, ultimately rests on belief. ('Belief' and 'faith' are the same word in German, *Glaube*. Hamann deliberately turns Hume's 'belief' into 'faith'.) For Hamann, all knowledge rests on believing your senses or trusting your system of logic; all knowledge rests on faith. One cannot escape this circle without falling into total scepticism.

> It is pure idealism to separate *believing* and *feeling* from *thinking*. *Companionship* is the true principle of reason and language, by which our sensations and representations are modified. This and that philosophy always separates things which by no means can be divided. Things without relationships, relations without things. There are no absolute creatures, as little as there is absolute certainty. . . . If we *believe* our sensations, our representations, then perhaps all divisions cease. We cannot dispense with these witnesses for ourselves, but can refute no one with their agreement.[49]

What this means for Hamann is that knowledge of God is not at all problematic, epistemologically. (It can be very difficult personally.) Knowledge of God arises in a personal relationship with one's creator. In one reworking of the Genesis creation story, he goes beyond the anthropomorphism of the text's portrait of God 'walking in the garden', and actually depicts God as 'playing with his human children'. We are made in God's image. He uses a quotation from Jesus – 'Whose is the inscription on this coin, whose likeness is on it?' – to indicate our belonging to, our intimacy with God. All knowledge rests on self-knowledge; and self-knowledge leads us to knowledge of God. But in fact the greatest knowledge consists in 'being known' – above all, being known by God. 'All things, even the Being of beings, are there for enjoyment, and not for speculation.'[50] Our existence, our being, is due to and remains constituted by a relationship; a relationship above all to the divine but which plays itself out in numerous other relationships with ourselves, among ourselves and between ourselves and the rest of creation.

Although you may never have heard of Hamann, he was actually very influential in German thought in the ensuing centuries. In the twentieth century several thinkers, including the two Jewish philosophers Martin Buber and Franz Rosenzweig, absorbed this 'relational' or 'dialogical' stance. In their work they mount similar critiques of dominant trends in European philosophy, and seek to ground knowledge and philosophy in relationship, above all in our intimacy with God.[51]

You might almost say that these thinkers, from al-Ghazālī to Buber, while interested in a kind of 'grounding', are interested in grounding reflection in faith in God, and not the other way round. What gives justification for beliefs, for claims, or assertions of truth is a relationship, or many relationships: a relationship with a text, which is itself the signifier of a relationship with its divine Author; a relationship with that Author; a relationship with the reality that is also the 'text', the creation, of the divine Author. Of course, the notion of the world as a text of which God is the author is not an uncommon idea. As Muṭahharī, in his essay *The World View of Tauhid*, expounds it:

The Noble Qur'ān designates sensed and cognized beings as signs (*ayat*), meaning that each being in turn is a sign of this unlimited Being and of the divine knowledge, power, life, and will. According to the Glorious Qur'ān, all of nature is like a book composed by a knowing, wise Author, of Whose boundless knowledge and wisdom its every line, its every word, is a sign. According to the Qur'ān, the more man learns through the power of science, the more aware he grows of the effects of divine power, wisdom, providence, and mercy.

Every natural science, just as from one point of view it is a science of nature, from another, more profound, point of view is a science of God.[52]

For this approach, the idea of relationship becomes the fundamental datum of philosophy, and all the topics of philosophy can be re-interpreted in this light. Knowledge becomes a relationship. Instead of being a matter of perception, inference, and the making of claims, knowledge itself is seen as a relationship between the knower and the known. The view of knowledge as a relation between the knowing subject and the known object was ascribed to al-Rāzī (d. 1209), but Muṭahharī ascribes this view to the earlier pioneer of kalām and the Asha'rite school, al-Ash'arī (d. *c*.941).[53] Allāma Muhammad Bāqir As-Ṣadr, a twentieth-century Iraqi Shi'a scholar, responding to the same two trends in Western philosophy that Hamann opposed,[54] defended a view of knowledge that is strikingly similar. Reality has the quality of 'disclosure',[55] and reveals knowledge to us. We do not construct what we see and know, it is shown to us, given to us. (This is in explicit repudiation of Kant.)

Even 'Being itself' can be seen as a relationship. Hamann was gently critical of his friend Jacobi, who was swept away by reflections on Being Itself. Hamann gently rebuked Jacobi in a letter, saying:

Being, belief and reason are pure relations, which cannot be dealt with absolutely, and are not things but pure scholastic concepts, *signs* for understanding, not for worshipping, aids to awaken our attention, not to fetter it, as Nature is the *revelation* not of itself, but of a higher Object. . . .[56]

Of course Hamann was not the only one keen to heal the divisions in philosophy. Mullā Ṣadrā is credited with unifying the divisions in Islamic thought, resolving the oppositions between the two styles of philosophy and '*irfān* and *kalām*. The name given to his system was 'sublime wisdom'; it sought to reconcile rational argument with direct awareness and mystical familiarity.

Muṭahharī 's decription of Mullā Ṣadrā 's scheme

Mullā Ṣadrā's organization of the philosophical topics concerning the intellectual and irrational way paralleled the manner in which the 'urafā' *(those who know; singular 'arif') had propounded the way of the heart and spirit. The* 'urafā' *hold that the wayfarer accomplishes four journeys in carrying through the method of* 'arif.

The journey from creation to God. At this stage, the wayfarer attempts to transcend nature as well as certain supernatural worlds in order to reach the Divine Essence, leaving no veil between himself and God.

The journey by God in God. After the wayfarer attains proximate knowledge of God, with His help the wayfarer journeys through His phases, perfections, names and attributes.

The journey from God to Creation by God. In this journey, the wayfarer returns to Creation and rejoins people, but this return does not mean separation and remoteness from the Divine Essence. Rather, the wayfarer sees the Divine Essence with all things and in all things.

The journey in Creation by God. In this journey, the wayfarer undertakes to guide the people and lead them to the Truth.

Mullā Ṣadrā, considering that philosophical questions constitute a 'way', if an intellectual one, sorted them into four sets.

Topics that constitute a foundation or preliminary to the study tawhīd. *These (the ordinary matter of philosophy) constitute our mental journey from Creation to God.*

Topics of tawhīd, *theology, and divine attributes – the journey with God in God.*

Topics of the divine acts, the universal worlds of being – the journey with God from God to Creation.

Topics of the soul and the Destination (ma'ād) *– the journey in Creation with God.*

The Asfāri Arba'a, which means 'the four journeys', is organized on this basis.

Mullā Ṣadrā distinguished between his own philosophical system of 'sublime wisdom' and what he called common or conventional philosophy, whether illuminationist or peripatetic.[57]

Concluding remarks

Between different religious traditions and systems of philosophy there are strikingly different controversies. If we are to remain true to the history of philosophy, one cannot speak simply of what philosophy is, therefore of what philosophy of religion is. At the same time, there are striking resonances across the traditions, systems, eras and continents. Time and again thinkers have grappled with a problem that has presented itself to them, sometimes not knowing that a forebear of another creed or language has been confronted by the same challenge.

So there are strongly divergent views, yet broad lines of approach and similarities of philosophical style. How would you characterize the ones you have met so far? What criteria would you use to categorize them? Here are some questions you can ask about the different thinkers, philosophies and schools of thought that you encounter here and elsewhere. How do they regard the use of different sources of knowledge (experience, sensory data, texts, reasoning etc.) and what authority do they have? What do they think reasoning consists in, and what worth do they give it? What value do they place on what cannot be proven by appeal to the five senses, or appeals to logic and argument?

For my part, I think the model of a relationship is a useful analogy for reflection on religious matters: a very good relationship, with lots of facets and different aspects. This brings not only focus but also richness to our thinking. We have different relationships to the sources that we use. If 'reason' as opposed to faith means we can only use a single cognitive function and we must disregard the world of texts, and the world of human traditions – other people's use of 'reason' – then we lose a great deal in our reflection. We have different relationships to the subject matter of our study. If 'reason' means that we stand in only one relationship to religious claims, we are impoverished.

We have different cognitive activities (not different mental 'things' or faculties) that we can bring to bear on the issues. We may be deluding ourselves if we think 'reason' can be divorced from our desire to prove one conclusion rather than another. There is also the question of philosophical etiquette, as the example of our Baghdad circle, at the opening of this chapter, demonstrated. Sometimes to speak of 'reason' is a way of insisting on mutual respect and making our deliberations accessible to someone of another faith. There 'reason' does not oppose 'faith' but is a way of showing other people respect. 'Reason' and philosophy can also signify openness to new ideas, willingness to explore and to question, the refusal to rule out an opinion or idea just because it is different. Above all, it can stand for self-criticism, analysing and questioning yourself – not only being critical of your beliefs but also of your 'reasoning'.

Faith – recall Smith's reading of *īmān* and *taṣdīq* – is not opposed to reason or to knowledge, on this view. Faith and knowledge both consist in a relationship to the truth: reasoning to knowledge is its investigative moment; faith is its moment of personal commitment to acknowledge that truth and live accordingly. Faith and reason, on this model, need each other, as Hamann argued. To conceive them as hostile opposites 'contradicts the unity' that is in the nature of things.

There is architecture and there is illumination.[58] A beautiful building needs both. It needs form and structure; it needs its parts to relate coherently, one thing to be supported by another, it needs decent foundations. Without that it will fall down. On the other hand, the architecture is there to glorify light: in its empty spaces, or reflected off its planes. An intricately crafted structure with no openness to illumination is a failure as a building. Systematic, disciplined reflection is the architecture; inspiration and engagement is the illumination.

From Jose Pereira

Thus arises a plurality of theological systems – a fact for which we cannot be sufficiently grateful. Reality has a richness far in excess of the power of the imbecile human mind to grasp it, and the order that this mind can impose on the complexity of things can never be absolute or complete, especially if the dimensions of the reality it seeks to understand exceed its understanding. Our insight into reality can thus be said to grow with the number of viewpoints from which it can be apprehended. The harmony perceptible from one viewpoint is what we may loosely call a system. The other systems may be erroneous in the view of any one of them, but error, if nothing else, serves to focus attention on a certain aspect of reality, through, shall we say, overemphasis – an aspect which might have otherwise eluded the human mind, a faculty notoriously incapable of giving equal attention even to the few aspects of reality known to itself.[59]

Draw your own conclusions

On reason, faith, and having constructive conversations

Do you agree with the 'Baghdad circle' that 'reason' or 'the intellect' forms a common ground on which people can agree, avoiding religious authority?

Does 'reason' or 'reasoning' give a guarantee against dogmatism or prejudice in religious debates?

When it comes to sharing your beliefs, do 'rational grounds' make a better way to justify your beliefs than your own personal experience?

If open-mindedness and tolerance are virtues in philosophical debates, what is the best way to achieve them?

Analysing your own context – the foundation of critical thinking

In your college, or your class, what is the 'tradition' – APA, AAR or something else? This may not be stated explicitly. See if you can analyse your lecturer. Or try interviewing somebody.

Which cultures are not represented in your intellectual environment? Why do you think that is?

Which intellectual history or culture are you the heir of, whatever the climate in your current college? Do you see yourself as continuing in that vein or changing?

Which thinkers, ideas or approaches described in this chapter attracted you, and which annoyed or repulsed you?

Create a visual representation of the tradition in which you are studying (perhaps using a diagram or map, or design a Powerpoint presentation). Include the negative influences and pet hates.

'Reasonable' vs. 'unreasonable' beliefs

In a group, think up some beliefs to fit in the following three categories:

> Something that is rational or reasonable to believe without proof.
>
> Something that is irrational to believe without proof.
>
> Something that you think is 'borderline', which people can either believe or not believe without being considered irrational.

Can you identify any pattern for the differences between the three groups of beliefs?

Discuss these experiments. Consider, perhaps, the following questions:

> Is there a consensus in your group about what (or what kind of) things are reasonable to believe without proof?

Are there things that cannot be *proved*, but that are silly or even crazy to doubt?

Which category do religious beliefs or beliefs about God(s) belong in your view?

Evidence for beliefs

Think through the following question: Is evidence or proof necessary to justify beliefs?

If YES ask yourselves:

What if there are no proofs of a belief? Must the believer either give up the belief or be considered irrational?

Aren't there beliefs that we cannot do without that we nevertheless cannot prove?

Such as: all universal or general statements or statements relating to the future.

Can we prove every assumption that we operate with?

If NO ask yourselves:

Then how else can you justify what you believe?

Or do you need to? Can you just believe anything you like without justification or reason?

Isn't it a bad idea for people to hold irrational beliefs with no justification?

What if someone believes something that is harmful to themselves or others?

Further reading

Cohn-Sherbok, D. (2001) *Interfaith Theology: A Reader*, Oxford, Oneworld

Cohn-Sherbok, D. (2003) *Fifty Jewish Thinkers*, Key Concepts, London, Routledge

G. Griffith-Dickson, 2000, *Human and Divine: An Introduction to the Philosophy of Religious Experience*, London, Duckworth

Guttmann, J. (1973) *Philosophies of Judaism: A History of Jewish Philosophy from Biblical Times to Franz Rosenweig*, trans. D. W. Silverman, New York, Schocken Books

Kalupahana, D. J. (1994) *A History of Buddhist Philosophy*, Delhi, Motilal Banarsidass

Kumar, F. L. (1991) *The Philosophies of India: A New Approach*, Studies in Asian Thought and Religion 14, Lampeter, Edwin Mellen Press

Muṭahharī, M. (2002) *Understanding Islamic Sciences: Philosophy; Theology; Mysticism; Morality; Jurisprudence*, London, ICAS Press

Pereira, J. (1991 (1976)) *Hindu Theology: Themes, Texts and Structures*, Delhi, Motilal Banarsidass

Ṭabāṭabā'ī, S. M. H. (2003) *The Elements of Islamic Metaphysics (Bidayat al-Hikmah)*, London, ICAS Press

Notes

1 J. Guttmann (1973) *Philosophies of Judaism: A History of Jewish Philosophy from Biblical Times to Franz Rosenweig*, trans. D. W. Silverman, New York, Schocken Books, pp. 59–60.

2 Wilfred Cantwell Smith (1979) 'Faith as Taṣdīq', in P. Morewedge (ed.), *Islamic Philosophical Theology*, Albany, State University of New York Press, pp. 106–7.

3 M. Muṭahharī (2002) *Understanding Islamic Sciences: Philosophy; Theology; Mysticism; Morality; Jurisprudence*, London, ICAS Press, p. 19.

4 K. Yandell (1998) *Philosophy of Religion*, London, Routledge, pp. 13–14, 17–18.

5 R. Rorty (1980) *Philosophy and the Mirror of Nature*, Princeton, Princeton University Press, pp. 369–70.

6 Wayne Proudfoot in W. J. Wainwright (ed.) (1996) *God, Philosophy, and Academic Culture: A Discussion between Scholars in the AAR and the APA*, American Academy of Religion: Reflection and Theory in the Study of Religion, Atlanta, Ga., Scholars Press, p. 71.

7 Philip Quinn in Wainwright, *God, Philosophy, and Academic Culture*, p. 49.

8 Quinn in Wainwright, *God, Philosophy, and Academic Culture*, p. 51.

9 Stephen Crites in Wainwright, *God, Philosophy, and Academic Culture*, p. 41.

10 For detailed discussion of this text and these issues, see P. Adamson (2002) *The Arabic Plotinus: A Philosophical Study of the 'Theology of Aristotle'*, London, Duckworth.

11 Muṭahharī, *Understanding Islamic Sciences*, p. 20.

12 Muṭahharī, *Understanding Islamic Sciences*, p. 26.

13 Muṭahharī, *Understanding Islamic Sciences*, p. 27.

14 Sayyid 'Alī Qulī Qarā'ī in his preface to his translation of S. M. H. Ṭabāṭabā'ī (2003) *The Elements of Islamic Metaphysics (Bidayat al-Hikmah)*, London, ICAS Press, p. xiii.

15 Guttmann, *Philosophies of Judaism*, pp. 3–5.

16 'Philo Judaeus', in H. A. Wolfson (1973) *Studies in the History and Philosophy of Religion*, Cambridge, Mass., Harvard University Press, p. 60. This essay is a useful short overview of Philo's views.

17 Guttmann, *Philosophies of Judaism*, p. 53.

18 There is a reason that Wolfson's monumental work on the the philosophy of kalām (H. A. Wolfson (1976) *The Philosophy of the Kalam*, Cambridge, Mass., and London, Harvard University Press) is followed by a work on the repercussions of the kalām in Jewish philosophy (H. A. Wolfson (1979) *Repercussions of the Kalam in Jewish Philosophy*, Cambridge, Mass., and London, Harvard University Press)! Nasr and Leaman's large compendium on the history of Islamic philosophy contains a whole section on Jewish philosophers.

19 This nickname in the Jewish tradition is taken from the initials of his name: Rabbi Moses Ben Maimon.

20 J. Pereira (1991 (1976)), *Hindu Theology: Themes, Texts and Structures*, Delhi, Motilal Banarsidass, p. 42.

21 From Pereira, *Hindu Theology*.

22 F. L. Kumar (1991) *The Philosophies of India: A New Approach*, Studies in Asian Thought and Religion 14, Lampeter, Edwin Mellen Press, p. 501.

23 S. Dasgupta (1997) *A History of Indian Philosophy*, 5 vols, Delhi, Motilal Banarsidass, vol. 1, pp. 127–8.

24 Dasgupta, *A History of Indian Philosophy*, vol. 1, p. 166.

25 B. Davies (1993) *An Introduction to the Philosophy of Religion*, Oxford, Oxford University Press, p. 1.

26 'To sum up: it is wrong always, everywhere, and for anyone, to believe anything upon insufficient evidence.' W. K. Clifford (1879) *Lectures and Essays*, reprinted in various places, including B. A. Brody (ed.) (1974) *Readings in the Philosophy of Religion: An Analytic Approach*, Englewood Cliffs, NJ, Prentice-Hall, p. 246.

27 Robert Pargetter, 'Experience, Proper Basicality, and Belief in God', reprinted in R. Douglas Geivett and Brendan Sweetman (eds) (1992) *Contemporary Perspectives on Religious Epistemology*, Oxford, Oxford University Press, p. 151.

28 See, for example, Alvin Plantinga, 'Is Belief in God Properly Basic?', reprinted in R. Douglas Geivett and Brendan Sweetman (eds) (1992) *Contemporary Perspectives on Religious Epistemology*, Oxford, Oxford University Press, pp. 133–41.

29 Nicholas Wolterstorff, 'Is Reason Enough?', reprinted in R. Douglas Geivett and Brendan Sweetman (eds) (1992) *Contemporary Perspectives on Religious Epistemology*, Oxford, Oxford University Press, p. 149.

30 P. Feyerabend (1996) *Farewell to Reason*, London and New York, Verso.

31 L. Wittgenstein (1969) *On Certainty*, trans. D. Paul and G. E. M. Anscombe, Oxford, Basil Blackwell, § 122.

32 Wittgenstein, *On Certainty*, § 115.

33 D. Z. Phillips, *Faith and Philosophical Enquiry*, a chapter of which is usefully reprinted as 'Faith, Skepticism and Religious Understanding', in R. Douglas Geivett and Brendan Sweetman (eds) (1992) *Contemporary Perspectives on Religious Epistemology*, Oxford, Oxford University Press, pp. 81–91 (the quotation can be found on p. 90).

34 Norman Malcolm, 'The Groundlessness of Belief', in Stuart Brown (ed.) (1977) *Reason and Religion*, Ithaca, NY, Cornell University Press, or in R. Douglas Geivett and Brendan Sweetman (eds) (1992) *Contemporary Perspectives*

on Religious Epistemology, Oxford, Oxford University Press, , p. 98.

35 Thomas Aquinas, 'On Being and Essence', in T. Aquinas (1998) *Thomas Aquinas: Selected Writings*, ed. R. McInerny, London, Penguin Books.

36 Muṭahharī, *Understanding Islamic Sciences*, p. 31.

37 S. M. H. Ṭabāṭabā'ī (2003) *The Elements of Islamic Metaphysics (Bidayat al-Hikmah)*, London, ICAS Press, p. 1.

38 Aquinas, 'On Being and Essence', p. 44.

39 Ṭabāṭabā'ī, *Elements of Islamic Metaphysics*, pp. 36–7.

40 Brahma-Sutra-Shankara-Bashya (1960) *Brahma-Sutra-Shankara-Bashya: Badrayana's Brahma-Sutras with Shankaracharya's Commentary*, trans. V. M. Apte, Bombay, Popular Book Depot, pp. 1–2.

41 *Brahma-Sutra-Shankara-Bashya*, p. 11.

42 al-Ghazālī (2000 (1997)) *The Incoherence of the Philosophers (Tahafut al-Falasifah)*, trans. M. E. Marmura, Provo, Utah, Brigham Young University Press, p. 6.

43 David Kaufmann has argued this extensively in his monumental work first published in 1877. D. Kaufmann (1967) *Geschichte der Attributenlehre in der Judischen Religionsphilosophie de Mittelalters von Saadja Bis Maimuni* UND *Die Spuren Al-Batlajusi's in der Judischen Religionsphilosophie Nebst einer Ausgabe der herbraischen übersetzungen seiner Bildlichen Kreise*, Amsterdam, Philo Press, pp. 119–40.

44 For Hamann's letters see the English translation in G. Griffith-Dickson (1995) *Johann Georg Hamann's Relational Metacritism*, Berlin and New York, de Gruyter, p. 343.

45 Griffith-Dickson, *Johann Georg Hamann's Relational Metacritism*, p. 345.

46 Griffith-Dickson, *Johann Georg Hamann's Relational Metacritism*, p. 346.

47 Griffith-Dickson, *Johann Georg Hamann's Relational Metacritism*, p. 345. 'Sensuousness' translates *Sinnlichkeit* (Kant's 'sensibility').

48 Griffith-Dickson, *Johann Georg Hamann's Relational Metacritism*, p. 338.

49 Griffith-Dickson, *Johann Georg Hamann's Relational Metacritism*, p. 344.

50 Griffith-Dickson, *Johann Georg Hamann's Relational Metacritism*, p. 354.

51 M. Buber (1970) *I and Thou*, trans. W. Kaufmann, New York, Charles Scribner's; F. Rosenzweig (1985) *The Star of Redemption*, trans. W. W. Hallo, Notre Dame, Ind., Notre Dame Press.

52 M. Muṭahharī (1985) *Fundamentals of Islamic Thought: God, Man and the Universe*, trans. R. Campbell, Contemporary Islamic Thought: Persian Series, Berkeley, Mizan Press, p. 79.

53 Ṭabāṭabā'ī, *Elements of Islamic Metaphysics*, p. 157. This view is contrasted with Ṭabāṭabā'ī's own, which is that quiddities can have a 'mental existence'. The idea that knowledge of an external object consists in a special relation between the object and the 'soul' Ṭabāṭabā'ī feels is refuted by the knowledge of non-existent objects; 'for the soul's relation to something non-existent is meaningless' (p. 22).

54 He is equally critical of two, opposite Western views: idealism, subjective relativism, as he analyses it in philosophers like Berkeley and Kant; and positivism and materialism, in particular as it is found in Marxism.

55 As-Ṣadr, Allāma Muhammad Bāqir (1989) *Our Philosophy*, trans. S. C. Inati, London, Muhammadi Trust, pp. 90–1 *et passim*.

56 Cited in Griffith-Dickson, *Johann Georg Hamann's Relational Metacritism*, p. 345. Jacobi was intoxicated with the notion of Being-in-itself; Hamann found this prosopopoeic and described it as a 'superstition'. '– Affirmation of *Being in itself* – the most abstract relation, that does not serve the intuition and understanding of the *things*, let alone *particular things* . . .' (Hamann's letters, vol. 7, p. 166: 19–20). He might have had the same reaction to Ferdinand Ebner, not to mention Heidegger.

57 Muṭahharī, *Understanding Islamic Sciences*, pp. 28–9.

58 I am adapting a metaphor from Jose Pereira, which he uses in a theological context (*Hindu Theology*, pp. 34–5).

59 Pereira, *Hindu Theology*, p. 35.

3

Ways of Talking About Religion

The problem of what we can know is closely bound up with the question of what we can say. It is only thought as expressed in words that can be understood, communicated and criticized. Language is not an accidental, dispensable garb which could be put on and put off. It grows with thought, or rather thought grows with it. In the ultimate analysis they may be identical. (T. R. V. Murti)[1]

For centuries in religious-philosophical debates epistemological questions had been dominant. At the beginning of the twentieth century, the primary question shifted from: 'What can we *know*?' to 'What can be *said*?' A leader in this discourse, Ludwig Wittgenstein stated his aim in his first work as 'to draw a limit to thought' (which 150 years previously had also been Immanuel Kant's aim in *The Critique of Pure Reason*).

But then Wittgenstein corrects himself: 'or rather – not to thought, but to the expression of thoughts', for it is 'only in language that the limit can be drawn, and what lies on the other side of the limit will simply be nonsense'.[2] Kant's Enlightenment project – to question whether we can think about and know things, like God, which are held to be beyond our sensory experience – has been transformed into a linguistic question about what can be talked about meaningfully.

Curiously, this concern with language is not as new as some of its recent practitioners believed, going back at least to Augustine in the fourth century. Nor is it a uniquely Western problem, as the debates in Indian philosophy and religion began even earlier.

What does a word 'refer' to, and is that reference what gives meaning to the word? This general problem is known in the West as 'the problem of reference'. How do words attach onto things in the world so that we can talk about them?

If language in general has become a problem, the problem is more acute for language applied to religious thought and experience. If we find it difficult to agree on how to talk about the table we can see before us, what about talking about a God whom we cannot see?

If words mean something by reference to the objects to which we point, then words about 'God' and similar religious insights or entities cannot mean anything, for we cannot point to a God in our world. Religious utterances cannot make sense, and anything 'transcendent' cannot be talked about.

Being thus ejected from discourse, twentieth-century philosophers of religion have taken up 'the problem of reference' with considerable anxiety. The aim is to find some grounding for speaking of the transcendent. They try to find answers to such questions as: What do religious words refer to, if anything? What gives meaning to words that name what you cannot display? Sallie McFague worries about the Scylla of idolatry and the Charybdis of irrelevance that confronts language about God: either we take it literally or find it meaningless. Can we refer to God without identifying our language exhaustively with the divine? Does religious language refer to anything? If it does – how?[3]

The Advaita Vedāntin Sureśvara maintains that words cannot directly denote Brahman, the ultimate reality. His predecessor Śaṇkara even went so far as to say that language is the instrument of ignorance. Both agree that it is impossible to use language directly to designate reality; ultimate reality still more so.[4] (This, however, is not their last word on the subject.)

There is another challenge to religious language, however, which was widely recognized for several millennia by religious believers themselves, well before sceptics took it up. I shall call it 'the problem of effability'. Religious thinkers have struggled with the question of whether the transcendent reality which they believe exists can be adequately expressed in human language. Mystics of every faith have repeatedly stressed that what they experienced in contemplation was beyond words; although they have nothing but words with which to communicate their experience of the ultimate. Śaṇkara and Sureśvara both maintain that the highest knowledge is a direct intuition without words; this finds its ultimate expression in the famous Upaniṣadic saying that Brahman is not this, not this (*neti neti*). So even believers can be sceptical about the utility of language about religious truths. Arindam Chakrabarti articulates the problem as it confronts the Advaita Vedāntin:

> A word denotes an object in virtue of some feature of the object. This feature . . . can be a universal (a natural kind), a quality (or unrepeatable attribute), an action or a specific relation. Thus the word 'apple' denotes any one instance of the universal *appleness* [= universal]. The word 'red' applies to anything which is of the colour red, although each red surface has a distinct hue of red [= quality or attribute]. The word 'singer' picks out any one who performs the act of singing [= action]. The word 'mother-in-law' obviously would apply to a lady only in so far as she is related to someone in the appropriate way [= relation]. Now Brahman . . . which is the ground of identity between the Absolute cause of the Universe and the individual person is said to be

devoid of any universal or particular property, any action or relation. How then can any word or phrase . . . apply to or denote or stand for Brahman?[5]

In this chapter we will survey the variety of responses to the problem. We will look first at some influential theories of meaning. Then we will reflect on the problem of whether human language needs to be cleaned up before it can refer to the divine or ultimate reality. We will consider whether figurative language holds the answer to the problem, before looking at recent views of language that suggest that language does not just say things and depict the world, it does things in the world.

Simon Blackburn suggests that philosophy of language is an attempt to achieve some understanding of a triangle of elements: speakers, language and the world.[6] (He doesn't say whether listeners might not be a fourth element to be taken into his geometry.) The task of the philosopher is to obtain some stable conception of these three and their relationships.

Blackburn's 'triangle' of speech

Each corner of the triangle has a philosophical discipline that deals with it: 'psychology' deals with the speakers; 'metaphysics' deals with the world, and 'meaning' is the philosophical issue of language. Next, each side of the triangle, or each relationship between each of the three, has a theoretical discipline. The relationship between speakers and the world is the domain of the 'theory of knowledge'; between speakers and language, 'theory of meaning'; and between language and the world, 'theory of truth'.

The history of philosophy has shown varying emphases on one or another corner of this triangle. The European tradition from Descartes until now has emphasized the individual and his or her capacities for experience and reasoning. The aim of metaphysics then is to attain a conception of the world which would enable the individual to know something about it. The nature of the mind then determines what kind of language this individual can speak; and Locke's and Kant's prime investigations therefore have been into what kind of mind the individual has.

In the nineteenth and twentieth centuries, philosophy has been dominated by 'scientific naturalism': the conviction that the science of psychology would provide the only real advance in our understanding of logic, language, and thought. The same attitude persists in much empiricist philosophy of language this century, he argues; although which discipline is thought to bring the best understanding of language shifts: from psychology, to formal logic, to formal semantics, to structural linguistics. The really notable change has been the shift to concentration upon language itself, to give it priority over the other elements of the triangle.[7]

How do words 'mean'?

In this section we will look at different theories of meaning.

In the beginning of the twentieth century in Europe, one of the most powerful influences on philosophy as a whole was a theory of meaning. In this theory, language is seen as a system of signs; words are signs referring to objects, language involves propositions and assertions of fact pertaining to these objects. Meaning is found in the object to which the word refers.

In the *Tractatus Logico-Philosophicus*, the Austrian philosopher Ludwig Wittgenstein's attempt to draw a limit to the expression of thoughts is summed up: 'What can be said at all can be said clearly, and what we cannot talk about we must pass over in silence.'[8] Language has a logical structure, and if we understand it we see the limits of what can be said meaningfully. Beyond this, both language and thought become nonsense.

In this account the structure of language mirrors the structure of the world.

Wittgenstein's first theory of language[9]

Names are the ultimate constituents of language. Names make up 'elementary' propositions, which in turn make up propositions. Correspondingly, objects make up states of affairs, which make up the world; the world thus consists in the totality of facts.

Each level of the structure of language matches a level of structure in the world. The arrangement of the names logically mirrors or pictures the arrangement of the objects in the states of affairs. A proposition, Wittgenstein tells us, is a picture of reality, a model of reality as we imagine it. It is because of this picturing relation that the propositions have sense. The meaning of a proposition is found in the situation it depicts; whether it is true or false depends on whether the situation it depicts exists or not.

Tying together these theses about the structure of language, the structure of world, and the 'picture theory' of meaning results in a set of assertions about the limits of language, and therefore of thought. The only significant propositions (and hence thoughts) are those which are pictures of reality. This means that the only significant discourse is factual discourse – discourse about things that can be pointed to. That which does not fall within the realm of facts is non-sense: such signs or strings of signs fail to express a proposition; they say nothing at all because they fail to picture anything in the world and hence have no connection with the world. 'Most of the propositions in philosophy', Wittgenstein tells us, are in this class.[10]

Only when there is that picturing connection to things in the world do our signs have sense. Thus, because many things that we do talk about – ethics, religion and 'the problems of life' – lie 'outside the world' (that is, outside the realm of facts and their constituent states of affairs) nothing can be said about them. They 'show' themselves, Wittgenstein asserts, but they cannot be stated. 'There are, indeed, things that cannot be put into words. They make themselves manifest. They are what is mystical.'[11]

Wittgenstein's picture theory may seem like plain common sense to you. Let us look briefly at a directly contrasting theory of meaning, put forward by the Indian philosopher Bhartṛhari approximately four centuries after the death of Christ. The basic unit of meaning is not the individual word, which has meaning because it 'pictures' a thing; for Bhartṛhari it is the whole sentence. The sentence is the basic, unanalysable unit of speech. The meaning of a sentence, in the mind of its speaker and when heard by a fluent listener, occurs in a 'flash' which is experienced by both as a whole (*sphoṭa* theory). A fluent speaker (or listener) does not take the meaning word by word and then add it up; it is experienced and understood as a unity. For Bhartṛhari, *sphoṭa* exists in each person, and *sphoṭa* itself bursts with pent-up energy in the mind and seeks expression.

Wittgenstein was never a member of the 'club' called the Vienna Circle which began in 1925, although he shared many of its attitudes. Its principal members had largely come from disciplines other than philosophy, chiefly science and mathematics.[12] A. J. Ayer spent some time with them as a young man, and returned to splash Logical Positivism across British philosophy in *Language, Truth and Logic* in 1936, when he was only 25.[13] Its approach and attitudes dominated Anglo-American thinking for decades, even though specific tenets were gradually dispensed with. His fundamental aim was to destroy 'metaphysics' once and for all – that is, any attempt to speculate or discuss anything beyond the material world. This rules out talk of God or an afterlife, as well as 'souls'. That was all right with the Logical Positivists but it also threatened talk of things that they *did* want to talk about, like ethics and aesthetics, for these are difficult to articulate in purely material terms.[14]

The Logical Positivists' chosen tools were logic and science. All sensible utterances for them had to be either what Hume called 'relations of ideas' (connections between abstract concepts as in logic or mathematics) or else 'matters of fact' (the domain of science). In later life, Ayer commented that it was not so much that they used science in their philosophy, as that they thought all knowledge was science.[15] Science for them is the correct way to describe and understand the world, and there isn't anything but the world to be known. All philosophy has to do, as Wittgenstein suggested, is criticize and refine the statements of science.

With the 'picture theory of meaning' at its base, Logical Positivism put forward its principle doctrine: the Verification Principle, which determines which sorts of statements have meaning. Any statement that isn't either empirically verifiable or else a formal statement (in logic or mathematics) is nonsense. Anything that cannot be confirmed by observation is nonsense, unless it is a tautological proposition as (they asserted) the statements of mathematics and logic essentially are. This clearly excludes any talk of God or religion, for how can these assertions be verified in material terms?

The Verification Principle

As formulated by Schlick, the Verification Principle runs:

The meaning of a proposition is the method of its verification.

This has the further corollary that what a proposition means can be described by saying what would verify it, which amounts to a reduction of all statements to statements of immediate observation. They originally thought that you could 'translate out' all statements into statements about sense data, but it proved impossible to put this into practice. General statements, like 'All ravens are black', are ultimately impossible to 'translate out' into sense perceptions because the subject extends to infinity. Who wants to undertake the arduous and tedious task of observing 'all ravens', even if that is possible?

Moreover, this tends to reduce any statement about other people to observations about their behaviour, which is contentious. But even in dealing with its own ideal subject-matter, scientific enquiry, it is difficult to translate out very high-level items like electrons into visual sensations observed by the scientist. So the principle was weakened and it was simply required that the proposition, to be significant, should be confirmable by sense observation. Ayer later admitted that this led to some unconvincing views, particularly about the past. One had to assert that a statement about a past event actually means 'If you look it up in a history book you will see it written that . . .' – a view which Ayer asserted in Language, Truth and Logic, *but later found desperately implausible.*

Ayer's later verdict on the Verification Principle is that it was never well formulated. He said that in his various attempts, he 'always let in either too little or too much'. This leads me to ask what his real motivation was: to draw the line where the line should be drawn, or just to exclude what he disliked and include what he fancied?

The Verification Principle faces another embarrassing hurdle in trying to pass its own test. It is not a mathematical statement, nor a tautology of logic. How could you possibly verify the Verification Principle in the material world? It trespasses on a realm of non-empirical reality which it refuses to recognize as significant. Therefore, it follows that the Verification Principle itself must be meaningless.[16]

The Logical Positivist has a fall-back position, such as the one taken by Antony Flew in the 'University Debate': if one cannot demand the possibility of verification, one can at least require that sensible statements can be susceptible of falsification.

He tells the story of two people in a clearing in the forest. One asserts that this wild place is actually tended by a gardener. The second insists that he has never seen such a person. 'Ah,' says his friend. 'He is invisible.' So traps and wires are set, but no gardener is caught. As each successive test is set, and failed, the one who believes in the Invisible Gardener has an excuse ready to hand.[17]

Flew maintains that it is the unwillingness of believers, like the man in the forest, to let anything count as evidence against their belief which gives rise to the suspicion that in the end this is empty and meaningless. If religious believers would at least be willing to allow that in principle, under some condition or circumstance, their beliefs could be falsified, we would have more confidence; but as it is their assertions 'die the death of a thousand qualifications'.

Flew's objection that believers refuse to allow anything to falsify their belief can be turned back on Logical Positivism. The same complaint can be made of analytic statements, such as 'a bachelor is an unmarried man'. These too are unfalsifiable by empirical considerations. If for example someone claimed to falsify that definition by claiming to know a married bachelor, I would say (or 'qualify' in Flew's terms) 'then he isn't a bachelor', or 'that isn't what I mean by a bachelor' or 'you don't understand what the term "bachelor" means or how it is used'.

Flew might insist on keeping such analytic statements separate from those that are empirical, and insist that those about God's existence are empirical statements. But certainly some religious discourse (such as the ontological argument) seems to function as if it thinks of itself as expressing necessarily true propositions.

Stephen Davis counters Flew's claim that believers will not allow anything to count against religious faith, by claiming that many believers do have a psychological limit to their acceptance of religious claims. Secondly, he maintains that religious statements can conceivably be verified in the future; if, for example, someone invents a new, successful proof. It may still remain the case that the statement may not be falsifiable, but there are other statements recognized as possessing cognitive meaning, which can be verified if true but not falsified if false. He gives 'There are three successive sevens in the decimal determination of pi' as an example.[18]

Despite his own criticisms of Logical Positivism in later life, Ayer still maintained there was something right in the approach. We still want to be able to say how we go about testing what people say to see if it is true. There has to be some backing to the 'currency' of our language. The early Logical Positivists erred in thinking we could maintain the gold standard – that we could present our words like bank-notes and cash them in for the gold of objects and methods of verification. While this is not possible, we can still have legitimate concerns about counterfeit notes and counterfeit speech.

In striking contrast to Logical Positivism, the theory of the Indian logicians of the Nyāya and Vaiśeṣika traditions was that the meanings of words, the connection between words and their referents, significative power, is willed and established by God. This would not satisfy many today, but it also did not satisfy all ancient Indian philosophers.

Some philosophers instead took the view that the meaning of a sentence comes from its parts. This view is known as the *khaṇḍārtha* theory. The Bhāṭṭa Mīmāṃsākas and the Nyāya–Vaiśeṣikas held that the meaning of a sentence comes from the individual words in it, and one understands the meaning of a sentence by understanding the words first. The Prābhākara Mīmāṃsākas believed that although the meaning of a sentence is composed of the individual word meanings, nevertheless one understands the meanings of the sentence immediately on hearing the words. One doesn't have to understand the meanings of the individual words first and then synthesize them.

But this theory was countered by a more holistic approach to meaning and the relation of a sentence to its constituent words, the 'partlessness' thesis (*akkhaṇḍārtha*), or the 'Synthetic' or 'Holistic' approach. The syllables of a word do not 'add up' to make its meaning; analogously, Bhartṛhari believed that the meaning of a sentence was manifested in its constituent words, but not made out of them. Maṇḍana Miśra followed this holistic approach to meaning.

Maṇḍana's discussion of what words 'aim at'

Since 'meaning' in Sanskrit, artha, *literally means 'target' or 'aim', Maṇḍana asks, do words only 'aim at', 'mean' the objects to which they refer? Or do they aim at a union with the thing to be done that is urged in speech? Or a union with the meanings of the other words in the sentence? It cannot be only the first, that words mean their objects. Otherwise there could be no understanding of the purpose of a sentence, especially such injunctions as make up much of the sacred scriptures of almost any religion, perhaps. And then words would be pointless.*

On the other hand, they must nevertheless aim at their objects in order to be explicable and so that knowledge of the object can arise. Otherwise, meaning becomes solely dependent on a speaker's intention. That is counter-intuitive; one could mean whatever one liked by a word, simply by intending it, whereas words carry with them a limitation of possible meaning. Also, in situations where there is no speaker (as in scriptures) there could be no meaning.

Words cannot aim simply at the action which they enjoin, without the mutual word-to-word connections; otherwise meaning would hang solely on the verb, and no qualification of action is possible. Consequently, words must 'aim at' a number of levels: things to which they refer, actions or purposes which they convey, and connections of meaning that arise from their relationship with other words.[19]

It seems that Maṇḍana Miśra would cope much better than Ayer in accounting for the meaning of words. To which objects do 'if' 'nothing' 'of' refer? And how do you verify 'pass the salt'? Theories of meaning which ignore the importance of action and motivation, not least the function of relations between words, cannot take us very far in understanding our everyday language. Perhaps Maṇḍana's multilayered theory of meaning, or 'aiming', is a shrewd tactic.

Unlike Ayer, Wittgenstein later turned against his own early theory. In *Philosophical Investigations* he deconstructs it patiently, using as a crowbar the idea of 'ostension' – of pointing to something to indicate the meaning of a word. The later Wittgenstein observes that, far from being the clear and obvious gesture he once thought, every ostensive definition can be interpreted in a variety of ways. Ostension can only make the meaning of a word clear 'when the overall role of the word in language is clear';[20] in other words, when you already have a good idea of what the person is talking about.

'Point to a piece of paper. – And now point to its shape – now to its colour – now to its number (that sounds queer). – How did you do it?'[21]

In any act of pointing, how do we know which feature is being indicated for our understanding?

Augustine – whose theory of language Wittgenstein thinks he is refuting – got there centuries before him in a work called *De Magistro*.[22] He discussed language with his son Adeodatus and wondered about how to define 'walking' ostensively when one is already 'walking'. 'Walk faster,' Adeodatus suggests. But maybe that would be taken as defining 'speed' or 'acceleration' or 'hurrying'. Augustine suggested that maybe nothing can be known by words, except what is already known. Words refer to other words;[23] this applies even to 'things' and 'activities', the easiest words point to or demonstrate. Augustine and Adeodatus consider the example of a fowler teaching the art of bird-catching, and conclude that every form of demonstration requires a prior, shared context of understanding.[24]

Maṇḍana similarly disputes that all language learning can arise from such situations.[25] – What 'ostension' in fact would require is for us to be able to step outside language, outside a shared world, in order to teach the meaning of a word. But this Archimedean desire is quite impossible, according to Maṇḍana Miśra, Augustine, Wittgenstein or Jacques Lacan. The latter writes: 'Either we already know the truth in question, and it is not, then, the signs which teach it to us, or we do not know it, and we cannot locate the signs which relate to it.'[26]

The value of such discussion, suggests Lacan, is that it shows 'that it is impossible to deal with language by referring the sign to the thing term by term'.[27] The Logical Positivists' picture of language and meaning is one that Lacan, like Augustine and the later Wittgenstein, finds inadequate. 'Language cannot be conceived of as the result of a series of shoots, of buds, coming out of each thing. The name is not like the little asparagus tip emerging from the thing.'[28] According to these thinkers, we must look elsewhere for an understanding of language, meaning and reference.

Dirty language

The German eighteenth-century thinker Johann Gottfried Herder complained about trivializing God through the lowest, most unworthy anthropomorphism. It is a common and understandable complaint. If language in general is not entirely up to the job of describing a transcendent Ultimate Reality, then language which looks all-too-human certainly isn't.

His friend Johann Georg Hamann came to the defence of what he called 'privileged anthropomorphism'. He was even happy to speak anthropomorphically of God, as Creator, having genitalia. One reason he did so was, paradoxically, to call attention to the inadequacy of *all* language about God. At least anthropomorphism is so obviously inadequate that one will not be misled by it. In contrast, if we clean up our dirty anthropomorphic language, the use of abstract terms can mislead us. Our language is grounded in particular terms, in ordinary language; every word has an empirical root.[29] But then we strip the 'particularity' from the word's field, generalizing it to enable it to fit all cases. The danger in this, however, is that we begin to believe that the existence of the abstract word demonstrates that the abstract objects to which these words refer have some independent real existence of their own. (Hamann argued that this was the case with the word 'Reason'.)[30]

The demand that language about God must be decently abstract in order to avoid gross theological misunderstanding plays upon our shame about the earthy vigour, the life, what Hamann daringly calls the 'pudenda' of our language. But it strikes a death blow at language to castrate it, he argues: 'The purity of a language deprives it of its richness; a correctness that is too rigid, of its strength and virility.'[31] The way to revive language is not to aim at philosophical purity, abstraction and obsessive correctness and precision. The way to bring language back from the dead is through 'hyperbole', poetic exaggeration, and creative provocation; to court the humble language of the people who experience and believe.

Anatole France made a similar point about the purification of language, with a different (less dirty) simile:

> the metaphysicians, when they make up a new language, are like knife-grinders who grind coins and medals against their stone instead of knives and scissors. They rub out the relief, the inscriptions, the portraits and when one can no longer see on the coins Victoria or Wilhelm or the French Republic, they explain: these coins now have nothing specifically English or German or French about them, for we have taken them out of time and space; they now are no longer worth, say, five francs, but rather have an inestimable value, and the area in which they are a medium of exchange has been infinitely extended.[32]

Anatole France's simile calls our attention to this conflict between the 'universal', the abstract, the general; and the particular, individual, concrete. Our language, some would argue, is a language of the particular. The way we speak is heavily conditioned by contingent factors, our race, class, gender, tastes in music even; and this affects how we speak. Others prefer to see language as having a universal validity. The metaphysician's 'solution', so say critics like George Berkeley in the Enlightenment, is to strip language of all particularity: of all the features that locate it in a history, a culture, a context, and make it as abstract as possible. Then it does not refer specifically to a place, a date, a value. What Anatole France recognizes is that this supposed neutrality does not make a coin (or a word) universal. A defaced coin does not have an infinite worth all over the world in every century; on the contrary, by losing all its particularity, it loses all its value.

Is this what happens with religious language when it struggles against its problem of reference? The believer wants to refer to something that is not an object; using everyday language nevertheless but tugging at it to make it fit. The Christian says 'God is a Father' and this often seems to work well enough in the framework of that religious tradition. But from time to time questions arise, and once the comparison has to be explained, it gets so wrapped around with qualifications, restrictions, and alterations that it has neither meaning nor use left to it. The dilemma seems to be: either human language is allowed to retain its meaning, drawn from human experience of the finite, in which case it can't be about a transcendent God; or, language is 'purified' of its anthropomorphic roots and threatens to be as 'purified' of any meaning.

Indian philosophers took a variety of stances on the question of the particular and the universal, and how it interacts with form. The Mīmāṃsākas held that the universal is the primary meaning; the logicians of the Nyāya and Vaiśeṣika traditions that the particular is, although it is characterized by the universal and by the form. Since the Buddhists reject universals they required a different theory, as we shall see shortly.

Religious philosophy has a tradition of different solutions to this problem. Aristotle distinguished 'univocal' and 'equivocal' uses of words. A word is used univocally when it is used in exactly the same way in two cases: as when one says the ace of clubs and the ace of spades are both cards. It is used equivocally if it is used in two completely different ways, like an ace of hearts and a wartime flying ace.

There are some who believe that univocal assertions are possible in religious language. The evangelical theologian Carl Henry claims that only univocal knowledge is real knowledge, so language must be used univocally about us and God if we claim to have knowledge about God. 'The logical difficulty with the theory of analogical [word use] lies in its futile attempt to explore a middle road between univocity and equivocacy. Only univocal assertions protect us from equivocacy; only univocal knowledge is, therefore, genuine and authentic knowledge.' There must be some literal truth about God, there must be some similarity between man and God; otherwise we cannot have genuine knowledge of God.[33]

Another tradition, however, asserts that language about the divine must be equivocal. This is not only a philosopher's position, but also a mystic's, and it is found in many different religions. 'Negative theology' in a strict form maintains that nothing or next-to-nothing can be said about God. Plotinus insists repeatedly that The One is beyond all knowing and saying. The Tao te Ching informs us that the Tao that can be spoken about is not the real Tao.

The milder version says that while we cannot necessarily make positive assertions about what God is, we can at least make confident assertions about what God is not. Maimonides warns us of the great danger in applying positive attributes to God. Every perfection we can imagine – even if God possesses it – would not in reality be in God the way we conceive it. It might be called by the same name, but it would in fact amount to a negation. Truth becomes manifest, Maimonides tells us, when we realize that language can only be used equivocally of God.[34]

The role of negation is prominent in Upaniṣadic thought; most of the attempts to speak about Brahman do so by means of negations: sometimes pithy: 'This Self is not this, not this'; sometimes in lengthy chains of negations:

> It is neither gross nor fine; it is neither short nor long; it has neither blood nor fat; it is without shadow nor darkness; it is without air or space; it is without contact; it has no taste or smell; it is without sight or hearing; it is without speech or mind; it is without energy, breath, or mouth; it is beyond measure; having nothing within it or outside of it.[35]

Maṇḍana combined a kind of optimism, compared with the austerity of Śaṇkara and Sureśvara, about the possibility of speaking about the ultimate, with an espousal of what Christian tradition was to call the 'via negativa'. An entity which is unknown by any form of knowledge (pramāṇa) can nevertheless be described by the negation of all particulars. Although one does not know Brahman or how Brahman connects with the word 'Brahman', nevertheless one knows the words of particulars – and the word 'not'. Thus the scriptures can teach us about Brahman.[36]

Negation then, paradoxically, can be taken as the basis for a theory of meaning. This was the point reached by some Buddhists: universals do not exist. On the other hand, particulars are transitory, fleeting, and have no stable existence. How and to what can words refer? In the understanding known as apohavāda, words function by exclusion: by cutting out everything to which the word does not apply.

Paradoxical language of a less playful sort than Hamann's is found more in theology, particularly in the Christian Protestant traditions, than in analytical philosophy.

However, it is theologians such as Luther or Karl Barth, and religious philosophers like Kierkegaard, who are masters in deploying paradox. For such thinkers, the Being of God is and remains a mystery; our affirmations then must have the paradoxical character of statements in which contraries are declared to be inseparable and equally necessary. These statements are not logically self-contradictory, as are statements about 'square circles'. Rather they are evocative images: such as 'losing life and finding it' or 'God everywhere present and nowhere included'. The negating or combining of images or words functions as an indication that the speaker is aware of the impropriety or impossibility of making affirmations about God. The justification for being able to make either an affirmation or a negation is strictly dependent on a religious attitude: a strongly 'existential' one, resting on a perceived relationship with God in which God communicates with the individual. Another way to put it is that one believes in the possibility of God's self-revelation as the source and ground of the claim made.

If one is not satisfied with univocity or equivocity, however, there is a third possibility, famously associated with Thomas Aquinas.[37] He agrees with his more mystical colleagues that a word, such as 'good', cannot be used univocally of us and of God because God is so utterly different to us that his goodness cannot be the same as ours, differing only in degree. My 'goodness' may consist in such acts as paying my taxes and not beating my husband. God's doesn't. On the other hand, when speaking of God our use of language cannot be purely equivocal, he argues. If God's goodness, for example, is completely unlike mine in every respect, as unlike each other as a fruit bat and a cricket bat, how can we know what we mean by saying 'God is good'? Isn't there anything in common between God's goodness and mine?

The middle route lying between these two extremes is 'analogy'. Words are neither used with completely the same sense nor with a completely different one; the analogical use of words is sort of the same and sort of different.

To see how analogy works in this way, I can say that God is good and my husband is good. But theirs are not the same 'kind of goodness'. My husband did not create or maintain the world out of his overflowing goodness. God's goodness does not mean coming home in time to collect the children from school like he promised. However, if the analogy works, we can see similarities. Both can be called 'loving Fathers', who care for their 'children' and strive to bring about the best for them. They are not good in exactly the same way, but there is a kind of common ground.[38]

Analogy has been taken up in a novel direction by Barry Miller with his discussion of God's existence and simplicity.[39] Miller distinguishes a 'limit case' from a 'limit simpliciter'.

Limit simpliciter and limit case

A limit simpliciter *differs only in degree from the things of which it is a limit, but it is still one of those things, a member of the set or series. The upper limit of speed, the speed of light, is itself a speed, and so this is a limit simpliciter.* A limit case, *on the other hand, draws a limit without being a member of that group. So the bottom limit of speed, 0 kilometres or miles per hour, is not actually a speed, it is the absence of any speed. So it is a limit case of speed. A series of lines getting shorter and shorter might be 'stopped' with a point; but a point is not a line, not even a tiny one, so it is a limit case of the set of lines. A series of polygons, with a progressively greater number of sides, becomes 'rounder and rounder' and closer and closer to a circle. A circle, then, is that to which such a progressive series points, or 'implies', as it were – but a circle is not a polygon and does not actually belong to the series, and so a circle is the limit case, not the limit simpliciter, of a series of polygons. (A triangle would be the lower limit simpliciter.) The limit case, then, 'is that in which a defining characteristic of the members has been varied to the point of extinction', in other words, it does not belong to the series at all.*[40]

Miller uses this distinction to understand God's attributes, and it could be called a kind of theory of analogy. God's attributes are not limits simpliciter, e.g. maximal goodness, although this is how they are often dealt with by philosophers of religion whom Miller describes as 'perfect-being theologians'. Perfect-being theologians have 'ensured the falsity of their claims about the nature of God . . . by ignoring the possibility of there being anything similar to, but beyond, the maximum of a series'.[41] God's is not the greatest possible goodness, on a scale that embraces the moral goodness of dogs, humans, angels, and God. God's attributes are outside the series, as a limit case is. And yet the series clearly points to its limit case, and gives an indication of what it is like, though an imperfect or inexact one; just as a many-sided polygon can give a hint of what a circle is like, although the polygon is not round. Practitioners of negative theology, Miller suggests, also err in the opposite direction, in 'not recognizing the possibility of some likeness between that entity and the members of the series beyond which it lay'.[42]

So God's existence and attributes are limit cases and not 'instances' of their creaturely counterparts; hence they are neither univocal nor equivocal. Univocal language is not possible for God. Meanwhile, there is some community of meaning between words for God and words for created things, so they are not equivocal.

The fig leaf of figurative language

Perhaps poetic language can provide a discreet cover-up for the problem of language about the divine. One can use colourful phrases or imagery to convey an impression, while denying that they are to be taken literally.

Metaphor

Aristotle said that the ability to create a good metaphor is a sign of genius, for it implies that someone can grasp the similarity that exists in dissimilarity. Nelson Goodman just says it is a matter of teaching an old word new tricks.[43] Although most are acquainted with metaphors as ornaments in language, as 'near relations' of other figures of speech, such as simile, metaphor is linguistically and epistemologically a much more complex and rich phenomenon than school lessons in grammar and literature ever suggested.[44] Among the various theories of metaphor, the simplest view is that it is another way of saying what can be said literally. A metaphor is a substitution for a more straightforward expression. I could say of a child, 'he is badly-behaved' but I say instead, 'he is a monster'. It is not difficult to translate my metaphor into more direct speech. This is the view of metaphor usually attributed to the ancients.

Janet Martin Soskice objects that this makes the value of metaphor negligible; not only does it reduce metaphor to the level of a riddle; it also reduces the intelligibility of language.[45] You could misunderstand my unkind reference to the little boy as meaning 'he is exceedingly large for his age', perhaps. This explains Thomas Hobbes's negative evaluation of metaphor; it is an abuse of speech 'when they use words metaphorically; that is, in other senses than that they are ordained for; and thereby deceive others'.[46]

Soskice argues that this view is untenable. A metaphor extends the meaning beyond what is contained in a single literal translation. Her strongest objection to this simple view is that it suggests that those who use metaphors as part of their art, like the poet, the theologian or the scientist, are 'doing no more than translating from a prior and literal understanding into an evocative formulation'. But actually the thinking itself is undertaken as metaphor.[47] 'What interests us in metaphor is precisely that we find in it an increment to understanding,' Soskice writes.[48]

This, then, is the direction that thinking about metaphor has taken in recent decades: metaphor is not something you can easily replace; often it cannot be reduced to literal speech for it has its own cognitive content.[49] Metaphor holds two ideas together and the meaning results from their relation. This permanent tension or interaction is crucial in understanding how metaphor works. It is not a question of substituting one word for another, but bringing into connection two different regions or contexts. Thus metaphors are not merely rhetorical devices, but can be new and unconventional ways of interpreting reality, or even creating reality.

In the hands of such thinkers, metaphor becomes a model for how we understand, as well as how we embody our understanding in speech. When we encounter something new, we begin by partly assimilating it to what is known, as well as pointing up the differences with what is already familiar. This plays on the tension of similarity/dissimilarity that exists in metaphor, and extends it to a view of the method of understanding, or a way of seeing the world, or indeed the way in which the human mind itself works. 'Metaphor is as ultimate as speech itself, and speech as ultimate as thought. . . . Metaphor appears as the instinctive and necessary act of the mind exploring reality and ordering experience.'[50]

If this viewpoint is accepted, then religious language is not unique in using language about God that is fundamentally metaphorical. The same has even been said of scientific language, as here by Bronowski:

> The whole of science is shot through and through with metaphors, which transfer and link one part of our experience to another, and find likenesses between the parts. All our ideas derive from and embody such metaphorical likenesses.[51]

If this is the case with science, then religious language, which attempts to refer to the Transcendent with metaphors, is not different in principle to other forms of discourse.

One corollary of this is that the assumption that univocal language comes first, and that metaphor is a later supplementation or ornamentation, is virtually reversed. We perceive or understand first metaphorically, and univocal propositions are later developments, refinements, clarifications of the initial 'metaphorical' perception. This has been stressed by various modern thinkers; Nietzsche and Derrida both suggest that all language is metaphorical. Lacan takes this understanding of metaphor as fundamental to epistemology further; he uses metaphor and metonymy not just to indicate how conscious thinking and language operate, but primarily and fundamentally how the unconscious operates as well. 'What need is there to talk of a reality which would sustain the so-called metaphorical usages? Every kind of usage, in a certain sense, is always metaphorical.'[52]

In contrast, the contemporary German philosopher Hans Blumenberg's 'metaphorology' is thoroughly historical and not simply theoretical.[53] With an impressive range throughout the history of ideas, he examines particular, concrete metaphors (such as metaphors of truth), as well as engaging in theoretical reflection on metaphorology. For example, he asks can metaphors be true? They cannot be verified. The issue cannot be decided theoretically, at least according to dominant contemporary understandings of truth and meaning. What Blumenberg is after, then, is the historical truth of metaphors, which is pragmatic. They answer to the question: what genuine guidance does it give? They give the world structure; they allow us to do what is impossible, that is, gain an overview over the totality of reality: 'the fundamental, enduring certainties, conjectures, valuations, from which the attitudes, expectations, activities and idleness, longings and disappointments, interests and indifference of an epoch are regulated'.[54]

Metaphor as Rhetoric

Metaphor as a 'mere' figure of speech in ancient Greece has its roots in rhetoric. While 'rhetoric' is not a term of approbation for most modern philosophers, it was held in considerable esteem in Greek philosophy – indeed, as Blumenberg points out, it was so important that Plato named the decisive phase of mythical cosmogony in Timaeus as the rhetorical act of persuasion. The power of persuasion was a quality of reality itself, extended into the arts and methods of rhetoric.[55]

It could be argued, then, that claiming it is a greater dignity for metaphor to be a way of perceiving and representing the world than being a rhetorical device actually rests on modern Western assumptions that the primary task of philosophy is description of material reality, and the primary task of language is to service thought by representing its cognitions accurately.

Talking about 'mere figures of speech' and the 'greater importance' of metaphor as cognitive makes epistemology more important than communication, interpersonal interaction, social change and transformation. But is that what you think? Perhaps the point of metaphor is not to teach an old word new tricks, as Goodman suggested, but to teach a new world old tricks. We might then see that metaphor as a device of rhetoric is more powerful than if it is viewed as a mode of private cognition.

Symbol

'Man's ultimate concern must be expressed symbolically, because symbolic language alone is able to express the ultimate,' so Paul Tillich claims, when it comes to speaking about the divine. According to Tillich, symbols give us access to levels of reality which we cannot reach scientifically. At the same time, they unlock hidden depths of our own being. Tillich's 'symbol' is characterized partly in distinction to the 'sign'.[56] Both point beyond themselves to something else. They are given a special meaning by convention. The decisive difference is that signs do not 'participate in the reality of that to which they point', while symbols do; they 'participate in [the] meaning and power' of what they symbolize. Signs can be changed by conscious decision, or replaced for reasons of expediency or convention, while symbols cannot. Symbols' relationship to what they symbolize is more than arbitrary or conventional. Although changing Stop-signs might cause some initial confusion, it would not have the impact of changing a country's flag, which is not a 'sign' of the country but a 'symbol'. Changing a flag may mean that the country made such a profound change that it must be embodied by a new symbol. The same thing can happen within religions, as, for example, Protestants felt it necessary to destroy Catholic symbols to signify a change in theology.

Tillich applies his account of symbols to religious faith by naming God as the fundamental symbol of our ultimate concern. 'God is a symbol for God.' We need therefore to distinguish the ultimacy, which is not symbolic itself, from the concreteness of the symbol, which is taken from ordinary experience and applied to God. Faith, then, does not require belief in these concrete images from earthly life, 'but it is the acceptance of symbols that express our ultimate concern in terms of divine actions'. These are not susceptible to empirical criticism; their truth lies in the adequacy to the situation for which they are created.

Randall has used an account of symbol and myth to highlight the non-representational function of religious language in particular.[57] Religion, he argues, is an activity which makes its own special contribution to society. It works with a body of symbols and myths that are non-representative and non-cognitive, that is, they do not symbolize some external thing that can be indicated apart from their operation; but rather it is a question of what these symbols and myths actually do.

Religious symbols, according to Randall, have a fourfold function: they arouse emotions and stir us to action, and thereby may strengthen our practical commitment; they stimulate co-operative action and thus bind a community together through a common response to its symbols; they are able to communicate qualities of experience that cannot be expressed by the ordinary literal use of language; they evoke, and also clarify our experience of an aspect of the world that can be called the divine. As artists can teach us to use our senses in a new way, so can prophets and saints open our hearts to new qualities in the world, the religious dimension of the world. Randall, however, does not believe that God or the divine exists as a reality independent of the human mind. God is rather an 'intellectual symbol' for the religious aspects of the world, our ideals, our values, what Tillich calls our 'ultimate concern'.

Paul Ricoeur observes that the symbol gives rise to thought. It is prior to philosophy, theology, even myth. It has a 'double intentionality', that is, points in two directions: the first, the literal intention, is the only way into the more cryptic meaning. There is always more to symbols (and myths) than in the whole of philosophy.[58]

But Ricoeur also calls our attention to a danger. We continually seek to make the Wholly Other into an object; 'metaphysics makes God into a supreme being; and religion treats the sacred as a new sphere of objects'[59] – with the result that sacred *signs* become sacred *things*. This is how 'idols' arise. The sacred can be a meaningful bearer of the Wholly Other, or can be a set of idols as one group of things in our culture alongside others. 'The ambiguity is inevitable: for if the Wholly Other draws near, it does so in the signs of the sacred; but symbols soon turn into idols.' For the symbols to live, the idols must die.[60]

Such accounts of symbol may seem to take us further than one expects to go when dealing solely with language.[61] Or do they? The symbol, apparently, makes something present. The symbol gives access to what we otherwise could not reach. The symbol gives rise to thought, or so they tell us. It points in two directions at once. Isn't all this what 'language' does? Jacques Lacan's realm of 'The Symbolic' is basically coextensive with language, and perhaps we can see why. Instead of being a part of language, such accounts tempt us to ask what part of language is *not* a symbol. We shall return to more complex ideas of symbolization shortly.

Myth

Rudolf Bultmann claimed that much of the Bible is 'mythological'; by which he did not mean 'untrue', but rather that it belonged to the genre of myth. The New Testament cosmology of the world, for example, three-tiered as it is with heaven, God and his angels above, hell with Satan and his devils below, and the earth in the middle, is clearly, according to Bultmann, mythological.[62]

When preachers confront people with the gospel message of redemption, Bultmann asserts, they have often done so within this mythical view of the world which the New Testament presupposes. But this makes the gospel message unbelievable to modern people, who (Bultmann says) cannot believe in this cosmos of demons and angels. Do we expect our converts not only to accept the essential message of salvation, but also the mythical view of the world in which it is set? And if we do not, does the New Testament embody a truth which is independent of its mythical framework? If it does, theology must undertake the task of stripping the message from its mythical setting, of 'demythologizing' it.

We cannot, Bultmann tells us, simply subtract the bits of the Bible we find mythological and believe what is left over: the sophisticated wisdom, the inspiring ethical exhortations, or whatever takes our fancy. We must reinterpret the myth because the real purpose of myth is not to present an objective picture of the world as it is, but to express our understanding of ourselves in the world in which we live. Myth speaks of the power or the powers which we suppose we experience as the ground and limit of our world and of our activity and suffering. We describe these powers in terms derived from the visible world and from human life. Myth is an expression of the human conviction that the origin and purpose of the world in which we live are to be sought not within it but beyond it. It is also an expression of our awareness that we are not the lord of our own being. The importance of the New Testament mythology lies not in its imagery but in the understanding of existence which it enshrines. This means that mythology needs to be reinterpreted existentially. We have to discover whether the New Testament offers us an understanding of ourselves which will challenge us to a genuine existential decision.

Bultmann's explanation of what demythologizing is not, and what it is

> *The purpose of demythologizing is not to make religion more acceptable to modern man by trimming the traditional Biblical texts, but to make clearer to modern man what the Christian faith is. He must be confronted with the issue of decision. . . . Such an attempt does not aim at reassuring modern man by saying to him: 'You no longer have to believe this and that' . . .; not by showing him that the number of things to be believed is smaller than he had thought, but because it shows him that to believe at all is qualitatively different from accepting a certain number of propositions.*[63]

What are the presuppositions of language and meaning underlying Bultmann's account? It presumes that meaning can be separated from the language in which it is dressed and we can extract the meaning as if removing old-fashioned clothing, which might contain but also conceals it.[64] It is this notion of the relation of meaning to the language which gives it expression that has aroused some of the most energetic criticism of Bultmann's programme.[65]

However, Bultmann's programme, although it was a central focus for twentieth-century theology and religious thought, is only part of a larger tradition that has developed in Europe over the last several centuries. Odo Marquard characterizes the fundamental attitude to myth of modern Europe as 'demythologizing', whether one is referring to Bultmann or not. Myth is what we have left behind us; we are in the course of progress from 'mythos to logos' by which is meant from myth to rationality. Opinions divide as to whether this is a bad or good thing. But this history of the processes of demythologizing is itself a myth, Marquard argues; the fact that 'the death of myth' has itself become a myth shows the relative immortality of myth.

For Marquard, myth is what we cannot do without. We cannot take it off like clothing, an image which Marquard develops with pleasing frivolity. Mythic nakedness – and Marquard reminds us of Blumenberg's investigation into the metaphor of the '*naked* truth'[66] – is a nakedness that doesn't exist for us. Marquard is sceptical about the striptease of demythologizing; the more that myth takes off, the more that it seems to keep on. A little child in the crowd might cry out that the Emperor of Logical Positivism still has myths on! Mytho-nudism is simply impossible.[67]

Blumenberg, in his monumental *Work on Myth*, suggests that myth is needed not just by so-called 'primitive' peoples but by all of us; we need it to prevent the 'absolutism of reality'.[68] Our knowledge is always only partial, but the absolutism of reality is total. Knowledge of the 'scientific' kind is not enough; we need something more than knowledge to cope. He disputes the myth of the progress from 'mythos' to 'logos' and claims that scientific rationality is not the end-state. Rationality and myth are both indispensable to us, from the start and forever afterwards.

What comes to light in Blumenberg's examination is that people oppose rationality to myth in a relatively hostile (he might have added: 'indiscriminate') manner: they assume that whatever contrasts with rationality is 'myth'. We might point out that 'myth' is colloquially used today for a story that isn't true. So, for example, discussions of Nazi propaganda often speak of it as 'myth' with an air of acceptance that 'myth' is what their stories truly were, although by the same token Nazi ideas of race and health are not considered 'philosophy' and 'science'.[69] Setting myth and rationality against one another in this way makes myth subject, at best, to carrying the blame for the failures of rationality, or at worst, a kind of demonization. This is ironically 'the mythicization of the difference between myth and rationality'![70]

Blumenberg chronicles modern attempts to bring myth to an end, suggesting that they are trying to end myth by means of myth itself. If the work of myth is to counter the absolutism of reality, then myth comes to an end when we have solved that problem – when our knowledge is complete; when the absolutism of reality is replaced by the absolutism of the subject. The German Idealists and those who succeed them (Nietzsche, Heidegger) compete to create the final myth, the story which is so complete that there is room for no other. 'To bring myth to an end was once supposed to have been the work of logos. This consciousness of itself on the part of philosophy – or better, the historians of philosophy – is contradicted by the fact that work aimed at putting an end to myth is again and again accomplished in the form of a metaphor of myth.'[71]

Marquard warns us against the dangers of 'monomythia', the domination of a single myth. What we need is the plurality of myths, polymythia, for our own protection; for some myths, like some mushrooms, are poisonous. His strategy, therefore, is to counter myths with a pluralism of myths, from which we can choose the healthy ones, rather than to try to strip language of myth altogether.

Language strips for action

Bring on the elephants

In the first year of his seminars, Lacan observed, by way of example, that the word 'elephant' allows us to take decisions about elephants in their absence, 'even before touching them', and these have much greater impact on them than our immediate presence can. Once he had alluded to elephants, he observed: 'It is clear, all I need do is talk about it, there is no need for them to be here, for them really to be here, thanks to the word elephant, and to be more real than the contingent elephant-individuals.'[72] Later he referred to himself as having brought an elephant 'into the room the other day by means of the word elephant'.[73]

What happened when Lacan talked about elephants? He was not *describing* some unusually large and noticeably grey members of the student body in the room, either in literal assertions of existence or in metaphors. He was *doing* something – making elephants present – by means of language.

In contrast to the emphasis on the 'representing' function of language, on description, report, and assertion, there are recent accounts that prioritize instead the non-representational aspects of language. These suggest that it does not merely *say* things, it *does* things. John Searle tells us that there are five things we can do with language. 'You can tell people how things are (assertives); tell them to do things (directives); commit yourself to doing things (commissives); express your feelings and attitudes (expressives); and bring about changes in the world through your utterances (declarations).'[74] Searle's approach has come to be known as 'Speech-Act Theory'.

Terrence Tilley claims that this schema can be used to throw light on much of religious language. He suggests as examples that petitionary prayer is a 'directive', that preaching is an 'assertive', that pledging is 'commissive', that swearing is 'expressive', and confession a 'declarative'.[75] Doubtless readers can reflect on the praxis of religious individuals they know to flesh out Searle's taxonomy still further.

What Speech-Act Theory does, first of all, is to underline that language is *act*, as well as 'speech'. Further, it asserts the right of language to be diverse. One needs to recognize the plurality of functions it possesses. However, I question whether a tidy list of five is the best way to encourage the recognition of diversity. The enumeration of a list always begs questions – and where it does not irritate listeners, it sometimes silences them. I remember sitting in a lecture in which a distinguished Catholic psychotherapist and marriage counsellor said solemnly: 'There are five reasons why married people have sex.' No doubt he wanted get away from theologies of sex which stressed only one purpose. However, I wondered if he considered someone repressed if they could only come up with four reasons; and whatever would he say about the fact that I could think of six?

J. L. Austin claimed that whenever we say something, we perform a number of acts. Contrary to representationalist views, much of what we say does not match the world; we say it in order to do something: to swear an oath or to make a vow does not describe the world, and yet such utterances are not meaningless. Austin called attention to 'performative utterances' – times when speech is effective, when it brings something about. Much religious language does not describe; there are times of worship, of making commitments, in which the action rather than the assertion is the important thing.[76]

Ian Ramsey similarly asserted that there are certain situations in which taking religious language as not propositional makes sense. He characterized these as 'discernment' and 'commitment'. Discernment is used in situations where we recognize an important insight, what he calls 'disclosure situations'. Religious language is the right currency for this. Commitment means that one sees one's whole life in terms of an insight. There is a point at which argument stops: some actions are self-justifying, and at such times we use phrases like: 'Duty is duty'. Although in analytical terms these appear to be empty and uninformative, they are 'significant tautologies' which point to a commitment. 'God is love' he suggests is such a tautology.[77]

It is, however, the later Wittgenstein's account of language that has had the most impact on non-representational understandings of language. Having repented and done penance for his earlier positivist leanings, he was born again into the new life of ordinary language. Wittgenstein had decided that the search for the ideal logical scientific language was misguided and that ordinary language would do very nicely. In fact, many philosophical problems can be untangled by paying attention to it. This was observed earlier by the Nyāya theoreticians,[78] not to mention Johann Georg Hamann.[79] Many traditional philosophical problems arise because we don't see the real nature of language; these problems arise when language is being used 'out of gear'.

What we see when we examine ordinary language is that it is much more complex than Logical Positivism allows. It is not just a tool for making assertions – '. . . As if there were only one thing called "talking about a thing". Whereas in fact we do the most various things with our sentences.'[80]

With an expansion of his view of what language does, Wittgenstein has to revise his earlier theory of meaning – his own picture theory. The word is not a unit of meaning, he now sees, nor is the sentence composed of word-units. 'If' 'there' 'now' only have their meaning in their use in language. So as compared to the *Tractatus*, where the meaning of the word was the thing to which it referred, in *Philosophical Investigations* the meaning of language is to be found in the many uses to which it is put.

While in the *Tractatus* using language correctly consisted in following certain rules, in *Philosophical Investigations* this is replaced by the idea of 'language games'. This contains the recognition that there are a variety of different systems of rules governing how we speak, and that these do not have a universal, objective, eternal validity, but are agreed, and apply to the matter at hand, without external justification. 'If you do not keep the multiplicity of language-games in view you will perhaps be inclined to ask questions like: "What is a question?" – Is it the statement that I do not know such-and-such, or the statement that I wish the other person would tell me . . .? Or is it the description of my mental state of uncertainty?'[81]

Wittgenstein's 'language games'

But how many kinds of sentence are there? Say assertion, question, and command? – There are countless kinds: countless different kinds of use of what we call 'symbols', 'words', 'sentences'. And this multiplicity is not something fixed, given once for all; but new types of language, new language-games, as we may say, come into existence, and others become obsolete and get forgotten. . . . Here the term 'language-game' is meant to bring into prominence the fact that the speaking of language is part of an activity, or a form of life. Review the multiplicity of language-games in the following examples, and in others: giving orders, and obeying them – Describing the appearance of an object, or giving its measurements – Reporting an event – Speculating about an event – Play-acting – Guessing riddles – Asking, thanking, cursing, greeting, praying. – It is interesting to compare the multiplicity of the tools in language and of the ways they are used, the multiplicity of kinds of word and sentence, with what logicians have said about the structure of language. (Including the author of the Tractatus Logico-Philosophicus.*)*[82]

Maṇḍana also asserted that children learn the meaning of words from their use in 'language-games', although he did not describe them as such; however, he disagreed with a hypothetical objector that the sole use from which they learned was in the form of injunctions.[83]

The corollary of this for religious language is that, if language functions in all kinds of different ways, then one can claim that religious language performs its own function. Religious language can be its own language game, or set of language games, with its own purpose, meaning and internal justification. This has, initially, the comforting consequence that religious believers can no longer be derided for being unable to display an object 'God' that corresponds to the word.[84] Moreover, language cannot be considered apart from other aspects of life and behaviour; language is always embedded in a 'form of life'. The corollary is that one cannot make the rash assumption that religious statements function in the same way as mathematical propositions and scientific assertions of fact. To understand a religious statement as a philosopher, one must take into account the whole context in which the statement occurs.

An early attempt to expand these insights was by R. Braithwaite. He adopted Wittgenstein's principle that meaning is found in use, and tried to consider the meaning of religious language with this as the starting-point. He argued that the primary element in the use of religious statements is the making of moral assertions, an ethical function. He further presupposes that moral statements are not verifiable propositions but express the attitude of the person making the statement and the speaker's adherence to a certain policy of action. To say one 'ought' to do something is to say that one intends to do this. Religious statements, then, express the intention to live life in a particular way. So, for example, a Christian's assertion that 'God is love' means 'I intend to follow an agapeistic way of life.'[85] Differences in ritual between religions are essentially unimportant; as is the fact that they tell different stories, which need not be true in order to inspire. To assert the doctrines of a religion is both to tell its doctrinal story and to confess allegiance to its way of life.

For an account that claims to base itself on Wittgenstein, this is strikingly un-Wittgensteinian. Braithwaite reduces the complex phenomenon of ethics to a single function, and the even more elaborate and multivalent phenomenon of religion to a single purpose. The particular force of Wittgenstein's later position, especially his rejection of his own earlier theory, is precisely to eschew such single-mindedness and assert the primacy of diversity and plurality. If language does not have a single function, or a single nature, how can ethical or religious language be so ruthlessly singular?

We met D. Z. Phillips in the previous chapter, when he suggested that religion does not need to be externally 'grounded' as the evidentialist claims. His view on rationality and 'grounding' religious claims is part of his Wittgenstein-inspired view that religious belief forms its own framework (like a language-game) and must be understood in its own context.

> It has been far too readily assumed that the dispute between the believer and the unbeliever is over a *matter of fact*. Philosophical reflection on the reality of God then becomes the philosophical reflection appropriate to an assertion of a matter of fact. I have tried to show that this is a misrepresentation of the religious concept, and that philosophy can claim justifiably to show what is meaningful in religion only if it is prepared to examine religious concepts in the contexts from which they derive their meaning. A failure to take account of the above context has led some philosophers to ask religious language to satisfy criteria of meaningfulness alien to it. They say that religion must be rational if it is to be intelligible. Certainly, the distinction between the rational and the irrational must be central in any account one gives of meaning. But this is not to say that there is a paradigm of rationality to which all modes of discourse conform.[86]

Gareth Moore has also thought through belief in God from the standpoint of how the language of religious believers functions, in a Wittgenstein-inspired account that does not however rely as heavily on the notion of the language-game as a system that escapes external scrutiny.

> Christian belief in and language about God is logically linked to the way Christians live and see their lives. It is through the attitudes and dispositions and activities of Christians that their language gets its meaning. It is not that belief in God . . . is somehow given an independent, theoretical meaning, and that we are then exhorted to develop the attitudes appropriate to such a being. . . . The attitudes, dispositions and activities are not just appropriate in the light of the beliefs we hold about some being called God, they are what gives sense to our belief in God and what we believe about him. Our religious beliefs and language have their place within the context of a particular kind of human life, a life in which gratitude, generosity, lack of self-seeking, a sense of dependence and mystery, among other things, play an important, even a defining part.[87]

Moore takes seriously the context of belief and real life against which religious utterances have meaning. He is like a metalworker trying to restore the place, date and value to neutralized coins to reinstate their value. His account could be subtitled 'God as Nothing'. Again and again he drives home the point that to say God did something is to say that no-one did it. Paradoxically, however, the absence to which Moore continuously refers is overlaid with the presence of a name, which makes sense in the absence of its bearer, which introduces its bearer into the room by means of the word, as did Lacan's elephant.

Picking up cats

A philosopher and a theologian were at a party engaging in the usual jousting. 'You philosophers', complained the theologian, 'are like blind men in a darkened room, looking for a cat that isn't there.' 'That may be so,' retorted the philosopher; 'but you theologians find the cat.'

For the accounts of language we have considered thus far, it is clear what language does when it announces: 'The cat sat on the mat'. But what can it do about a cat like the theologian's cat, which isn't there?

Freud described a baby playing his own little game of throwing a cotton reel away, saying 'Here!' while it is gone, then pulling it back to himself, saying 'Gone!' once it is present again. Lacan takes this game as the phenomenon of symbolization taking shape: making something present in its absence, by means of the word. 'When the object is there he chases it away, when it isn't there he calls it. Through these first games, the object passes . . . on to the plane of language. The symbol comes into being and becomes more important than the object.'[88]

On this account, the word makes the absent present, like cats and elephants. Less commonly observed is that it can also make the present absent, as those from despised social or ethnic groups can feel when language used by others doesn't include them. This notion of the word as making-present (or absent) is arguably a more comprehensive basis for understanding how language refers to the world than accounts of language as representational and picture theories of meaning. The word is not the label of what it names; the relation of word to object is the symbolic function of making something present in its absence. Lacan actually says that the word is the thing itself.[89] In his thought the object is almost the incarnation of the word.

In Lacan's conception, words are joined into a 'signifying chain', which links one signifier or word to another. With this image, the focus shifts off the connection of each word to its appropriate thing; now the attention is on the connection between one word and the next.

A graphic example may illustrate the impact that such a paradigm shift may have on something's meaning.

A friend who is a Roman Catholic priest (let's call him 'Johannes') was at my house for dinner. Johannes found himself in the company of psychotherapists and made the mistake of relating a dream that he had had several times lately, and canvassing opinion. He dreamed that he desperately wanted a pet cat. He reflected that he could go out in the street and pick one up, a stray, and pet it. But what he really wanted was one of his own to cuddle and take home and keep by him all the time for company.

The Jungian psychotherapist present observed that around the world, cats are symbols or archetypes for the underworld. The underworld is the image of the unconscious. Johannes was now at the time of life where it was time to make that descent of self-examination into the unconscious. This is not to be done casually ('pick up one in the street'); one needs to make a commitment to do this ('take the cat home with you and keep it'). What the dream was trying to tell Johannes was that he should now embark on a Jungian psychoanalysis.

The Lacanian was not interested in connecting the word 'cat' to an object, to then interpret the symbolism of the object – what that animal symbolizes, as the Jungian had. Her focus was on a word-to-word connection: not what the word 'cat' brings to mind, but what word the word 'cat' brings to mind. One word came immediately to her mind: 'Pussy.'

With this an entirely new direction of interpretation opened up.[90]

The Lacanian account of meaning does not grapple with the question of how the word attaches to the thing. It examines the way that words connect to other words. In this way, it is 'Augustinian' – it echoes the insight of Augustine and Adeodatus that words do refer, despite our sceptical doubts; but what they refer to is other words. This also recalls Maṇḍana's suggestions. Every signifier only leads to another signifier; 'no signification can be sustained other than by reference to another signification'. [91] Language is not supported by the existence of things outside it. 'So, you will get caught up in paths which are always dead ends . . . if you fail to take account of the fact that signification only ever refers back to itself, that is to say to another signification.'[92] Language is not justified by its connection with the 'real world'.

Language consists of signifying chains, which are made up by two structures: 'metaphor' and 'metonymy'.[93]

Metonymy and metaphor

Metonymy is the device in which one word stands in for, or replaces, another; almost like a euphemism. They are so common in everyday language that they may go unnoticed. Reporters say 'Downing Street announced' and are not telling us about a talking road, but the Prime Minister's spokesperson.

Metonymy is a word-to-word connection. Metaphor Lacan conceives as a substitution of one signifier for another; 'the occulted signifier remaining present through its (metonymic) connection with the rest of the chain'.[94]

In the signifying chain of Johannes' dream,[95] 'cat' was a metaphor, blocking out the metonymic 'pussy', the occulted signifier. But because 'pussy' is metonymy for something else which I don't need to name, what is blocked out is nevertheless still present in the signifying chain through this metonymic connection. This arrangement of things, so we are to understand, allows you simultaneously to block something out and to let it resonate in your listener's mind. By saying 'cat' we can include the thing 'pussy' is slang for without naming it.

Metonymy, in those languages and cultures which encourage it, allows an extraordinary depth and richness to one's speech. The Hawaiian language enjoys a phenomenal degree of polysemy (multiple meanings to a single 'word'); and Hawaiian poetry makes extensive use of the possibilities inherent in both polysemy and metonymy. Most songs and poems contain more than one meaning: it includes the most obvious, but also a '*kaona*' or hidden meaning. Once Hawaii was invaded by a different culture which was somewhat hostile and critical of its mores, yet desirous of enjoying it aesthetically, a kind of inter-lingual metonymy took place and still does. The original multiple meanings of poems and songs can be occulted behind a single translation – or lack of one. When certain things are forbidden and cannot be said, they can still find expression. The biblical genre of 'apocalyptic' functions in a similar way, to allow one to speak to those who will understand, when under conditions of repression or censorship.

For example, a Hawaiian prince, Lele-iō-Hoku, had written a love song in the Hawaiian language which unreservedly describes making love in the sea ('we two in the spray, oh joy two together, embracing tightly in the coolness' it begins). In my childhood it was sung at tourist shows, but in the original Hawaiian, never translated or sung in English. It was described to the tourists as 'The Hawaiian War Chant'. Lele-iō-Hoku's secret was safe.

Wittgenstein's problem at the end of the *Tractatus* – 'I need to say something that my rules won't permit me to say' – is the problem faced by religious believers, even if they reject Logical Positivist restraints. If they hold fast to the affirmation of divine transcendence, how can they do the impossible and say the unsayable? By metonymy and *kaona*, would be one answer. It allows you to allude without claiming to describe.

Lacan is adamant that it is not 'picturing' which justifies language:

> We will get no further as long as we cling to the illusion that the signifier [word] answers to the function of representing the signified [what it refers to], or that the signifier has to answer for its existence in the name of any signification whatever. For even reduced to this latter formulation, the error is the same – an error that leads to logical positivism in search of the 'meaning of meaning', as its objective is called in the language of its devotees.[96]

The later Wittgenstein similarly asserted, 'When we say: "Every word in language signifies something", we have so far said nothing whatever.'[97] Neither thinks that language can be explained simply by reference to the things or situations in the world that it is supposed to mean, or represent. If we reject the picture theory, and maybe even a sense of language as representational, what are we left with? Words lead only to still more words, never things; language is a blind alley from which there is no exit into the real world.

Wittgenstein's and Lacan's ideas, along with Nietzsche and Derrida, have influenced some thinkers in Britain towards a stance of 'non-realism'. Non-realism stoutly rejects the idea that words work by referring to things 'out there'. The non-realist is scornful of the 'out there'. Language is a bubble in which we live, as the British theologian Don Cupitt put it, with nothing outside it.[98]

In the view of Don Cupitt, language is endlessly on the move, sliding, transient, slipping by 'at such a rate that the object of our desire never fully arrives'.[99] It is a closed system from which there is no escape, a language-bubble, with nothing, no 'external reality' outside it. This could be seen as the linguistic corollary of Cupitt's earlier views of God, the approach which has come to be referred to as the Sea of Faith, 'the view that there is nothing beyond or outside human beings, neither God nor some other notion like "Ultimate Reality" that gives life and meaning and purpose'.[100] Now the challenges of the problem of reference in religious language, as previously with the problem of knowledge of God, are met with a solution that is purely self-referential: there is nothing beyond or outside language to which language refers, no external reality to act as the guarantee of truth in language.

That is not, however, where Lacan ends up. He recognizes the 'lure' of the picture theory and commonsensical notions of language as depicting reality: 'this lure is structural to human language and, in a sense, the verification of every truth is founded on it'.[101] In Lacan's view, words just point you to other words, not things; but if this order of language is a blind alley with no exit, it would be an order without meaning. Truth requires something 'beyond' signification. 'But it is in relation to truth that the signification of everything which is expressed is to be located.'[102] Like Wittgenstein, he needs a ladder to climb out of the threatened confines of his own theory.

His 'ladder' is the insistence that language ('the Symbolic' in his vocabulary) does have a strong relation to what he calls 'the Real'. Language, says Lacan, 'introduces the dimension of truth into the real'.[103] It throws a net over things, and thus brings them to us for speech; it is the way the world of things is brought into the human world of speaking. So although it does not 'picture' or simply 'mirror' reality, what language does to 'things' is to bring them into being for us, reveal them and their significance for us. Aristotle says that 'voice', as the expression of pleasure and pain and emotion, is something we share with animals. But 'language' makes clear what is expedient, what is harmful, what is good or evil, what is just and unjust, and so on.[104] Thus according to Aristotle, language does not passively describe the world, it interprets it according to human interests, needs, and desires.

'All speech always possesses a beyond.'[105] The beyond of signification is of course beyond language; but it is not a-linguistic and utterly ineffable. 'When you understand what is expressed in the signs of the language, it is always, in the end, on account of light coming to you from *outside* of the signs. . . . The truth is *outside* of the signs, elsewhere.'[106] It is significant, perhaps, that Cupitt may have modified his stance somewhat and now seems to suggest that 'Being' is outside language, that language is no longer a closed circle.[107]

Lacan's linking of Symbol and Reality

'We are talking about things, and not about some eternally unidentifiable I know not what.'[108] For although one word may always send us off after another, 'all our experience runs counter to this linearity'. There are 'anchoring points' for language. 'There is no signifying chain that does not have, as if attached to the punctuation of each of its units, a whole articulation of relevant contexts suspended "vertically", as it were, from that point.'[109] Although each signifier is linked to the next signifier in the chain, each signifier is also grounded, anchored – but not in a simplistic word-to-thing, one-to-one correspondence. The anchors are contexts, and what anchors the signifiers are associations. We cannot say, ' "cat" symbolizes x' – but even if 'cat' connects to another word like 'pussy', a context and associations still exist to anchor these words in our world and our desires.

Weaving some strands together

Let us take forward some of these ideas for an understanding of religious language; in particular, those that have been neglected in mainstream philosophy of religious language; of the importance of communication and not just representation; of metonymy, as the possibility for saying the unsayable; the idea of the word as making present what is seemingly absent or occulted; and of the signifying chain, which does not look to the world of things for its meaning – or its justification.

To begin with, we might restore the primacy of 'communication' to our ideas about language. Some time ago, I was involved in language therapy training for small children with language disorders. These seminars focused entirely on the question of communication as what language is all about. 'Reference' was never mentioned. Our concerns were: What does communication presuppose, what does it consist in, what facilitates it? It was striking that I could not think of contemporary Western philosophers of language who put this issue at the top of their agenda, or saw the challenges that exist in communicating with someone else as 'the problem of religious language'. In this view, the establishment of relationships and empathy were seen as critical in the child's ability to communicate and thus to learn the system of a language.

Lacan suggests:

> A creature needs some reference to the beyond of language, to a pact, to a commitment which constitutes him, strictly speaking, as an Other, a reference included in the general, or, to be more exact, universal system of interhuman symbols. No love can be functionally realizable

> in the human community, save by means of a specific pact, which . . . [is] at one and the same time within language and outside of it. That is what we call the function of the sacred. . . .[110]

Language then presupposes a tacit commitment, a 'pact'; with a family, with a community. Children cannot learn language without it. It is in this community that we are initiated into a shared symbolic system that unites us in solidarity with other human beings, both in language and beyond it. It is this pact that, first, converts 'The Other' into 'another human being', as Blumenberg comments; but further, allows us to undergo the sometimes humbling experience of becoming an Other to someone else.

This pact connects us with a tradition; a relation to our forebears is presupposed in the very existence of daily life. The Ṛgveda speaks of language 'as grain is shifted through the sieve and becomes clear of cockle' over time. This is accomplished through the tradition, 'after many labours and efforts', 'for the benefit of all the initiated, so that they could communicate by this language, so enriched and ennobled, in their gatherings'.[111] Above all, without this pact, this community and tradition, language is not possible.

This is why I suggested earlier that rhetoric was important in considering metaphor; perhaps more important than epistemology. This pact commits us to engagement with our community with all that entails: conflict; the need for change, for persuasion in the resolution of conflict and the maintenance of solidarity. Metaphor, myth and symbol are only important as ways of representing the world if we are trying to convince, persuade, inspire. Why else should we spend our time 'representing the world', what for? We want to 'represent the world' above all when we want to persuade someone to help us to engage with it, indeed to change it.

The picture of language can change considerably if we stop thinking of meaning as a label and start thinking of it as '*artha*', almost literally as a target. Language 'aims at' something; words don't sit permanently attached to their objects. Language does not possess meaning, but aspires to it. It is not a given, something we can thoughtlessly assume and just knock together words as in a game of Scrabble. Rather, it is an achievement when our sentence strikes its target.

To speak of meaning as a target brings out the emphasis on language as communication, rather than representation; for the understanding of the listeners is the target. It also makes clear that communication is a venture and it points up the risk. One can never be certain in advance of success; neither of its 'reference' nor its reception.

If meaning is a target, it also reminds us of the idea of the 'beyond' of signification and language. Miller's notion of God as a limit case brings out the fact that linguistic reference to the divine is a pointing-to, a pointing-beyond-itself-to, which never really arrives at its destination. Like the Greek philosopher Zeno's paradox of arrows, language of the divine then can be seen as flying accurately towards its target, thus indicating clearly where its aim lies – but never reaching it. Both its power to reveal, and its inability to master, are clearly expressed in this image.

If meaning can be understood as a target, then it only emphasizes again how important a community is for understanding meaning. This is how it reaches the target. Lacan's 'anchoring points' of the word in a context of meaning and associations, that keep language connected and prevent the Cupittian 'incessant sliding', presuppose a community. 'All knowledge is interpenetrated with words, and it is impossible to have a cognition free from word association',[112] as Bhartṛhari believes. Those of us English-speakers who are old enough to know, all share the same associations to the word 'pussy' and can hear its different meanings. We get the joke about Johannes' dream, but if a little child says, 'Here, pussy pussy!' the ladies in the room are not offended.

The more dramatic theory of meaning that Bhartṛhari and Maṇḍana Miśra propose – that meaning is *sphoṭa*, it bursts forth – also demonstrates the need for a prior interpersonal understanding for any understanding to take place. Bhartṛhari tells us that *sphoṭa* will not work if someone does not know the language sufficiently well. Then they do have to work it out word by word. But for those who are fluent, the sentence is an integral symbol. This insight is not meant simply to express the banal truth that people need to know your language in order to understand what you say. Bhartṛhari wants us to see that what 'bursts' into my mind, bursts into yours in a successful communication event.

> Sentence meaning is produced by word meanings but is not constituted by them. Its form is that intuition, that innate 'know-how' awareness possessed by all beings. It is a cognitive state evident to the hearer. It is not describable or definable, but all practical activities depend on it directly or through recollection of it. It comes to a person through maturing, just as animals and birds know innately how to act.[113]

With the idea of a community's understanding as the ground for explaining the phenomenon of meaning, the prospects for reference to what is not material improve greatly. Meaning, explanation and understanding don't have to come from pointing at objects while saying words, or justifying your utterance by producing a *thing* that it is talking about. We can make use of metonymy, or Hawaiian *kaona*. Metonymy has good prospects for reference to the transcendent. Metonymy removes the imperialist remnants of positivism, the insistence that language can only be justified by the existence of something solidly material. Metonymy makes it possible to refer to the immaterial; it can cope with the absence of what it names because its function is to replace, or even displace. It stands in for what is missing; it is the locum for the absent target. Moreover, its fluidity means that it resists idolatry; as significance shifts easily onto it, so too it can easily shift off and onto another signifier.

The Hawaiian device of the *kaona*, perhaps familiar in different names to other cultures and traditions, also allows the speaker to say the unsayable, to refer to what one is not allowed to name. It allows discourse on at least two levels, which are not unrelated to one another, but do not reduce one to the other. (Its closest European relative is perhaps the way that Lacan speaks of the way one discourse takes hold of another and uses it as a support, when describing the activities of the unconscious, in dreaming, for example.) An utterance can validly be about my experience, about human existence, and can make perfect sense as the *mana'o*, the primary layer of meaning. But those who know how to understand such things can hear, at the same time, a second layer of communication about divine action in my life.

The community of those who know and understand are what is necessary to make non-literal language work, whether figurative or non-representational. As an illustration, Hawaiian elder Mary Kawena Pukui gave this explanation of how *kaona* works: 'When all the Hawaiians in the audience start laughing, you know there's a *kaona*.' Some might feel this is too insecure to justify the claim that a sentence has meaning, compared to pointing at a material object and thus providing evidence. But to demonstrate that a sentence has meaning (whether it is true or false), is it not enough that you are understood? And even ostension, the game of pointing at things and naming them, still presupposes a prior understanding from your listeners, as Augustine argued in *De Magistro*. People need to know already what you are doing, to understand that you are intending to teach them a word by pointing to its object. (Maybe he wants you to pick it up? Or lie down on it?) Even the picture theory of meaning requires a community's understanding to work.

We saw earlier that the Nyāya philosophers of language supposed that reference was given by God (except for technical terms, which are established by human convention and agreement). To Westerners this may sound eccentric, even to believers. But there are ways of unpacking this claim that make it more familiar to the ears of the Western monotheist.

Maṇḍana Miśra maintained that all the universe is accompanied by speech, because everything is known by cognition, and cognition always has the 'tincture of speech'. Here Maṇḍana weaves together two relationships: the relationship of speech to cognition, and of language to the universe.

On the first point, Maṇḍana tells us that cognition or thinking cannot appear 'without a support'. Even babies' activities, in reaching for their mothers' breast, for example, show the 'tincture of speech': 'This!' is the baby's target. Even if you maintain that some cognition is possible in advance of speech, it becomes more vivid and distinct after language has been learned: the examples he gives are notes of the scale and herdsmen naming their animals. And when language has been lost, things are as good as unknown.[114] Some Indian philosophers spoke of ultimate knowledge, *śāstra*, as *śabda*, the spoken (or spoken word), others as *vāc*, speech; thus solidly identifying language and knowledge.[115] Hamann similarly reminded us that the ability to think, along with other things such as emotional development and social interaction, all rest on language.[116] As Bhartṛhari insists, 'There is no cognition without the operation of words; all cognition is shot through and through by the word. All knowledge is illumined through the word.'[117]

In the Jewish and Christian creation account, the world is created by language; by the word. Hamann, in his reworking of the biblical creation myth, suggests an identification between the world and speech which smoothes away the difficulties in their relationship:

> Every phenomenon of nature was a word, – the sign, symbol and pledge of a new, mysterious, inexpressible but all the more intimate union, participation and community of divine energies and ideas. Everything the human being heard from the beginning, saw with its eyes, looked upon and touched with its hands was a living word; for God was the word. With this word in mouth and heart the origin of language was as natural, as near and as easy as child's play.[118]

On this view, language is part of creation – part of *God's* creation. Language is the agency of the divine, in scriptural stories that anthropomorphically depict God speaking. It is the means by which God communicates with human beings in these scriptural stories. Adam is enjoined to participate in the creation of language by naming the animals – establishing 'reference', one might say facetiously. There is then in the West a theological narrative, if by no means a linguistic-philosophical account, that founds the relationship of language to the world in God's creation.

Indian traditions join the creation of the cosmos and language or speech in their own way.

> The meaning of *śabda* (lit. 'what-is-spoken') is able both to create everything, and to make everything known. It follows therefore, that the closest correlation between *śabda* and *artha*, the spoken matter and its referent . . . must pertain to the original condition of the world. Identity is certainly the strongest form of this pertinence. And indeed, it was proclaimed that Transcendent Speech is the Universe; both of them shape knowledge of Reality as itself, i.e. as it is. At the same time, to have a structured cosmic shape means to be *vāṅmaya*, 'made of words' or 'manifested in words.[119]

The Indian tradition goes one step further. Bhartṛhari is credited with systematically equating Brahman, the one reality without a second, with language; although this utterance is found earlier in the Vedas and the Upaniṣads. Maṇḍana Miśra develops the idea that Brahman *is* language. Brahman is consciousness, consciousness is the power of speech, so Brahman is of the nature of speech, whose universe is a manifestation of speech. Brahman is the word. The word is Brahman itself, and not just a symbol of Brahman.[120] As we shall see in later chapters when the concept of Brahman is discussed, Brahman is not different from all of creation, so this equation of Ultimate Reality, what is real, and language is an easy move to make for these Indian thinkers.[121] Moreover, Brahman is self-illuminating. 'Being the real self of every being, in a way, Brahman is self-evidently ever-manifested and obvious to everybody all the time.'[122]

The Indian philosophers remind us of what they think the central purpose for religious language is: enlightenment and liberation. For although both Śaṇkara and Sureśvara, as Advaita Vedāntins, are pessimistic about the ability of language to create knowledge and describe ultimate reality, both are adamant that it is indispensable in attaining enlightenment. Although Śaṇkara even goes so far as to say that the Upaniṣads are ultimately false because language is an instrument of ignorance, we can still be liberated by something that is false. Sureśvara asserts that although words cannot directly denote Brahman, they can help to dispel ignorance, just as someone can be woken from sleep by words even if she doesn't understand their meaning.[123]

The conflicting schools of Advaita Vedānta and of Bhartṛhari and the Nyāya grammarians are all consonant on one point, and that point is utterly lacking in Western philosophies of language. It is that a most fundamental point is how to become a better listener, a true understander of religious language. Moreover, how to do that *is* properly the subject of philosophy and not some separate category of 'faith' or 'religion'. When we talk about understanding an utterance of 'religious language', such as the Vedantic insight 'You are That' [Brahman], Chakrabarti tells us,

> we are not speaking of any ordinary uptake of [the] utterer's meaning of a sentence. There are elaborate moral and psychological preparatory conditions which have to be satisfied before the competent listener can begin to ponder about the individual purported meanings of the crucial words 'That', 'You', and 'are'. The rareness of such a competent listener is emphasized time and again in sacred texts. Listening is followed by rational reflective thinking of which sincere philosophical argumentation is an acknowledged part.[124]

As Coward and Raja observe, not all will be convinced by the spiritual vision of the Hindu philosophers of language. But, they argue, we do find here a view of language that makes sense of poetry, revealed scripture, science, and the mystical chanting of mantras, and which in addition strongly resonates with our ordinary everyday experience of coffee-cup chat. It is a way of seeing language that effectively explains why it is that sometimes when we listen we do not hear. It also teaches how to remove the obstructions in one's consciousness so that real hearing becomes possible and suggests in a different way the ultimate wisdom of the observation. 'In the beginning was the Word, and the Word was with God, and the Word was God' (John 1.1).[125]

Draw your own conclusions

Carry out a conversation with someone challenging everything they say that cannot be verified or falsified. How well does ordinary language face up to the verificationist challenge?

Do you prefer your language about Ultimate Reality to be dirty or pure? Why? Is anthropomorphism desirable or dangerous?

Think of an example to fit Anatole France's 'coin' simile – a word that has been made abstract. Is that word useful or misleading in disclosing or describing reality? Why?

When you want to persuade someone, do you find yourself using metaphors? Similes? Analogies? Why do you think that British judges are not permitted to use metaphors in their summing-up?

Think of a religious symbol that was changed forcibly, or that died of natural causes. Analyse the circumstances.

Is there a poisonous myth in circulation in your world? Is 'polymythia' or 'demythologizing' the antidote to it?

Give examples of religious speech acts that are 'assertives', 'declaratives', 'directives', 'commissives' and 'expressives'. Having done so, do you think this framework is the best way of understanding these religious utterances?

Think of a religious statement that is hard to justify or explain in terms of 'representation'. Does it do any better under the interpretive framework of 'communication'?

Further reading

Ayer, A. J. (1978) *Language, Truth and Logic*, Harmondsworth, Penguin Books

Blackburn, S. (1984) *Spreading the Word: Groundings in the Philosophy of Language*, Oxford, Clarendon Press

Burrell, D. (1973) *Analogy and Philosophical Language*, New Haven and London, Yale University Press

Cupitt, D. (1994) *After All: Religion without Alienation*, London, SCM Press

Macquarrie, J. (1967) *God-Talk: An Examination of the Language and Logic of Theology*, London, SCM Press

McFague, S. (1982) *Metaphorical Theology: Models of God in Religious Language*, London, SCM Press

Miller, B. (1996) *A Most Unlikely God: A Philosophical Enquiry into the Nature of God*, Notre Dame, Ind., University of Notre Dame Press

Moore, G. (1996) *Believing in God: A Philosophical Essay*, Edinburgh, T & T Clark

Ramsey, I. (1957) *Religious Language*, London, SCM Press

Ross, J. (1981) *Portraying Analogy*, Cambridge, Cambridge University Press

Soskice, J. M. (1987 (1985)) *Metaphor and Religious Language*, Oxford, Clarendon Press

Stiver, D. R. (1996) *The Philosophy of Religious Language: Sign, Symbol and Story*, Oxford, Blackwell

Wittgenstein, L. (1993) *Philosophical Investigations*, ed. G. E. M. Anscombe, Oxford, Blackwell

Notes

1 T. R. V. Murti (1974) 'Some Comments on the Philosophy of Language in the Indian context', *Journal of Indian Philosophy* 2, pp. 321–31.

2 L. Wittgenstein (1961) *Tractatus Logico-Philosophicus*, trans. D. F. Pears and B. F. McGuinness, London, Routledge & Kegan Paul, from the Preface.

3 S. McFague (1982) *Metaphorical Theology: Models of God in Religious Language*, London, SCM Press.

4 See the summaries in K. Potter (ed.) (1981) *Encyclopedia of Indian Philosophies*, vol. 1: *Advaita Vedānta up to Śaṇkara and His Pupils*, Princeton, Princeton University Press, pp. 525 and 54 respectively.

5 A. Chakrabarti (1995) 'Sleep-Learning or Wake-up Call? Can Vedic Sentences Make Us Aware of Brahman?', in Sibajiban Bhattacharyya and Ashok Vohra (eds), *The Philosophy of K. Satchidananda Murty*, New Delhi, Indian Council of Philosophical Research, pp. 159–60.

6 S. Blackburn (1984) *Spreading the Word: Groundings in the Philosophy of Language*, Oxford, Clarendon Press, pp. 3–5.

7 Blackburn, *Spreading the Word*.

8 Wittgenstein, *Tractatus Logico-Philosophicus*, from the Preface.

9 Wittgenstein, *Tractatus Logico-Philosophicus*.

10 According to Wittgenstein, propositions represent the existence and non-existence of states of affairs [4.1]. The totality of true propositions is the whole of natural science (or the whole corpus of the natural sciences) [4.11]. Philosophy is not one of the natural sciences [4.111]. Philosophy aims at the logical clarification of thoughts. Philosophy is not a body of doctrine but an activity. A philosophical work consists essentially of elucidations. Philosophy does not result in 'philosophical propositions', but rather in the clarification of propositions [4.112].

Philosophy sets limits to the much disputed sphere of natural science [4.113]. It must set limits to what can be thought; and in doing so, to what cannot be thought [4.114]. It will signify what cannot be said, by presenting clearly what can be said [4.115]. Its task is therefore 'elucidation' – the process of clarifying our thought and our talk. It is *not* to add a body of doctrines or true statements to our knowledge – that is a matter for the natural sciences (Wittgenstein, *Tractatus Logico-Philosophicus*).

11 Wittgenstein, *Tractatus Logico-Philosophicus*, 6.522.

12 Important members were Moritz Schlick, Otto Neurath, Rudolf Carnap, as well as Friedrich Waismann, Herbert Feigl, Viktor Kraft, Philipp Frank, Kurt Gödel, Hans Hahn.

13 See A. J. Ayer (1978) *Language, Truth and Logic*, Harmondsworth, Penguin Books.

14 They found two broad ways to speak about the unspeakable when they wanted to. One was the naturalistic route: ethics could be understood as statements about what is or is not conducive to human happiness – a kind of Utilitarianism. Schlick in *Fragen der Ethik* (*Questions of Ethics*) suggests that ethics is about what human beings want, and how these desires are to be satisfied. In this way 'ethics' becomes a matter of the social sciences, and is decided on the basis of psychology, sociology, anthropology. Another route for discussing ethics is either to see it as a form of imperative statement, so that ethical statements are not fact-stating, a matter of truth or falsity (Carnap); or to see it as emotive statements, expressions of feelings (Ayer). Both these sorts of statements were permitted by the Logical Positivists.

15 In an interview with Brian Magee.

16 There are further problems. Something which could not possibly be verified 100 years ago, therefore is meaningless, we might now accept as scientific truth. Was it meaningless 700 years ago that the world was round, and now true? Schlick sought to find a way to make the VP independent of the current state of affairs in scientific knowledge. He attempted this by saying a statement is meaningless if it is 'unverifiable in principle', 'logically impossible'. So the Verification Principle judges matters on *logical* grounds, not empirical ones? Schlick tried to harmonize the two, by saying there was no conflict between logic and experience, and that every logician must be an empiricist; but this position is not convincing to many.

To avoid some of these problems, Neurath reached the conclusion that we can never measure up sentences against reality or 'the facts' to see if the one fits the other. Sentences can only be compared with sentences. Therefore verification is a relation between sentences, not between sentences and experiences. Sentences are verified by 'protocol sentences'. These are direct reports of experience. These reports are translatable into 'the language of physics' – my experience of seeing red might be translated into physiological statements about the activity of certain nerves or my retina. Experience can also be translated behaviouristically, so that my experience of pain can be translated into a statement about my writhing and moaning. It may be possible to *postpone* the connection between the sentence and experience in this way, but it is difficult to see how it can be *prevented* – as long as the sentences still claim to be 'empirical'. Someone must be observing the activity of the retina or the moaning.

This leads to a third area of difficulty. In the end, something can only be verified by someone having an experience of some kind – seeing and feeling if it is raining, checking the reading on a laboratory instrument, etc. Usually, this comes down to someone's sensory perceptions; and this (following Russell) boils down to someone experiencing or having sense-data. But sense-data are ultimately private. We may all look at the same object and all utter the same description, but we cannot swap our sense-data. The ultimate result will be that the verification of a statement can only be checked by the person whose experience it is. And on this, it could be argued, a person must be infallible. You cannot be wrong that you are experiencing what you are experiencing, even if your judgements and assessments about the situation are. Certainly no-one else can tell. – Either such statements of personal experience are 'incorrigible', as Carnap thought; which amounts to (as he admitted) a kind of 'solipsism' (though he tried to pass it off as merely 'methodological'). Or else they are not, as Neurath thought. This means not only that we have to allow the possibility that we can be wrong about what we are in fact experiencing, it also seems to subvert the very possibility of 'verifying' anything. But either position leads to a problem in the total 'privacy' that it maintains. All statements boil down to a purely personal experience that can never be checked or confirmed by another human being. Even the existence of other human beings translates into my experience of seeing other objects, and nothing more. And yet what Logical Positivism was attempting to do was provide a philosophy of *science*, a public objective and verifiable discourse. How do you make a transition from private experience to the public world within this framework? Schlick first attempts to solve this problem with a distinction between 'structure' and 'content'; like a colouring-book, where the structure is the outline, the content is the colouring. We all have the same colouring-book, which each of us colours in for ourselves. We cannot communicate the 'content', the actual experience, to anyone else. But if we cannot communicate *content*, we can observe that our two different worlds share the same *structure*. I can observe that when I look at this card I say red, and when you look at the same card you say 'red' too, though I cannot see what you are seeing to know if you see the same thing. I can see that when you say you are in pain you wince and cry 'Ow!' just as I do, although I cannot feel your pain. This is all we need to communicate with each other. But is this distinction permissible, and what would pure structure be? Neurath and Carnap rejected this position. The fundamental verifiable statements must be intersubjective and somehow refer to public physical events. Neurath's move is to espouse 'physicalism', or 'behaviourism', that translates human experiences into observable behaviour. Carnap attempts to solve this problem by suggesting that all empirical statements can be expressed in a single 'language', which is the language of physics. So every statement of personal experience can be translated into a statement of my body: which can be physically tested in some way. 'I am seeing red' = 'Body G was told to push the button if she saw red, and on being shown the red-coloured card she pushed the button.' But do these two sentences *mean* the same thing? Carnap maintained that they did; any difference between them was one of purely personal associations. They are logically equivalent, therefore they mean the same thing. (But imagine 'I am in pain' being taken as identical to pain behaviour; then imagine someone faking.)

17 See Antony Flew, R. M. Hare and Basil Mitchell, 'Theology and Falsifi-

cation: A Symposium', in B. Mitchell (ed.) (1971) *The Philosophy of Religion*, Oxford, Oxford University Press, p. 13.

18 S. Davis (1978) *Faith, Skepticism and Evidence: An Essay in Religious Epistemology*, Lewisburg, Bucknell University Press. See the argument concluding pp. 210–21.

19 See the discussion in Maṇḍana Miśra, *Brahmasiddhi*, particularly at I.26. For a paraphrase, see Potter, *Encyclopedia of Indian Philosophies*, vol. 1, p. 362.

20 L. Wittgenstein (1993) *Philosophical Investigations*, ed. G. E. M. Anscombe, Oxford, Blackwell, §30.

21 Wittgenstein, *Philosophical Investigations*, §33.

22 Augustine, *De Magistro*, in Augustine (1953) *Earlier Writings*, trans. J. H. D. Burleigh, Library of Christian Classics, London, SCM Press, §33. Wittgenstein alludes to a passage in Augustine's *Confessions*, I. 8. Ironically, he seems unaware of *De Magistro*. As I have discussed elsewhere, this analysis by Augustine foreshadows Wittgenstein's later critique: 'Are you inclined still to call these words "names of objects"?' (Wittgenstein, *Philosophical Investigations*, §27). This is ironic, since the view that Augustine rejects in *De Magistro* is the view which Wittgenstein attributes to him, precisely in order to reject it on the same or similar grounds. See Gwen Griffith-Dickson (1996), '"Outsidelessness" and the "Beyond" of Signification', *Heythrop Journal* 37, pp. 258–72.

23 G. O'Daly (1987), *Augustine's Philosophy of Mind*, London, Duckworth, p. 172, observes that the pointing in ostension is a sign as much as a word is.

24 Augustine, *De Magistro*, §32.

25 *Brahmasiddhi* I.15, in Potter, *Encyclopedia of Indian Philosophies*, vol. 1.

26 J. Lacan (1988) *The Seminar of Jacques Lacan*, Cambridge, Cambridge University Press, vol. 1, p. 259.

27 Lacan, *Seminar*, vol. 1, p. 253.

28 Lacan, *Seminar*, vol. 1, p. 262.

29 Hamann calls Berkeley (and Hume) to his support. See George Berkeley (1988) *Principles of Human Knowledge*, London, Penguin, Introduction, §§18ff.

30 In Hamann's view, there are a variety of ways we reason, varieties of activities we perform; but there is no such 'thing' as 'Reason'. Having created this word as an abstraction from our reasoning processes, we can debate whether 'Reason' is universal, pure, what 'it' can do, whether savages or other races or women have 'it'. The way we use language, then, conditions our thinking. This is why Hamann suggested that language is the crux of 'reason's misunderstanding with itself'. If we resist the lure of thinking that this abstract noun denotes the real existence of a thing, however, and remember that reasoning is something we do, we are more likely to realize that we do it differently after a heavy meal than on an empty stomach; we might reason differently when we are in a rage than when we are in love; we might be able to observe people of other cultures (or genders) actually doing it. In Hamann's 'Metacritique of the Purism of Reason', his review of Kant's *Critique of Pure Reason*, the remedy urged for this temptation to reify is to pay attention to ordinary language – as Wittgenstein was to urge two centuries later. See Johann Georg Hamann, 'Metacritique of the Purism of Reason', in G. Griffith-Dickson (1995) *Johann Georg Hamann's Relational Metacritism*, Berlin and New York, de Gruyter, pp. 517–25, see in particular p. 520.

31 J. G. Hamann (1950) *Sämtliche Werke*, 6 vols, Vienna, Herder, vol. 2, 136:3–4. Translation mine.

32 Anatole France, *The Garden of Epicurus*, cited in R. Rorty (1980) *Philosophy and the Mirror of Nature*, Princeton, Princeton University Press, p. 368.

33 C. Henry (1979) *God, Revelation, and Authority*, Waco, TX, Word Books, p. 364.

34 M. Maimonides (1969) *The Guide of the Perplexed*, trans. S. Pines, Chicago and London, University of Chicago Press, see III. 20.

35 Bṛhadāraṇyaka Upaniṣad, 3.8.8. *Upaniṣads* (1998) Oxford World's Classics, p. 45.

36 *Brahmasiddhi* I.26, in Potter, *Encyclopedia of Indian Philosophies*, vol. 1.

37 Cf. the discussions in D. Burrell (1973) *Analogy and Philosophical Language*, New Haven and London, Yale University Press; and J. Ross (1981) *Portraying Analogy*, Cambridge, Cambridge University Press.

38 Aquinas grounds this similarity and difference in two ways: in 'attribution' and 'proportion'. To illustrate the analogy of 'attribution', I'll adapt Aquinas's example and speak of people and a diet as 'healthy'. One possesses the attribute 'formally', the other causally: the diet is 'healthy' because it causes people to be healthy. One can also possess the attributes to a different degree or 'proportion'.

39 B. Miller (1996) *A Most Unlikely God: A Philosophical Enquiry into the Nature of God*, Notre Dame, Ind., University of Notre Dame Press, see ch. 8.

40 Miller, *A Most Unlikely God*, pp. 9f.

41 Miller, *A Most Unlikely God*, p. 10.

42 Miller, *A Most Unlikely God*, p. 10.

43 N. Goodman (1976) *Languages of Art*, Indianapolis, Hackett, p. 69.

44 See Janet Martin Soskice's chapter 'Metaphor Amongst Tropes' for an examination of metaphor alongside its 'near relations', in Soskice (1987 (1985)) *Metaphor and Religious Language*, Oxford, Clarendon Press, pp. 54–66. This work is the most useful and comprehensive study of the topic.

45 See Soskice, *Metaphor and Religious Language*, p. 25.

46 T. Hobbes (1997) *Leviathan*, Cambridge, Cambridge University Press, pt. I, ch. 4, p. 26.

47 For a discussion of the 'emotivist' theory of metaphor, in which metaphor is seen as lacking in cognitive content, but having an emotional impact or import, and for a discussion of Donald Davidson's complex theory of metaphor, see Soskice, *Metaphor and Religious Language*, pp. 26–30.

48 Soskice, *Metaphor and Religious Language*, p. 25.

49 This is sometimes referred to as the 'Incremental' view. See Soskice for lucid descriptions of its varieties and exponents, such as Monroe Beardsley's controversion theory, Max Black's interactive theory, the interanimation theory of I. A. Richards. Soskice, *Metaphor and Religious Language*, pp. 31–53.

50 J. M. Murry (1931) *Countries of the Mind*, Oxford, Oxford University Press, p. 1.

51 J. Bronowski (1978) *The Visionary Eye*, Cambridge, Mass., MIT Press, cited in Sallie McFague (1982) *Metaphorical Theology: Models of God in Religious Language*, Philadelphia, Pa., Fortress Press, p. 35. See also Soskice, *Metaphor and Religious Language*; M. Hesse (1980) *Revolutions and*

Reconstructions in the Philosophy of Science, Bloomington, Indiana University Press; and I. Barbour (1974) *Myths, Models and Paradigms: The Nature of Scientific and Religious Language*, London, SCM Press.

52 Lacan, *Seminar*, vol. 1, p. 238.

53 H. Blumenberg (1999) *Paradigm zu einer Metaphorologie*, Frankfurt, Suhrkamp.

54 Blumenberg, *Paradigm*, p. 25.

55 Blumenberg, *Paradigm*, pp. 8f.

56 P. Tillich (1958) 'Symbols of Faith', in *Dynamics of Faith*, Harper Torchbooks, World Perspectives 10, New York, Harper, p. 41. See also pp. 41–54.

57 J. H. Randall (1986) *The Role of Knowledge in Western Religion*, Lanham, Md., University Press of America.

58 Paraphrased from P. Ricoeur (1970) *Freud and Philosophy*, trans. D. Savage, New Haven, Yale University Press, p. 527.

59 Ricoeur, *Freud and Philosophy*, p. 530.

60 Ricoeur, *Freud and Philosophy*, p. 531. See also pp. 524–31.

61 D. R. Stiver (1996) *The Philosophy of Religious Language: Sign, Symbol and Story*, Oxford, Blackwell, pp. 123f., and Soskice, *Metaphor and Religious Language*, p. 55, hint as much. See also the work of Langdon Gilkey, who understands 'symbol' very broadly: Jesus, the Exodus, creation, incarnation, redemption, etc. are all 'symbols'. The purpose of theology is to reflect on this symbolic system. L. Gilkey (1979) *Message and Existence: An Introduction to Christian Theology*, New York, Seabury Press.

62 See R. Bultmann (1941) 'New Testament and Mythology', in H.-W. Bartsch (ed.), *Kerygma and Myth*, vol. 2, London, SPCK; and R. Bultmann (1960) *Jesus Christ and Mythology*, London, SCM Press.

63 R. Bultmann (1953) 'The Case for Demythologizing: A Reply', in H.-W. Bartsch (ed.), *Kerygma and Myth*, vol. 2, London, SPCK, pp. 182f.

64 In a letter to Karl Barth, 11–15 November 1952, Bultmann declared: 'Naturally it is easy to argue against me from the statements of the NT, but only because the christological statements of the NT are clothed in the language of mythology which I want to strip off.' B. Jaspert (ed.) (1982) *Karl Barth – Rudolf Bultmann: Letters 1922–1966*, Edinburgh, T & T Clark, p. 93.

65 See C. W. Kegley (1966) *The Theology of Rudolf Bultmann*, London, SCM Press, for an excellent selection of critical essays on Bultmann's work as well as a reply by Bultmann. Also see A. C. Thiselton (1980) *The Two Horizons: New Testament Hermeneutics and Philosophical Description with Special Reference to Heidegger, Bultmann, Gadamer, and Wittgenstein*, Exeter, Paternoster Press, *passim*.

66 In Blumenberg, *Paradigm*.

67 Odo Marquard (1996) 'Lob des Polytheismus', in Hans-Joachim Höhn (ed.), *Krise der Immanenz: Religion an den Grenzen der Moderne*, Frankfurt, Fischer, pp. 154–8.

68 H. Blumenberg (1985) *Work on Myth*, trans. R. M. Wallace, Cambridge, Mass., MIT Press.

69 A starting-point for this was E. Cassirer (1946) *The Myth of the State*, Oxford, Oxford University Press.

70 See the introduction to Blumenberg, *Work on Myth*, pp. xxivff.

71 Blumenberg, *Work on Myth*, p. 629.

72 Lacan, *Seminar*, vol. 1, p. 178.

73 Lacan, *Seminar*, vol. 1, p. 243.

74 J. R. Searle (1983) *Meaning*, Berkeley, Center for Hermeneutical Studies in Hellenistic and Modern Culture, p. 44.

75 See T. W. Tilley (1991) *The Evils of Theodicy*, Washington, D.C., Georgetown University Press, particularly ch. 3.

76 J. L. Austin (1976) *How To Do Things with Words*, Oxford, Oxford University Press, *passim*.

77 I. Ramsey (1957) *Religious Language*, London, SCM Press.

78 Cf. D. B. Zilberman (1988) *The Birth of Meaning in Hindu Thought*, Dordrecht, Reidel, p. 71.

79 See Hamann, 'Metacritique of the Purism of Reason'.

80 Wittgenstein, *Philosophical Investigations*, §27.

81 Wittgenstein, *Philosophical Investigations*, §24.

82 Wittgenstein, *Philosophical Investigations*, §23.

83 *Brahmasiddhi* I.22, I.25; see also III.41; for convenience see the paraphrases in Potter, *Encyclopedia of Indian Philosophies*, vol. 1.

84 'We said that the sentence "Excalibur has a sharp blade" made sense even when Excalibur was broken in pieces. Now this is so because in this language game a name is also used in the absence of its bearer.' Wittgenstein, *Philosophical Investigations*, §44.

85 R. B. Braithwaite (1971) 'An Empiricist's View of the Nature of Religious Belief', in B. Mitchell (ed.), *The Philosophy of Religion*, Oxford, Oxford University Press, pp. 72–91.

86 D. Z. Phillips, *Faith and Philosophical Enquiry*, a chapter of which is reprinted as 'Faith, Skepticism and Religious Understanding', in R. Douglas Geivett and Brendan Sweetman (eds) (1992) *Contemporary Perspectives on Religious Epistemology*, Oxford, Oxford University Press, pp. 81–91 (the quotation can be found on p. 83).

87 G. Moore (1996) *Believing in God: A Philosophical Essay*, Edinburgh, T & T Clark, pp. 147f.

88 Lacan, *Seminar*, vol. 1, p. 178.

89 Lacan, *Seminar*, vol. 1.

90 From Gwen Griffith-Dickson (2000) *Human and Divine: An Introduction to the Philosophy of Religious Experience*, London, Duckworth. For non-native English speakers: 'pussy' is coarse slang for the female genital.

91 Jacques Lacan, 'The Agency of the Letter', in J. Lacan (1997) *Écrits: A Selection*, London, Routledge, p. 150.

92 Lacan, *Seminar*, vol. 1, p. 238, cf. also pp. 247f.

93 Cf. the complex discussion in Lacan, 'The Agency of the Letter'. The specific reference here is to p. 164.

94 Lacan, 'The Agency of the Letter', p. 157.

95 As my example shows, this structure of language mirrors the structure that Freud and Lacan imagine for the unconscious, and the Freudian theory of dream interpretation operates in this fashion. Lacan translates his terms into Freud's: 'condensation' is the superimposition of signifiers, in other words, metaphor; 'displacement' is metonymy.

96 Lacan, 'The Agency of the Letter', p. 150.

97 Wittgenstein, *Philosophical Investigations*, §13.

98 See D. Cupitt (1994) *After All: Religion without Alienation*, London, SCM Press, *passim*; (1986) *Life Lines*, London, SCM Press; (1987) *The Long-Legged Fly*, London, SCM Press.

99 Cupitt, *After All*, p. 57.

100 David A. Hart (1993) *Faith in Doubt: Non-realism and Christian Belief*, London, Mowbray, p. 7. See also Colin Crowder (1997) *God and Reality: Essays on Christian Non-Realism*, London, Mowbray.

101 Lacan, *Seminar*, vol. 1, p. 248.

102 Lacan, *Seminar*, vol. 1, p. 259.

103 Lacan, *Seminar*, vol. 1, p. 263.

104 See Aristotle (1988) *Politics*, ed. S. Everson, Cambridge, Cambridge University Press, I. 2.

105 Lacan, *Seminar*, vol. 1, p. 243.

106 Lacan, *Seminar*, vol. 1, p. 262. Italics mine.

107 See Don Cupitt (1998) *The Religion of Being*, London, SCM Press; and (1998) *The Revelation of Being*, London, SCM Press.

108 Lacan, *Seminar*, vol. 1, p. 243.

109 Lacan, 'The Agency of the Letter', p. 154.

110 Lacan, *Seminar*, vol. 1, p. 174.

111 Ṛgveda X.71.2. Cited in Zilberman, *The Birth of Meaning in Hindu Thought*, p. 93.

112 Coward's and Raja's description of Bhartṛhari's view, citing *Vākyapadāya* 1.123. Harold G. Coward and K. Kunjunni Raja (2001) *Encyclopedia of Indian Philosophies*, vol. 5: *The Philosophy of the Grammarians*, Delhi, Motilal Barnarsidass, p. 27, see the text on p. 133.

113 In Coward and Raja, *Encyclopedia of Indian Philosophies*, vol. 5, p. 144.

114 See *Brahmasiddhi* I.17 *et passim*, in Potter, *Encyclopedia of Indian Philosophies*, vol. 1.

115 '*Śabda* is described . . . as a slight vibration or disturbance in the field of Reality. It is conducive to the everlasting self-revelation of Reality as its first and ceaseless vexation. *Vāc*, Speech, is ever ready to express some-*thing* and relate it to some-*body*.' Zilberman, *The Birth of Meaning in Hindu Thought*, pp. 75ff.

116 'Metacritique of the Purism of Reason'. See the translation, notes and discussion in Griffith-Dickson, *Johann Georg Hamann's Relational Metacritism.*

117 Coward and Raja, *Encyclopedia of Indian Philosophies*, vol. 5, p. 51.

118 Hamann, 'The Last Will and Testament of the Knight of the Rose-Cross', N III, 32:21–8, in G. Griffith-Dickson (1995) *Johann Georg Hamann's Relational Metacritism*, Berlin and New York, de Gruyter, p. 468.

119 Zilberman, *The Birth of Meaning in Hindu Thought*, p. 76.

120 *Brahmasiddhi* I.16 in Potter, *Encyclopedia of Indian Philosophies*, vol. 1.

121 Although compare this phrase from Lacan: Lacan tells us: 'For the human being, the word or the concept is nothing other than the word in its materiality. It is the thing itself. It is not just a shadow, a breath, a virtual illusion of the thing, it is the thing itself.' Lacan, *Seminar*, vol. 1, p. 178.

122 Chakrabarti, 'Sleep-Learning or Wake-up Call?, p. 162.

123 *Taittirīyopaniṣadbhāsyavārtikka*; cf. Potter, *Encyclopedia of Indian Philosophies*, vol. 1, pp. 595–614.
124 Chakrabarti, 'Sleep-Learning or Wake-up Call?'.
125 In Coward and Raja, *Encyclopedia of Indian Philosophies*, vol. 5, p. 50.

Part 2

All That Is

4

Creation

From speaking to knowing

As with the problem of speaking about what is beyond us, the problem of knowing the transcendent appears in the major religions as a central preoccupation. In Hindu philosophy, the question is: 'What could be a pramāṇa – a mode of knowledge – for Brahman?' In the Western (Islamic, Christian, Jewish) philosophy, the problem is, 'How can one know a transcendent God?'

In the West, it was not uncommon in ancient times to believe that everyone has an 'innate' knowledge of God; inborn, within us, is an awareness of God, and we can thus arrive at a knowledge of God naturally, even spontaneously. Another approach is that represented by 'ontologism' – that we naturally have an inner innate intuitive awareness of God. Since we have this immediate knowledge of God, no demonstration of God's existence is necessary. Such was Malebranche's approach, combining themes from Augustine and Descartes. Others might want to say that God is equally present at all times, in all events and experiences; in other words, whatever our capacity to experience God, God is always immanent in all our experiences. On this latter view, a religious experience could be, at most, an unusual insight into what is always true. Somehow or other, one can discern God in the world, in nature, as well as in ourselves and each other. It is not uncommon to find twentieth-century theologians suggesting that something is present in the human person, which leads on to a deeper and wider knowledge of God. Rudolf Bultmann maintained that in the human being there is an existential awareness of God's existence which takes the form of a searching question concerning the meaning of life.[1] Karl Rahner also emphasizes the human capacity to experience and know God. While God is absolutely transcendent, and knowledge of God comes through God's self-revelation, nevertheless that revelation is not alien to us but something which we are already attuned to, by grace.[2]

Aquinas was sceptical of the possibility of 'innate' knowledge of God; what we have heard about from childhood, and which seems self-evident to us, should not be confused with what is 'naturally known'. As we have seen, although experience was the ground of Aquinas's philosophy, he felt that something further was needed to arrive at a knowledge of God: reason or revelation. In Luther's view, the God 'arrived at' by reason was a false God. God can only reveal God's Self, above all in the Bible. Knowledge of God is not something human beings can decide to obtain for themselves, whatever their sources or methods for doing so.

One way to begin to explore the question of the transcendent, then is through what we do experience: the world.

Anthropomorphism in speaking and knowing the divine

Anthropomorphism is a constant embarrassment for sophisticated thinkers in Judaism, Christianity and Islam; that on the one hand God is above all creatures, and yet the Scriptures continually portray him using imagery drawn from human beings. It gets worse when ordinary religious believers go on to take such language literally. God sees, hears, is angry, jealous, bares his holy arm, is a man of war, and so on. It is a particular problem whenever belief in God is ridiculed, and people who do believe in God have to add health warnings against an old man with a long white beard in the sky.

Stewart Guthrie, in what he offers as a new theory of religion, says that religion just is anthropomorphism.[3] Anthropomorphism is a basic perceptual strategy we have – we see it in our propensity to see faces in the clouds or the moon, to see the face of Jesus in a tortilla, to imagine human emotions in our pets, human figures in root vegetables and so on. We find it in literature, art, advertising and, of course, concepts of God. Since according to Guthrie religion is anthropomorphism, he thinks any attempts to create a notion of God without being anthropomorphic are doomed to failure. But clearly he thinks that this anthropomorphism, and therefore belief in God, are illusory.

Given that the norm in elevated discussions is to decry anthropomorphism, I want to make a different suggestion. There is, I suggest, something we can call 'deanthropomorphism'. By this I mean language about God which has not successfully escaped anthropomorphism, but has just stripped away its tell-tale signs.

Its forerunner is Ludwig Feuerbach, who lets us see that the deanthropomorphized God is the essence of reason. Feuerbach intends this as a compliment. But I think it shows us what has happened here. We have still made God in our own image; we have just selected a different aspect to deify: reason. Human reason, human logical requirements have been made divine and Maximally Great; God is that than which nothing more reasonable can be conceived.

This little lapse is characteristic, I represent, of much of present-day philosophy of religion. In discussions of whether or not God can suffer, be acted upon, or feel emotions – God's impassibility – we find, reasonably enough, suggestions that it is anthropomorphic to suggest that God can. But can it not also be anthropomorphic to say that God must not?

Brian Davies, OP, as a follower of Thomas Aquinas, would certainly want to rise above crude anthropomorphism. Indeed, one of his reasons for opposing the idea that God can feel emotions or be affected by anything is that such an idea is anthropomorphic. As we shall see later, here is how he argues against the idea that God could be affected by another: 'God would seem to be something vulnerable and defective.'[4] 'If that were true, then God could be out of control and something could have its way with him and be capable of acting independently of him.'[5]

Can we still see here the embodiment of human fantasy? Not, as Freud would have it, the fantasy of Big Daddy. The anthropomorphism is less infantile but perhaps more adolescent than that: God as James Bond, neither shaken nor stirred, never out of control. It is the *morphe* [form] of a different *anthropos* [person], that is all; one who fears loss of control, and who equates receptivity with vulnerability, and openness with defectiveness.

At the same time, much contemporary philosophy of religion fails to do away with a crude anthropomorphism that can still take hold where human reason can invent a logical problem for God, as in problems concerning the compossibility of attributes. One example of this is the 'stone paradox'. This is a logical trap for God's omnipotence: can God make a stone that is too heavy for him to lift? – Either way you answer it, if you play the game by its rules, God is not omnipotent. – But do you think a transcendent God puts together rocks – let alone picks them up? Do you think God is in trouble, as a being lacking in power, if He does neither? The worst temptations to idolatry may be words like 'Perfect Being', 'Being Itself' or 'Ultimate Concern' rather than carved statues.

The Indian Muslim Nagendra Singh writes: 'When God is named it means that he is brought into the human context and we talk about Him in terms which have relevance for us. Thus anthropomorphism in some form or other cannot be dispensed with.'[6] If that is so, it may not be so foolish to follow the strategy which Johann Georg Hamann called 'privileged anthropomorphism', which we touched on in the last chapter. 'Privilege' here means not social status or wealth, but something bestowed though undeserved. In Hamann's theology, speaking of God in anthropomorphic terms has been explicitly licensed and welcomed by God. For Hamann the Christian, it finds its ultimate justification in God's incarnation in Jesus: it was God's own choice to speak of himself in human terms. Why are we too squeamish to do so? Hamann's theology stresses God's 'condescension'; a thoroughly positive term here, it portrays God everywhere as reaching out to us, at our level, communicating to us in ways and manners as lowly and unworthy as necessary for us to understand and respond.

This theme of divine condescension or accommodation is not a uniquely Christian idea. It is also part of Rāmānuja's picture of God.

> How can a lame man climb on an elephant if you tell him to do so? Likewise how can an insignificant soul in this imperfect world . . . approach the Lord of All . . .? The answer is surely that the elephant can accommodate itself, kneeling down so that the lame man can mount. God likewise makes Himself very low so that He can be worshipped by the soul in this imperfect world.[7]

For Rāmānuja, interestingly, as for Hamann the Christian, God's willingness to lower himself for the sake of communicating for us is seen preeminently in his willingness to become incarnate:

> But being a shoreless ocean of compassion, gracious condescension, motherly love and generosity, while still not losing his own inherent nature and attributes, he has assumed his own bodily form, which on each occasion has the same generic structure as one of the various classes of creatures, and in these various shapes he has descended again and again to the various worlds where they dwell, where having been worshiped by these different kinds of creatures, he has granted them whatever they prayed for, whether meritorious action, wealth, physical pleasure, or deliverance, according to their own desire.[8]

Deliberately provocative language is a crucial part of the strategy of privileged anthropomorphism: use anthropomorphic language which is so concrete or inappropriate that we cannot possibly deceive ourselves about our incapacity to describe God in adequate ways. Draw the imagery of God not from those aspects of ourselves which are most abstract or most refined; draw on those gifts which are devalued or scorned: our embodiment, our childish play.

Current research has shown that 'baby talk' or 'motherese', even when ungrammatical, actually facilitates language learning. Those parents who refuse to 'talk down' to their babies can actually make it more difficult for their child to learn to speak. But by accommodating their speech style to the level of the child, 'The adult shows an awareness of the child's level and seems to unconsciously promote the linguistic development by using structures slightly more advanced than those used by the child.'[9]

Perhaps there is another aspect to our ambivalence about anthropomorphism. Whose religions are anthropomorphic? – Do you find it plausible that the sun is a white cockatoo? Do you think it reasonable to suppose that a God you could believe in takes the form of a sweet potato?

Anthropomorphism is the language of the 'primitive'; the child, the uneducated, the 'native'. It is found in so-called 'indigenous religions'. It is a reason for rejecting the religious beliefs of those whom you intend to convert, or if necessary, to conquer. It is the religion, the theology or the spirituality of those who should not be allowed to keep it.

There is, I suggest, a connection between well-educated scorn of anthropomorphism and a tacit imperialism or even racism. Anthropomorphism is the foolishness of The Other; it does not mark our own thinking. Euro-American Christians who believe in the Real Presence of Jesus in bread and wine laugh at the idea that the Hawaiian god Lono could take the *kino* (body form) of a sweet potato. The civilized rejection of anthropomorphism therefore becomes a mode of superiority, cultural, personal or otherwise. One can, as Jean-Luc Marion for example does, distinguish 'idols' (which are bad, of course) from 'icons', which are good and revelatory of God. But one cannot entirely escape the impression from some treatments of this distinction that icons are what Europeans and Americans have, and idols are the religious imagery of the developing world and its religions. Anti-anthropomorphism thus becomes a mode of superiority, cultural, personal or otherwise.

A nicer way of saying it comes from Radhakrishnan:

> The monotheists are quite certain that the gods of the polytheists are symbolic if not mythological presentations of the true God, but they are loath to admit that their own God is at bottom a symbol. All religion is symbolic, and symbolism is excluded from religion only when religion itself perishes. God is a symbol in which religion cognises the Absolute.[10]

Monotheists may not agree that God is 'symbol' (not if what is meant is that the Divine Being is 'mere' symbol). Yet many philosophers are guilty of thinking they have come up with the linguistic formula which adequately states how God must be, while the poets and provocateurs like Hamann do not forget the inappropriateness of their language.

Attributes of God?

Controversy arose early in Islamic reflection on the question of God having attributes. In the first half of the eighth century, a movement arose which denied the reality of attributes in God.[11] The Mu'tazilite argument runs like this: anything eternal must be a God; there can only be one God; if you postulate eternal attributes in God you are asserting the existence of other 'gods', which is impossible and impious. The Attributists believed in the relative unity of God; so in God there could exist eternal real attributes. The Anti-attributists variously denied that attributes were real things, but may also have denied that they were mere names and therefore were modes. This had not initially been a problematic area for Judaism, but in the Arabic milieu, the questions entered into Jewish philosophy and were dealt with energetically by Maimonides.[12]

This was one of the areas of debate between al-Ghazālī and Ibn Rushd, and they identified the impact on two areas: God's unity and simplicity, and God's (alleged) necessary existence. There are several issues at stake:

Where speaking about God having attributes suggests diversity in God, or a composite nature, this seems to threaten God's absolute oneness.

Where language of attributes suggests dependence on something outside Godself, it seems to threaten God's aseity or self-sufficiency.

Without attributes, however, it seems to threaten assertions people want to make about God (can't we say God is good or powerful?) and God seems to lack qualities.

More fundamentally: it raises the question of knowledge of God, or predication of God: it strikes at the core issues of epistemology and language. Even when or where we claim to know: how can we begin to speak without falling into contradictions?

One tactic we find among religious thinkers in many traditions is to draw a division between the knowable and the unknowable God; or the God with and the God without attributes; or the God which can be spoken about and the God that cannot, or barely can. This distinction is clearest in the distinction in Hinduism. The concept of Brahman we will explore in this and the next chapter, but briefly, Brahman is ultimate reality, identified with everything. Nirguṇa Brahman is ultimate reality, even beyond all attributes. Saguṇa Brahman is Brahman with attributes. Another term used is Īśvāra (often translated into English as 'Lord'). Īśvāra is a mode of Brahman's expression which is the cause of the world and makes the empirical world possible. One way of describing Īśvāra is as Brahman when viewed from the perspective of ignorance. When viewed through the veil of ignorance, Brahman is seen 'as it were' (Śaṇkara's phrase) as Lord, Creator, one with qualities. It is no longer an impersonal absolute, but takes on the qualities of the Governor of the Universe. So the Advaita Vedāntin tradition allows them to have it both ways: to have a conception of the ultimate so transcendent that it is beyond all the kinds of distinctions and qualities that we can imagine; but also to be able to talk about it and ascribe attributes to it, acknowledging all the while that these are attributed to it by our ignorance. Even Rāmānuja, who does not go in for this distinction in the way that Śaṇkara does, has a polarity in his picture of God, between the God that is unknowable and the God that reaches out to us, above all in making himself incarnate.

A distinction roughly of this kind is not unknown in the West. Meister Eckhart makes a rather controversial distinction between 'God' and 'the Godhead'. Thomas Aquinas distinguishes between God's Real Being and God's Intentional Being. 'Real being' is God as God is in himself, intrinsically. 'Intentional being' is something as it is perceived, known, experienced (intentional here signifying not 'deliberate' but 'as an object of someone's perception'). God's real being may be unchanging and impassible, while God's intentional being we can experience as responding to us in our pain.

Even Islam, so insistent on the unity of God, finds occasion to portray God in this twofold way.

> Ibn 'Arabī and his school were fully cognizant of this nominal dimension of the Godhead and His creation-oriented dimension and accordingly distinguished between *wahid* and *ahad*, God as manifest and God as supreme mystery beyond our reach. It is His transcendental absence which defies understanding. Only when God comes as a person, as a self in His I-ness, that we can talk about Him and He talks to us. And as a consequence a dialogical relationship ensues between God and [humanity]. . . .[13]

But Singh, as a Muslim among Hindus, also goes on to observe:

> The distinction between nirguṇa brahman and saguṇa brahman is familiar to Hindu thought. But in the Qur'ān the personal aspect of reality is not an illusion superimposed on a nameless reality, but its manifestation. Whatever we can say of God, we can say only in His personal dimension.[14]

So in a characteristically monotheist way, he alludes to the transcendent unknowability of God, but also maintains that human language cannot but speak of a God who communicates in a personal way. This is not an inferior mode of God for Singh, but how the unknowable God manifests and reveals himself.

In this book we will not investigate God taken as a series of attributes. First, in this chapter we will begin to explore concepts of the divine through the existence of the world. Then, in the next chapter, we shall explore different views of the relation between the divine and the world. In the chapters that follow, we will see how this divine–world relationship has given rise to arguments that may purport to prove the existence of God.

In Part 3 we will continue our investigation of the divine by identifying two areas in which God's 'attributes' (or not) are seen to impact particularly on human existence and activity: knowledge and power. These have an immediate impact on the question we will explore subsequently, one of the most difficult problems of all: the problem of evil and suffering. The other side of the coin, however, is the positive or blissful experiences that people claim to have, which will be our final topic.

Science, religion and creation: one false assumption

Because questions of the material world are also investigated by science, it is now often asserted that all these questions of philosophy and theology should be replaced by the natural sciences. People sometimes assume that folk of earlier ages invented religious views because they didn't realize that there could be purely scientific views, and they had to invent a god to explain the existence of the universe. However, in both ancient India and ancient Greece there were purely materialist, non-theistic explanations for the origin of the universe; accounts which tried to explain its origin and existence in purely material terms (what we might call now 'scientific' terms). In India, the Cārvāka tradition and the Presocratic philosophers often called the Milesian Naturalists are two examples of early attempts to give a purely 'scientific', or purely 'natural' origin to the universe. In ancient times, people forged their religious accounts because for some, at least, purely material accounts were intellectually unsatisfying; or could answer only certain questions – 'how', perhaps, but not 'why'; 'through which mechanisms' but not 'why this exists to function that way in the first place, rather than nothing ever existing'.

Creation

The Judaeo-Christian Bible, Christian creeds, and catechisms traditionally begin with establishing God as the Creator for the basis of what else will be said about divinity. Modern non-believers in the West, on the other hand, frequently begin by asserting that advances in scientific knowledge have made God redundant for the world and its evolution. Thus for both viewpoints, the question of how the universe came to be and whether there is something or Someone beyond the world as we perceive it, is a concern for philosophy of religion. We will begin looking at the nature of God by considering what various religions have had to say about the world and its relation to God, and how this relates to other issues to be considered in philosophy of religion.

Science, religion and creation: another false assumption

Another common but false assumption is to think that scientific accounts necessarily conflict with and therefore replace religious ones. Many, perhaps most religious believers in the West, for example, accept theories of the Big Bang (or the rival steady state theory) for the origin of the universe, and Darwin for the origin of species.

Although many (supporters of science or supporters of religion) insist that this must be the case, not everyone agrees.

Here is Ayatullah Murtaḍā Muṭahharī writing about creation as evolution:

> *The logic of the Qur'ān is premised on life's being wholly a sublime emanation from a plane above that of sensible bodies, by means of whatever law and reckoning the emanation takes place. Therefore, the evolution of life is creative and perfective. According to this logic, it makes no difference whether life appeared on earth in an instantaneous creation or gradually, in successive creations. . . . According to the Noble Qur'ān, creation is not an instantaneous phenomenon. An animal or a human being continuously undergoes creation in traversing the stages of evolution. The whole universe is continuously undergoing creation.*[15]

To understand the fundamental framework of a religious tradition's concept of God (or whatever they call the creative force), we can ask two questions:

Whence – how did the universe come to be? Was it created in a free conscious act by the deity? Did it emanate or evolve from the boundless Absolute? Or is there no divine origin?

When – is it eternal, or did it have a beginning?

The possible views on Creation and the divine

1. *It was created by God (or whatever name is used for the creative force):*
   - *from nothing, at a moment in time;*
   - *from nothing, eternally (without beginning);*
   - *from something, eternally;*
   - *from something, at a moment in time.*
2. *It emanated from the Absolute (or whatever It is called).*
3. *The world does not come from God: It evolved without divine intervention.*
4. *It is an illusory product of our own consciousness.*

Any of the views set out in the textbox can be theistic – including those asserting that the world is *not* created by God. It is not so much an attempt to find explanations where no scientific ones are available; it is rather a question of the *relation* that exists between God and the world. Thus religions that don't include a belief that God created the universe can still maintain a belief in God; those who think that the universe is eternal can still believe God created it.

1. The universe was created by God from nothing, at a moment in time

In the Semitic monotheistic religions the mainstream concept of the creation is that the universe was created out of nothing, *ex nihilo*. This means that there was not some pre-existing inchoate substance or matter on which God acted. There was absolutely nothing; then God brought something into existence. Often this is given a scriptural basis; for Jews and Christians, it is the creation story (or stories) in the early chapters of Genesis, and for Muslims the similar story told in the Qur'ān.

Creation *ex nihilo* means that the existence of the world is totally dependent on God. This belief also usually emphasizes the freedom of God in the act of creating; the universe does not emanate in some unconscious process from God but by God's free decision. Believers also often emphasize that creation continues to be totally dependent on God; that God conserves all things in being moment by moment.

For the medieval philosopher-theologian Thomas Aquinas, God is the cause of the universe. This is based on Aristotle's four ways of speaking about 'causes', which are not all what we in ordinary English would consider 'causes'. Thinking about 'source' might be a good alternative to the language of 'cause'. There is the 'material cause' which is the 'stuff' from which the thing is made. Bronze is the material cause (we commonly would say simply the material) of a bronze statue. The 'formal cause' is the source of the form of a thing. A woman's figure, as the visible image of the goddess Athena, is the formal cause of a bronze statue of Athena. The 'efficient cause' is 'the source of the first beginning of the change'; the sculptor is the efficient cause of the statue. The 'final cause' is the purpose of the thing, 'that for the sake of which something is done'; the 'end', as Thomas sometimes says. The final cause of the statue would be to provide a focus for devotion.

You might assume that 'creation *ex nihilo*' means that God is only the efficient cause of universe – the universe is not made of God (the material cause), in God's form (the formal cause), or made for the purpose of God (the final cause). But that is not what Aquinas thinks.

For him, God is of course the 'efficient cause' of the universe – the one who made it, the one who 'acted' as it were in bringing everything into existence. Matter, the material substance of the universe, is created by God. Curiously, however, Thomas uses two words here for God's making. Along with the word 'creation', he uses a second term, 'emanation'. Aquinas writes, 'But here we are speaking of things according to their emanation from the universal principle of being; from which emanation matter itself is not excluded.' This is interesting, because it is so often said that monotheists believe in creation *ex nihilo*, while other religions (such as Indian ones and Neoplatonism) believe that the universe is an *emanation* from God. 'Creation' – which suggests a sort of separation from God – and 'emanation' – which suggests something coming forth from God – are supposed to be mutually exclusive.

Thomas also considers that God is the 'first exemplar cause of all things', even material or natural things[16] and thus God is also the formal cause of all things. God is also the final cause of things, Aquinas argues.[17] This may seem unlikely to many believers who hold that God does not need anything; so God does not need a purpose for creating the universe.[18] Aquinas replies that God 'intends only to communicate His perfection, which is His goodness; while every creature intends to acquire its own perfection, which is the likeness of the divine perfection and goodness. Therefore the divine goodness is the end of all things'.[19] He concludes then that 'God is the efficient, the exemplar and the final cause of all things and since primary matter is from Him, it follows that the first principle of all things is one in reality.'[20]

Al-Ghazālī from a Muslim perspective forms an interesting comparison to Aquinas here. Without specific reference to the Aristotelian divisions, he provides his own distinctions of aspects in God's act of creation, but anchors them to specific 'divine names' taken from the Qur'ān. Thus he seeks to articulate the meanings of calling God (or rather, God calling himself) *Al-Khāliq* – the Creator, *Al-Bārī* – the Producer, and *Al-Muṣawwir* – the Fashioner. These, al-Ghazālī says, might casually be taken as synonymous but need not be. 'Rather, everything which comes forth from nothing to existence needs first of all to be planned; second, to be originated according to the plan, and third, to be formed after being originated. God . . . is creator inasmuch as He is the planner, producer inasmuch as He initiates existence, and fashioner inasmuch as He arranges the forms of things invented in the finest way'.[21]

In light of these two different explanations, it is simplistic to see creation *ex nihilo* as always and inevitably 'opposed' to something called emanation; or to make the point another way, emanation and creation may be two different ways of speaking about the universe's origin from God which can be deployed at different times for the sake of different emphases. If you want to emphasize God's freedom or infinite superiority to the world, you might speak of 'creation'. If you want to emphasize God's intimacy with creation, or stress that there is nothing outside

God with its own self-sufficient existence, you might choose the word 'emanation'. This is not always the case, however, for there exist understandings of either creation or emanation that preclude the other, as we shall see.

2. The universe was created by God from nothing, eternally

Stephen Hawking famously suggested that the universe was eternal and consequently there was 'nothing for a God to do'. Many centuries earlier, Indian critics of the Nyāya theistic arguments also asked why a Creator was needed for a beginningless cycle of universes. But as great minds in different parts of the world have made clear, the universe being eternal doesn't preclude God creating it. Nor does the idea that God creates the world as an eternal production contradict the belief that God created the universe from nothing.

The suggestion that the universe is eternal did not have to wait for Hawking's era. This view was found in ancient Greece, in Aristotle's time, and still earlier was the majority view among India's religious philosophers. We also find in Islamic thought, following Aristotle, the idea that the universe is an eternal production of God, an eternal creative process.

One reason for arguing that God creates eternally is that, if God is eternal and unchanging, no particular moment could have been selected as the right moment for creating the universe. As Davidson observes, the paradox that 'what exists cannot have come into being' goes back at least to Parmenides and is articulated by Aristotle: 'Why, after not existing for an infinite time, would the thing be generated at a particular moment?'[22] although neither makes an explicit reference to the problem of a Creator. But once you add the idea of an eternal and immutable Creator, the problem sharpens:

> On the assumption of creation, no given moment in an undifferentiated eternity could, as distinct from any other moment, have recommended itself to the cause bringing the world into existence as the proper time for it to create the world; the cause that would, on the assumption of creation, have had to create the world could not therefore have acted at any moment whatsoever.[23]

This argument is rehearsed in Islamic, Jewish and Christian medieval thinkers.

A variety of responses were made, by all three communities of monotheists. The simplest response perhaps is to say a moment was selected by God's will, albeit in a somewhat arbitrary fashion. Saadia and al-Ghazālī stress the importance of will, al-Ghazālī adding that it is the nature of a willing agent to select, to differentiate. Indeed, Augustine, Proclus and

Saadia all argued in various ways that since there was no time before creation, strictly speaking, one cannot say that a moment was selected out of infinite time. Al-Ghazālī, Augustine and Aquinas all point to an analogy with space, which ought to raise equal problems; but in Aquinas's view, for example, to ask the analogous question about space simply points to the foolishness of the question: 'Why did God create the universe in this particular spot rather than another?'[24] In short, rolling together these observations, one who does not assert the eternity of the universe can answer this point by saying that with the universe, space and time were also created. There was not an infinity of 'moments' and 'spots' from which God arbitrarily (or incoherently) selected one, at which to create the universe.

It is sometimes argued that certain attributes of God contraindicate creation at a point in time and that therefore God's creation must be eternal. The most popular argument of this kind invokes God's immutability. If God is unchanging, it claims, God could not have created the universe, because that implies a temporal sequence: at one point God did not create a universe, then did, and then ceased doing so – all changes which some deem impossible for the divine nature. This was maintained by Ibn Sīnā and Ibn Rushd. The Aristotelian distinction between actuality and potentiality may be used; God, as pure actuality, cannot have had an unactualized potential to create which was later actualized at the time of creating. Indian philosophers also debated this point. The Buddhist Dharmakīrti said at the moment of creation, God would have to change from being a non-cause to being a cause and therefore God cannot both be a creator and be unchanging.[25]

Those who take a different view can simply maintain that creation, in the case of God, does not entail change (and then explain why not); or alternatively they may claim that God is eternally and immutably creating, but the world nevertheless comes into existence in time and is not eternal with God's act. Philosophers across various traditions – Ibn Hazm, Philoponus, Shahrastānī, Gersonides, Maimonides, Aaron ben Elijah, Crescas, Aquinas, and Bonaventure – all put forward arguments of this kind. God's action itself is distinguished from the changing development of the world.

Other attributes of God have been used, less frequently, to carry forward the idea that the universe is eternal. One can claim that divine *goodness* suggests that God would always want to give the universe the gift of being. God's perfect and unchanging *knowledge* can be said to entail an eternal object of knowledge, that is, the universe; divine *omnipotence* requires that God always is capable of creating the universe and therefore does so eternally. Some have responded to this sort of belief by saying that God has no 'attributes' which have to be taken into consideration; this is a characteristically Islamic solution. Others deny that eternal attributes need to express themselves in an eternal world, or else they set out to show that it is impossible for them to do so.

How have thinkers responded to the basic objection of Hawking and others, that the eternity of the world means it cannot have been *created by God*? Ibn Rushd concedes that if the world existed eternally *of itself*, then it would not need a creator. 'But if the meaning of "eternal" is that it is in everlasting production and that this production has neither beginning nor end, certainly the term "production" is more truly applied to the one who brings about an everlasting production than to one who procures a limited production.'[26] 'The philosophers' theory, indeed, is that the world has [a creator] acting from eternity and everlasting, i.e. converting the world eternally from non-being into being.' (Ibn Rushd observes that this very question proved to be a point of disagreement between those who followed Plato and those who followed Aristotle.[27]) The reason the world is eternal, Ibn Rushd says, is not based in the fact that it has eternal constituents, for the actual world consists of motion, something which is in the process of gradual change from potentiality to actuality. 'Therefore the term "eternal becoming" is more appropriate to the world than the term "eternity".'[28] He goes on to explain, 'Therefore the world is during the time of its existence in need of the presence of its agent for both reasons together, namely, because the substance of the world is continually in motion and because its form, through which it has its subsistence and existence, is of the nature of a relation, not of the nature of a quality . . .'[29] Eternity of the world in this view does not negate its relationship to God; it characterizes it.

In the twentieth century, we see Muṭahharī moving in a similar thought world, with the post-Darwinian terminology of evolution:

> The universe has as its reality the properties of from Him-ness and to Him-ness. On the one hand, it is proven that the universe is not a moving, fluid reality; rather, it is motion and flux itself. On the other hand, research on motion has proven that unity of source, unity of end, and unity of course impart to motions a kind of unity and singularity. Therefore, considering that the whole universe runs on one evolutionary course from one source to one end, it necessarily takes on a kind of unity.[30]

3. *The universe was eternally created from something*

The idea that the universe is in eternal production can, however, be maintained in a way that opposes the idea of a single eternal creation *ex nihilo*. In many of India's religious philosophies, the universe exists in an eternal cycle of creation, dissolution and creation again. The universe is seen as eternal and without a beginning, a 'first moment'. Alternatively, it can be said that the universe has an infinite number of beginnings. When a divinity is given a role in creation, the god's role is to assemble the universe again and again, using the eternal atoms left over from the last dissolution like a never-ending Lego set. In discussing this theory, Uddyotakara in the *Nyāyavarttika* creates a dialogue which I paraphrase:

Objection: Does God create the world out of something or out of nothing? If God creates the world out of something, then He cannot be the creator of that something. If out of nothing, human efforts are useless and liberation impossible.

Answer: A man makes an axe out of wood and iron and then with the help of the axe he makes lumber. Just so God makes the instruments with which He creates.

Objection: But what about the first thing He makes – is it made out of nothing?

Answer: There was no first thing.[31]

This is an enigmatic response. In Udayana's *Nyāyakusumanjali*, an opponent says that as the universe is eternal and continues in process without a break, there is no scope for creation and therefore none for a creator (which is, of course, exactly the point Hawking makes in our time). Udayana finds a series of ways to argue against the idea. He does *not* dispute the idea that the universe is eternal, but disputes that its eternity means that it is self-sufficient and self-explanatory.[32] Even if the universe does not have a single, once-for-all beginning, and even if it is comprised of pre-existing ingredients, it can no more assemble itself than a store-bought cake mix can.

Vaiśeṣika or 'Atomism' in Indian Thought

'Atomism conceives reality as made up of unchanging particles rearranged but never altered. . . . According to the Indic Atomists, atoms exist only singly, and need to be combined by a mind to give rise to the complex structure of the visible world.'[33]

How Praśasta Pāda, a Vaiśeṣika thinker, describes creation:

I shall now describe the creation and destruction of the four Great Elements. After a hundred years, by Brahma reckoning, the moment draws near for the present Brahma's liberation. It is then that the supreme Lord, Master of the worlds, wills to destroy, so that living beings, weary of transmigration, might find repose. All the unseen forces of karma, which manifest the bodies and organs of beings and the Great Elements, and which inhere in souls, are suppressed. Impelled by the Supreme Lord's will, the actions deriving from the union of soul and atoms, and the differences in the atoms that underlie bodies and organs, together destroy that union, so that the bodies and organs are reduced to the atomic state. Then the four Great Elements, earth, water, fire and air, in that order, are dissolved – each previous element being destroyed before the others. After that the separated elements remain, and to that moment also survive the souls, permeated with merit and demerit.

Afterwards the Supreme Lord wills to create, so as to make experience possible for living creatures. Atoms combine with all the souls, through the karmas – whose powers have been restored – implanted in those souls.[34]

Activity begins to stir in the atoms of the four elements one by one. The atoms of fire combine with those of earth to form a great egg, in which the Supreme Lord creates the four-faced Brahma. Commanded by the Supreme Lord, Brahma creates creatures.

4. *The universe was created from something in time*

In Process Theology, which grows out of the philosophy of the American Alfred North Whitehead, God is in a mutually dependent and coeternal relation with the world. The world is in evolution and God is involved in this process. God's uniqueness from the world lies principally in contributing the initial aim of the universe. Thereafter, each occasion involves its own creative synthesis of what it 'prehends of the divine', as David Pailin puts it, which includes the possibilities God envisages, as well as its own aim.[35] God does not act in a coercive way but as a 'lure', to attract or persuade creation in the divine direction, which is not a material goal but the situation of greatest aesthetic satisfaction. God's influence does not strictly and exclusively determine events. In each situation there is a range of states possible to actualize, graded in importance. Creation uses its freedom on each occasion to actualize either God's goal or another. Pailin writes:

> God thus influences each momentary event. But while God's ordering of the structure of reality ensures that to a massive extent each concrescing occasion conforms to its immediate predecessor, the divine presentation of alternative possibilities provides the ground for minute changes in each occasion's self-creation. Each actual occasion composing the enduring object which is a DNA molecule is thus able to contribute to the evolutionary development of that molecule (and so to the creature genetically produced by that molecule) by its own particular synthesis of what it prehends of what Whitehead refers to as the 'consequent' and 'primordial' aspects of the divine reality.[36]

This luring depends on a 'panpsychic' view of the constituents of reality: that is, that there is a mental or psychic aspect to every entity, whether conscious or not. Whitehead suggests that we overcome mind–matter dualism in this way, by realizing that each entity has both a mental and a physical aspect; it 'feels' its environment. There is no such thing as 'pure matter'. In this way, it becomes possible for Process theologians to speak of choices and decisions made by molecules. These statements do, however, raise the question of how far this way of speaking is meant as a metaphor or intended with absolute literalism. Are molecules really exercising choice or is that a colourful description of indeterminacy?

5. The universe emanated from the Absolute

The Hellenistic philosopher Plotinus speaks of 'The One', who does not create the world the way the Jewish, Christian or Muslim God does. Instead, timelessly rather than at a point in time, It 'overflows' – this term Plotinus wants us to understand as metaphorical: 'Seeking nothing, possessing nothing, lacking nothing, the One is perfect and, in our metaphor, has overflowed, and its exuberance has produced the new.'[37] This 'new', as it turns back to contemplate the One, becomes what Plotinus calls *Nous*, or the Intellectual principle. The Intellect in turn overflows in a vast power and this Form or Idea (in the Platonic sense) becomes the third principle, Soul (*psyche*). Soul continues this 'downward' movement and generates Sense and Nature. This process of ongoing overflowing or emanation is what gives rise to all being, in which nothing is severed from its predecessor. It is spontaneous and yet necessary, not a conscious willed activity on the part of the One. It takes place in eternity; the sense of succession or 'phases' which Plotinus suggests is not to be understood as stages in time, but in levels of dependence of being on the One. It goes on forever and endlessly from the One, which is never exhausted or spent.

This account had a tremendous influence not only on the 'pagan' strands of philosophy which succeeded it, but also on philosophers in Islam, Christianity and, though to a lesser extent, Judaism. The early conduit for Neoplatonism into Islam was al-Fārābī, who made use of this scheme of emanationist creation in his own account. In his story, he absorbs Aristotle's idea that God is an intellect in self-contemplation and self-understanding. Thus in this self-contemplating there is an emanation or overflow into a second intellect. This second intellect self-contemplates but also contemplates God. In thinking about God, it overflows into a third intellect, and in its own self-contemplation it generates the first heaven. The process continues in this way, with each new intellect generating the next intellect and the next celestial sphere, finally generating ten intellects and spheres in total, with the last being our own world.

Al-Fārābī's account was taken up and elaborated by his renowned successor, Ibn Sīnā. Ibn Sīnā retains the concept of an emanation proceeding by Divine Necessity, rather than a Qur'ānic free act of creation *ex nihilo*. The Necessary Being's thinking itself is the first emanation and First Intelligence which begins the process of creation, and is how one moves from the one to the many. Again, there is a generation of ten intellects, plus celestial spheres and celestial souls at which point the sublunar world is created.

This schema had an afterlife in several Islamic circles, notably in the portrait painted by the 'master of illumination', Suhrawārdī, of God as pure light, giving perfect and constant illumination and thereby bringing all things into existence. This creation of 'light from light' happens in a complex hierarchical scheme which includes angels and others. But this Neoplatonic view (with Aristotelian riffs) was hardly the mainstream Muslim view. It was sharply criticized by al-Ghazālī, not purely on grounds of Qur'ānic orthodoxy but also for its alleged incoherence.[38] Even when Ibn Rushd came to the defence of 'the philosophers' against al-Ghazālī, he often refrained from defending and espousing these further shores of Neoplatonist cosmology.

The casual assumption that all Hindus take an emanation view is a false one. Nyāya views espouse creation explicitly, while in views where Brahman is thought to be the material cause of the world, often the world of things is not regarded simply as ontologically dependent on God, but also as ontologically questionable. It may be that Western readers have tended to read Indian texts through a Neoplatonist filter.

Sri Aurobindo on creation

For Sri Aurobindo, the world comes from the Supreme Reality in a manner that is neither 'emanation' nor straight-up 'creation'. He uses the word 'evolution' but coupled with the word 'involution'. Supreme Being (Saccidananda) veils itself voluntarily and descends to the level of matter, in order for matter (which is therefore veiled consciousness) to be able to evolve into life and then into sentient and intelligent beings. Evolution then is not a matter of chance but is guided by the immanence of Supreme Spirit within material reality. This involution, followed by evolution, takes place in six stages; for evolution *in the following order, and in reverse order for the* involution *of Saccidananda: matter – life – psyche – mind – super-mind – existence.*[39] *These two processes are always going on in an endless cosmic cycle of play and delight for supreme reality – the delight of becoming. The personal ascent and spiritual development of human beings is part of this process of evolution.*

Aurobindo's The Life Divine *indicates at once his dependence on*

Indian traditions, but his difference from non-dualist Advaita Vedāntin thinking:

> *Existence that acts and creates by the power and from the pure delight of its conscious being is the reality that we are, the self of all our modes and moods, the cause, object and goal of all our doing, becoming and creating. As the poet, artist or musician when he creates does really nothing but develop some potentiality in his unmanifested self into a form of manifestation and as the thinker, statesman, mechanist only bring out into a shape of things that which lay hidden in themselves, was themselves, is still themselves when it is cast into form, so is it with the world and the Eternal. All creation or becoming is nothing but this self-manifestation. . . .*
>
> *. . . Therefore whatever comes into the world, seeks nothing but this, to be, to arrive at the intended form, to enlarge its self-existence in that form, to develop, manifest, increase, realise infinitely the consciousness and the power that is in it, to have the delight of coming into manifestation, the delight of the form of being, the delight of the rhythm of consciousness, the delight of the play of force and to aggrandise and perfect that delight by whatever means is possible, in whatever direction, through whatever idea of itself may be suggested to it by the existence, the conscious-force, the delight active within its deepest being.*[40]

6. The world does not come from God

The Hawaiian creation chant, the *Kumulipo*, speaks of the beginning of the world as deepest darkness, intense heat as the heavens turn inside-out, and thereafter a long evolution of the species of the earth, described in 2,000 verses. In this chant, the creation of the universe is not described as the act of a god.

> At the time when the earth became hot
> At the time when the heavens turned about
> At the time when the sun was darkened
> To cause the moon to shine
> The time of the rise of the Pleiades
> The slime, this was the source of the earth
> The source of the darkness that made darkness
> The source of the night that made night
> The intense darkness, the deep darkness
> Darkness of the sun, darkness of the night
> Nothing but night.[41]

The source of life on earth Hawaiians felt to be the stuff at the bottom of the sea. This ancient view has a recent echo from scientists in Düsseldorf and Glasgow, who suggested that life on earth began in tiny metal spheres, formed in total darkness on the ocean floor near hydrothermal vents.[42]

The gods and goddesses arise too as part of this scheme of evolution. Such a view can still be 'religious', part of a spiritual world view and a response of respect; and indeed it can still lead to an attitude of praise and wonder.

The Sāṃkhya philosophers of India did not believe in a God although they accepted the authority of the scriptures. As far as the universe is concerned, they believed in the ultimate reality of a primal substance which pervades everything, is eternal and indestructible. It is what forms the basis of all that the universe is, despite its variety. They call it *prakṛitī*. Sometimes you will find this translated as 'matter', but that is misleading as it is not just material substance. It is not conscious, still less personal. *Prakṛitī* is the source of the world; creation is an unfolding of different effects of the original *prakṛitī*. It is not so much a stuff as a force, a state of tension between its three constituents: *sattva* (potential consciousness which produces pleasure), *raja* (source of activity, which produces pain), *tamas* (source of that which resists activity, which produces indifference). In different proportions, they constitute all things which are the products of *prakṛitī*. The different ways in which they interact explains the diversity found in the world. When they are perfectly balanced, there is no action; but when the equilibrium is upset, the process of evolution begins.

The evolution of unconscious *prakṛitī* can only take place through the presence of conscious *puruṣa*, a Sanskrit word often translated as 'spirit'. This sets the *prakṛitī* into activity, upsetting the balance of *gunas*, and so the process of evolution can begin.

Sāṃkhya gets a vigorous critique from Śaṇkara and the Vedāntins, as well as Nyāya thinkers. Śaṇkara asks: How can unconscious matter give rise to consciousness and spirit? 'You think that the potential form is independently capable of producing the world, whereas our view is that its capacity is dependent on God.'[43] The Nyāya school agrees: we need a conscious creator, even if that creator acts with or through matter. The cake mix cannot bake itself, no matter how upset its equilibrium is. Uddyotakara says that God creates the tool before using it; the Nyāya picture is that God works through material causes. God doesn't zap the cake mix either; but follows the recipe and does the stirring. Self-agitation of *prakṛitī* just won't do as an explanation of the universe for the Nyāya thinker.

7. The world as illusory product

Sāṃkhya thinkers assert that the effects pre-exist in the cause. (The cake is inherent in the powdered mixture.) Advaita Vedāntin philosophers agreed, but parted company on an interesting point. For the Vedāntin does not think that the effects are a transformation of the cause. Rather the difference between cause and effect is only apparent. Śaṇkara argues that this is true to our perception. When we perceive cloth, we perceive the threads that make it up – nothing more and nothing less, even though the threads may be in a new arrangement. We do not view some different substance than the threads.[44]

The effect can thus be seen as the cause in another form, but not ultimately a different *thing*. This means that Brahman as the cause of the world of effects is both the material *and* the efficient cause of the world, to use the Aristotelian terms. The non-dualist school of Advaita Vedāntin says that Brahman is what the origin, maintenance and destruction of the world proceeds from. Śaṇkara writes:

> That omniscient omnipotent cause from which proceed the origin, subsistence and dissolution of this world – which world is differentiated by names and forms, contains many agents and enjoyers, is the abode of the fruits of actions, these fruits having their definite places, times and causes, and the nature of whose arrangement cannot even be conceived by the mind, – that cause, we say, is Brahman . . .[45]

If this is so of the world and its material and efficient cause, Brahman, then the world must be nothing other than Brahman, only looking rather different from this viewpoint; just as fabric is nothing more than the threads from which it is woven, only appearing in a different form, and the cake is nothing other than its ingredients. The Advaita Vedāntin, therefore, sees the world identical with Brahman which only *appears* to us to be an entirely different thing or collective of things.

Advaita Vedāntins say that only Brahman is ultimately real, and that therefore this appearing world and all its creatures and objects are not really real in themselves. So they differ utterly from the Sāṃkhya view that, although the object exists in its cause, it is a transformation of it. For Śaṇkara and his fellow Advaitins, the effect (the world) is only an apparent manifestation of the cause (the one true reality, Brahman).

What the Advaitin particularly has to explain to the sceptic are two paradoxes: how you get the many from the undifferentiated one, or the different from the same; and how the world can be in some sense real and unreal at the same time.

For, despite Western caricatures of Indian 'acosmism', even these so-called 'monists' say the world is real. If it is an illusion, it is not one we make up for ourselves which can swiftly disappear on enlightenment or just be thought away. The snake you wrongly think you see lying on the road is only unreal if the rope that you're actually seeing *is* real. This analogy, for the Advaita Vedāntins, illustrates how we can construct a false world of appearances for ourselves. But it is false not because it is a hallucination or a figment of our imagination (it's not), but because it is not *ultimately* real.

Some of the West's many misunderstandings of the East can be cleared up if you stop to ask what these thinkers mean by 'real' or '*ultimately* real'. For these thinkers, if a thing is real this means it exists independently, in its own nature. Anything that exists through dependence on another is unreal. Only Brahman exists entirely of itself, in its own nature. All other things are dependent on Brahman or God. So only Brahman is *ultimately* real.

This is a quite different criterion for reality than the one many Western philosophers use, and it approaches what Western philosophers mean by 'self-existent'. Theistic philosophers believe that, while we are all real, only God is self-existent. But if 'only Brahman is real' means, in Western terms, 'only Brahman is self-existent', then 'Western' and 'Eastern' metaphysics may not be as different as people often suppose.

Śaṇkara clarifies: 'There could be no non-existence because external entities are actually perceived. . . . An external entity is invariably perceived in every cognition such as pillar, wall, a pot or a piece of cloth. It can never be that what is actually perceived is non-existent.'[46] This point is important because, as Eliot Deutsch observes, Śaṇkara is concerned to oppose the school of Buddhism (Vijñanavāda), which grounds the existence of external objects in the actions of consciousness alone.[47]

How then does our apparent mistaken perception of the world come to be? The appearance of the world as independent and self-existent comes about through illusion (māyā) or ignorance (*avidyā* – the two terms are sometimes used almost interchangeably in this discussion). *Māyā* is our superimposition onto reality, Śaṇkara observes, as when we superimpose a memory of something else onto what we currently perceive. We see a rope lying across the road at dusk and project onto it our memories of seeing snakes and therefore perceive the rope to be a snake. In this way, we superimpose onto the one ultimately real Brahman the variety of the world, which is however ultimately not different from Brahman.

The first thing to say about Buddhist views of the origin of the universe is that there shouldn't be any. The Buddha resisted offering explanations for the origin of the world, feeling strongly that issues about the world and the existence of a God or first cause were an undesirable distraction. They do not aid religious insight, they lure us away from the spiritual progress we should make, and it would be false to either confirm or deny such questions.

Buddhism, like Advaita Vedānta, denies to the material world any objective and independent reality. A fundamental thrust in Buddhism, however, is to deny Vedānta's assertion that effects pre-exist in their causes. Since everything is impermanent, there can be no lasting cause or effect. One change is affected by another – and given that there is no permanent underlying reality, one can only say, 'one thing happened, then another'.

Everything is momentary and in flux; nothing is permanent, whether the object of our perceptions or indeed ourselves as perceivers. Buddhists do not think in terms of substance but rather in terms of process. This means that the relation between cause and effect must not be between two things, but two events.

This belief in transience, momentariness and rejection of substance means that a belief in creation is impossible for Buddhists, just as it makes belief in an enduring and immutable Creator God impossible. 'The assumption that an Īśvara is the cause is based on the false belief in an eternal self. This belief is untenable as soon as it is recognized that everything is (impermanent and therefore) subject to suffering.'[48] Buddhists also typically deny that there was, or need be, a First Cause. If the first cause need not have a cause or creator, then neither do other phenomena of the universe that the theist thinks require an explanation in terms of cause.

The causality that the Buddha was most interested in was not the causation of a putative material world, but the causality of suffering. This concern is seen in the Buddhist doctrines of the Four Noble Truths and the Principle of Dependent Origination. The principle of conditionality puts it succinctly: When that is present, this comes to be; on the arising of that, this arises. When that is absent, this does not come to be; on the cessation of that, this ceases.[49]

The Principle of Dependent Origination is used to explain the arising of suffering, and therefore of existence.[50] It asserts that all things are relative, conditioned states that arise dependent on certain conditions. When the conditions that support it do not exist, that phenomenon will not arise. Thus the phenomena of the world are all dependent on certain conditions, but when those cease, the apparent objects will cease. Thus the Principle of Dependent Origination describes how from ignorance, volitional impulses arise, with volitional impulses as a condition, consciousness; with consciousness, body and mind or name and form (*nama-rupa*); with name and form, the six senses (their sixth sense is mind); with the six senses, sense contact; with contact, feeling; with feeling, craving; with craving, clinging; with clinging, becoming; with becoming, birth; and with birth as condition, ageing and death, sorrow, lamentation, pain, grief, despair. But in abandoning ignorance, volitional impulses cease, and when volitional impulses cease, so does consciousness, and so on through the cycle. The cycle is without beginning, so 'ignorance' is not as it were a first cause. This emphasizes the interrelated, interdependent character of all things, and the fact they are part of a process or a continuum. This continuum, it should be noted, is clearly in the realm of our experience rather than as some metaphysical process taking place outside the universe.

The Buddhist interest in causality then is in what causes the *experience* of the world. What is striking about their approach is that the 'causation' under discussion is no longer causation as applied to matter or material entities – such as whether God or a Big Bang caused the formation of galaxies. It is rather causality as applied to human subjects, to psychology, to consciousness and human experience. It is as if 'the world' for most other philosophical systems means nature and matter, but for Buddhist systems, the origin and existence of 'the world' to be explained is a largely human one: the world of our experience, perception, and suffering.

The existence of things for Buddhists is explained by the psychology of human perception. As perception and consciousness are constantly changing, so analogously physical objects are impermanent and dependent on causes without any lasting nature or substance.

The emphasis of Buddhist psychology means that material objects do not have independent objective reality. Particularly in the development of Mahāyāna Buddhism in the writings of Nāgārjuna and of Vijñanavāda Buddhism, the world itself is depicted as an illusion, as a dream, or figuratively as a flash of lightning or a drop of water. All experience of the world is subjective; the fact that we experience objects does not entail that they exist out there. The fact that all co-arises in dependent relation on something else means that finite objects are not independent or self-subsistent but exist temporarily by virtue of their dependence on something else. 'Neither the effect, nor the cause can be regarded as an isolated unitary event. Thus all things are only processes, not entities. Identities are nothing but analyzable sequences, and independence an illusion.'[51]

Conclusion

In summary, Christian (or Jewish or Islamic) philosophers often sharply distinguish their belief in creation *ex nihilo*, from theories of 'emanation' that they think are held by Neoplatonist 'pagans' like Plotinus, or Eastern thinkers like the Advaita Vedāntins. But when you dig deeper into the language used by each, some of these absolute differences don't look so absolute. As I've noted, Thomas Aquinas himself wants to use the word 'emanation' for how the universe proceeds from God. By this he does not mean that God oozes or extrudes the universe out of his own 'stuff', but neither do Śaṅkara or Plotinus mean that. They are all concerned with finding some way of insisting simultaneously that the material universe has no other source than God; and that all that exists is dependent on God. At the same time they want to maintain that the material world is not just the same as God (as Stoics or pantheists might do). They choose different emphases and images, and they court different dangers of misunderstanding. Creation accounts emphasize God's freedom and consciousness in creating, and worry that Plotinus' 'emanation' implies necessity and unconsciousness in the Creator. But these views can suggest that creation is an arbitrary choosing that does not flow essentially from the unstoppable love and goodness of the Ultimate One. David Burrell sums up his requirement nicely as 'a One that need not create and from which all that is emanates'.[52] Thomas Aquinas simply says he is talking 'about the emanation of all being from the universal cause, which is God; and this emanation we designate by the name of creation'.[53]

But is the most urgent question the origin of planets, or the end of human selves? The most important difference between the emanation of Brahman and the Christian God's creation *ex nihilo* is not so much the beginning as the end. Do we merge seamlessly back into, or do we remain eternally distinct from but very, very intimate with, the Source of all Being?

Draw your own conclusions

Do you think God is personal or impersonal? How would you describe the difference?

Even if science could explain everything material about the universe, would there still be room for something else? How would you describe that something else?

Do you think 'superimposition' does explain some of our perceptions, whether or not you are an Advaita Vedāntin – that we overlay what we actually see and hear with our expectation of something else, and misperceive reality? Does this occur with spiritual matters or only physically perceptual ones?

What do you think the difference between 'creation' and 'emanation' amounts to? What is the significance of the distinction?

Are you more persuaded of arguments for the eternity of the universe, or for the universe having a beginning in time?

Do you think matter is eternal, or do you think it came into being at some point? And do you think this is a question only for science?

Do you think, like the Buddhists, that everything is in eternal flux and nothing is permanent? What are the consequences of this view, desirable or undesirable?

Further reading

Averroës (Ibn Rushd) (1969) *Tahafut al-Tahafut*, trans. Simon Van den Bergh, London, Luzac

Deutsch, E. (1973) *Advaita Vedānta*, Honolulu, University of Hawaii Press

al-Ghazālī (2000 (1997)), *The Incoherence of the Philosophers (Tahafut al-Falasifah)*, trans. M. E. Marmura, Provo, Utah, Brigham Young University Press

al-Ghazālī (1999 (1992, 1995, 1997)) *The Ninety-Nine Beautiful Names of God*, trans. David B. Burrell and Nazih Daher, Cambridge, Islamic Texts Society

Kalupahana, D. J. (1994) *A History of Buddhist Philosophy*, Delhi, Motilal Banarsidass

Pailin, D. A. (1989) *God and the Processes of Reality: Foundations of a Credible Theism*, Routledge Religious Studies, London and New York, Routledge

Pereira, J. (1991 (1976)) *Hindu Theology: Themes, Texts and Structures*, Delhi, Motilal Banarsidass

Plotinus (1991) *The Enneads*, trans. S. MacKenna, London, Penguin

Vattanky, J. S. J. (1993) *Development of Nyāya Theism*, New Delhi, Intercultural Publications

Wolfson, H. A. (1976) *The Philosophy of the Kalam*, Cambridge, Mass., and London, Harvard University Press

Notes

1 See R. Bultmann (1969) *Faith and Understanding*, trans. Louise Pettibone Smith, London, SCM Press.

2 See Karl Rahner (1978) *Foundations of Christian Faith*, trans. W. Dych, New York, Seabury Press.

3 S. Guthrie (1993) *Faces in the Clouds: A New Theory of Religion*, Oxford, Oxford University Press.

4 B. Davies (1985) *Thinking About God*, London, Geoffrey Chapman, p. 156.

5 Davies, *Thinking About God*, pp. 157–8.

6 N. K. Singh (1996) *God in Indian Islamic Theology*, New Delhi, Sarup, p. 50.

7 Vadakku Tiruvidi Pillai, *Idu* 1.3 intro., cited in J. B. Carman (1994) *Majesty and Meekness: A Comparative Study of Contrast and Harmony in the Concept of God*, Grand Rapids, Eerdmans, p. 93.

8 Introduction to Rāmānuja's commentary on the Bhagavadgita, reprinted in Carman, *Majesty and Meekness*, pp. 96ff; this on p. 97.

9 Law in James Law (ed.) (1992) *The Early Identification of Language Impairment in Children*, London, Chapman & Hall, p. 49. See the seminal work by R. Brown (1973) *A First Language: The Early Stages*, London, Penguin Books, in opposition to Chomsky's suggestion that the parent's style of speech is a defective model for language learning. Brown demonstrated that 'motherese' differs from other speech styles consistently and predictably.

10 S. Radhakrishnan and C. A. Moore (eds.) (1957) *A Source Book in Indian Philosophy*, Oxford, Oxford University Press, p. 630.

11 See the lengthy discussion in H. A. Wolfson (1976) *The Philosophy of the Kalam*, Cambridge, Mass., and London, Harvard University Press.

12 See the discussion in H. A. Wolfson (1979) *Repercussions of the Kalam in Jewish Philosophy*, Cambridge, Mass., and London, Harvard University Press.

13 Singh, *God in Indian Islamic Theology*, p. 49.

14 Singh, *God in Indian Islamic Theology*, p. 51.

15 M. Muṭahharī (1985) *Fundamentals of Islamic Thought: God, Man and the Universe*, trans. R. Campbell, Contemporary Islamic Thought: Persian Series, Berkeley, Mizan Press, pp. 202–3.

16 'Now it is manifest that things made by nature receive determinate forms. This determination of forms must be reduced to the divine wisdom as its first principle, for divine wisdom devised the order of the universe, which order consists in the variety of things. And therefore we must say that in the divine wisdom are the types of all things, which types we have called ideas – i.e. exemplar forms existing in the divine mind. And these ideas, though multiplied by their relations to things, in reality are not apart from the divine essence, according as the likeness to that essence can be shared diversely by different things. In this manner therefore God Himself is the first exemplar of all things. Moreover, in things created one may be called the exemplar of another by the reason of its likeness thereto, either in species, or by the analogy of some kind of imitation.' Thomas Aquinas (1947) *Summa Theologica*, Benziger Brothers edition, I, Question 44, article 3, answer to objections.

17 Aquinas, *Summa Theologica*, I, Question 44, article 4.

18 Aquinas, *Summa Theologica*, I, Question 44, article 4, objection 1.

19 Aquinas, *Summa Theologica*, I, Question 44, article 4, answer to objections.

20 Aquinas, *Summa Theologica*, I, Question 44, article 4, reply to objection 4.

21 al-Ghazālī (1999 (1992, 1995, 1997)), *The Ninety-Nine Beautiful Names of God*, trans. David B. Burrell and Nazih Daher, Cambridge, Islamic Texts Society, p. 68.

22 See *On the Heavens* I. 12. 283^a11–12; cf. *The Physics* VIII. I. 252^a15–16. Aristotle (2000) *The Works of Aristotle*, trans. T. Taylor, Thomas Taylor series 19–26, Frome, Prometheus Trust.

23 H. A. Davidson (1987) *Proofs for Eternity, Creation and the Existence of God in Medieval Islamic and Jewish Philosophy*, New York and Oxford, Oxford University Press, p. 52.

24 Thomas Aquinas (2002) *Summa Contra Gentiles*, Notre Dame, Ind., University of Notre Dame Press, II.35.5.

25 See the discussion of Dharmakīrti's critique in J. S. J. Vattanky (1993) *Development of Nyāya Theism*, New Delhi, Intercultural Publications, pp. 50–7.

26 Averroës (Ibn Rushd) (1969) *Tahafut al-Tahafut*, trans. Simon Van den Bergh, London, Luzac, pp. 96–7.

27 Averroës, *Tahafut al-Tahafut*, p. 103.

28 Averroës, *Tahafut al-Tahafut*, pp. 103–4.

29 Averroës, *Tahafut al-Tahafut*, pp. 100–1.

30 Muṭahharī, *Fundamentals of Islamic Thought*, p. 116.

31 Uddyotakara, *Nyāyavartikka*, Book Four, Portion One, Topic XXXVII. See the summary of the discussion in Karl H. Potter (ed.) (1977) *Encyclopedia of Indian Philosophers*, vol. 2: *Indian Metaphysics and Epistemology: The Tradition of Nyāya-Vaiśeṣika up to Gaṅgeṣa*, Delhi, Motilal Banarsidass, p. 332.

32 Udayana, *Nyāyakusumanjali*, Book Two. See the summary of the discussion in Potter, *Encyclopedia of Indian Philosophers*, vol. 2, p. 572.

33 J. Pereira (1991 (1976)) *Hindu Theology: Themes, Texts and Structures*, Delhi, Motilal Banarsidass, pp. 105–7.

34 Pereira, *Hindu Theology*, pp. 106–7.

35 D. A. Pailin (1989) *God and the Processes of Reality: Foundations of a Credible Theism*, Routledge Religious Studies, London and New York, Routledge.

36 Pailin, *God and the Processes of Reality*, p. 139.

37 Plotinus (1991) *The Enneads*, trans. S. MacKenna, London, Penguin, V.2.1.

38 al-Ghazālī (2000 (1997)) *The Incoherence of the Philosophers (Tahafut al-Falasifah)*, trans. M. E. Marmura, Provo, Utah, Brigham Young University Press.

39 The terms in Sanskrit are *jada* (matter), *prana* (life), *caitanya-purusa* (psyche), *manas* (mind – or inner sense; mind may not be the best translation), *vijnana* or *Rtacit* (super-mind), *sat* (existence). See the discussion in P. Chatterji (1982) 'Plotinus and Sri Aurobindo: A Comparative Study', in R. B. Harris (ed.), *Neoplatonism and Indian Thought*, Albany, State University of New York Press.

40 Aurobindo (1996) *The Life Divine*, Pondicherry, Sri Aurobindo Ashram, pp. 105–6.

41 Martha Beckwith's translation, M. W. Beckwith (1981 (1951, 1972)), *The Kumulipo: A Hawaiian Creation Chant*, Honolulu, University of Hawaii Press, p. 58. She discusses problems with the translation and previous attempts in pp. 42–9. The Kalakaua text of the original is given from p. 187.

42 Reported in *The Independent*, 4 December 2002, article by Steve Connor, abstract at http://www.independent.co.uk/story.jsp?story=358265.

43 Śaṇkara, *Brahma-Sūtra Shankara-Bhāshya: Bādarāyaṇā's Brahma-Sūtras with Shankarāchāryā's Commentary*, translated by Vasudeo Apte, I.4.1–7.

44 Śaṇkara, *Brahma-Sūtra Shankara-Bhāshya*, II.1.15.

45 Śaṇkara, *Brahma-Sūtra Shankara-Bhāshya*, I.1.2.

46 Śaṇkara, *Brahma-Sūtra Shankara-Bhāshya*, II.2.28.

47 E. Deutsch (1973) *Advaita Vedānta*, Honolulu, University of Hawaii Press, p. 31. 'The realism of Advaita is in opposition to this position both on theoretical and practical grounds. It is argued theoretically that subject/object experience means precisely a distinction between subject and object, which distinction can be overcome only through transcendence; and practically that any doctrine of subjectivism becomes a barrier to this act of transcendence.'

48 Abhidarmakosha, cited in H. von Glasenapp (1970) *Buddhism – A Non-theistic Religion*, trans. I. Schloegl, London, Allen & Unwin, p. 35.

49 Kalupahana's translation: D. J. Kalupahana (1994) *A History of Buddhist Philosophy*, Delhi, Motilal Banarsidass, p. 56.

50 Or of the world, as it is rendered in some Pali texts 'Thus does this world arise', 'thus does this world cease', Sutra II.78.

51 G. C. Pande (1997, 1999) 'Causality in Buddhist Philosophy', in E. Deutsch

and R. Bontekoe (eds), *A Companion to World Philosophies*, Oxford, Blackwell, p. 373.

52 David Burrell (2004) *Faith and Freedom*, Challenges in Contemporary Theology, Oxford, Blackwell, p. 87.

53 Aquinas, *Summa Theologica*, I, Question 45.

5

Relation

'I' and 'you' are but the lattices,
In the niches of a lamp,
Through which the One Light shines.
'I' and 'you' are the veil
Between heaven and earth:
Lift this veil and you will see
No longer the bonds of sects and creeds.
When 'I' and 'you' do not exist.
What is mosque, what is synagogue?
What is the Temple of Fire?[1]

Differing views on creation, as we pointed out in the previous chapter, suggest different ways God is seen in relation to the world. The issues around identity and difference between the divine and the world of our experience have more ramifications and, as before, we will find different answers to the questions raised. Is God identical to all that we see, One Light shining through the lattices in a lamp, as Shabistarī describes it? Or is God a different being altogether, 'wholly other'? Or is neither of these options the answer, or can God be somehow both? At the heart of these questions are different concepts of deity. For example, to speak of creation out of nothing at the beginning of time is already to specify that God is a being not identical with the world. And that implies that God is transcendent of the world, and philosophers are led from this point to draw some related conclusions. Does this suggest that God is infinite, therefore eternal? Does it perhaps mean that God is all-powerful?

David Burrell argues:

> Without a clear philosophical means of distinguishing God from the world, the tendency of all discourse about divinity is to deliver a God who is the 'biggest thing around.' That such is the upshot of much current philosophy of religion cannot be doubted. . . . The wary will note that talking about a God distinct from the world will inevitably involve one in analogical forms of speech . . .[2]

Burrell argues that God's simplicity and God's eternity are the 'formal features' of divinity, which can be cognitively distinguished from God's attributes; and that an understanding of God's simplicity and eternity is the best way to ground an understanding of the difference of God from the world.

In this chapter we will look at this fundamental question of the identity or difference of God to the world, discussing some possible views of the divine, and reviewing strategies for entwining both transcendence and immanence together as aspects of God.

Some possible views of the divine

No God (but still a religion, spirituality, ethic or world view)
Identity of the divine and the world
- *'Monism'*
- *'Pantheism'*

Absolute difference between God and the world
- *Transcendental monotheism*
- *Indian dualism*

Immanence of God in the world
- *Enworlded gods*
- *Boundless permeation*
- *Immanent personalism*

Non-theism

Are there cases where a set of beliefs is deemed a 'religion' but does not include belief in God? Yes. Indian systems like Buddhism, Jainism, Mīmāṃsāka and Sāṃkhya all have a base in some sacred scriptures, and have a code of ethics and a theory of liberation or salvation and they follow a spiritual path without feeling the need of a God. To take Buddhism as an example of a religion without a God, we find that disputes surround the question of whether this tradition should be called atheist, agnostic, non-theist, polytheist or monist. The Buddha himself steadfastly refused speculative theological issues of divinity, on the grounds that they are non-questions which, moreover, hinder spiritual discipline and progress. After his death, this refusal to take a position led to different tendencies and ideas which were claimed by differing thinkers as the 'real' stance of Buddhism. Walpola Rahula, in the Theravāda tradition which traditionally has been firmly atheistic, insists that Buddhism has always rejected belief in a God and is thus atheistic.[3] Buddhism has argued against the existence of a God because of the horrors of evil and suffering. It also has put forth logical arguments against God as the cause of the world, because of an understanding of causality as a multiple affair, requiring a number of factors and indeed a number of decisions which must be involved in the making of a universe whereas God, in some accounts, is said to be single, simple, eternal and changeless.

Charles Wei-hsun Fu, on the other hand, writes, 'If the Buddhist principle of a Middle Way is strictly applied to the problem of God or the Absolute, the only possible conclusion one can draw is that Buddhism must naturally lie midway between theism and atheism. If the Buddhists themselves truly abide by the principle of the Middle Way, they must consistently avoid any propositional assertion about the existence or non-existence of God or the Absolute.'[4] He cites Kenneth Inada with approval: 'It should be remembered that the denial of atheism does not bring forth theism just as the denial of theism does not bring forth atheism. These are not mutually identifiable or mutually refutable concepts; and thanks to this, Buddhism is neither of the two.' Rather than force Buddhism into one of the other -isms – atheism, agnosticism, etc., – we should simply call it 'Buddhism'. A neat solution. Fu grants the greater plausibility of seeing Buddhism as atheistic but still maintains that 'it is not in perfect accord with the genuine spirit of the Middle Way'.[5] That Middle Way and the refusal to speculate should just as surely preclude arguments *against* the existence of God.

There is at the same time theistic or goddish talk in other strands of Buddhism. This takes several forms. First of all, there are in Pure Land Buddhism or in Tantric and Tibetan traditions a number of texts which, in the words of von Glasenapp, 'confirm unmistakably and authoritatively that since the oldest times Buddhists believed in the existence of gods (*deva*)'.[6] The panoply of Bodhisattvas and saints in Buddhist practice can take on divine traits. This is even truer of the Buddha himself, around whom after his death pious speculation began to weave superhuman characteristics. These tendencies have given rise to the ascription of 'polytheism' or indeed 'monotheism' to some traditions of Buddhism. Finally, the Mahāyāna ideas of 'Buddha-nature' have a whiff of pantheism to some interpreters. Buddha-nature is the original nature of the Buddha, the seed which can develop into Buddhahood. It is said to be possessed by all sentient beings, and indeed according to some by non-sentient beings like plants. In the T'ien-t'ai school it is even said that 'Every grass or every tree, every country or every land, all attains Buddhahood.'[7] Nevertheless, according to Fu, such ' "theological" talk' is 'constructed pedagogically and conventionally for the sake of those who lack keen insight into what is ontologically non-differentiable and epistemologically non-conceptualizable in the light of the principle of the Middle Way'.[8]

Religions are composed of many strands, and any attempt to reduce them to a single essential ingredient distorts the reality of that which we are trying to study. Certainly there can be religions without a belief in God. What is clear from the example of Buddhism is that a pretty robust and satisfying stance needs to be taken to address those many issues and problems to which God seems to be an answer for so many religious people: the origin of what there is, the meaning of my life and how I should live it now, the ultimate goal of my existence.

Identity of the divine and the world

'Monism' – Advaita Vedānta

Monism is the name often given to the belief that there is only one fundamental reality, and God and the world are not ultimately different. This is one way that you can interpret some passages in the Indian scriptures that form the sacred texts for the many strands of belief that we call 'Hinduism', especially the Upaniṣads. The strand known as Advaita Vedānta is a prominent 'non-dualist' tradition.

'Truly, this whole world is Brahman, from which he comes forth, without which he will be dissolved and in which he breathes.'[9] The non-dualist way of interpreting and expounding the Upaniṣads maintains that all conceptual distinctions that we apply to reality, such as the belief that you are fundamentally different from me and both of us from the divine, are ultimately false. It is ignorance and false perceptions that lead to this mistaken distinction. Just as we see a rope lying across the road at night and perceive it as a snake, we perceive but misperceive or misunderstand the nature of what is. The world we see does exist, but as an 'appearance'. The ultimate principle, Brahman, underlies all reality as its true Self, and individual human selves are not fundamentally to be distinguished from Brahman.

Brahman, which is what is most real, contains no differentiation; for example, consciousness and bliss are not separate qualities of Brahman. Brahman transcends all distinctions, even the distinction of subject and object, Itself and Not-Itself. What is true above all is that the Self (*atman*), one's own truest self, is not different from Brahman, nor is anything else. It is this knowledge that leads to liberation and enlightenment. As the Chāndogya Upaniṣad puts it: 'this is the self of mine within the heart . . . It is Brahman. On departing from here after death, I will become that.'[10]

Śaṇkara compares it to the situation where a crystal is seen in front of a red flower, and so the observer thinks the crystal is red. The observer was not hallucinating; but she has not seen the true nature of the crystal. Instead, perceiving the redness of the flower, she takes the crystal to be red, and thus misses its transparency. When one learns to discriminate, one will perceive the true nature of Brahman as distinct from its adjuncts.[11]

This is a highly nuanced position; and it is not right to understand it as saying that the material world is unreal and a hallucination. Maṇḍana Miśra points out in the *Brahmasiddhi* that even the monist cannot say that Brahman is literally identical with *everything*, as it says in Scripture.[12] For Scripture denies that there is diversity; if there is diversity in the world and in Brahman's nature, there can be no liberation, for one cannot separate a thing and its nature. There would also be no difference between liberated and unliberated selves. 'Therefore Brahman is not identical with the diversity of the world, but the diversity is simply the display, the play of ignorance.'[13] Maṇḍana also maintains that the unreality of diversity is not the highest truth; if so, 'this would be equally so in bondage and in liberation, and so everyone would be freed from all eternity'.[14] Everything has a positive reality in the positive reality of Brahman; this distinguishes the Advaita view from the Buddhists' view that all is *śūnya* (emptiness).

On the whole, to describe Brahman accurately in positive statements, to state what Brahman is, cannot be done. It is easier and more accurate to say what Brahman is not. Three properties only can be ascribed to Brahman positively: *sat*, *cit* and *ananda*. *Sat*, sometimes translated as 'being', is the 'nature of reality inferred from what it is not; not composite, subject to origination and destruction, relations, change'.[15] *Cit* is awareness; Brahman is self-luminous, perfectly aware but not itself an object of thought (not even to itself). *Ananda* is bliss, which makes Śaṇkara reluctant to ascribe it to Brahman without some clarification, for bliss is of course a temporary state as far as we are concerned. Sureśvara explains that this bliss is not a content of consciousness. The Upaniṣads say that Brahman's bliss lies in its 'fullness', its lack of lack.[16] In a manner reminiscent of the West's 'negative theology' or 'apophatic' tradition, it is easier to say what Brahman is not. 'About this self, one can only say "not ——, not ——". He is ungraspable, for he cannot be grasped.'[17]

As we saw when considering views of creation, the Advaita Vedāntins believe that we superimpose difference and dualism on our perceptions of the world. The divine itself is superimposed upon, they believe, as the perceived creator of the world, Īśvāra. Here Advaita Vedānta speaks with Nyāya of Īśvāra's creation, but with the important difference from Nyāya that Īśvāra remains the material cause of the world, not the re-arranger of pre-existing atoms. And for the Vedāntin, Īśvāra is not Brahman as it really is, but Brahman with ignorance or illusion imposed on it (by our perception). Brahman is what is real; we superimpose our idea of God, Īśvara, onto Brahman.

From the *Bṛhadāraṇyaka Upaniṣad*

Then Vigardha Śākalya began to question him. 'Tell me, Yājñavalkya – how many gods are there?' Saying, 'As mentioned in the ritual invocation within the laud to the All-gods', he answered in accordance with this very ritual invocation: 'Three and three hundred, and three and three thousand.'

'Yes, of course,' he said, 'but really, Yājñavalkya, how many gods are there?'

'Thirty-three.'

'Yes, of course,' he said, 'but really, Yājñavalkya how many gods are there?'

'Six.'

'Yes, of course,' he said, 'but really, Yājñavalkya, how many gods are there?'

'Three.'

'Yes, of course,' he said, 'but really, Yājñavalkya, how many gods are there?'

'Two.'

'Yes, of course,' he said, 'but really, Yājñavalkya, how many gods are there?'

'One and a half.'

'Yes, of course,' he said, 'but really, Yājñavalkya, how many gods are there?'

'One.'

. . . 'Who is the one god?'

'Breath. He is called "Brahman" and "Tyad".'[18]

Because what they are trying to talk about resists ordinary speech, the Advaitins usually resort to analogies or metaphors to communicate to us intuitively how it can be true.

> It is like this. When a chunk of salt is thrown into water, it dissolves into that very water, and it cannot be picked up in any way. Yet, from whichever place one may take a sip, the salt is there! In the same way this Immense Being has no limit or boundary and is a single mass of perception. It arises out of and together with these beings and disappears after them.[19]

One venerable analogy is to point to seawater and to the foam that appears on its surface. You are not deluded if you think you perceive foam on the seawater; it can be distinguished in perception from the water itself. And yet it is not *something else* than that water; it comes from the water and dissolves back into it. So too with Brahman and the world and the many selves that we are. They are non-different and yet can be distinguished, just as sea foam and seawater.

Advaitins also use the analogy of space and a pot. Space is apparently single, continuous, undifferentiated. Now imagine a pot. Compare the space around a pot with the space enclosed by the empty pot. Once the pot is created, you can differentiate the space inside and outside the pot, but these are not two different 'things' any more than they were before. When a pot is destroyed, the space 'inside' it is simply merged back with the rest of space. Gaudapāda uses this image to explain the relation of Brahman and individual selves; when a soul is liberated it simply returns to oneness with Brahman, but even before that, though you can isolate it, it is not really a different 'thing' from Self.

From the *Bṛhadāraṇyaka Upaniṣad*

Then Uṣasta Cākrāyaṅa began to question him. 'Yājñavalkya,' he said, 'explain to me the Brahman *that is plain and not cryptic, the self that is within all.'*

'The self within all is this self of yours.'

'Which one is the self within all, Yājñavalkya?'

'Who breathes out with the out-breath – he is the self of yours that is within all. Who breathes in with the in-breath – he is the self of yours that is within all. Who breathes across with the inter-breath – he is the self of yours that is within all. Who breathes up with the up-breath – he is the self of yours that is within all. The self within all is this self of yours.'

Uṣasta Cākrāyaṅa retorted: 'That's a fine explanation! It's like saying "This is a cow and that is a horse!" Come on, give me a real explanation of the Brahman *that is plain and not cryptic, of the self that is within all.'*

'The self within all is this self of yours.'

'Which one is the self within all, Yājñavalkyaya?'

'You can't see the seer who does the seeing; you can't hear the hearer who does the hearing; you can't think of the thinker who does the thinking; and you can't perceive the perceiver who does the perceiving. The self within all is this self of yours. All else besides this is grief!'

Thereupon, Uṣasta Cākrāyaṅa fell silent.[20]

'Pantheism'

Although pantheism is much talked about, and some suggest it is about to undergo a revival in New Age religious thinking, it is not that easy to define precisely. Nor is it easy to draw up an identity parade of genuine pantheists.

Pantheism means identifying God totally with the material world. This might be taken as saying either that matter itself is somehow divine; or that the material and the divine or spiritual are fully unified. It is surprisingly difficult to find thinkers who assert that matter itself is fully divine. More often texts which are cited as examples of pantheism actually slide off subtly in a different direction. You find them saying that the divine is fully within the material world, but matter itself is not divine;

or there is some 'first principle' or 'inner principle' underlying all things but not identical with them. Those who truly believe there is nothing above and beyond nature often find nature itself sufficiently wondrous and worthy of reverence to need no divine spin (leaving the '-theism' out of 'pantheism', as it were).

Views which refuse to oppose matter and spirit are a little easier to identify. If they deny the reality of either matter or spirit, they are not what I call here 'pantheists' but are one or another kind of 'monist'. Those who say only matter is real and there is no such thing as a 'spiritual dimension' are materialist monists, and lie outside the scope of this book. Those who say matter is an illusion and all is spiritual could be called idealist or acosmic monists; these would include Advaita Vedānta, already examined. What we are after here are those few who totally and without reserve unite the physical and the spiritual.

An ancient example of a way that unifies matter and spirit is the thinking of the Greek Stoics. Their central tenet is the unity of all things despite the apparent diversity and opposition of elements; and more important still, they saw a single rational or spiritual principle which is within all things, intellectual or material. So one can say at once that everything is corporeal and material – even God – and therefore Stoics are sometimes (misleadingly) called materialists. At the same time, everything, even lifeless matter, is animated by an inner principle which is spiritual. In plants it is found as a natural organizing principle, in humans as a rational soul; but it is the same seminal principle (*spermatikos logos*) found in all. So if the Stoic God is corporeal, their God is also rational (*logikos, Logos*) and spiritual.

Stoicism is described by Caird as 'a philosophy which clings to the idea of the unity of all things, but which in its exposition of that unity passes abruptly from materialism to spiritualism, from individualism to pantheism, from sensationalism to idealism, as the occasion may require'.[21]

This central principle, when Stoics want to talk matter, is described as fire. The physical universe had its origins in fire, which gives rise to the paired oppositions we find in all things, which they characterize as fire/air vs. earth/water, and which holds them together in tension. As this tension gives out eventually, all will ultimately collapse back into its source, fire. This world-creating fire, 'from everywhere hence streaming all around, encircling and embracing all'[22] of course is another way of speaking about what we are calling God; 'source of all',[23] the one who made the world, 'the same as the Father of all'.[24] This fire is also described as spirit (*pneuma*) or breath penetrating all and encompassing all.[25] But because this pervades all and is not a separate entity from matter, the Stoics constantly tell us that you can call the world and all its parts God.[26]

The Dutch Jewish philosopher Spinoza is a 'pantheist' for logical reasons; he believes that there can only be one substance, because he understands the 'independence' entailed in the idea of 'substance' very powerfully: it is something which is conceived through itself, and does not need the conception of another thing from which it must be formed. Something is a 'substance' only if it is capable of absolutely independent existence. In this he is of the same view as the Advaita Vedāntin. As nothing else is this independent, it is immediately clear that God can be the only substance for Spinoza, a single substance, 'God or Nature', in which all things and events are determined by the eternal and immutable nature of God.

Spinoza's argument for pantheism

If two substances have nothing in common, one cannot cause the other (III); there cannot be two substances with the same nature or attributes (IV) therefore one substance cannot produce another. It is the nature of substance to exist (VII) and every substance is necessarily infinite (VIII), because it could only be limited by another substance of the same nature, and Spinoza has already argued that two substances of the same nature cannot exist. 'God, or substance consisting of infinite attributes, each one of which expresses eternal and infinite essence, necessarily exists' (XI). Substance is indivisible (XII, XIII) so 'Besides God, no substance can be nor can be conceived' (XIV). 'Whatever is, is in God, and nothing can either be or be conceived without God' (XV). From the necessity of God's nature, infinite numbers of things must follow (XVI), but all this takes place by God acting through the laws of his own nature, under compulsion from no-one (XVII). God is immanent; He is the cause of all things through himself, and is not the 'transitive cause' of things; i.e. He does not act by acting on other things outside Himself (XVIII). God and God's attributes are eternal (XIX) and God's essence is the same as God's existence (XX); so God and His attributes are immutable and eternal. So whatever follows from God's nature is also eternal, infinite, and necessary (XXI, XII). God is the cause of the essences as well as the existence of things, and God alone determines them (XXV–XXVIII). So in nature, all things are determined and could not be otherwise than how they are (XXIX, XXXIII). God possesses both the attributes of thought (although he does not have an intellect or will) (Part 2, I) and the attribute we see in the material world, extension (meaning it takes up space) (Part 2, II). Spinoza, Ethics, *Part 1. All citations are from Part 1 unless specified otherwise.*

Absolute difference between God and the World

Transcendental Monotheism

What I call transcendental monotheism conceives of God as a personal or quasi-personal being rather than an impersonal absolute. But 'person' should not be misunderstood. God is beyond all that we are. This has several corollaries.

The first is that the difference between God and everything else is absolute. 'There is nothing like Him', both the Bible and the Qur'ān tell us.[27] The language, imagery and philosophical claims all try to mark off the divine from what is experienced in concrete ways in the world. Where figurative speech or anthropomorphic language are used, and indeed may be abundant as it is in the Bible, the more philosophically minded monotheist is anxious to point out that such talk should not be taken literally.

Another corollary of this absolute difference is that God is also beyond what we can comprehend. Believers in a God who is Wholly Other insist that God's transcendence means a transcendence of human cognition, knowledge, understanding, as well as language.

This absolute transcendence implies perfection; God's attributes (if the language of attributes is used) are taken to be unlimited and unconditioned, essential and not subject to change or chance, and therefore eternal. The absoluteness of God is also taken to imply a oneness and uniqueness. This absolute difference is something that cannot be shared with another being. God's attributes cannot shared, therefore; at least not in their infinite and absolute forms.

As the Qur'ān puts it:

> In the name of God, the Merciful, the Compassionate. Say (O Muhammad) He is God the One God, the Everlasting Refuge, who has not begotten, nor has begotten, and equal to Him is not anyone.
>
> He is God; there is no god but He, He is the Knower of the unseen and the visible; He is the All-Merciful, the All-Compassionate. He is God, there is no God but He. He is the King, the All-Holy, the All-Peace, the Guardian of Faith, the All-Preserver, the All-Mighty, the All-Compeller, the All-Sublime. Glory be to God, above that they associate! He is God the Creator, the Maker, the Shaper. To Him belong the Names Most Beautiful. All that is in the heavens and the earth magnifies Him; He is the All-Mighty, the All-Wise.[28]

This God is the creator of all, another reason for stressing absolute difference from creatures. If the divine was of the nature of a creature, God too would be something subject to the power of another, subject to change, and it would then be reasonable to ask if God too needed a maker. God is not caused. This means self-sufficiency, self-subsistence; God does not require any other for existence. Nothing can therefore damage or bring an end to God.

Indian Mādhva Dualism

The Indian philosopher Mādhva asserted a dualism of God and the world. In contrast to the view of Advaita, for the Mādhva dualist Hindu, the individual may reflect God, but is not identical with God. Even when meeting God at the time of salvation the individual never loses her own identity and personhood. This God is not the Brahman without qualities and attributes of the Advaita Vedāntin monist; for Mādhva, such a God in the end is no different from the śūnya or nothingness of the Buddhist. One cannot prove the thesis of the monists, he claims, because all argument relies on difference and thus even arguments for monism must be false, which is an interesting charge.

For Mādhva, God is personal, omniscient, omnipotent, blissful and the maker of the world. All things, beings, selves, time depend for their existence on God. This, he argues, is the knowledge of God that is given in the Vedas, and in experience; both of which contradict the monism of the Śaṇkarite Vedāntin. However, one cannot prove the existence of this God, as the Naiyāyika tries to do; equally convincing inferences can be drawn against the existence of God. It is only by knowing God that one can devote oneself to him, and only devotion to God can bring salvation. According to Mādhva, such devotion is not possible to what is identical to oneself.

Immanence of God in the world

Enworlded gods

Religions who place their gods within creation are usually given short shrift within the realms of philosophy. They may be seen as primitive; superseded or supplanted by later religious developments, as in Greece, or subject to conversion by missionary activity, if not yet, then they should be soon. Where they still remain, they may be known tactfully as 'indigenous religions' – perhaps implying that anyone not born into one couldn't possibly believe in it. Thus they are not usually treated as religio-philosophical systems whose beliefs merit *philosophical*, as opposed to anthropological, investigation.

Hesiod was a Greek poet who lived in approximately 700 BC. He is credited with writing the Theogony, *about the origin of the world and the gods. He is one of our principal sources for Greek mythology.*

Jaeger describes the original Greek gods as 'stationed *inside* the world', and subject to what he calls natural law. But in Hesiod there is already the beginning of a search for a 'single, natural principle' such as later Greek philosophers desire. When Hesiod's pagan thought eventually yields to philosophy, the divine that is sought is understood to be what gives rise to the natural world. (This is presumably why Jaeger is happy to call it philosophy – because it seeks rational explanation.) This means then that the divine is sought inside, and not outside, the world.[29] Thales, the earliest named Greek philosopher, on the one hand does not engage in myth-writing accounts of gods and the origin of the universe, and believes that everything comes from water. On the other hand, he is recorded as saying that 'everything is full of gods'. Clearly 'gods' here are not beings that go about disguised as bulls or showers of gold and seducing young ladies; it marks a clear difference in how the gods are conceived and spoken of. Jaeger interprets this gnomic quasi-pantheism as 'everything is full of mysterious living forces; the distinction between animate and inanimate nature has no foundation in fact; everything has a soul'.[30] There is a famous story about Heraclitus warming his hands by the fire, saying to guests hesitating on the threshold, 'Enter. Here, too, are gods.' It marks perhaps a shift from a pantheon of mythic mighty personalities to principles, forces, that lie unseen but powerful within the world of visible things. Jaeger's account implies that the transition from mythology to theology, from stories of many gods to the rational reflection on The Divine, is precisely the philosophical impulse that seeks scientific explanations for things (although that is not how he puts it).

The impulse to move beyond mythic gods as what counts as 'the divine' would only be heightened when Parmenides introduces a stark contrast between 'Being' and 'Becoming'. The world of 'becoming' is clearly changing, impermanent, and implicitly imperfect. Perhaps here we see what makes it possible to develop the idea of transcendence. For the first thing the idea of transcendence requires is a metaphysical basis for asserting the absolute ontological superiority of one kind of thing, or one set of properties or qualities, over another. If it is better to exist in an eternal realm of Being rather than a changing world of Becoming, we have the starting-point for the evolution of what one might call rational or philosophical theology, which leads from the world of myths eventually to transcendent monotheism.

Now if this is so, one could also throw the engines in reverse, or challenge the tacit philosophical decisions that led to this development in the first place. Are there metaphysical or spiritual commitments or values that are lost in this Greek/Western history that might nevertheless be valuable ones to recover? Might these suggest that it is worth reflecting philosophically on enworlded gods, if I may coin a term less pejorative than 'pagan'?

A prefatory remark is that enworlded divinity is not necessarily the same thing as polytheism. They often do go together, as in many 'indigenous religions'. That may be so because being enworlded means that the gods often lack attributes that are ascribed to a transcendent God and are usually thought to be exclusive. It is commonly argued that there can only be one omnipotent being, for example. (This will be discussed in the next chapter.) But if such exclusive attributes are not ascribed to the enworlded god, such logical problems do not arise and the conceptual way is clear to enjoy as many gods as seem right to a community.

For the same reason, there seems in practice to be no trouble in conceiving a relation between enworlded gods or goddesses and an Absolute with less of a personality. This is the situation for many Hindus, who believe that the gods and goddesses in their pantheon are all manifestations of nirguṇa Brahman. It can also mean that enworlded theologies can be more hospitable than monotheisms, and can accommodate into the existing religion an *arriviste* God brought by missionaries, much to the discomfiture of the evangelizing exclusivist. This can happen simply by welcoming the new god in to join the party, or by giving the new god an identity already found within the host religion.

What sort of metaphysics is the philosophical condition of possibility for enworlded divinity?[31] One value found in many indigenous religions like that of Hawai'i is the value placed on the earth itself. In such a world view the earth is not an inferior realm characterized by ontological or metaphysical inferiority or inherent lack or evil, and the divine need not be defined as the opposite of the earthly.

What is it that makes a goddess distinguishable from a woman? Are enworlded theists working with a completely different notion of the divine?

It seems not. Enworlded goddesses share many features with transcendent gods. They are generally invisible, though they may be symbolically represented (but so too may be a transcendent god).[32] They are generally incorporeal, although they may have a unique kind of embodiment in geographical or other features in the world, and they may have bodily experience in some of its aspects for narrative purposes. Understanding this embodiment requires interpretative sensitivity; which we take for granted with 'anthropomorphic' monotheistic narratives we may refrain from granting to the devotees of polytheist or 'pagan' deities. The Hawaiian goddess Kapo has a sort of detachable, flying vagina, a *kohelele*, which, when you learn more about what it can do in a difficult situation, is clearly an arrangement to be envied. If you go to the right place on O'ahu, you can see the appropriately shaped crater where it once hit the earth. But this does not entail that the Hawaiians thought that if you went to the right place on O'ahu at the right time, you would perceive Kapo herself in the flesh, with or without all her relevant attributes in place. If we assume that the ancient Israelites did not expect to *see* the Lord baring his holy arm (Isaiah 52.10), are we right to assume the Hawaiians *did* naively expect to see Kapo bearing her sacred *kohelele*? Hawaiians believed that gods could take at will particular body forms. Lono could have the *kinolau*, as it is called, of a sweet potato. But first, this does suggest that the gods are otherwise incorporeal, and temporary corporeality is a matter of sovereign choice. Second, what a Hawaiian expects to see when she sees Lono in his *kinolau* of a sweet potato is not some divine form, but – a sweet potato. If there is something different about seeing this sweet potato and seeing others, it is not to be found in the sensory perception of a divine body. It is transignification – a change in meaning of the perception of a sweet potato (or a communion wafer) which looks much like any other.

One day, the goddess Pele and her sister Kapo were taking a walk on the Hawaiian island of O'ahu. They were spied by Kamapua'a (literally 'son of pig'). He desired Pele and began to chase Pele and Kapo, who ran away as fast as they could. (It should be noted that Kamapua'a, even when in man form, had thick, rather unsightly bristles on his back.)

'It's no good,' said Pele. 'We can't run fast enough. He's going to get us.'

'Don't worry,' said Kapo. 'I have my kohelele. *You know men. They are only interested in one thing.'*

Kohe = *vagina*

Lele = *flying, detached, separatable*

So Kapo threw her kohelele *and it went – that way. Meanwhile the two goddesses ran – this way. Kamapua'a ran up and went . . . that way. (Kapo was right.) The two goddesses escaped. Kapo went and retrieved her* kohelele *later.*

Although Jaeger speaks of enworlded gods as 'stationed in the world', any facile opposition of gods inside vs. outside of the material world could surely be interrogated with more scepticism. What does a Hawaiian mean when she seems to locate Laka in a waterfall or speaks of Pele making her home in a volcano? Is this language to be interpreted as fundamentally different from God being 'in' a burning bush, or 'in' a sacramental wafer? For those who believe in it, the bush and the wafer are not God's material body. God is not contained by them. It seems that this is a privileged, powerful but temporary revelation of God, for the moment spatially located but only as far as our reception is concerned. The waterfall and the volcano are not the goddesses' bodies either, and their being does transcend that place – they are not confined there like naiads or water sprites. They choose to reveal themselves in that way to the *haumana* (hula initiate) or to the witness of an eruption. The waterfall and the volcano do not imprison the goddesses, nor are the places divine, though they may be 'sacred' in a way that requires the removal of footwear.

So I am suspicious of the idea that talk of non-monist, non-pantheist divinity as 'inside' the world or of a transcendent god as 'outside' is not still metaphorical, as much for the 'pagan' as the monotheist. To ask an enworlded theist if her deity is 'outside the world' is like asking a Muslim if 'Allah is subject to karma as Shiva is. It is a question that implies a complex framework of assumptions and beliefs which are not shared by the believer. If you do not share those prior beliefs – here, an oppositional world view – the question is not one that you can answer meaningfully. For if Pele is not material but can be present in the world, is she inside or outside it? As spirit, is she not both immanent in and transcendent of the world? Our later discussions of immanence might clarify the suggestion that talk of inside and outside are less fixed properties of an entity, but rather are *discourses*, ways to emphasize features in our relations with the one(s) we worship. And certainly the spatial terms are metaphors, and can misguide us.

So enworlded gods share with transcendent gods the facilities for incorporeality, invisibility, and in some cases omnipresence, as well as their own kind of transcendence and immanence. Enworlded goddesses are more powerful, more knowledgeable and wiser than women. This suggests that the desirable features ascribed to a Monotheos are often ascribed, though maybe not all at once, to enworlded deities. They may or may not be *omni*-all-these-things – their knowledge, power or wisdom may not be described as without limit. What enworlded gods might *not* enjoy in some cases are certain attributes ascribed to the transcendent Monotheos: infinity, uniqueness, absolute difference from humanity. So what makes an enworlded deity different from a human being is partly what distinguishes the transcendent god from humanity. However, it is a question of greater possession of these qualities, or maximal possession of them; but not an absolute qualitative, ontological difference, as is the difference between 'Allah and Ali.

This suggests that the reasoning in theologizing about enworlded gods differs in one respect from at least some monotheistic or monist thinking. Positive attributes are intensified, maybe purified (depending on the enworlded god's morals and deportment) when they are ascribed to the one who is worshipped. The human version of these attributes is not negated by way of comparison in this process. In contrast, a central feature of the more aspirational forms of transcendent monotheism underlines the divinity of God by negation of anything resembling human finitude or imperfection.

Reasoning based on negation, on avoiding contradiction, on analysis that consists of paring-down of concepts – all these may be features of certain cultures' logic. It may be that such thinking leads to the kind of abstraction that prioritizes the One over the Many as ontologically prior; that sees 'Being Itself' devoid if need be of any attributes as the ultimate, rather than as empty and dull. But where some people's sophisticated mental work consists in analysis and stripping-down, others' can consist of synthesis and combination. Hawaiian thinking patterns were less concerned with contradiction and avoiding it than with the union of opposites and the relating of many strands in a lokāhī, a harmony of diverse elements. It is more worthwhile and profound from this point of view to enumerate the *many* micro-environments that exist where the wave meets the sand, or 20-odd kinds of rain, than it is to identify a *single* principle which allegedly lies behind all things.

Perhaps those cultures that give rise to monotheisms have philosophical systems that are founded on oppositional thinking, and those that give rise to enworlded, and maybe multiple gods, do not. Or maybe they just give a different answer to the question: What is it to be holy?

Boundless permeation

Taoism is sometimes described as 'pantheist', but caution must attend on interpreting the *Tao te Ching* and other Taoist thinkers in this way, which is based on our more precise definitions. It is clear that the Tao is in everything – even in excrement, as the texts of Chuang Tsu tell us. But the Tao is not 'nothing but' the universe, rather, it is all-pervading. It pre-existed the material world and is that from which heaven and earth came forth infinite and eternal, it gives birth to infinite worlds. It is not personal or a being; it is beyond being and not-being. And it is also something that is not visible or audible, which we fail to grasp in material things though it exists in them.

Passages from the foundational text of Taoism, the Tao Te Ching, *which describe the fundamental principle, the Tao:*

The Tao is like a well:
Used but never used up.
It is like the eternal void:
Filled with infinite possibilities.

It is hidden but always present.
I don't know who gave birth to it.
It is older than God.
(Chapter 4)

The Tao is called the Great Mother:
Empty yet inexhaustible,
It gives birth to infinite worlds.

It is always present within you.
You can use it any way you want.
(Chapter 6)

The Tao is infinite, eternal.
Why is it eternal?
It was never born;
Thus it can never die.
Why is it infinite?
It has no desires for itself;
Thus it is present for all beings.
(Chapter 7)[33]

You might call that view something like 'boundless permeation'. The divine (or the ultimate) is salient in all that is. That is one way of conceiving the 'immanence' of the divine.

We have seen interpretations of Vedic religion and the Upaniṣads that are monist, and others which resolutely insist on difference. But there is also a style of interpretation, sometimes categorized as 'difference in identity', which asserts the reality of Brahman within all things without necessarily exhaustively identifying Brahman with the diverse world, and implying the illusory nature of the former.

The Upaniṣads can be interpreted in a non-monist way. There are passages which speak of Brahman as 'inner controller', the 'thread that holds the world together'. Such Upaniṣadic texts suggest the *immanence* of Brahman or the Supreme Self in one's own self and in the world, without necessarily asserting an absolute *identity* between Brahman and creation. The *Śvetāśvatara Upaniṣad* contains a number of images that evoke the idea of presence within, without annihilating the character of the host. 'Like oil in sesame seeds, and butter in curds, like water in the river-bed, and fire in fire-drills, so when one seeks it with truth and austerity, one grasps that self in the body – that all-pervading self . . . That is brahman.'[34]

Rāmānuja and the tradition which followed him rejected Śaṇkara's assertion of absolute non-difference; Rāmānuja in fact claimed there was no scriptural text that maintained it. The famous Upaniṣadic saying, 'thou art that' is 'not meant to indicate absolute unity of non-differenced substance'. Individual existence is not illusory but real. The personality of the Absolute is unchanging but the *embodiment* of the Absolute does change. Rāmānuja's view of the relationship between Brahman and the rest of us is 'identity in and through and because of difference'.

Rāmānuja on Brahman and the self

There is a highest Brahman which is the sole cause of the entire universe, which is antagonistic to all evil, whose essential nature is infinite knowledge and blessedness, which comprises within itself numberless auspicious qualities of supreme excellence, which is different in nature from all other beings, and which constitutes the inner Self of all. Of this Brahman, the individual selves – whose true nature is unlimited knowledge, and whose only essential attribute is the intuition of the supreme Self – are modes, in so far, namely, as they constitute its body.[35]

The divine Supreme Person, all whose wishes are eternally fulfilled, who is all-knowing and the ruler of all, whose every purpose is immediately realized, having engaged in sport befitting his might and greatness and having settled that work is of a two-fold nature, such and such works being good and such and such being evil, and having bestowed on all individual selves bodies and sense-organs capacitating them for entering on such work and the power of ruling those bodies and organs, and having himself entered into those selves as their inner self, abides within them, controlling them as an animating and cheering principle.[36]

The desire to mediate between absolute identity and difference is still seen in modern thinkers like Radhakrishnan, of whose thought Charles A. Moore writes:

> The Divine is both in us and out of us. God is neither completely transcendent nor completely immanent. To bring about this double aspect, contradictory accounts are given. . . . The unity of man and God is the fundamental thesis of the great philosophic tradition which has come down to us from the Upaniṣads and Plato.[37]

Looking West to find similar notions, one of the earliest Greek philosophers we know of, before the time of Socrates, was Anaximander. In seeking to name the source of everything, that which must be able to give rise to all things but be identical with none of them, he decided its distinguishing property must be that it is unbounded, so he calls it this – *apeiron*. Aristotle tells us that this means an 'endless inexhaustible reservoir or stock from which all Becoming draws its nourishment'.[38] It must have no beginning, and be unable to pass away and have an ending, otherwise it would have a boundary – and thus not be The Boundless. Repeatedly the Presocratics tell us that this unborn and imperishable is that which 'governs' and 'encompasses' all things. This moment in Anaximander is the first time we find a notion of 'The Divine'.[39]

The Greek notion of what is boundless and divine is clearly fully ripe in Plotinus.

'The One is all things and not one of them; the source of all things is not all things; all things are its possession – running back, so to speak, to it – or, more correctly, not yet so, they will be.'[40]

Plotinus, who was fascinated by Eastern thought, speaks about the One in language reminiscent of the Upaniṣads' language about nirguṇa Brahman:

> The First is no being but precedent to all Being; it cannot be a being, for a being has what we may call the shape of its reality but The Unity is without shape, even shape Intellectual. Generative of all, The Unity is none of all; neither thing nor quantity nor quality nor intellect nor soul; not in motion, not at rest, not in place, not in time: it is the self-defined, unique in form or, better, formless, existing before Form was, or Movement or Rest, all of which are attachments of Being and make Being the manifold it is. . . . Note . . . that, when we speak of this First as Cause, we are affirming something happening not to it but to us, the fact that we take from this Self-Enclosed: strictly we should put neither a This nor a That to it; we hover, as it were, about it, seeking the statement of an experience of our own, sometimes nearing this Reality, sometimes baffled by the enigma in which it dwells.[41]

For Plotinus, all things are embodied in an immortal soul, and not the other way around – all entities are 'ensouled'. This makes for a remarkable picture of universal identification and sympathy:

> . . . this All is one universally comprehensive living being, encircling all the living beings within it, and having a soul, one soul, which extends to all its members in the degree of participant membership held by each; secondly, that every separate thing is an integral part of this All by belonging to the total material fabric – unrestrictedly a part by bodily membership, while, in so far as it has also some participation in the All-Soul, it possesses in that degree spiritual membership as well, perfect where participation is in the All-Soul alone, partial where there is also a union with a lower soul. But, with all this gradation, each several thing is affected by all else in virtue of the common participation in the All, and to the degree of its own participation. This One-All, therefore, is a sympathetic total and stands as one living being.[42]

Plotinian Neoplatonism then is one style of distinguishing the Absolute from the material world, while insisting that our world is thoroughly permeated by it.

One can speak of God or the divine as unboundedly within creation:

panentheism. One can just as well speak of all that exists as being within God. Krishna tells us in the *Gita* that in his unmanifested form he is immanent in the entire creation; everything rests in him, not he in them.[43] Everything is 'strung' in him as pearls are strung on a thread.[44] God, as what is ultimate, contains the world; the world does not contain God.

Immanent personalism

Many believers, in particular monotheists like Muslims, Jews and Christians, feel that God is not so much 'something' as 'someone'; and moreover, someone separate from us, yet somehow unbelievably close. Thus the way they speak about God's presence in the world takes different terms within the language of 'immanence'. They struggle to speak of God as no less close than Rāmānuja's Brahman; but are more concerned to give God a separate identity or person-hood. Their infinite God has nevertheless what we may call an outline of personality.

This discourse of immanence describes God as thoroughly present in the universe in its entirety, rather than standing apart from it. But as the universe does not exhaust God – there is more to God than the material universe – God is not *only* the spirit within things. In this view, God isn't just the same thing as the world. On the other hand, all things only exist within God and have no independent existence from God. There is a God outside the world, but no world outside God.

The Jewish philosopher Martin Buber, after an initial attraction to mysticism, rejected a theology or metaphysics of identification with God in favour of a different approach inspired by Ḥasidism; in short, he rejects *identification* with God in favour of *relationship* with God. Explaining the language of mystics, he suggests that we view it as we view the language of lovers,

> who in the passion of erotic fulfillment are so carried away by the miracle of the embrace that all knowledge of I and You drowns in the feeling of a unity that neither exists nor can exist. What the ecstatic calls unification is the rapturous dynamics of the relationship; not a unity that has come into being at this moment in world time, fusing I and You, but the dynamics of the relationship itself . . .[45]

So when you consider the phrase 'I am one with God', you can distinguish the language of the ecstatic theist who gets carried away, from the monist, who is making a sober, metaphysical assertion. The Indian Islamic Sufis, living as they were in close quarters with monists, were also concerned to make the distinction. Absolute union with God was not possible; what is possible is 'the subjective state of the lover in relation to the beloved (God), in which the lover imagines himself to be united with God. . . . This stage is the outcome of the ecstatic mood of the creature. It does not efface the distinction between the creature and the Creator.'[46]

The monists' metaphysical assertion of real absolute identity is rejected by Buber. To assert an underlying unity of all, of the Self, has nothing in common with 'lived actuality', and can only be maintained by asserting the unreality of the world. In real life as it is lived, the world, God and I are not one. Nevertheless, the world and so-called worldly life do not separate us from God. Instead, he calls us to love the world and not annul it. Monist metaphysics is a 'delusion of the human spirit bent back into itself', rather than moving between humanity and what we are not which would be a relationship. The deepest truth is not identity but reciprocal activity; 'The strongest and deepest actuality is to be found where everything enters into activity – the whole human being, without reserve, and the all-embracing God; the unified I and the boundless You.'[47] 'God embraces but is not the universe; just so, God embraces but is not my self.'[48]

So Buber, in effect, calls for a way of speaking about God's relatedness to the world in a way that maintains a difference between them.

Christian theological language of immanence speaks of God present within creation, of working in and through creatures to achieve the good. At the same time, this assertion of God's presence is often countered with an assertion that God is unbounded, perhaps to prevent any possible implication of pantheism. This often results in paradoxical utterances as God is 'everywhere present and nowhere included'; or Augustine's famous metaphor: 'God is a circle whose centre is everywhere and whose circumference is nowhere'. As Meister Eckhart wrote: 'The One descends into each and every thing, always remaining one and uniting what is divided.'[49] God is fully immanent within the whole of creation, without abolishing the distinct identity and uniqueness of each entity.

Christian religious language frequently uses language of God animating what exists, in order to assert God's relation, both intimate and almighty, to the world. Mystics and spiritual writers can often carry off this manoeuvre particularly well. Hildegard of Bingen portrays God as saying:

> I, the highest and fiery power, have kindled every spark of life . . . I, the fiery life of divine essence, am aflame beyond the beauty of the meadows, I gleam in the waters, and I burn in the sun, moon, and stars. With every breeze, as with invisible life that contains everything, I awaken everything to life. The air lives by turning green and being in bloom. The waters flow as if they were alive. The sun lives in its light, and the moon is enkindled, after its disappearance, once again by the light of the sun so that the moon is again revived . . . And thus I remain hidden in every kind of reality as a fiery power. Everything burns

> because of me in the way our breath constantly moves us, like the wind-tossed flame in a fire.[50]

Strategies for entwining transcendence and immanence

Are these different ways of speaking about God in conflict? Must the believer choose whether God is beyond all things or within all things, and not have it both ways? Monism and absolute, exclusive transcendence can never be consistently combined. However, there are ways of believing in a God everywhere and contained nowhere.

Strategies for entwining transcendence and immanence

God is omnipresent
God is incorporeal; the world is God's body
No opposition between God's transcendence and immanence
Language is limited (so why not flaunt it?)

Omnipresence

One of God's claimed attributes can be seen as a strategy for portraying God as present in the world. The Qur'ān teaches: 'Whichever way you turn, there is 'Allah's face.'[51] An Indian Islamic story tells of Moses calling out, asking God where he is. God answers: 'I am in front of you and behind you, to your right and to your left, and everywhere. When any creature remembers me, I am by his side, and when he calls Me, I am near him.'[52] Religious philosophers then have often used the attribute of omnipresence as a way of representing God's boundlessness, while remaining present everywhere; just as theologians have used it as a way of asserting God's simultaneous transcendence and immanence: 'This All is universal power, of infinite extent and infinite in potency, a God so great that all his parts are infinite. Name any place, and he is already there.'[53] Meister Eckhart also spoke of God's omnipresence as ensuring both an immanent and a transcendent relation to the world:

> God is infinite in his simplicity and simple by reason of his infinity. Therefore, he is everywhere and everywhere entire. He is everywhere by his infinity, but entire everywhere by reason of his simplicity. God alone flows into all created beings, into their essences; nothing of other beings flows into anything else. God is in the inner reality of each thing, and only in the inner reality. He alone 'is one'.[54]

Anselm, however, was troubled by certain logical difficulties he thought were involved in omnipresence, and struggled to overcome them. The Supreme Being 'exists either everywhere and always, or merely at some place and time, or nowhere and never: or, as I express it, either in every place and at every time, or finitely, in some place and at some time, or in no place and at no time.'[55] Of these options, surely the first is true: the Supreme Being must exist always and everywhere. But logical considerations seem to rule that such a being cannot exist as a whole, at one time, in all individual places, without being many different things. This forces Anselm to the apparently contradictory conclusion:

> In no place or time, that is, nowhere and never does it exist. For it cannot exist, except in every or in some place or time. But, on the other hand, since it is irrefutably established, not only that it exists through itself, and without beginning and without end, but that without it nothing anywhere or ever exists, it must exist everywhere and always.[56]

Anselm resolved the difficulty by claiming that one can predicate a 'place' to an object only if a place can include and contain it; and time, likewise. So if a being cannot be bounded by spatial extent or temporal duration, no place or time can be properly attributed to it. 'For, seeing that place does not act upon it *as place*, nor time *as time*, it is not irrational to say, that no place is its place, and no time its time.'[57] Thus the laws of space and time cannot compel it, place limits on it, or restrain it. So the usual laws that apply to place, that one cannot be in more than one place at a time, do not apply to the Supreme Being: it must be simultaneously present in every individual place and time. Anselm further observes that existing in a certain place or time usually means two things: being present in those places and times, and being contained by them. Of the Supreme Being, we can only mean 'present in' in the first sense: God is present, but not contained in place and time.

> If the usage of language permitted, it would, therefore, seem to be more fittingly said, that it exists *with* place or time, than that it exists *in* place or time. For the statement that a thing exists *in another* implies that it is contained, more than does the statement that it exists *with another*.
>
> In no place or time, then, is this Being properly said to exist, since it is contained by no other at all. And yet it may be said, after a manner of its own, to be in every place or time, since whatever else exists is sustained by its presence, lest it lapse into nothingness. It exists in every place and time, because it is absent from none; and it exists in none, because it has no place or time, and has not taken to itself distinctions of place or time, neither here nor there, nor anywhere, nor then, nor now, nor at any time; nor does it exist in terms of this fleeting present,

> in which we live, nor has it existed, nor will it exist, in terms of past or future, since these are restricted to things finite and mutable, which it is not.
>
> And yet, these properties of time and place can, in some sort, be ascribed to it, since it is just as truly present in all finite and mutable beings as if it were circumscribed by the same places, and suffered change by the same times.[58]

Aquinas, addressing the question of God's omnipresence, spoke in the first instance of God as being; it is this that places God everywhere, so to speak:

> But being is innermost in each thing and most deeply inherent in all things since it is formal in respect of everything found in a thing. Hence it must be that God is in all things, and most intimately. . . . He acts immediately in all things. Hence nothing is distant from Him, as though it did not have God in itself.[59]
>
> God fills every place, not indeed as a body, for a body is said to fill place in so far as it excludes the presence of another body; but by God being in a place, others are not thereby excluded from it; rather indeed He Himself fills every place by the very fact that He gives being to the things that fill that place.[60]

But he gave substance to his discussion of omnipresence by relating God's presence to all that is, in three vectors: 'God is in all things by His power, inasmuch as all things are subject to his power; He is in all things by His presence in all things, inasmuch as all things are bare and open to His eyes; He is in all things by His essence, inasmuch as He is present to all as the cause of their being.'[61] Thus, by virtue of other attributes that relate God to the world, God is seen to be omnipresent, as knowing all, controlling all, causing all. Aquinas also spoke of God's relation to all places as a 'contact of power'.[62] Thus the first idea of God as being unfolds into a further elaboration that invokes knowledge and power as God's way of being present.

Omnipresence then can be interpreted as 'present with all'. Plotinus expresses perhaps a similar sentiment: 'It has not deserted its creation for a place apart; it is always present to those with strength to touch it.'[63] This notion of omnipresence as 'ever present to everyone' suggests that the 'spatiality' of the notion is somewhat metaphorical, or at least, not the point. The point of omnipresence is neither power nor knowledge, neither cause nor control, nor even is it about location. It is about the kind of relationship with each creature that it makes possible. 'Omnipresent' means continual availability to everyone, without restriction by anything. The very attributes that suggest God's transcendence of the world at the same time ensure all the more intimate a contact with creation. Seeing omnipresence as an absence of limit in the presence and availability of the divine interprets immanence as the mode of relationship that allows for the closest possible intimacy.

Incorporeality

God's limitlessness involves a lack of bodily limit, but need not be the antithesis to what is bodily or physical. It is not to be conceived as opposed to matter, as some conceive mind or spirit as 'opposed' to the body. It means that nothing can limit God's presence to, presence in, or indeed presence *with* all matter, all places, all bodily beings. To suggest that God does not '*have* a body' means that not even matter itself restricts God's perfect presence in the world.

The fundamental reason for asserting that God is incorporeal is that bodiliness is thought to conflict with other divine attributes. Matter is said to be essentially limiting, but God suffers no limitation; matter or material bodies suffer change, but God does not; God is Absolute Being or Existence Itself but bodies are contingent and particular; God is eternal, matter is not.[64] Currently, Western thinkers are reconsidering many of these divine attributes; perhaps there are aspects of contingency to God, perhaps God is not timeless, perhaps God can suffer and change. At the same time, recent thinking in physics is challenging traditional views of matter, suggesting for example that the material universe might be eternal.

One is fairly new or at least unusual in Western reflection, though familiar in the East. Rāmānuja used the analogy of the mind–body relationship to portray the relationship of the Lord to the world. Just as one's own spirit is present to all of one's body, and identified with it, but more than it, so too is the Lord to the universe.

> The Brahman is concentrated goodness, abhorrent of all imperfection, diverse from all things other than Himself. He is all-knowing, the realizer of all His wishes, fulfilled in His desires, limitless and sovereign joy. Embodied as the mass of all conscious and unconscious beings that subserves His cosmic play, He becomes the soul of that body. Then [at dissolution] – through the successive regression of Matter's evolutes, the Elements, Egoism and Instinct – the universe that has become His body survives as an unconscious substance extremely subtile, known as Darkness. With this body of Darkness, now arrived at a state of subtlety so extreme that it can hardly be called different, the Supreme Brahman attains a condition of oneness. [At the time of creation] He conceives the thought 'Let me become the world body, composed of conscious and unconscious beings, differentiated, as previously, in

> conceptual and corporeal fashion' – and then transforms Himself, in His world body, through entering one evolute of Matter after another. This is the doctrine of transformation in all the Upaniṣads.[65]

A similar idea is suggested in Indian Islamic theology, but clearly as an analogy: the being together of God with his creatures is not like that of a body with other bodies, or a substance with other substances, or an attribute with other attributes; it is understood analogically as the omnipresence of the soul to the body. 'He is with his creatures, but at the same time, He is separate from them. In other words, God is immanent in His creatures, but at the same time, He is also transcendent.'[66]

Two Western thinkers have happened on a similar analogy and interpreted God's omnipresence to the world analogously with the mind and the body. Thus Charles Hartshorne suggests that God has immediate, direct knowledge of the entire universe as we have immediate and direct knowledge of our own body; indeed, Hartshorne suggests that the world *is* God's body. Swinburne suggests a 'limited embodiment' of God, also beginning from the idea of a mind–body analogy. To some extent he also follows Aquinas in choosing to understand God's relation to the world in the twofold terms of God's ability to act everywhere directly, and to know everything directly, without inference or indirectly through a causal chain.[67]

This discussion allows us to see how the doctrine of God as incorporeal functions as a correlate of omnipresence. If the mind–body relationship is an analogy for the God–world relationship, then either that God must be incorporeal, that is, lacking a body (as Anselm and Aquinas would hold); or alternatively the world just is God's body, as Hartshorne suggests.

In an early work, Grace Jantzen offers a critique of the idea of God's bodilessness, which she grounds in a Cartesian mind–body dualism and a theological suspicion of the body.[68] A theology based on this dualism has nefarious consequences, which she believes should and would be overcome by viewing the world as God's body. Her argument is that the relationship between God and the world is 'analogous'[69] to the relationship between human person and his or her body when viewed in a holistic, not a dualist, fashion. Just as human persons have a kind of 'transcendence', that is, they cannot simply be reduced to their physical aspects, in this way the world can be viewed as the embodiment of a transcendent God.[70] God is not exhaustively identified with the material world in her system, God is not *dependent* on the universe; but God is not composed of two parts, world and spirit, either. God's embodiment in the universe means the world is God's self-expression, self-formation, while 'it remains the case that there is a difference between God and the world'.[71] This difference exists for humans and their bodies. Reduction in either case is false.

> If pantheism is reductionism, it is unacceptable. But the claim that the universe is God's body in the sense I have described does not entail that variety of pantheism, and is compatible with the doctrine of divine transcendence analogous to the way human embodiment is compatible with human transcendence.[72]

Rejecting opposition between transcendence and immanence

Certainly one can challenge the idea that transcendence and involvement with the world are mutually exclusive. Many assume that the more involved the deity is with the world, the less transcendent it is, and vice versa. The reverse I believe is the case. The more you insist that transcendence means the negation of involvement in the world, the more you limit God's being and action. God becomes finite because there is a limit set for God precisely where the world starts. On a different view, what makes God radically different from every creature is God's ability to be intimately connected with every creature, transcending all opposition.

Kathryn Tanner observes that transcendence and involvement with the world seem to be mutually exclusive. However, Tanner then distinguishes 'contrastive' views of transcendence, which get their meaning from being defined in opposition to the non-divine, from 'non-contrastive' accounts. In a non-contrastive Hellenistic view,

> God transcends the world as a whole in a manner that cannot properly be talked about in terms of a simple opposition within the same universe of discourse. Direct contrasts are appropriate for distinguishing beings within the world; if God transcends the whole world, God must transcend that sort of characterization, too.[73]

She claims, then, that there is an opposition between God's transcendence and God's involvement with the world only when God's transcendence is defined contrastively.

Paradoxically, she claims that a contrastive account of God's transcendence is limiting for God. God is limited by what is opposed to it, so in the end 'God is as finite as the non-divine beings with which it is directly contrasted.'[74] On the other hand, a non-contrastive understanding of God's transcendence suggests both an extreme of divine involvement and an extreme of divine transcendence.

> [W]hat makes God radically different from every creature . . . is exactly what assures God's direct and intimate relation with every creature *in the entirety* of its physical and particular being. Because divine

> transcendence exceeds all oppositional contrasts characteristic of the relations among finite beings – including that of presence and absence – divine transcendence, according to Irenaeus, does not exclude but rather allows for the immanent presence to creatures of God in his otherness.[75]

So perhaps we are looking through the wrong end of the telescope when we ask if God transcends or is within the universe. Perhaps if we say the universe is immanent in God, there is no contradiction between God's perfect availability to us and God's transcendence.

Language straining

Although the 'orthodox' view in Judaism, Christianity and Islam is that there remains a distinction between God and the world, as we have seen with Buber's reflections, one also finds texts, particularly among the writings of mystics, that suggest oneness with God. The strongest statements of immanence within monotheistic writers in fact look indistinguishable from the language of monists, who assert an absolute unity of human selves with the divine Self. When trying to convey an extreme of intimacy, intimacy strains towards identity and perhaps crosses the line. This does not only happen with respect to the individual relationship between the creature and God, but also when discussing the relationship between God and the world, as we see in this Jewish writer, Moses Cordovero: 'The essence of divinity is found in every single thing – nothing but it exists.'[76]

As we have seen, Buber wants to explain such utterances about the unity of God and the believer as exaggeration, the enthusiasm of the lover. This interpretation could be applied to those apparently asserting an identity between God and the world. But perhaps monist writing from other religious traditions should be interpreted with equal delicacy and caution? What justifies exercising caution and a refusal of literalism in the case of the monotheist, while taking the language of Eastern writers at face value as ('falsely') asserting an unnuanced sameness – what, beyond a conviction that all religious thinkers must, whatever their language, remain within the bounds of *our* notions of *their* orthodoxy?

Conclusion

'Identity' vs. 'immanence', 'pantheism' vs. 'panentheism' – perhaps these are all-important religious distinctions for setting bounds to orthodoxies, but they are also surprisingly fine ones. If you want to decide from their writings where thinkers stand on these questions, you may be asking for a precision and certainty about language that in most cases does not exist. Do they mean it literally or figuratively? When you are talking about God, where does the difference between literal and poetic really lie? Not where we often think it lies in our speech – in having some empirical backing. To pronounce upon this matter we need the writers (a) to make clear whether or not their language is intended literally, and (b) to bring a similar *ontological* transparency to their discourse: are they stating how things *are* or just how it *feels*? We need them, for example, to make clear exactly what the word 'one' means. Is there any differentiation at all between God and material beings and things (and almost all would say there is on some level, even Śaṅkara)? If so, what exactly is the nature of this differentiation: is it in large part illusory (and even monotheists might assert this too)?[77]

When confronting issues on the edges both of philosophy and of mysticism, it is not so easy to say what the difference between 'literal' and 'figurative' speech actually is. If you ask a mystic *or* a philosopher whether their language on this question is perfectly adequate to express exactly what they are trying to convey, they are likely to say 'No!' And that is not much help. 'Is what you say *literally* how God really is? Or is it just your way of expressing yourself? Are you saying you are really one with God or does it just feel like that?' Such philosophers as we have been discussing – and their mystical counterparts – would view such questions as evidence of our lack of understanding. Whether God is *literally* or 'physically' in all things, or it just feels like that, is just not a question that makes any sense if you have really absorbed what they are trying to tell you.

These are not issues to do with substance, as if the crucial religious question concerns the stuff-ness of God and the universe. Rather, they are attempts to convey the experience of a relationship, or insights into its nature. As such, it would be odd if they did not differ. But even the monist and immanentist monotheist seem to agree in their desire to assert a perfect intimacy between God and the world; not even difference itself can bound or limit the perfect relatedness and perfect availability of the Absolute with creation.

I suggest then that we see these contrasting, often conflicting discourses as ways of describing a relationship that has many aspects. The language of God's transcendence, ultimate reality as beyond anything we can know, describe, or capture, is a powerful way to assert the ultimacy of the divine – but also its freedom. In the end, many religious thinkers assert that God escapes our formulae and is free of our dogmas.

At the same time, the discourses of identity and immanence are valuable for those who want to assert God's intimacy and availability to us. To be God is to be perfection *in relation*; while never controlled or manipulated, always there; while unknowable, yet perfectly intimate. This dynamic relation of transcendence and immanence also points the way to solve the philosopher's (and the mystic's) age-old problem about knowing God. It is God's transcendence or difference above all that problematizes human knowledge of the divine. But perhaps God's immanence or identity can also suggest a theological solution. Hildegard tells us that it is God whom we know in every creature. This was one of Hamann's most oft-repeated insights: that the whole of creation, nature and humanity with it, are revelations of God, the 'sensuous revelation of God's majesty',[78] the key to understanding our own nature,[79] the revelation not of itself, but of something higher.[80] If one holds that God is identified with or immanent in the world, then the world itself becomes what Indian philosophers call a *pramāṇa*, a possible mode of knowledge, a way of knowing God.

If so, for such believers, then God – even as Wholly Other – is also then 'Other' to God's own Otherness.

Draw your own conclusions

Of the possible views of the divine, which view did you have before you read the chapter? Which view did you have after you read the chapter? If you are an atheist, which view did you have in mind that you didn't believe in?

Do you think a belief in God is an essential part of a religion, or do you think you can have a 'religion' without a belief in God? Would you prefer to call such traditions (like Buddhism or Jainism) a spirituality, world-view, or something else other than religion?

Do you think the monist view of Brahman as not different from all things would have spiritual and ethical benefits? Is it a view that you find persuasive?

Are 'enworlded gods' primitive or are there insights that indigenous religions have that monotheism does not have?

If you find the view that God is somehow 'in all things' attractive, which of the many models do you find best articulates your intuitions? Why?

Is 'the world is God's body' a metaphor or a more literal assertion? Do you find it persuasive?

Does the mystic really 'become one' with something, or does it just feel like that?

Choose your most favourite and your least favourite model from this chapter. Explore the advantages and disadvantages.

Are there poems, pieces of music or works of art that express the insights some of these models are trying to convey?

Further reading

Anselm (1966) *Monologion and Proslogion: A New Interpretive Translation of St. Anselm's Monologion and Proslogion; by Jasper Hoskins*, Minneapolis, Minn., Banning

Aquinas, T. *The 'Summa Theologica' of St. Thomas Aquinas*, London, Burns Oates & Washbourne

Aquinas, T. (2002) *Summa Contra Gentiles*, Notre Dame, Ind., University of Notre Dame Press

Jaeger, W. (1960) *The Theology of the Early Greek Philosophers*, trans. E. S. Robinson, Oxford, Oxford University Press

Jantzen, G. M. (1984) *God's World, God's Body*, London, Darton, Longman & Todd

Laozi/Lao-tzu (1988) *Tao Te Ching*, trans. S. Mitchell, London, Macmillan

Pereira, J. (1991 (1976)) *Hindu Theology: Themes, Texts and Structures*, Delhi, Motilal Banarsidass

Plotinus (1991) *The Enneads*, trans. S. MacKenna, London, Penguin

Rahula, W. (1997) *What the Buddha Taught*, Oxford, Oneworld

Swinburne, R. (1993) *The Coherence of Theism*, Oxford, Clarendon Press

Tanner, K. E. (1988) *God and Creation in Christian Theology: Tyranny or Empowerment*, Oxford, Blackwell

Upaniṣads (1998) trans. P. Olivelle, Oxford World's Classics, Oxford, Oxford University Press

Notes

1 Mahmud ibn 'Abd al-Karim Shabistarī (1920) *The Secret Rose Garden of Shabistarī*, Grand Rapids, Phanes Press.

2 D. Burrell (2004) *Faith and Freedom*, Challenges in Contemporary Theology, Oxford, Blackwell, pp. 4–5.

3 W. Rahula (1997) *What the Buddha Taught*, Oxford, Oneworld.

4 C. W.-h. Fu (1977) 'Buddhist Approach to the Problem of God', in S. A. Matczak (ed.), *God in Contemporary Thought: A Philosophical Perspective*, Philosophical Questions Series 10, New York, Learned Publications, p. 158. Citing Kenneth Inada (March 1969) 'Some Basic Misconceptions of Buddhism', *International Philosophical Quarterly* 9/1, p. 111.

5 Fu, 'Buddhist Approach to the Problem of God', p. 160.

6 H. von Glasenapp (1970) *Buddhism: A Non-theistic Religion*, trans. I. Schloegl, London, Allen & Unwin, p. 1.

7 Fu, 'Buddhist Approach to the Problem of God', p. 177.

8 Fu, 'Buddhist Approach to the Problem of God', p. 170.

9 *Chāndogya Upaniṣad* 3.14.1. The translation of the Upaniṣads used is *Upaniṣads* (1998), trans. P. Olivelle, Oxford World's Classics, Oxford, Oxford University Press, p. 123.

10 *Upaniṣads*, p. 124: *Chāndogya Upaniṣad* 3.14.4.

11 Karl Potter (ed.) (1981) *Encyclopedia of Indian Philosophies*, vol. 1: *Advaita Vedānta up to Śaṇkara and His Pupils*, Princeton, Princeton University Press, pp. 135–6: I.3.19.

12 *Brahmasiddhi* I.19. See the summary in Potter, *Encyclopedia of Indian Philosophies*, vol. 1, pp. 358–9.

13 *Brahmasiddhi* I.19. See Potter, *Encyclopedia of Indian Philosophies*, vol. 1.

14 *Brahmasiddhi* I.19. See Potter, *Encyclopedia of Indian Philosophies*, vol. 1, p. 359.

15 *Brahmasiddhi* I.19. See Potter, *Encyclopedia of Indian Philosophies*, vol. 1, pp. 74–6.

16 *Brahmasiddhi* I.19. See Potter, *Encyclopedia of Indian Philosophies*, vol. 1, pp. 74–6.

17 *Upaniṣads*, p. 68: *Bṛhadāraṅyaka Upaniṣad* 4.4.22.

18 *Upaniṣads*, p. 46: *Bṛhadāraṅyaka Upaniṣad* 3.9.1ff.

19 *Upaniṣads*, pp. 29–30: *Bṛhadāraṅyaka Upaniṣad* 2.4.12.

20 *Upaniṣads*, p. 39: *Bṛhadāraṅyaka Upaniṣad* 3.4.

21 E. Caird (1904) *The Evolution of Theology in the Greek Philosophers*, Glasgow, James MacLehose and Sons, vol. 2, p. 82.

22 H. F. v. Arnim (1905, 1964) *Stoicorum Veterum Fragmenta*, vol. 1: *Zeno et Zenonis discipuli*, Stuttgart, Teubner, p. 530. In the following passages, the translation is mine.

23 Arnim, *Stoicorum Veterum Fragmenta*, vol. 1, p. 153.

24 H. F. v. Arnim (1903, 1964) *Stoicorum Veterum Fragmenta*, vol. 2: *Chrysippi fragmenta logica et physica*, Stuttgart, Teubner, p. 1021.

25 Arnim, *Stoicorum Veterum Fragmenta*, vol. 2, p. 1051.

26 See Arnim, *Stoicorum Veterum Fragmenta*, vol. 1, p. 155; vol. 2, pp. 528, pp. 1022, etc.

27 Qur'ān 42; 112:1–4.

28 Qur'ān 59:22–4.

29 W. Jaeger (1960) *The Theology of the Early Greek Philosophers*, trans. E. S. Robinson, Oxford, Oxford University Press, pp. 16–17.

30 Jaeger, *The Theology of the Early Greek Philosophers*, p. 21.

31 See the discussion in C. Crittenden (1997) 'In Support of Paganism: Polytheism as Earth-Based Religion', in P. A. French, T. E. Uehling and H. K. Wettstein (eds), *Philosophy of Religion*, Midwest Studies in Philosophy 21, Notre Dame, Ind., University of Notre Dame Press. His discussion differs from mine; he is performing a socio-psychological thought-experiment, imagining the sort of life a polytheist would lead. I am doing a philosophical experiment.

32 Marion's attempt to distinguish 'icons' from 'idols' is unsuccessful, in my view, in marking a workable boundary between representations of enworlded deities and supra-worldly ones. J. L. Marion (1991) *God Without Being*, Chicago, University of Chicago Press.

33 Laozi/Lao-tzu (1988) *Tao Te Ching*, trans. S. Mitchell, London, Macmillan.

34 *Upaniṣads*, pp. 254–5: *Śvetāśvatara Upaniṣad* 1.15–16.

35 Rāmānuja's commentary on I.ii.12; see Sarvepalli Radhakrishnan and Charles Moore (eds) (1957) *A Source Book in Indian Philosophy*, Oxford, Oxford University Press.

36 Rāmānuja's commentary on II.ii.3; see Radhakrishnan and Moore, *A Source Book in Indian Philosophy*, p. 553.

37 Radhakrishnan and Moore, *A Source Book in Indian Philosophy*, p. 628.

38 See the discussion in Jaeger, *The Theology of the Early Greek Philosophers*.

39 'The phrase "the Divine" does not appear merely as one more predicate applied to the first principle; on the contrary, the substantivization of the adjective with the definite article shows rather that this is introduced as an independent concept, essentially religious in character, and now identified with the rational principle, the Boundless. That this expression is of epoch-making importance in Greek philosophy is clear from the frequency with which we encounter similar statements both in the other pre-Socratics and in later philosophers. Taking the natural world as their starting-point, they develop the idea of some highest principle (for instance, the *ens perfectissimum* of Aristotle and the world-forming fire of the Stoics) and then proceed to assert of it that "this must be the Divine".' Jaeger, *The Theology of the Early Greek Philosophers*, p. 31.

40 Plotinus (1991) *The Enneads*, trans. S. MacKenna, London, Penguin, 5.2.1.

41 Plotinus, *Enneads*, 6.9.3.

42 Plotinus, *Enneads*, 4.4.32.

43 Bhagavadgita (1994) *The Bhagavadgita*, trans. W. J. Johnson, Oxford World's Classics, Oxford, Oxford University Press, IX.4.89.

44 *Bhagavadgita*, V.2.6–7.

45 M. Buber (1970) *I and Thou*, trans. W. Kaufmann, New York, Charles Scribner's, p. 135.

46 N. K. Singh (1996) *God in Indian Islamic Theology*, New Delhi, Sarup, pp. 103–4.

47 Buber, *I and Thou*, p. 141.

48 Buber, *I and Thou*, p. 143.

49 M. Eckhart (1986) *Teacher and Preacher*, trans. B. McGinn, Classics of Western Spirituality, New York, Paulist Press, p. 224: Latin sermon 29.

50 Hildegard (1987) *Book of Divine Works*, trans. M. Fox, Santa Fe, Bear & Company, pp. 8–10: Vision 1:2.

51 Qur'ān 2:115.

52 Singh, *God in Indian Islamic Theology*, pp. 148 *et passim*.

53 Plotinus, *Enneads*, 5.8.9.

54 Eckhart, *Teacher and Preacher*, p. 224.

55 Anselm (1966) *Monologion and Proslogion: A New Interpretive Translation of St. Anselm's Monologion and Proslogion; by Jasper Hoskins*, Minneapolis, Minn., Banning, ch. 20.

56 Anselm, *Monologion and Proslogion*, ch. 21.

57 Emphases mine. Anselm, *Monologion and Proslogion*, ch. 22.

58 Emphases mine. Anselm, *Monologion and Proslogion*, ch. 22.

59 Thomas Aquinas, *The 'Summa Theologica' of St. Thomas Aquinas*, London, Burns Oates & Washbourne, I.8.1.

60 Aquinas, *Summa Theologica*, I.8.2.

61 Aquinas, *Summa Theologica*, I.8.3.

62 Thomas Aquinas (2002) *Summa Contra Gentiles*, Notre Dame, Ind., University of Notre Dame Press, III.68.3.

63 Plotinus, *Enneads*, 6.9.7.

64 See Taliaferro's concise discussion in P. L. Quinn and C. Taliaferro (eds) (1997) *A Companion to the Philosophy of Religion*, Oxford, Blackwell, pp. 271–8.

65 J. Pereira (1991 (1976)) *Hindu Theology: Themes, Texts and Structures*, Delhi, Motilal Banarsidass, p. 287.

66 Singh, *God in Indian Islamic Theology*, p. 148.

67 R. Swinburne (1993) *The Coherence of Theism*, Oxford, Clarendon Press, pp. 99–129.

68 G. M. Jantzen (1984) *God's World, God's Body*, London, Darton, Longman & Todd, p. 20.

69 Jantzen, *God's World, God's Body*, p. 20.

70 Jantzen, *God's World, God's Body*, p. 127.

71 Jantzen, *God's World, God's Body*, p. 150.

72 Jantzen, *God's World, God's Body*, p. 150.

73 K. E. Tanner (1988) *God and Creation in Christian Theology: Tyranny or Empowerment*, Oxford, Blackwell, p. 42.

74 Tanner, *God and Creation*, p. 46.

75 Tanner, *God and Creation*, pp. 56–7.

76 D. C. Matt (1995) *The Essential Kabbalah*, Mystical Classics of the World, New York, Quality Paperback Book Club, p. 24.

77 Maṇḍana Miśra, glossing a verse which asserts that Brahman is 'not everything' and at the same time asserts Brahman is 'everything', explains it thus: Brahman is not everything insofar as Brahman is not identical with the diversity of the world. Brahman is everything insofar as it is true that although Brahman does not have everything as Its self, everything has Brahman as its Self. *Brahmasiddhi*, I.7. See the summary in Potter, *Encyclopedia of Indian Philosophies*, vol. 1.

78 Hamann's works, N II, 198:1–2; see the translation in G. Griffith-Dickson (1995) *Johann Georg Hamann's Relational Metacritism*, Berlin and New York, de Gruyter.

79 Hamann's works, N II, 206:32–207:2; 198:3–5; see Griffith-Dickson, *Johann Georg Hamann's Relational Metacritism*.

80 Hamann's letters, ZH 7, Nr. 1060, 173:8–17, to Jacobi, 27.4–3.5.1787; see Griffith-Dickson, *Johann Georg Hamann's Relational Metacritism*.

6

An Issue About the World

Whether God exists, clearly, is not a controversy concerning God. It is an issue about the world. (Arindam Chakrabarti)[1]

We have looked at questions of identity and difference between God and the world, but there are further issues that depend on how this distinction is made. There are philosophers who see difference as basic to reality and believe that the sheer existence of the universe requires a creator, and that therefore in the universe we can find proof that God must exist.

There are a family of arguments, often known in a generic way as 'The Cosmological Argument', which purport to offer this proof.

As we have seen, the possibility of accounting for the world in purely naturalistic terms was well known to the most ancient Greek and Indian philosophers. The problem is more complex and subtle than this makes it seem; the Cosmological Arguments did not arise merely from inadequate scientific knowledge.

On the other hand, those who reject the arguments based on cosmology are not necessarily atheists. Some believers in creation are opposed to the idea of proving the existence of a divine creator as a matter of principle; usually as part of a platform which opposes faith to reasoning. Then there are those curious and contrary characters like al-Ghazālī, who can argue against proofs for the existence of God on some occasions, yet seem to appeal to them on others, depending on the ideological or polemical purpose to which they are put. Al-Ghazālī, whose deconstructive and critical points will appear often below, could be seen simply as an opponent of the arguments. Although a believer, he was a ruthless critic of philosophical arguments purporting to prove the existence of God, in his attempt to deconstruct the activities of the believing 'philosophers'.

Al-Ghazālī's ire is not reserved for the atheist (considered as the materialist) so much as for 'the philosophers' who are believers and claim both that the world is pre-eternal (as do the materialists) and that it has a maker. In other words, he views them as neither Muslims following the Qur'ān nor honest Aristotelians, but those illegitimately trying to combine aspects of both.

Arguments for the existence of a creator, supported by the existence of the world, were found in the Indian Nyāya philosophers. Three verses in Gautama's Nyāyasutras gave the impulse to constructing a case, with aphorisms stating that God is the cause of the universe, because human beings are pretty ineffectual.[2]

On Gautama's Nyāyasutras

Gautama is the name usually given to the author of the Nyāyasutras; it is a very common name in India (and the Nyāya Gautama is not to be confused with Gautama Siddhārta, the Buddha). Its authorship and its date are disputed by scholars; the estimated date varies as widely as from the sixth century BC to the second century AD. They are the primary foundational source for early Nyāya philosophical theism. The three foundational verses:

> *God is the cause because we find fruitlessness in the actions of human beings.*
>
> *It is not so because no fruit appears without the actions of human beings.*
>
> *This reasoning is not correct since it (human action) is influenced by Him (God).*

John Vattanky writes:

> *What is the distinct contribution of Gautama? Wherein does lie his originality? Although the contribution of Gautama to the problem of existence of God does not extend beyond a few lines, it has been of decisive importance in the history of Nyāya for, in one way or another, all the subsequent Nyāya authors speak of God as 'cause'. The intuition of Gautama that God is to be considered the cause of the world has remained the cornerstone of Nyāya theism and for this reason alone Gautama deserves to be called the father of Nyāya theism. Further, his reference to God as cause has the implied meaning . . . that God actually confers on man the fruit of his endeavours. Therefore, God stands supreme not only over the world but even over the inexorable law of karma, at least in some sense. This would point out that the God of the Nyāya system even right at the beginning of the formation of the system is, at least by implication, a transcendent God.*[3]

The elliptical nature of these verses gave birth to numerous commentaries and debates which began to develop a more sophisticated argument. Equally formative on the argument were concerted Buddhist attacks on it, for it became ever more precise and subtle as Nyāya philosophers and commentators responded to the critiques of their Buddhists opponents.

Early commentators interpreted these mysterious sutras as asserting that God is the cause of the universe, including human action. This formed the foundation stone for the argument. Uddyotakara takes up the task of a serious argument, setting it in the context of controversy over the origin of the world: some say it is time, some God, some *prakṛitī*. He is primarily concerned to move against the view of Sāṃkhya, that the world originates from primal matter without an intelligent agent, but under the influence of the purpose of the 'soul' (puruṣa). He is also concerned to outmanoeuvre those who say that pre-existent atoms, led by the merit and demerit of individual souls, give rise to the world. The argument he first sets out runs:

> Prime matter, atoms and fruits of actions become active in as much as they are activated by an intelligent cause because they are not themselves intelligent like an axe. Just as an axe and so on work only when brought into action by an intelligent carpenter, even so prime matter, atoms and fruits of actions being non-intelligent work only when brought into action by an intelligent agent.[4]

As for merit, demerit and the bodies of individual souls, he goes on to argue, these too must be activated by an intelligent agent and cannot themselves give rise to the world. They can be known by the senses and hence are products, not the ultimate cause. Almost as a throwaway line, Uddyotakara at the end of his discussion introduces an element that becomes an important part of later Nyāya reasoning: that some phenomena have the quality of 'being an effect'. We shall see later the use that is made of this. These writings came under sharp attack from the Buddhists; and under their fire the arguments of Nyāya theism were further refined and developed.

The major players in the Hindu and Buddhist debate

Hindu proponents of the argument	Buddhist opponents of the argument
Gautama (?)	
Vātsyāyana (450–500)	
	Vasubandhu (dated variously from AD *270–500)*
	Diṇnāga
	Dharmakīrti
Uddyotakara (550–610)	
	Śāntarakṣīta (700)

Kamalaśīla
Vāscapati Miśra
Udayana (1050–1100)

The earliest versions of the arguments in the West were found in Plato and Aristotle. They took on a new life and a new importance when the early Christian writers sought to disprove Aristotelian arguments for the eternity of the world, culminating in the thought of the sixth-century Christian John Philoponus. The arguments lived on in the Islamic world, and developed in the ninth and tenth centuries. Al-Kindī was the initiator of the argument in Islamic thought. As in the early Christian apologetics, a prime motivation in some of the Kalām arguments is to prove the temporality of the world as contained in the Qur'ān against the thesis of the world's eternity; which is one reason why those, like Ibn Rushd, who asserted the eternity of the world were so bitterly refuted. Fakhry credits Ibn Hazm with being the first to advance arguments for the temporality of the world.[5] Given then that the world is temporal, something had to bring it into being, given the 'principle of particularization' or of 'determination'. We will consider aspects of this argument in more detail in the chapter on the design argument; here, the principle was used to argue that something had to happen to bring the world into existence rather than not. Versions of this argument were developed by Al-Fārābī, Al-Juwaynī, Al-Baqillānī, Al-Baghdādī and others, reaching a high watermark in the arguments of Al-Rāzī. A version of this argument was even made by the paradoxical al-Ghazālī. One should note here that the polemical point for al-Ghazālī is not to use philosophical proofs to replace the act of faith – an activity he detests – but rather to attempt to crush the idea of the eternity of the world – a view he detests. It will be seen shortly that he also deconstructs versions of the argument.

From these Islamic incarnations, the arguments disseminated back again into Jewish and Christian thought. Cosmological arguments are most famously associated in the Christian tradition with Thomas Aquinas, and they received continued attention up to and including the Enlightenment.

Of the various arguments for the existence of God, the cosmological argument was the one used most heavily by Jewish philosophers, who knew it as the proof from creation. Wolfson argues that it progressed in three stages: an initial phase in which it was essentially the same as Plato's proof in the Timaeus; a second Aristotelian phase; and a third development by Hasdai Crescas.[6] Even in its early phase, its Platonic roots were apparently not recognized, and Maimonides credits the Muslim theologians, the Mutakallimūn, with its invention. Outlining its use by Saadia, Maimonides, Baḥyā, Judah Halevi, Joseph ibn Zaddik, Abraham ibn

Daud and Hasdai Crescas, Wolfson suggests the reason for its salience among Jewish thinkers:

> The popularity of this type of cosmological argument, the readiness with which it was generally accepted, was due to the fact that it chimed in with the traditional method of reasoning which had come down from the Scriptures. To argue from the fact that the world had come into existence to the existence of a Creator was simply to translate into a syllogistic formula the first verse of the book of Genesis or to rationalize the emotional appeal of the Prophets to look up into heaven and ask who had created it all. It is thus that for a long time this argument passed for the standard proof of the existence of God and God's existence was made dependent upon a belief in the created world.[7]

A similar reason may underlie the ambivalent place the argument has had in Islamic thought, and the apparent contradictions seen in the thought of a thinker like al-Ghazālī. The Qur'ān has a number of passages which invoke the existence of creation as an indication that a creator exists. A number of different aspects are taken as signs of the creator: among them, the sheer fact that something exists,[8] or the fact that things change. Abraham is depicted as observing change in the movements of the sun, moon and stars, and concluding that because they change, they are unworthy of consideration as gods.[9] This principle was formulated by Muslim thinkers as an argument from change or contingency: things change and thus need an unchangeable creator, different from them, to explain their creation. The verse maintains, 'This is the argument we gave to Abraham.' The Qur'ān gives support to the philosophical impulse not only to marvel at creation but also to reflect on it and infer that it has been created. Insofar as this is the case, cosmological arguments could be seen as scriptural, as grounded in revelation. Insofar as philosophy is seen as an attempt to replace faith or revelation, it provokes opposition in some theologians of a traditional stripe.

The arguments are more diverse than is sometimes recognized and their internal workings are different. They all have a common logic, however: to argue that the existence of the universe raises questions which it itself cannot answer. There can only be a satisfactory answer to these questions if there is a creator, is the argument's central claim.

While the underlying conviction is that the universe is not intelligible without a creator, here are some of the other assertions that we find in cosmological arguments:

> The universe, in common with most or all the material things we know, must have been caused by something, but cannot have been caused by

> itself. That notion is unintelligible; for it requires that something exist before it exists, in order to bring itself into existence. Therefore, there must be some other cause of all material things.
>
> Something must explain why *this* universe, with *these* particular features and not others, has been selected for existence, and at one particular point in time rather than another.
>
> The world is contingent; it could have been or not been. Something must have made all things be rather than not be.
>
> An 'infinite regress' is impossible. You cannot keep going back forever saying A was caused by B and B by C, *ad infinitum*. There must be a stopping point. This intuition that there cannot be a series stretching *backwards* into infinity, even if one can stretch forwards to infinity, can be based on an intuition about logic or on an intuition about time. But either way, the claim is that one cannot explain this state of the universe by the prior state of the universe forever; eventually there must be a first item.

Intelligibility

Many people have the intuition that there must be reasons and explanations for the way things are. Why are my eyes brown? Why does my friend have a cancerous tumour in her lung? – To all such questions we seek answers, in genetics, upbringing, the immediate circumstances, behaviour, diet, or God's will. Our assumption is that things happen, and things exist, for a reason. They do not happen or burst into existence spontaneously, uncaused, totally without explanation.

This intuition, unconscious and unthinking in most of us, is dignified in philosophy with the name 'The Principle of Sufficient Reason'. This principle holds, simply, that for every state of affairs, there is a reason or set of reasons why it is so and not otherwise. As Leibniz formulated it, there must be a reason why anything happens at all, there must be a reason why things exist, and a reason why one thing exists rather than another:

> Our reasonings are founded on *two great principles, that of contradiction*, in virtue of which we judge that to be *false* which involves contradiction, and that *true*, which is opposed or contradictory to the false. And *that of sufficient reason*, in virtue of which we hold that no fact can be real or existent, no statement true, unless there be a

> sufficient reason why it is so and not otherwise, although most often these reasons cannot be known to us.[10]

As Craig observes, 'sufficient reason' has a variety of senses for Leibniz: cause, purpose, but also 'rational basis' or 'ground of intelligibility': a true statement must have a reason for being true.[11] When one of two possibilities comes to pass, there must be some reason why it was this one and not the other. So can we ask these questions, or apply this intuition, not just to states of affairs in the universe, but also to the universe itself? Can we not ask why the universe exists, rather than timeless nothingness?

The Jesuit philosopher Frederick Copleston, in a famous radio debate with Bertrand Russell, articulated this intuition as an argument for the existence of God:

> COPLESTON: First of all, I should say, we know that there are at least some beings in the world which do not contain in themselves the reason for their existence. For example, I depend on my parents, and now on the air, and on food, and so on. Now, secondly, the world is simply the real or imagined totality or aggregate of individual objects, none of which contain in themselves alone the reason for their existence. There isn't any world distinct from the objects which form it, any more than the human race is something apart from the members. Therefore, I should say, since objects or events exist, and since no object of experience contains within itself the reason of its existence, this reason, the totality of objects, must have a reason external to itself. That reason must be an existent being. Well, this being is either itself the reason for its own existence, or it is not. If it is, well and good. If it is not, then we must proceed farther. But if we proceed to infinity in that sense, then there's no explanation of existence at all. So, I should say, in order to explain existence, we must come to a being which contains within itself the reason for its own existence, that is to say, which cannot not-exist.

In the debate that developed, Russell accurately diagnosed:

> RUSSELL: So it all turns on this question of sufficient reason. . . . What do you mean by sufficient reason? You don't mean cause?

> COPLESTON: Not necessarily. Cause is a kind of sufficient reason. Only contingent being can have a cause. God is his own sufficient reason. And he is not the cause of himself. By sufficient reason in the full sense I mean an explanation adequate for the existence of some particular being.

RUSSELL: But when is an explanation adequate? Suppose I am about to make a flame with a match. You may say that the adequate explanation of that is that I rub it on a box.

COPLESTON: Well, for practical purposes – but theoretically, that is only a partial explanation. An adequate explanation must ultimately be a total explanation to which nothing further can be added.

RUSSELL: Then I can only say that you're looking for something which can't be got and which one ought not to expect to get.

COPLESTON: To say that one has not found it is one thing; to say that one should not look for it seems to me to be rather dogmatic. What I am doing is to look for the reason, in this case the cause of the objects, the real or imaginary totality of which constitutes what we call the universe.

RUSSELL: Well, I don't know. I mean, the explanation of one thing is another thing which makes the other thing dependent on yet another, and you have to grasp this sorry scheme of things entire to do what you want, and that we can't do.

COPLESTON: But are you going to say that we can't, or we shouldn't even raise the question of the existence of the whole of this sorry scheme of things – of the whole universe?

RUSSELL: Yes. I don't think there's any meaning in it at all . . .

COPLESTON: . . . What I'm doing is to look for the reason, in this case the cause of the objects – the real or imagined totality of which constitute what we call the universe. You say, I think, that the universe – or my existence, if you prefer, or any other existence – is unintelligible?

RUSSELL: . . . I shouldn't say unintelligible. I think it is without explanation. Intelligibility to my mind is a different thing; intelligibility has to do with the thing itself intrinsically and not with its relations.

COPLESTON: My point is that what we call the world is intrinsically unintelligible, apart from the existence of God.[12]

What could explain the universe as a whole? The first physical event can explain the second, the second can explain the third. But what can explain why the *first* physical event occurred, and thereby explain why there is something rather than nothing?

Perhaps the existence of the world is after all a 'brute fact', with no reason, no intelligibility to it.

Causation

The first reason proposed for why the universe is thought to be unintelligible without a creator is the idea that the universe must be *caused* by something. (Note however that some versions of the argument make no reference to the idea of causality; Spinoza does not, and Leibniz does not involve efficient causality.[13])

The oldest argument of this sort is found in Plato, who reasoned, 'What comes into existence must perforce come into existence through some cause.'[14] For many, the suggestion that the world could cause itself is nonsensical. Nothing can possibly bring itself into existence, for if it did, it would exist before coming into existence, which is absurd. This intuition was often treated as self-evident by Jewish, Islamic and Christian philosophers in the medieval period; either they justified it or illustrated it with simple analogies to the world of individual things.[15] As the Jewish thinker Saadia notes, we see that things which come into existence are dependent on a cause; so too must be the things beyond our experience. The Muslim Maturidi writes, 'Building, writing, and ships testify to what we have said. For they can come into existence only through an existent agent, and the present instance must be similar,' and he adds, 'In the world as perceived, nothing exists which combines or separates by itself. It follows that such must have been true of the state of the world which cannot be perceived.'[16]

The idea that material causes are good enough causal explanations is also rejected by the early Nyāya thinker Uddyotakara, as we have seen. For him, they can be causes only if they are activated by an intelligent agent. Nyāya logic following Uddyotakara uses a kind of analogical reasoning to establish that the world must have God as its creator. The form of this pattern of inference in Nyāya logic runs like this:

> Because A and B share a property *g*, they also share a property *f*. A fire in a kitchen and a fire on the hill both share the property of producing smoke, so they likely share other properties as well, such as needing to be ignited in order to start. The latter (*f*) are known as 'inferable properties' (*sadhya*). A and B thus belong to a class, members of which can be inferred to share a number of properties if invariable concomitance can be shown between *f*, the inferable property, and *g*, the *hetu* or 'reason', 'mark', or 'ground' of the inference.[17]

The terse form in which we usually find such arguments is:

> A has *f*
> Because it has *g*
> Like B.

What is necessary for the inference to work is invariable concomitance – these must always found together, without exception. Otherwise the case in question could just be one of the exceptions and the proof fails. There is not invariable concomitance between having black hair and having brown eyes, so one cannot say that every member of the class 'Has black hair' must also therefore have brown eyes, even though some do.

This form of Nyāya syllogism is used to establish the existence of God as the creator of the world. Great precision was given to defining the elements in the syllogism, above all by the Nyāya sage Gaṅgeśa. Broadly speaking, the argument infers the existence of a creator of the world from the fact that the world has the 'mark' of something that has been produced, like other objects we observe being created. (The subject (A) is the world, the *hetu* or mark (*g*) is 'being an effect', and (*f*) or the property to be inferred is 'having-an-[intelligent]-agent-as-cause'.) What the Nyāya logician has to show is that there is invariable concomitance between 'having an agent' and 'being an effect'.

For al-Ghazālī, invariable concomitance between one particular event and another was not enough to establish the existence of *causality*.[18] Putting cotton near fire and seeing the cotton burn does not prove that the fire *caused* the cotton to burn. This argument will be familiar to Western philosophers as it is similar to Hume's famous critique of the notion of causality. Al-Ghazālī beat Hume to it by hundreds of years, maintaining that our observation does not establish necessary causation, but rather a regularity of natural events. As he puts it, 'the continuous habit of their occurrence repeatedly, one time after another, fixes unshakeably in our minds the belief in their occurrence according to past habit'.[19]

According to al-Ghazālī, however, the real cause of any such event is God (thus, clearly, al-Ghazālī parts company from Hume's atheistic account). Al-Ghazālī performs this manoeuvre in order to leave room for the possibility of divine miracles. Since God continually creates the events we expect in what we consider to be the regularity of nature, or the workings of natural laws, all God has to do in a miracle is to allow the unexpected possibility to occur.

One reading of the history of Islamic arguments is that this deconstruction of the alleged necessity of natural causality had an impact on the use of arguments for the existence of God based on causality; which largely thanks to al-Ghazālī did not have the popularity in Islam that they had in Christianity; and not least because of the Aristotelian (therefore not orthodox Muslim) overtones that discussions of causality typically had. If you no longer argue that every material thing necessarily has a cause, it makes the deployment of aetiological arguments for the existence of God poor etiquette at least. Nevertheless there was a lively, ongoing tradition of metaphysics and philosophical theology in Shi'a Islam.

The Islamic discussion of the eternity vs. the temporality of the universe, as contested in their arguments for the existence of God, bears on one set of modern objections raised against the Cosmological Argument: that its notion of a First Cause or a First Mover is incoherent because the universe has no beginning in time. Either the universe is infinite in time, or else the universe is like a circle, finite, but without a beginning or end. Either way it is a series of events with no first member, but every event has a cause. So any argument for a 'First' mover, cause or creator fails. Alternatively, the universe might have a beginning, but based on modern theories about time, the notion of a Creator pre-existing the universe is incoherent. Time might have a beginning, coinciding with the beginning of the universe; but then there can be no 'cause', for nothing pre-exists the universe. Or, there was a finite period of time before the beginning of the universe. Then the universe has a cause; but so must time. 'But, by definition, nothing can occur before time itself. Time cannot have a cause for its existence, and so it provides a counter-example to the premise that everything that begins to exist has a cause.'[20] Or, third, there was an infinite period of time before the universe began. Then the universe can have a cause, but it would simply be the last member of an infinite chain of causes. Why could that member not be God? Because, if God willed the universe to exist, why did it not come into existence sooner? There must be something that obtained just before that event; then we are led back to the causal regress the argument tries to avoid. In fact these objections are nothing new, and formed a large and complex debate in Islamic thought as well as an avenue in Buddhist critiques. As we have seen, there were Islamic scholars who argued that the material universe was eternal, such as Ibn Sīnā and Ibn Rushd; just as Nyāya thinkers were able to maintain both that the world is created and that it is without a beginning in time.

Modern Western atheists, the heirs of Hume rather than al-Ghazālī, baulk at the idea of the material universe as a whole needing an overriding transcendent cause. In his famous debate with Copleston, Russell is happy to allow that one can seek to 'explain' any particular object, if that means finding a cause for it. But he sees no reason to think that there is a single cause for the existence of all objects. 'The whole concept of cause is one we derive from the observation of particular things. I see no reason whatever to suppose that the total has any cause whatsoever. . . . I should say that the universe is just there, and that's all.'[21] Copleston will not agree that this allows us to rule out the question; the absence of a cause (if that is the truth) should be the conclusion of an investigation, not an attempt to prevent it. 'The fact that we gain our knowledge of causality empirically, from particular causes, does not rule out the possibility of asking what the cause of the series is.'[22]

Robin Le Poidevin, objecting to arguments for the existence of God, sensibly raises the question of what counts as a good explanation. A good explanation, he suggests, is one that is genuinely informative and not just descriptive. So, to take his example, a good explanation of 'Why is there smoke coming out of that house?' is *not* 'Because there is a smoke-producing effect going on inside.' That simply re-describes the state of affairs without really *explaining* it. 'Burning of furniture' as an explanation adds to your knowledge and therefore deserves to be called an explanation.[23] Le Poidevin demands moreover that a good causal explanation describes the cause so as to bring out its connection with the effect. So to explain the burning of furniture by saying 'because relatives are visiting' may be true, but it does not make clear the connection of events. In his view, an explanation of the universe with the supposed existence of a first cause or creator is not a good causal explanation; it may be true, but is a 'dead loss' as an explanation. It tells us nothing about the first cause other than it is a cause. 'It is on the same level as "smoke is coming from that house because some smoke-producing event is going on inside".'[24] However, it is only informative if there is already agreement that there is an event that is causing the smoke; but in the case of the Cosmological Argument that is precisely the point in question, whereas it is assumed in Le Poidevin's analogy. If it is unclear whether there is an event producing smoke or just naturally occurring fog drifting by, such an assertion does inform and is the first step in an explanation. It may be comparatively uninformative, as a first stage, to conclude cautiously only that it must be a 'smoke-producing event', but on the other hand it is proper to go no further with the inference than the evidence warrants. This is why Jewish uses of arguments were often composite: to use cosmological arguments simply to argue for 'creation', and to use design and similar arguments to infer the characteristics of the creator.[25]

Contingency

Sayyid 'Alī Qūlī Qarā'ī puts his finger on a key issue in understanding one aspect of the argument, and one which forms a critical question in the interpretation of Thomas Aquinas's 'Third Way':

> A salient feature of Islamic metaphysics is its conception of cause. The efficient cause stands on a higher existential plane than the effect. In other words, the cause–effect relationship is a vertical one, not horizontal. Some modern Western philosophers appear to conceive the First Cause as standing on the same existential plane as that of the world of material phenomena, as if the First Cause were first by virtue of its being first in a temporal causal sequence. [He cites Bertrand Russell in this respect.] These remarks show that Russell considers the

> concept of the First Cause to be the result of the denial of the possibility of a series without a first term! However, he has misconstrued the First-Cause argument, for it does not state that every series must have a first term, but that the character of the terms involved in the present series, which consists of effects, requires that it must have a first term, a cause that is not an effect. Moreover, it is not a temporal series in which subsequent terms are effects of antecedent causes. The metaphysical conception of causality involved here should not be confused with the common-sense conception of causation, nor with the scientific notion of it (as the determination of an event by antecedent events). Further, Muslim philosophers have generally held the universe to be beginningless, thus positing the admissibility of a series of physical events which has no first term. Therefore, the First-Cause argument does not rest on a lack of mathematical imagination, as implied by Russell.
>
> The priority of the First Cause derives from its being the absolute source of all existence. Formless and without quiddity, It transcends becoming, time and space, wherein the lower forms of being enfold. The very existence of effects, for coming into existence as well as for their continued existence, depends on their attachment to the cause, which is not separate from the being of the effects. The effect cannot exist for a moment in separation from its cause.[26]

This long passage illustrates that the idea coiled hidden at the heart of the concept of causality is the duality of contingency and necessity. Russell interpreted the 'causal' question as being one that applies to time. Qarā'ī maintains that what is at stake is contingency; that as long as something is merely possible, it can never come into being until it is caused to come into existence by something else, and thus made necessary. (This particular understanding of necessity and contingency deriving ultimately from Ibn Sīnā we will explore in Chapter 8.)

Other versions of the Cosmological Argument, then, turn on the claim that the universe is contingent, that is, its existence is possible and not necessary. One contingent thing or cause may explain another; but ultimately something more is required to make the existence of the universe intelligible. If arguments based on causality are the 'classical' Christian arguments, contingency arguments can be said to be the 'classical' Islamic argument.[27] These were often coupled with Islamic arguments about the 'newness' [non-eternity] of the universe as a crucial doctrine to be defended. If the universe began at some point, it is contingent and does not possess necessary existence, and therefore requires a creator as explanation. Related arguments are examined later under the aspect of 'determination'; they can be distinguished as Al-Rāzī did by differentiating between 'The argument from the possibility of the universe to the existence of a necessary being', and 'the argument from the possibility of *qualities* of the universe to the necessity of one who determines them'.[28]

Contingency arguments can be structured in two ways. An argument from contingency can be coupled with 'infinite regress' arguments, or it can stand on its own. Where it is coupled with arguments against the possibility of an infinite regress, it is important to distinguish an infinite regress argument based on the impossibility of an infinite regress of cause or contingency, from one arguing against an infinite regress *in time*. These are different issues. Ibn Sīnā is the best example of this, as he believed, on the one hand, that the world was eternal – thus, to the irritation of al-Ghazālī, he believed in the infinity of past time – yet at the same time he rejected an infinite regress of contingent causes. So the universe has gone on forever but that cannot explain how or why it has come to exist. An infinite *temporal* chain of events cannot explain its existence.

Most familiar to Christians is Thomas Aquinas's Third Way,[29] which couples the issue of contingency with the impossibility of an infinite regress:

Thomas Aquinas's 'Third Way' (to prove the existence of God)

The third way is taken from possibility and necessity, and runs thus. We find in nature things that are possible to be and not to be, since they are found to be generated, and to corrupt, and consequently, they are possible to be and not to be. But it is impossible for these always to exist, for that which is possible not to be at some time is not. Therefore, if everything is possible not to be, then at one time there could have been nothing in existence. Now if this were true, even now there would be nothing in existence, because that which does not exist only begins to exist by something already existing. Therefore, if at one time nothing was in existence, it would have been impossible for anything to have begun to exist; and thus even now nothing would be in existence – which is absurd. Therefore, not all beings are merely possible, but there must exist something the existence of which is necessary. But every necessary thing either has its necessity caused by another, or not. Now it is impossible to go on to infinity in necessary things which have their necessity caused by another, as has been already proved in regard to efficient causes. Therefore we cannot but postulate the existence of some being having of itself its own necessity, and not receiving it from another, but rather causing in others their necessity. This all men speak of as God.[30]

However, even if we assert the possibility of an infinite series, we still find a few stubborn thinkers in our path insisting on the inadequacy of contingent things as an explanation. Leibniz argues that even an *infinity* of contingent or finite things is insufficient to explain the universe. It is not the quantity of causes, as it were; it is the metaphysical clout that they have. Ibn Sīnā makes the point that the cause of all the causal chain must lie outside the group; it must be of a different kind or nature, and not be caused itself.

Copleston tried to articulate the point in this way in his debate with Russell:

> COPLESTON: My point is that what we call the world is intrinsically unintelligible, apart from the existence of God. You see, I cannot believe that the infinity of the series of events – I mean a horizontal series, so to speak – if such an infinity could be proved, would be the slightest degree relevant to the situation. If you add up chocolates you will get chocolates after all and not a sheep. If you add up chocolates to infinity, you presumably get an infinite number of chocolates. So if you add up contingent beings to infinity, you still get contingent beings and not a necessary being. An infinite series of contingent beings would be, to my way of thinking, as unable to cause itself as one contingent being.[31]

So for some, it is the very contingency of the world which demands an explanation that points beyond itself.

For others, the distinction between contingency and necessity, and the way it is deployed in this argument, is illegitimate. 'Necessity' and 'contingency', in their view, cannot be applied to entities, only propositions. Al-Ghazālī criticized the way that Ibn Sīnā made the distinction: as between those things which were caused and those which were not. He pointed out that an infinite series of contingent causes, if the series itself was uncaused, therefore must count as 'necessary' and no longer in need of a different necessary being to explain it:

> We say: Each member of a causal series is possible in this sense of 'possible', namely, that it has a cause additional to its essence, but the whole series is not possible in this sense of 'possible'.[32]

The individual beings or states of affairs might be contingent, but the aggregate not; it could have an internal cause; at any rate, thc series itself no longer needs an external cause.

It was a criticism Ibn Rushd had to concede, and he did not follow Ibn Sīnā's distinction of 'possible' and 'necessary' as defined by having a cause or lacking one.[33] Rather, necessary existence is found in a being 'identical with its existence', whereas a possible being is one which comes into being.[34]

Some would object that, as an explanation, a 'necessary being' is no better than an 'uncaused universe'; that is, it is no more intelligible or satisfactory. Indeed, some argue that it is incoherent.

More precisely, problems may attend on the alleged relation between the necessary and the contingent. Le Poidevin argues that necessary facts cannot be used to explain contingent ones. Necessary facts are always there, in all possible worlds, and therefore they cannot explain why *some* possible worlds contain the relevant contingent fact (like the existence of the universe) and some do not:

> If there is an ultimate explanation, a fact which calls for no further explanation, then it must be a necessary fact, one which obtains in all worlds. . . . Since the very problem was to explain why the *actual* world, but not all worlds, contained a universe, i.e. what it was about this particular world that made the crucial difference, appeals to a feature which all worlds share will not advance our understanding any further at all. . . . Necessary facts, then, cannot explain contingent ones, and causal explanation, of any phenomenon, must link contingent facts. That is, both cause and effect must be contingent. Why is this? Because causes make a difference to their environment: they result in something that would not have happened if the cause had not been present. . . . So one of the reasons why necessary facts cannot causally explain anything is that we cannot make sense of their not being the case, whereas causal explanation requires us to make sense of causally explanatory facts not being the case. Causal explanation involves the explanation of one contingent fact to appeal to another contingent fact.[35]

The theist might respond – and this is even if they concede the validity of using the possible worlds ontology which Le Poidevin employs – that a necessary cause, presuming that is God, does not entail necessary creation. A 'necessary' divine Being might will creation in those possible worlds that have it and will to abstain from creating in those that do not. 'Necessity' in the divine being does not constrain the being's action.[36]

Rowe is also troubled by the relation between contingent things and a necessary one:

> Consider the huge conjunctive fact whose conjuncts are all the other contingent facts that there are. This huge conjunctive fact must itself be a contingent fact, otherwise its conjuncts would not be contingent. Now what can be the sufficient reason for this huge conjunctive fact? It cannot be some necessary fact. For the sufficient reason for a fact is another fact that entails it; and whatever is entailed by a necessary fact is itself necessary. The huge conjunctive fact cannot be its own sufficient reason since only a necessary fact could be self-explanatory.

> So, the sufficient reason for the huge conjunctive fact would have to be one of the contingent facts that is a conjunct of it. But then that conjunct would have to be a sufficient reason for itself, since whatever is a sufficient reason for a conjunctive fact must be a sufficient reason for each of its conjuncts. It follows, then, that the huge conjunctive fact cannot have an explanation. It thus appears that PSR is false.[37]

As we have seen, Copleston agrees that 'the huge conjunctive fact cannot be its own sufficient reason', and this is precisely why he argues for the necessity of a cause outside the series. The quest for a sufficient reason within the series of contingent facts is pointless; but does not so much disprove the PSR as point to a cause (or sufficient reason) outside the scheme of contingent things, the 'huge conjunctive fact'. So Copleston would say. As for Rowe's point that a necessary fact as cause would make the contingent facts necessary, the theist could say that God is not a necessary 'fact' whose causing is unconscious and necessary. God is a free agent who chooses to bring about states of affairs that are *intrinsically* contingent.

Here is how Ibn Rushd deals with a cognate argument in al-Ghazālī. He uses the concept of 'necessary through another'.[38] Something can be possible in itself, but its existence can become 'necessary' because something else has caused it to happen; a distinction which derives from Ibn Sīnā and which we can see is handled as mainstream and uncontroversial in contemporary Iranian metaphysics, as demonstrated by Ṭabāṭabā'ī. To say that something is merely 'possible' is to claim 'that its essence determines that its existence can become necessary only through a cause; what is meant, therefore, is an essence which will not be by itself necessary in its existence when its cause is removed and therefore is not a necessary existent, i.e. it is denied the quality of necessary existence'.[39] So in fact any contingent thing becomes necessary through another when it is caused, even by a contingent cause; not merely when it is entailed by a 'necessary fact' as Rowe says. It would be an unnecessary confusion, however, to construe this as a complete change of modality in all its aspects. So Rushd's response to Rowe would be: the huge contingent fact that is the universe becomes 'necessary through another', though contingent in itself, when caused by a necessary being. If that is impossible, as involving some kind of illegitimate transfer of necessity, then no kind of causality is possible even in the purely material world.

It can be argued that the Cosmological Argument falls prey to something like the 'quantifier shift fallacy'; that is, it takes something (a quantifier) applicable to one group and shifts it to another group. Russell seems to imply something like this criticism in a charge against Copleston:

> RUSSELL: I can illustrate what seems to me to be your fallacy. Every man who exists has a mother, and it seems to me that your argument is

that therefore the human race must have a mother, but obviously the human race hasn't a mother; that is a different logical sphere.

COPLESTON: Well, I really cannot see the parity. If I were saying 'every object has a phenomenal cause, therefore the whole series has a phenomenal cause', there would be parity, but I am not saying that; I am saying that every object has a phenomenal cause if you insist on the infinity of the series; but a series of phenomenal causes is an insufficient explanation of the series. Therefore the series has not a phenomenal cause but a transcendent cause.

RUSSELL: Well, that is always assuming that not only every particular thing in the world has a cause but that the world as a whole must have a cause. For that assumption I see no ground whatsoever. If you give me a ground I will listen to it.

COPLESTON: The series of events is either caused, or it is not caused. If it is caused there must obviously be a cause outside the series. If it is not caused, then it is sufficient to itself and if it is sufficient to itself it is what I call necessary. But it cannot be necessary since each member is contingent and we have agreed that the total has no reality apart from its members, therefore it cannot be necessary.[40]

In fact the argument coursing between Ibn Sīnā, al-Ghazālī and Ibn Rushd centuries earlier already raised this point. Al-Ghazālī anticipates Russell by objecting that what is true of each unit in a collectivity need not be true of the collectivity. Thus one can ask for the cause or the sufficient reason for individual things; but that does not entitle one to assume that just because each individual has a cause or a sufficient reason, that therefore the whole group must also have one of its own.

But one might ask whether in fact this objection begs the question. Russell complains that the Cosmological Argument, by analogy, uselessly asks for the mother of the human race. However, it is a perfectly legitimate exercise to investigate the origin of the species. Palaeontology cannot be addressed by providing a genealogy for everybody; it is perfectly legitimate to raise the question of origins on another level than can be provided for the individual. The question of the origin of *homo sapiens* is a different question from the question of my personal genealogy and has a different methodology, and so too, Copleston would maintain, does the Cosmological Argument. Palaeontology, like the Cosmological Argument, asks for the origin of the whole, and maintains that it must be on a different level of explanation than that which exists for each individual.

The Nyāya philosopher Uddyotakara raises an objection not commonly met in Western philosophy. Even if these proofs establish the existence of God at the beginning of the world, it doesn't mean He exists afterwards. Uddyotakara's response is to argue that God's divine creative activity is needed on an ongoing basis to activate the karma of souls just dying and join them to an appropriate new body. God's activity is also needed for things to continue the functions for which they have been created – God has to sustain as well as create.[41]

Infinite regress

Sometimes the argument that the existence of the universe requires a cause has another ingredient in it to block the sceptic's recourse to an infinity of causes. Cosmological arguments are often seen as depending on the notion that an infinite regress is impossible. The situation is actually more complex than that, as we have seen. Some make no reference to the idea of an infinite regress. Some appeal to the alleged possibility of an infinite regress, on the differing bases of time, cause or contingency.

Philoponus' set of proofs contained some which rely on the impossibility of an infinity.[42] He sets forth these arguments to show that the past cannot be infinite: The first, derived from Aristotle, argues that if the world was eternal, the past transformations of states of affairs leading up to now would amount to an infinite series. However, an infinite number cannot 'actually' exist – to talk of numbers being 'infinite' is not to say that there is a particular number which is infinite, but rather to deny that one can reach an upper maximum. This is another way of saying that one cannot traverse an infinity. Therefore, if the world had no beginning but was eternal, an infinite series of changes and states of affairs would lead up to the creation of a given thing. However, such an infinite series could never be completed, so this thing would never come into being.

Philoponus' second argument takes a principle from the Greek Peripatetic tradition: an infinite cannot be exceeded. One infinite cannot be larger than another. Since each thing or change adds to and increases the number in existence in the history of the universe, it would constitute adding more to infinity, which is impossible. So what has been accumulated already cannot be infinite.[43]

The Islamic philosopher al-Kindī and the Jewish philosopher Saadia both adopted and adapted these arguments from Philoponus. Al-Kindī argued in a threefold fashion that past time must be finite because an infinite interval cannot be traversed; that bodies must be finite and as they come into being they would add to the infinity of those already in existence, but an infinite cannot be increased; and that a supposedly infinite past time would increase as time goes on, which is also absurd. Saadia argues similarly that an infinite past time could not be traversed, as do Iskafi and Naẓẓām, two Mu'tazilite thinkers who were approximate contemporaries of al-Kindī.[44]

Such thinkers then object to the idea of an infinite regress in *time*, insisting that time cannot go backward infinitely. One cannot traverse an infinite distance, whether of space or time. If an infinite distance of time existed *before* the present moment, we would never have reached the present moment: for that requires arriving at the other side of infinity, so to speak. Imagine a magic arrow which, when shot, goes on for infinity. We can imagine it flying onwards forever, never stopping. But try to imagine a different kind of magical arrow. Imagine an arrow that is said to have flown an infinite distance now reaches its target: for example, St Sebastian. Can we make sense of the idea of something having traversed an infinite distance and now, as it were, completing it by arrival at the present point?[45]

Once upon a time, a young and inquisitive Prince lost his way while hunting in a forest. In the forest, inside two adjacent caves, he came across two strange sorts of persons. In the first cave, he found a team of young boys with a lot of energy together chanting the following mantra: 'Zero, one, two, three, four, five, six' . . . . . . and so on. Since they never stopped, the Prince, clever as he was, figured out that these boys were wanting to recite the names of all the natural numbers starting with zero. Little do these boys know, the Prince thought, that they will never come to the end of their task. But more surprise awaited him in the second cave where he saw a group of very ancient men with their beards and matted hair touching the ground. He could hear them muttering together under their breath, '. . . Eight, seven, six, five, four, three, two, one, zero'. Then, suddenly, they heaved a sigh of relief and stopped. Picking up courage, the Prince asked one of these old men, 'Venerable Sir, what on earth have you been doing all these years sitting in this cave?' 'We were counting the natural numbers, my boy!' replied the sage. 'We were counting them backwards and we have just finished with zero.' 'But when did you begin this counting?' asked the puzzled Prince. 'Never my child, we never began,' was the answer. [This story was] inspired by a thought experiment invented by one of the greatest Western philosophers of this century, Ludwig Wittgenstein. It runs in the oral tradition and has never, as far as I know, been written down.[46]

Some object to the idea of an infinite regress of *causes*. It is specifically a *causal* series which cannot regress indefinitely. When tracing causes backwards in the series, therefore, you must ultimately reach a first cause.

The idea that an infinite regress of causes is impossible was argued by

Aristotle[47] and therefore was followed by the majority of monotheists who were subsequently influenced by him. In considering a series of causes, Aristotle divides the causes into a 'first' cause, a 'final' cause, and any number of 'intermediate' causes, which could be infinite or finite. This raises the interesting possibility, not often explored, that a causal series could be *infinite*, but it could not *regress infinitely*. It must have a first cause, even if it has an infinity of intermediate causes. (Exponents of an infinite universe could avail themselves of this possibility.) Aristotle's argument is that if there were no first cause, there would be no 'true' cause; an infinite regress would entail a causal series with no first cause, therefore without a true cause.

Ibn Sīnā's focus, following Aristotle, and Ibn Rushd's (following both) is not just on the nature of infinity but on the nature of causality, in particular, the different characters of the three parts of the Aristotelian causal series: first, intermediate and final. The first cause is the cause of everything, whereas the intermediate causes are mere links, whether finite or infinite in number.[48] The intermediate causes are both effects and causes; but without a first cause, a causal series is a series of effects without a cause. Here is how the argument is summarized by al-Ghazālī – who challenges it:

> The world (with its existents) either has a cause or does not have a cause. If it has a cause, then: 'Does this cause have a cause or is it without a cause?' The same applies to the cause of the cause. This would either regress infinitely, which would be impossible, or terminate with a limit. The latter, then, is a first cause that has no cause for its existence. We call this the First Principle.[49]

Ibn Rushd responded in the following way, with a restatement of the argument he attributes to Ibn Sīnā:

> Possible existents must of necessity have causes which precede them, and if these causes again are possible it follows that they have causes and that there is an infinite regress; and if there is an infinite regress there is no cause, and the possible will exist without a cause, and this is impossible. Therefore the series must end in a necessary cause, and in this case this necessary cause must be necessary through a cause or without a cause, and if through a cause, this cause must have a cause and so on infinitely, and if we have an infinite regress here, it follows that what was assumed to have a cause has no cause, and this is impossible. Therefore the series must end in a cause necessary without a cause, i.e. necessary by itself, and this necessarily is the necessary existent. And when these distinctions are indicated, the proof becomes valid.[50] [Otherwise, he concedes, it is invalid.]

Aquinas's Second Way does not deal with the impossibility of an infinite past time, but with the nature of the causal series. The reasoning is familiar from Aristotle,[51] Ibn Sīnā, Ibn Rushd: there must be first, last and intermediate members of the series. Without a first term, the series never comes into existence. It is only the first cause that has causal power; the others all derive their efficacy from it. If you remove a cause, you remove its effects; so if you remove a first cause, you remove all the subsequent effects – and their effects, for in a causal chain they are also causes in turn. Thus, if there were no first cause, there would be nothing.

When he criticizes Ibn Sīnā, al-Ghazālī observes that the impossibility of an infinite regress is not self-evident. It has to be established by argument, he insists. Moreover, it cannot, in his view, be used by those (such as Ibn Sīnā) who believe in the eternity of the world, that is, in an infinity of past time. One can only reject it by rejecting every kind of infinite series. Modern philosophers also question whether an actual infinite series of past events is impossible, as for example Quentin Smith does here:

> By acknowledging that events are given successively *in reality*, are we not admitting that *in reality* they can never add up to an infinite collection? Is it not true that for an infinite class to be given at all, whether in thought or reality, it must be given all at once?
>
> The reply is that the collection of events cannot add up to an infinite collection in a finite amount of time, but they do so add up in an infinite amount of time. And since it is coherent to suppose that in relation to any present an infinite amount of time has elapsed, it is also coherent to suppose that in relation to any present an infinite collection of past events has already been formed by successive addition.[52]

It should be noted that, as with causality, both Spinoza and Leibniz frame versions of the argument which do not rely on the impossibility of an infinite regress.

Conclusion

Does it work? Well, what would 'working' look like? If 'working' consisted in producing conviction in the sceptic, clearly it does not work. If 'working' means it is logically watertight; is the logic infallible? It depends on whose framework of logic and metaphysics you are using. Whether it is question-begging and illegitimate, or whether it sets creation in a context which makes it meaningful and intelligible, depends on your intuitions and beliefs about the nature of cause, necessity, time and intelligibility. Its proponents seek a context of meaning in which creation becomes comprehensible only when it is seen in relation to something which transcends it. You may not agree.

Draw your own conclusions

Is looking for a proof for the existence of God contrary to faith? Is it part of faith? Is faith unreasonable without it?

Are you convinced by the Principle of Sufficient Reason? Do you think it is necessary for all knowledge? Do you think it is useful for common-sense affairs, but may not have universal validity? Or do you think it is a human construct that we can easily discard?

Do contingent things need an explanation outside themselves to be intelligible?

Does the universe need an explanation as a whole, or can we explain it bit by bit until we get a complete, if composite, answer?

If the universe has no beginning, does it still need a creator?

Is an infinite regress of causes possible? Is an infinite regress in time possible?

Do you think the argument works? What do you mean by 'work' here?

Further reading

Aquinas, T. *The 'Summa Theologica' of St. Thomas Aquinas*, London, Burns Oates & Washbourne

Chakrabarti, A. (1989) 'From the Fabric to the Weaver?', in R. W. Perrett (ed.), *Indian Philosophy of Religion*, Studies in Philosophy and Religion 13, Dordrecht, Boston and London, Kluwer Academic

Craig, W. L. (1980) *The Cosmological Argument from Plato to Leibniz*, London, Macmillan

Davidson, H. A. (1987) *Proofs for Eternity, Creation and the Existence of God in Medieval Islamic and Jewish Philosophy*, New York and Oxford, Oxford University Press

Everitt, N. (2004) *The Non-Existence of God*, London, Routledge

Fakhry, M. (1994) *Philosophy, Dogma and the Impact of Greek Thought in Islam*, Aldershot, Variorum

Hick, John (1964) *The Existence of God*, New York, Macmillan

Le Poidevin, R. (1997) *Arguing for Atheism: An Introduction to the Philosophy of Religion*, London, Routledge

Sobel, J. H. (2004) *Logic and Theism: Arguments for and Against Beliefs in God*, Cambridge, Cambridge University Press

Vattanky, J. S. J. (1993) *Development of Nyāya Theism*, New Delhi, Intercultural Publications

Yaran, C. S. (2003) *Islamic Thought on the Existence of God: Contributions and Contrasts with Contemporary Western Philosophy of Religion*, Cultural

Heritage and Contemporary Change, Series IIA: Islam 16, Washington, D.C., Council for Research in Values and Philosophy

Notes

1 A. Chakrabarti (1989) 'From the Fabric to the Weaver?', in R. W. Perrett (ed.), *Indian Philosophy of Religion*, Studies in Philosophy and Religion 13, Dordrecht, Boston and London, Kluwer Academic, p. 21.

2 Nyāyasutras IV.1.19–21 in my flippant paraphrase. See the discussion in J. S. J. Vattanky (1993) *Development of Nyāya Theism*, New Delhi, Intercultural Publications, p. 16.

3 Vattanky, *Development of Nyāya Theism*, pp. 22–3.

4 *Nyāyadarsanam*, cited in Vattanky, *Development of Nyāya Theism*, p. 30.

5 M. Fakhry (1994) *Philosophy, Dogma and the Impact of Greek Thought in Islam*, Aldershot, Variorum, pp. 137f.

6 H. A. Wolfson (1973) 'Notes on Proofs of the Existence of God in Jewish Philosophy', in *Studies in the History and Philosophy of Religion*, Cambridge, Mass., Harvard University Press, pp. 571ff.

7 Wolfson, 'Notes on Proofs of the Existence of God in Jewish Philosophy', p. 571.

8 'Were they created by nothing, or were they the creators of themselves, or did they create the heavens and the Earth?', Qur'ān 52:35–6.

9 Qur'ān 6:74–80.

10 G. W. von Leibniz (1951) 'The Monadology', in P. P. Wiener (ed.), *Leibniz Selections*, New York, Charles Scribner's, p. 539. Cf. G. W. von Leibniz (1951) *Theodicy: Essays on the Goodness of God and the Freedom of Man and the Origin of Evil*, trans. E. M. Huggard, Rare Masterpieces of Philosophy and Science, London, Routledge & Kegan Paul, p. 147.

11 W. L. Craig (1980) *The Cosmological Argument from Plato to Leibniz*, London, Macmillan, pp. 260–2.

12 John Hick (1964) *The Existence of God*, New York, Macmillan, pp. 173–4.

13 Craig, *The Cosmological Argument*, pp. 241, 276 *et passim*. 'Leibniz's God is, of course, the efficient cause of the world, but his proof for God's existence does not proceed along the chain of efficient causes to a first cause, but seeks a reason for the whole world.'

14 Plato (1971) *Timaeus and Critias*, trans. H. D. P. Lee, London, Penguin, 28C, cf. also 28B.

15 Davidson claims that Kalām writers who take it to be self-evident include al-Ghazālī, Galen, al-Rāzī, Tusi, Ījī, Kindī, Joseph ibn Saddiq, and Baḥya. H. A. Davidson (1987) *Proofs for Eternity, Creation and the Existence of God in Medieval Islamic and Jewish Philosophy*, New York and Oxford, Oxford University Press, p. 164. However, there was serious controversy in medieval Islam over the idea of causality, which muddies the waters for this kind of causal argument. See Fakhry, *Philosophy, Dogma and the Impact of Greek Thought in Islam*.

16 Davidson, *Proofs for Eternity, Creation and the Existence of God in*

Medieval Islamic and Jewish Philosophy, p. 156.

17 Chakrabarti translates *hetu* as 'mark', Vattanky as 'reason'. See Chakrabarti, 'From the Fabric to the Weaver?' and Vattanky, *Development of Nyāya Theism*.

18 al-Ghazālī (2000 (1997)) *The Incoherence of the Philosophers (Tahafut al-Falasifah)*, trans. M. E. Marmura, Provo, Utah, Brigham Young University Press, Question 17, beginning p. 166.

19 al-Ghazālī, *The Incoherence of the Philosophers*, p. 170.

20 R. Le Poidevin (1997) *Arguing for Atheism: An Introduction to the Philosophy of Religion*, London, Routledge, p. 13.

21 Hick, *The Existence of God*, pp. 174–5.

22 Hick, *The Existence of God*, p. 175.

23 Le Poidevin, *Arguing for Atheism.*

24 Le Poidevin, *Arguing for Atheism*, p. 37.

25 See Wolfson, 'Notes on Proofs of the Existence of God in Jewish Philosophy'.

26 S. M. H. Ṭabāṭabā'ī (2003) *The Elements of Islamic Metaphysics (Bidayat al-Hikmah)*, London, ICAS Press, p. 164.

27 So claims Fakhry, *Philosophy, Dogma and the Impact of Greek Thought in Islam*, p. 135.

28 Al-Rāzī, in *Kitab al-Arba'īn*, see Fakhry, *Philosophy, Dogma and the Impact of Greek Thought in Islam*, p. 6.

29 Although Craig, when considering what Thomas has contributed to the argument, concludes that it was little. 'After one has studied the history of the cosmological argument, one realises that Aquinas has said little with regard to it that was not said before him by Aristotle, al-Fārābī, ibn Sīnā, and Maimonides. The principal contribution of Aquinas comes in his conception of existence as the act of being of a particular essence. Prior to Thomas existence was conceived as an accident added to the essence of a thing, but Aquinas denied the accidentality of existence.' Craig, *The Cosmological Argument*, p. 195. Although it depends on how one understands Ibn Sīnā's understanding of existence as a happening which instantiates essence, in which case Thomas's contribution is even less. Craig, *The Cosmological Argument*, p. 196.

30 Thomas Aquinas, *The 'Summa Theologica' of St. Thomas Aquinas*, London, Burns Oates & Washbourne, I.2.3.

31 Hick, *The Existence of God*, pp. 173–4.

32 As portrayed by Ibn Rushd, in Averroës (1969) *Tahafut al-Tahafut*, trans. Simon Van den Bergh, London, Luzac, pp. 165–6.

33 See Ibn Rushd, in Averroës, *Tahafut al-Tahafut*, pp. 163–67, 252. 'The objection which can be directed against Avicenna is that when you divide existence into possible and necessary and identify the possible existent with that which has a cause and the necessary existent with that which has none, you can no longer prove the impossibility of the existence of an infinite causal series, for from its infinite character it follows that it is to be classed with existents which have no cause and it must therefore be of the nature of the necessary existent, especially as, according to him and his school, eternity can consist of an infinite series of causes each of which is temporal. The fault in Avicenna's argument arises only from his division of the existent into that which has a cause and that which has none. If he

had made his division in the way we have done, none of these objections could be directed against him' (p. 166).

34 See the discussion, Averroës, *Tahafut al-Tahafut*, pp. 117f.

35 Le Poidevin, *Arguing for Atheism*, pp. 40–1.

36 The fashion for considering problems in terms of a multitude of 'possible worlds' was of course not present among the Islamic thinkers; but the question of necessity of creation certainly was. 'But existence which is linked up with non-existence only exists as long as the producer exists. The only way to escape this difficulty is to assume that the existence of the world always has been and will always be linked together with non-existence, as is the case with movement, which is always in need of a mover.' Averroës, *Tahafut al-Tahafut*, p. 98. Note the assumption about movement comes from Aristotle.

37 P. L. Quinn and C. Taliaferro (1997) *A Companion to the Philosophy of Religion*, Oxford, Blackwell, pp. 335–6.

38 Averroës, *Tahafut al-Tahafut*. Sec p. 91, also 118.

39 Averroës, *Tahafut al-Tahafut*. See p. 118.

40 Hick, *The Existence of God*.

41 Vattanky, *Development of Nyāya Theism*, p. 37.

42 For a translation of Philoponus, see J. Philoponus (1987) *Philoponus: Against Aristotle, on the Eternity of the World*, trans. C. Wildberg, Ancient Commentators on Aristotle, London, Duckworth.

43 His third argument makes use of the same logic, applied to multiplication, and addresses the revolutions of the heavenly spheres. See Davidson on all three arguments, *Proofs for Eternity, Creation and the Existence of God in Medieval Islamic and Jewish Philosophy*, pp. 88–9.

44 See Davidson, *Proofs for Eternity, Creation and the Existence of God in Medieval Islamic and Jewish Philosophy*, pp. 106–7. For Kindī's text, consult Y. q. i. I. al-Kindī (1974) *al-Kindī's Metaphysics / a Translation of Ya'qub ibn Ishaq al-Kindī's treatise 'On first philosophy' (fi al-Falsafah al-ula) with Introduction and Commentary by Alfred L. Ivry*, trans. A. L. Ivry, Studies in Islamic Philosophy and Science, Albany, State University of New York Press. Wolfson credits Abraham ibn Daud with being the first to introduce what he calls 'the second form' of the cosmological argument in Jewish philosophy, in which the block to an infinite regress is invoked. Wolfson, 'Notes on Proofs of the Existence of God in Jewish Philosophy', p. 574.

45 Paul Helm uses this reasoning not to create a cosmological argument, but to argue for God's atemporality. P. Helm (1988) *Eternal God: A Study of God without Time*, Oxford, Oxford University Press, pp. 37–8.

46 Told by Arindam Chakrabarti.

47 Aristotle (1998) *Metaphysics*, trans. H. Lawson-Tancred, London, Penguin, II.2.

48 Crescas rejected the possibility of an infinite number of intermediate causes, but still maintained the validity of the proof of God's existence, in that he agreed that an uncaused cause is still necessary for the series. See Davidson, *Proofs for Eternity, Creation and the Existence of God in Medieval Islamic and Jewish Philosophy*, pp. 365–6. In criticism of Ibn Sīnā, al-Ghazālī observes that the impossibility of an infinite regress is not self-evident. It has to be established by argument. Moreover, it cannot, in his view, be used by those (such as Ibn Sīnā)

who believe in the eternity of the world, that is, in an infinity of past time. One can only reject it by rejecting every kind of infinite series. On this point, see Davidson, *Proofs for Eternity, Creation and the Existence of God in Medieval Islamic and Jewish Philosophy*, pp. 367–70.

49 al-Ghazālī, *The Incoherence of the Philosophers*, p. 79 (Discussion 4).

50 Averroës, *Tahafut al-Tahafut*, p. 165.

51 Aquinas attributes this proof to Aristotle in the *Summa Contra Gentiles*, ch. 13. Thomas Aquinas (2002) *Summa Contra Gentiles*, Notre Dame, Ind., University of Notre Dame Press, p. 86.

52 Q. Smith (1987) 'Infinity and the Past', *Philosophy of Science* 54/3, p. 72.

7

How the World Seems

The Nyāya arguments for the existence of a creator as we saw in the last chapter foreshadow the pattern of reasoning which is found, initially less formally and with far less rigour in its formulation, in Western arguments often classed as 'design' arguments. These too draw an analogy between the world and some made artefact, and infer from this a creator of the world.

Western 'design' arguments can focus on an alleged pre-existent plan for the universe – thus focusing on the beginning – or they can, so to speak, focus on the end or 'ends' of things. Aquinas's 'Fifth way' is an archetype of the latter kind of argument, based on the notion of the 'ends' or goals to which things progress. He suggests that whenever we confront a being the question always arises, 'What is its purpose?', which is just as necessary a question as 'What began it?' or 'What keeps it existing?' (the question of the Cosmological Argument). In other words, the existence of a thing involves its end, its purpose. So, the argument runs, whatever exists acts towards an end. Non-intelligent things cannot propose their own end. Therefore their end must come from an intelligent being which directs all natural things to their end. This being we call God.

A modern Islamic version of this 'teleological' version of the argument is offered by Ismail Rājī al-Farūqī, in *Al Tawhid: Its Implications for Thought and Life*:

> Nature is equally a realm of ends where everything fulfils a purpose and thereby contributes to the prosperity and balance of all. From the little inanimate pebble in the valley, the smallest plankton on the surface of the ocean, the microbial flagellate in the intestine of the woodroach, to the galaxies and their suns, the giant redwoods and whales and elephants – everything in existence, by its genesis and growth, its life and death, fulfils a purpose assigned to it by God, which is necessary for other beings. All creatures are interdependent, and the whole of creation runs because of the perfect harmony which exists between its parts.[1]

Of course, the argument has been criticized and rejected throughout its history. With arguments whose structure is 'teleological', like the Fifth Way of Aquinas, one can object to the notion of teleology itself. Why see things in terms of 'purpose'? Does the state of the world necessarily imply an 'end' or 'purpose', or could it be the accidental result of random activity? Why view things in terms of 'ends', rather than beginnings? Rather than seeing a pre-existing plan to which the universe is created to conform, we tend since Darwin to reverse the equation and imagine that forms of life evolved to exist in the pre-existing conditions as they were.[2] Rather than saying that exactly the right atmospheric conditions were created to sustain human, animal and plant life, we tend to think that such life as exists developed under the pre-existing conditions which could sustain it. We are less likely to say: 'How extraordinary that the ozone layer is (or was) exactly the right thickness to protect life on earth! Such a miracle could not have arisen by chance!' than we are to say: 'The thickness of the ozone layer is a "given"; such life as exists on earth evolved as precisely the life that could exist under the prevailing conditions.'

If one speaks in terms of purposes or ends, then the problem of evil becomes a pressing one for this argument. Would evil then ultimately be the responsibility of the being which directs everything to their end? Do we have to allow that evil is part of God's design? This can also be viewed in an evidential way: does the universe give evidence, not merely of *design*, but of *good* design? Couldn't God have done better, if he was setting out to design such a world from scratch?

Or indeed, do we need a God? From Buddhist critics of Nyāya arguments, through David Hume to Richard Dawkins, one standard criticism of the design argument is that God is simply redundant and everything can be explained in some other, perhaps simpler, way.[3] The argument supposes that the order in nature can only be explained if it is traced back to a plan, that is, a mind, in this case a divine mind. But why is the order in a mind any more explicable than the order in the material world? And is a Supreme Designer as much in need of explanation as apparent design in the universe? A modern proponent of the argument, William Dembski, counters that

> The problem with this criticism is that it can be applied whenever scientists introduce a novel theoretical entity. When Ludwig Boltzmann introduced his kinetic theory of heat back in the late 1800s and invoked the motion of unobservable particles (what we now call atoms and molecules) to explain heat, one might just as well have argued that such unobservable particles do not explain anything because they themselves need to be explained.[4]

The argument in various versions has been known for centuries in India, Islamic thought, and Europe. It has also been criticized in all those cultures. In the West, Hume through his character 'Philo' and Darwin between them have long been seen as having defeated the Design Argument for any rational thinker. However, it has made a comeback in the last few decades – not so much *in spite of* developments in science as *because of* them. These arguments less resemble the inferential approach of Nyāya than a different forerunner, in the Islamic arguments based determination.

Uses of probability in design arguments

Unlike cosmological arguments, design arguments often rely on notions of probability, though often (especially in early versions) that reliance on probability is tacit, and the appeal is to our intuitive sense of what is likely rather than using more explicit probabilistic arguments. One such appeal is to create an analogy between the universe and examples where we know a designing agent has been involved, and argue or imply that that analogy is a tighter one than the analogy between the universe and some non-designed object.

When we calculate probabilities, we generally ask, 'What is the probability that *x* will happen, given *y*?' When we want to ask how plausible a hypothesis is, we ask, 'What is the probability that this hypothesis is true, given the observations we have made?' Design theorists want to argue that the hypothesis that an intelligent (or divine) designer is responsible for the universe is more likely and/or more probable than the hypothesis that the universe came to be by chance or by some form of non-intelligent necessity.

Some thinkers use a tool from probability calculus, Bayes' Theorem, to construct their arguments. Bayes' Theorem allows us to take account of background knowledge and new further knowledge in order to revise our estimates of the probability of something.[5]

Let us say you join me waiting at a bus stop served by three bus services, A, B and C. What is the probability that the next bus that arrives will be the one I want, bus A? You suggest that it looks like the odds are one in three.

But then I tell you that bus A is scheduled to run every 8 minutes, bus B runs every 5 minutes, and bus C runs every 10 minutes. Now their chances do not look so equal because their frequencies are different. I intuitively imagine that bus B will probably be next.

But then a lady at the bus stop tells us that a bus B just went by a minute ago.

And then again, buses rarely follow their advertised timetable, especially when you are late and in a hurry; and given our shared perception that you wait for ages and then three buses arrive at once, we decide sarcastically that probably the next two buses will be Bs.

Then the helpful lady at the bus stop tells us there is a wildcat strike of bus drivers and many of them did not turn up for work today, leading to a reduced service on buses B and A.

However we decide to calculate the probability now, it is unlikely that it remains at one in three. All these different factors affect our calculations of probability. Bayes' Theorem is a formula that lets the user calculate the probability of a given hypothesis, given the evidence, the background knowledge, the prior probabilities of these things, to give your estimate. Some (most famously Richard Swinburne) use Bayesian style reasoning to calculate that the probability of God's existence is high, given the evidence that the universe as it is exists and the background of scientific knowledge from cosmology to show how improbable it is that exactly such a universe exists. However, as you can see, this approach requires assigning probabilities (explicitly or tacitly) to God's existence before and after you consider the evidence, and similar judgements about the probability of the universe existing as it is. In other words, the scope for disagreement is great.

The design argument need not be Bayesian (in fact, relatively few use Bayesian theory explicitly). Others view it as a kind of inference; the existence of a divine designer is inferred from the existence of the world as it is. Hume's 'Philo' claimed that our inference is based on experience; and that the argument from design therefore is really an inductive generalization:

> When two *species* of objects have always been observed to be conjoined together, I can *infer*, by custom, the existence of one wherever I *see* the existence of the other. And this I call an argument from experience. But how this argument can have place, where the objects, as in the present case, are single, individual, without parallel, or specific resemblance, may be difficult to explain. And will any man tell me with a serious countenance, that an orderly universe must arise from some thought and art, like the human; because we have experience of it? To ascertain this reasoning it were requisite, that we have experience of thc origin of worlds.[6]

This problem is an epistemological one. According to Hume, all reasoning and knowledge must be grounded in experience. It is true that we have experience of the world, but we only have experience of *one* world, so we cannot compare it to other possibilities to determine its likelihood. And we don't have experience of the *origins* of worlds, so we cannot say anything about how they come about. Dharmakīrti and other Buddhist critics arrived at this critique centuries before Hume. This was exposed by the long and detailed debate between the Naiyayikas and the Buddhists:

> The Naiyayikas and Buddhists of the Dharmakīrti school have different concepts of inference and the implication of their various theories can best be seen when they apply their logic to the proofs for the existence of God.
>
> According to Buddhists, human knowledge is restricted to what is directly experienced and we can establish the existence of something unknown only if that unknown belongs to the class of things which could be directly experienced. The Nyāya system developed by Vācaspati Miśra, Udayana and Gaṅgeśa rejects the position of the Buddhists and establishes that on the basis of what is known, we can legitimately arrive at the existence of something unknown, even if that unknown does not belong to the class of what is known. Therefore the inherent nature of inference lends itself to the possibility of establishing the existence of God.[7]

If, however, design arguments could be viewed as a kind of 'inference to the best explanation' then it may escape this criticism.[8] Sobel and Dembski argue that we should in fact see the design argument as an instance of 'inference to the best explanation'. An explanation does not need to be an inductive generalization in order to be the best explanation, and there may be only one instance for it to engage with. After all, Hume's argument would militate against scientific investigation of the Big Bang. The scheme of 'inference to the best explanation' indicates that such arguments are competitive; the champion can change with time, circumstances and the arrival of new competitors. Before Darwin, design may have been the best explanation of certain phenomena in living organisms. After Darwin, it may not be. (And of course, if the design argument evolves and improves under the pressure of competition for resources and wins out in natural selection, and Darwinian theories stumble, it could in theory become the best current explanation again.)

Wolfson tells us that the design argument, when it was used by Jewish philosophers, was not used to prove the existence of God:

> *It was used either as a reinforcement of the cosmological argument from creation or as evidence of divine goodness, unity, intelligence, and the like, after existence had already been demonstrated on some other ground. Baḥya introduces the argument from design as a refutation of those who 'had maintained that the world came into being by accident'. The allusion is no doubt to the Epicurean view, which, unlike admitting a temporal beginning of the world, denied the*

existence of a Creator, explaining the origin of the world as the result of the interaction of blind mechanical forces. The argument is thus used by Baḥya in conjunction with creation; in no way does he attempt to prove thereby the existence of God if the world were assumed to be eternal. Likewise Judah ha-Levi makes the argument dependent upon creation, proving thereby, after having shown that the world was created and that consequently there must be a Creator, that creation was an act of wisdom and will and justice and not merely that of blind chance and accident. Averroës and Maimonides, too, use design as evidence of divine knowledge, unity, and the purposiveness of creation. Joseph Albo puts the situation in a nutshell when he says something to the effect that the act of creation itself proves the existence of God; the fact that creation was performed after a certain manner proves that it was an act of purpose and forethought.[9]

Analogies of agency

William Paley put forward one of the most famous versions of the Design argument in the West.[10] If in the desert we find a rock, we may reasonably suppose it to have come there by chance. If we find a watch, however, we cannot reasonably account for it in this way. It is utterly implausible to suppose it has come into existence there by chance and natural forces; it is obviously designed and created with intention, for a particular purpose. We are obliged to postulate an intelligent mind to account for it. The world is as complex a mechanism and as manifestly designed as any watch; therefore it too must have been designed. Paley develops much cumulative evidence by pointing to the complexity of phenomena such as the planets, the brain, the eye. He argues that it would not weaken the inference if we had never seen the watch before; or if it doesn't always work perfectly; or if there were some parts whose function we could not discern.

The analogy of agency was also used by al-Kindī, who writes:

> In the order of this world, in its structure . . . in the mutual action and interdependence of its parts . . . and in the perfection of its constitution, to the effect of the most suitable condition for everything, there is the greatest proof for the most exact organisation and for the most perfect wisdom. Organisation and wisdom need, by necessity, a wise organiser on the basis of logical correlation.[11] . . . Just as the visible signs of the designed order in the human body cannot be without an invisible designer, so the signs of designed order in the Universe cannot be without a designer who is 'Allah.[12]

Hume's character Philo in his *Dialogues*, the most famous critic of this argument, wouldn't allow an analogy at all between the world and things that are designed and produced. The world is in fact so dissimilar to 'houses, ships, furniture, machines', he claims, that 'the great disproportion bars all comparison and inference'. One might as well say that the world is like a vast vegetable or crustacean, Philo objects. We won't wait for an answer, far from obvious, to the question: In which respects does the world resembles a giant lobster? For the point is made less as a piece of rhetoric and more like a logical argument by the Buddhist critics of Nyāya arguments, Dharmakīrti and Śāntarakṣīta. They claim that insufficient grounds are given for claiming that there is a strong analogy between things that are made and things in nature; a jar and a tree. The fact that both are formed by a conjunction of parts is not enough. We have not seen instances of trees being made as we have with pots. We can see instances of houses being made by human agents, and infer that temples are also made by human agents; but we cannot infer that therefore hills are too. Nyāya thinkers cannot validly move from the 'parts' to the 'whole' in the way that they do. Mere 'conjunction of parts' is not enough of a similarity to form the valid basis of an analogy between human artefacts and objects in the natural world. The fact that jars and trees may have some qualities in common is insufficient. Otherwise we could infer, from the fact that we observe potters making pots, that anthills are also made by potters because they too are orderly arrangements of soil. The Nyāya philosopher Vācaspati develops a portfolio of subtle and complex arguments in response; but also pithily observes: we cannot infer that a potter makes an anthill, but we can correctly infer that *someone* does. That is the nature of the Nyāya arguments.

Can this argument prove the existence of the God that the theist believes in? 'Philo' claims it cannot. The cause must be proportionate to the effect. Otherwise, we open the door to groundless and boundless speculation. But then, we are not entitled to predicate either perfection or infinity to the Creator, since experience does not show the world to be either perfect or infinite. The same is true of the other attributes: simplicity, unity, immutability, etc. All that can be conceded is:

> *A man who follows your hypothesis is able, perhaps, to assert, or conjecture, that the universe, some time, arose from something like design: But beyond that position he cannot ascertain one single circumstance, and is left afterwards to fix every point of his theology, by the utmost licence of fancy and hypothesis. This world, for aught he knows, is very faulty and imperfect, compared to a superior standard; and was only the first rude essay of some infant Deity, who afterwards abandoned it, ashamed of his lame performance; it is the*

> *work only of some dependent, inferior Deity; and is the object of derision to his superiors: it is the production of old age and dotage in some superannuated Deity; and ever since his death, has run on at adventures, from the first impulse and active force, which it received from him.*[13]

The world could have been put together by a Demiurge; the 'end' of natural things could be provided by some finite intelligent creature. Flew suggests:

> *The result of such calculations could, I am prepared to allow, provide some premises for an argument to construction by some immensely powerful yet nevertheless still finite and limited Fabricator – a Being out of the same stable as the Demiurge of Plato's* Timaeus.[14]

Again, the Buddhist critics went after this weak spot with arguments on the lack of parity that are tighter, more technical and more focused than the looser rhetoric of Hume's Philo. In particular, they home in on the concept of the agent who is inferred. The Buddhists were quite happy, as Dharmakīrti points out, to allow the inference that the world is produced by an intelligent agent, for the Buddhist too believes that something unseen, not material causes, produces the world of our experience (our own minds for example). The problem is in arguing that this agent must be eternal and changeless. To cause something produces a change in the agent: to be first a non-cause and then a cause entails a change. So God cannot be both changeless and the cause of the universe.

Further, as Śāntarakṣīta and Kamalaśīla point out, we have no other examples of an omniscient creator. How can we then argue that there is an invariable concomitance in acts of creation by omniscient agents? Nyāya thinkers such as Vācaspati Miśra however boldly infer attributes of the creator from aspects of the creation. The creation is so vast and diverse it could not have been produced by any but an omniscient agent, they claim.

Order, function and their implications

Why is it then that people observe the world and think that it must have been created – that it must have been designed? Because, some claim, it exhibits certain features that seem unlikely if the universe was the result of a random process or mindless cause. Hume's character 'Philo' put his finger on one of these features when he asked: Can you infer 'design' from 'order'? The universe may be *orderly*, but it requires a further argument to prove that it is therefore *designed*, by a conscious and intelligent mind. Order could have arisen by chance. It is not enough to point to the ordered state of the universe; any universe must be stable and coherent in order to exist. 'It is vain, therefore, to insist upon the uses of the parts in animals or vegetables, and their curious adjustment to each other. I would fain know how an animal could subsist, unless its parts were so adjusted?' 'Philo' suggested the 'Epicurean hypothesis': that the universe consists in finite atoms moving about at random. If any possible combination of these atoms constitutes a self-maintaining order it is inevitable that in infinite time they will sooner or later fall into this combination – and once there, stick.

Anyway, 'Philo' wonders, how are we entitled to claim 'intelligence' as the principle behind the universe? 'Thought, design, intelligence is no more than one of the springs and principles of the universe', and it is illegitimate 'to take the operations of one part of nature upon another for the foundation of our judgment concerning the origin of the whole'. Indeed, it is dubious to 'selcct so minute, so weak, so bounded a principle as the reason and design of animals is found to be upon this planet' for the source of all order. 'What peculiar privilege has this little agitation of the brain which we call thought, that we must thus make it the model of the whole universe?' This is an illusion springing from 'our partiality in our own favour', which 'sound philosophy ought carefully to guard against'.[15]

However, even some modern scientists cannot renounce the perception that some kinds of organization just seem too wondrous to be the products of chance.

The physicist Paul Davies writes:

> *You might be tempted to suppose that any old rag-bag of laws would produce a complex universe of some sort, with attendant inhabitants convinced of their own specialness. Not so. It turns out that randomly selected laws lead almost always either to unrelieved chaos or boring and uneventful simplicity. Our own universe is poised exquisitely between these unpalatable alternatives, offering a potent mix of freedom and discipline, a sort of restrained creativity. The laws do not tie down physical systems so rigidly that they can accomplish little, nor are they a recipe for cosmic anarchy. Instead, they encourage matter and energy to develop along pathways of evolution that lead to novel variety, what Freeman Dyson has called the principle of maximum diversity: that in some sense we live in the most interesting possible universe.*
>
> *Scientists have recently identified a regime dubbed 'the edge of chaos,' a description that certainly characterizes living organisms, where innovation and novelty combine with coherence and co-operation. The edge of chaos seems to imply the sort of lawful freedom I have just described. Mathematical studies suggest that to engineer such a state of affairs requires laws of a very special form. If*

we could twiddle a knob and change the existing laws, even very slightly, the chances are that the Universe as we know it would fall apart, descending into chaos. Certainly the existence of life as we know it, and even of less elaborate systems such as stable stars, would be threatened by just the tiniest change in the strengths of the fundamental forces, for example. The laws that characterize our actual universe, as opposed to an infinite number of alternative possible universes, seem almost contrived – fine-tuned some commentators have claimed – so that life and consciousness may emerge. To quote Dyson again: it is almost as if 'the universe knew we were coming.' I can't prove to you that that is design, but whatever it is it is certainly very clever!

Now some of my colleagues embrace the same scientific facts as I, but deny any deeper significance. They shrug aside the breathtaking ingenuity of the laws of physics, the extraordinary felicity of nature, and the surprising intelligibility of the physical world, accepting these things as a package of marvels that just happens to be. But I cannot do this. To me, the contrived nature of physical existence is just too fantastic for me to take on board as simply 'given'. It points forcefully to a deeper underlying meaning to existence. Some call it purpose, some design. These loaded words, which derive from human categories, capture only imperfectly what it is the Universe is about. But it is about something, I have absolutely no doubt.[16]

One feature that has led people to suggest that a part of the world exhibits 'design' is function – that fact that some things seem so suited to their apparent tasks that their form and function seem purposive. One reason Darwin's theory of evolution had such a deconstructive impact on design arguments is that he gave an alternative explanation of how even very complex biological systems or functions could have arisen by chance; originally at random and then accelerated in a particular direction by natural selection. Some highly complex phenomena, however, seemed to hold out against such explanation, such as the eye. However, in more recent times the biologist Richard Dawkins in a series of highly accessible and popular works has set out an argument for how even highly complicated things could have arisen by chance: step by step, so long as there is sufficient time postulated for this evolution.[17]

Astonishingly, to its critics, this never-say-die argument not merely lives on but has taken on a renewed vigour in precisely its most contentious arena: biology and evolution. The biochemist Michael Behe has bravely taken on Darwin and reformulated the biological version of the Design Argument.[18] His argument from 'intelligent design' is restricted in scope compared to its predecessors in history, for it only seeks to argue for an 'intelligent' designer, not an omnipotent, omniscient, omnibenevolent one – in other words, not the familiar God of the theists. However, he maintains, it is all the more resilient for it because he is burdened with less baggage – less burden of proof – than Paley. Moreover, Behe insists, it is a scientific theory, not a theological one (although it has theological implications) because it uses physical data, not religious, to justify itself.

Darwin himself suggested that the way to falsify his theory was to find any complex organ that could not have arisen from 'numerous, successive, slight modifications'. As we have seen, Dawkins has shown how such a process might work in specific cases. Behe argues that what one needs to find is a system that is 'irreducibly complex' – in other words, a single system which is composed of several well-matched, interacting parts that contribute to the basic function, and where the removal of any one of the parts causes the system to effectively cease functioning.[19]

In other words, an irreducibly complex thing is something complicated, with different elements, but you cannot reduce it down to something a little simpler and have it still work. Take away one of its many parts and it is not that it functions less well; rather it does not function at all. All the different parts need to be there together simultaneously from the beginning in order to have the item work. You couldn't have the others hanging about performing their function while waiting for the last member to evolve by blind chance and finally turn up. They couldn't be doing anything while their missing member was as yet non-existent.

A bicycle might be one example of something irreducibly complex; if you tried to simplify it by removing any one of its fundamental parts (wheel, chain, frame) none of the other parts would function without it. Behe argues that irreducibly complex things 'are headaches for Darwinian theory, because they are resistant to being produced in the gradual, step-by-step manner that Darwin envisioned'.[20] Something irreducibly complex is without a function as long as one of its parts is missing. Natural selection therefore cannot produce such a system gradually, each part evolving in its own time, one by one. They would have no function until the gang was all together, and if they are non-functional there is nothing for natural selection to be getting on with, for it can only select functioning systems. In his various writings, Behe gives examples from biology of phenomena that are irreducibly complex, and therefore which (he argues) resist Darwinian explanation for their origin. This undermines Darwin's evolutionary theory for *some* phenomena, and as long as *some* phenomena in the natural world cannot be explained by evolution and show signs of design, Behe reckons he has done his work.

Now there is a problem with this. What if, before bicycles were invented, the wheels and chains existed doing other things (rolling carts, restricting prisoners) before the frame came along? If the different components have *other* jobs to do before they do a job together, they could evolve separately, and once the new part joins them, they have a great new idea to do together and change their function. Imagine a human team brought together by the employer for a specific project, each with a unique and necessary role. The team can't exist and do their project before they are all assembled; and if any one of them goes, the project falls apart and they can't work. But if they were seconded to the team from different roles, it is clear that they could all have been employed doing other things and progressed along different paths until they were brought together to do something new and irreducibly complex.[21] So Behe's claims of irreducible complexity may be real, but do not justify the assertion that individual parts of an irreducibly complex system must be without function prior to their involvement in a system. If that is so it seriously weakens Behe's inference to design, as evolution and natural selection still seem able to account for everything.

The Nyāya thinker Uddyotakara almost seems to engage with this point, or at least a related one. He refutes certain Vaiśeṣika theists, as well as those such as Sāṃkhya philosophers who believe that prime matter is the source of the universe, without an intelligent agent. According to Uddyotakara, if atoms act, then as they always exist, they should always act. But if at some point in time they act differently or particularly, then another agent – an intelligent agent – is necessary to make them act.[22] Whether an intelligent Boss is necessary to redefine elements' job descriptions, or whether they can fall into these new roles without intelligence, design, or teleology, is precisely the point at issue.

Determination and design

One contribution made by the Islamic thinkers to the arguments from creation is a principle known variously as the principle of determination or principle of particularization. Given that the universe could have come into being at any time, given that any number of different possible universes could have arisen, there must be some reason/cause for *this* particular universe coming into being at *this* particular time. To use the Islamic image, something had to 'tip the scales' in one direction rather than another. This concept of God as the one who determines is a distinct notion from the idea of a cause, creator, actualizer, or prime mover. This style of argument finds examples in the universe where one alternative has come into being rather than another possible one, and argues that this determining implies an agent performing the selection.

This pattern of argument can be applied to different aspects of the universe and its existence. Determination arguments can focus on the beginning of the world, and thus be inextricable from arguments for the world's temporality against its putative eternity. Alternatively these arguments can focus on contingency and thus resemble cosmological arguments of that nature. Determination arguments can be applied to the very existence of the universe: something had to tip the scales to bring the world into being at all. Thus al-Ghazālī, al-Rāzī, al-Baqillānī and Ījī all argue that the selection of the existence of the world over its non-existence demands an explanation in the form of a determining agent. Something possible, or contingent, as the world is, can only come into being if some agent 'tips the scales' in favour of its existence.[23] As Leibniz observed in his European context, it needs someone intelligent to fix on one of the possibilities.[24]

Or they can centre on the fact that particular qualities exist in contingent beings which are unable to determine these for themselves. Islamic thinkers applied this argument to every individual thing: the coming into being of each of which required such an explanation. Muāmmār, Baqillānī and Juwaynī, for example, argued that many features of the universe could have been otherwise, and that natural forces and laws cannot explain why they have realized the options that they have. An agent is necessary to explain the selection or actualization of certain possible qualities and not others. Ash'arīte thinking, picking up Qur'ānic themes, argues that the transformations of the world – from sperm to embryo to man, for example – require an 'agent of transformation' for their explanation.[25] This is clearly dependent on a particular strand of Ash'arīte thinking, which denies any natural causation at all and sees God as the creator and enactor of all.[26]

Ibn Rushd identifies two premises in this argument. The first is that the world and all that it contains might have had different characteristics than it has; while the second is that an agent must therefore be responsible. Ibn Rushd admits neither premise. As far as the first is concerned, it cannot be assumed that particular attributes, qualities or states of affairs could have been otherwise. Perhaps some form of necessity has operated in the natural world. There may therefore be no need for a selecting or determining agent. Moreover, an agent who is eternal, and whose will is eternal, might not have particularized creation at a specific point in time.

With typical perspicacity, Maimonides identifies a further premise that lies behind this argument, indeed, behind what he characterizes as Mutakallimūn thinking as a whole. It is a notion of possibility as that which can be imagined – whether it can be found in reality or not; whereas the impossible is that which is inconceivable: 'Thus it has already been made clear that that which can be imagined is, according to them, something possible, whether something existent corresponds to it or not. On the other hand, everything that cannot be imagined is impossible.'[27] He complains that they apply this way of thinking to 'the whole world', 'and they say this without paying attention to the correspondence or lack of correspondence of that which exists to their assumptions'; as a criterion for what is possible, reality is disregarded in favour of what can be imagined.[28] One wonders what he would have made of possible worlds ontology.

It is clear that this premise identified by Maimonides is one which Ibn Rushd does not share – nor would Spinoza – nor would anyone who believes that there is a high degree of necessity or determinism in the natural world. However, the 'outdated' scientific world view of the determination argument would actually go well with some versions of 'chaos' theory, which even in a godless universe allows for an element of indeterminacy. It therefore has a curious affinity with aspects of Process thought, or suggestions such as Keith Ward's that God acts in the world at quantum level to determine what otherwise would be undetermined.

Islamic thinkers also used this argument from determination to deal specifically with the question of the time at which the universe came into being. Al-Juwaynī argued: 'If the temporality of the world is established and if it is established that it has a beginning, since the temporal can equally exist or not exist, reason requires that it must have a determinant who determined its actual existence.'[29] The determinant is God. Māturīdī argued that if the world came into being spontaneously, no one time would have been more suitable than any other. The fact that the world came into existence at a given time proves that an agent must have been responsible for fixing that time.[30] Maimonides observed that this was no use at all against one who believes in the eternity of the universe. The question of who tipped the scales to bring the universe into existence can only be asked by one who believes that the universe came into existence. But this precisely is a disputed point – then, among Islamic thinkers, as now, among scientists. If one believes the universe had no beginning, such an argument carries no weight. 'For the adversary who believes in the eternity of the world is of the opinion that our imagining its non-existence is similar to our imagining any impossible thing whatever that occurs to the imagination.'[31]

These Islamic arguments foreshadow an interesting new turn in Western design arguments, which is to suggest that the fundamental physical constraints under which the universe came to be seem to be so 'finely tuned' that it is improbable that this life-permitting universe could have arisen by chance. The physicist Paul Davies writes:

> Some scientists have tried to argue that if only we knew enough about the laws of physics, if we were to discover a final theory that united all the fundamental forces and particles of nature into a single mathematical scheme, then we would find that this superlaw, or theory of everything, would describe the only logically consistent world. In other words, the nature of the physical world would be entirely a consequence of logical and mathematical necessity. There would be no choice about it. I think this is demonstrably wrong. There is not a

shred of evidence that the Universe is logically necessary. Indeed, as a theoretical physicist I find it rather easy to imagine alternative universes that are logically consistent, and therefore equal contenders for reality.[32]

If the Cosmological Argument based itself on the simple fact that the world exists, new versions of the design argument that trade in cosmology focus on *what makes it possible* for the world to exist. Early in the twentieth century, F. R. Tennant embraced evolutionary theory into a new version of the design argument, taking as his fundamental datum the very fact that the world is one fit to set the conditions for the evolution of life.

No explanation is contained in the assertion that the world is an organic whole and consequently involves adaptiveness. That is only a re-statement of the occult and wondrous fact that cries for explanation. The world's 'thusness' is explained, however, if it be attributed to the design and creativeness of a Being whose purpose is, or includes, the realisation of moral values. Further back than a creative Spirit it is neither needful nor possible to go.[33]

Science has of course become much more sophisticated in the last one hundred years, but that has only fuelled cosmological versions of the design argument. Paul Davies argues:

The evidence suggests that in its primordial phase the Universe was in a highly simple, almost featureless state: perhaps a uniform soup of subatomic particles, or even just expanding empty space. All the richness and diversity of matter and energy we observe today has emerged since the beginning in a long and complicated sequence of self-organizing physical processes. What an incredible thing these laws of physics are! Not only do they permit a universe to originate spontaneously; they also encourage it to self-organize and self-complexify to the point where conscious beings emerge, and can look back on the great cosmic drama and reflect on what it all means.

Now you may think I have written God entirely out of the picture. Who needs a God when the laws of physics can do such a splendid job? But we are bound to return to that burning question: Where do the laws of physics come from? And why *those* laws rather then some other set? Most especially: Why a set of laws that drives the searing, featureless gases coughed out of the Big Bang towards life and consciousness and intelligence and cultural activities such as religion, art, mathematics, science?[34]

Recent proponents of this argument include John Leslie, William Lane Craig and William Dembski. Just as 'irreducible complexity' signals a new initiative in the biological wing of the design argument, 'fine-tuning' is the slogan for new thinking on design on the macro level, the origin of the universe.

> The scientific community has been stunned by its discovery of how complex and sensitive a nexus of conditions must be given in order for the Universe to permit the origin and evolution of intelligent life. The Universe appears, in fact, to have been incredibly fine-tuned from the moment of its inception for the production of intelligent life.[35]

The 'fine-tuning' version of the design argument needs to give us grounds for thinking that the best explanation for that is intelligent design, rather than the randomness of chance. The core strategy is to emphasize just how improbable is the state of cosmological affairs that gives rise to life. If possible, it might also help to cut out the possibility of rival explanations: sheer chance, or some kind of physical necessity (as Ibn Rushd suggested so long ago as an explanation for how physical things are). However – given the resilience of religious believers when they are determined to keep believing – if the universe were such that *only this* life-permitting universe were possible, that paradoxically might be taken by some to be a strong reason for believing in a creator God.

William Lane Craig, using ideas from Dembski, outlines the argument like this:

1. One learns that the physical constants and quantities given in the Big Bang possess certain values.

2. Examining the circumstances under which the Big Bang occurred, one finds that there is no theory that would render physically necessary the values of all the constants and quantities, so they must be attributed to sheer accident.

3. One discovers that the values of the constants and quantities are fantastically fine-tined for the existence of intelligent, carbon-based life.

4. The probability of each value and of all the values together occurring by chance is vanishingly small.

5. There is only one universe; it is illicit in the absence of evidence to multiply one's probabilistic resources (i.e. postulate a World Ensemble of universes) simply to avert the design inference.

6. Given that the universe has occurred only once, the probability that the constants and quantities all possess the values they do remains vanishingly small.

7. This probability is well within the bounds needed to eliminate chance.[36]

8. One has physical information concerning the necessary conditions for intelligent, carbon-based life (e.g. a certain temperature range, the existence of certain elements, certain gravitational and electromagnetic forces, etc.)

9. This information about the finely tuned conditions requisite for a life-permitting universe is independent of the pattern discerned in step 3.

10. One is 'warranted in inferring' that the physical constants and quantities given in the Big Bang are not the result of chance.[37]

One way that critics of the argument have countered the appearance of overwhelming improbability in the existence of *this* universe is to suggest that maybe lots of universes exist (a 'multiverse' or many-worlds hypothesis). An outstanding no-trumps hand for bridge, randomly dealt, may be somewhat improbable. However, if a million hands were dealt, we would rather be surprised if such a hand never turned up. Or as Cambridge cosmologist Martin Rees puts it succinctly, if a shop has a huge stock of ready-to-wear suits, we are not surprised to find one that fits us. Similarly, if our universe is just one in a multiverse of many universes, its apparent fine-tuning turning up on one occasion is not so surprising.[38]

Since an observation first made by Ian Hacking, defenders of fine-tuning, such as Craig, Mellor or White, suggest that this is a form of the Gambler's Fallacy.[39] The odds of throwing double sixes when throwing a pair of dice is one in 36. Knowing this, if a gambler throws the dice 35 times and never gets a double six, he is inclined to think 'It's *bound* to be a double six *this* time!' If a woman has had six girls and is pregnant again, her friends and family are likely to think that this time, it's got to be a boy. But the odds against double sixes are 36 to one for every throw, no matter what has been thrown before; the dice have neither a memory nor a sense of fairness. So as far as the multiverse is concerned, say fine-tuning believers, the existence of lots of other universes with different universal constants that don't give rise to life don't actually give a higher probability to this one existing.[40] Anything improbable could be rendered probable if you multiply the number of opportunities. Now if the gambler rolling dice rephrased his belief, he would be right. That is: the chances of rolling a double six *at some time* increase the longer you roll them. That would suggest that if you roll a pair of dice just once you are less likely to roll a double six at least once than if you had a thousand throws.

This could work to your advantage if you intend to cheat at poker. Having deceptively dealt yourself amazingly good hands ten times in a row, you can counter your opponents' suspicions by saying: 'an infinite number of universes exist, so it stands to reason that in one of them a person has this outstanding good luck by pure chance. I'm just so happy that this is that very universe.' See if you get away with it.[41] All the same, Thrush and Manson think that this defence against the multiverse theory is not persuasive. The same argument is not usually applied to other situations where there are a great many replications. For example, the question is not raised by fine-tuners: 'Why is *this* planet uniquely suited to permit life?'[42]

Let us take this statement from a fictional defender of fine-tuning: 'It nevertheless remains surprising that the universe we are in is one that permits life.' Is that true? It has been suggested that it is not at all surprising, as if the universe did not permit life, we would not be here to be impressed at its improbability. This is known as 'the anthropic principle', formulated by Brandon Carter and developed in an influential work by Barrow and Tipler.[43] It unpacks the implications of the 'observational selection effect' proposed by Eddington;[44] when musing on the probability of what you have observed, you have to take into account what your experiment or your equipment allows you to observe. If your fishnets have big holes and you *can* only catch big fish, you can't infer from the fact that you only catch big fish, that there *are* only big fish.

Barrow and Tipler have unpacked the implications of this insight for our problem; and point out that given that we're here, it is not so astonishing that the universe permits life, no matter how finely tuned. Our existence as observers is playing the role of the instruments in the observational selection effect. There could be other universes that are not life-permitting, which would not have students of philosophy of religion to raise the question of the improbability of *their* universe.

> We should emphasize once again that the enormous improbability of the evolution of intelligent life in general and *Homo sapiens* in particular does not mean we should be amazed we exist at all. . . . Only if an intelligent species does evolve is it possible for its members to ask how probable it is for an intelligent species to evolve.[45]

This seems true; but is it a truism? The principle and its use have been highly controversial. Some have distinguished epistemic from physical probability. Craig claims:

> They have confused the *true* claim
>
> 1. if observers who have evolved within a universe observe its fundamental constants and qualities, it is highly probable that they will observe them to be fine-tuned to their existence
>
> with the *false* claim

2. it is highly probable that a universe exists that is finely tuned for the existence of observers who have evolved within it.

An observer who has evolved within a universe should regard it as highly probable that he will find the basic conditions of the universe fine-tuned for his existence; but he should not infer that it is therefore highly probable that such a fine-tuned universe exists.[46]

It is worth asking more precisely what should or should not surprise us. If a large firing squad, well armed with functioning equipment in good light, tries repeatedly and always fails to execute me, should I be surprised to find myself still alive? Most people's intuitions say yes; anthropically principled people and fine-tuning sceptics, as we have seen, say no. But the conflict could perhaps be resolved by unpacking precisely what is and isn't surprising.

I should be surprised to observe that I am alive (because it seems *prima facie* improbable).

I should not be surprised not to observe that I am dead (because if I was dead, I would not be able to observe that fact).

So to say, 'You should not be surprised to find yourself still alive because if you weren't, you couldn't observe it' misses the point. I should not be surprised at not observing that I am dead, true enough. But that does not banish my legitimate surprise at my improbable escape.

What this discussion brings out in my view is less a question of probability than an issue of meaning, or indeed, wonder. What needs explanation? What is surprising? This is what all such arguments hinge on. The chance that I win the British lottery is something like 14 million to 1. It is thus highly improbable. However, more or less every week someone *does* win the lottery. The arguments' defenders' reaction to the existence of the world is like that of the winner of the lottery: given that the probability of this happening is 14 million to 1, it seems like a miracle. To the organizers of the lottery, however, it is an everyday event; and this is the attitude taken by the arguments' critics: *any particular* state of affairs is wildly improbable, but one of them had to be the case. It is improbable that I can toss a coin ten times and get 'tails' each time. But any other pattern is equally improbable. However, the other patterns or possibilities, although statistically equally unlikely, are uninteresting and meaningless to us. Therefore we do not marvel at them and call them improbable.

Probability debates show, if anything, how questionable it is to attempt to quantify or give an objective value or numeration to the existence of the universe as it is, and the fact that we exist. The mathematical calculations are not the point; the point is the significance that the existence of the universe has. Expressions of its improbability are exclamations of wonder; perhaps more doxology than cosmology; but importantly, one in which atheists also can share.

Draw your own conclusions

In principle, can Bayes' Theorem or any way of calculating probability be used to calculate the existence of God?

Is the design argument a 'proof' or an inference to the best explanation?

Is 'design' or 'order' an objective fact about a thing, or our perception, or a way of seeing something which we impose on the object?

Do you find the 'fine-tuning' of the universe persuades you to think that there must be an omniscient creator? Is this persuasion intuitive, a gut reaction, or a logical conclusion?

Can you think of a system that is 'irreducibly complex'? What can you infer from it about design and the purpose of its designer? Will this work as an analogy for a divine creator?

If I say I have had a 'miraculous escape', what do I mean by that? Should I regard it as surprising or self-evident, given my survival?

Do you think the argument works? What do you mean by 'work' here?

Further reading

Behe, M. J. (1998) *Darwin's Black Box: The Biochemical Challenge to Evolution*, New York, Touchstone Books

Davidson, H. A. (1987) *Proofs for Eternity, Creation and the Existence of God in Medieval Islamic and Jewish Philosophy*, New York and Oxford, Oxford University Press

Davies, P. (1983) *God and the New Physics*, London, Dent

Dawkins, R. (1986) *The Blind Watchmaker*, New York, Norton

Dawkins, R. (1995) *A River out of Eden*, New York, Basic Books

Dembski, W. A. (1998) *The Design Inference: Eliminating Chance through Small Probabilities*, Cambridge, Cambridge University Press

Dembski, W. A. (1999) *Intelligent Design: The Bridge Between Science and Theology*, Downers Grove, InterVarsity Press

Everitt, N. (2004) *The Non-Existence of God*, London, Routledge

Hume, D. (1991) *Dialogues Concerning Natural Religion*, in *Dialogues Concerning Natural Religion in Focus*, new edn, ed. Stanley Tweyman, Routledge Philosophers in Focus, London, Routledge

Le Poidevin, R. (1997) *Arguing for Atheism: An Introduction to the Philosophy of Religion*, London, Routledge

Manson, N. A. (2003) *God and Design: The Teleological Argument and Modern Science*, London and New York, Routledge

Sobel, Jordan Howard (2004) *Logic and Theism: Arguments for and Against*

Beliefs in God, Cambridge, Cambridge University Press

Vattanky, J. S. J. (1993) *Development of Nyāya Theism*, New Delhi, Intercultural Publications

Wolfson, H. A. (1973) 'Notes on Proofs of the Existence of God in Jewish Philosophy', in *Studies in the History and Philosophy of Religion*, Cambridge, Mass., Harvard University Press

Yaran, C. S. (2003) *Islamic Thought on the Existence of God: Contributions and Contrasts with Contemporary Western Philosophy of Religion*, Cultural Heritage and Contemporary Change, Series IIA: Islam 16, Washington, D.C., Council for Research in Values and Philosophy

Notes

1 Cited in C. S. Yaran (2003) *Islamic Thought on the Existence of God: Contributions and Contrasts with Contemporary Western Philosophy of Religion*, Cultural Heritage and Contemporary Change Series IIA: Islam 16, Washington, D.C., Council for Research in Values and Philosophy, p. 90.

2 Le Poidevin suggests that Dawkins's selfish gene theory takes the place of a teleological explanation for the atheist (though Dawkins is careful to avoid teleological language). R. Le Poidevin (1997) *Arguing for Atheism: An Introduction to the Philosophy of Religion*, London, Routledge, pp. 62f.

3 R. Dawkins (1986) *The Blind Watchmaker*, New York, Norton.

4 W. A. Dembski (1999) *Intelligent Design: The Bridge Between Science and Theology*, Downers Grove, InterVarsity Press, p. 255.

5 For an introduction to Bayesianism, see C. Howson and P. Urbach (1993) *Scientific Reasoning: The Bayesian Approach*, Chicago, Open Court Press.

6 David Hume (1947 (1779)) *Dialogues concerning Natural Religion*, ed. Norman Kemp Smith, 2nd edn, Edinburgh, Nelson.

7 J. S. J. Vattanky (1993) *Development of Nyāya Theism*, New Delhi, Intercultural Publications, p. 187.

8 For an introduction to this concept see P. Lipton (2004) *Inference to the Best Explanation*, International Library of Philosophy, London and New York, Routledge.

9 H. A. Wolfson (1973) 'Notes on Proofs of the Existence of God in Jewish Philosophy', in *Studies in the History and Philosophy of Religion*, Cambridge, Mass., Harvard University Press, pp. 568–9.

10 W. Paley (1802) *Natural Theology: or, Evidences of the existence and attributes of the deity, collected from the appearances of nature*, London, R. Faulder.

11 Y. q. i. I. al-Kindī (1978) *Rasa'il al-Kindī al-falsafiyah / li-Abi Yusuf Ya'qub ibn Ishaq al-Kindī; The Philosophical Treatises of al-Kindī*, al-Qahirah, Matba'at Hassan, pp. 214–15.

12 al-Kindī, *The Philosophical Treatises*, p. 174.

13 D. Hume (1991) *Dialogues Concerning Natural Religion*, in *Dialogues Concerning Natural Religion in Focus*, new edn, ed. Stanley Tweyman, Routledge Philosophers in Focus, London, Routledge.

14 J. P. Moreland and Kai Nielsen (1993) *Does God Exist? The Debate between Theists and Atheists*, Buffalo, New York, Prometheus Books, p. 163.

15 Hume, *Dialogues Concerning Natural Religion*, new edn, p. 148.

16 P. Davies (2003) 'The Appearance of Design in Physics and Cosmology', in N. A. Manson (ed.), *God and Design: The Teleological Argument and Modern Science*, London and New York, Routledge, p. 152.

17 See for example Dawkins, *The Blind Watchmaker*; and (1995) *A River out of Eden*, New York, Basic Books.

18 M. J. Behe (1998) *Darwin's Black Box: The Biochemical Challenge to Evolution*, New York, Touchstone Books.

19 Behe, *Darwin's Black Box*, p. 39.

20 M. J. Behe (2003) 'The Modern Intelligent Design Hypothesis', in N. A. Manson (ed.), *God and Design: The Teleological Argument and Modern Science*, London and New York, Routledge, p. 280.

21 Kenneth Miller uses the discoveries of Enrique Melendez-Hevia and others on the Krebs cycle to show that something like this could show how Behe's cases of irreducible complexity could have arisen by chance, step by step. K. R. Miller (2003) 'Answering the Biochemical Argument from Design', in N. A. Manson (ed.), *God and Design: The Teleological Argument and Modern Science*, London and New York, Routledge, p. 296.

22 See Vattanky, *Development of Nyāya Theism*, p. 32, Uddyotakara's commentary on the Nyāyasutras.

23 See Davidson for details of these arguments, H. A. Davidson (1987) *Proofs for Eternity, Creation and the Existence of God in Medieval Islamic and Jewish Philosophy*, New York and Oxford, Oxford University Press, p. 162.

24 Leibniz wrote, 'this cause must be intelligent: for this existing world being contingent and an infinity of other worlds being equally possible, and holding, so to say, equal claim to existence with it, the cause of the world must needs have had regard or reference to all these possible in order to fix upon one of them . . . to fix upon one of them can be nothing other than the act of the *will* which chooses.' G. W. von Leibniz (1951) *Theodicy: Essays on the Goodness of God and the Freedom of Man and the Origin of Evil*, E. M. Huggard, Rare Masterpieces of Philosophy and Science, London, Routledge & Kegan Paul, pp. 127–8.

25 M. Fakhry (1994) *Philosophy, Dogma and the Impact of Greek Thought in Islam*, Aldershot, Variorum.

26 Davidson, *Proofs for Eternity, Creation and the Existence of God in Medieval Islamic and Jewish Philosophy*, pp. 177–8.

27 M. Maimonides (1969) *The Guide of the Perplexed*, trans. S. Pines, Chicago and London, University of Chicago Press, I. 73. 113b, p. 207. Maimonides goes on to observe that this premise is only true if nine preceding premises are true.

28 Maimonides, *Guide of the Perplexed*, I. 75. 113a, p. 206.

29 Fakhry, *Philosophy, Dogma and the Impact of Greek Thought in Islam*, p. 140.

30 Davidson, *Proofs for Eternity, Creation and the Existence of God in Medieval Islamic and Jewish Philosophy*, p. 160.

31 Maimonides, *Guide of the Perplexed*, I. 74, p. 220.

32 Davies, 'The Appearance of Design in Physics and Cosmology', p. 148.

33 F. R. Tennant (1928) *Philosophical Theology*, 2 vols, Cambridge, Cambridge University Press, vol. 1, p. 113.

34 Davies, 'The Appearance of Design in Physics and Cosmology', p. 150.

35 W. L. Craig (2003) 'Design and the Anthropic Fine-Tuning of the Universe', in N. A. Manson (ed.), *God and Design: The Teleological Argument and Modern Science*, London and New York, Routledge, p. 155.

36 Dembski has offered a ten-step Generic Chance Elimination Argument to nail down when we can reasonably say something can or cannot have happened by chance. See W. A. Dembski (1998) *The Design Inference: Eliminating Chance through Small Probabilities*, Cambridge, Cambridge University Press, and a brief discussion in Craig, 'Design and the Anthropic Fine-Tuning of the Universe'.

37 Craig, 'Design and the Anthropic Fine-Tuning of the Universe', pp. 164–5.

38 M. Rees (2003) 'Other Universes: A Scientific Perspective', in N. A. Manson (ed.), *God and Design: The Teleological Argument and Modern Science*, London and New York, Routledge, p. 214.

39 Craig, 'Design and the Anthropic Fine-Tuning of the Universe'; I. Hacking (1987) 'The Inverse Gambler's Fallacy: The Argument from Design. The Anthropic Principle Applied to Wheeler's Universes', *Mind* 76; D. H. Mellor (2003) 'Too Many Universes', in N. A. Manson (ed.), *God and Design: The Teleological Argument and Modern Science*, London and New York, Routledge; R. White (2003) 'Fine-Tuning and Multiple Universes', in N. A. Manson (ed.), *God and Design: The Teleological Argument and Modern Science*, London and New York, Routledge.

40 For more on the multiverse, see Rees, 'Other Universes: A Scientific Perspective'; Mellor, 'Too Many Universes'; White, 'Fine-Tuning and Multiple Universes'; and W. A. Dembski (2003) 'The Chance of the Gaps', in N. A. Manson (ed.), *God and Design: The Teleological Argument and Modern Science*, London and New York, Routledge.

41 The example is adapted from Craig, 'Design and the Anthropic Fine-Tuning of the Universe', p. 173. 'The error made by the Many-Worlds Hypothesis is that it multiplies one's probabilistic resources without warrant. If we are allowed to do that, then it seems that *anything* can be explained away.'

42 See the discussion in N. A. Manson (2003) *God and Design: The Teleological Argument and Modern Science*, London and New York, Routledge, pp. 20–1.

43 J. D. Barrow and F. J. Tipler (1986) *The Anthropic Cosmological Principle*, Oxford, Oxford University Press.

44 A. Eddington (1939) *The Philosophy of Physical Science*, Cambridge, Cambridge University Press.

45 Barrow and Tipler, *The Anthropic Cosmological Principle*, p. 566.

46 Craig, 'Design and the Anthropic Fine-Tuning of the Universe', p. 169.

8

Being – and the Alternative

The Ontological Argument is utterly different to its cousins. Unlike the Cosmological and Design Arguments, it is *not* one that the average believer would hit upon intuitively. If the Moral Argument has a certain dull but annoying worthiness to it, the Ontological Argument strikes fresh hearers as decidedly shifty. It is therefore the most provocative of the arguments. Sceptics of the Cosmological Argument can at least, when feeling generous, see why some are naturally taken in by it; but to most of them, the Ontological Argument looks like a deliberate sleight of hand. But even some who think that the Ontological Argument doesn't 'work' (and probably all of those who do) find it sleek, elegant and clever.

The various arguments gathered here under the rubric 'Ontological' all want to argue that God's existence is evident simply from the divine nature, essence or being (hence its name from the Greek *onto-*, referring to being). Its proponents hold that it is self-contradictory to affirm who or what God is and yet to deny that such a God exists. It does not appeal to mere 'probability', as does the Design Argument, but goes for the vitals of deductive certainty. To pull it off would be such a bold feat that it ranks as the Holy Grail of philosophical theists, but a resemblance to puzzles of the 'can you make 4 squares from 6 matchsticks' type hangs over some of its formulations.

The most important, fundamental way that the Ontological Argument differs from its stablemates is its character as an *a priori* argument. As we have seen, the other runners start their races with an empirical (or *a posteriori*) observation – an appeal to our shared experience. The Ontological Argument in contrast launches itself on no such solid earth, but seems to operate in the pure ether of logic; necessity, the definition of concepts and what they entail. The very nature of God, our understanding of the concept (even if we are, in fact, atheists) entails God's existence.

Those medieval thinkers who first formulated it operated with certain presuppositions. The fact that these presuppositions are not so often shared by us today is responsible for the sceptical reaction many have on their first encounter with the Ontological Argument. Medieval philosophers also thought about 'Being' rather differently than most contemporary analytic philosophers. For most philosophers 'existence' simply means a thing is instantiated rather than not. For earlier ages, Being not only *is* something, it is something rich, not minimal. Why this is so important to appreciate, if you want to understand the minds that conceived it rather than just squabble over the Meccano-like structure, will be clear shortly. Another notion that may be unfamiliar is the idea of 'necessary existence'. To possess necessary existence would mean that a thing must exist, could not *not* exist. God's necessary existence is said to have an *absolute* necessity and not the relative kind of necessity pertaining to finite causes (i.e. if *x* happens *y* must happen; but *y* is not an intrinsically necessary event). It is also an *ontological* necessity, pertaining to the being of God; not a *logical* necessity pertaining to our affirmations about God. All this is perhaps another way of saying, as Aquinas does, that in God essence and existence are identical.

Another facet to this 'necessary existence' is elaborated in the idea of God's '*self*-existence' or 'aseity' – that God, unlike us, does not depend on the existence of anything else. Creatures exist *per se* (by or in themselves); God exists *a se* (from or of God's own self). It signifies independence in God's being of anything else, and the notion clearly seems to derive from the conviction of God's transcendence. Although this can seem an abstract idea, not an attribute perhaps which a believer readily warms to in prayer, it became religiously powerful for Thomas Merton one day:

> In this one word, which can be applied to God alone, and which expresses His most characteristic attribute, I discovered an entirely new concept of God – a concept which showed me at once that the belief of Catholics was by no means the vague and rather superstitious hangover from an unscientific age that I had believed it to be. On the contrary, here was a notion of God that was at the same time deep, precise, simple and accurate and, what is more, charged with implications which I could not even begin to appreciate. . . . *Aseitas* – simply means the power of a being to exist absolutely in virtue of itself, not as caused by itself, but as requiring no cause, no other justification for its existence except that its very nature is to exist. There can be only one such Being: That is God. And to say that God exists a se, of and by and by reason of Himself, is merely to say that God is Being Itself. *Ego sum qui sum.* [I am who I am.] And this means that God must enjoy 'complete independence not only as regards everything outside but also as regards everything within Himself.'
>
> This notion made such a profound impression on me that I made a pencil note at the top of the page: 'Aseity of God – God is being *per se*.'[1]

Although Merton associates this concept with Catholicism, it is certainly a fundamental conviction in Indian religious philosophy. Numerous verses in Upaniṣadic texts struggle to express this religious insight about the ultimate; the dependency of the world on it, and its lack of dependence on anything else for its existence. Plotinus also uses the phrase 'self-sufficing' to refer to it.[2]

Before examining the argument in detail, it is worth briefly sketching its history. The fundamental concept really has its origin in a brief argument by Aristotle in his *Physics* and *Metaphysics*. This is that there must be a first source for motion in the world, since an infinite regress of 'movers' is impossible (by motion/movement, *kinesis*, Aristotle means the fulfilment of what exists potentially). After Aristotle, subsequent commentators such as Proclus or Simplicius suggested that Aristotle's bare proof from motion, in itself a slim entity, implied the proof of a cause of the existence of the physical universe itself.[3] Ibn Sīnā picks up an observation, almost a throwaway line, from Aristotle's *Metaphysics* – that the unmoved mover can in no way be otherwise than it is, that it is something that exists from necessity – and suggests (as Ibn Rushd did after him) that the proof from motion, which has become the 'Cosmological Argument', implies – but does not by itself provide – a further and more fundamental proof.

Ibn Sīnā describes his proof of the first cause of the universe as a 'metaphysical' proof. He distinguishes two kinds of proofs: one which examines nothing but existence itself, and derives its proof from the nature of existence in general; and another which derives proof of God's existence not from the generality of existence itself but from a particular part of it: creation. In short, he distinguishes what we, since Kant, call 'ontological' from 'cosmological' proofs.

Ibn Sīnā distinguishes between 'possibly existent' and 'necessarily existent'. The latter he further subdivides: what is 'necessarily existent by virtue of another and possibly existent by virtue of itself', vs. what is 'necessarily existent by virtue of itself'. The former kind of thing or being could conceivably not exist; but becomes 'necessary' when caused to exist. So, for example, 'combustion' may or may not occur; but when a match is tossed into kerosene it necessarily occurs. The kerosene, the match or 'combustion' do not have a choice in the matter.

For Ibn Sīnā all the things that exist are necessary. *Either* a thing is 'necessarily existent by virtue of another and possibly existent by virtue of itself', or else it is 'necessarily existent by virtue of itself'. Something that is hanging around being merely possible cannot come into existence. You cannot imagine that it could come into existence by an external agent permitting but not requiring it to exist, and after which it just *chooses* to exist; for nothing can cause itself. If something *causes* it to exist, it becomes necessary and not merely possible. So *if* something exists, it became necessary at some point. Therefore everything that exists is necessary; the question is whether it is made necessary by external causation or whether it is 'necessarily existent by virtue of itself'. Properly speaking, such things as horses or trains or you yourself are *necessarily* existent once they exist, and *impossible* until that point. So the live difference is really between what only becomes necessary by the power or causality of another, and what is necessary by virtue of its own self. Here we can see this concept's relation to the Islamic arguments for 'particularization', examined in the previous two chapters; that something needs to be the determining cause to bring a merely possible thing into existence.

Ibn Sīnā's careful formulation 'necessarily existent by virtue of itself', especially given the idea that other contingent things can come to exist necessarily, is not the same as logical necessity. It is not the same as saying 'existence is part of the concept or definition of God, therefore necessarily, God exists'. What Ibn Sīnā does *not* do is to unpack the concept of 'necessarily existent by virtue of itself' into an ontological argument. What he does instead is to explore the other category of being – what is only necessary by virtue of another, being merely possible in virtue of itself – and use *that* to establish the necessity of one who is necessarily existent by virtue of itself. In other words, he constructs a kind of cosmological argument, one which is a clear forerunner of Aquinas's Third Way. For things that are necessary by virtue of another cannot cause themselves. Even if some cause others, and you add them up to a totality, still the totality must be either necessary or possible by virtue of itself. It cannot be necessary, for these things we are talking about are the things that are *possible* by virtue of themselves. Therefore, Ibn Sīnā claims, they must be possible, but if so the *totality* of things unable to cause themselves are as unable to cause themselves as a single thing. So the totality of all that exists, even if individual things are causing other individual things, must be caused by another. (Ibn Sīnā thinks there can be no infinite regress of finite causes.) So if anything exists, there must be something necessarily existent by virtue of itself. As this is really a cosmological argument, very like that of Maimonides and Thomas, we will not consider it further here.[4]

The hybridity (from our perspective) of Ibn Sīnā's argument means that it was taken in different directions by those who followed him. The very concept of something that necessarily exists of itself is a profound legacy to leave for those who would later construct the Ontological Argument from it. Other strands were disentangled and taken up into cosmological arguments by other thinkers, Islamic, Jewish and Christian.

From the idea of 'necessarily existent by virtue of itself', Ibn Sīnā can conjure forth the essential attributes of the Deity, as had al-Fārābī before him. 'Necessary Existence' for Ibn Sīnā then is not a bare proof but the foundation for a more systematic theology of the divine. He develops it from remarks in Aristotle – that a necessary being cannot have more states than one and must be 'simple', that its role as unmoved mover means it must be eternal and immovable. In Proclus' analysis, such a being must also be self-sufficient, self-subsistent and indestructible. Al-Fārābī adds to this chain of deduced attributes that it must not be caused by anything and must not be divisible. And there can only be one. As the First, it must be immaterial and pure intellect, Truth itself, of the greatest beauty, enjoying the highest conceivable pleasure and being the prime object of love and desire.[5] Ibn Sīnā conducts a similar analysis, adding goodness to al-Fārābī's list.

In Islamic metaphysics this tradition continues into the present century, as seen in Ṭabāṭabā'ī's metaphysics. From his initial (very brief) proof of the necessarily-existing-by-itself he provides proofs of its unity and simplicity. He then provides proofs that the Necessary Being is the source of every being and every existential perfection.[6] From this he goes on to give an account of the attributes of the Necessary Being.

Dissenting from this tradition, al-Ghazālī maintained against Ibn Sīnā that the attributes of God could not be analysed from his concept of 'necessarily existent by virtue of itself'. At best, he claimed, these arguments establish the termination of the regress and nothing more. But the Islamic thinkers who used such arguments saw the need to add to the minimal Cosmological Argument further arguments for the unity and the incorporeality of this First Cause. These connect the concept of First Cause (operative in the Cosmological Arguments) with that of Necessary Existence (operative also in the Ontological Argument); but also with the other 'attributes' of God.

Although there are important forerunners such as Ibn Sīnā who contribute key moves and concepts, most see Anselm of Canterbury as the first proposer of an ontological argument, while he was prior of the Abbey of Bec in Normandy. The first work for which we know him, *Monologion*, is a philosophical meditation on the Christian understanding of God, written in 1077. He wrote *Proslogion* in 1078 when he discovered a more streamlined and elegant approach, starting from a single premise from which to unpack not only the nature but also the very existence of God. What is taken by later readers as the Ontological Argument appears in chapters 2 and 3. Briefly, he notes that in Psalm 14, 'the fool says in his heart there is no God'. But even 'the fool', i.e. even an atheist who does not believe that God exists, can still understand the concept. The concept Anselm chooses to use to signify God is 'that than which nothing greater can be conceived'. An imagined God that exists only in the mind is not as great as one which exists in reality. So the God who doesn't exist isn't 'that than which nothing greater can be conceived'. The God who exists in reality is. Second (chapter 3), it is greater to be something that cannot *not* exist than to be something merely possible. A merely possible God is not 'that than which nothing greater can be conceived' either. So God who exists in reality is that than which nothing greater can be conceived.

These arguments came in for criticism immediately by another monk, Gaunilo, in *On Behalf of the Fool.* Discussion and criticism was lively throughout medieval times, with Alexander of Hales, William of Auxerre, Richard Fishacre, Bonaventure, Duns Scotus accepting it, others, such as Gaunilo or Thomas Aquinas, offering significant criticism or rejecting it outright.

After a brief lull, the Ontological Argument returned with the work of René Descartes, who put forward in his *Meditations* a simpler version than Anselm's. (It is unclear whether Descartes knew Anselm's.) Naturally, criticism revived again immediately, with detractors (Gassendi, Berkeley, Locke, Hume, Kant) and supporters who defended or reformulated it (Leibniz, Malebranche, Spinoza, Baumgarten, Wolff). Kant's refutation had such force that the Ontological Argument wilted again, briefly if bizarrely finding favour in a *jeu d'esprit* of Russell, who had to admit it worked.[7] It could hardly flourish in the atmosphere of Logical Positivism in the twentieth century, being as deeply unfashionable as a philosophical argument could be. And yet being odious can be a very good way of getting attention, and at least the Ontological Argument was not neglected. Even its critics just couldn't leave it alone. With the development of analytic philosophy of religion came renewed interest in medieval philosophical theology in the English-speaking world (in the German-speaking world, attention from Karl Barth meant that it was thought worthy of examination). This, combined with developments in modal logic, meant that the Ontological Argument was dusted off, found fascinating once more, and redesigned by Hartshorne, Malcom and Plantinga, and most extraordinarily by the mathematician Kurt Gödel. It has even come to life again in the Islamic world in the thinking of the political Islamist Mohammed Abduh.[8]

What is the Ontological Argument?

Different arguments labelled as 'ontological' are often lumped together; so too are criticisms commonly made of them. The arguments are different and a criticism tellingly made of one may not afflict another version in the same way, and this is not always made clear. Often the contemporary discussion is handled as if Kant is criticizing Anselm – the more historically aware imagine Kant's target is Descartes – but in fact it is Baumgarten, whom you may never have heard of. Specific formulations have specific weaknesses and invulnerabilities and it requires sensitivity to sort them out.

Descartes' statement of the Ontological Argument is the simplest. Existence is part of the concept of a supremely perfect being; therefore necessarily (as an analytic truth) a supreme being possesses existence. In other words, necessarily, God exists.

A triangle may or may not exist; but if it does, it will have three sides and three angles. One thing has got to be true of a triangle – that it has three sides, because that is an indispensable part of the definition of a triangle. Descartes is treating God's existence like the three-sidedness of a triangle. In an analogous way to the triangle, one thing has got to be true of God: that God exists; because that is an indispensable part of the definition of a supremely perfect being.

Descartes' Fifth Meditation:

. . . For example, when I imagine a triangle, even though there may perhaps be no such figure anywhere in the world outside of my thought, nor ever have been, nevertheless the figure cannot help having a certain determinate nature, or form . . . which I have not invented and which does not in any way depend on my mind. This is evidenced by the fact that we can demonstrate various properties of this triangle. . . . Whether I wish it or not, I recognize clearly and evidently that these are properties of the triangle, even though I had never previously thought of them in any way when I first imagined one. And therefore it cannot be said that I had imagined or invented them.

. . . Now, if from the very fact that I can derive from my thoughts the idea of something, it follows that all that I clearly and distinctly recognize as characteristic of this thing does in reality characterize it, can I not derive from this an argument which will demonstrably prove the existence of God? It is certain that I find in my mind the idea of God, of a supremely perfect Being, no less than that of any shape or number whatsoever; and I recognize that an actual and eternal existence belongs to his nature no less clearly and distinctly than I recognize that all I can demonstrate about some figure or number actually belongs to the nature of that figure or number. . . . The existence of God should pass in my mind as at least as certain as I have hitherto considered all the truths of mathematics, which deals only with numbers and figures.

And this is true even though I must admit that it does not at first appear entirely obvious, but seems to have some appearance of sophistry. For since in all other matters I have learned to make a distinction between essence and existence, I am easily convinced that the existence of God can be separated from his essence, and

> *thus I can conceive of God as not actually existing. Nevertheless, when I consider this with more attention, I find it manifest that we can no more separate the existence of God from his essence than we can separate from the essence of a rectilinear triangle the fact that the size of its three angles equals two right angles, or from the idea of a mountain the idea of a valley. Thus it is no less self-contradictory to conceive of a God, a supremely perfect Being who lacks existence – that is, who lacks some perfection – than it is to conceive of a mountain for which there is no valley.*

What, if anything, is wrong with this argument?

First of all, you may be unhappy that it seems somehow to beg the question, or that it seems circular. An argument might be said to beg the question if it *assumes* what it is claiming to *prove*; the conclusion is an illegal stowaway in the premises. The Ontological Argument seems to some to be obviously guilty of this charge, as God's existence seems clearly to be smuggled into the definition of God as a supremely perfect being.

Actually it is harder than you might think to make this charge stick. All valid arguments have conclusions that are contained in some way within their premises.[9] If the Ontological Argument's conclusion simply unpacks what is entailed by the premise, then it is just behaving like a well-bred analytic argument. Russell's temporary acceptance of the Ontological Argument shows that it knows how to behave in philosophical company as far as premise-circularity is concerned. The question-begging problem is not so much in the muscular-skeletal system of the argument. It is more of an interpersonal problem (or dialectical, if you prefer – as Oppy phrases it). It does not 'work' in the psychological sense of producing conviction, and is resented by the sceptics rather than producing converts. In that is its interpersonal question-begging character. The resentment comes from the definition itself. It is taking liberties with the good will of the opponent. Oppy, for example, suggests that a proper form of the argument (in the version he calls 'definitional') might be

1. By definition, God is an existent supremely perfect being. (Definition.)
2. (Hence) According to the preceding definition God exists. (From 1.)[10]

But many atheists would grant that the argument above *is* valid, but go on to say: 'Yes, *according to that definition*, it would follow validly that God exists – but so much the worse then for that definition, which I won't accept as the starting-point for an argument.' Oppy does state that making the inference from 2. to a proposition 3. 'God exists' is invalid. Are such objections just bloody-minded?

Existence

No. Another allergic reaction which the Ontological Argument provokes is brought on by the way it handles 'existence', seeming to stick it onto the concept of God. After all, if you build into the definition of anything that it exists, then you can prove *a priori* that it does exist. Unicorns, the philosopher's stone, Atlantis, the fountain of Eternal Youth, your dream lover – the world of fantasies is your oyster. Your ontological magic wand works like this:

> A unicorn is a being which is equine, four-legged, and which possesses a horn and existence.

Now if that is the definition of a unicorn, it becomes a contradiction to deny that a unicorn exists. But this is ontologically promiscuous, if you prove the existence of just anything that takes your fancy; there ought to be a law against it. Gaunilo, one of the first critics of the Ontological Argument when it made its debut under Anselm, launched a protest against this kind of definitional hanky-panky. In his response to Anselm, *On Behalf of the Fool*, he tries to create an analogy of a most perfect island, and objects that one cannot argue it into existence via a definition.

The most famous and heavyweight objection along these lines comes from Immanuel Kant. Kant's most weighty blow against the Ontological Argument is to claim that 'being is not a real predicate'. Existence is not a quality that we have, or a property that we possess. You can't legitimately tot up a list of the attributes of a unicorn *or* of a horse and include 'existence' along with 'hooves, mane, tail'. When we say that something exists, we do not 'add anything to the concept' – we simply say that that concept with all its properties is instantiated.

This objection has been treated almost with reverence since Kant, and taken as virtually axiomatic since Russell. Indeed, it is almost treated like a biblical proof-text when it is bandied about to put a stop to further discussion of the Ontological Argument. But is it so?

First of all, existence and non-existence are sometimes treated as if they *are* part of a concept, and a defining characteristic at that. Compare the two notions of 'a historical figure' and 'a fictional character'. If you remove from the one concept that the person existed, and remove from the other that they did not, and then say of both of them that they may or may not be instantiated and that is irrelevant to the concept, then the distinction between them vanishes and the whole tent collapses. But if one says 'Queen Elizabeth I of England is a historical figure, therefore unlike the fictional Guinevere she once existed' – is one illicitly 'defining Queen Elizabeth into existence'? No, one is validly drawing a conclusion from the concept of 'historical figure'. And if we say that Guinevere never existed because she is fictional, we are not cruelly denying her the right to a life she might otherwise have had. We are just explaining in more detail what it is to be fictional or historical. So, *pace* Kant, if we do stipulate that existence is or is not part of the concept of historical or fictional persons, we *are* adding something important to that concept. Take Kant's analogy of '100 Thaler' (Thaler were his currency). 100 real Thaler, Kant says, do not contain one penny more than 100 imaginary Thaler. But *pace* Kant, compared to the concept of '100 Thaler', '100 imaginary Thaler' does add something to the concept – albeit not a penny. Kant is right that the existence of something is not quantifiable as pennies and thalers and it does not add to the sheer quantity of an entity, make it one centimetre taller or the like. But expounders of the Ontological Argument would agree that 'existence' does not *add in quantity* to the concept of God, not least because God is simple and it would violate the idea of divine simplicity to think that his attributes are additive; as if adding or expanding an attribute makes God one kilogram heavier. 'A being who exists' is not a taller, larger, more numerically enhanced or heavier one than 'a being who does not exist'. It is a *different* one.

Anselm, as we shall see later, does not explicitly claim that existence is a predicate, as Descartes can be seen to do by making existence analogous to the possession of angles and sides. Anselm just claims that it is greater to exist than not to (or that it is greater to exist in reality than in the imagination), and prima facie that is harder to deny. One hundred real Thaler may not have one penny more than 100 imaginary Thaler, but they have much greater purchasing power, and given the choice between the real and imaginary, I know which I prefer. Imagine Kant trying to pay a bill with Monopoly money, painstakingly pointing out to the salesperson that 100 Monopoly dollars contains not one penny less than 100 US dollars. A being that exists is clearly greater than one who doesn't – not numerically, but in ontological clout.

Does that mean that we can legitimately render anything into existence by definitional sleight of hand? No, because the sceptic is right to complain that such definitions do 'beg the question' dialectically. *Sometimes* existence or its absence can be seen to be essential to a definition, as in 'mythical beast' or 'historical personage'. Sometimes, as in the description of a colour, it can be seen to have no legitimate place in a definition. The problem is that the question of God is contentious on this very point. Is it or is it not the case that being or existence is an intrinsic part of what absolute transcendence – unsurpassable perfection – total actuality with no unrealized potentiality *means*? That is the question that believers and not-believers will never agree on, and that is the foundation of the argument; the subsequent logical moves are relatively unproblematic.

Does this explain *Proslogion* 3? Anselm's argument that necessary existence is greater, and therefore *does* belong to the concept of God, now clearly has an important function in the ecology of the debate. Perhaps we can now see better the importance of Ibn Sīnā's foundation stone: his insight that the essentialness of 'necessity' in the understanding of God is what needs to be established above all.

God and being

David Burrell writes:

> . . . if God's 'necessity' is defined by what makes such a creator unique, namely that God's very essence is to-exist, then the primacy of existing will be confirmed in the clearest way possible. The One from which all-that-is comes to be exists in and by itself. What it bestows in creating will be a share in that perfection of existing, so that the very existence of the creature will consist in 'a relation to the creator as the origin of its existence.' [Aquinas, *Summa Theologica* I.45.3] Even if the formulation of necessity as 'being true, or obtaining in, all possible worlds' were an adequate account of the modal notion [of necessity] . . ., it would hardly succeed in formulating what it is about God's being necessary that further identifies such a One as the creator, indeed, as the free creator of all-that-is.[11]

Taken out of the context of argument or proof, 'being' or 'existence' has throughout the ages been seen by some as the most fundamental statement of what God is. Exodus 3.13–15 depicts God as identifying himself to Moses as 'I am who am'. Christians unite this biblical inheritance with a heritage from Greek metaphysical speculation, and with their own tradition of recounting the 'divine names'. One result is to see 'Being' as the ultimate designation of what God is. St Bernard writes:

> Who is he? I cannot think of any better way to put it than to say that he is 'He who is' (Exod. 3.14). This is what he wanted to be said of him. . . . Rightly indeed. Nothing is more fitting to the eternity which God is. If you say that God is good or great or blessed or wise or anything of that sort, it is all summed up by saying that he 'is.' For him, to be is what it is to be all these things. If you were to add a hundred such things you would not have gone beyond saying that he is. If you said

those things you would not have added anything. If you did not mention them you would have subtracted nothing.[12]

Thomas Aquinas puts 'Being' at the top of his list of how to think about God. Being is what God is, first and foremost. God is being itself, not a something that *has* being, like the rest of us. (Thomas's phrase is *ipsum esse subsistens*: subsistent being itself.[13]) God is not caused to exist by anything; God alone is the first cause. So in Thomas's understanding, God's existence cannot be other than God's nature.[14] Existence is what beings *have*; God's existence is what God *is*.[15] Aquinas does not imply that existence is a property that one can have, and that in God's case being is identical with this property.[16] Instead, he means God's existence and God's essence are identical, while they are distinguished in creatures. *What* a creature is, is not identical to *that* it is. I am a human, but that is a separate issue from the fact that I exist. Many others are humans also and I share that nature or essence with them, but I do not share their existence, nor does my sharing in the human essence entail that I exist necessarily. Knowing what a creature is does not answer the question of its existence. But in God, *what* God is, is identical with *that* God is. This foundational idea is shared by other monotheist metaphysicians, like Ṭabāṭabā'ī.

The idea of Being as the Ultimate, and moreover as what the Ultimate is, rather than a quality it possesses, is also a fundamental conception in Indian philosophy. Radhakrishnan writes: 'He does not have "being" as other things have being. He is his own being. Being is, is God. It is prior to all things. All other things are from being, live in it and end in it.'[17]

'Being' (just on its own as it were) became a focus of study in twentieth-century Continental philosophy, in a way quite foreign (even repugnant) to Anglo-American analytical philosophy. This has largely been an evolution from phenomenology.

Heidegger asserts that 'the question of the meaning of Being' is the fundamental question of philosophy. This he sees as representing an important shift in Western philosophy from 'What is knowledge?' or 'What is possible to know?' to 'What is being?' or 'What does it mean to be?' The whole history of metaphysics from Plato to Hegel has been 'forgetful' of this fundamental question, he maintains. I suppose it does depend on whose history you read. The question of his early work – 'What does it mean to be?' – is examined through an analysis of the only being that is capable of asking this question, human being; thus he seeks to grab hold of Being in characterizing the nature of human being. In his later work, he finds two ways to extend this investigation of Being: through deconstructive readings of the metaphysical tradition from Plato to Nietzsche, and through reflection on language as the means *par excellence* of disclosing Being, because 'language is the house of Being'. But in this later work on Being, the primacy of Being-itself over individual 'beings' is further established, and approaches identification with God. The essence of the holy can only be thought from the truth of Being. Being is given a kind of theological ultimacy. Being is what lets God be. Thus, to describe Being as the fullest characterization of God almost understates the case with Heidegger. Whereas most theists might worry about the adequacy of 'Being' as a description of God, a snide critic might say that Heidegger seems more prone to anxiety that God might not be quite up to the task of being Being.

But there have been suggestions, repudiating both Heidegger and mainstream monotheistic metaphysicians, that Being-as-such or Being-in-itself is not the best or most fundamental framework in which to understand God. Plotinus has this to say on the issue: 'The One is all things and yet no one of them. It is the source of all things, not itself all things, but their transcendent Principle. . . . So that Being may exist, the One is not Being, but the begetter of Being.'[18] Perhaps then we need a notion of 'God beyond Being', or even, as a provocative book by Jean-Luc Marion suggests, 'God Without Being'. There are several different angles from which this case has been made.

First, the observation comes from Indian philosophy that Being is *opposed* to something: to non-being; and that the Ultimate Reality is that which transcends all opposition, all dualism. So, insofar as 'Being' is still delimited as a concept by 'Non-being', God must even transcend 'Being'. Sri Aurobindo writes:

> Only the positive and synthetic teaching of the Upaniṣads beheld *sat* [existence] and *asat* [non-existence] not as opposites destructive of each other, but as the last antinomy through which we look up to the Unknowable. And in the transactions of our positive consciousness, even unity has to make its account with multiplicity; for the many also are *Brahman*. It is by *vidya*, the knowledge of the oneness, that we know God; without it *avidya*, the relative and multiple consciousness, is a night of darkness and a disorder of ignorance. Yet if we exclude the field of that ignorance, if we get rid of *avidya* as if it were a thing non-existent and unreal, then knowledge itself becomes a sort of obscurity and a source of imperfection. We become as men blinded by light so that we can no longer see the field which that light illumines.[19]

The Upaniṣads speak of Brahman both as being and as non-being, although the latter was contested.[20] As Radhakrishnan comments on the Māṇḍukya Upaniṣad:

> This verse affirms what Parmenides, Plato and Hegel assumed that the opposition of being and not-being is the original duality from the ontological standpoint. Being is *a priori* to non-being. The negation pre-

supposes what it negates. Though being is *a priori* to non-being, being itself cannot be conceived without an opposite. Being could never be being without being opposed to not-being. But there is something which is a priori to the opposition of being and non-being and that is the unity which transcends both. Thought cannot grasp and determine this spirit beyond the opposition. There is no concept or substance that could be thought of as being the unity without any opposition whatsoever. We cannot even call it unity for it suggests the opposite category of diversity. But we are in the sphere of oppositions, dualities and yet the positive side of the opposition brings out the content of the spirit. We have to seek the ultimate truth, goodness and beauty in its direction.[21]

Thus in this perspective Being is not the highest, there is something still higher: that which transcends it, unites it with its opposite. This is a view shared by Taoism. The *Tao te Ching* says the Being and non-Being produce each other; that non-Being is that from which Heaven and Earth sprang, whereas Being is the mother of all things.

When Maṇḍana Miśra appears to suggest that Brahman is to be identified with being , even though he seems to feel this comment is metaphorical, he is still taken to task by his fellow Advaita Vedāntin Sureśvara. Sureśvara's objection is that this seems to introduce a distinction into the nature of Brahman, and thus violates Brahman's unity.[22]

Alternatively, one might object that 'Being' or 'Existence', no matter how expansive the concept seems to us, is too limited a notion to use for God; certainly not to exhaust what the Ultimate Reality is. Maimonides was prepared to deny even that God has existence, as the human mind understands it.[23] Plotinus spoke of the Absolute as 'beyond Being', as transcending it,[24] as Plato described It as 'beyond Reality'[25] and Plotinus as 'the absolute no-thing which is above all reality'. Similar language often comes from the experience of mystics. Eckhart writes, 'If I have said that God is not a Being and is above Being, I do not mean to deprive him of Being, but to honour Being in Him.'[26] Thus the refusal to equate, or even impute, Being to God is not a statement of theistic disbelief so much as an insistence that the divine transcends even Being Itself.

This is the spirit also behind French theologian Jean-Luc Marion's book, *God Without Being*. There he writes of Being as an 'idol', which fixes or freezes God into our own conceptualizations, whereas his aspiration is to free God from being. His explicit critique of Heidegger is that the latter puts Being anterior, prior, to God. He describes Heidegger's view as: 'In the beginning and in principle, there advenes neither God, nor a god, nor the logos, but . . . Being',[27] which is the starting-point for all other beings, including God, one must suppose. He calls to his support many Heideggerian passages of which he is critical, which seem to him to indicate that Being is the ultimate in which God finds existence, such as: 'Even God is – if He exists – a being, and stands as a being within Being.'[28]

This scepticism about 'God as Being' can also come about through a critique of the way the notion is formed and deployed. Hamann found himself contending with his friend Jacobi in their letters on precisely this point. Jacobi was writing enthusiastically on the idea of 'Being-in-itself'. Hamann dubbed this a 'superstition'. '– Affirmation of *Being in itself* – the most abstract relation, that does not serve the intuition and understanding of the *things*, let alone *particular things* . . .'[29] Hamann's argument is that 'Being' is abstracted from the actual being or existence of real things, smuggled into the status of a concept, and then promoted into being some-*Thing*. '*Being, belief and reason* are pure relations, which cannot be dealt with absolutely, and are not things but pure scholastic concepts, *signs* for understanding, not for worshipping, aids to awaken our attention, not to fetter it, as Nature is the *revelation* not of itself, but of a higher Object . . .'[30]

A distinction can be drawn between Aristotle's position and those who see God as the source of being for others and the cause of their existence. This can be seen clearly in the difference between Ibn Sīnā and Aristotle who influenced him.[31] For Aristotle, there is no need for a source of all being to be the ground of unity of all things. A thing and the fact that it exists are identical. For Ibn Sīnā, on the other hand, God is that from which everything receives its being. But in contrast to Plotinus, this source is not the One beyond being. God is being to the supreme degree, and is not outside it. The question is whether there is really an irresolvable dichotomy between those who see God as the source of being that is Being Subsisting In Itself, and those who see God as the source of being and therefore beyond even being itself. Burrell argues that Aquinas's identification of God as the One whose essence is to-be 'effectively brings him into alignment with Plotinus, whose One is said to be "beyond being" '. By disallowing talk of God as an item in the universe (even a necessary one), 'we are forbidden to think of *being* as a category spanning the uncreated and the created; indeed as a category at all'.[32] So perhaps one could speak of God as beyond both 'the being of beings' and 'non-being'. The contingency of beings is not just a metaphysical mode, but, as 'createdness' suggests, their dependence on what gives being. This is the reason that Hamann moves from a dismissal of the abstraction of metaphysics' talk of Being and anchors it to nature as revelation: 'being' is a sign to aid worship, as nature is the revelation of a creator, to whom created beings relate. On this understanding, 'non-being' is not an opposition to (still less 'in') God but is the space for God's creativity.

Tao Te Ching 11
We join spokes together in a wheel,
But it is the centre hole
That makes the wagon move.

We shape clay into a pot,
But it is the emptiness inside
That holds whatever we want.

We hammer wood for a house,
But it is the inner space
That makes it livable.

We work with being,
But non-being is what we use.

Draw your own conclusions

Do you think there are significant differences between different versions of the argument; say Anselm's and Descartes'? Or do you think they would all suffer under the same criticisms?

Do you think Kant's argument about 'existence is not a predicate' is a damning criticism, or do you think existence can sometimes add something to the concept of a thing?

Is existence, or 'being', part of your understanding of what The Ultimate is?

If you believe in a God or transcendent reality, do you see he/she/it as Being Itself or Beyond Being, or as something else?

Do you think we can talk about 'Being As Such', or can we only talk in a common sense way about things existing or not existing?

Do you think the argument works? What do you mean by 'work' here?

Further reading

Aquinas, T. *The 'Summa Theologica' of St. Thomas Aquinas*, London, Burns Oates & Washbourne

Aurobindo (1996) *The Life Divine*, Pondicherry, Sri Aurobindo Ashram

Davidson, H. A. (1987) *Proofs for Eternity, Creation and the Existence of God in Medieval Islamic and Jewish Philosophy*, New York and Oxford, Oxford University Press

Davies, B. (1992) *The Thought of Thomas Aquinas*, Oxford, Clarendon Press
Griffith-Dickson, G. (1995) *Johann Georg Hamann's Relational Metacriticism*, Berlin and New York, de Gruyter
Inge, W. (1929) *The Philosophy of Plotinus*, 2 vols, London, Longman
Maimonides, M. (1969) *The Guide of the Perplexed*, trans. S. Pines, Chicago and London, University of Chicago Press
Marion, J. L. (1991) *God Without Being*, Chicago, University of Chicago Press
Oppy, G. (1996) *Ontological Arguments and Belief in God*, Cambridge, Cambridge University Press
Owens, J., CSsR (1992) 'The Relevance of Avicennian Neoplatonism', in P. Morewedge (ed.), *Neoplatonism and Islamic Thought*, Albany, State University of New York Press
Plotinus (1991) *The Enneads*, trans. S. MacKenna, London, Penguin

Notes

1 T. Merton (1975 (1948)), *The Seven Storey Mountain*, London, Sheldon Press, pp. 172–3.

2 Plotinus (1991) *The Enneads*, trans. S. MacKenna, London, Penguin, V.4.1.

3 See Davidson for discussion of the history of interpretation of Aristotle's argument. H. A. Davidson (1987) *Proofs for Eternity, Creation and the Existence of God in Medieval Islamic and Jewish Philosophy*, New York and Oxford, Oxford University Press, pp. 281–3.

4 For criticisms see the earlier chapter on the Cosmological Argument, especially Copleston on his chocolates/sheep argument for this kind of reasoning about the totality of contingent things still being contingent. Davidson thinks that the proof fails because Ibn Sīnā didn't consider the possibility that the totality of things merely possible in themselves, while each being contingent, as a totality could be necessary. But I think that is why Ibn Sīnā has recourse to the 'no infinite regress' argument (which Davidson thinks is an unnecessary step here) – to imagine the totality being responsible for all causation, Ibn Sīnā pictures it as a chain and not a contemporary mass, therefore something that extends in time.

NB that Ibn Sīnā does not only speak in terms of causing the origins of something – for there could be eternal things that are nevertheless still dependent on another for their existence. So Ibn Sīnā speaks not only of the *generation* of existence but also of what *maintains* things in being.

5 For a brief account of this history see Davidson, *Proofs for Eternity, Creation and the Existence of God in Medieval Islamic and Jewish Philosophy*, pp. 293–8.

6 S. M. H. Ṭabāṭabā'ī (2003) *The Elements of Islamic Metaphysics (Bidayat al-Ḥikmah)*, London, ICAS Press, pp. 133–7.

7 G. Oppy (1996) *Ontological Arguments and Belief in God*, Cambridge, Cambridge University Press, p. 6.

8 Mohammed Abduh (1966) *The Theology of Unity*, London, Allen & Unwin, translated from the Arabic by Ishaq Masa'ad and Kenneth Cragg.

9 See the useful discussion in Oppy, *Ontological Arguments and Belief in God*.

10 Oppy, *Ontological Arguments and Belief in God*, p. 49.

11 D. Burrell (2004) *Faith and Freedom*, Challenges in Contemporary Theology, Oxford, Blackwell, p. 87.

12 Bernard of Clairvaux (1987) 'On Consideration' VI. 13, in *Selected Works*, trans. G. R. Evans, Classics of Western Spirituality, New York, Paulist Press, pp. 157–8.

13 Thomas Aquinas, *The 'Summa Theologica' of St. Thomas Aquinas*, London, Burns Oates & Washbourne, I.11.4.

14 Aquinas, *Summa Theologica*, I.3.4.

15 Aquinas, *Summa Theologica*, I.12.4.

16 B. Davies cautions: 'Nor is it to say that existence is a property identical with God, as some readers of Aquinas take him to be arguing. It is to say that God depends on nothing for his existence. . . . Aquinas, in fact, does not think of existence as a property at all, let alone one identical with God.' B. Davies (1992) *The Thought of Thomas Aquinas*, Oxford, Clarendon Press, p. 56.

17 S. Radhakrishnan (1953) *The Principal Upaniṣads*, London, George Allen & Unwin, p. 448.

18 Plotinus, *Enneads*; this passage is Book 5, 2nd Tractate, 1: 'The Origin and Order of Being'.

19 Aurobindo (1996) *The Life Divine*, Pondicherry, Sri Aurobindo Ashram, pp. 34–5.

20 As in the Chāndogya Upaniṣad 6.2.1–2.

21 Radhakrishnan, *The Principal Upaniṣads*, pp. 700–1.

22 Karl Potter (ed.) (1981) *Encyclopedia of Indian Philosophies*, vol. 1: *Advaita Vedānta up to Śaṇkara and His Pupils*. Princeton, Princeton University Press, p. 75.

23 M. Maimonides (1969) *The Guide of the Perplexed*, trans. S. Pines, Chicago and London, University of Chicago Press, I.56.

24 Cf. Plotinus, *Enneads*, V.4.1. *et passim*; Cf. W. Inge (1929) *The Philosophy of Plotinus*, 2 vols. London, Longman, vol. 2, p. 111.

25 J. L. Marion (1991) *God Without Being*, Chicago, University of Chicago Press.

26 Inge, *Philosophy of Plotinus*, vol. 2, p. 112.

27 Marion, *God Without Being*, p. 41.

28 Cited in Marion, *God Without Being*.

29 G. Griffith-Dickson (1995) *Johann Georg Hamann's Relational Metacritism*, Berlin and New York, de Gruyter, 166:19–20. ZH 7, Nr. 1060, 165:7–11, 27.4–3.5.1787.

30 Griffith-Dickson, *Johann Georg Hamann's Relational Metacritism*, ZH 7, Nr. 1060, 165:7–11, 27.4–3.5.1787.

31 See the discussion in J. Owens, CSsR (1992) 'The Relevance of Avicennian Neoplatonism', in P. Morewedge (ed.), *Neoplatonism and Islamic Thought*, Albany, State University of New York Press.

32 Burrell, *Faith and Freedom*, pp. xviii–xx.

Part 3

The Divine and the Human Relationship

9

The Knowledge of All

On 11 September 2001, a group of men hijacked aeroplanes and flew them into symbolic buildings, killing thousands of people. Was it true on 10 September that they would do this? If so, then nothing – a change of heart, better security, intercepting jets, or even divine intervention – could have prevented it. Otherwise, it would have been false on 10 September. But if it was true in advance, it was inevitable.

In chapter 9 of *On Interpretation* Aristotle raises the problem of statements about the future. Can we say that these are either true or false? Is it true or false now, he asks, that a battle will start tomorrow? As Aristotle sees it, a problem arises if you claim that the Principle of Bivalence – that a proposition is either true or not true – applies to propositions involving the future. If a proposition is true, necessarily, reality must correspond to it. If a future proposition is true, then reality in future must turn out the way the proposition claims. Everything then is predetermined – even what we think of as our free will. If what we do is determined and when the time comes we have no choice, we are not morally responsible for what we do, because we couldn't do otherwise. So if it was true on 10 September that those atrocities would occur, then those who committed them are not morally responsible for their actions because even if they had tried to change their mind, they couldn't have changed their acts. – Is that right?

The dilemma is it seems that either nothing can truly be said about the future, or else the future is wholly fixed and determined and there is no freedom, choice or chance. Aristotle's way out was to decide that statements about the future which are not true by necessity are *neither true nor false* now. He may have resolved the paradox in a common-sense way, if you are thinking about human knowledge which is bound by time. But the monotheist philosophers of Islam, Judaism and Christianity spotted the problem for believers in God. It is one thing to say that a future statement is not true now and cannot be known by human minds. But what if you claim that there is a God who is all-knowing – a God who *ought* to know the future? Is God ignorant of what lies ahead? Or if God knows what will happen tomorrow, are we human beings bound to a predetermined course of action?

If God does know my future actions, surely reward and punishment cannot be just because my future is predestined and I have had no choice. On the other hand, if God cannot know the future, God cannot exercise providence and arrange things for our benefit or divine justice. So if God is omniscient, how can human beings possess free will? Or if not omniscient, is God still worthy of the name 'God'?

These problems arose in exegetical discussions within Judaism. Jewish commentators had long exercised their skills on the story contained in Genesis 22.1–14, known in Jewish circles as the Binding of Isaac, when God commands Abraham to take his son Isaac up a mountain and offer him as a sacrifice. Did God know in advance what Abraham would do? If not, and this was a genuine 'test', then God is not all-knowing.[1] If God did know what Abraham would do in the future, God's knowledge being certain, it would certainly come to pass. So, if there is no question of what Abraham will do, in what sense is Abraham still 'free' to perform or not perform his actions when the time comes? It also bears on the value and import of the Torah: what sense is there in enjoining someone to uphold and follow the Law if they cannot do otherwise than what they in fact do?

This question had a different history in Islam, in a wider Islamic debate over predestination and libertarianism (belief in an effective human free will). The Qur'ān gives indications of both. There are Qur'ānic texts which imply predestination, and also texts which imply free will.[2] This left scope for thinkers to take either path. As far as predestination and God's foreknowledge are concerned, although the Qur'ān implies that God is omniscient, it does not say that God knows what humans will do in the future. The way was open for those for thinkers to marshal their arguments accordingly.

The underlying moral worry for Islam is the same as the Jewish one, as al-Fārābī observed:

> It then becomes necessary in all religions that in his doing of anything man has basically no choice. Thus what comes to him by way of punishment in this world and the next is not due to something of his doing that has come about through his will and choice. Thus God, who rewards and punishes, would not then be just in His action. But these things also are all repugnant and reprehensible according to all the religions and very very harmful for people to believe.[3]

In Christian thought, the problem was raised by Augustine, and later by Christian medieval philosophers, some aware of the discussion in Jewish and Islamic circles, some well versed in Aristotle, but some following the purely Christian tradition found in Augustine and Boethius. The logical dilemma was put pithily by Aquinas: 'Whatever is known by God must be; for whatever is known by us must be, and God's knowledge is more certain than ours. But nothing which is future and contingent *must* be. Therefore, nothing which is future and contingent is known by God.'[4] Again, the moral implication is identified, as here by Boethius:

> In vain is reward offered to the good and punishment to the bad, because they have not been deserved by any free and willed movement of the mind. That which is now judged most equitable, the punishment of the wicked and the reward of the good, will be seen to be the most unjust of all; for men are driven to good or evil not by their own will but by the fixed necessity of what is to be.[5]

Within Christianity, the problems surrounding God's knowledge were perhaps most bitterly contested in the Reformation in disputes between Catholics and Protestants. The issue moved from God's omniscience to the predestination of salvation or damnation.

Christian theological spats on human freedom

When Erasmus and Luther clashed on the subject, Erasmus challenged Luther's theological position on the grounds that it denied human free will. Luther was willing to embrace the possibility that all events in the world are necessary, because all happens through God's willing, which is not contingent or changeable. Even though our actions are in some sense necessitated, however, so long as we willed them they happen in accordance with our will. Erasmus's response was to depict this scenario as God willing us to sin then punishing us for it, which is unjust. Thus the question of what human freedom consists in was highlighted as a central question in the debate, both in the philosophical debate about the logical problem, and in the theological disputes between Catholics and Reformers. The Catholic response in the Counter-Reformation consisted in part of a heightened sensitivity to any position resembling the Reformers', as can be seen in the controversies between the Dominicans and the Jesuits which we will visit when we consider Molina's theory of 'Middle Knowledge'. The Jesuits thought that the Dominicans' view, derived from Aquinas, was rather too close to Luther's for comfort; the response of the Spanish Jesuit Molina was to formulate an account of God's knowledge in an attempt to preserve God's omniscience combined with a strong notion of human freedom that is not close to Luther's.[6]

The controversy was revived again in our times with the work of Arthur Prior and an article by Nelson Pike. A wearying number of articles and books have been written in the last few decades on the question of whether or not divine foreknowledge and human free will are incompatible. Some have tried to generate new positions which escape the problems. Some have revived medieval positions on the question, sometimes knowingly and sometimes not. The Islamic and Jewish contributions, however, are often overlooked in contemporary Anglo-American, mostly Christian, debates.

The dilemma of foreknowledge and human freedom contains within it all the other major issues and puzzles afflicting divine omniscience: what does omniscience mean and what does it cover, how does God know, can God be omniscient timelessly, can God know the future, can God know empirical, temporal, physical or particular things? It therefore makes a good frame in which to examine these puzzles, often abstruse, because the dilemma of divine foreknowledge and human freedom has a religious pertinence to it – which is more than can be said for some other questions. If I believe in a God, one can easily see that it matters whether or not God has foreknowledge of my actions, and whether or not my actions are free and I am fully responsible for them.

Responses to the dilemma

The easiest way out of a dilemma is to give up or nuance one of the two apparently incompatible claims: in this case, either God's omniscience, or human freedom. Those who would do so outright are in the minority; more often, one redefines one term or the other.

Reconsidering God's foreknowledge

Some Islamic thinkers did not assert that God knew future free choices. Sometimes this was for reasons of piety: the mystic Abū Yazīd al-Bisṭamī denied that God possessed knowledge, because only something known or knowable can have the possession of knowledge ascribed to it. Only a heretic or unbeliever would claim that God is knowable Himself; thus we cannot ascribe knowledge to God.[7] Strict reverence and respect for transcendence precludes such description.

Some thinkers transformed this apparent limit into a compliment. Medieval Jewish and Islamic thinkers were squeamish about attributing knowledge of trivia to God. A God who doesn't do details seems like a more regal and exalted figure. Thus Gersonides suggested that, while God knows some 'particulars' (specific individuals, concrete events) God does not know them *all*. What God knows is the general pattern of things – a qualified knowledge of particulars, through knowing their form and the principles they follow, their order. So God knows them in one respect, but not in another. Individual things and events are ordered in one sense, yet contingent in another sense.[8] So the sense in which God knows them is that in which they are ordered and determined, on the other hand, the sense in which God doesn't know them is that in which they are contingent; knowledge of this is not possible.

Gersonides on God's foreknowledge

> *We do possess such knowledge insofar as such events are ordered. Yet they remain contingent by virtue of the factor of choice. . . . Since we have claimed that God has knowledge of these events insofar as they are ordered, it is not strange that they are still contingent with respect to human choice. In this way, the difficulty that has continually plagued men – i.e., how can God know future events without these events being necessary – disappears; for these events exhibit two aspects, and not just one aspect.*[9]

The result is that divine knowledge, in some respects, is not so very different from human knowledge. This conclusion, which would horrify Maimonides, seems almost an advantage to Gersonides. God knows all the options which exist for people and events, and God also knows that the result is contingent – hence, Gersonides claims, God *does* know reality, because it is true that the result is contingent.[10] This solution, he feels, not only avoids philosophical problems but is identical to the doctrine of the Torah.[11]

Ibn Sīnā in the Islamic tradition had a slightly different way of handling this notion. He suggested that God knows particulars 'in a universal way'. through an intellectual, not sensory, mode; eternal, even if what is known is transient; and this knowledge remains the same before, during and after, otherwise that would entail change on God's part. God knows things via his self-knowledge, as effects of divine causality. (So far this has much in common with Thomas Aquinas.) Ibn Sīnā's concern is to identify what is seemly for a transcendent being to know; which does not in his view include facts about the world, which is not merely transient, but also full of decay and corruption. It would surely be far more appropriate for God to know universals, rules of logic, abstract things, the relations between them. However, that leaves a lot of particulars which God can't know.

But this view could also be maintained as a philosophical position. Aristotle's view, that future propositions are neither true nor false now, means that the future is not an object of knowledge. This denial was maintained by some Islamic and Jewish thinkers. One cannot 'know' if the object of knowledge does not exist.[12]

Various modern philosophers agree. One way philosophers put this is: '"Future contingent propositions" are neither true nor false.' Peter Geach, for example, says that the future is not real, and cannot be an object of knowledge; so how can it be either true or false?

Hasker suggests that God's knowledge of the future consists of everything that it is possible to know in advance: 'all of the future outcomes that are objectively possible, *as well as* knowledge of the objective likelihood that each outcome will occur, and in cases where one choice is overwhelmingly likely (though not as yet absolutely certain) to be made, God will know that also'.[13]

But is this not a restriction on God's omniscience? Their response would be: God's omniscience means that God can know everything that is knowable. Future free choices are not knowable. As Swinburne defines omniscience, it is the knowledge of everything true which is logically possible to know.[14] Thus, God knows everything that is or has happened, and the future insofar as it is necessitated by physical causes.

A stance along these lines has recently been created, principally among US Protestant thinkers; it is often described as 'Open Theism'. On this view, some aspects of the future remain 'genuinely open' and God does not know what will happen. The view seems to be derived both from an attempt to solve dilemmas of foreknowledge and human freedom, together with intractable problems like God allowing evil to exist, and the difficulties around human action; but also from certain interpretations of biblical texts. Its proponents claim that it is not a restriction on God's omniscience, but a specification of what is knowable. If some events or actions in the future are truly 'open' to human free will, then the results cannot be known in advance and it is a logical contradiction to say that God knows them. Boyd puts it this way:

> The view I shall defend agrees unequivocally with the classical view that God is omniscient, but it embraces a different understanding of creation. It holds that the reality that God perfectly knows not only excludes some possibilities as what might have been, but also includes other possibilities as what might be. Reality, in other words, is composed of both settled and open aspects. Since God knows all of reality perfectly, this view holds that he knows the possible aspects as possible and knows the settled aspects as settled. In this view, the sovereign Creator settles whatever he wants to settle about the future, and hence he perfectly foreknows the future as settled *to this extent*. He leaves open whatever he wants to leave open, and hence he perfectly foreknows the future as possible *to this extent*.[15]

Boyd mainly defends this view using the Bible. This is awkward, not only because this is in general a problematic method in philosophy, but also because the Bible contains many different sentences on this subject which have not been forced together into a synthetic unity. There are passages he does not note which assert or imply that God has an exhaustive knowledge of the future. Anyone resorting to biblical 'proof texts' therefore has to explain why texts supporting his position should be taken literally while the conflicting texts should not be interpreted in an equally straightforward fashion. I have not seen any argument (including Boyd's) which does this convincingly, and which has a consistent and plausible hermeneutic approach.

As we have seen, it is accepted practice to distinguish those aspects of the future which are plausibly fixed and those that are not; those that are 'necessary', caused, from those that are contingent. Boyd's language differs, since he refers to the 'open' vs. the 'settled'. The distinction between the two is not made on philosophical grounds (such as 'necessary' vs. 'contingent') but on religious or theological ones: it is a question of God's choice to settle or leave open as God wants. In practice this does not pan out as the difference between natural causes and human free will. Boyd presents some human decisions as 'settled', such as Peter's betrayal of Jesus (Boyd has to include this, since Jesus predicts it in the Bible), or God's declarations about certain individuals' accomplishments in advance (e.g. Josiah and Cyrus). Boyd thinks it is unwarranted however to extrapolate that God knows *every* individual's *every* future action. God's foreknowledge restricts the freedom these individuals can exercise regarding certain events, but in other respects they remain self-determining and free. 'These examples certainly show that [God] is the sovereign Lord of history and can predetermine and thus foreknow whatever he pleases. But they do not justify the conclusion that he desires to predetermine or foreknow the whole of the future.'[16] Other future human actions might not be 'settled' by God's decree but by a person's own character, which becomes increasingly settled over time. God's reading of our character enables him to foreknow the future free choice. He goes on to say:

> In my view, this is how we should understand the wicked activity of individuals who played foreordained roles in the death of Jesus. . . . Scripture never suggests that these specific individuals were destined or foreknown to carry out these wicked deeds. It only teaches that these specific deeds were destined and foreknown to take place. Saying that someone carried out a predestined or foreknown wicked event is much different from saying that someone was predestined or foreknown to carry out a wicked event. Scripture affirms the former but not the latter.[17]

In his discussions of Peter and Judas and Jesus' apparent knowledge in advance of their free actions, Boyd provides us with two things: an explanation of *how* this could be known in advance (through a perfect understanding of character) and an assertion that Jesus' (or God's) prior knowledge does not remove Judas' or Peter's freedom and responsibility. These are the two things that must be provided in order to defend the classical view that Boyd says he rejects: that God foreknows future free choices while the human remains free and responsible and not predestined. On the other hand, although Boyd is strongly opposed to the Calvinist view that God foreordains and predetermines all things, it seems to me that he tacitly accepts the assumption that God's foreknowledge implies God's coercive control by stating that when God does foreknow an event, that amounts to a restriction on the individual's freedom.

So: Boyd's account of Open Theism contains three elements:

1. The Calvinist view that God foreknows, hence predetermines human action which is not free (e.g. those of Josiah and Cyrus);

2. The 'classical' view that it is *possible* for God to foreknow human action without determining it (e.g. Peter and Judas); and

3. The assertion that God sometimes chooses not to know at all.

4. The implicit assertion that these (normally opposing) views are all tenable together if each only applies to *some* events.

Now (4) is probably true. But why would one want to hold this view, or rather, all of these views at once? It seems to combine all the disadvantages of these views without any of the advantages of holding only one of them. By asserting (1) at times, he asserts that God sometimes does predestine individuals' actions; thus compromising our freedom. By holding (2), he is subject to all the problems of theodicy and challenges to divine sovereignty that belief in efficacious human free will give rise to. It is not clear that asserting (3) gives him any advantage at all in the 'God highly values our freedom' stakes. Since God *can* foreknow things without compromising human freedom anyway, why should God choose to not-know if there is no compromise of human freedom? And if God is willing to compromise our human freedom by predestining us *sometimes*, his liberality is already compromised. Surely it compromises God's reputation as a liberal *more* to say God predestines than to say God foreknows. So if Boyd is prepared to say the former, why baulk at the latter? It seems the worst of both worlds for God's reputation as a nice guy, and at the price of sacrificing some conceivable foreknowledge God might have.

Philosophically speaking, the nub of the issue for Open Theism is this: do statements about the future or about what might have been in the past or the present have any truth value or not? If they have a truth value, then an omniscient divinity must know them; and if the Openness God does not, then that God is not omniscient. Discerning Boyd's view on this precise question is difficult since he only uses his term 'open' and 'settled', which as we have seen do not correspond to 'contingent' and 'necessary', and thus do not address the central epistemological point.

I am not just playing Scrabble with Boyd's terminology. It does have a theological impact. One difficulty about denying *tout court* that such counterfactuals can have even a whiff of truth about them, and that God can know about them, is that it presents problems for one's conceptions about God's creation, providence, judgement or discernment. If God deliberately creates things in a certain way, was God able to conceive of different options, foresee the consequences of certain decisions, and choose accordingly? (Granted some – including me – might feel squeamish that this is an anthropomorphic way of describing the mind of God; but as Boyd feels it literally true that God can experience regret and frustration, and change his mind, he presumably does not.) If God cannot know the likely results of his decisions, how can the right choice be made? Mind you, since Boyd considers that God (as portrayed in the Hebrew scriptures) seems to feel He made some mistakes, then perhaps Boyd feels that God is not infallible in this decision-making. Clearly then the revision to a 'classical' view of the Supremely Perfect Being then involves more than adjustments to God's omniscience. But on what epistemological foundation does Boyd believe God makes his plans?

There is one further repercussion to this view, in my opinion. In those 'genuinely open' situations which God does not foreknow, God finds out as it happens. So – in general – where does God get this knowledge from? On this account, God must receive knowledge passively – by observation, as it were, or its divine equivalent. This makes God dependent on creation for God's own knowledge. Is God truly transcendent if God receives divine knowledge just as we do – by finding out from events? There are other alternatives, as we shall see later.

Reconsidering free will

Alternatively, you can examine the question of human freedom, and how to make it fit uncontroversially with divine prescience. You might deny human freedom, and opt for a strong vision of predestination, a tendency that existed in both Islam and Christianity. You can, as Luther did, interpret human freedom in such a way as to coexist with a strong view of omniscience and foreknowledge, by distinguishing the 'liberty of spontaneity' and the 'liberty of indifference'. Those who think freedom consists in the 'liberty of spontaneity' claim that freedom consists in *choosing* to do something, even in the absence of other options. Those who think freedom only fully exists as the 'liberty of indifference', however, insist that freedom consists in the choice exercised in a situation when one has the power to perform an act *and* the power not to. Someone in a locked room can decide not to leave the room, and with the liberty of spontaneity they have chosen freely. Freedom understood as the liberty of indifference would argue that such a person is not free to *leave* the room, so no matter how much she wants to remain in it, one cannot really speak of her as enjoying freedom.

Duns Scotus and Luther both understood freedom as spontaneity. Duns Scotus, the medieval theologian, argued that if one decides to jump off a cliff, necessarily one falls; but if one willed and continues to will the fall, one falls both by necessity and by one's free choice. So an action can be both free and necessary. Luther maintained that one can be foreordained to sin, but insofar as one wills it when one does it, one does it freely and culpably. So God's knowledge of our future action may entail that necessarily it happens; but insofar as we have chosen them we are free and therefore responsible for the consequences.

A current proponent of this view is Paul Helm. His view is that the problem of divine foreknowledge and human freedom can be resolved in no other way than by taking a compatibilist view of human freedom; that is, to be free and responsible is compatible with one's choice being necessitated in some way. That this introduces a degree of causal determinism into human action is an advantage rather than a disadvantage, in that it 'extends the idea of causal explanations of events, which all recognize is fundamental to natural science, into the realm of human action'.[18] This flirts with the danger of making God the cause of evil, in particular evil human action. Here Helm draws a distinction between 'causing' and 'permitting' evil. But is there really an important moral distinction here? Whether God reluctantly allows me to act with cruelty or permits me with relish to do so, the end result is the same: creaturely suffering. One can also question whether this violates divine simplicity: does God do lots of different things, or continuously exercise one creative relation with the world?

For many this position undermines our intuitions about human freedom, and the moral responsibility that is felt to rest upon it; and it remains one of those questions resolved only by philosophical and theological taste.

God's knowledge is not causal

One response to the problem is to deny that God's knowledge in some way *makes* me do what he knows I will do. This was commonly the Jewish philosophers' position.

Jewish philosophers on God's knowledge and causation

Rabbi Akiba is said to have proclaimed, 'Everything is foreseen, yet freedom of choice is given.' Unfortunately, history has not preserved how he thought this was possible. The issue was kicked off by Saadia, who argued (rather dangerously): 'If God's foreknowledge of anything could be the cause of its coming into being, then all things would have to be eternal, having existed always since God has always known of them.' This is unfortunately a neat way of denying divine foreknowledge at all, which is the use that Hisham al-Hakam made of it. Abraham Ibn Daud, wanting to preserve God's omniscience, cites Christian thinkers for support: John of Damascus telling us 'God foreknows all things but does not predetermine them' and Abucara maintaining that, 'So also it is impossible that God's foreknowledge should transform into necessity that free will with which He had equipped man'; a free will that Abucara feels that God ordered for our good. Judah Halevi's paraphrase of the Islamic theologian runs: 'God's knowledge does not compel things yet to be generated – they are, despite His knowledge of them, possible either to be generated or not to be generated, for the knowledge of that which may be generated is not the cause of its being generated . . .' Hai Gaon puts it: 'God's foreknowledge is not the cause for the coming of a thing into being.'[19]

In the Christian tradition Origen argued that God's knowledge does not cause things to be true, rather, that something is true is what causes God's knowledge of it. Aquinas would not like the idea of God's knowledge being caused by events in the world; but he did observe that if I see Socrates sitting, I know that Socrates is sitting, but my knowledge doesn't make Socrates sit; thus knowing something is not causing it. Vardy writing in our time comments:

> God does, indeed, timelessly know what we shall do in the future, but his knowledge is *not causal*. God timelessly sees our future free actions, but what He sees is the result of our freedom – God does not cause us to act in any particular way.[20]

Unfortunately this is not enough to dispose of the problem (as Aquinas, at least, knew). The problem is not just that God's knowledge, in itself, is thought to be causal. (Although as we shall see some thinkers, including Aquinas, think that it is, but in a sense more profound than just logical necessity.[21]) The problem is that something can only be 'known' if it is already true. So, it is claimed, future events can only be known if they are in some way necessary or determined; because how else could they be already true? The compromise to my freedom comes not from God's knowledge itself, but from the implication that my action is caused by factors that are wholly predictable, like natural laws, therefore knowable in advance. For this reason, many do not find the simple disavowal of any causal factor involved in God's knowledge a sufficient solution to the foreknowledge dilemma. It needs to be conjoined with an understanding of God as timelessness, which we will investigate below.

Investigating necessity

Why is God's foreknowledge thought to make my act 'necessary'? It could be that a fallacious slide is taking place somewhere in the way the dilemma is formulated, and if it is unmasked, then it might disappear. Aquinas is most often cited on this point, but he was not the first to suggest it. Almost three centuries earlier, in Islam al-Fārābī distinguished different senses of necessity. Events in the past and the present are in some sense 'necessary': that is, they cannot be otherwise, because they cannot now be changed. Such events might be called 'temporally necessary', as they are in Aristotelian discussions. This kind of necessity is also referred to as 'accidental necessity'. No-one forced me to marry my husband, but now it is irrevocable that I did. If I divorce him, it can never change the fact that I had gone through that prior process of marriage.

One can also, however, use the term 'necessary' when speaking of the relation between a statement and the state of affairs it describes. A true statement 'necessarily' implies the fact that it describes, otherwise it wouldn't be true. This, al-Fārābī argues, is a purely logical necessity, not a causal one. The solution to the dilemma of foreknowledge, in his view, is to distinguish between what is necessary in itself, and what is necessary simply as a consequence of a proposition. If we know that tomorrow Zaid will travel, then it is necessarily true that he will travel. That does not mean that his travel is itself intrinsically necessary. So something can be necessary in one respect while remaining contingent in another. Divine knowledge that Zaid will travel does not remove his ability to decide to stay at home.[22]

As we saw with Aristotle, even human knowledge of a situation suggests fatalism if one does not attempt to distinguish different types of 'necessity'.

It is not surprising therefore that a number of Jewish, Muslim and Christian thinkers after al-Fārābī attempted to differentiate between different notions of necessity. We find arguments in Crescas and Boethius, and most notably, Aquinas.[23] Aquinas tackles this aspect of the problem in two ways. The first is to make a distinction between *de dicto* and *de re* necessity: between necessity as it applies to statements (what is said, *de dicto*); and as it applies to things (*de re*).

> The proposition 'whatever is known by God must be' can be analysed in two ways. It may be taken as a proposition *de dicto* or as a proposition *de re*. . . . As a *de re* proposition, it means: Of everything which is known by God, it is true that that thing must be. So understood the proposition is false. As a proposition *de dicto* it means: The proposition 'whatever God knows is the case' is necessarily true. So understood, the proposition is true.[24]

If John is a bachelor he cannot be married according to *de dicto* necessity. Otherwise we could not say he was a bachelor. But this does not mean that John can never marry, or that it was impossible for him to marry in the past. We could distinguish, then, between:

> Necessarily, a bachelor is unmarried.
> (Which explains what the term means.)

And:

> A bachelor is necessarily unmarried.
> (Which implies no woman would have him).

In the same way, we could distinguish between true (if vacuous) statements and misleading ones in our present case:

> Whatever God knows is, necessarily, true.
> (Otherwise we would have to say: 'God wrongly believes that . . .')

> Whatever God knows is necessarily-true.
> (Which, according to Aquinas, is false.)

Otherwise, all the things which not merely God but you or I know, such as my height, are 'necessary truths', which seems absurd to most people.

The second way Aquinas distinguishes aspects of necessity is to differentiate the necessity of the *consequence* from the necessity of the *consequent*, not unlike Boethius. That is, the 'consequence' of 'If p, then q' might follow *necessarily*; but that does not mean that the 'consequent' of that statement, q itself, is a necessary truth. The *consequence* 'If John is a bachelor, then John is unmarried' may be 'necessary'; but that does not mean that the *consequent*, 'John is unmarried', is a necessary truth. Whatever John's marital state, in theory he could have done otherwise.

The claim, then, is that the 'necessity' in the foreknowledge dilemma is misunderstood. It may be a necessary truth (*de dicto*) that if God knows I will do x, I will do x. But that does not mean that 'I will do x' is itself a necessary truth. If, however, necessity is removed from my action, then the dilemma vanishes, according to those who advocate this solution. My acts are not necessary, so I am free, whatever God knows.

Craig has sought to deconstruct the alleged incompatibility of divine foreknowledge and (incompatibilist) human freedom along similar lines.[25] The 'necessity' of the *inference* from 'Necessarily, if God foreknows *x*, then *x* will happen' and 'God foreknows *x*' to 'Therefore, *x* will happen' does not transfer to the conclusion itself. There is a mistaken tendency to confuse epistemological certainty with the logical necessity of propositions. 'But it is muddle-headed to think that because *x* will certainly happen then *x* will necessarily happen.'[26] Yandell also reminds us of the distinction between 'entailment' and 'truth determination', to create the following observation:

> we should distinguish between *direction of entailment* and *direction of truth determination. Entailment* is defined this way: *Proposition P entails Proposition Q* if and only if *'P is true but Q is false' is a contradiction. Truth determination* is defined this way: *A's obtaining determines B's truth* if and only if *The explanation that B is true is that A obtains.* ('To obtain' is 'to be the case' or 'to be a fact'.)[27]

In the case of God knowing what I will do tomorrow, the entailment goes in this direction: from the proposition expressing God's knowledge to the proposition expressing my action. But the direction of truth determination goes the other way around. My action is what makes the proposition expressing God's foreknowledge true, and not the other way around. My freedom as the explanation of my action is perfectly compatible with this. The explanation of the proposition expressing God's foreknowledge being true is that God is omniscient and the proposition expressing my action is true; and Yandell considers that divine foreknowledge is compatible with human freedom.

Necessity and the past

But maybe a muddle over necessity and propositions isn't really the only problem. For many, the problem is that if God foreknew what I am currently doing, his knowledge of my current activity is past, and so unchangeable. One could say that what is past becomes 'necessary' because it is no longer changeable, and nothing can be done about it.

William of Ockham's account, which takes on this problem of the past and necessity, has also received considerable attention today from analytic philosophers. He deems 'accidental necessity' to apply to statements which are only about the past, pure and simple, without a component that refers to the future. The date of my birth, known the year after, is accidentally necessary. But statements that refer in part to the future remain contingent and are not accidentally necessary. So if God knew, in the year of your birth, the future details of your love life, those events do not become accidentally necessary when you are a babe in arms.

According to Ockham, God's knowledge, although it is unchangeable, is also contingent. That means it could have been otherwise. And so that proposition is *unchangeable*, and yet is not a *necessary* proposition but a contingent one. Therefore, in contrast to Aquinas, Ockham believed that God's knowledge about the future was itself contingent. Therefore it does not make my future action necessary.[28]

Thus some things, apparently about the past, are now fixed, and others, also apparently about the past, are not, according to Ockham and those who would follow him. The debate raging in contemporary philosophy has largely centred on how those two groups can be distinguished in a way that is not arbitrary. Some distinguish 'hard' from 'soft' facts about the past. Hard facts are entirely about the past, over and done with. 'I was born 60 years before my death', given that I am still alive, is only a 'soft fact' about the past: although it refers back to a past event, it also refers to the future which has not happened yet. Plantinga locates the crucial difference in what an agent has the power to change, or not. Broadly, if an agent has power to change it, it is not accidentally necessary. Accidentally necessary facts are not fixed until a later time, after which they are fixed forever.[29] These manoeuvres are attempts to prise open past knowledge, in order to allow room for future change. They are not, ostensibly, trying to claim that one can *change* the past. The hope is that it might be possible to assert that we have the power to do something, such that if we were to do it, God would have had a different belief to the one that God did have in the past. It suggests that there might be something now called 'backward counterfactual dependency'; that past propositions are somehow dependent and open to change from the future. It is claimed to differ from outright 'backward causation', the ability to make something be the case in the past. Whether in fact backward counterfactual dependency can escape backward causation is a debated point.[30] There is an Irish joke about an English motorist pulling over to the side of the road and asking an old fellow: 'How do I get to Lisdoonvarna from here?' 'Ah now,' replied the Irishman, 'if I was going to Lisdoonvarna I wouldn't start from here in the first place.' The pattern of reasoning is similar: if God 'foreknew that I would decide A' and then I changed my mind and chose B, God wouldn't have foreknown A in the first place. God would have foreknown B instead; or as Craig puts it, 'it does lie within my power to freely perform some action *a*, and if *a* were to occur, then the past would have been different than it in fact is'.[31] This view of the nature of the past clearly will have its own problems in winning converts. Does it cohere with your intuitions? (Plantinga says, 'it certainly seems possible', but this may not be enough to satisfy everyone).[32]

Attempts to distinguish different modes of the past have attracted much criticism. The distinctions themselves are difficult to formulate in a reliable and satisfying way, and no clear agreement can be reached on what these concepts should cover and what they should exclude.[33] Craig even questions whether it is valid to mix this *temporal* necessity with the *logical* necessity of the proposition 'Necessarily, if God foreknows *x*, then *x* will happen.' How do we know that temporal necessity is passed on from premises to conclusions in the way that logical necessity is? Anyway, even if it is temporally necessary, how do we know that temporal necessity is incompatible with being free? 'So long as a person's choice is causally undetermined, it is a free choice even if that person is unable to choose the opposite of that choice.'[34] As far as Craig is concerned, no-one has given an adequate account of what temporal necessity is anyway.

Timeless knowledge

Very well, then: If it is the 'time' aspect which creates the problem, let's just cut that part out. (In fact, Aquinas maintains not merely that God is eternal, as if that is some quality God possesses; but that eternity is God. 'Eternity is nothing else but God Himself. Hence God is not called eternal, as if He were in any way measured; but the idea of measurement is there taken according to the apprehension of our mind alone.'[35]) If God exists outside time, as is frequently asserted, God does not have 'fore'-knowledge. Instead, God has 'timeless' knowledge. This has an immediate impact on our problems. First, it might solve the dilemma of human freedom. God does not 'know in advance' what I will do, but 'knows' in some kind of continuous eternal present. God's knowledge is not 'future' (at least to God). Second, it might solve the 'source problem' of how God knows, for as Aquinas writes: 'Just as he who goes along the road, does not see those who come after him; whereas he who sees the whole road from a height, sees at once all travelling by the way',[36] so God knows by simple intelligence what is future to us as well as what is present to us. Earlier, Boethius wrote:

> His knowledge, too, transcends all temporal change and abides in the immediacy of his presence. It embraces all the infinite recesses of past and future and views them in the immediacy of its knowing as though they are happening in the present. If you wish to consider, then, the foreknowledge or prevision by which He discovers all things, it will be more correct to think of it not as a kind of foreknowledge, but as the knowledge of a never-ending presence.
>
> People see things but this certainly does not make them necessary. And your seeing them doesn't impose any necessity on the things you see present, does it? . . . And if human and divine present may be compared, just as you see certain things in your present time, so God sees all things in his eternal present. So that this divine foreknowledge does

> not change the nature and property of things; it simply sees things present to it exactly as they will happen at some time as future events. . . . The divine gaze looks down on all things without disturbing their nature; to Him they are present things, but under the condition of time they are future things.[37]

As Aquinas constructed it, something that is contingent in itself becomes 'certain' in our knowledge as it happens. In an analogous way, because God knows all things as present, God can know them as certain, without this removing their contingency. In the divine vision, in eternity, all things are as present, and are 'seen' so to speak.

> Now God knows all contingent things not only as they are in their causes, but also as each one of them is actually in itself. And although contingent things become actual successively, nevertheless God knows contingent things not successively, as they are in their own being, as we do but simultaneously. The reason is because His knowledge is measured by eternity, as is also His being; and eternity being simultaneously whole comprises all time, as said above. Hence all things that are in time are present to God from eternity, not only because He has the types of things present within Him, as some say; but because His glance is carried from eternity over all things as they are in their presentiality. Hence it is manifest that contingent things are infallibly known by God, inasmuch as they are subject to the divine sight in their presentiality; yet they are future contingent things in relation to their own causes.[38]

Aquinas also uses the image of a circle: all the points on the circumference are all 'present' to the centre at once.[39] This view, then, which was also put forward by Ibn Sīnā and by Crescas, seeks to explain the certainty entailed in God's knowledge in such a way that the knowledge does not itself *create* the certainty, *make* the event happen, but merely witnesses it eternally and continually, even though from *our* point of view, it hasn't happened yet.[40]

This proposed solution met with criticism from an early stage. Duns Scotus rejected timelessness as a solution to the foreknowledge dilemma for several reasons. The idea that past, present and future can all be present to 'eternity' implies that they can be simultaneous, which to his mind is incoherent. He thinks a thing must exist in order to 'coexist' or 'be present to' something else. The past and the future do not exist, and cannot therefore 'be present' to an alleged 'eternal now'. To say that past, present and future are all 'present to God in eternity' implies that the past, once it has happened and is over and done with, continues to exist somewhere and somehow, and the future likewise is out there somewhere existing before it comes into existence as present. Similarly, Ibn Rushd in criticism of al-Ghazālī claimed that if God knows an event before it comes about, then there is no difference between the actualization and the non-actualization of a particular event; God must be knowing both at once. Such timeless knowledge used to resolve the dilemma implies that 'the existent and the non-existent are one and the same'. Anyway, 'it can hardly be conceived that the knowledge of a thing before it exists can be identical with the knowledge of it after it exists'.[41]

So the success of the timelessness solution depends on your intuitions about eternity and its relation to the temporal sequence we experience. However, even if it solves the 'foreknowledge' dilemma, it leaves behind a problem in its wake: am I free if God knows *in eternity* what I will do?[42]

A timeless knowledge dilemma?

Zagzebski wonders if solving the 'foreknowledge' dilemma with God's timeless, eternal knowing just shifts the problem of necessity to a different point: from God's necessitating foreknowledge to God's necessitating eternal knowledge. Eternity is just like the past in being irrevocable and unchangeable. If the foreknowledge dilemma consists in the fact that I cannot affect the past, and thereby change God's prior knowledge, eternity creates the same situation: if it has been known timelessly by God from all eternity that I would marry my husband, I hardly seem more free to change my mind at the church door than I was when it was claimed that God merely 'fore'knew that I would marry him.

Zagzebski does not think the problem insoluble; our intuitions about eternity are less deeply entrenched than our intuitions about the past, so this problem might be easier to solve. But it does, in her view, show that the timelessness solution is not a complete solution in itself.[43]

Molina had a further problem with this timeless view of God's knowledge. If God's knowledge arises from his timeless contemplation of all, is God dependent on the created world for this knowledge? If God 'knows' things from observation, then it does rather imply God is having to learn about the world from the world itself. Those who hold a Thomist/Maimonidean line have an answer for this anxiety, as we shall see shortly.[44]

But can a changeless, timeless God know everything?

Kretzmann has argued that omniscience and immutability are incompatible. A perfect being, one who is not subject to change and who knows everything, must know what time it is. But a being that always knows what time it is, is subject to change. Therefore there must be no perfect being of this kind.[45] This was also a charge made by Ibn Rushd against al-Ghazālī.

Al-Ghazālī claimed that changes in the relationship between subject and object did not necessarily entail changes. He pointed out that the pillar does not move or change if it was previously on the right of me, and is now on the left once I've moved. Knowledge is a relation between the one who knows and the one who is known; the latter can change while the former does not.[46]

In our own century, Geach took up al-Ghazālī's suggestion (in apparent ignorance of the Islamic predecessor). He argues for a distinction between 'real' and 'apparent' change. The truth-value of a proposition about something can change without the thing itself changing. For example:

I was taller than my sons but now I am shorter.

Or

Butter has become more expensive.

I have not shrunk, nor has butter undergone a change in its inner nature. These kinds of 'changes', where what we say about something has changed but the thing itself hasn't, are what Geach calls 'Cambridge' changes.[47] One could argue that 'changes' in God's knowledge are not changes in God, but in the objects of his knowledge; as far as God is concerned, they are Cambridge changes (that is, not real changes at all).

Kretzmann also maintained that a perfect being can't just know the whole plan of history, but also has to know what stage it is at *now*. An omniscient God must know what I am doing *now* or is not omniscient.[48] A proposition which contains a time in it can't be known timelessly, 'because it just isn't true timelessly', as Prior put it.[49] So can a timeless being not be omniscient, because such a being cannot know 'Today is Saturday, tomorrow is Sunday'?

Is this something a timeless being can't know – or are these just words which an omniscient being couldn't use to express knowledge?[50] Perhaps an omniscient being could know timelessly all that a time-bound being knows at a given time; it just needs to be expressed differently.[51]

Davies however argues that if you know the man upstairs committed a crime, and I knew the father of Michael committed the crime, I do not know what you know – even if the man is the same person.[52] Kenny similarly argues that ' "Today is Friday" on Friday does not express the same knowledge as "Yesterday was Friday" on Saturday. . . . If a changeless being cannot know the time, then it cannot know either what is expressed by tensed propositions. . . . A believer in divine omniscience must, it seems, give up belief in divine immutability.'[53]

Here it might be useful to remember the difference between 'sentences' and 'propositions'. Sentences are the words used, propositions the truths (or falsehoods) expressed. The two sentences may not be the same, but the propositions (who committed the crime; which day was Friday) can be. Does omniscience mean 'knowing the truth-status of every proposition' or does it entail 'expressing propositional knowledge in every possible sentence'? Aquinas did not know the proposition: 'My brain stem is functioning'. Does that mean that he did not know he was alive?

Aquinas asserted that it would be false to say 'Whatever God knew He [now] knows' if that refers to 'what is enunciated' – the way it is expressed.

> For as it is without variation in the divine knowledge that God knows one and the same thing sometime to be, and sometime not, so it is without variation in the divine knowledge that God knows that an enunciation is sometime true, and sometime false. The knowledge of God, however, would be variable if He knew enunciations according to their own limitations, by comparison and division, as occurs in our intellect. Hence our knowledge varies either as regards truth and falsity, for example, if when a thing is changed we retained the same opinion about it; or as regards diverse opinions, as if we first thought that someone was sitting, and afterwards thought that he was not sitting; neither of which can be in God.[54]

So, on this account, God can know the date of your marriage, the date of the birth of your children, and the order in which these events occurred. But God cannot know it in the experiential form: 'Reza and Gazala are *now* getting married.' 'Gazala is *now* going into labour.' 'Gazala has *just* had her second son.' God could know that *Gazala* is knowing these sentences at a certain time; but knowing as the divine knows it does not require that God either knows temporally, or changes as events change.

Of course, one need not accept that God's knowledge is propositional. In which case, the charge that because God cannot know every proposition we know, God must not be omniscient, is like saying the fact that a divinity cannot have headaches like we have indicates that God is not omnipotent.

Another way to analyse this problem is like this:

> 'My husband says I am beautiful.' Who is said to be beautiful? The husband or the wife?
>
> 'Yesterday you said you would finish that job today.' On which day would the job be finished?

Probably you have no difficulty in understanding which person or which day was intended by the speaker. But what was probably said by the husband was: 'You are beautiful' and 'I will finish that job tomorrow' – not 'I' or 'today', as quoted. In fact, if the wife had quoted her husband more literally and said 'My husband says "you are beautiful"' it might have caused a misunderstanding. Although this shiftiness in everyday speech causes no confusion, even to small children, this is the philosopher's problem known as 'indexical reference' – reference to times, places, events, objects or persons by means of demonstrative or personal pronouns or adverbs.[55] As far as our God problem is concerned, according to an argument from Castañeda the problem is the word 'now' (or other markers of time).

When we report the speech, knowledge, beliefs or whatever of someone else, the indicators we use are often our own and not the other's. Kretzmann's statements of what an omniscient being cannot know ('It is now 10:00') use Kretzmann's own indexical references, not the omniscient knower's. But if the content of the knowledge is the same but the indexical reference to time is reportedly different, is this not the innocuous shift of saying 'Yesterday you said you would finish that job today'? If so, although it would strictly be inaccurate to say a timeless being knows 'what time it is now', God can know timelessly what goes on in what order, as well as what temporal beings experience and know.

Middle knowledge

Luis de Molina created a new solution to the dilemma, in an attempt to preserve both God's omniscience and human freedom. He did this by distinguishing three kinds of knowledge that God has. First, God has 'natural' knowledge: this is a knowledge of all the necessities of creation, and all the possibilities of what could happen, in all possible combinations. This knowledge is part of God's essential omniscience. God also has 'free' knowledge: knowledge of the actual world as it exists; that is, of all the possibilities that have been actualized. If they have been actualized, it is as a result of God's free will, which is why this kind of knowledge is called 'free': it is the result of free choice and exercise of will. It is the knowledge with which God knows what will or won't happen. This knowledge comes after the divine act of will, and this knowledge is contingent, since it is dependent on the decisions and choices God makes in the creation of the world.

In between these two forms and contents of knowledge comes God's act of will. God's decisions are 'informed', so to speak, by a third kind of knowledge, which Molina calls 'middle knowledge', coming as it does in the middle of the other two: after God's knowledge of what must and might be, but before knowledge of what has been actualized.[56] This middle knowledge is knowledge of 'what would happen if'. This is the knowledge of what finite free wills would do if placed in certain conditions, for example. Molina says it is that knowledge by which God sees, in his own essence, what each person would freely do in a given situation, even though one would really be able to do the opposite. God does not acquire this middle knowledge, however, from the creatures – that would compromise transcendence – but rather from God's own self-knowledge. Because of the 'depth of his knowledge which surpasses all creatures' – what Molina calls his 'supercomprehension' – God can foreknow beings' free choices in a way impossible for us. Molina also makes clear that in his view if the antecedent of a conditional clause is temporally necessary, it does not entail that the consequent is temporally necessary. If there is a necessity about God's knowledge which is purely temporal – not causal or logical – then if the state of affairs God knows about is contingent, it remains so despite God's knowledge.

Middle knowledge, then, supplies an answer to the foreknowledge dilemma: it provides a sort of epistemological halfway-house wherein God can know our free choices before they exist, in a way in which it is still possible for them to have been otherwise. It leaves my acts uncaused by God's knowledge, and God's knowledge uncaused by my acts.

Molina's doctrine of middle knowledge was the topic of furious debate. It has won some adherents in the modern revival of the foreknowledge debate and has also attracted fierce criticism.[57] What, asks Adams, are the grounds for middle knowledge: how does one know it to be true? Either the grounds for the truth of what is known are necessitating, in which case it cannot be the result of freedom, or the grounds can only confer probability, and not certain knowledge. Once you have eliminated logic and causes as guarantees for certainty, the only basis for knowing 'what will happen if' are human character. But knowledge of this is uncertain; we can always act out of character.

> Molina seems to want to say that what free creatures would do under various possible conditions is not there, objectively, to be known, but that God's mind is so perfect that He knows it anyway. But that is impossible. The problem to be solved is how the relevant subjunctive conditionals can be true, and nothing that may be said about the excellence of God's cognitive powers contributes anything to the solution of that problem.[58]

Can the appeal to God's super-comprehension form a successful response to these objections? Molina would be quite happy to agree with these objections, as applied to human knowledge. We cannot have certain middle knowledge. But God's super-comprehension is precisely the ability to read human intentions, desires, motivations and characters infallibly. *Pace* Adams, Molina clearly thinks 'the excellence of God's cognitive powers' is precisely the point. Some think that God's excellent cognitive powers can encompass the future, despite objections to the truth-status of future contingent propositions. If so, then Molina's middle knowledge is a subcategory of this.

Molina's position comes closest to the immediate response of most philosophically untutored people to the foreknowledge dilemma. 'If you know someone really, really well, you *do* know what they would do in certain hypothetical situations. God being God, has knowledge more perfect than ours, so God can be 100 per cent certain, whereas I can only be 95 per cent certain. But the fact that I know what my husband would do in certain circumstances doesn't mean that he isn't free when he does it.' *How* God knows is by knowing human characters even before their creation; with greater accuracy, however, than we can possess.[59] It is more sophisticated of course. What is critical for Molina, in preserving human freedom, is the timing; God's knowledge of counterfactuals comes *before* God's creation.[60] This exempts what humans *would* do from God's decree in creation, or as Craig – a defender of Middle Knowledge – puts it,

> the Molinists, by placing God's counterfactual knowledge prior to the divine decree, made room for creaturely freedom by exempting counterfactual truths from God's decree. In the same way that necessary truths like 2 + 2 = 4 are prior to and therefore independent of God's decree, so also counterfactual truths about how creatures would freely choose under various circumstances are prior to and independent of God's decree.[61]

Craig's understanding of God's relationship to necessary truths is an interesting one; apparently they are not created by God and enjoy independence. It may be true that God does not decide on a daily basis that today 2 + 2 = 4; but most theists do believe that necessary truths like this are part of God's plan. So creatures' free choices, the content of middle knowledge, would also be part of that plan. It may pre-exist God's execution, but not God's conception.

Adams and Kenny in different ways also accuse Molina of circularity. In middle knowledge there must be something there to be known; whereas middle knowledge is supposed to exist before anything actual exists. Middle knowledge must be there, as it were, for purposes of divine consultation, to advise God on any decisions in creating. 'Middle knowledge' then suggests that God knows something that isn't real, that isn't there to be known. Not merely do my actions not yet exist; I don't yet exist to have a character to be known in advance. So this runs aground on the familiar objection that what does not exist (like the future) cannot be an object of knowledge. Kenny's claim is:

> The difficulty is simply that if it is to be possible for God to know which world he is actualizing, then his middle knowledge must be logically prior to his decision to actualize; whereas, if middle knowledge is to have an object, the actualization must already have taken place.[62]

This rests on the assumption that God's knowledge must be of existent things or states of affairs; and the problem is that what is counterfactual does not in fact exist. However, if all knowledge entails an existent object, then one cannot know the proposition 'The dodo is extinct.' So is it possible to know the truth about abstract things, unreal things, fictional things, or historical things, that once existed but now do not?

The tacit model of God's knowledge that lies behind this objection is a passive one: God beholds things and knows them by perceiving them, analogously to our seeing or perceiving. God's knowledge is acquaintance with what is. But there are other ways of conceiving God's knowledge to consider before revisiting Molina's suggestion.

Can God know what is not actually real and existing? Aquinas gives this answer:

> *I answer that, God knows all things whatsoever that in any way are. Now it is possible that things that are not absolutely, should be in a certain sense. For things absolutely are which are actual; whereas things which are not actual, are in the power either of God Himself or of a creature, whether in active power, or passive; whether in power of thought or of imagination, or of any other manner of meaning whatsoever. Whatever therefore can be made, or thought, or said by the creature, as also whatever He Himself can do, all are known to God, although they are not actual. And in so far it can be said that He has knowledge even of things that are not.*
>
> *Now a certain difference is to be noted in the consideration of those things that are not actual. For though some of them may not be in act now, still they were, or they will be; and God is said to know all these with the knowledge of vision: for since God's act of understanding, which is His being, is measured by eternity; and since eternity is without succession, comprehending all time, the present glance of God extends over all time, and to all things which exist in any time, as to objects present to Him. But there are other things in God's power, or the creature's, which nevertheless are not, nor will be, nor were; and as regards these He is said to have knowledge, not of vision, but of simple intelligence. This is so called because the things we see around us have distinct being outside the seer.*
>
> Objection!
> *Something that does not exist or is not actual is not true, and so cannot be known.*

Reply:
Those things that are not actual are true in so far as they are in potentiality; for it is true that they are in potentiality; and as such they are known by God.

Objection!
The knowledge of God is the cause of what is known by Him. But it is not the cause of things that are not, because a thing that is not, has no cause. Therefore God has no knowledge of things that are not.

Reply:
The knowledge of God, joined to His will is the cause of things. Hence it is not necessary that what ever God knows, is, or was, or will be; but only is this necessary as regards what He wills to be, or permits to be. Further, it is in the knowledge of God not that they be, but that they be possible.[63]

How does God know?

Where then does God get knowledge from? Things that do not (or do not yet) exist aren't there for God to know them, or so the argument goes. But this picture of how God knows makes God's knowledge dependent on creatures, which is theologically and religiously repugnant for some thinkers, such as Ockham. So *how* can we explain that God knows what I will do in the future?

Many philosophers see God's knowledge as propositional. God's knowledge takes the form of statements, and God knows if they are true or not. So omniscience is defined in such ways as 'if that being believes all and only what is true, and justifiably believes all and only what he believes' (Kvanvig) or a being is omniscient if it knows the truth value of every proposition (Zagzebski).[64]

Alston suggests that the fact that our knowledge is propositional could be seen as a result of our limitations, which need not apply to God. We cannot grasp the whole, we can only grasp certain features at a time, which we then form into propositions. In this case, propositional knowledge is really a limitation which we suffer. But God's knowledge is not partial in this way. So perhaps God knows things by immediate intuition. As we immediately perceive a scene and take it all in at once, without dividing it into separate facts, God's knowledge is similar, only perfect. Such intuitive knowing is the most perfect form of knowing; we reject it as a model for ourselves, not because it is inadequate, but because it is too great. As Alston puts it,

> If we could be continuously directly aware of every fact of which we have knowledge, that would be splendid; but we must settle for

something more modest. Immediate awareness of facts is the highest form of knowledge just because it is a direct and foolproof way of mirroring the reality to be known.[65]

For Aquinas God's knowledge does not consist of the entire body of true propositions. There is no distinction between God's knowledge and what God knows; what God knows is the divine knowledge, which is known by knowing His own self perfectly. God knows everything by understanding the essence of each thing.[66] Just as God knows material things immaterially, things that we know expressed as propositions, God knows by 'simple intelligence'. Precisely *how* God pulls this off we cannot know. But one thing it has to recommend it (if your views run in this direction) is its harmony with the doctrine of divine simplicity. If God is simple, God cannot have complex knowledge, that is, knowledge built up of different bits or facts. Instead divine omniscience knows all by knowing God's own self – not by knowing this or that proposition.

Aquinas is in part following an Aristotelian tradition that sees the proper object of God's knowledge as God Himself. Another heir to this is Ibn Rushd; and one notion he would like to obliterate with this Aristotelian idea is the implication that God needs to discover from reality what is going on. Ibn Rushd protested against al-Ghazālī on this account:

> Ghazālī's objection . . . is that it is possible that God's knowledge should be like the knowledge of man, that is that the things known should be the cause of this knowledge and their occurrence the cause of the fact that he knows them, just as the objects of sight are the cause of visual perception and the intelligible the cause of intellectual apprehension.[67]

But the idea that God must obtain his information in this way, that God is thereby dependent on created entities for knowledge, Ibn Rushd rejects absolutely.

> It is impossible, according to the philosophers, that God's knowledge should be analogous to ours, for our knowledge is the effect of the existents, whereas God's knowledge is their cause, and it is not true that eternal knowledge is of the same form as temporal. He who believes this makes God an eternal man and man a mortal God, and in short, it has previously been shown that God's knowledge stands in opposition to man's, for it is his knowledge which produces the existent, and it is not the existents which produce his knowledge.[68]

So for Thomas Aquinas, Ibn Rushd and also Maimonides – all conscious of Aristotelian views of God and knowledge – the task is not to explain how God finds out what is going on in the world. Rather, what goes on in the world is itself dependent on, a function of, God's knowledge. As Augustine puts it: 'It is not because things are what they are that God knows them, it is because he knows them that they are what they are.'[69] Aquinas describes God's knowledge as the cause of how things are. Ibn Rushd maintains that, as their maker, God knows the structure and principles of the universe. God doesn't need observation of particular instances to possess full knowledge. The relation between God's knowledge and how things are is like the relation between a craftsman's knowledge and his products.

On this view – contrary to the picture suggested by Adams' and Kenny's objections to Middle Knowledge – God's knowledge is not that of a perceiver, but of a creator: we might characterize aspects of it as the imagination of what might be, and the contemplation of those possibilities, in order to exercise wisdom and discernment in creation. We could (courting trouble) invoke an analogy with how an author knows what her characters will do. Mary Weston, writing *The Escape Plan*, knows what Hoku will do not by knowing her character so well that she can predict his action; but because it is in her power to create the plot.[70] Weston's plot, however, is one in which Hoku acts *freely* in the way that he does, because it is in harmony with his character. Although the novel is entirely dependent on Weston's will, it is a novel in which all the characters choose to act the way they do – including the occasions when Tiger acts rather compulsively. When Tiger's choices in life appear constrained, they are not constrained by the author but by his inner tensions, and he never is heard to complain about the grip that Weston has on him.

Now if you believe God transcends time, this knowing and creating by God takes place timelessly. Molina's ordering of natural knowledge–middle knowledge–free knowledge is meant to be 'logical' and not 'chronological'; and yet, Molinists firmly hold that middle knowledge comes before God's decree and not after. Our freedom is meant to hang on this timing. Craig claims, '. . . if counterfactuals of creaturely freedom were known only after the divine decree, then it is God who determined what every creature would do in every circumstance'.[71] But if God *really* creates timelessly, it is not clear what is really signified by 'logically prior' (or 'after the divine decree'). There is no gain in 'freedom' anyway, no matter the timing of the counterfactual knowledge. For God is the cause of all creatures, no matter when he knows or creates them. It is surely not the case that once God creates them, all their acts are dependent on God, but before that they escape divine control. Before that they are not independent; they are non-existent. And whether or not God knows the truth about them when they are non-existent, part of that truth (for the Thomist–Averroëan theist) is that they can never be independent of God's knowledge and creative power.

'For through knowing the true reality of His own immutable essence, He also knows the totality of what necessarily derives from all His acts.'[72] In this way, Maimonides maintained that God knows as a creator who does not need to watch and see how things will turn out. A clockmaker's knowledge, which is based on the principles of the design and execution, does not require observation in order to work out how the clock functions. An onlooker, on the other hand, must learn and understand by watching. In an analogous way, God knows by knowing the form and the principles of creation; God knows the design, all the possibilities of the future which will be realized. Maimonides is critical of the Islamic philosophers' notions of 'possibility' – as that which is conceivable, that which is not a contradiction. For Maimonides, merely logical possibility is not real possibility. Only what is willed by God is possible. God's essential will is to will being, to let things be, guided by divine wisdom, which is characterized by goodness. This leads Maimonides to the principle of plenitude: that every genuine possibility will one day be realized. God as pure goodness would not want to deprive any good thing of existence, or deprive the universe of the existence of any good thing. There is no category that is the 'unactualized possible'. What is possible is not simply dependent on the absence of contradiction; but on God's will. Something that is 'theoretically' or 'logically possible' but not God's will is theologically not possible. It cannot and will not ever be actualized.

As Ibn Rushd maintains, God's thinking and creating are the same; the universe reflects God's thought. 'For His knowledge is the cause of being and being is the cause of our knowledge. . .'[73] As Mullā Ṣadrā wrote,

> Just as His Being – May He be exalted! – is not mixed with privation of anything at all, likewise His Knowledge of His Essence, which is the Presence of His Essence, is not mixed with the absence of anything at all. This is because His Essence is That Which makes all things to be those things and Which gives all realities their reality.[74]

This line can be seen in contemporary writers of a broadly Thomist persuasion. Brian Davies' way of solving the foreknowledge dilemma is to say:

> One may therefore suggest that God can know the future by knowing himself as Creator of whatever goes to make up the universe as time goes on. . . . In terms of this view, God can know the future by knowing himself and thereby knowing what in the universe will come to pass by virtue of him.[75]

Miller argues in a similar vein that God knows the events in the world by being their cause; even including the free choices of human beings.[76]

> God could know the free activities of his creatures in exactly the same way as he knows their unfree activities in causing or bringing it about that they occur. Human freedom could therefore co-exist quite happily with divine simplicity – and with the omniscience and omnipotence that it entails.[77]

Affirming transcendence

The thinkers we have just been considering, as an alternative to Molinism, tend to deny that we *can*, still less *must*, work out a tidy account in human terms of how an almighty, transcendent God can be omniscient. Maimonides denies that we could even attempt to comprehend it. God's knowledge is identical with God's essence and this essence cannot be comprehended. He observes that 'philosophers' have insisted that

> His knowledge is His essence, and His essence His knowledge. As we have explained, they were those who have demonstrated that our intellects are incapable of apprehending the true reality of His essence as it really is. How then can they think that they can apprehend His knowledge, seeing that His knowledge is not a thing that is outside of His essence? For the selfsame incapacity that prevents our intellects from apprehending His essence also prevents them from apprehending His knowledge of things as they are. For this knowledge is not of the same species as ours so that we can draw an analogy with regard to it, but a totally different thing.[78]

Because God's knowledge is identical with God's essence, it is likewise incomprehensible, and therefore the way in which free will and divine foreknowledge are compatible is also incomprehensible to us.[79] What we *can* know of God's knowledge is that

> He does not apprehend at certain times while being ignorant at others. I mean to say that no new knowledge comes to Him in any way; that His knowledge is neither multiple nor finite; that nothing among all the beings is hidden from him; and that His knowledge of them does not abolish their natures, for the possible remains as it was with the nature of possibility.[80]

As far as the foreknowledge problem is concerned, God's knowledge does not change the nature of the possible to the necessary. Maimonides simply asserts this, without feeling the need to explain exactly how this can be so; the support he gives it is textual support from the Torah. Indeed, it would be inconsistent of him to attempt to spell it out, given his insistence on the folly of such a procedure.

> All the contradictions that may appear in the union of these assertions are due to their being considered in relation to our knowledge, which has only its name in common with His knowledge. . . . It is accordingly true that the meaning of knowledge . . ., when ascribed to us, [is] different from the meanings of [this] term when ascribed to Him. When, therefore, the two . . . knowledges . . . are taken to have one and the same meaning, the above-mentioned difficulties and doubts arise. When, on the other hand, it is known that everything that is ascribed to us is different from everything that is ascribed to Him, truth becomes manifest. The differences between the things ascribed to Him and those ascribed to us have been explicitly stated . . . in its dictum *Neither are my ways your ways.*[81]

Feldman has recently observed that, 'In essence, Maimonides' "solution" to this classic dilemma is to make the dilemma its own answer.'[82] Maimonides' triumph (unless you think it an evasion) is to make the contradictions we find themselves into an affirmation of God's transcendence.

> What I myself say is that all these difficulties . . . have as their cause the fact that they established a relation between our knowledge and His, may He be exalted; for every sect considers the things that are impossible for our knowledge and consequently thinks that this also holds necessarily with regard to His knowledge or else that the thing is obscure for it. The philosophers ought to be blamed more strongly than anyone else with regard to this question.[83]

Omniscience and personal knowledge

In many of these debates, it looks as if the thinkers have ceased to think about this question as an aspect of God's relationship to creatures, and instead made it a question about God's *capabilities*. 'What can God know, and how? And given our answer, does God still deserve to be called God?' Need we take problems about truth-value, future contingent propositions, counterfactuals, subjunctive conditionals, and other philosophical paraphernalia as the only way to examine the problem? What if we explore God's knowledge using the model of a relationship? What if we recognize that the problem of divine foreknowledge is really a question about how God knows us?

Use of a personal model of knowledge as a way of understanding how God knows has been swiftly dismissed for two reasons. Some dismiss this humble analogy because the certainty or otherwise of God's knowledge is not felt to be the point at issue: the point at issue is taken to be the logical problem, that if in some way it is true beforehand, then there is no possibility of it turning out otherwise.

The other reason for dismissal is that, although we 'loosely' speak of such convictions as 'knowledge', really they are not, according to some philosophers. They are firmly held beliefs, perhaps with some warrant and evidence, but they do not possess the requisite certainty to qualify as knowledge. It isn't really possible to *know* what your spouse or best friend or dog would do, if he, she, or it were placed in certain circumstances. Thus the analogy fails, unless one wants to speak of God holding a firm belief in what I will do.[84] Hasker is one who does think God has beliefs and that the dilemma just might be solved if we speak not of God's knowledge but of God's beliefs, for 'no-one supposes that a human being's believing something entails the truth of what is believed'.[85] But does it solve the problem to say that I am free if it is possible that God has false beliefs about what I will do?

It is tempting to respond that this is simply to forget what an analogy is; moreover, to forget what an analogy must be when it, however clumsily, is drawn between divine and human experience. If an analogy does not break down at some point, it is not an analogy but an identity. It seems perfectly reasonable to argue that the point at which an epistemological analogy between the divine and human breaks down is at the degree of certainty or perfection of one's knowledge. I feel I can be quite certain that if my husband was offered a large sum of money to kill our children, he would refuse. I would generally say 'I *know*'; although some strict philosophers would only count this as a firmly held belief. Nevertheless, there seems no good reason why this 'relational' knowledge of another person must be fallible in God. It seems reasonable to say, given that God is transcendent, that one of the differences between us is that whereas I possess a 'high' degree of certainty in my comprehension of someone else, God possesses complete certainty in his supercomprehension (to use Molina's word). Meanwhile, my 'knowing' what my husband would do does not make it necessary that he does so, even if I turn out to be right. In the same way, God's knowledge of possibilities future to us based on intimate supercomprehension, rather than the necessity of propositions, is certain but does not change the modal status of their action.

What grounds this supercomprehension of creatures? Just supreme intelligence? We could return to an inspiration from Aristotle, who thought that what God knows is God's very self – His divine essence and ideas. Many believers after Aristotle found that unsatisfying, and rather cold or even egotistical for a personal God. But it was taken up by philosophers in all three of the Abrahamic faiths: Ibn Rushd, Maimonides and Aquinas all argued that God knows all by knowing God's own essence, which reflects the whole of reality. As we have seen, they (and a long tradition after them) believe that God knows all by creating all. If we see ourselves not as an alien object opposed to God, but as taken up in

God's essence and God's creation, God knows what it is *we* are knowing and experiencing – simply in the act of being a self-contemplating God who knows what he creates. This is also one way to address the problem of how a timeless God can know time-bound events: through intimacy with me God is aware of what I experience, as I experience it.

God creates and conserves all things in being, including human free action, and that is how God knows. – Surely this makes the problem worse? God knows all things, including my future free action, by creating them – this makes God the cause of my acting. This doesn't solve the problem of freedom; it brings it to a head.

What this account in fact does is reveal what lies at the root of the divine foreknowledge problem: the relation between God and human action, between divine and creaturely power. For it declares that we are free, yet utterly dependent on God for our being, our action, *and* for our freedom. Does human freedom require human independence from God? To these questions we shall now turn.

Draw your own conclusions

Does God know what I will do tomorrow? What do you think are the consequences of your view?

Are some parts of the future genuinely open? Does God not know them?

Are you free if you have only one alternative, but you want it?

If you do what you want but had no choice between options, are you morally responsible for what you have done?

Does God exist within time, or outside time? If God is eternal, need that mean 'timeless'?

Can God know things by knowing that I know them?

Can God know everything by knowing Himself?

Does the image of an author, or an artisan, provide a useful analogy for how God knows creation?

Is interpersonal knowledge a workable model for God's knowledge?

Further reading

Aquinas, T. *The 'Summa Theologica' of St. Thomas Aquinas*, London, Burns Oates & Washbourne

Boethius (1978) *The Consolation of Philosophy*, ed. V. E. Watts, Harmondsworth, Penguin

Craig, W. L. (1987) *The Only Wise God: The Compatibility of Divine Foreknowledge and Human Freedom*, Grand Rapids, Mich., Baker Book House

Craig, W. L. (1988) *The Problem of Divine Foreknowledge and Future Contingents from Aristotle to Suarez*, Leiden, Brill

Craig W. L. (1991) *Divine Foreknowledge and Human Freedom: The Coherence of Theism: Omniscience*, Brill's Studies in Intellectual History 19, Leiden, Brill

Davies, B. (1985) *Thinking about God*, London, Geoffrey Chapman

Fischer, J. M. (1989) *God, Foreknowledge, and Freedom*, Stanford, Calif., Stanford University Press

Hasker, W. (1989) *God, Time, and Knowledge*, Cornell Studies in the Philosophy of Religion, Ithaca and London, Cornell University Press

Hughes, G. J. (1995) *The Nature of God*, London and New York, Routledge

Kvanvig, J. L. (1986) *The Possibility of an All-Knowing God*, Basingstoke, Macmillan

Swinburne, R. (1993) *The Coherence of Theism*, Oxford, Clarendon Press

Zagzebski, L. T. (1991) *The Dilemma of Freedom and Foreknowledge*, New York, Oxford University Press

Notes

1 For example, v. 12 can be interpreted to mean that it can now be made known to everyone else that Abraham passed the test (Saadia and Maimonides interpret v. 12 in this fashion). Maimonides further interprets v. 1 as God will 'make Abraham a paradigm', which is a possible translation of the Hebrew. One can also say that it was a 'trial': God knew that Abraham would pass the test, but Abraham could not be *rewarded* for passing the test if he had not actually done it. And, of course, the words in v. 12 are attributed to an angel. So some have suggested that God foreknew Abraham's behaviour, but the angel did not. Gersonides, however, sees the challenge as a true test, whose result not even God knew. On the history of interpretation of the binding of Isaac, see S. Feldman (1985) 'The Binding of Issac: A Test-Case of Divine Foreknowledge', in T. Rudavsky (ed.), *Divine Omniscience and Divine Omnipotence in Medieval Philosophy: Islamic, Jewish and Christian Perspectives*, Synthese Historical Library 25, Dordrecht, Boston and Lancaster, Reidel. The problem of God's foreknowledge was often raised in terms of prophecy in the Jewish literature. Indeed, Gersonides (ben Gershom) devotes Book II of his *Wars of the Lord* to the problem of prophecy, before turning to the more explicit philosophical problem of divine foreknowledge in Book III. L. G. ben Gershom (1987) *The Wars of the Lord*, trans. S. Feldman, Philadelphia, New York and Jerusalem, Jewish Publication Society, vol. 2.

2 For predestination, see: 10:100; 7:29–30; 6:125; 2:6; 63:11; for free will, 18:28; 20:84.

3 al-Fārābī (1960) *Alfarabi's Commentary on Aristotle's [Peri hermeneias] (De interpretatione)*, trans. W. Kutsch and S. Marrow, Beirut, Université Saint

Joseph, Institut de lettres orientales, Recherches 13, Beirut, Imprimerie catholique, p. 97, line 27 and p. 98, line 19.

4 Thomas Aquinas, *The 'Summa Theologica' of St. Thomas Aquinas*, London, Burns Oates & Washbourne, I.14.3.3.

5 Boethius (1978) *The Consolation of Philosophy*, trans. V. E. Watts, Harmondsworth, Penguin, p. 153.

6 On this history, see D. C. Langston (1986) *God's Willing Knowledge: The Influence of Scotus' Analysis of Omniscience*, University Park and London, Pennsylvania State University Press. For their texts, see Luther and Erasmus (1969) *Luther and Erasmus: Free Will and Salvation: Erasmus: De libero arbitrio, Luther: De servo arbitrio*, trans. and ed. E. Gordon Rupp in collaboration with A. N. Marlow *et al.*, London, SCM Press.

7 Cited in F. Rosenthal (1970) *Knowledge Triumphant: The Concept of Knowledge in Medieval Islam*, Leiden, Brill, p. 120.

8 ben Gershom, *The Wars of the Lord*, vol. 2, Bk II, ch. 2.

9 ben Gershom, *The Wars of the Lord*, vol. 2, pp. 133–4.

10 ben Gershom, *The Wars of the Lord*, vol. 2, p. 118.

11 So he argues in Bk III, chs 5, 6.

12 Hisham al-Hakam writes: 'one cannot properly be a knower, unless an object of knowledge is already existent'. Cited in H. A. Wolfson (1976) *The Philosophy of the Kalam*, Cambridge, Mass., and London, Harvard University Press, p. 661. The Jewish thinker Abraham ben Daud believed that God foreknew that someone would be faced with a choice, but not what he would choose. H. A. Wolfson (1979), *Repercussions of the Kalam in Jewish Philosophy*, Cambridge, Mass., and London, Harvard University Press, p. 217.

13 W. Hasker (1989) *God, Time, and Knowledge*, Cornell Studies in the Philosophy of Religion, Ithaca and London, Cornell University Press, p. 188.

14 R. Swinburne (1993) *The Coherence of Theism*, Oxford, Clarendon Press, p. 175.

15 See Boyd's essay in J. K. Beilby and P. R. Eddy (eds) (2001) *Divine Foreknowledge: Four Views*, Downers Grove, Ill., InterVarsity Press, p. 14.

16 See Boyd's essay in Beilby and Eddy, *Divine Foreknowledge*, p. 20.

17 See Boyd's essay in Beilby and Eddy, *Divine Foreknowledge*, p. 22.

18 See Helm's essay in Beilby and Eddy, *Divine Foreknowledge*, p. 178.

19 For texts, sources and discussion, see Wolfson, *Repercussions of the Kalam in Jewish Philosophy*, p. 214. And see also Wolfson, *Philosophy of the Kalam*, p. 662.

20 P. Vardy (1999) *The Puzzle of God*, London, Fount, p. 124, using Boethius.

21 Aquinas explicitly says that the knowledge of God is the cause of all things, in *Summa Theologica*, I.14.8.

22 Barry Kogan formalizes al-Fārābī's argument in this way:

1. Statements about future contingent events are necessarily either true or false at some time, i.e. when they are determinate.
2. God foreknows as determinate all true statements about future contingent events, e.g. human free choices.
3. What God knows to be true will necessarily happen.
4. What necessarily happens, occurs either (4a) because it is necessary in

itself, or (4b) because it is necessarily caused or (4c) because it is necessary as a consequence of a true statement.

5. Only events which are necessary in themselves or necessarily caused [(4a) and (4b)] are incompatible with contingency or freedom.
6. Therefore, what happens as a consequence of God's knowing a true statement [(4c)] is fully compatible with contingency and freedom.

B. S. Kogan (1985) 'Some Reflections on the Problem of Future Contingency in Alfarabi, Avicenna, and Averroes', in T. Rudavsky (ed.), *Divine Omniscience and Divine Omnipotence in Medieval Philosophy: Islamic, Jewish and Christian Perspectives*, Synthese Historical Library 25, Dordrecht, Boston and Lancaster, Reidel, p. 96.

23 Crescas distinguished what is necessary or contingent in itself from a third category, that which is contingent in itself but necessary because it has been caused. This is a threefold distinction which derives from Ibn Sīnā. God's knowledge makes the act 'necessary', but only in a trivial sense – as anyone's knowledge would. Even if God's knowledge is causative, according to Crescas, it doesn't annul the contingency of the act. See Feldman, 'The Binding of Issac'. Boethius had earlier distinguished 'simple' from 'conditional' necessity. Propositions which are governed by 'simple necessity' are necessarily true by virtue of the necessity of essential attribution (which Boethius associates with causal necessity). But conditional necessity follows on conditional statements like, 'If you know that John is married, he is married.' But this does not confer simple necessity on such a state of affairs. To say that something is temporally necessary means only that it is impossible to perform it and the opposite. Arguably it does not threaten human freedom. W. L. Craig (1988) *The Problem of Divine Foreknowledge and Future Contingents from Aristotle to Suarez*, Leiden, Brill, p. 97.

24 Aquinas, *Summa Theologica*, I.14.3.3.

25 W. L. Craig (1987) *The Only Wise God: The Compatibility of Divine Foreknowledge and Human Freedom*, Grand Rapids, Mich., Baker Book House; W. L. Craig (1991) *Divine Foreknowledge and Human Freedom: The Coherence of Theism: Omniscience*, Brill's Studies in Intellectual History 19, Leiden, Brill; see also his pieces in J. K. Beilby and P. R. Eddy (eds) (2001) *Divine Foreknowledge: Four Views*, Downers Grove, Ill., InterVarsity Press.

26 Craig, *The Only Wise God*, p. 127.

27 K. Yandell (1999) *Philosophy of Religion: A Contemporary Introduction*, Routledge Contemporary Introductions to Philosophy, London, Routledge, p. 336.

28 See Ockham's text in M. M. Adams (1969) *Ockhams' 'Predestination, God's Foreknowledge and Future Contingents'*, New York, Meredith.

29 Plantinga argues that '*p* is accidentally necessary at *t* if and only if *p* is true at *t* and it is not possible both that *p* is true at *t* and that there exist agents $S_i \ldots$, S_n and actions $A_i \ldots, A_n$ such that (1) A_i is basic for S_i, (2) S_i has the power at *t* or later to perform A_i, and (3) necessarily, if every S_i were to perform A_i at *t* or later, then *p* would have been false.' In A. Plantinga (1986) 'On Ockham's Way Out', *Faith and Philosophy* 3, p. 209.

30 Zagzebski argues: 'Either God's past belief is not *really* past, in which case my causing it is not really backward causation, or it *is* really past, in which case

backward counterfactual dependency seems to be ruled out just as well as backward causation, for how can the hard past counterfactually depend on the future any more than it can be caused by it?' L. T. Zagzebski (1991) *The Dilemma of Freedom and Foreknowledge*, New York, Oxford University Press, p. 31.

31 Beilby and Eddy, *Divine Foreknowledge*, p. 131.

32 Plantinga, 'On Ockham's Way Out', p. 254.

33 For detailed proposals and criticisms of the hard/soft distinction and of 'accidental necessity', see the volume edited by Fischer whose essays almost without exception deal with the Ockhamist solution. J. M. Fischer (ed.) (1989) *God, Foreknowledge, and Freedom*, Stanford, Calif., Stanford University Press. See also Zagzebski's criticisms of the effort, Zagzebski, *The Dilemma of Freedom and Foreknowledge*, pp. 74ff. G. Hughes makes the novel suggestion that the views of Aquinas and Ockham are closer together than is often supposed; the difference is largely verbal, each using 'necessary' in a different sense. 'Aquinas's criterion is the immutability of the state of the knower: Ockham's is the actual occurrence of the event known.' In fact, he thinks, the two views are compatible. G. J. Hughes (1995) *The Nature of God*, London and New York, Routledge, p. 89.

34 See his piece in Beilby and Eddy, *Divine Foreknowledge*, p. 130.

35 Aquinas, *Summa Theologica*, I.10.2 reply to objection 3.

36 Aquinas, *Summa Theologica*, I.14.13.

37 Boethius, *The Consolation of Philosophy*, pp. 165–6.

38 Aquinas, *Summa Theologica*, I.14.13.

39 In the other *Summa*, Thomas Aquinas (2002) *Summa Contra Gentiles*, Notre Dame, Ind., University of Notre Dame Press, I.66.7, p. 219. 'The divine intellect, therefore, sees in the whole of its eternity, as being present to it, whatever takes place through the whole course of time. And yet what takes place in acertain part of time was not always existent. It remains, therefore, that God has a knowledge of those things that according to the march of time do not yet exist.'

40 More recent exponents of this view, in addition to those inclined to modern Thomism, are E. Stump and N. Kretzmann (1981) 'Eternity', *Journal of Philosophy* 78, pp. 429–58. (Cf. T. Morris (ed.) (1987) *The Concept of God*, Oxford, Oxford University Press, pp. 219–52.)

41 Cited in O. Leaman (1988) *Averroes and his Philosophy*, Oxford, Clarendon Press, p. 76.

42 See Zagzebski, *The Dilemma of Freedom and Foreknowledge*, pp. 61–3.

43 Zagzebski, *The Dilemma of Freedom and Foreknowledge*, pp. 61–3.

44 Zagzebski also offers a response: 'The doctrine of providence requires that nothing goes on without God's willing, or at least permitting, that it be so. But the vision model is not incompatible with this doctrine. Suppose that God timelessly wills to go along with whatever humans choose. I would not be able to choose without God's so willing, although God could still know what I will do in the future *because* he sees me do it from his eternal perspective.' This, to her mind, is an acceptable degree of passivity. Zagzebski, *The Dilemma of Freedom and Foreknowledge*, p. 58. I prefer the idea of creation, rather than a twofold picture of contemplation and willing what is seen.

45 N. Kretzmann (1966) 'Omniscience and Immutability', *Journal of Philosophy* 63.

46 Averroës (1969) *Tahafut al-Tahafut*, trans. Simon Van den Bergh, London, Luzac, p. 459.

47 He gives this explanation of the name: 'The only sharp criterion for a thing's having changed, is what we may call the Cambridge criterion (since it keeps on occurring in Cambridge philosophers of the great days, like Russell and McTaggart): the thing called "x" has changed if we have "F(x) at time t" true, and "F(x) at time t1" false. . . . But this account is intuitively quite unsatisfactory. . . . Of course there is a "Cambridge" change whenever there is a real change, but the converse is not true.' P. Geach (1969) *God and the Soul*, London, Routledge & Kegan Paul, p. 71.

48 Geach, *God and the Soul*, pp. 370–1.

49 A. Prior (1962) 'The Formalities of Omniscience', *Philosophy* 37, pp. 114–29.

50 So N. Pike (1970) *God and Timelessness*, London, Routledge & Kegan Paul. See also H. N. Castañeda (1967) 'Omniscience and Indexical Reference', *Journal of Philosophy* 64, pp. 203–9; and Swinburne, *The Coherence of Theism*, p. 165.

51 Swinburne, *The Coherence of Theism*, p. 165.

52 B. Davies (1985) *Thinking about God*, London, Geoffrey Chapman, p. 187.

53 A. Kenny (1979) *The God of the Philosophers*, Oxford, Clarendon Press, pp. 46–7.

54 Aquinas, *Summa Theologica*, I.15.

55 H. N. Castañeda (1992) 'Omniscience and Indexical Reference', in B. A. Brody (ed.), *Readings in the Philosophy of Religion: An Analytic Approach*, 2nd edn, Englewood Cliffs, NJ, Prentice Hall, p. 377.

56 This is not the same as either natural or free knowledge, though it has some aspects in common with each of these. It is not the same as natural knowledge, because the content of natural knowledge is essential to God while the content of middle knowledge is contingent, resulting as it does from particular beings' choices. It is different from God's subsequent free knowledge in that it is not under his control; God cannot change what I would freely choose to do under certain circumstances, although God could change the circumstances to affect the end result. It also comes *before* his act of will and decision, indeed is presupposed by his decision.

57 Modern supporters include William Craig and Thomas Flint; detractors include William Hasker and Robert Adams.

58 R. Adams (1997) 'Middle Knowledge and the Problem of Evil', *American Philosophical Quarterly* 14, p. 111.

59 This solution, a modified Molinism, has been suggested by B. Leftow (1991) *Time and Eternity*, Cornell Studies in the Philosophy of Religion, Ithaca and London, Cornell University Press, p. 262.

60 The Dominican view was that God's knowledge of counterfactuals comes *after* creation; it is then uncontroversial *how* God knows and Adams' and Kenny's criticisms would fall well wide of the mark. Before creation, God knows all that is

necessary and all the possibilities. Counterfactual truths are created along with what is actual, at the time of creation. Molinist views were held by the Jesuits (Molina himself was a Jesuit).

61 Beilby and Eddy, *Divine Foreknowledge*, p. 122.

62 Kenny, *The God of the Philosophers*, pp. 68–71.

63 Aquinas, *Summa Theologica*, I.14.9.

64 J. L. Kvanvig (1986) *The Possibility of an All-Knowing God*, Basingstoke, Macmillan, p. 71; cf. also p. 33. See also Zagzebski, *The Dilemma of Freedom and Foreknowledge*.

65 W. P. Alston (1989) *Divine Nature and Human Language: Essays in Philosophical Theology*, Ithaca and London, Cornell University Press, p. 190.

66 Aquinas, *Summa Theologica*, I.14.14, in *The Basic Writings of Saint Thomas Aquinas*, trans. Laurence Shapcote OP, ed. Anton C. Pergis, vol. 1, New York, Random House, 1945, p. 158.

67 Averroës, *Tahafut al-Tahafut*, p. 284, nos. 467–8.

68 Averroës, *Tahafut al-Tahafut*, p. 285, no. 468.

69 Augustine (1963) *The Trinity (De Trinitate)*, trans. S. McKenna, Washington, D.C., Catholic University of America Press, XV.13.

70 See her wonderful debut novel: M. Weston (2001) *The Escape Plan*, London, Quartet.

71 Beilby and Eddy, *Divine Foreknowledge*, p. 143.

72 M. Maimonides (1969) *The Guide of the Perplexed*, trans. S. Pines, Chicago and London, University of Chicago Press, p. 485.

73 Averroës (1984) *Ibn Rushd's Metaphysics: A Translation with Introduction of Ibn Rushd's Commentary on Aristotle's Metaphysics, book l-am*, trans. C. Genequand, Islamic Philosophy and Theology: Texts and Studies 7, Leiden, Brill, 1707–8, trans. p. 197.

74 J. W. Morris (1981) *The Wisdom of the Throne: An Introduction to the Philosophy of Mullā Ṣadrā*, Princeton Library of Asian Translations, Princeton, Princeton University Press, Part I §6, trans. p. 105.

75 Davies, *Thinking about God*, pp. 184–5.

76 B. Miller (1996) *A Most Unlikely God: A Philosophical Enquiry into the Nature of God*, Notre Dame, Ind., University of Notre Dame Press, pp. 127–41.

77 Miller, *A Most Unlikely God*, p. 141. Kvanvig rejects such accounts (though not Miller by name) because of the implications he sees for human freedom: if God is the cause of my action I am not free, so this does not solve the problem for God's omniscience. I suggest this rests on an inadequate understanding of God's causal action; but the reconciliation between divine power and human action we will turn to later.

78 Maimonides, *Guide of the Perplexed*, p. 482.

79 See the discussion in Wolfson, *Repercussions of the Kalam in Jewish Philosophy*, p. 215, on *Shemonah Perakim* and *Mishneh Torah*.

80 Maimonides, *Guide of the Perplexed*, p. 483.

81 Maimonides, *Guide of the Perplexed*, pp. 483–4.

82 In his translation of ben Gershom, *The Wars of the Lord*, vol. 2, p. 78.

83 Maimonides, *Guide of the Perplexed*, p. 481.

84 Which is the language of many, since Pike. Many in the foreknowledge debate talk about God's 'beliefs', not God's knowledge.

85 W. Hasker (1989) 'Foreknowledge and Necessity', in J. M. Fischer (ed.), *God, Foreknowledge, and Freedom*, Stanford, Calif., Stanford University Press, pp. 220–1.

10

The Power of All

When the USA originally announced a war on Afghanistan as a consequence of the events of 11 September 2001, it was given the name 'Infinite Justice'. What were the military planners thinking of, giving the operation this name? Did they mean to say that this war was in reality being undertaken by God? Or did they actually believe that it was the United States which was capable of discerning and dispensing *infinite* justice? The reason that the name was changed to the more modest (but still highly aspirational) 'Enduring Freedom' was that it was pointed out that calling the war 'Infinite Justice' would be 'offensive to Muslims'. What was astonishing is that they didn't see, as Christians, that it was no less an offence to their own faith. Christians, no less than Muslims, believe that Infinite Justice can only be predicated of God. Jews would be offended by the hubristic name, as would Hindus and Sikhs. Buddhists, even if not theistic, would find the attribution of 'justice' to such war-making highly immoral. As for atheists – they should find its implications ridiculous.

But this theological slip is very revealing. What the phrase 'Infinite Justice' unconsciously indicated is the connection, sometimes inextricable, between people's view of their God and their view of themselves. When the philosopher of religion Brian Davies considers the possibility that God might not be impassible, in other words God might be affected by something, he protests that this means that God would be 'vulnerable and defective'[1] and 'God could be out of control and something could have its way with him'.[2] The latter sounds more like a drunken young lady in the back of a taxi than God. Although this possibility is certainly theologically worrying, it is not clear that a God conceived as responsive is necessarily at risk.

Our understanding of divine power, perhaps more than any other divine attribute, shows us who *we* are. What does power consist in? What is it about power that we admire? Gareth Moore shows a scepticism about what is involved in seeing omnipotence as an important attribute of God: 'To worship one who is powerful in this way can seem a very dubious thing to do; it comes close to power-worship.'[3] The process theologian David Pailin goes so far as to say that omnipotence should be given up 'as an inappropriate quality of the proper object of worship. It implies that God is capable of being a despot and that we may believe that the divine does not act despotically at present either because we are ignorant of the strings that are pulling us like puppets or because God is at present not sufficiently bothered to take control.' Pailin maintains that, 'Such views of divine power probably owe more to human limitations than to insight into the divine nature. When we find ourselves frustrated we are tempted to react like children and think that "if only" we had the power then we would not put up with such nonsenses.'[4]

Before we return to these reflections, let us begin with the succinct account of omnipotence given by Thomas Aquinas, who was a believer in God's infinite power. Because God's existence is infinite, 'it is necessary that the active power in God should be infinite'. The difficulty is in explaining precisely what God's omnipotence consists in; 'for there may be doubt as to the precise meaning of the word "all" when we say that God can do all things'. For Aquinas there are two areas which 'all' does not include: what is evil, and what is *logically* impossible. Doing evil or sinning is not within the scope of God's power, because in Thomas's reckoning it is not so much an accomplishment as a failure, and that would be a sign of weakness or ignorance. 'To sin is to fall short of a perfect action; hence to be able to sin is to be able to fall short in action, which is repugnant to omnipotence. Therefore it is that God cannot sin, because of His omnipotence.'[5]

Second, what is impossible absolutely, as he describes logical impossibility, is not just a very difficult task or a mere miracle. It is just non-sense and is incoherent. It is like a square circle, which we cannot even imagine; not the Philosopher's Stone, which we can.

> For such cannot come under the divine omnipotence, not because of any defect in the power of God, but because it has not the nature of a feasible or possible thing. Therefore, everything that does not imply a contradiction in terms, is numbered among those possible things, in respect of which God is called omnipotent: whereas whatever implies contradiction does not come within the scope of divine omnipotence, because it cannot have the aspect of possibility. Hence it is better to say that such things cannot be done, than that God cannot do them . . . For whatever implies a contradiction cannot be a word, because no intellect can possibly conceive such a thing.[6]

Thomas has introduced us to two important questions. The first concerns God's power over the laws of logic and necessity. Can God do what is logically impossible? If God cannot, it is not through any fault or failure and God is absolved, for example, of being unable to change the past, or from other such illogical obligations on God's goodness and creativity that raise philosophical problems for the believer when God apparently fails to act as desired. This opens out in Aquinas to the religiously more important second question of whether God, if omnipotent yet good, can do what is evil, which will be taken up below.

Maimonides opens his discussion of the topic by stating firmly:

> The impossible has a stable nature, one whose stability is constant and is not made by a maker; it is impossible to change it in any way. Hence the power over the maker of the impossible is not attributed to the deity.[7]

In Maimonides' treatment, any debate centres on what is or is not to be considered possible – not on what God does or does not have the power to do. In other words, he is firmly in Aquinas's camp. God cannot do what is impossible. More surprisingly, also in Aquinas's camp, having pitched his tent there earlier, is al-Ghazālī. In the very book that pours scorn on 'philosophy' (suitably titled *The Incoherence of the Philosophers*) al-Ghazālī independently produces a similar account to Aquinas, the arch-philosopher. Al-Ghazālī's fundamental affirmation is that if God wills, nothing is impossible for Him; but that certain alleged acts are simply incoherent and do not therefore lie within God's power.[8] Al-Ghazālī writes:

> The impossible is not within the power. The impossible consists in affirming a thing together with denying it, affirming the more specific while denying the more general, or affirming two things while negating one [of them]. What does not reduce to this is not impossible, and what is not impossible is within [divine] power.[9]

What on strict logical grounds is impossible, what is incoherent and has no meaning – that God does not do. But what is impossible for *us*, God could do if God chose – like making a dead man sit up and write.[10] Al-Ghazālī's reasoning is: God is the agent of all. And once that is understood about what normally happens, it is seen that God can also choose not to create the normal, expected event. God also creates our knowledge of those events, as well as our perception of the norm and of natural laws.

> We did not claim that these things are necessary. On the contrary, they are possibilities that may or may not occur. But the continuous habit of their occurrence repeatedly, one time after another, fixes unshakeably in our minds the belief in their occurrence according to past habit.[11]

There is nothing to stop God altering the habitual course of nature and altering our perceptions and memories accordingly.

> There is, therefore, nothing to prevent a thing being possible, within the capabilities of God, [but] that by His prior knowledge He knows that He would not do it at certain times, despite its possibility, and that He creates for us the knowledge that He will not create it at that time.[12]

Most modern philosophers are broadly 'Thomist' on this question (we could as well say Ghazālīan or Maimonidean).[13] The logically impossible, like making a square circle, God cannot do because it is nonsense. There is also a further category of things that God cannot do due to his nature as a perfect and incorporeal being – like go swimming or perform in a feeble manner.[14] The most explicit rejection of any logical constraints on God's power comes not from al-Ghazālī (as we would expect) but from Descartes, who is normally very fond of logic with its sense of clarity and certainty. In Descartes' view, however, the eternal truths, truths of logic and mathematics, are created by God; and as such, God cannot be bound by them. One cannot say that they would exist no matter what, or even if God did not exist.[15] The absolute limits to necessity are found only in God's nature; perhaps in a few other laws such as causality. There are other 'necessary' truths whose necessity, as it were, is not independent of God. They may be unchanging and eternal, but they are willed so by God. We can discover and know them, we can see that their contraries are impossible or contradictory; but none of this restricts God. Descartes makes clear in his letters that he is not positively asserting that God can fashion a square circle, or that such a feat is possible. He maintains that, though he can make no sense of logical impossibilities existing, though such things are unintelligible, it is incumbent on him not to deny that God could achieve such things, if God wanted to. 'In general we can assert that God can do anything that is within our grasp, but not that he cannot do what is beyond our grasp. It would be rash to think that our imagination reaches as far as his power.'[16]

G. Hughes, in our time, attempts to mediate between the combatants. On the one hand, we cannot describe an action we think God can do except in conformity with our experience and the interpretation of it. We can only express it in conformity with the rules of logic. 'To that extent, Aquinas was right to suggest that God can do anything provided there is no true description of it which can be expressed only by a contradiction.' However, non-contradiction is not a way of discovering what God can do, nor a criterion for assessing any such claim. Insofar as Aquinas implied that, he was wrong; insofar as Descartes rejected that, he was right. Hughes maintains, 'For all we know, God has it in his power to bring it about that something occur which, given our existing beliefs, can be described only by a contradiction. . . . We simply do not have any *a priori* method of determining with any certainty what does and does not lie within the absolute power of God.'[17]

Perhaps it is best to put it in this circumscribed way: God does not create what does not exist. If what is logically impossible is non-existent, God does not do it – and if not, does it matter? If we believe in the unity of God's attributes, then God's power is not different from divine wisdom, or divine benevolence. The key criterion for God's power is not the total sum of describable tasks; the key criterion for reflecting on God's power to act is its conformity with what is all-knowing, wise, good and all-loving.

That conclusion could guide discussion on our second question: Can God do wrong? Two thinkers, separated by culture, creed and era, put forward the assertion that God *cannot*. Abu Ishaq al-Naẓẓām (d. 836), a Mu'tazilite theologian, maintained that God was actually *unable* to do evil. His argument runs in this way: God performs actions purely for their own sake; that is, God does them because of their own intrinsic value. But clearly this can only be thought of with respect to good and just actions; it could not possibly apply to evil or unjust deeds. Deeds that are intrinsically evil form a separate class of actions, which cannot be chosen by God. – But if God cannot do otherwise – if, so to speak, God is only inadvertently good, then why should God be praised? And then is God obliged to grant paradise and eternal happiness to all? Al-Naẓẓām's response was that the role of God's choice was not eliminated. There are a number of good options that God could choose being only unable to opt for the bad. Therefore God is still praiseworthy.[18] In a similar fashion, the medieval theologian Peter Abelard maintained that, when God lacks the will to do something, then God is unable to do it. Certainly God lacks the will to do evil, so it remains impossible.[19]

Both these positions were rejected by the majority in their traditions. Al-Murdar argued that God was able to do evil, but certainly never will. Abelard's view was condemned at the Council of Sens. However, among modern philosophers, Pike and Geach revive these two broad styles of resolving the dilemma. Geach advocates a restriction in the notion of omnipotence in order to maintain that God *cannot* do evil.[20] Pike argues that that represents a restriction on God's power, and therefore one ought to maintain that God has the power, but certainly never will use it.[21]

But what does it mean 'to be able to'? Most commentators distinguish different senses of the word, thus making clear where, if anywhere, God's impotence might lie. Thus Pike distinguishes a logical impossibility, a limitation on power, and what in English we call 'cannot bring myself to do'.[22] God is not limited in power; but 'cannot bring Himself' to do evil. Morris distinguishes the three conditions: 'God cannot sin'; 'It is impossible that God sin'; and 'God lacks the power to sin.' Hughes distinguishes, not between notions of inability, but notions of wrongness: doing something when you know there are reasons you shouldn't, doing what is forbidden by God, and further, if God does something we think is wrong, we ought to change our views of what it is to act wrongly. (In this he echoes not only Plato in the dialogue *Euthyphro* but also the Asharite–Mu'tazilite dispute over whether an act is just because God does it, or whether God does what is just because it is just.)

The discussion of the Iraqi Basrian philosophers' views on moral action is an illuminating way to examine this question. The view from Basra was that an agent's ability has as its object not individual actions but classes of actions. The power to do something refers to an indefinite number of actions, not a single unique action. If one has the power to use a knife to slice, one can use a knife to slice cabbages or throats. One cannot have 'the ability to cut cabbages but not throats', or 'to slice tomatoes but not my finger'. All the moral attributes an action may have come from its performance by a certain agent with certain intentions, how it is done, why, when, in what context – but not from the mere kind of activity it is. My ability to slice is neither good nor bad. A slicing-event which I enact derives its goodness or badness from my intentions, what I slice, the context, and so on. But the ability to perform such acts is not restricted to its performance under certain conditions. If one is able to do something, one can do it in a way that is ethically good or ethically bad.[23] An agent possesses the power to speak; whether she uses it to tell the truth or lie, do good or harm with her words; and the morality of the business lies not in the ability to speak, is not indeed a question of power but of intention and cognition.

In God's case, the Basrians argued, the categories of divine ability to act are unrestricted. Therefore, God possesses the ability to perform an action absolutely, whatever the divine intentions or the context. However, God's absolute possibility to do something does not entail the concrete possibility of doing it in a certain manner or context. For we do what is wrong either in error of the facts, or in error of the rightness or wrongness of the act, or in hopes to achieve some benefit or avoid some harm by doing it. None of these things is possible in God's case; so it becomes concretely impossible for God to do evil. This, however, does not mean there is a class of actions God cannot perform, and that therefore means, they said, there is no restriction on God's omnipotence.[24]

In the thought of the Dvaita Vedāntin Mādhva, the understanding of God's power is approached through the description of what God *actually* does, rather than considering whether or not God *could* do this or that. God is the instrumental cause of all. God is the creator, sustainer, destroyer of worlds. God's omnipotence is shown in number and variety of worlds created: this is without limit. It is also shown in God's governance of the world; for which the word 'control' is often used. The principal medium of God's power, control and action is through natural laws and the workings of nature. Narain puts it this way: 'The inviolable laws of nature with their unerring control on all that is in time and space indicate the workings of an inscrutable power . . . in whose absence such a complex accomplishment would have been impossible.'[25] So where some Western monotheists discuss a God who acts in specific activities, tasks or intervention, the tacit picture here is of divinity's continual, subtle and mediated power, rather than isolated actions.

God's power is also shown in relation to human beings, 'directly concerned with the trials and tribulations, with the joys and sorrows of the individual souls'.[26] God is the source of the ignorance (māya) which veils us; in this Mādhva departs from Śaṇkara, who does not attribute māya to nirguṇa Brahman. But God is also the cause of knowledge and of deliverance, the way out of suffering. In conscious repudiation of the schools of Indian philosophy that speak of self-realization as the route to knowledge and liberation, Mādhva insists that God – Brahman – implants knowledge in the hearts of those who love God, and redemption is part of God's power and not part of the potentiality or potency of the human being.

In Indian thought the word for God is Īśvāra. The root of the word, īś, means 'the power to will' – not, significantly, the will to power as in Nietzsche. When you find references to divine power in the texts of Indian thinkers, you often find it in a particular context: the creation, maintenance and dissolution of worlds by the will of the Lord (Īśvara).

The word for power in Sanskrit is śakti. Śakti is a word with many interesting uses. It refers, in particular, to the feminine, generative, creative aspect of Īśvara. It refers to the God Śiva's feminine aspect, or the Divine Mother. So as Arindam Chakrabarti comments, 'Isn't it interesting that while in Semitic religion God's masculinity is constituted by his power, the Śakti-power of God is constituted in Indic Theism by his/her femininity!' (In a private communication.)

The Nyāya tradition, like Mādhva, sees Īśvara's creation and dissolution of endless worlds as the vehicle of omnipotence. Īśvara brings about the destruction of the world not out of cruelty but in order to give creatures some rest and respite from the sufferings of existence. Then the constructive process of world-creation from the integration and unification of atoms begins again, by the action of Īśvara's will. But in Nyāya, the most important power of God is the power to impart saving knowledge. For that reason, there can be no sharp division between God's omnipotence and omniscience. Islam would agree, and perhaps refine the point this way: given the unity and simplicity of God, God's omnipotence is not different from God's omnisicence. Ṭabāṭabā'ī in fact explains power this way: 'the attribute of power means that an entity be a knowing source of its acts. It is known that contingent existents derive from the Divine Essence, for there is nothing beyond contingent existents except the unconditioned Necessary Being. Hence God is the source of everything and His knowledge is identical with His Essence, which is the source of contingent effects. He has power and it is identical with His Essence.'[27] We could certainly say omnipotence is not different from God's *wisdom*. That alone could send packing silly questions about whether or not God *can* do something pointless, for God never *will* do anything so manifestly lacking in wisdom.

What comes to the fore in these manifold discussions is that in Indian philosophy, divine power is seen in what God actually *does*. If the aim is to understand God or one's faith, how else would you go about it? Why waste time on situations that philosophers call 'counterfactual'? 'God wouldn't want to create a square circle but could if He wanted to' – what spiritual use is that and how does it contribute to real *knowledge*?

Now what if your aim is different – *not* seeking to understand faith, or God as God is, but to show that the very concept of God is incoherent? Then a whole new philosophical activity can be created: trying to create impossible situations and logical dilemmas to explode the concept of 'omnipotence' as internally incoherent. So in an age where English-speaking philosophy of religion has become an ideological battle-ground, perhaps it is no wonder that there is increasing interest *not* in what God does, but in what God can or can't do; all this in the interests of arguing that there can be no omnipotent God.

One of the questions to attract the greatest number of English-language articles in recent decades is the paradox of the stone. As formulated by C. Wade Savage, it goes like this:

> Either God can create a stone which he cannot lift, or God cannot create a stone which he cannot lift.
>
> If God can create a stone which he cannot lift, then he is not omnipotent.
>
> If God cannot create a stone which he cannot lift, then he is not omnipotent.
>
> Therefore God is not omnipotent.[28]

If you are a believer, you might stop and reflect on whether the making or lifting of stones counts among the important abilities you want your God to have. If you are not a believer, you might like to consider whether you think, in fairness, that religious believers are obliged to think that a transcendent God engages in hands-on geological activity and weight-lifting.

If, as I am assuming will be the case for the majority, you cannot see that there is any profound spiritual significance or problem in this issue, you might now be wondering why so many articles and chapters have been written on such an ostensibly silly question. But as Savage explains: 'What the argument really tries to establish is that the existence of an omnipotent being is logically impossible.'[29]

There are ways of tackling the stone paradox head-on. Swinburne defends God against this slur by rejecting statement 3 above. God is not omnipotent unless and until God actually creates that stone. God could have the ability to create the unliftable stone without exercising it; and if so, God is not omnipotent (because the stone that God cannot lift does not exist). Being omnipotent 'includes the ability to make himself no longer omnipotent'.[30] However, if you think God is *essentially* omnipotent – that it is an essential feature of God and not changeable – then this solution cannot be made to work for you. (If *essentially* omnipotent, God cannot cease to be omnipotent, not even by God's own ostensibly omnipotent action. So here is another thing an essentially omnipotent Being cannot do.)

You can, as Mavrodes does, dismiss the stone paradox by claiming that the suggestion is self-contradictory. 'For it becomes "a stone which cannot be lifted by Him whose power is sufficient for lifting anything." But the "thing" described by a self-contradictory phrase is absolutely impossible and hence has nothing to do with the doctrine of omnipotence.'[31]

Of course this rests on the belief that God cannot do the logically impossible. For those who will not allow this, there are get-outs. You can say, as Frankfurt does: If God can do something self-contradictory, then God can do two self-contradictory things: create the stone, and lift it. 'After all, is there any greater trick in performing two logically impossible tasks than there is in performing one? If an omnipotent being can do what is logically impossible, then he can not only create situations which he cannot handle but also, since he is not bound by the limits of consistency, he can handle situations which he cannot handle.'[32]

If this is not enough to do down the sceptic (and we will find that it isn't), Mavrodes opines that God possesses infinite lifting power, which means that God can also possess infinite stone-making power without outstripping his infinite lifting power. 'And if God's power to lift is infinite, then His power to create may run to infinity also without outstripping that first power. The supposed limitation turns out to be no limitation at all, since it is specified only by reference to another power which is itself infinite.'[33] So the stone paradox is no real limitation to God's omnipotence. Another way out is to say (as Savage does) 'For if God is omnipotent, then He can create stones of any poundage and lift stones of any poundage. And "God can create stones of any poundage, and God can lift stones of any poundage" entails "God cannot create a stone which He cannot lift."'

But what are we to make of this whole debate? It would seem that some philosophers have become obsessed with God's *capabilities* rather than with understanding the relationship of God to creation and ourselves. Aquinas *or* al-Ghazālī *or* the Naiyāyikas would have thrown up their hands at the idea that God is the sort of being that has capabilities, as if God were a military force or a very hi-tech weapon. For such thinkers, God doesn't perform *tasks*, and the point of philosophical reflection is to understand our relationship to what is real and important – not to nail down what is admitted to be counterfactual and is undeniably trivial. Thomas puts his finger on what he sees as the tangles you can find yourself in when you ask and answer the question in the wrong register:

> Now God cannot be said to be omnipotent through being able to do all things that are possible to created nature; for the divine power extends farther than that. If, however, we were to say that God is omnipotent because He can do all things that are possible to His power, there would be a vicious circle in explaining the nature of His power. For this would be saying nothing else but that God is omnipotent, because He can do all that He is able to do.[34]

To return to the musings that opened this chapter, it is tempting to suggest that certain unexamined notions beset discussions of divine power:

> to be affected is to be vulnerable, defective and out of control, and then something can have its way with you
>
> power is measured in capabilities – the more unrestricted your capabilities, the greater your power
>
> and power must be demonstrated in acting out these capabilities whenever challenged

These propositions suggest that the God of Infinite Justice is a Divine Superpower. The Bhagavad-Gita suggests that people are made of faith, and that we *are* what we have faith in. If so, then the Divine Superpower suggests not only an image of God but also of ourselves: the Divine Superpower then grounds the 'Infinite Justice' meted out by earthly superpowers.

Here we could reflect on some insights offered by Arindam Chakrabarti. Commenting on the activities of Hindu extremists, he observes that violence on behalf of faith is a *loss* of faith in religious obligation (*dharma*) or in God; it is *loss* of faith that makes a religious community turn violent. 'If Hindus really believed that Rama or Śiva is omnipotent and omnipresent then they would not have taken up arms to protect

Rama.'[35] We can extend his point to say, if religious terrorists really believed in the rule of God, and the reach of God's justice beyond the grave, they would not commit the acts they do. Nor would religious politicians feel it is down to them to dispense 'infinite justice'.

It is easy to imagine (updating Feuerbach's thought) a cycle of projection and appropriation of a concept of God. A certain view of infinite divinity, based on fantasies of human perfection, is projected outwards. When that deity fails to react in an expected action, overt loss of faith does not occur; but a reappropriation of that now deified image takes place. Not God's, but *our* desires to create, sustain, control and destroy the world are named as 'Infinite Justice'. But what happens when there is a human appropriation of the power which, for the conventional believer, should properly be God's – the taking of life? In a different context, Chakrabarti derives this lesson from the *Mahabhārata*: when religious obligation is violated, it itself becomes a killer.[36]

On the other hand, as Chakrabarti observes, 'In the Indian bhakti tradition, the greatest power ascribed to Īśvara is the power to shower grace, *reasonlessly* and often undeserved.'[37] This suggests a different conception of divine power; perhaps one in which omnipotence is shown in infinite generosity and giving, or which understands being all-powerful as meaning indefatigably loving. 'Majesty' need not mean domination. In the Qur'ān, 'majesty' and 'generosity' are conceptually united in a single Divine Name, *Dhu 'l-Jalal w 'l-Ikram*. Al-Ghazālī explains, 'For majesty is His by nature while generosity emanates from Him to His creation.'[38]

On this view – far from mainstream, and yet historical and steeped in some traditions – God's power is not separate from God's knowledge and wisdom, and neither is omnipotence anything other than all-conquering love or Infinite Mercy. As Thomas Aquinas wrote: 'God's omnipotence is particularly shown in sparing and having mercy, because in this is it made manifest that God has supreme power.'[39] Why? Because by doing so, God leads us into the participation of an infinite good, 'which is the ultimate effect of the divine power', and because the effect of divine mercy/power is the foundation of all divine works. 'In this way the divine omnipotence is particularly made manifest, because to it pertains the first foundation of all good things.'

Whether divine power is coercive or compassionate, how is it exercised?

Does God somehow act *directly* in the world as we perceive it? As you have by now learned to expect, there is a range of answers to be considered. At one end of the spectrum on this matter is the view known historically as Deism. It is still widely held, in some way, although few people call themselves deists, for the word has an eighteenth-century ring to it, as if it commits you to wearing a powdered wig. Some refer to contemporary quasi-deistic views as 'theistic evolutionism'.[40]

The deist thinks that God set the world up and has since taken early retirement to leave it and its inhabitants to get on with things without His active assistance. Thus, while this was a belief that came to prominence during the Enlightenment, it is not unlike a view held by many today who think that there must some ultimate creator, but not one who engages in hearing and answering prayers, knows us each by name, and performs miracles when absolutely necessary. This God may well have fine-tuned the universe then left it to nature to run, without sticking his hand into the fishbowl to manipulate events or solve problems.

At the other end of the spectrum come views described variously as 'occasionalism', 'universal divine sovereignty', or 'omnideterminism'. These hold that nothing at all lies outside the scope of God's activity. (For some proponents this means not even evil is excluded.) God's hand is in some way behind every event, including those in which we dirty our own hands.

Is the universe 'closed' or 'open' to divine action?

The first question this raises is whether you see the universe as 'open' or as 'closed' to divine action. Can God reach into the world somehow to do things in it, or is the universe a tightly sealed web of purely material cause-and-effect which God created and cannot pull apart?

Maurice Wiles in his Bampton Lectures argued that God does not act directly in the world in particular, isolated events.[41] God doesn't maintain a tight control over every happening. Instead, God gives us freedom, even over against God Himself. God has chosen to be limited in creation, especially in creating human beings with free will. This is necessary in order to have the stability of the material universe, so that we can not only act but also see the consequences of our actions. God intervening constantly on any significant scale would undermine the meaning of free will.

The point of divine self-limitation is necessary, not only for the possibility of wrong choice, but also to create a stable background where actions give rise to consequences that are not subverted by special divine actions which change the expected consequences in such ways that the good will be rewarded and the evil punished.

Clearly divine intervention across the board to alter undesirable consequences would undermine the point of the creation as the free-will defence envisages it.[42]

Wiles maintains his view for two reasons: first, because it is demanded by an understanding of the origin of evil as found in human free will.[43] Second, the regularity of nature shows that it is impossible that God be intervening on certain occasions, but not others.

At the other extreme of Christian views, Vernon White holds the stronger, bolder thesis of universal divine sovereignty – God's control over every event. White says the very fact of the regularity of nature *does not* preclude divine action and involvement in it. Divine involvement is a different order of explanation; it is not an explanation for any gaps in the scientific accounts given. God's action is 'transcendent and hidden within all worldly occurrences'.[44] It transcends the events, yet is implicit within them; it is a cause of worldly events, but in a different way from material causes.[45] God then can act, that is, express intentions, in and through the world in a way analogous to the way that we can move our bodies and thereby 'invest them with meaning and purpose'. This can happen both through events in the world, but also as God acting through other agents, such as human beings.

In a work on divine action in 1990 Keith Ward, who was concerned to bring scientific insights into line with Christian theology, maintained that the closed universe is an idea whose time has gone.[46] Drawing on concepts from modern physics, he rejects the view of the world as a self-contained system closed to the presence and action of God. He argues on purely scientific grounds that the 'closed universe view' is not tenable nowadays. The understanding now of how we use scientific models is that no single model fits the world exactly; nor is any complete explanation ever possible.[47] It is false to suppose there is a nearly complete model with a few gaps in it in which God might work. Rather, 'there is no consistent and complete model at all; so gaps do not become apparent in the model'. They lie outside it. God's action, Ward thinks, may be invisible in the way that laws of physics are.[48] God's action is not, however, completely invisible and impossible to detect or assert; for aside from the visible fact that the universe exists at all, God is also continually bringing new states of the universe into being, leaving many alternatives open to our free choice. Ward suggests that there are at least five kinds of divine action: the act of bringing the universe into being; particular acts of imaginative development which shape the universe in contingent ways; acts in response to 'chance' permutation of natural forces and creatures' free choices; acts by which God relates in a distinctively personal way to created persons, in revelation, etc.; acts of redemptive shaping of good out of evil to achieve a final consummation.[49] Thus, he holds, we can unite the contemporary scientific view of the world with the theistic view:

> The acts of God in nature will be those hidden but all-pervasive causal influences which shape the emergent processes of physical reality towards goals which take specific form only in the process itself, but the general character of which are laid down as archetypes in the being of God.[50]

Thomas Tracy similarly argues that God's action can be seen in those areas of reality which modern physics suggests are indeterminate. God can act indirectly, but God can also act directly, and work through natural indeterminacies which we know to exist within the regular structures of nature. Some events are not determined through causal sequences; either because they are incomplete or because they are the result of free human actions. God could act in events of either kind.[51]

> Note that the integration of chance into the order of nature provides a structure within which God's particular providential actions need not involve any miraculous suspension of natural law. In selectively determining events that occur by chance on the finite level, God does not displace natural causes that would otherwise have determined that event, and God's activity could be entirely compatible with whatever the sciences may tell us about the distribution of such events in regular probabilistic patterns. In this way, the world God has made could display both a reliable causal structure and an inherent openness to novelty, allowing for a seamless integration of natural law and ongoing direct involvement by God in shaping the course of events.[52]

Thus both Ward and Tracy find a niche for God's action in the physical universe in the theories of modern physics which hold that events occur which are not entirely determined by their causes. On this plane God can intervene to effect results in the material world, without being judged to 'violate natural laws'. For them, this could provide an account of God's agency in the world which will satisfy the mainstream monotheist, without giving offence to modern scientific sensibilities. But the attempt does look a little apologetic; as if they are trying to find nooks and crannies for God's action in areas where science will not make serious objections. There are other ways and different paths to deal with the same underlying issue.

In line with its revision of God's power following the ideas of Whitehead, Process Theology reconceives God's action in the world not as coercive, but 'as the luring influence of a love which respects the proper integrity and intrinsic value of all others'.[53] This model is said to allow the non-divine greater autonomy; God acts in the world without overt force, but rather 'in the patient operation of the overpowering rationality of his conceptual harmonization'.[54]

Process Theology maintains that God is involved in evolution, by being present in every occasion. What happens in each occasion as it becomes concrete 'involves its own creative synthesis of what it "prehends" of the divine'. This 'prehension' includes both 'the divine valuation of previous actual occasions', and what the divine envisages for future possibilities. God therefore influences every event, ordering the structure of reality so that each moment develops smoothly from what precedes it, but also presenting alternative possibilities for each moment; allowing minute changes to take place. The evolutionary developments that occur arise from such moments.

> Each actual occasion composing the enduring object which is a DNA molecule is thus able to contribute to the evolutionary development of that molecule (and so to the creature genetically produced by that molecule) by its own particular synthesis of what it prehends of what Whitehead refers to as the 'consequent' and 'primordial' aspects of the divine reality.[55]

While God can be said to be 'the necessary ground of all changes', the divine influence is not deterministic, because it is not coercive. It is an 'influence', which lures each occasion to actualize the situation which God envisages from among the possibilities. 'God's creativity is hence conceived to be an unceasing activity which is effected through the divine luring of each concrescing occasion. Nothing at all happens without God being involved in it and, in the consequent nature of the divine, being totally aware of it.'[56] However, the idea of God 'luring' an occasion presupposes that an occasion can, in some way, choose and respond to a 'lure' – as opposed to being compelled, as unconscious matter would need to be. It requires Whitehead's 'panpsychic view' of reality: Whitehead urged us to overcome mind–matter dualism by seeing everything as 'essentially bipolar', possessing both a mental and a physical aspect. Thus even entities which we think of as not sentient can somehow 'feel' their environments. (This is only conscious in the minority of beings; in the rest, it is unconscious.) However, some such metaphysic is necessary for the success of the idea of God luring, and molecules choosing.

Timeless and changeless action?

A further problem to divine action in the world comes from the notions of God's timelessness and changelessness. Richard Swinburne argues that actions take place in time. If we say someone does something, we can reasonably ask, '*When* does He do so?' So the idea of God acting, creating, or bringing something about seems to entail the idea of time. This would be particularly true if some of God's actions are said to be in response to human actions, for then they must occur *after* the human deeds.

One way philosophers of religion have countered this is to distinguish between agency and effects of that agency; the event which God brings about is in time, but God is not. Brian Davies claims that Swinburne is wrong to suppose that the notion of God acting entails that God is within time, or that God changes in Himself. If God brings something about at a certain time, that does not mean that God must have been 'undergoing some sort of process' at that time. 'It need only mean that at 2 o'clock last Friday such and such came to pass by virtue of God.'[57]

E. L. Mascall makes a similar point. God's act is timeless at his end ('at its subjective pole') and temporal at our end ('at its objective pole').

> God timelessly exerts a creative activity towards and upon the whole spatio-temporal fabric of the created universe. This will be experienced as temporal by each creature who observes it and describes it from his own spatio-temporal standpoint; but it no more implies that God is in time . . . than the fact that I describe God in English means that God is English.[58]

Even if one can find a way of defending 'timeless action', a further knot remains. If God has a will and if God acts or does things, then God must change. That God can decide to do something, then do it, implies some kind of change or development or at least progression in God. However, the tradition that God is changeless has been dominant in a number of the most ancient religious traditions precisely because it is so consistent. It is difficult to challenge unless one wants to reject, or redefine, God's simplicity, eternity, and perfection.

Some have sought to formulate conceptions of agency that can cope with changelessness and timelessness. Others have sought to clarify, and perhaps slightly modify, the 'classical' Christian position to take account of the problem in a way more satisfying than some modern believers find in rigorous Thomism.

Richard Creel has argued that we must distinguish different 'aspects' of God: God's nature, knowledge, will and feeling.[59] For God to be God, an absolutely perfect being, God's nature must be absolutely unchanging. So too must God's will be immutable.[60] Not even implementation of the divine will changes God.

> It seems more compatible with the notion of God as infinite pure act to think of ourselves as continually wrapped in the unchanging will of God, so that neither God's decision nor God's will ever changes. What changes is the way we experience the will of God. How we experience it is contingent on how *we* change in relation to God's unchanging will.[61]

Norris Clark reminds us of Aquinas's distinction between 'intentional being' and 'real being'.

Intentional being and real being

'Intentional being' is something as it is perceived, known, experienced. The word 'intentional' here signifies not 'deliberate' but 'as an object of someone's perception'. 'Real being' is something as it is in itself, intrinsically.

Clark maintains that this distinction, if accepted, solves dilemmas to do with God's eternity and immutability, by allowing us to assert a timeless, changeless absolute being, who nevertheless seems to *us* to change as needed. The *expression* of God's loving concern for us should constantly develop, and God's consciousness could be contingently other than it is.

> But that the intentional content of God's loving consciousness should be contingently other because of the unfolding expression of unchanging personal love for us does not entail that God's own intrinsic real being, the level of his own intrinsic perfection, in any way undergoes real change to acquire some new higher mode of perfection not possessed before.[62]

Second, he observes that in Thomist metaphysics, causality does not take place in the agent, but in the recipient; not in the cause, but in the effect. To *cause* is to make another be, it enriches the other, not the agent. *Change*, however, enriches the agent, 'it is enriching *oneself*, acquiring something new for *oneself*, and it says nothing at all about any enrichment of another'.[63] So a causal action doesn't affirm any new 'intrinsic being' in the agent. Thus, he suggests, we do not need to assert that God *changes* in order to love effectively, authentically, in accordance with our changing needs. God does not need to change *in God's own self* to do so. So, he argues, the problem is *not* that God's real response to us or real effective expression of divine causality must take place in time. They do. However, we must remember that the effects of God's causing occur *within* the recipient.

> This is precisely where it should be, where we would *want* it to be, immanent *in us*, communicated *to us*, not consisting of some moving-around of inner wheels in God or change in his own intrinsic real being. A response should be precisely *in* the one to whom the response is being given. So the real being of God's action on and response to us occurs down in our temporal process. Causality is the ecstasy of the agent present by its power *in* its effect. The failure to understand this key metaphysical point in the nature of causality invalidates a large amount of what seems to me simply uncritical 'common sense' criticism of the

divine-immutability position, as though it were obvious that to do something, to produce any change, in time necessarily puts change and time in the doer.[64]

Recalling the distinction between different kinds of change such as 'Cambridge change', perhaps we can distinguish intrinsic or essential change from 'intentional' or 'relational' change. I might change as the object of your feelings when you change your views of me or your feelings towards me. I might now be 'beloved' to you, when I was not before. Yet in changing 'in your eyes' I do not have to change intrinsically at all. Perhaps, a stickler might say, since the change is in the perceiver, you ought only to speak of your feelings as changing. And yet, that may not sum up everything you might wish to say when you fall in love or come to treasure someone as a friend. You may, understandably enough, find it inadequate simply to say: 'My feelings for her have become precious to me.' You might insist that only: '*She* has become precious to me' will do as an expression of the state of affairs.

Divine and human action

In different eras, the most difficult question was to conceive of a way that an immaterial God can act in a material world, because this was felt to be either contradictory or unseemly. Our attitude towards matter is more dynamic nowadays;[65] and meanwhile, our attitude to our own human freedom, independence and power is more assertive than it once was. That means that today in some ways, the more intractable problem in Western monotheist circles is not how to understand God's action in the material world; but how to square it with human freedom and agency.

Many seem to assume that if we say that God did something, then a human being did not do it. Typically, though, the middle-of-the-road theist wants to assert all the following things: that there is human free will and moral responsibility; that our actions are effective; and therefore we bear the responsibility for them and their effects; and at the same time, that God does act in the world too and moreover is all-powerful. If all of these are to be true, the middle-of-the-road theist has some explaining to do. How can such divine action and human action exist side by side, so that God is unhindered yet human beings are completely responsible and accountable?

Austin Farrer created a concept called 'double agency'. The idea of 'double agency' allows both God and a human being to cause an event, because the nature of God's action is to work in and through other agents. Farrer writes: 'God's agency must actually be such as to work omnipotently on, in or through creaturely agencies without either forcing them or competing with them.'[66] The agency of God and creatures must be understood as being on two different levels.

In one event both the divine and creaturely agents are fully active. God has not overwhelmed the finite agent so that it is merely a passive instrument, and God is not simply the creator and sustainer who allows the creaturely agent to act independently of divine agency. Furthermore, the divine and finite agents are not merely complementary, that is, they do not contribute distinct parts to the one event. As many authors have put it, God acts in and through the finite agent which also acts in the event.[67]

'Double agency' is not *a number of things:*

> *A case where two agents co-operate, each one contributing part of the action, as when two people pull a boat out of the water. One does not want to suggest that God needs help, nor that the human being doesn't really accomplish the act.*
>
> *A case of two people doing two different things to create one effect, as when one person has a hand on the tiller and another holds the sails.*
>
> *Nor something like a state of affairs in which I 'give my younger son some chocolate' by handing it to his older brother and asking him to pass it on. There must be some identity in the actions of the two agents, whereas in this example my elder son and I are actually doing different things. Yet at the same time, what is done by God and by the human cannot be entirely the same.*

It can be seen that this strong demand for identity of the action coupled with a strong demand for distinctness in the action is difficult to fulfil.[68]

'Double agency' means the two agents are doing the same thing – not humans and God each doing different things to contribute to the same event. It is hard to see how in double agency the freedom of one of the agents is not denied, or the action not divided between them. Yet there must be some distinction between the divine and the human action. If there is a genuine unity of action, there is no duality of causes, and if there is duality of causes, there is no unity of action, no single event.[69] Or are God's act and the human act each thought to be a 'sufficient cause' itself, and if so, is not the idea of two sufficient causes for one event self-contradictory? But perhaps one could speak of 'modal overdeterminism'. There are plenty of events in everyday life in which more than one sufficient cause happens to exist, in flagrant disobedience of philosophers' laws of parsimony. – In the end, I wonder if Farrer was really striving after the notion of action that can be found in Aquinas or Ṭabāṭabā'ī?

White also wants to see God as acting through everything, even human action. He observes that even in the purely human sphere, we can act through another's action without coercion or reducing the other to utter passivity. 'This is especially true in intimate personal relations where the straightforward category of cause and effect will not contain what actually happens.'[70] He offers the analogy of trustees acting to make sure a client's wishes are carried out. In God's case, this happens universally, perfectly and with aseity. He insists that this does not compromise human freedom. God arranges reality so that whatever I decide to do, God still makes it carry God's ultimate intentions. Every sequence of events begins with God's will, and is developed in interaction with our own intentions and acts, 'so that it develops both in accordance with its own nature and the divine intention which knows what each interaction will in fact produce'. If a human being acts in a way contrary to God's ultimate purposes, 'all other relevant interlocking sequences will have accommodated this fact "from the beginning" '.[71] 'Whatever happens is encompassed without uncertainty, within a higher meaning of God's intention.'[72]

Tracy is less comfortable saying that God is the direct and total cause of every finite event. He worries that this might make creatures just the opportunity for God exercising power; so the action is really God's, and not the human's. So although he speaks of God acting directly and also indirectly, he writes: 'If our acts are directly enacted by God, then there is an important sense in which they are not free, and if they are free in this strong sense, then they cannot be direct acts of God. In his view, we must continue to grapple with what he calls the 'mutually limiting character of claims about human freedom and divine agency'.[73]

There are thinkers who draw on traditions found in Thomas Aquinas, which see divine providence as working *through* creatures, 'from the abundance of divine goodness imparting to creatures also the dignity of causing'.[74] The Thomist view sees God's activity *first* as bringing everything into existence, which also means that every thing is not just created, but created as it is, with the activity and desires that it has. So David Burrell maintains that Tracy is wrong to allege that on this account, the only power and efficacy exercised are God's and not humans', and he notes, 'For the divine agency effects particular actions *through* the proper modality of creatures, as befits the creator, whose proper effect is the very *existing* of things.'[75]

God's action then does not 'vastly exceed' our own (the language found in Tracy). God's action is nothing like our own. It is not the far part on a continuum, it is something else entirely. The language used of our action cannot be used of God's univocally.[76] From Burrell's critique, we can begin to speculate that the secret core of this issue is the understanding of how language operates in religious discourse. Let us look at several other writers whose accounts of God's action bring this to fore, and use a conscious understanding of how language functions to clarify the question of the relationship between God and humanity.

The Dominican theologian Gareth Moore points to a Gospel story where Jesus stills a storm, as a reminder that talking of God's action does not mean that God *acts on* things. The story indicates an 'alternative kind of language that has always been prominent in the Christian tradition'; one not of causality but of command, not of power so much as authority. God is said to create by command, which

> makes clear that God does not do anything to things, does not act upon them, does not interfere with them, make them different from what they would otherwise have been. There is no temptation to postulate an invisible agent behind the scenes who brings about events as causes bring about their effects. To understand events as having been brought about by God is, on this model, to see them not as effects of somebody with great power, great strength, but as signs of somebody with great authority.[77]

In miracle stories, there is no divine causal mechanism at work. In fact, the essential point is that *no* causal mechanism is involved, and that is precisely why we are inclined to call it a miracle.[78] To ask 'how' the miracle happened and treat that as the meaning of the story is to reduce God's action to a series of tricks. But when we say 'God acted', we do not work out by a process of elimination that God must have done it. Nor are there two things whose relation we must understand: God's command and the event. *They are not separate events.* To see something happening in the natural world is precisely to see God's command being obeyed. According to Moore, 'I cannot suspect, for instance, that the snow is not really obeying God but was going to fall anyway, or that it misheard or misread the command.'[79] This just *is* the language that we use to describe the relation between God and the world. So if snow falls in London in January, we do not imagine that fortuitously its agenda and God's agenda agreed. Nor do we think that God didn't want it to snow but the snowflakes, ready to jump with their little white parachutes, didn't get the order right. To see something happen in the natural world, for the believer, is to see God's will being realized.

So to say something has been done by God is to react to it in a particular way, not 'to infer that the event in question was brought about by an undetectable agent with a particular identity'.[80] So to describe events as 'natural' is not to deny God's action or involvement. It is rather a way of saying about some events: ' "Don't wonder at them, don't think of them as significant or extraordinary. They are perfectly ordinary, so don't pay any particular attention to them".'[81] To explore this suggestion, let us say that the spots on a burned chapati resemble a bearded face like

Jesus'.[82] If we say, 'This was not some divine act but a natural event, not a miracle', what are we saying? We are not saying that it was God's will that the chapati should *not* burn, and the chapati defied God by burning. On Moore's account, we are also not saying that the natural world is independent of or irrelevant to God and so the chapati escapes God's control. What we are saying is, 'If the chapati burned, it must have been part of God's will in some unimportant sense, but forget the chapati, it doesn't mean anything. Focus on something that *does* have spiritual significance.'

From the BBC's website:

> *Hundreds of Christian pilgrims and other curious onlookers have been making their way to a church in Bangalore in India to see a chapati which has the image of Christ burnt into it.*
>
> *The chapati – a loaf of unleavened bread – is one of dozens that Shella Anthony bakes in her oven in Bangalore every day. But this one she thought was different.*
>
> *Burnt into it was what looked like the image of the face of Jesus Christ.*
>
> *Shella Anthony took the loaf to a local church and word spread like wildfire.*
>
> *Church officials say nearly 20,000 Christians have already visited the Renewal Retreat Centre to pay homage in front of the chapati, which has now been mounted in a glass case, and to offer prayers.*
>
> *Father Jacob George of the Renewal Retreat Centre is convinced it is a miracle.*

Mixed feelings

'We believe in miracles. Devotees are feeling blessed on witnessing it,' he said.

Pilgrims have come from Bangalore and surrounding towns and villages, and it is not just Christians who have made the odyssey.

Hindus, too, have come to look at the eight-centimetre (five-inch) loaf.

Anil Philip, a young freelance journalist, says initially he was sceptical about the shape of Jesus emerging on the surface of a chapati.

'But after a couple of visits, I experienced a different feeling,' he said.

'Christians are coming here out of devotion, the others are coming out of curiosity,' said Anil Philip.

BBC Delhi correspondent Adam Mynott says that while some believe it to be a miracle others have ridiculed the apparition as a load of eyewash.

On the other hand, to attribute an event to God's intervention is to say, as Moore puts it, 'See this event as significant; don't think of it as ordinary but as charged with meaning, and be impressed with it.'[83] This can be true even when there is a plausible scientific explanation for something. With Moore's suggestion of a shift from cause and effect to command and obedience comes a shift in the understanding of the greatness of God. We do not worship God's power; we respect his authority. 'To acknowledge somebody's authority is to see him as great; and that, without resigning your freedom.'[84]

Barry Miller maintains that God's agency is not simply a more powerful version of human agency, but exists on a different logical plane altogether. Miller asserts that the relation between God's and a creature's activity is that God brings it about that the creature does it. This does not reduce creatures to being instruments rather than agents; for 'God brings it about that (someone does something)' does not imply 'God brings someone to do something' or 'God makes someone do something'. Nor does this infringe the creature's freedom.

To understand how this can be so, one must bear in mind the radical difference between the action of creatures and a creator. Creatures must act *on* things; whereas the distinctive feature of the divine creative act is that it can produce its effects without acting on anything at all. Just as God does not create *from* something, but creates *ex nihilo*, so too God does not act *on* things but brings them about *ex nihilo*.

On this description of God's action, the direct effect of God's causing has my causing built into it. 'God brings about the situation in which I decide to do it' is how we should understand God's activity; not 'God makes me decide to do it.' Far from compromising my freedom and efficacy, expressed in this way, God's causality *includes* my free action; God is the cause of the situation in which I choose and cause my activity.

So the difference between God's and my causality is not that God's is 'greater' or 'more powerful'. The difference between God's and creatures' causality is absolute.

But if God's action is sufficient, how can it coexist with creaturely action? Miller is forthright: there is no causal role for me in bringing about Gwen-deciding-to-marry-Andrew. However, 'there most certainly is a causal role' for me in deciding. If God brings it about that I decide to marry Andrew, God is bringing about more than the marrying of Andrew – God is also bringing it about that I decide to marry him. It is plainly impossible that God exclude me from any causal role in that particular event, for God can bring it about that I decide to marry Andrew, only if it is I who decide. Cf. Aquinas: 'Those words of the Apostle are not to be taken as though man does not wish or does not run of his free choice, but because the free choice is not sufficient for this unless it be helped and moved by God.'[85]

The fact that God, unlike us, does not act on anything means, to Miller, that the logical form of propositions expressing God's causation is different from that expressing the causation by creatures. The logical form of a proposition expressing a creature's action states what can affect the result; whereas nothing can affect God's end result, so it would be misleading to express God's activity in the same logical form. What is required is a logical structure which does not portray God as acting on anything. The way to achieve this, he suggests, is simply shift the causal operator from inside the proposition to outside it. The causal operator is the phrase expressing God's causing; the proposition is the state of affairs effected. What Miller proposes is that the logical form that expresses God's causality is not: 'God caused S to do x' but: 'God caused it that (S did x).' In other words, God did not cause Socrates to raise his leg; God caused the state of affairs, 'Socrates raising his leg'. The causal operator, Miller explains, is like modal and tense operators: it can have both an internal and an external use, and the meaning changes accordingly. The placement of the phrase expressing God's causation affects the meaning of what is asserted. 'Outside' the state of affairs, it suggests that God 'makes be' the situation; brings and supports it in existence. 'Inside' the description of the state of affairs, it implies that God makes the agents described do what is asserted. The crucial difference between the two, therefore, is that in the internal use, X would act on Socrates – which is precisely how a creator God could never act. In the external use of the causal operator, Socrates is not acted upon, which is how God would always act.

As Miller puts it, God does what only God can do: produce an effect ex nihilo*; Socrates does what only a creature can do,* ex aliquo*, from something. Then in what way should we conceive of the 'how' of God's production? Perhaps, he suggests, as a 'limit case'; that is, the ultimate point to which lesser approximations point in a series. In this case, the series is one of 'productions', in which progressively less and less of the 'product' stems from the materials used, and more and more from the manufacturer; until one reaches the 'limit case' in which nothing at all is required by the* ex-nihilo*-creator in order to create. Such creation, causing or acting is not a greater version of the 'same thing' as ours; it is the absolute to which other forms of creating, causing and acting point, but never reach.*[86]

What, in effect, Miller is doing is providing the logical back-up for a theory of analogical language about God. Thus Burrell and Miller, in very different ways, emphasize the importance of an adequate understanding of analogical language, while Moore and Tanner, again quite different in style, both assert that a proper understanding of the function and workings of theological discourse reveal that there is no competition between divine and human action.

Now in Islam you find, possibly exposed with even greater clarity, the same structuration of the problem. Ash'arītes, the followers of al-Ash'arī, said there is no creator but 'Allah. Not only human beings themselves, but also every one of their actions is created by God. Human beings do not have a choice, nor any power over their actions. Any power held by any creature would compromise the omnipotence of God.

The Mu'tazilites, whom we might describe in Western terms as the 'liberal' wing of Islamic theology, took exception to this account. To their mind, it may have preserved God's omnipotence but at the price of 'Allah's justice. For it entails that God wills someone to do evil, then punishes him for it. So they believed in a kind of 'delegation' – *tafwid* – in which God creates us with power and intelligence and entrusts us with using them according to our own will, at our own risk, on our own responsibility. We have real independence and power from 'Allah and 'Allah does not influence us in a particular direction. – You can see how, from the Ash'arīte point of view, this creates an unacceptable picture of human beings having independence and therefore power over against God.

Maimonides suggested that God's way of working indirectly was to influence our minds. Maimonides had a highly intellectualized picture of our relations to God; it is through our intelligent souls that we unite with God, and in that quasi-mystical, quasi-intellectual union, God influences us to do the divine will. Maimonides had a theological son, Rabbi Abraham ben Moses ben Maimon, who, interestingly, was powerfully influenced by the Islamic Sufi tradition, and that suffuses his thinking. In particular, this Sufi influence overtakes the influence from his father on this very point of divine action. He nuances his father's picture of an intellectual unity with God. Theoretical knowledge and reflection is important, but is balanced by the need for a purification of heart and soul. The question of divine activity then becomes the place for special trust in God. Rabbi Abraham does not reject God's special activity in miracles; God can work in this way. But he does reject omnideterminism or predestination, which deny to human beings and to nature their own agency. The real difference between the believer and the unbeliever, he suggests, is not in their attitude to miracles but in their attitude to natural events and causes. The believer sees God at work also in these ordinary, non-miraculous events, the unbeliever does not. But for the believer, whether a natural event can even take place or a natural law take effect depends on God's will that it do so.

Islamic theology also developed its own complex and closely reasoned middle way, between the predestination and omnideterminism of the Ash'arītes, and the delegation view of the Mu'tazilites. We find this in particular in the early Shi'ite thinkers of Twelve-Imam Shi'ism. A ḥadīth (tradition) about Imam al-Sadiq, one of the great lights of Shi'ism, has a man tackle the Imam on this question. Imam al-Sadiq rejects the Ash'arīte position, saying, 'God is more just than to make people commit misdeeds then chastise them for what they have done.' He also rejects the Mu'tazilite view: 'If He had delegated it to them, He would have not confined them to enjoining good and forbidding evil' (a Qur'ānic phrase). When the man asks if there is any possible station or position between these two viewpoints, the Imam exclaims, 'Yes, wider than the space between heaven and earth!'

This 'station between the stations', or Muslim middle way, argues that human beings have free will and possibility of action, for which they are responsible, precisely because they are created that way by God and maintained in existence and empowered to act in that way by God. In that way, human actions are their own, and at the same time can be seen as actions of God, for there is no affair, no action, no authority but God's, and every power comes from God. Their position is essentially the one sought also by Moore, Miller and Tanner which we investigated earlier, possibly even what Farrer was after with his 'double agency'; in other words, Imam al-Sadiq is the forerunner of the account later given by St Thomas Aquinas.

Ṭabāṭabā'ī draws on the Islamic concept of something contingent in itself, but necessary through another, to articulate an understanding of the relation between human action and divine power. Something purely contingent cannot come into being without being caused, and at that point it becomes necessary. In that way, a free human action must be 'caused' and become 'necessary' – in that sense and only that sense, which would apply just as much to a random throw of dice. It is evident, he goes on, that something necessary-through-something-else does not actualize without ultimately terminating in that which is necessary-by-itself – which is only God. 'Hence His power is all-encompassing and includes even the acts of free will.'[87] So on one hand voluntary acts are caused by God; 'the existence of an effect is relative in relation to its cause, and is not realized except through dependence on something independent that may sustain it. There is nothing that is independent-in-itself except that which is necessary-in-itself. Hence God is the primary source of all effects dependent for their existence on a cause, and He has power over all things.'[88] However, that does not mean human acts are compelled, nor, for that matter, that divine foreknowledge makes their occurrence necessary. The divine will relates to human actions as they are in themselves, 'and as such they remain attributed to the person who is part of the complete cause. Their being subject to the Divine does not change what they are. Hence the subjection of the actions to the Divine will is through man's free choice.' It is God's will that someone should perform an act through their own free will. As for divine foreknowledge and human action, 'acts of free will are subject to God's knowledge as they are, that is, as voluntary actions which one can perform or refrain from performing, and the knowledge of something does not alter its reality'.[89]

So on this multi-faith view, divine and human action – or divine power and knowledge (which are identical, and identical to divine compassion) – are related to human action through the primordial relationship of creation: the gift of being created and being known, and being empowered to act freely while being sustained in being throughout our acting.

So on this view, can God act in the world? Yes. Why? Because *we* can. How does God do it? Through our action. But is that then also God's action? Yes, because that is what God made us to be like, and God keeps us in being, and acting this way. What does the difference between God's action and our action *look* like then? Nothing at all.

This stance is often expressed in spiritual traditions, usually through tales or anecdotes. In the Sufi tradition there is a story that describes a man going through the world seeing evil, suffering, and horror – crime, sickness, death, and war. Finally he rounds on God, demanding: 'God, why did you not *do something* about it?!' God replies: 'I *did* do something about it. I made you.'

Draw your own conclusions

What is it about power that you admire? Which of those aspects would you ascribe to God if you believe in one?

Do you think it makes sense, and is important to say, that God can do the logically impossible? Why or why not?

If there are things that God cannot do, is God not omnipotent?

What is your view of the stone paradox?

Do you think God acts directly in the world? Are there any problems created by your view? How would you deal with them?

Would God's action in the world be visible? How?

Are miracles, if there are any, God's action in the world while natural laws are not? Or are they different? How?

How do you relate divine and human action? Do any of the views represented in this chapter attract you?

Further reading

Aquinas, T. *The 'Summa Theologica' of St. Thomas Aquinas*, London, Burns Oates & Washbourne

Davies, B. (1985) *Thinking about God*, London, Geoffrey Chapman

Geach, P. T. (1973) 'Omnipotence', *Philosophy* 48

al-Ghazālī (2000 (1997)) *The Incoherence of the Philosophers (Tahafut al-Falasifah)*, trans. M. E. Marmura, Provo, Utah, Brigham Young University Press

Harrison, J. (1999) *God, Freedom and Immortality*, Avebury Series in Philosophy, Aldershot, Ashgate

Hebblethwaite, B. and E. Henderson (eds) (1990) *Divine Action: Studies Inspired by the Philosophical Theology of Austin Farrer*, Edinburgh, T & T Clark

Hughes, G. J. (1995) *The Nature of God*, London and New York, Routledge

Kenny, A. (1979) *The God of the Philosophers*, Oxford, Clarendon Press

Maimonides, M. (1963) *The Guide of the Perplexed*, ed. S. Pines, Chicago and London, University of Chicago Press

Miller, B. (1996) *A Most Unlikely God: A Philosophical Enquiry into the Nature of God*, Notre Dame, Ind., University of Notre Dame Press

Moore, G. (1996) *Believing in God: A Philosophical Essay*, Edinburgh, T & T Clark

Narain, K. (1986 (1962)) *An Outline of Mādhva Philosophy*, 2nd edn, Allahabad, Udayana

Pailin, D. A. (1989) *God and the Processes of Reality: Foundations of a Credible Theism*, Routledge Religious Studies, London and New York, Routledge

Pike, N. (1969) 'Omnipotence and God's Ability to Sin', *American Philosophical Quarterly* 6

Savage, C. W. (1967) 'The Paradox of the Stone', *Philosophical Review* 76

Swinburne, R. (1993) *The Coherence of Theism*, Oxford, Clarendon Press

Tracy, T. F. (ed.) (1994) *The God who Acts: Philosophical and Theological Explorations*, University Park, Pa., Pennsylvania State University Press

Wierenga, E. R. (1989) *The Nature of God: An Inquiry into Divine Attributes*, Cornell Studies in the Philosophy of Religion, Ithaca and London, Cornell University Press

Ward, K. (1990) *Divine Action*, London, Collins

White, V. (1985) *The Fall of a Sparrow: A Concept of Special Divine Action*, Exeter, Paternoster

Wiles, M. (1993) *God's Action in the World: The Bampton Lectures for 1986*, London, XPRESS Reprints

Wiles, M. (1994) 'Divine Action: Some Moral Considerations', in T. F. Tracy (ed.), *The God who Acts: Philosophical and Theological Explorations.*, University Park, Pa., Pennsylvania State University Press

Notes

1 B. Davies (1985) *Thinking about God*, London, Geoffrey Chapman, p. 156.

2 Davies, *Thinking about God*, pp. 157–8.

3 G. Moore (1996) *Believing in God: A Philosophical Essay*, Edinburgh, T & T Clark, pp. 248–9.

4 D. A. Pailin (1989) *God and the Processes of Reality: Foundations of a Credible Theism*, Routledge Religious Studies, London and New York, Routledge, p. 95.

5 Thomas Aquinas, *The 'Summa Theologica' of St. Thomas Aquinas*, London, Burns Oates & Washbourne, I.25.3.

6 Aquinas, *Summa Theologica*, I.25.3.

7 M. Maimonides (1963) *The Guide of the Perplexed*, trans. S. Pines, Chicago and London, University of Chicago Press, p. 459.

8 al-Ghazālī ((2000 (1997)) *The Incoherence of the Philosophers (Tahafut al-Falasifah)*, trans. M. E. Marmura, Provo, Utah, Brigham Young University Press, Discussion 17.

9 al-Ghazālī, *The Incoherence of the Philosophers*, p. 170.

10 In the discussion of miracles, he first engages in a Hume-like refutation of the necessity of causation. Where the connection is not logically necessary, where the affirmation or negation of one entails the affirmation or negation of the other, the causal connection of events is not a necessary one. 'Their connection is due to the prior decree of God . . . not to its being necessary in itself' and it lies within God's power to create one without the other. al-Ghazālī, *The Incoherence of the Philosophers*, Discussion 17, pp. 16ff.

11 al-Ghazālī, *The Incoherence of the Philosophers*, p. 170.

12 al-Ghazālī, *The Incoherence of the Philosophers*, p. 171.

13 For example, Swinburne on why a restriction of the notion of omnipotence to what is logically possible is not a significant theological loss: 'A logically impossible action is not an action. It is what is described by a form of words which purport to describe an action, but do not describe anything which it is coherent to suppose could be done. It is no objection to A's omnipotence that he cannot make a square circle. This is because "making a square circle" does not describe anything which it is coherent to suppose could be done.' R. Swinburne (1993) *The Coherence of Theism*, Oxford, Clarendon Press, pp. 153–4.

14 This receives discussion in, for example, E. R. Wierenga (1989) *The Nature of God: An Inquiry into Divine Attributes*, Cornell Studies in the Philosophy of Religion, Ithaca and London, Cornell University Press; and a lengthy list of what God can't do, like 'make people sleep more slowly than they do', 'do mental arithmetic' or 'alter the past', is found in J. Harrison (1999) *God, Freedom and Immortality*, Avebury Series in Philosophy, Aldershot, Ashgate, pp. 282–3.

15 Letter to Mesland, R. Descartes (1991) *The Philosophical Writings of Descartes*, vol. 3: *The Correspondence*, ed. R. S. J. Cottingham, D. Murdoch and A. Kenny, Cambridge, Cambridge University Press, 3 2.5.1644.

16 Letter to Mersenne, Descartes, *The Philosophical Writings: The Correspondence*, 3 15.4.1630.

17 G. J. Hughes (1995) *The Nature of God*, London and New York, Rout-

ledge, pp. 150–1. Hughes suggests that the real question about omnipotence is not about coherence and non-contradiction, but about 'what is, in some absolute sense, causally possible'; which 'is an empirical, not a logical, matter', and moreover, 'one where due agnosticism seems to be entirely proper'.

18 J. van Ess (1985) 'Wrongdoing and Divine Omnipotence in the Theology of Abu Ishaq An-Nazzam', in T. Rudavsky (ed.), *Divine Omniscience and Divine Omnipotence in Medieval Philosophy: Islamic, Jewish and Christian Perspectives*, Synthese Historical Library 25, Dordrecht, Boston and Lancaster, Reidel, pp. 53ff.

19 See Kenny for a discussion of Abelard's view, A. Kenny (1979) *The God of the Philosophers*, Oxford, Clarendon Press.

20 Geach thought that the believer would be well advised to steer clear of the assertion that God is omnipotent. It gives rise to too many logical incoherences. Instead, the believer should claim that God is 'almighty'. 'Omnipotent' means the ability to do everything, while 'almighty' refers simply to power over all things. P. T. Geach (1973) 'Omnipotence', *Philosophy* 48.

21 N. Pike (1969) 'Omnipotence and God's Ability to Sin', *American Philosophical Quarterly* 6.

22 Pike, 'Omnipotence and God's Ability to Sin'.

23 E. L. Ormsby (1984) *Theodicy in Islamic Thought: The Dispute over al-Ghazālī's 'Best of All Possible Worlds'*, Princeton, Princeton University Press.

24 Perhaps in ignorance of this Islamic argument, Morris makes a parallel point in his defence of God's perfection and power. T. V. Morris (1987) *Anselmian Explorations: Essays in Philosophical Theology*, Notre Dame, Ind., University of Notre Dame Press, pp. 70–5.

The claim that God cannot sin is not, he argues, tantamount to 'God lacks the power to sin'. Indeed, is there such a thing as a discrete power of sinning, which we have but that God lacks? There are powers needed in order to commit a sin, 'But there is no discrete power of sinning, no distinct power to sin, no power the exercise of which is, in itself, *sufficient* for doing evil or sinning' (p. 73). With reference to causal powers, to say either 'God is able to sin' or 'God is unable to sin' is highly misleading. What theists claim is that 'God cannot do evil because he cannot intend to do evil.' That does not entail, nor do they maintain, that 'God could not do evil even if he intended to'. That, Morris, like Pike, seems to accept would constitute a restriction in power.

25 K. Narain (1986 (1962)) *An Outline of Madhva Philosophy*, 2nd edn, Allahabad, Udayana, p. 112.

26 Narain, *An Outline of Madhva Philosophy*, p. 113.

27 S. M. H. Ṭabāṭabā'ī (2003) *The Elements of Islamic Metaphysics (Bidayat al-Hikmah)*, London, ICAS Press, p. 144.

28 C. W. Savage (1967) 'The Paradox of the Stone', *Philosophical Review* 76, pp. 74–9.

29 Savage, 'Paradox of the Stone', p. 74.

30 Swinburne, *The Coherence of Theism*, p. 158.

31 G. I. Mavrodes (1963) 'Some Puzzles Concerning Omnipotence', *Philosophical Review* 72, pp. 221–3.

32 H. Frankfurt (1964) 'The Logic of Omnipotence', *Philosophical Review* 73, pp. 262–3.

33 Mavrodes, 'Some Puzzles Concerning Omnipotence', p. 342.

34 Aquinas, *Summa Theologica*, I.25.3.

35 A. Chakrabarti (2000) 'The Cloud of Pretending', *India International Centre Quarterly*, Spring, p. 97 *et passim.*

36 *Dharma eva hato hanti.* Chakrabarti, 'The Cloud of Pretending', p. 95.

37 In a private communication.

38 al-Ghazālī (1999 (1992, 1995, 1997)) *The Ninety-Nine Beautiful Names of God*, trans. David B. Burrell and Nazih Daher, Cambridge, Islamic Texts Society, p. 140.

39 Aquinas, *Summa Theologica*, I.25.3.

40 N. A. Manson (2003) *God and Design: The Technological Argument and Modern Science*, London and New York, Routledge, p. 15.

41 M. Wiles (1993) *God's Action in the World: The Bampton Lectures for 1986*, London, XPRESS Reprints.

42 M. Wiles (1994) 'Divine Action: Some Moral Considerations', in T. F. Tracy (ed.), *The God who Acts: Philosophical and Theological Explorations*, University Park, Pa., Pennsylvania State University Press, p. 22.

43 Alston does not accept that Wiles has demonstrated that a more interventionist God does in fact compromise human freedom. The problem of evil is a greater one than just relating to God's action. He has further elaboration of the issue. W. P. Alston (1994) 'Divine Action: Shadow or Substance?', in T. F. Tracy (ed.), *The God who Acts: Philosophical and Theological Explorations*, University Park, Pa., Pennsylvania State University Press.

44 V. White (1985) *The Fall of a Sparrow: A Concept of Special Divine Action*, Exeter, Paternoster.

45 White, *The Fall of a Sparrow*, p. 108.

46 K. Ward (1990) *Divine Action*, London, Collins, p. 98. Other more recent treatments of the religion-science issue on an accessible level include (2004) *God, Faith and the New Millennium: Christian Belief in an Age of Science*, Oxford, Oneworld. See also his Gresham Lectures on religion and science, posted at www.gresham.ac.uk.

47 Nor, for that matter, is certainty possible he claims, invoking Heisenberg's Uncertainty Principle. Ward, *Divine Action*, p. 99.

48 Ward, *Divine Action*, p. 105.

49 Ward, *Divine Action*, p. 111.

50 Ward, *Divine Action*, p. 118.

51 T. F. Tracy (1997) 'Divine Action', in P. L. Quinn and C. Taliaferro (eds), *A Companion to the Philosophy of Religion*, Oxford, Blackwell, pp. 304–5.

52 Tracy, 'Divine Action', pp. 304–5.

53 Pailin, *God and the Processes of Reality: Foundations of a Credible Theism*, p. 94.

54 A. N. Whitehead (1979) *Process and Reality: An Essay in Cosmology*, Gifford Lectures 1927–8, London, Collier Macmillan, p. 346.

55 Pailin, *God and the Processes of Reality: Foundations of a Credible Theism*, p. 139.

56 Pailin, *God and the Processes of Reality: Foundations of a Credible Theism*, p. 140

57 Davies, *Thinking about God*. He complains that 'in general, Swinburne

confuses "God brings it about that X is true at t" and "God, occupying some moment of time, brings it about at that time that X is true" ' (pp. 153–4).

58 Davies, *Thinking about God*, p. 166.

59 R. Creel (1986) *Divine Impassibility*, Cambridge, Cambridge University Press.

60 Creel accommodates problems of temporality by suggesting that God could know all possibilities eternally, and 'God can index his will to all possibilities that can be actualized in the world that he intends to create, and he can do this independently of the existence of the world.' R. Creel (1997) 'Immutability and Impassibility', in P. L. Quinn and C. Taliaferro (eds), *A Companion to the Philosophy of Religion*, Oxford, Blackwell, p. 316.

61 Creel, 'Immutability and Impassibility', p. 317.

62 W. N. Clark (1994) *Explorations in Metaphysics*, Notre Dame, Ind., University of Notre Dame Press, p. 187.

63 Clark, *Explorations in Metaphysics*, p. 190.

64 Clark, *Explorations in Metaphysics*, p. 198.

65 Although there is a 'matter' problem today, which doubts whether God can act if he is incorporeal. Our notions of action, it is said, are so bound up with our physicality that it is incoherent to suppose that God, as a bodiless being, can be an agent in the physical world. Kenny has argued that a body is necessary for a being to act. (Kenny, *The God of the Philosophers*, last chapter.) Kenny's notion of action rests on Danto's analysis: that actions are made up of or reduce to 'basic actions'. That I close a window is an action, but the basic action it reduces to is raising my arm. These basic actions seem inescapably bodily, and this is what fuels Kenny's argument.

Basil Mitchell, however, contends that rather than presupposing a body, the notion of action merely 'presupposes a conscious agent with intentions and purposes which he attempts to realize in his environment as he sees it' (B. Mitchell (1981) *The Justification of Religious Belief*, New York, Oxford University Press, pp. 7–8). Tracy argues, similarly, that 'agency' and 'action' may be inextricably linked; but not 'agency' and 'bodiliness'. 'We may not be able to explain *how* an incorporeal agent brings about physical effects, but talk of such agency poses no readily discernible problem of internal consistency' (Tracy, 'Divine Action', p. 302).

Holzer tries to deconstruct Kenny's claim by rejecting Danto's account. He thinks that there is too much phenomenological evidence against Danto's account: 'raising my arm' is not basic, for there are too many intervening steps involving the brain, nerves, etc. Action cannot be analysed adequately by reduction to single fundamental physical acts. Where does one draw the line, in a complex neurology? Thus, he suggests Kenny's challenge is defeated. S. W. Holtzer (1987) 'The Possibility of Incorporeal Agency', in W. J. Abraham and S. W. Holtzer (eds), *The Rationality of Religious Belief: Essays in Honour of Basil Mitchell*, Oxford, Clarendon Press, pp. 189–209.

Grace Jantzen, however, has argued that the idea of God as incorporeal is analogous to a Cartesian dualism of mind as opposed to body, as applied to human beings; and thus attributing incorporeality to God is not so much philosophically incoherent, as theologically undesirable (G. M. Jantzen (1984) *God's World, God's Body*, London, Darton, Longman & Todd). She wonders how a disembodied agent could have any 'basic actions'. 'There are difficulties with the notion that an incorporeal spirit could perform any basic actions whatsoever which would result in physical movement; on the other hand, God can perform *any* physical action, and any such action of God's part is direct, basic' (p. 87).

If it is theologically unacceptable to say that God has a finite body, the logical alternative is not to say that God is incorporeal, but to assert that the *whole world* is God's body. In her view, the idea of God's action in the world makes more sense within that model. 'Such a model also has the advantage of illuminating the notions of providence and miracle. If the world is God's body, and every part of it is sustained by his will, then he can arrange the natural order to suit his purposes (providence) and alter it in individual "miraculous" instances if he so chooses' (p. 90). The whole unfolding of nature, including human action, can then be seen as the manifestation of divine activity; but there is no need for a concept of miracle as an intervention from 'outside' the world.

66 Austin Farrer (1967) *Faith and Speculation,* Edinburgh, T & T Clark, p. 79.

67 Owen Thomas, in B. Hebblethwaite and E. Henderson (eds) (1990) *Divine Action: Studies Inspired by the Philosophical Theology of Austin Farrer*, Edinburgh, T & T Clark, p. 46.

68 For example, Tracy has suggested variously that we might loosen the definition of double agency, or speak of a 'limited' double agency. (T. F. Tracy (1994) 'Divine Action, Created Causes, and Human Freedom', in T. F. Tracy (ed.), *The God who Acts: Philosophical and Theological Explorations*, University Park, Pa., Pennsylvania State University Press; Tracy, 'Divine Action'.

Neither the divine nor the creaturely agent is a sufficient cause of the event; there may be a duality of causes but no unity of action. The two causes are complementary, and each contributes a distinct part to the event (Tracy, 'Divine Action'). As he observes, we can ascribe an event to someone even when the actions are brought about by an instrument or intermediary (Tracy, 'Divine Action, Created Causes, and Human Freedom'). 'God's causal activity goes much deeper, of course, because God brings about and sustains the very existence of finite causes themselves. But in addition to this direct divine agency, events that flow from the network of finite causes that God has established can be attributed to God as indirect divine acts. God brings about these events by bringing about creatures that produce them' (Tracy, 'Divine Action, Created Causes, and Human Freedom', pp. 88–9).

On this view, creaturely freedom and its causal context exist by God's action and permission. So God not only establishes the agent's capacity for free action, but also plays a unique role in setting the conditions under which it is exercised. Our action everywhere presupposes this indirect form of divine action. But God can also act directly to bring about various events. One can imagine situations where one person plays so crucial a role in enabling or inducing something done by another, that one can also attribute a role to the inducer. 'God's agency envelopes and pervades our own' (Tracy, 'Divine Action, Created Causes, and Human Freedom', p. 100).

69 So argues F. Dilley (1983) 'Does the "God who Acts" Really Act?', in Owen C. Thomas (ed.), *God's Activity in the World: The Contemporary Problem*, Chico, Calif., Scholars Press, pp. 55–7.

70 White, *The Fall of a Sparrow*, p. 111.

71 White, *The Fall of a Sparrow*, p. 117.

72 White, *The Fall of a Sparrow*, p. 120. White recognizes that the potential undoing of his account is the existence of evil, events which seem to be not the enactment but rather the frustration of God's purposes and intentions. Far from taking the easy or moderate way out, such as declaring such events are a means to the divine good end, White takes the bull by the horns and declares that 'every event is in some sense "end" and never purely "means".' Even unhappy or evil events are 'in some sense an intended action of God in relation to those involved, bearing some intended end for them. These events are not simply made a means to some general and external end, rather, those involved may find some specific end within the event for themselves' (p. 128).

Of course such events can still be part of a wider context of meaning; but without simply being a means to an end. White insists that there is no class of events which frustrate God's purposes. Although there are evil events, no event is evil in itself; for evil is never the whole context. See the discussion in White, *The Fall of a Sparrow*, 133–36.

73 Tracy, 'Divine Action, Created Causes, and Human Freedom', p. 97.

74 Aquinas, *Summa Theologica*, 1.22.3.

75 D. B. Burrell (1994) 'Divine Action and Human Freedom in the Context of Creation', in T. F. Tracy (ed.), *The God who Acts: Philosophical and Theological Explorations*, University Park, Pa., Pennsylvania State University Press, p. 106.

76 To speak of God's mode of agency as 'exceeding' – even 'vastly' – obscures 'the distinction' of God from the world, 'the infinite qualitative difference'. It is to suggest that Creator and creature are on a continuum, with the Creator at one end. 'That simply will not do,' Burrell objects, 'for the notions that can span "the distinction" do so only because they are able to function analogously'. In all talk of God's agency or causing and ours, the words function analogously. Burrell, 'Divine Action and Human Freedom in the Context of Creation', p. 105.

77 G. Moore (1996) *Believing in God: A Philosophical Essay*, Edinburgh, T & T Clark, p. 247.

78 Moore, *Believing in God*, pp. 240–1.

79 Moore, *Believing in God*, p. 251.

80 Moore, *Believing in God*, p. 262.

81 Moore, *Believing in God*, p. 263.

82 http://news.bbc.co.uk/2/hi/south_asia/2484195.stm (accessed 4 September 2004).

83 Moore, *Believing in God*, p. 264.

84 Moore, *Believing in God*, pp. 248–9.

85 Aquinas, *Summa Theologica*, I.83.1, reply to objection 2.

86 B. Miller (1996) *A Most Unlikely God: A Philosophical Enquiry into the Nature of God*, Notre Dame, Ind., University of Notre Dame Press, p. 131.

87 Ṭabāṭabā'ī, *Elements of Islamic Metaphysics*, p. 145.

88 Ṭabāṭabā'ī, *Elements of Islamic Metaphysics*, p. 145.

89 Ṭabāṭabā'ī, *Elements of Islamic Metaphysics*, p. 146.

11

Explanations of Evil

On any day when I was writing this book the news was full of stories of human suffering, natural disasters, and violent acts of evil; and – I sorrowfully expect – any day you are reading this it will be the same. And every day somewhere someone, out of the depths of their personal suffering, cries, 'Why, God, do you allow this to happen to me?' Someone struggling to find the meaning of what they see and hear, will be asking, 'Why this evil, why this pain, why does God let it happen to our world?' And someone else will be saying, 'God cannot exist if our world is so disordered by evil.' Even the atheist philosopher Sidney Morgenbesser, a renowned wit, is reported to have said shortly before he died, 'Why is God making me suffer so much? Just because I don't believe in him?'

Faced with the horrors of today and the atrocities recorded in human history, it seems reasonable enough to doubt that a good God exists. Non-theistic traditions in Buddhism made this point repeatedly against the Hindus. If all good and evil is the creation of a supreme god, then it must be the achievement of that god that people become liars, thieves, unchaste, heretical, murderers. Modern-day Western atheists issue the challenge of evil against believers in newspaper columns as well as in books of philosophy. It is a not a new dilemma, and in its long histories in all religions of the world, no believer has come up with answers which everyone can accept. What we will attempt is to analyse the problems – for they are multiple – and the thinking that arises out of them, and see where that leaves us.

Is evil real?

Some religious traditions believe that evil is an illusion, and that the aim of the spiritual life is to rise above the level of superficialities of ordinary living and see reality as it truly is and see suffering and evil for the illusions they are. Hinduism and Buddhism have traditionally used this metaphysic. The Upaniṣadic view, developed particularly in the non-dualist or monist schools such as Advaita Vedānta, is that the variety of beings we perceive and the experiences we undergo are not ultimately real. From this it follows that – like all else in our experience – evil and suffering are not ultimately real. Despite their unreality, they are seen, paradoxically, as of value, for they can further spiritual growth and enlightenment by helping detach us from worldly things and experiences.

A summary of Indian ideas of the non-reality of evil

The tangible realm of māyā, which is the veil that occludes Truth, is at the same time the self-revelation of truth. Everything is a mask, a gesture of self-revelation. The dark aspects of life . . . counterbalance the bright.

Suffering, therefore, is only a problem so long as it appears to be a final and inescapable truth. But when it is realized that the self is not bound for ever to the transient world of suffering, but rather that it is Brahman, then suffering can no longer occur.[1]

The idea that evil does not have positive existence in itself is also present in the Christian tradition. Augustine and Aquinas, following Aristotle in part, maintained that evil is fundamentally the lack of some good quality that an entity ought to have. Evil is 'the privation of good' and represents an element or a tendency towards non-being. All created being, since it was created by God, is good, and becomes evil insofar as it becomes defective. Moral evil, according to Augustine, is a human choice not to fulfil the true nature and being that God has intended for us. This evil originates in basically good, rational creatures (in Augustine's thinking, angels and human beings) whose will falls short of the 'unchangeable good'.

What is called 'evil' can also be seen as resulting from a point of view. Nature can be used to show how in a diverse world, some conditions favour one species at the expense of another, so what seems evil to one will be good to the other; the whole system of eating and being eaten is one example, and earth processes that cause human suffering, like earthquakes and floods, have a role to play in the continuation of the planet. It can be argued that human pleasures and judgements are not necessarily coextensive with 'the good' that God intends. Viewed as a whole, it is sometimes claimed, creation is good, even if aspects of it are not desirable from the point of view of a particular individual or a particular species. Spinoza maintained this, saying that in nature there is no good and no evil; rather things exist the way they are necessarily. Calling things good and evil is an act of the imagination, and it reflects our own concerns and interests, not their own intrinsic natures. Therefore, there is no philosophical problem of why there is evil in the world.

Buber relativizes the evilness of evil in a different manner, suggesting that we reject the notion of evil and goodness as opposites. 'Good' is the orientation and motivation towards God (or 'home', as he puts it) while 'evil' he sees as 'the aimless whirl of human potentialities without which nothing can be achieved and by which, if they take no direction but remain trapped in themselves, everything goes awry. If the two were indeed poles the man who did not see them as such would be blind; but the man would be blinder who did not perceive the lightning flash from pole to pole, the "and".'[2] In this way evil appears as just a misdirection of good, or of a good impulse, drive, or motivation. This becomes clearer in Buber's 'Images of Good and Evil'.[3] The evil urge is more important than the good one because of its creative potential, and is identified with passion – it is only evil if misused. In a similar vein Mordecai Kaplan suggests that evil is chaos and good is the purposive force that produces the cosmos out of chaos.[4]

Buber's views were disputed by Eliezer Berkovits, who feels that the account does not fit most people's experience; instead 'evil and wickedness, sorrow and suffering, failure and sin' seem much more than mere unformed nature or chaos.[5] Perhaps those who can accept the non-existence of evil need read no further, but Berkovits's feelings may be closer to more people in the modern Western world.

Does evil come with the creation of the world?

First a distinction is helpful: there are two forms we have to deal with,

'moral evil' resulting from human actions

'natural evil' usually seen in such events as earthquakes, floods, droughts that become a source of human suffering.

Although these may be separated, there is some interpenetration; for one thing, much of 'natural' evil has humanly caused aspects, even if only through ignorance. The effects of floods may be magnified by destructive logging. Poor building quality has been blamed for increasing the damage and deaths when earthquakes strike. Sometimes human malice or evil has played a part, but in addition, when we see imperfections in the natural world, humanity is included as part of nature. Where does evil of either kind originate?

In the Judaic and the Christian traditions, some thinkers maintain, when God created the universe, God had to create what was 'Other' than God's own being. If creation is differentiated from God, who is perfect, the universe as not-God cannot be perfect. There must be a metaphysical or ontological difference between God and the world, and it is from this inherent imperfection that evil arises.

Within the Jewish tradition, one way of conceiving divine creation evolves out of the notion of *tsimtsum*, or divine contraction, found in Lurianic Kabbala.

A Jewish mystical view

The Lurianic Kabbala speaks of Ein-Sof, *which is the name for God transcendent in all that is, God-in-God's-self as opposed to God's manifestations.*

> *[The] very essence of* Ein-Sof *leaves no space whatsoever for creation, for it is impossible to imagine an area which is not already God, since this would constitute a limitation of His infinity. . . . Consequently, an act of creation is possible only through 'the entry of God into Himself,' that is, through an act of* zimzum *whereby He contracts Himself and so makes it possible for something which is not* Ein-Sof *to exist. Some part of the Godhead, therefore, retreats and leaves room, so to speak, for the creative processes to come into play.*[6]

This absence-of-God's-presence is a necessary condition for the existence of other things, but also entails imperfection. It leads to the creation of 'vessels', one of which is 'primordial humanity', which then 'break' from the irresistible pressure of the divine light which they contain. This 'breaking of the vessels' leads to the roots of evil.

Some base this point, as Plato does, on the unavoidable imperfections in matter. Maimonides sees matter as limited and a source of deficiency, and deduces that this makes imperfections in the material order inevitable.[7] Both Augustine and Aquinas think the ontological difference between God and the world explains the existence of suffering and evil. To have a full range of good things, a hierarchy of goods must exist. This means there will be defective things at the bottom of the continuum, and moreover some things will arise from change, which of itself brings imperfection.

Kropf takes this Thomist tradition and works it into an evolutionary view:

> Perhaps evil, or what we take to be evil, especially in the course of natural events, exists primarily because creation, understood as an evolutionary process, necessarily begins with forms of existence that are as totally unlike God as possible. This would not deny God's immanence or presence within the working of the process, but rather offer a new, dynamic understanding of what Thomas Aquinas said long ago: that the basic reason for God's immanence within creation (sustaining

> things' existence and providentially guiding them toward their fulfillment) is to be found precisely in his total 'otherness' from them as the transcendent cause of their existence. In terms of good and evil, this would mean that created things, at least in their primitive evolutionary beginnings, would be at the same time as totally unlike God and as imperfect as could be imagined![8]

Evolution and the inevitability of metaphysical imperfection can also be used to explain the defects of the moral world, as well as nature. Modern thinkers are inclined to find such psychological and spiritual versions of 'evolution' more comfortable than earlier treatments of original sin. Psychological or biological traits may be morally neutral, but in human lives may predispose people to turn toward evil.

The social psychologist Ervin Staub in a study of genocide and mass violence examines the complex biological, psychological and sociological factors that can give rise to horrific evil-doing by ordinary people.[9] What is interesting about his account, for the point we are considering now, is how fundamental human traits which are useful can also be turned towards an 'evil' direction. Theories of evolution can take on a theological or spiritual colouring; such as the theodicy of John Hick which we will consider later, or the somewhat mystical vision of Teilhard de Chardin.

Here is a Talmudic story:

The Evil Tempter was captured. The captors started to kill it, but were warned that if they did, the entire universe would fall apart, so they contented themselves with imprisoning him instead. Three days later, they searched throughout the land trying to find a fresh egg, but could find none. When there is no sex drive, there can be no eggs. They were faced with a dilemma: if they did not release the Evil One, they could not continue with life as they knew it; if they did release him, evil would roam the land once more. They appealed to heaven for a 'half-mercy': the Tempter should live, but not tempt us with evil. A voice answered from above: 'They do not grant halves in heaven.'[10]

Is evil a necessary counterpart to good?

Another set of explanations for the reality of evil arises from logical construction, by looking at such questions as:

> Could we recognize and appreciate good if there was no evil?
>
> Is evil the logically necessary counterpart to good?
>
> Can some good results only arise by means of some bad things?

Is the world somehow better as it is, with some of what we consider 'evil' in it, than without evil?

The Islamic theologian al-Naẓẓām held that a just world requires a mixture of opposing components, which includes evil as well as good. This was further developed by his student, al-Jaḥīẓ, who argued that if creation were totally good, 'the requisite testing, the trial-and-error conducive to thought, would also cease'. He explains, 'It is the opposition of things within creation that provokes thought. Without thought, there would be neither discrimination nor choice. Knowledge itself would no longer be possible. . . . It is through the opposition of good and evil, perfect and imperfect, that we acquire knowledge.'[11] Richard Swinburne says that if we are to learn and develop morally, we need to experience the consequences of our good and bad actions: this development would not happen if there were no consequences. To make moral choices, we need to learn from past experiences, and 'if all knowledge of the future is obtained by normal induction, that is by induction from patterns of similar events in the past – then there must be serious natural evils occurring to man or animals.'[12] He sees it necessary that 'laws of nature must operate regularly' and that means that there will be 'victims of the system'.[13] What is interesting is that al-Jaḥīẓ extends this principle from the knowledge of good and evil, which is perhaps obvious, to all cognition. The capacity to think, judge and discriminate itself come from the ability to discern good from evil.

John Mackie thinks it is not necessary that everything have an opposite in order to exist: 'it is not really impossible that everything should be, say, red, that the truth is merely that if everything were red we should not notice redness'.[14] In the same way, 'God might have made everything good, though *we* should not have noticed it if he had.'[15] Try a little thought experiment: if we could not tell that God had made everything red, or good, how do we know that he hasn't? Perhaps he has and we, as Mackie says, can't tell . . .

The second question is whether good can exist without evil. One insight frequently adduced in a variety of traditions is to say that there is no evil that does not contain some good in it; Muslim thinkers refer to this frequently, often with such examples as the amputation of a gangrenous hand. 'God created nothing without there being wisdom in it, and He created nothing without there being blessing in it, either for all people or for some of them. Thus in God's creation of suffering, there is blessing, too, either for the sufferer or for someone else.'[16]

Mackie's objection to the claim that the universe is better with some evil in it

*First, he notes, goods which can be said to result from evil are only derivative, and why promote misery in order to maintain happiness? Mackie thinks with this idea, 'God is not in our sense benevolent or sympathetic: he is not concerned to minimize evil . . ., but only to promote good . . .; and this might be a disturbing conclusion for some theists.'[17] Despite Mackie's concern for their peace of mind, believers in most religious traditions profess a higher value for 'virtues' than for 'pleasures', and may be less troubled than he expects by the thought that God would allow some suffering because of its tendency to promote growth and maturity. His final point is that 'first-order evils' (suffering, discomforts) may be balanced by 'first-order good', i.e. pleasure. He claims that the theist invokes second-order good (virtues) that arises out of first-order evil and makes it worthwhile. But this is cancelled out by second-order evils (vices). So the theist has to posit 'third-order goods' to cope with those, 'and we should be well on the way to an infinite regress, where the solution of a problem of evil, stated in terms of evil (n), indicated the existence of an evil (*n + 1*), and a further problem to be solved.'[18]*

Mackie's construction of 'orders' may be questioned; it is a little artificial. In real life, virtues or 'second-order goods' respond both to pains and to vices (first- and second-order evils) and there is no 'further problem to be solved' with a different level of goods.

Mackie also objects to setting a limit to what a supposedly omnipotent God can do.[19] If God cannot create good without some evil, there is a limit to divine power. 'It would be a causal law that you cannot have a certain end without a certain means, so that if God has to introduce evil as a means to good, he must be subject to at least some causal laws.'[20] (In fact, this is not so much a causal issue as a logical one, and the question of whether God is bound by logic is a disputed one as we have seen in an earlier chapter.)

If it is logically impossible to have good without evil, God could not have arranged the world otherwise. (This view does require acceptance of the idea that God cannot do what is logically impossible.) But two questions arise:

Are evil and good really opposites, and precisely *logical* opposites?

Could God could have created a universe in which natural and moral evils were not necessary for the good things to arise?

To show how God could have created a world in which evil was *not* necessary for good, we could cite virtues that can exist without corresponding evils. Generosity is possible even without the need to relieve poverty. Empathy would allow us to enjoy one another's pleasures and rejoice in their joys, even when it was not necessary to sympathize with their suffering. For *certain* goods, however, *certain* evils might be necessary. Forgiveness is based on injury, courage on danger.

Mesle takes issue with any necessity of this sort, as well. 'With regard to friends it is loyalty which we value, not the fear of betrayal.'[21] But why *do* we value loyalty? Because we know there is an alternative, and so someone's loyalty is a valuable as well as a free gift of friendship. If there were no possibility of betrayal, loyalty would be unnoticed rather than held as a value, like Mackie's 'redness'. We wouldn't notice it, let alone value it.

So the existence of evil *is* logically necessary for some goods, because it is part of the definition or essence of those things that they respond to an evil. If there is no injury or offence, one is unable to forgive. The word indeed would have no meaning in such a world.

So might the world be better with some of what we call 'evil' in it, than if it were designed as we would like to see it? Al-Ghazālī saw the world as it is, as 'most wonderful'; because God has willed it and brings it into being moment by moment, it cannot be better. Even its defects contribute to its excellence; for it is what has been willed by God. Ormsby describes this view as 'the perfect rightness of the actual'.[22] Aquinas poetically stated a similar appreciation of what is: overstretch one harp-string and the melody is lost.[23]

The actual world is beautiful as it is

A Muslim view is expressed by al-Jaḥīẓ: 'Through the combination (of disparate things) divine beneficence is perfected.'[24] This suggests a different view of the world, one which recognizes it as full of diversity, a coincidence of opposites which cannot simply be reduced to one another, and whose total appraisal requires a level of insight and discernment that we humans lack. 'In the negation of a single one is the negation of all,' al-Jaḥīẓ maintained.[25] 'The cosmos is like a living body; to remove or alter one part is to damage all.'[26] To eliminate a part of it which we designate evil or injurious is to amputate a limb. God has created a universe, full of defect and yet perfect in its actuality, for the divine purpose. 'Do you not see that the mountain is not more indicative of God than the pebble and that the praiseworthy peacock is not more indicative of Him than the disapproved pig?'[27]

Hawaiian religion does not spend much time musing on the metaphysical problems of evil. It has a principle called lōkāhi*: unity,* *agreement, harmony. Lava is destructive of plant and animal life; but when its fire, its dryness, its barrenness is balanced with water, it makes a tremendously fertile soil, and the 'ōhi'a-lehua trees and the hāpu'u ferns move in and repopulate the renewed earth. For Hawaiians, the activity of the volcano was the act of the goddess Pele, in all her destructive power: a power for destruction, as so many stories tell, that often followed on human cruelty or hard-heartedness; but also the beginning of new creation and ever-increasing beauty. In Hawaiian thought, destruction is no less a witness to the divine than creation.*

Is there a purpose to evil?

The task of 'theodicy' is to explain, defend or justify God or the gods for allowing evil. This is usually aimed at showing that some greater good comes from it or because it is necessary for some good purpose.

Such theodicies are based, like the stance of Ibn Sīnā and al-Ghazālī, on the principle that God never wills evil with any intent of doing evil or bringing about suffering, but only wills it or allows it for the good that it contains or provokes. Stewart finds that a number of these defences and theodicies are related and calls them 'the greater good defence':[28] There are different ways of seeing that God only permits evil for the sake of a greater good, some tailored to meet specific challenges.[29] *Every* evil, some hold, is outweighed or counterbalanced by some corresponding good. This suggests that there is a causal or logical connection between the evil and the good, and that can be difficult to establish. So a fallback position is to see evils that are not matched by a specific good do, however, arise from (or are made possible by) other states of affairs which will lead to a greater good. Free will is often cited in such cases. Alternatively, the claim may be that the general aggregate of evil is outweighed by the aggregate of good in the universe, or evil is part of a long process which will lead triumphantly, despite the evil it contains in the interim, to a 'limitlessly good end-state'.[30]

Mesle argues that if good comes from evil, that means that evil is really good. It is not then a 'real evil' but only an 'apparent' one.[31] Christian theology, he thinks, by maintaining that all things work for the good 'implies that nothing is ultimately evil'.[32] What does 'ultimately' mean here? Christian theology, like Jewish and Islamic faith and the insights of the Indian religions, certainly maintains that good, not evil, is ultimate in the sense of being ontologically prior. Nor is evil 'ultimate' in the sense of being the final word, for redemption and transformation are possible. But things *can* be intrinsically – and really, really – evil. To say that rape, torture and war are not really and intrinsically evil would be abhorrent. That we can respond to human evil acts to turn them towards better state of affairs, however, seems to be a fact of life.

Trau distinguishes several points which bring some clarity to these confusing issues.[33] She sees a distinction between something being 'intrinsically' bad or good, and 'instrumentally' bad or good; 'instrumental' value comes from what it contributes in the realization of something else. The positive or *overall* value, however, comes from both intrinsic *and* instrumental value taken together. Something's intrinsic goodness can outweigh its instrumental badness (e.g. telling the truth even though it might hurt someone's feelings). Alternatively its instrumental goodness can outweigh its intrinsic badness (telling a lie to save someone's life). In either case, overall it has positive value. For the 'positive value' of something is not the same as its goodness. The result of Trau's argument is to show how something which may be intrinsically bad may still have overall positive value. So an act may be intrinsically evil, but if we can transform that into a far greater good, then overall the situation has positive value. The argument of the 'greater good defences' would be that even acts or states of affairs that are intrinsically evil can be taken up and transformed into a greater good, so that the end state has positive value.

Does the end-justifies-the-means doctrine apply to evil?

Stewart observes that, just as many defences have a greater-good core, all of these work with an end-justifies-the-means (EJM) principle.[34]

Although we do this in everyday life, some find it inappropriate or wrong to apply the EJM principle to God. D. Z. Phillips puts the objection this way:

> What then are we to say of the child dying from cancer? If this has been *done* to anyone, it is bad enough, but to be done for a purpose, to be planned from eternity – that is the deepest evil. If God is this kind of an agent, He cannot justify His actions, and His evil nature is revealed.[35]

In other words, it is bad enough that God *allows* evil to happen. If we suggest that God willingly makes use of evil to achieve certain aims, the moral implications are even worse. But does the greater good defence have that inescapable implication?

These issues can be considered with the doctrine of 'double effect'. An act may have two results, one good and one bad; it may be acceptable in some cases to perform that act to bring about the good result and suffer the bad, while it would have been unacceptable to create the bad result directly and as an end in itself. Thus, some people who are morally opposed to abortion in general are prepared to accept a medical procedure necessary to save a woman's life but which may result in the death of her foetus.

Double effect as a solution

J. M. Trau uses the doctrine of double effect as part of a solution to the problem of evil. The free will defence speaks of evil results as a double effect of free will, while natural evils can be a double effect of some natural good. The primary effect should not, she cautions, be seen as an 'aim' or an 'end', but rather as something that must occur if the universe is to exist as it is.

If it is true that there could be no other material universe, that this universe could not function any other way, and that it is better that this universe exist than it not, we can make this claim: the existence of the universe is a natural good and has positive value. Because the existence of the universe is a natural good and has positive value, the events involved in its existence also have positive value. If natural evils are necessary double effects of those events, then the double effects have positive value.[36]

The doctrine of double effect should be distinguished from the simpler claim that something evil can have positive value if it has sufficient instrumental *goodness; this might be true, but would only apply to certain cases. The double effect doctrine goes further, in her view:*

> *If we can show that evil exists as a double effect of the necessary condition for the existence of goodness, then we can show that all evil has positive value.*
>
> *The doctrine of the double effect allows us to make the claim that because the possibility of the existence of evil is* necessary *for the existence of free will and moral goodness, the positive value of evil can exceed its negative value, even when evil retains all its intrinsic badness.*[37]

To succeed as a justification, however, it must be the case that the bad effect is really unavoidable, and that the desired good result cannot be obtained in any other way. A sceptic might question whether this can ever be the case for an omnipotent God, whose ways and means ought not to be so constrained. Trau's view is that such limits lie in the nature of things, and not in God's power to realize other possible worlds. God could have realized other material worlds without the laws of this one, but they would be very different worlds. God could not actualize *this* world with *different* natural laws; that is impossible.

Thus, if this material universe is a great natural good, if we prefer that it exist, and if certain natural evils are necessary double effects of its existence, we cannot ask God to eliminate those evils. To eliminate the evils is to eliminate the natural goods. Thus another underlying claim is that it is a good thing that this world exists.[38]

Let us consider some of the ways that thinkers have suggested that good might come from evil.

Can evil be a source of human improvement?

The Egyptian Jewish thinker Saadia ben Joseph named three purposes for evil. It could be a punishment, or a test, or serve as a form of instruction to us. Answering the problem that the good often suffer while the evil prosper, Saadia distinguishes between the dominant tendency of someone's action, which is rewarded or punished in the hereafter, and the minority of one's acts. A good person might suffer while being punished *now* for minor evil acts; but will be rewarded later.[39] Saadia's Alexandrian predecessor Philo, however, rejected this reasoning and preferred the Stoic idea that virtue was its own reward and that God prefers us to choose virtue from desire rather than fear.[40] Much later, Moses Mendelssohn held that the idea of a punishing God is contrary to both reason and religion.[41] The German Jewish Neo-Kantian philosopher Hermann Cohen agrees that suffering as a form of punishment is an important part of self-development and redemption.[42] We can use it for ourselves, for we are in a better position to know what we have done. But this idea is not to be used to blame others for their suffering. Suffering, for Cohen, is the point at which religion emerges from ethics[43] and challenges us to a deeper understanding of life and a new relationship with our fellow creatures. 'In suffering, a dazzling light suddenly makes me see the dark spots in the sun of life.'[44]

In the Indian traditions, karma is used to explain suffering: why pain comes when we can see no apparent fault in this lifetime that could justify punishment. By stressing that previous faults are responsible, God is not held to be the source of the suffering that ensues. Śaṇkara says the Lord cannot be reproached with injustice; for apparent inequities are due to the merit and demerit of creatures themselves. For all of the Indian religions that accept the concept of karma, human agency and responsibility accounts for good or ill. It has another explanatory use as well, most clearly seen in its Buddhist manifestation: it gives an account of *why* we are disposed to act wickedly.[45]

Is evil a test?

In the book of Job in the Hebrew Bible, one of Job's friends tries to comfort him with the idea that suffering is a form of test. The 'test' of Abraham in Genesis 22 has also meant that this idea figures prominently in Judaism, Christianity and Islam. Saadia suggested,

> An upright servant, whose Lord knows that he will bear sufferings loosed upon him and hold steadfast in his uprightness, is subjected to certain sufferings, so that when he steadfastly bears them, his Lord may reward him and bless him. This too is a kind of bounty and beneficence, for it brings the servant to everlasting blessedness.[46]

But this theodicy creates problems for the traditional conception of God as all-knowing, all-wise and all-compassionate, as does the punishment theodicy. If God needs a test to find out what we will do, can God still be called omniscient? If God does know the result, what is the justification for subjecting people to hardship or pain as a 'test'? Jewish exegetes wrestled with these questions when interpreting the story of Abraham being commanded to sacrifice his son, Isaac (Genesis 22.1–12).[47]

Maimonides is not happy with this notion of God's providence, and argues that it is *not* found in the Bible, if rightly understood. 'Know that the aim and meaning of all the *trials* mentioned in the *Torah* is to let people know what they ought to do or what they must believe . . . the purpose being not the accomplishment of that particular act, but the latter's being a model to be imitated and followed.'[48]

The Islamic Ash'arite theologian al-Ghazālī was another who objected to the test theories, for it seemed to him that it makes God a capricious tyrant who first slaps his servant and then offers financial compensation. He preferred the idea that suffering is medicinal, and that, although human compassion may shrink from imposing a painful treatment, God who is all-wise will apply the remedy.

Karma, as understood by Jains, Buddhists and Hindus, also aims at self-improvement through suffering. The Sikh use of the concept, in a kind of theological pun, takes the word *karamu* (Punjabi for karma) but juxtaposes it to 'karma' now seen as from Arabic *karam*, meaning the grace of God. While 'karma' does exist, it can be overcome by 'karam' in the theological sense and bring us to union with God.

Views of evil as God's punishment, testing, and perhaps even as a way of purification or teaching, can be faulted on the grounds of God's compassion. For some they seem to make God more like a harsh disciplinarian than a kind and loving parent. They might, however, be taken as an insistence on *human* responsibility for human actions, and they call for human correction. They may also be a way to understand our inevitable sufferings within the framework of a relationship with God, a concept which can be further developed.

Can evil lead to redemption and union with God?

Stewart has argued that all versions of the greater good defence are ultimately incomplete: what theodicy needs is to recover an appreciation of the idea of redemption. Answering the question of whether evil is logically necessary for the existence of good, he writes: 'the good which logically requires the *existence* of evil is *redemption*'.[49]

The Orthodox Jewish theologian Michael Wyschogrod takes a similar view:

> The God of Israel is a redeeming God; that is the only message which we are justified in preaching, no matter how false it may seem in the eyes of unbelief. . . . If there is hope after the Holocaust, there is hope because for believers the voice of the prophets speaks louder than Hitler, and because the divine promise extends beyond the crematoria and reduces the voice of Auschwitz to silence.[50]

Future redemption which will justify present and past evils is not a concept that can be demonstrated empirically or logically to a sceptic; the standard taunt is 'there will be pie in the sky when you die'. Is there, however, a redemption which can be experienced here and now? Stoeber claims that mystics in all faith traditions have a uniquely 'mystical' response to the problem of evil and we can identify or create a 'mystical theodicy' across faith boundaries.[51] Mystics find in their powerful experience of God's love an ultimate good purpose for creation. 'Mystical theodicy does not merely point to a future spiritual eschaton that justifies teleology; but emphasises, on the authority of enlightened mystics, experiences of God's purposes in the context of the very transformative processes which are associated with the teleology.'[52] Moreover, the consolation for suffering is also found here and now in the mystical experience of God. Although mystics are traditionally thought of as in isolated cells or retreats, they are also inspired to active love and compassion towards practical responses to others' suffering. 'So in its treatment of the problem of evil, mystical theodicy offers a much more effective practical response than that which we find in non-mystical theodicy.'[53]

When we consider religious experience, it will be seen that using personal experience as evidence is philosophically problematic, particularly when it comes to persuading someone else of something. What happens in mystical experiences, or in what is recounted of them, does not so much impart any new information about God's purposes as reassurances of what was expressed, perhaps more theologically, in the mystic's religious tradition. It is difficult to see how anyone can claim a *verification* of the end of history here and now. A vivid impression or vision of the end of history may be intense and convincing to the person who experiences it but that is no proof of its truth or predictive power. I would not call Stoeber's view a new theodicy, but a footnote perhaps to the traditional forms of redemptive justification. Perhaps what we can say after Stoeber is this: for those who have set themselves on the paths of personal perfection there come moments when they are convinced that the suffering they encounter is paradoxically one way they experience God's redeeming love. This too points to a theodicy based on relationship.

The experience of redeeming love

At the end of his lengthy Guide of the Perplexed, *Maimonides finds that the understanding of evil is inextricable from the spiritual journey. As long as we are united with God through our intellect, God's providence over us is complete and no evil can befall us. Such evils can overtake us only when we abandon God and are consequently separated from Him. The ability to achieve perfect and continual contemplation of God increases with age; in addition the great love for God increases 'until the soul is separated from the body at that moment in this state of pleasure'. This is how Maimonides understands the deaths of Moses, Aaron and Miriam: 'the three of them died in the pleasure of this due to the intensity of passionate love'.*[54]

The Hebrew scriptures speak of God as 'like a refiner's fire'. The English poet Gerard Manley Hopkins, asking after the purpose of his suffering, answers his own question: 'Why? That my chaff might fly; my grain lie, sheer and clear.' Those who feel themselves in an intimate relation with God reckon their pain as part of the spiritual path. Before we can be united with God, we must be purified, which can be painful at times. These lovers of the divine urge us to believe that suffering can transform us; therefore it is to be attributed to God's will, God's providence, even God's love: 'It is Love, manifesting itself in different forms; in one, it is a beseeching need, in another, a Perfect withhold. When manifest on the face of the lover, it is all suffering, when veiling the Beloved, it is all music,' says the Sufi poet Eraqi.[55] *Sufi mystics like Junayd were explicit about the sufferings entailed in the mystic's development; a theme common in mysticism of most religious traditions.*

'Whoever does not take pleasure in the trials of love is not a lover,'[56] *comes from the Islamic tradition, while a Christian saying echoes it, 'There is no living in love without pain.'*

Is evil a means of personal development and soul growth?

In his teaching on Job, Saadia spoke of sufferings as 'instruction'; as 'visitations of love' from God. John Hick has created a theodicy of great influence in our time, based on the idea that suffering is necessary for our personal growth and development.[57] Rather than adopting the Fall theology of humanity as having an evil bent, he sees our state as one in which we need to grow and expand our capacities for good. The mixture of good and evil, he says, is because the world is a 'vale of soul-making', taking the phrase from the English poet Keats. For Hick, God's purpose for creation surely determines the nature of that creation and he thinks that atheistic writers assume a purpose which is at odds with Christian belief. God's intent is not to create a hedonistic paradise, filled with all earthly delights, but an environment in which we can grow into 'children of God'. Good parents who want their children 'to become the best human beings that they are capable of becoming' do not treat pleasure 'as the sole and supreme value'. In fact, as a parent trying to do my best I am sometimes disheartened by how often their desires for pleasure have to be frustrated for their betterment – from the age when they feel the addicting power of sugar. So Hick's analogy strikes home:

> To most parents it seems more important to try to foster quality and strength of character in their children than to fill their lives at all times with the utmost possible degree of pleasure. If, then, there is any true analogy between God's purpose for his human creatures, and the purpose of loving and wise parents for their children, we have to recognize that the presence of pleasure and the absence of pain cannot be the supreme and overriding end for which the world exists. Rather, this world must be a place of soul-making. And its value is to be judged, not primarily by the quantity of pleasure and pain occurring in it at any particular moment, but by its fitness for its primary purpose, the purpose of soul-making.[58]

Hick's theodicy has come under attack for its optimism; for not taking evil seriously enough, nor giving sufficient weight to the reality of massive evil. Critics make a telling point about the sense of proportion that can consider something like the Holocaust as an opportunity for moral development. It must make an appeal to 'mystery', perhaps all theodicies do.

Must this resort to mystery be considered a fatal flaw in a theodicy? The sceptic might accuse theodicists of failing to meet epistemic obligations if they fail to give a precise, logical and complete account of exactly what God is up to in the universe. The believer, on the other hand, might accuse theodicists of failing to meet both epistemic and the religious obligation to humility if they think that they have *succeeded* in penetrating the fullness of godhead.

Let us unpack these theological suggestions as they appear in cognate theodicies.

A Christian evolutionary theodicy

Richard W. Kropf, largely inspired by Teilhard de Chardin, has a theodicy which remains within the mainstream Christian tradition but weaves evolution into the account.[59] *Both the structure of the problem and the solution remain largely 'traditional' in that he insists on the reality and goodness of God, the reality of evil and the reality of human freedom and responsibility.*

God's activity is an evolutionary process. He takes the words in Genesis 1 that 'God saw all that He created was good' as referring more to the final end product than to the present state of affairs. For Kropf moral evil and natural imperfections are inevitable en route, *and our image and likeness to God is more God's intention than our present actuality.*

The necessary unlikeness of the universe to God (especially in the beginning, before it has evolved) is part of the reason for its defects. Kropf also stresses the role that chance and indeterminacy play in evolution. Randomness lies behind both the 'progress' of evolution and the failures; 'Statistically, the failures far outnumber the successes when we judge them as individual ventures or experiments of nature. That we should call these failures evils is, of course, a human judgement, which must be balanced by the realization that evolution as a whole has been a success.'[60] *The dimension of chance inherent in evolution brings great potential for things going wrong. 'Being ourselves the children of chance, it is not surprising that there also lurks, both within the void of the universe and within each one of us, a "dark storehouse" from which unknown potentialities may manifest themselves.'*[61]

In Kropf's view, there is no absolute distinction between moral and natural evil, because this world is one in which spirit and matter not merely coexist, but are indeed two aspects of a single reality. 'It is unreasonable' therefore 'to restrict what we call "suffering" to the purely human segment of creation.'[62] *In the evolutionary context, suffering is a basic condition of the universe. All forms of evil await redemption, 'incompleteness and defect on all levels of created being share a common travail until all things are consummated in one great ecstasy of union with God'.*[63]

Human suffering is the price of freedom. To accept the price of freedom indeed takes an act of faith.

Yet the pattern is clear. Freedom has emerged, and with it, sin, while life has always meant death, and any degree of sensitivity has brought suffering with it. None of these has been possible without the other, nor have any of these fated pairs existed over the eons of time without a direct relationship to the rest. It is all of one vast piece. There is a solidarity in sin, as well as in retribution for it, and there is a solidarity in freedom as well. But there is also a solidarity in suffering, which makes it one with life and death, sin, and freedom.[64]

Ultimately Kropf's solution is to posit a God who suffers with us, indeed more than all of us; and 'God's response to the problem of evil is to be found in the mystery of his own suffering in Christ.'[65] *The final answer for the Christian is the Resurrection, the redemption of all suffering.*

While Kropf is based on Christian traditions, David Birnbaum has created a 'Quest for Potential' theodicy from traditions in Judaism paired with ideas of human potential. In Birnbaum's view, this both answers the classic problems of theodicy, and also has an answer to the painful question of how in biblical tradition God intervened to save the Hebrews in Pharaoh's Egypt but in our times did not rescue them from Hitler's extermination.

Birnbaum expresses the core of his theodicy in the following five points:

1. The purpose of man [*sic*] is to quest for his potential – spiritual and other.

2. The greater man's freedom, the greater his ability to attain his potential.

3. Freedom requires privacy, responsibility, and selfhood.

4. In order to yield man greater freedom (along with greater privacy, responsibility, and selfhood), God has contracted His here-and-now consciousness, in correlation to mankind's ascent in knowledge.

5. With the Divine consciousness increasingly contracted from the here-and-now, and evil existent in the here-and-now, man is increasingly forced to confront evil on his own.[66]

The theory is a complex one, but remains solidly in the 'greater good' classification.

At the heart of Birnbaum's theodicy is the notion of potential, both human and divine. As long as we live in a 'gilded cage' existence, we will never fulfil our potential. A life of greater challenge is a life of greater dignity, growth, knowledge and fulfilment, but also brings with it greater potential for evil. We need the greatest possible freedom to achieve this.

Birnbaum uses the Lurianic idea explored earlier, of divine contraction or *zimzum*, to articulate his next theological step. In order to give us maximal freedom, God must 'contract' God's 'here-and-now consciousness' to give us freedom, privacy and responsibility – just as a parent does with a child as it grows up.

This means, however, that as God withdraws his providential care and control, not only are we given increasingly full rein; so too is evil unleashed. But this still leads to a greater good: 'For the ultimate Providence may be in securing mankind's freedom and potential for (primarily spiritual) growth and ultimate perfection, an attainment conceivably possible only in an environment of proportionate contracted real-time omniscience.'[67]

Are massive evils a special case for theodicy?

> One can still 'believe' in a God who allowed those things to happen, but how can one still speak to Him? (Martin Buber)[68]

There is a kind of suffering that is so far out of the range of 'ordinary life' that it seems to raise the problem of evil to a different level, harder even to discuss much less provide answers. Sometimes it feels not just a question of whether we can speak to God, as Buber puts it, but even whether we speak to anyone about such pain. Hick has named this 'dysteleological suffering'. (*Telos* is a Greek for 'end' and *dys* is a prefix which adds the meaning of 'hard, bad' to a word.) It is also called gratuitous evil. This is evil or suffering which leads to no good that we can see or imagine, suffering so vast and overwhelming that it seems impossible that there are any corresponding goods that can balance or redeem. Questions arise like, 'What are the greater goods that compensate for the degradations and deaths of eleven million people, including children, in the Nazi camps?' And we can add the catalogue of events that have continually piled up in the years following that war. How much compassion or courage or forgiveness or transformation would have to arise from the seeming endless list of horrors in history to justify such an appalling quantity of suffering? The existence of apparently off-the-scale evil that seems to lead to no good, or not enough good, seems to undermine any 'greater good' line of argument before it even gets started.[69]

Can karma deal with dysteleological evil?

In karmic theory Michael Stoeber sees some scope for working out a theodicy. He finds reincarnation a possible solution. It is 'a hypothesis of rebirth within which dysteleological evils might be understood as never utterly destructive. . . . This world, with all its terrible adversities, is justified as an appropriate realm of personal and spiritual progression to the divine life . . .'[70]

Does rebirth in this way really solve the problem of unjustified, and especially dysteleological, suffering? I suspect the theory of karma is not satisfactory as a theory of compensation if it is uprooted from the particular ethical soil in which Jaina and Buddhist thinking have planted it. Karma is above all the result of our own action, and does not serve to control the impact of others. In the traditional Indian understanding, you can only bring an end to this otherwise endless cycle of rebirth by your own ethical and spiritual endeavours in a life in which unjust suffering (as opposed to one's unjust action) is neither here nor there. If you suffer unjustly in a life which is blameless, that acceptance obtains the necessary release. One does not have to be reborn again to be compensated.

But if rebirth is to make up for all massive suffering, God or apūrva must somehow guarantee that in the end there will be some life in which no unjust affliction takes place which needs counterbalancing in still a later life.

Is one the same as the many in theodicy?

Eliezer Berkovits, in dealing with the Holocaust, makes the point that the death of one innocent person is no less morally or theologically problematic than the death of millions.[71] Oliver Leaman summarizes: 'The only difference between the Holocaust and previous disasters lies in the size of the former, and there is little theological significance in size. The issues surrounding the death of just one innocent person are the same as in the case of six million.'[72]

There are at least two ways that one can interpret this. 'The death of six million is no worse than the death of one' would misconstrue Berkovits, who intends something more like: 'One must be held accountable for a single murder no less than for genocide.' We may feel that a serial murderer has done something worse than one who has committed a single murder; nevertheless we call murderers to account, whether they have killed one or twenty. By analogy, then, if it is proper to hold God to account for human deaths, there needs to be theodicial justification for the death of one person, no less than for millions. The question is one of accountability, not of the qualitative or quantitative difference between horrible events, or the difference in emotional and psychological impact between single bereavements and atrocities.

The import of this issue, as I see it, is whether a *different* theodicial manoeuvre or piece of reasoning is required for 'dysteleological' evils than has been encountered already. The effect of Berkovits's claim would be to say that in principle 'dysteleological' evil does *not* ultimately require a different sort of theodicial justification than a single death. Nevertheless, the impact of massive evils on our reflection is different. It does force a different kind of consideration. As Arthur Cohen writes, 'The death camps are a reality which, by their very nature, obliterate thought and the human programme of thinking.'[73]

What epistemological assumptions are made about 'gratuitous' evil?

What is the basis for the claim that something is *dysteleological*? What do we do, when we say: 'No good can ever come of this,' or 'No good can ever outweigh or redeem this evil'? How do we *know*?

We might identify a good that has come out of a terrible situation, but find it trivial in comparison to the evil. Or we might operate on an intuitive sense of proportion, and simply declare that no good can be as big as this evil. Both are natural things to do, but there are nevertheless philosophical problems if they are more than a heartfelt exclamation. Can we know with certainty that all the results and evidence are in, and that it is time now to make a final judgement that the good has not, in fact, outweighed the evil? Can that be done at any point before 'the end of history'? Consider Roth's assertion: 'History refutes more than it confirms God's providential care.'[74] If this is really meant as an assertion, not a cry of anguish, one wonders what kind of method or historical analysis he could use in supporting this judgement.

First and most fundamentally, *all* such styles of reasoning, whether for or against religious belief, require the quantification of what can in no way be 'objectively' quantified: the extent and intensity of suffering and evil, on the one side, and on the other side the value of human existence and human freedom and the existence of the natural world as we know it. Plantinga coins the term 'turp' to signify a unit of evil, and Stewart the term 'ben' for a unit of goodness; but both seem to be aware of the absurdity of doing this.[75] How do you measure a turp, or allocate turps to acts of moral cruelty as compared to degrees of physical pain? Do pleasures and virtues rate equally on the ben scale?

The business becomes even more difficult when you come to the point of weighing turps against bens to see which is greater, and a great number of questions arise. Among them: How many bens cancel out one turp and thus justify God? How closely do the turp and the ben have to be connected to balance?

As a concrete case, consider Roth's claim that nothing can ever outweigh the Holocaust. How do you 'measure' the suffering of the Shoah to reach this conclusion? What goods, which joys and pleasures of existence, and *whose* existence, are allowed to count as relevant in the comparison between the good and the evil?

There is both a diachronic and a synchronic question in the process;

that is, a question of duration in time, and of breadth of relevance. Must every suffering be outweighed in the life of each individual? The sum total of outweighing goods might not manifest themselves in the lives of those individuals immediately involved and affected. May not the impact of something on many millions of people throughout history be included in the reckoning? There is the question of the appropriate cut-off point; a story can have a happy ending, or a sad one; it all depends on whether you put 'The End' after a happy bit or a sad bit. In the same way, is it plausible to fix a deadline for all resulting goods to have occurred, in order to be considered in the reckoning of the results of a particular evil? Two thousand years later, we are still learning from the example and teachings of Jesus; we are still learning from the example and teachings of Socrates and Buddha and Mahāvīr, who lived even longer ago, and people today still moderate their behaviour according to the teachings and examples of all four of these people. Perhaps 2,000 years from now, people might still be learning good moral lessons from the horrors and evils of the twentieth century, modifying their behaviour and thus preventing evils that might otherwise have occurred.

There is an obvious degree of debatable interpretation involved in deciding whether or not a good 'resulted from' an evil, whether it could have been achieved any other way (which involves 'middle knowledge', the certain knowledge of 'what if' cases).

Are 'theodicies' explanation, or justification, or both? Both explanation and justification can occur on different levels.

Levels of explanation and justification

Take a case of a forensic psychologist asking a serial killer: 'Why did you kill twenty women?' The man answers: 'Well, I killed the first victim because she was a prostitute and so she deserved to die, and the second one because she reminded me of my mother, and the third because I didn't like her hairstyle', and so on. In this way he 'accounts' for each individual murder on its own. Would it make sense for the psychologist to respond, 'Yes, but you haven't told us why you killed all twenty of them – you've only given a particular explanation for each, but not for the series of twenty.' Does the phenomenon of 'a series of twenty' need its own justification, over and above the account given of each?

Or alternatively: let us say that the whole series of twenty murders is 'accounted for' by the man's psycho-pathological hatred of women. Beyond that, he can't say why he killed this woman rather than that one; or killed on this night, but not on another. Have the deaths not been accounted for in the general explanation, or do we need to explain the man's behaviour with reference to each individual woman: some explanation maybe that derives from the woman's own characteristics, and not his?

These questions are intended to bring out the fact that different accounts can be given of the same phenomenon, when it is considered under different aspects: on its own, or as part of a category or classification which we create. A murder could be considered as the murder of one individual, or as one of a series of murders (and this interpretation might affect the detectives' investigation); it might require an explanation as one of a psychotic person's acts, or as part of a growing trend in 'violent crime', or as an example of misogyny and violence against women – and quite different accounts may be given of it under those different headings.

So for anyone trying to provide a theodicy for dysteleological evils or for anyone contending that it cannot be done, the question arises: on which level must an account be provided? We can ask for explanations to be given at every level or under every classification we can create. This can be informative when a new insight or critique is developed: feminist critique now allows one to re-examine history and a number of other disciplines and ask questions that have never before been answered. The answers to these questions bring new revelations. But when it is no longer of humanity and its world that we require explanations, but we ask for God's justification, does God need to be justified or explained on all levels we can devise?[76]

Does everything need at least two justifications, on the level of the individual evil and the aggregate of evils? But what is an 'aggregate of evils'? The sense that 'massive' evils are something over and above the individual evils and tragedies they embody is what some would call 'a human construct'. By this I do not mean that it is 'untrue'. Rather, we do not see the deaths in Nazi death camps as random events; instead, we link together certain events as meaningfully belonging together. In the Shoah itself, the discussion is often about the deaths of the 'six million'. But a further estimated five million were killed whom we often do not include because they were not Jewish. Meanwhile, more than these six million Jews died in those years. Presumably many other Jewish people around the world, including soldiers from Jewish communities in the Allied countries, also died in the war, yet their deaths are not included in the figure of the six million, because the circumstances of their deaths were different. *Certain* people in *certain* circumstances are joined in our mind as a meaningful group. Depending on the interpretative grid one lays over the events, different groupings could arise. One can divide up and group together individual persons or events in different ways.

It is a natural hermeneutical tendency of ours to gather events and look for explanations and causes not just of the individual events, but of the whole group we have marked out. But this is *our* interpretative activity, and it may not philosophically require a further divine justification. Let us consider six million traffic accident victims, or six million people who died by choking. God 'allowed' all these people to suffer and die too. But we do not see these as massive, dysteleological evils, because we do not see these as a single event. We do not ask for a special theodicy for these, asking why God lets *all* road traffic accident victims die or how can God be justified for allowing the creation of automobiles?

There seems to me to be no way that the measurement, definition, contextualization and interpretation of good and evil can be put on a universally agreed and public footing (made objective, in other words), in such a way as to justify a claim that there is some 'dysteleological' suffering which requires a special theodicy. Perhaps, if we were strictly logical, we would consider all human death as a dysteleological evil. God allows everyone to die someday in any case, and perhaps is no less 'guilty of mass-murder' in virtue of the fact that God allows billions of people to die peacefully of natural causes. God is either 'justified' or not for all human deaths. Certainly atrocities raise questions and demand explanations that natural or accidental death does not. But is it of *God* that we require the explanation? Is it not *human action* that marks the profound moral difference between accidental death and genocide, not God's apparent allowance of evil?

It may not be so much God's ways that are inscrutable, as humanity's. Evils and sufferings *can* be utilized by ourselves and by nature to transform hardship or wickedness into better states of affairs. This is not an excuse or justification for evil human action. The good may not 'outweigh' the evil in the life of the individual sufferer. It may not 'redeem' the situation, if this is understood as effecting a great transformation of the immediate state of affairs.

And I do not think myself that belief in God's existence should be seen as a guarantee that good will always come from evil. However, I say this not from scepticism or pessimism, but rather because such a guarantee reduces human responsibility and initiative. It is up to *us* to make sure that no evils are or become 'dysteleological', not up to God to eliminate this 'category' of evil. If good comes from such events, it is not a conjuring trick of God's, or some automatic mechanism that has been placed in the workings of the universe. 'Good comes from evil' should not be a phenomenon that can be merely observed nor waited for passively. Rather, it seems to me, it should be seen as an inspiration, an exhortation, even a command. To affirm this means a determination to take good as the overarching context for evil, not evil for good. For one who believes in a just, good and powerful God, this holds open the possibility that good, and still more good, may yet come from a tragedy or atrocity – better still, 'may yet be *made* to come from evil'. This attitude does not dismiss or minimize the horror of evil: what it does is to create room for the action required to make this affirmation true.

The task of theodicy is not to 'justify evil'; the word 'theodicy' refers rather to the 'justice of God'. In my view the believer should not seek to 'justify evil', and to ask if God is 'justified' in allowing massive evils is a category mistake. My own conviction is that humanity, not divinity, must be put in question and called to account in 'theodicy'. We must be challenged as to the origin, persistence, and certainly the extent and intensity, of evil. Any theological or philosophical reflection that encourages responsibility and prudent action is to be preferred, all else being equal, to one that does not.

Emil Fackenheim formulated this '614th commandment' (so-called because traditionally Jews believe that the number of commandments given by God in scripture is 613):

> *We are, first, commanded to survive as Jews, lest the Jewish people perish. We are commanded, second, to remember in our very guts and bones the martyrs of the holocaust, lest their memory perish. We are forbidden, thirdly, to deny or despair of God, however much we may have to contend with Him or with belief in Him, lest Judaism perish. We are forbidden, finally, to despair of the world as the place which is to become the kingdom of God lest we help make it a meaningless place in which God is dead or irrelevant and everything is permitted. To abandon any of these imperatives, in response to Hitler's victory at Auschwitz, would be to hand him yet other posthumous victories.*[77]

Draw your own conclusions

Do you believe evil is an illusion or really lies in the nature of things?

Is it conceivable that any natural world, following its natural laws, would never give rise to creatures' suffering?

Is it worth sacrificing some pleasure and experiencing some suffering for the sake of virtue, strength or goodness? Where would you draw the line, if anywhere, where it ceases to be worth it?

Do you think suffering can ever be a punishment or a test, or is that religiously repugnant?

Is God 'justified' in allowing evil from the fact that we grow and develop? (Consider it in terms of Hick's, Kropf's, or Birnbaum's theodicy.)

Is the principle that good comes from evil a matter of interpretation? An article of faith? Something that can be demonstrated? Or just plain false?

Under what circumstances does the end justify the means?

Is the doctrine of double effect a useful clarification or just fancy footwork with ethics?

Further reading

Birnbaum, D. (1989) *God and Evil: A Jewish Perspective*, Hoboken, Ktav

Bowker, J. (1970) *Problems of Suffering in Religions of the World*, Cambridge, Cambridge University Press

Buber, M. (1949) *Between Man and Man*, London, Routledge & Kegan Paul

Buber, M. (1982) 'The Dialogue between Heaven and Earth', in E. L. Fackenheim, *To Mend the World*, New York, Schocken

Davis, S. T. (1981) *Encountering Evil: Live Options in Theodicy*, Edinburgh, T & T Clark

Griffin, D. (1976) *God, Power and Evil: A Process Theodicy*, Philadelphia, Westminster

Hick, J. (1977) *Evil and the God of Love*, London, Macmillan

Kropf, R. W. (1984) *Evil and Evolution: A Theodicy*, Rutherford, NJ, Fairleigh Dickinson University Press

Leaman, O. (1995) *Evil and Suffering in Jewish Philosophy*, Cambridge, Cambridge University Press

Mackie, J. L. (1990) 'Evil and Omnipotence', in M. M. Adams and R. M. Adams (eds), *The Problem of Evil*, Oxford, Oxford University Press

Ormsby, E. L. (1984) *Theodicy in Islamic Thought: The Dispute over al-Ghazālī's 'Best of All Possible Worlds'*, Princeton, Princeton University Press

Staub, E. (1989) *The Roots of Evil: The Origins of Genocide and Other Group Violence*, Cambridge, Cambridge University Press

Stewart, M. (1992) *The Greater Good Defence: Essay on the Rationality of Faith*, London, Macmillan

Swinburne, R. (1979) *The Existence of God*, Oxford, Clarendon Press

Notes

1 H. Zimmer (1952) *Philosophies of India*, London, Routledge & Kegan Paul, p. 349, p. 214.

2 M. Buber (1949) *Between Man and Man*, London, Routledge & Kegan Paul, pp. 78–9.

3 M. Buber (1953) 'Images of Good and Evil', in M. Buber, *Good and Evil: Two Interpretations*, New York, Charles Scribner's.

4 See M. Kaplan (1947) *The Meaning of God in Modern Jewish Religion*, New

York, Behrman; and (1958) *Judaism without Supernaturalism*, New York, Reconstructionist Press.

5 E. Berkovits (1974) *Major Themes in Modern Philosophies of Judaism: A Critical Evaluation*, New York, Ktav, p. 161.

6 G. Scholem, 'Kabbalah', *Encylopedia Judaica*, vol. 10, cols 588–601, col. 589. See also A. Steinsaltz (1980) *The Thirteen Petalled Rose*, trans. Y. Hanegbi, New York, Basic Books, p. 37: 'The world becomes possible only through the special act of Divine withdrawal or contraction. Such Divine non-Being or concealment, is thus the elementary condition for the existence of that which is finite.'

7 M. Maimonides (1963) *The Guide of the Perplexed*, trans. S. Pines, Chicago and London, University of Chicago Press, p. 444, bk. III, ch. 12 (employing the principle of plenitude that every genuine possibility must at some time be instantiated).

8 R. W. Kropf (1984) *Evil and Evolution: A Theodicy*, Rutherford, NJ, Fairleigh Dickinson University Press, p. 41.

9 E. Staub (1989) *The Roots of Evil: The Origins of Genocide and Other Group Violence*, Cambridge, Cambridge University Press.

10 Babylonian Talmud Yoma, 69b. My paraphrase of H. M. Schulweis's paraphrase in (1984) *Evil and the Morality of God*, Cincinnati, Hebrew Union College Press, p. 137.

11 E. L. Ormsby (1984) *Theodicy in Islamic Thought: The Dispute over al-Ghazālī's 'Best of All Possible Worlds'*, Princeton, Princeton University Press, pp. 223f.

12 R. Swinburne (1979) *The Existence of God*, Oxford, Clarendon Press, p. 211.

13 Swinburne, *The Existence of God*, p. 210.

14 J. L. Mackie (1990) 'Evil and Omnipotence', in M. M. Adams and R. M. Adams (eds), *The Problem of Evil*, Oxford, Oxford University Press, p. 29.

15 Mackie, 'Evil and Omnipotence', p. 30.

16 Al-Ghazālī, *Iḥyā* IV. 111, lines 7ff. Cited in Ormsby, *Theodicy in Islamic Thought*, p. 255.

17 Mackie, 'Evil and Omnipotence', p. 32.

18 Mackie, 'Evil and Omnipotence', p. 32.

19 Mackie, 'Evil and Omnipotence', pp. 33–6.

20 Mackie, 'Evil and Omnipotence', p. 30.

21 C. R. Mesle (1991) *John Hick's Theodicy: A Process Humanist Critique*, London, Macmillan, p. 43.

22 Ormsby, *Theodicy in Islamic Thought*, pp. 221–5, 259–65, *et passim*.

23 Thomas Aquinas, *The 'Summa Theologica' of St. Thomas Aquinas*, London, Burns Oates & Washbourne, I.25.6, reply to objection 3.

24 al-Jaḥīẓ, *Kitab al-Hayawān* I, in Ormsby, *Theodicy in Islamic Thought*, p. 206.

25 al-Jaḥīẓ, *Kitab al-Hayawān* I, in Ormsby, *Theodicy in Islamic Thought*, p. 206.

26 al-Jaḥīẓ, *Kitab al-Hayawān* I, in Ormsby, *Theodicy in Islamic Thought*, p. 224.

27 al-Jaḥīẓ, *Kitab al-Hayawān* I, in Ormsby, *Theodicy in Islamic Thought*, p. 206.

28 M. Stewart (1992) *The Greater Good Defence: Essay on the Rationality of Faith*, London, Macmillan, p. 56.

29 See Stewart, *The Greater Good Defence*, ch. 3.

30 Thus Hick, defending himself against Mesle, insists that despite the enormous amount of evil which we would be better off without, nevertheless the world will finally fulfil God's purpose for it, in a 'limitlessly good end-state'. Hick, in Mesle, *John Hick's Theodicy*, pp. 130f.

31 Mesle uses Griffin's distinction of '*prima facie*' and 'genuine' evil. See D. Griffin (1976) *God, Power and Evil: A Process Theodicy*, Philadelphia, Westminster, p. 22.

32 Mesle, *John Hick's Theodicy*, p. 39.

33 J. M. Trau (1988) 'The Positive Value of Evil', *International Journal for Philosophy of Religion* 21, pp. 21–33.

34 Stewart, *The Greater Good Defence*, pp. 65f. Conditions are set on this: the means must be causally necessary or, for an omnipotent being (who is not bound by ordinary causality), logically necessary. If one could achieve the same end without using that undesirable means, one is not justified in using it. One might also add that the means must be proportionate to the goodness of the end. I may be justified in displeasing or angering my child in the course of raising him to be a moral and considerate person; but I am not justified in injuring him to attain the same end. There is an immediate logical problem: for almost any necessary evil means that leads to a good end, we can identify a different evil situation that could achieve the same result; therefore no *one particular* evil means could ever be logically necessary. Stewart deals with this objection by adding 'of equal negative value' to the specification (pp. 65–9).

35 D. Z. Phillips (1965) *Concept of Prayer*, London, Routledge & Kegan Paul, p. 93.

36 Trau, 'The Positive Value of Evil', p. 32.

37 Trau, 'The Positive Value of Evil', p. 29.

38 Trau, 'The Positive Value of Evil', p. 31.

39 For a thorough discussion of Saadia's philosophy and theology, see I. Efros (1974) *Studies in Medieval Jewish Philosophy*, New York and London, Columbia University Press.

40 Cf. Philo (1929–62) 'De decalogo', in *Works*, vol. 12, trans. F. Colson, G. Whitacker and R. Marcus, Loeb Classical Library, Cambridge, Mass., Harvard University Press; see also the discussion in O. Leaman (1995) *Evil and Suffering in Jewish Philosophy*, Cambridge, Cambridge University Press, pp. 37f.

41 M. Mendelssohn (1983) *Jerusalem, or On Religious Power and Judaism*, trans. A. Arkush, London, University Press of New England, p. 62.

42 See H. Cohen (1972) *Religion of Reason: Out of the Sources of Judaism*, trans. S. Kaplan, New York, Ungar; and the discussion of Cohen's views in Leaman, *Evil and Suffering in Jewish Philosophy*, pp. 157–64.

43 Cohen, *Religion of Reason*, p. 18.

44 Cohen, *Religion of Reason*, p. 19.

45 Wendy Doniger O'Flaherty suggests that this psychological explanation for sin is primarily a Buddhist tendency, whereas in Hindu texts, past sins are the starting-point for explaining present evil and suffering. W. D. O'Flaherty (1980) 'Karma and Rebirth in the Vedas and Puranas', in W. D. O'Flaherty, *Karma and*

Rebirth in Classical Indian Traditions, Berkeley, University of California Press, p. xxiii.

46 S. Gaon (1988) *Book of Theodicy: Translation and Commentary on the Book of Job*, trans. S. Rosenblatt, New Haven, Yale University Press, pp. 125f. See also Efros, *Studies in Medieval Jewish Philosophy*, pp. 96–100.

47 For an interesting examination of the history of Jewish interpretation of this passage, see S. Feldman (1985) 'The Binding of Issac: A Test-Case of Divine Foreknowledge', in T. Rudavsky (ed.), *Divine Omniscience and Divine Omnipotence in Medieval Philosophy: Islamic, Jewish and Christian Perspectives*, Synthese Historical Library 25, Dordrecht, Boston and Lancaster, Reidel, pp. 105–33. Saadia took verse 12, frequently understood as God meaning, 'Now I know you are a God-fearing man,' and reinterpreted it as, 'Now I have made known [to all people] that you are a God-fearing man.' Thus he could see the 'test' not imposed upon Abraham to inform God, but as a lesson and example for all. Hasdai Crescas took an Aristotelian idea, that virtuous action itself *makes one* virtuous to say that the purpose of testing is to strengthen, exercise, perfect one's virtue which otherwise would simply have remained in potential. Isaac Arama had a different take: 'God tested Abraham in order to teach him that rational, or philosophical, morality is not absolutely binding, that there are situations wherein this morality has to be "suspended". . . . By commanding Abraham to sacrifice his son God taught him that there is a "higher morality", determined by God's will.' This account is a striking forerunner of Søren Kierkegaard's idea that religion can place higher demands on one than rational morality (or 'the ethical', as Kierkegaard calls it). Kierkegaard's early work – (1986) *Fear and Trembling*, London, Penguin – uses the story of Abraham as a way of exploring these ideas. Perhaps the advocate of this position could also claim that, while God might know that Abraham *would have* passed the test if he had been subjected to it, he could not justly be rewarded for it if he hadn't had to undergo it. There is also a kabbalistic theodicy of the 'bread of shame' which picks up this idea: 'If the good bestowed by God is not deserved [as in a world with no challenge], the recipient's pleasure will be lessened, or even negated, by the feelings of shame which always accompany undeserved favors' (D. Birnbaum (1989) *God and Evil: A Jewish Perspective*, Hoboken, Ktav, p. 34).

48 Maimonides, *Guide of the Perplexed*, III.24, p. 498.

49 Stewart, *The Greater Good Defence*, p. 145.

50 Cited in H. Küng (1992) *Judaism Between Yesterday and Tomorrow*, New York, Crossroad, pp. 585f.

51 M. Stoeber (1992) *Evil and the Mystics' God: Towards a Mystical Theodicy*, London, Macmillan.

52 Stoeber, *Evil and the Mystics' God*, p. 188.

53 Stoeber, *Evil and the Mystics' God*, p. 189.

54 Maimonides, *Guide of the Perplexed*, III.51, p. 628.

55 From a poem by Eraqi, which begins, 'The instrument of the joy of Love, who knows it?', in an unpublished translation by Mehri Niknam.

56 Ja'far As-Sadiq's commentary on the Qur'ānic Moses, in M. A. Sells (ed.) (1996) *Early Islamic Mysticism: Sufi, Qur'an, Mi'Raj, Poetic and Theological Writings*, New York, Paulist Press, p. 82.

57 J. Hick (1977) *Evil and the God of Love*, London, Macmillan.

58 Hick, *Evil and the God of Love*, pp. 257–9.

59 Kropf, *Evil and Evolution.*

60 Kropf, *Evil and Evolution*, p. 108.

61 Kropf, *Evil and Evolution*, p. 109.

62 Kropf, *Evil and Evolution*, pp. 124f.

63 Kropf, *Evil and Evolution*, p. 125.

64 Kropf, *Evil and Evolution*, p. 136.

65 Kropf, *Evil and Evolution*, p. 159.

66 Birnbaum, *God and Evil*, p. 54.

67 Birnbaum, *God and Evil*, p. 146.

68 M. Buber (1982) 'The Dialogue between Heaven and Earth', in E. L. Fackenheim (ed.), *To Mend the World*, New York, Schocken, p. 196.

69 Stewart observes that Hick, Yandell and Peterson, all of whom offer defences that have a 'greater good' element, all seem to agree that there is such a thing as gratuitous evil; that is, evil that cannot be justified by any apparent good result. And yet, when their writings are examined, all three nevertheless seem to offer justifications for this allegedly unjustifiable evil. Peterson, for example, has a threefold justificatory scheme that includes free will, natural law and soul-growth defences. The point is even excessive suffering tends to be taken up into greater good justificatory patterns. Stewart, *The Greater Good Defence*, pp. 80f.

70 Stoeber, *Evil and the Mystics' God*, p. 189.

71 See E. Berkovits (1973) *Faith after the Holocaust*, Hoboken, Ktav.

72 Leaman, *Evil and Suffering in Jewish Philosophy*, p. 191.

73 A. Cohen (1981) *The Tremendum: A Theological Interpretation of the Holocaust*, New York, Crossroad, p. 1.

74 J. K. Roth (1981) 'A Theodicy of Protest', in S. T. Davis (ed.), *Encountering Evil: Live Options in Theodicy*, Edinburgh, T & T Clark, pp. 7–22, p. 17.

75 A. Plantinga (1982 (1974)) *The Nature of Necessity*, Oxford, Clarendon Press, pp. 190–5; Stewart, *The Greater Good Defence*, p. 58.

76 See G. Griffith-Dickson (2000) *Human and Divine: An Introduction to the Philosophy of Religious Experience*, London, Duckworth.

77 E. L. Fackenheim (1969) 'Transcendence in Contemporary Culture: Philosophical Reflections and a Jewish Theology', in H. W. Richardson and D. R. Cutler (eds), *Transcendence*, Boston, Beacon Press, p. 150.

12

Responsibility for Evil: Divine and Human

Robin Le Poidevin calls the problem of evil 'the most powerful and convincing argument for atheism':

> Certainly there is a case to answer if we believe in a deity who is all-knowing, all-powerful and perfectly good. If he is all-knowing, he will be aware of suffering; if he is all-powerful, he will be able to prevent suffering; and if he is perfectly good, he will desire to prevent suffering. But, clearly, he does not prevent suffering, so either there is no such deity, or, if there is, he is not all-knowing, all-powerful *and* perfectly good, though he may be one or two of these.[1]

Do believers have to give way before such claims of contradictions put forth by atheists? Do the defences they attempt have to be qualified in so many ways that they 'may thus be killed by inches, the death by a thousand qualifications', as Anthony Flew charges?[2]

This chapter will deal with the many ways believers have responded, and how the issues have gone back and forth in various traditions.

Can we hold God accountable for the evils of the world?

For some, God is off the hook if the world is necessarily as it is, although many have a reluctance to see their God subjected to necessity. Ormsby notes that, 'This is the hidden problem of theodicy: to affirm the necessary rightness of things without simultaneously subjecting God to necessity. . . . The problem is to assert the necessary rightness of things as they are, but to do so in a way that they are seen as proceeding from God's will, wisdom, and power, and not from a necessity of His nature.'[3]

Nevertheless, certain philosophical and theological schools have overcome any such qualms and do believe that God is subject to necessity, at least in some respects. Islamic Mu'tazilites, Christian scholastics and Jewish rationalists have all accepted the notion that God is bound at least by logic. An Indian variant is to wonder whether the gods are subject to karma.

A different tack is to ask what right humans have to call God to account. The case can be made that if God is the ultimate being and thus also is ultimate in justice, it follows that God should not be accountable to us who are God's inferiors as creatures of the Creator. We can claim that God is the standard for justice and not one who has to meet some prior, more ultimate, standard of justice. The Islamic Ash'arite school, in opposition to the more 'rationalist' Mu'tazilite school, took an uncompromising position on this. In a form of reasoning similar to the Western 'Euthyphro' dilemma (from Plato's dialogue of that name), the Ash'arites argued that God does not 'do what is just because it is just'; rather, what God does is just because 'just' is defined as 'what God does'. We cannot judge God, for we have no independent ability to discern 'good' and 'evil' apart from God's action.

'Whatever happens for good and evil in the world results from the eternal decree of God, but this decree itself has been issued in accord with what "wisdom demands." In the Islamic theodicy, divine wisdom is the final refuge of necessity.'[4]

The biblical Book of Job presents God as using this defence, in as it were a self-theodicy, with an impassioned poetic statement of how God's power and wisdom exceed Job's understanding.[5] (God in the words of this author makes no further defence against the charge of causing Job to suffer despite his innocence, though God ends by criticizing the theodicies of Job's friends.[6])

Using the Book of Job

Maimonides asserts that God's providence does not consist in arranging things for our convenience and comfort, or even our physical well-being. In Maimonides' opinion, the idea that God's providence means that He guarantees health, wealth and happiness for us is explicitly repudiated in the Book of Job; Job had previously held this opinion, and that precisely is what he learns to reject. The lesson that God teaches in his speech in Job is that the notion of His providence is not the same as the notion of our providence; nor is the notion of His governance of the things created by Him the same as the notion of our governance of that which we govern. The two notions are not comprised in one definition, contrary to what is thought by all those who are confused, and there is nothing in common between the two except the name alone.[7]

Maimonides concludes, 'If a man knows this, every misfortune will be borne lightly by him. And misfortunes will not add to his doubts regarding the deity and whether He does or does not know and whether he exercises providence or manifests neglect, but will, on the contrary, add to his love.'[8]

Aquinas took the view that God is not a moral agent, which is another way of removing 'accountability', though not 'goodness'. A moral agent would have moral obligations and duties, so that being good consists in meeting these. Brian Davies observes that discussions of the problem of evil frequently presuppose that God's goodness consists in God meeting moral obligations. 'We are in no position to say that God ought or ought not to have done something and that he is morally at fault or morally excusable for not doing it. In this sense, so one might argue, there is no problem of evil.'[9]

Why God is not a moral agent

In Thinking about God, *Davies provides three reasons why God is not a moral agent. First, God is changeless, whereas those who are subject to moral duties and obligations must be changeable, and have the chance of becoming something different as a result of their response to their duty. Second, to be a moral being depends on being a human being with the ability to choose between alternative courses of action. But God is not a human being, therefore He cannot be a moral being. Finally, with humans, one has moral obligations in a certain context: as a parent, as a doctor, and these differ. But God creates* ex nihilo, *which means there is no context or background against which God's act of creating can be evaluated. So God does not have duties and obligations.*[10]

The argument could be better formulated. God, on a Thomist understanding, cannot be subject to some pre-existing moral code or list of obligations, in fact cannot be subject to anything, because God is omnipotent and exists in absolute freedom. A moral code is, in a sense, something higher than the one who is bound by it. Nothing, however, is higher than God; the whole notion that there is something to which God could be bound is nonsensical. Second, God cannot be obligated to some moral code because God precedes anything and everything, temporally and ontologically, and there cannot be some prior moral code.

Davies gives another reason why God cannot be judged by the existence of evil in the world. Following his interpretation of Aquinas, he understands God's 'goodness' as consisting in perfection, which does not imply moral excellence.[11] 'Perfection' means perfectly actualizing all that something can or should be. He quotes Aquinas: 'For things are called perfect when they have achieved actuality, the perfect thing being that in which nothing required by the thing's particular mode of perfection fails to exist.'[12]

The second meaning Davies has for what the goodness of God means is that God is 'the maker of all creaturely goodness, which must therefore reflect him somehow'.[13] But creaturely goodness does include moral goodness. A more Aristotelian way to put this point is: 'God can be called "good" as the source of all that is attractive.'[14]

Many philosophers do tend to speak as if God in a rather human way is not living up to our moral obligations. Positions like Davies' offer some correction to setting ourselves up as God's judges. People, however, who are deeply troubled by the existence of evil, given their belief in God, may find this an almost glib by-passing of a real issue. If, as Davies claims, God 'is as divine as it takes divinity to be. It is for God to be fully God and, therefore, perfectly God,'[15] what part of divine perfection (much less 'attractiveness') is it to allow unjust and unavoidable suffering? Is there not a potential for omnibenevolence that we would expect God to actualize perfectly? Thomist accounts in other instances name a number of attributes that God fully is or actualizes, and omnipotent and omnibenevolent are two of them. How does unjust suffering coexist with divine perfection?

It seems to me that we have here an either–or choice. We can go for God as Unaccountable, and then follow the *via negativa* consistently, and accept that we will have no account of what God's goodness is, nor any reason to question God on this. Or we can go with Aquinas in positively predicating the goodness of God, in which case we have to find some way to show why imperfections and evils in the world do not likewise reveal evil and imperfection in God's nature. We will next look at efforts to do this.

Logical contradiction or a balance of probabilities?

To begin with, however, some have risen to the atheist's challenge of a logical contradiction. Alvin Plantinga has argued that, despite this traditional challenge put by Epicurus, Augustine and David Hume, there is no *contradiction* as such or *logical incompatibility* between the affirmations that the theist wants to make about God's omnipotence and omnibenevolence, and the proposition that evil exists.[16] Yandell has argued similarly.[17] 'God is good.' 'God is omnipotent.' 'Evil exists.' – None of these propositions are formally opposite to or the contradiction of any of the others, so the theist's set of propositions are not self-contradictory in a strict or formal sense. 'Atheologians', Plantinga remarks, have not been able to formulate a necessarily true proposition which renders the set of theistic propositions contradictory.[18]

Plantinga thinks that the theist can even forestall the looser claim that evil is a *contra-indication* for the existence of God. What is required to show that these propositions are consistent with one another is to formulate a third proposition that harmonizes them. This proposition must be consistent with one of the propositions (e.g. 'Evil exists') and entailed by the other (e.g. 'God is good').[19] It would look something like this: 'Because of God's goodness and omnipotence, God must necessarily *x*; and *x* is fully consistent with the existence of evil.'

Plantinga offers here a 'defence', which has recently been distinguished from a 'theodicy'. A defence of belief in God is considered more modest in scope and ambition; it merely tries to show (variously) that belief in God is not irrational, or is more probably true than false, or that the existence of evil is not incompatible with the existence of an omnipotent and omnibenevolent God. A 'theodicy' is a more ambitious attempt to 'justify God'; it goes beyond the task of minimal defence, and attempts to give some account of why God might allow suffering and evil events to happen. Plantinga's 'defence' is the idea that human beings have free will; we shall examine this idea in a later chapter.

Ground has shifted since these arguments, and philosophers of religion now often deal with the question of the probability of God's existence given the existence of evil. There is a burgeoning literature, much of it using Bayes' Theorem and therefore highly technical; consult the website therefore for more information on this.[20]

Is God the source of evil?

Some believers answer that question affirmatively, often because they do not want to question that God is all-powerful. God must be the source of all that is – what rival creator or power could have given rise to evil, which escapes God's control? There are verses in the Hebrew scriptures which say that God is the source of all, 'weal and woe' included. Christians tend to avoid any association between God and evil, but some Christian theologians, such as Oswald Bayer, do reflect on the position from the Hebrew Bible:

> the incomprehensible, terrible hiddenness of God, in which he conceals himself in an omnipotence both dark and endlessly distant and at the same time infinitely close – consumingly, burningly, oppressively close, closer than I am to myself; in that omnipotence which creates life *and* death, light *and* darkness (Isaiah 45.7), love *and* hate (Ecclesiastes 9.1f.), conservation *and* destruction, weal *and* woe (Amos 3.6; Isaiah 45.7), evil *and* good (Lamentations 3.38), in short: that he works all in all – inextricably and impenetrably to us.[21]

Many Islamic thinkers would rather face the tensions raised for God's goodness than compromise God's transcendence and power. Ash'ari wrote: 'Good and evil (occur) through the decree and power of God. We believe in God's decree and power – the good as well as the evil, the sweet as well as the bitter.'[22] The Ash'arite position was that God is the only agent, God alone 'creates acts', and this includes human action; from this it follows that God is the source even of evil.

A Christian mystic's view

*For Jakob Boehme, God is 'All' – as well as 'Nothing'. In his vividly described cosmogony, God is not so much the 'highest' as the 'lowest': everything, including matter and natural forces, rises up from this primal foundation (*Urgrund *or* Ungrund*) and sinks back into it. This origination from the unmanifested Godhead is threefold, a triad of thesis, antithesis and the synthesis that results from them. Thus the* inner *life of God is the original triad of 'Attraction', 'Diffusion', and what results from their interaction: 'Agony'! The life of God as* manifested *is the triad of Love, Expression, and their synthesis, Visible Variety. Human phenomena are explained with the same triadic structure: soul, body, spirit; and good, evil, and their resultant, free will.*

Boehme's attempts to account for the origin of evil are the outcome of this unusual metaphysical structure, and they also demonstrate that his thinking evolved as each attempt, presumably, was found wanting over time. In his earliest thought, he wants to maintain that nothing but good results from this Urgrund*. Later he suggests that good and evil, as an opposition, arise from the same creative source of the divine; as part of life and movement. Finally, he reaches the conclusion that evil itself becomes a consequence of the first, ultimate divine principle: the wrathful side of God.*

Why doesn't God intervene to prevent evil?

Perhaps you are willing to accept, for the sake of argument, that the existence of 'natural evil' arises from the nature of a material world, and the existence of 'moral evil' arises from human free will. That might 'justify' God on the question of why evil exists. But why does God *allow* reason to exist? Why doesn't God intervene to prevent horrible things from happening?

Reichenbach and Swinburne take the line that for the natural order to remain stable and predictable, it is undesirable for frequent divine interventions to take place to subvert the course of nature.[23] While many assume it would be better to have God avert evil consequences of human actions, Reichenbach and Swinburne argue that this would undermine our growth in causal and moral reasoning. If God intervened to protect such victims, Swinburne maintains, 'others will not take the trouble to help the helpless next time, and they will be rational not to take that trouble. For they will know that more powerful help is always available.'[24] This means that as an unfortunate but necessary consequence, serious evils will occur.

Problems that are seen to arise if God intervenes

Basinger observes that given the great number of widespread causal factors in our world, God cannot significantly lessen the amount of evil and death without having to intervene directly and continuously in our world.[25] Each intervention that upsets the causal apple-cart requires further interventions to right things again. Birnbaum thinks not even an omnipotent deity could intervene to overthrow natural laws without unravelling the cosmos.[26] Basinger further argues that if God were continually circumventing natural and psychological laws, it would destroy our belief that anticipated consequences will normally follow certain actions; in which case, 'we must seriously question whether we can retain a meaningful concept of "free choice".'[27] 'Continuous widespread divine intervention into our present natural system would make meaningful human choice impossible (or at least greatly lessen its meaningfulness).'[28] Could we function as rational people if natural laws were continually disrupted and our own decisions frequently undermined, with unpredictable results?

These points can still be defended by those who believe that God does sometimes intervene in the course of human history. Extraordinary and rare interventions ('miracles'), or God's action as a response to human prayer, would not have the same confusing effect. We can be occasionally confounded without having our sense of the intelligibility of things destroyed.

Basinger concludes that atheologians have not established that the relatively specific modifications that they demand to the natural order would result in a significant improvement in the world. He doubts whether such an undertaking could be done, and whether it would not represent a significant reduction in the integrity of human freedom. 'He or she must demonstrate that, in the context of the entire world system of which it would be a part, such modification would actually result in a significant increase in the net amount of good in comparison to the actual world.'[29]

Could God not intervene for at least the worst of evils?

If believers hold that God sustains the world in being, we can ask why divine power could not be used to cut off evil before the 'dysteleological' level. Why does God not prevent the worst evils from happening, or intervene before they deteriorate beyond a certain point? Why doesn't God offset the worst effects of abused free will, permitting the freedom but ameliorating the worst results? Parents may well let their toddler fall over on the floor when learning to walk; but would intervene to prevent a plunge down a long flight of concrete stairs, rather than say the fall was 'all part of the learning process'. What is suggested by this is that God could have built a kind of ratchet into the natural world, to prevent the worst evils from happening. Robert McKim, like Boër, has used this idea to claim that God could have created a world in which 'we can inflict considerable harm on each other, but we cannot destroy each other'.[30]

Swinburne argues that God *has* set limits on suffering. 'There is a temporal limit constituted by death to the amount a given man can suffer. And there is also presumably a limit to the intensity of possible suffering, set by the constitution of the brain through which suffering comes to man.'[31] Dilley takes a similar line:

> the limits McKim proposes look quite like those limits which the orthodox theist would accept as being *presently operative* in the real world. . . . God does put limits on the damage that can be done to us, the believer might say. . . . God allows evil-wishers to harm the flesh, but God does not allow the essential person, the spirit, to be slain by evildoers.[32]

The point that the length of time that one can suffer is limited by death or the onset of unconsciousness is not always consoling when you are in severe intractable pain; nor may one living under a ruthless dictator appreciate the observation that the amount of evil a human being can inflict is limited by their life-span. A sceptic is not reassured by the preservation of 'spirit'. But the logical point remains: in a finite world, suffering cannot be infinite. Nevertheless, I do not feel that this observation confronts the real issue. The complaint is not that suffering is infinite; but rather that though finite, the upper limit on suffering is set at too high a level. What can be said about that?

Perhaps God *has* built a ratchet into the system; perhaps God continually intervenes to ameliorate situations. *If that were so, we would not know it.* Not seeing a possible future which will never be realized, and never knowing for sure what would have been the case but isn't, we could never know what God may actually have prevented. Hitler and Stalin have become paradigms of ruthless evil in our era, but writers, like J. R. R. Tolkien with Sauron in *Lord of the Rings*, have imagined one more malevolent and destructive; if God has cut short the life of a potential Sauron we would not realize what we had been spared. Therefore we cannot object that God does not prevent the worst possible evils, for in fact he may be doing so all the time without our realizing it. What we could do is to object that he doesn't prevent the worst of the evils that remain, or protest the point at which God steps in.

It is clear from following this line of reflection that pain and vice form a kind of continuum; from scuffed knees to Aids; from lies to genocide. This means that a God who intervened would not so much 'eliminate the worst evils' in a general sort of way, as draw the line at a particular point.

'The worst' is not a separate category or different group of evils, but the furthest point on a continuous scale of our experience. We can ask why God does not eliminate a particular evil thing; but to eliminate 'the worst' would be like asking God to eliminate 'the largest number'. It is a task that could never be completed. Once the suffering or evil act at the top of the scale had been prevented, we would start asking about the next down the continuum, and this would go on and on. Where would a point be reached that we could say, 'Stop at this particular level of evil'? There may be different answers from different people, but to fix on any point in the continuum of evils is going to be seen as arbitrary and arguable to those who would want to have it stopped two notches further.

Mesle does not agree, and responds to a similar argument by Hick, which speaks of a 'slippery slope', by saying that there is a right place to stop: 'There is a stopping place on the slippery slope . . . and that is the kind of world best suited for raising children so as to be loving, trustworthy, and sympathetic people.'[33] This is ringing rhetoric – who wants to speak out against an environment that would produce such admirable people? To try to actually *conceive* what this means, however, is not as easy as it sounds. It is undermined first and foremost by the phenomenon of human diversity, which makes it look hopelessly simplistic to assert that there is one 'right' balance between fruitful hardship and overly severe suffering. Mesle may be confident in knowing what the *world* best suited for child-raising consists in; I am not confident in finding what such a *household* would consist in. Even if I were not frequently confounded by my own children as to what is the 'correct' balance between strictness and indulgence, ease and challenge, I would hesitate to assert that the best way to raise my child to be loving and sympathetic is the best way for everyone else's children.

Experience teaches rather that what works for one child is ineffective or inappropriate with another; what functions as a productive challenge for one is an insupportable burden for another. The same is also true for adults. To create an environment which did not crush some while leaving others insufficiently stimulated would require the ironing out of individual differences. Moreover, a sameness of life-experiences might also be necessary. An event that challenges and stimulates an adult, and from which she can draw greater good, might damage or destroy a child. So there would need to be metaphysical controls on certain events, like the death of parents, to prevent them occurring at the wrong time. What we must envision to make sense of Mesle's proposal is not 'an environment' designed to be supportive and beneficial, but a totally controlled and determined life-course for each individual.

Must God create the best possible world?

In Islamic philosophy, the notion of God's justice was taken by some to imply that God is *obliged* to provide the best for us. Details were disputed. The school of Basra restricted itself to the relatively modest claim that this applied only to religious matters, and the optimum that God is obliged to provide is defined in terms of 'benefit'. The Baghdad school in general made the more ambitious claim that God must lay on the best, not only in spiritual affairs but also in worldly situations – according to His wisdom and providence.[34]

The founder of the Baghdad school, Bishr ibn al-Mu'tamir, however, did say, 'It is not obligatory for God to do the best of things for man; indeed, this is absurd because there is no end and no term to the beneficence which God can perform.'[35] And here he has made a point lost on some modern Western commentators. Some object (or imply, perhaps using 'possible worlds' ontology) that this is not the best of all possible worlds and that God should have created a better. Others, Plantinga, Adams and Aquinas[36] among them, believe that the notion of a 'best possible world' is about as coherent as 'the largest possible prime number'. One can always push the frontiers back. Dream up the best of all possible worlds; now add a few more chocolates.

But, says the ratchet objector, I do not demand the *best* possible world; I just want a better world than this one. Aquinas maintained, in unknowing accord with al-Mu'tamir, that as an important affirmation of God's omnipotence, whatever world is actual, God *could* always have created a better one. Aquinas felt it would be a compromise of God's power to claim that God could not, so to speak, outdo himself. The result of this, paradoxical for God's omnipotence, is that *precisely because* God is omnipotent, he can never create a 'best of all possible worlds'. To Mesle's boast that he can conceive of a better world than this for God to create ('An omnipotent God with values like mine would have created us with better natures, a better environment and better freedoms'[37]), Aquinas might have responded dryly, 'So can God.'

If this point is accepted, one could formulate a kind of mini-theodicy out of it: God cannot be blamed for not creating a best of all possible worlds, for that is logically impossible. No matter how good the world and our natures were, so long as they were not perfect, human beings could (and probably would) always complain about such evil as existed. The relativity inherent in human perceptions and reactions to our experience means that we would find any evil or lack of a possible good to be something worth complaining about. And if the world, and we, were perfect, we would be God.

Is rethinking God a way out of an impasse?

We have seen so far how many theodicies have to struggle with the balance of two concepts about God: that God is all-powerful (and some insist as well all-knowing) but God is also 'good' or loving. One simple way out of this apparent conflict of attributes is to get rid of one or more of them. Some philosophers have taken this line, and this can go in three directions: rejecting or redefining God's power, or God's goodness, or keeping both of these in play while modifying God's superintendence of the world.

Omnipotence

Within Judaism and Christianity, there has been considerable discussion on the question of whether we should continue to think of God as omnipotent. Hans Küng, in writing about the work of Hans Jonas, a Jewish philosopher of religion:

> Against God's omnipotence Jonas sets *God's impotence*, that of a God who in Auschwitz and elsewhere kept silence and did not intervene, 'not because he did not want to, but because he could not'. In other words, Jonas maintains God's goodness and his comprehensibility even after Auschwitz. The omnipotence of God must be sacrificed.[38]

Process Theology took the lead in rethinking God's power. One reason some find their idea so attractive is precisely the way it deals with the problem of evil. One process theologian, David Ray Griffin, goes so far as to say that the problem of evil is 'unique' to those who believe in absolute omnipotence and creation out of nothing.[39] (Well, perhaps not.) If instead of nothing, God acted on some pre-existent actualities, we could understand these to have powers of their own which they could use independently of God. There could also be eternal and necessary principles that govern the potentialities of such entities in states of affairs. These entities Griffin sees as having power to determine themselves, at least in part, and as well power to influence others. God does not have the kind of power that would override that of these entities. More importantly, God's power is understood as *persuasive*, not coercive, or all-controlling. God seeks to persuade, but cannot force, people to act morally. In this view expecting God to avert effects of all the evils we experience is to misunderstand the nature of God's power. As Lewis Ford describes it,

> Divine persuasive power maximises creaturely freedom, respecting the integrity of each creature in the very act of guiding that creature's development toward greater freedom. The image of God as the craftsman, the cosmic watchmaker, must be abandoned. God is the husbandman in the vineyard of the world, fostering and nurturing its continuous evolutionary growth throughout all ages; he is the companion and friend who inspires us to achieve the very best that is within us. God creates by persuading the world to create itself.[40]

One corollary of the process view, which Ford concedes, is that it offers no assurance that good will triumph.[41] Some believers will be reluctant to give up this conviction. A variant in Madden and Hare is that God's power is persuasive in some respects, but they do not accept that it must be persuasive in *all* respects.[42] There are other problems with Process thought; one is that it does not explain why so many remain unpersuaded. We may also ask if persuasive power for *evil* is at work in the world, as persuasive power for good, given the evidence?

What is valuable, perhaps, even for those who are not attracted by the whole line taken in Process Theology, is the suggestion that God's omnipotence be reconsidered. We need not reject omnipotence outright in order to step back for a moment and reflect on what divine power might consist in, or how it might (or might not) be evident in the world. The process idea of God's acting with persuasive love might be taken as part of a theodicy explaining why God has not overcome by coercive power all the evils we see around us.

Does the existence of evil mean that God is not good?

While questioning which conception of God's power fits more easily into Judaeo-Christian theology, a more revolutionary act is to wonder if God is good in any sense that we understand the term. A survivor of the Holocaust, Elie Wiesel, found God guilty, and responsible for the suffering of the Jews. But despite this, Wiesel did not suggest that Jews should abandon traditional belief in God. But R. Rubenstein asks how it is possible, to continue to believe in an omnipotent and beneficent God:[43]

> If I believed in God as the omnipotent author of the historical drama and Israel as His Chosen People, I had to accept . . . that it was God's will that Hitler committed six million Jews to slaughter. I could not possibly believe in such a God nor could I believe in Israel as the chosen people of God after Auschwitz.[44]

Giving up belief in God, Rubenstein says, does not mean that Jewish identity and Jewish values should also be jettisoned and Judaism without

God. Others have not opted for atheism, but instead rejected the concept of an all-good God. From within the Christian tradition, John Roth has proposed 'a theodicy of protest'.

On the basis of what he calls the 'slaughter-bench of history', Roth questions the assumption that God cares about history. 'This result testifies that such a wasteful God cannot be totally benevolent. History itself is God's indictment.'[45] The responsibility for all evil (including human moral evil) cannot be placed on humanity alone; God too is responsible – as the one who started everything. Moreover, human freedom, far from constituting a defence of God, is part of the offence. We have both too much and too little of it: we do not have enough freedom to overcome our limitations, but we abuse the freedom we have and thus have too much.

> Freedom's defense for God looks more and more like a ploy by the devil's advocate. That defense cannot avoid saying: only if freedom has the potential to be what it has become can there be a chance for the highest goods. But can the end justify the means? – that is the question. A protesting theodicy is skeptical because it will not forget futile cries. No good that it can envision, on earth or beyond, is worth the freedom – enfeebled and empowered – that wastes so much life.[46]

Roth believes in an omnipotent God who *could* intervene (because he thinks that a God who isn't omnipotent isn't worth bothering about), but who chooses not to. Roth's God does not predetermine the future, and the past cannot be undone. Therefore, Roth's God is responsible for all evils: 'Thus, in spite and because of his sovereignty, this God is everlastingly guilty and the degrees run from gross negligence to murder.'[47]

Roth's call for action is complex. On the one hand, he advocates despair. Noting Rubenstein's observation that 'the Holocaust bears witness to *the advance of civilization*', Roth considers that there can only be worse to come. We can also only despair over the hope that there will be a future good that will justify what has happened so far. 'The irretrievable waste of the past robs God of a perfect alibi. Only if he obliterates truth by wiping out the memory of victims can a protesting "Why?" be stilled forever. So long as that question can sound, the whole human experience stands as less than acceptable.'[48]

Yet Roth also advocates trust and even hope – albeit the ambivalent hope of Wiesel: 'to have hope in God is to have hope against God'.[49] Rather than inaction, we should be fuelled by dissent against God to fight; for 'it is given to man to transform divine injustice into human justice and compassion'.[50]

Such a God has no simple nature. He is tugged and pulled by multiple

> desires, but he is not at their mercy. They are controlled by his own acts of will. This God is no bumbler. He knows what he is doing, and that reality [*sic*] is the problem. Our protests do him no harm. Indeed, his license gives us a mandate to say what we feel, and we must . . . so long as we speak for the sake of human well-being. When dissent is raised in that spirit, its rebellious care may grip God's ear.[51]

Frederick Sontag has an even more robust indictment of God:

> 'Freedom' and 'will' as divine attributes become essential to any picture of a holocaust God. 'Contingency' and 'chance' are equally important. We must be dealing with a God who takes great risks and whose mode of control is at best quite loose. We face a God with a policy of non-interference, one who consciously created humans with a greater capacity for evil and destruction than any aim to enhance good can account for. And God did this by rejecting other options open to him, some of which are preferable from a human point of view. Such a God, certainly, is not easy or comfortable to believe in, but that is not so great a difficulty for organized religion as it might seem. . . . Only a God more difficult for us to deal with seems likely to account for a harsh world, once our romantic views of life have been exploded by passing through a holocaust.[52]

Is this a good answer to the problem? My inclination is to say either we find an answer with an all-good God, or we adopt the perspective which says that we cannot justify God to ourselves, or we abandon belief in God altogether. There seems to be little sense in worshipping a God whose moral standards fall short of ours. Griffin's response to this view is to suggest that it will eventually undermine our own moral goodness.[53]

This is not to say that it is inappropriate to quarrel and rail against God. But the paradoxical statements of writers like Wiesel should be understood with the appropriate degree of irony, and the recognition of ambivalence that they represent – not as one-sided denunciations. 'The Jew has found it possible to simultaneously protest and praise.'[54] We might note how frequently voices in the Hebrew Bible, such as some of the Psalms, take the mode of accusing God, but with the hope of being heard. Wiesel himself expresses a complex and subtle ambivalence, as this quotation indicates:

> I do not believe that we can speak *about* God; we can only – as Kafka put it – speak *to* God. It all depends on who is speaking. What I am attempting is to speak *to* God. Even if I speak *against* him, I am speaking *to* him. And even if I am angry with God, I am attempting to show him my anger. But that in itself contains a confession of God, not a negation of God.[55]

If one is to let go of the notion that God is straightforwardly good in the way that human beings are good, I think that rather than adopting the idea that God might be at least partly bad, the theist would be better off following Aquinas, and claim that God's goodness is not identical but *analogous* to ours. God's goodness may not consist in arranging the world to our satisfaction, allowing us decent freedoms and rights but intervening when necessary; it may not consist in eliminating even horrendous sufferings. Thus the existence of evil is not necessarily incompatible with the existence of a God who is *transcendently* good in ways non-transcendent humans will find it hard to comprehend. This in effect is the position of those who worship the Unaccountable God.

Do we need a meticulous Providence?

Perhaps we can solve the problems by giving up the painstakingly controlling deity, the god who intervenes continuously to work things out for the good.

Oliver Leaman summarizes the Jewish philosopher Arthur Cohen's argument: 'To suggest that God could have prevented such events is to want him to intervene in the running of the world on our behalf, which would prevent us from exercising our freedom.'[56] God cannot be held responsible for the evil acts of humanity, in Cohen's view, because God no longer acts directly in the world. God gave us guidance on the right way to live; if we ignore this, what happens can be painful or disastrous, but that is not because God is not to be blamed for our disobedience. God's goodness does not consist in willingness to intervene, but in creating the world.

Although many find these theodicies which whittle away at God's omnipotence or God's goodness unsatisfactory, they do offer a useful insight: there may be a problem with the concept of God used in the usual questions about why God allows evil.

Asking such questions as 'Why didn't God intervene to stop this suffering, or at least mitigate it?' pictures God as a glorified social worker who is expected to remove the vulnerable in danger to a place of safety. But as anyone knows who has had to handle a determined two-year-old, humans from a young age fiercely resent any restriction of their actions by someone of greater power. They object even if the intervention is 'for your own good'. I wonder if God were to carry out moment by moment the sort of intervention some call for, would we be any more satisfied with God than we are now? Might we not claim that having our wills thwarted and our freedom compromised was a new reason for questioning God's omnibenevolence? Some of our suffering might be a different kind, but we could still see it as a problem.

Should we just give up 'theodicy'?

Kenneth Surin and Terence Tilley argue that theodicy itself is an evil to be resisted:

> [T]he usual practice of academic theodicy has marginalized, homogenized, supplanted, 'purified,' and ultimately silenced those expressing grief, cursing God, consoling the sorrowful, and trying practically to understand and counteract evil events, evil actions, and evil practices. I have come to see theodicy as a discourse practice which disguises real evils while those evils continue to afflict people. In short, engaging in the discourse practice of theodicy *creates* evils, not the least of which is the radical disjunction of 'academic' philosophical theology from 'pastoral' counsel.[57]

Tilley contends that theodicy is purely theoretical, addressed to abstract individual intellects, when what should be offered is something practical. If someone conjures up an abstract problem, and an even more abstract 'solution', it is of course galling to those who suffer. However, to treat the distinction between 'practical' and 'theoretical' as a clear-cut distinction is simplistic. Those who reflect also suffer, and those who suffer also reflect.

Moreover, to demand that those who write on the problem of evil display a practical approach instead of dealing in abstractions actually makes a self-contradictory demand. There is no practical action or response to 'the problem of evil', because there is no 'practical problem of evil'. There is rape, war, torture, child abuse, betrayal of a friend, drug addictions. These are the experiences that give rise to our tortured reflection on what we generalize as 'the problem of evil'. Clearly there is no one 'practical' answer to all of these. But we find some similarities between them that are necessarily 'abstracted' from the practical details of pain and cruelty. The fact that, from all these diverse experiences, we distil a common core, is precisely what gives rise to the perception that we have a philosophical problem. We feel we need to sort it out in our own minds.

But sorting out what we think and believe is not somehow in opposition to feeling, experiencing, being angered by evil, or being moved to compassion or action. On the contrary, such reflection is a necessary accompaniment to action that is effective and compassion that is wise. The implicit anti-intellectual, anti-academic prejudice is ultimately founded on a faulty anthropology, one that opposes thinking to feeling, experiencing to reflecting, suffering to pondering. Theodicies like the 'greater good' can offer the suffering reasons for having hope that good is the overarching context for evil, rather than seeing good events as sporadic and inadequate in an overarching context of pain and cruelty.

What is the nature of God's love for us?

> Someone tells us that God loves us as a father loves his children. We are reassured. But then we see a child dying of inoperable cancer of the throat. His earthly father is driven frantic in his efforts to help, but his Heavenly Father reveals no obvious sign of concern. Some qualification is made – God's love is 'not a merely human love' or it is 'an inscrutable love', perhaps – and we realize that such sufferings are quite compatible with the truth of the assertion that 'God loves us as a father (but, of course . . .)'. We are reassured again. But then perhaps we ask: what is this assurance of God's (appropriately qualified) love worth, what is this apparent guarantee really a guarantee against?[58]

This is one of Antony Flew's famous challenges to theism. In Gareth Moore's opinion, this misses the point of what Christians say about the love of God.[59] Flew wants to know what such a love is a guarantee against; Moore wonders why love must be taken as a 'guarantee'. One who says that 'God loves me' does not thereby claim certain things cannot happen; 'for he may say it when every conceivable misfortunate *has* afflicted him'. In fact, he may say it precisely *because* such things have happened.

> To one who trusts in God, one who says things like 'God loves me', what actually happens to him is irrelevant to the love of God for him. He has confidence in God, but that is not because he has learned by experience that God is loving, trustworthy and solicitous for his welfare. To say that God is loving is an expression of confidence in God, and so of a disposition to live in a certain way – not to despair, take to drink or commit suicide, in the face of adversity. While he has that confidence, nothing is going to count as evidence of God's not loving him. . . . And to say that is not to convict him of irrationality; it is to make a comment on the meaning, that is the use, of the phrase 'the love of God'.[60]

The reason Flew's challenge cannot be answered on its own terms, Moore suggests, is because it falsely construes the love of God as being just like the love of a human being. Instead Flew's challenge is really a challenge to his own false conception of the love of God. Rather than to look and see how religious believers actually use the sentence and therefore to understand what it means, Flew has assumed he knows what it means because he thinks God is logically the same as a human being.

> Hence he wants to say that one of the central and typical situations in which talk of the love of God is used – comforting people in great

anguish – is one where it is not to be used at all. But this is like saying that it is illegitimate to use a hammer to bang nails . . .

To continue to believe in God means still to see a certain way of life as possible, and one who is that badly hurt may be unable to see it as possible. But if that is so, he has not been swayed by evidence; he has been affected, by what has happened in his life. A man may lose faith because of the death of his son; he is not likely to lose faith over the death of a stranger thousands of miles away . . ., for it does not enter his life in the same way. . . . Belief in the love of God is not based on evidence, and so neither is the loss of that belief.[61]

Religious believers are not merely entitled but compelled to question the existence of God; and not just that but also the particular *conception* of God that they have. If God is conceived as a divine social worker who constantly intervenes to prevent us from doing harm, then that God is either incompetent, or apathetic, or non-existent. But is that the inescapable conclusion? Or does it rather suggest that such a notion of divine action is fundamentally misconceived? And it is time to look at the other partner in the relationship?

Does evil come from a Fall from original blessedness?

Some traditions report the human origin of evil in narrative or mythological form. The story told in Judaism, Christianity, and Islam, is that an omnibenevolent God created a peopled world, but human free choice destroyed this and the evils of the present world are a result of turning against God. In the Mahābhārata, the sage Mārkaṇḍeya gives an account of karma and *samsāra* in a story of human origins that parallels the Semitic 'Fall' mythology within a thoroughly Indian metaphysical framework.[62] In the primal age, human beings lived in 'pure' bodies, were free of physical and moral imperfections, were godlike, honest and pious; were able to commute between heaven and earth and to see the gods directly, without any aid or special procedures. But over their lifespans of thousands of years, they succumbed to wrath and lust, became subject to delusion. After that they were reborn in such unfortunate incarnations as demons, animals and mere human beings, and accumulated a store of evil and good deeds. The result was karma, when our past actions 'follow us like a shadow'. But even in this fallen state, the wise may get insight into this history and by living piously gain control over their fates through good and wise action.

Fall accounts can be said to work only by pushing the origin of evil further back in human history. So the question that arises becomes, 'Why did the godlike creatures of the Mahābhārata fall prey to vice; or why did Lucifer sin?' Without an answer to this initial puzzle, evil remains anthropologically inexplicable. In the present time, the role of the Devil has become questionable (although both Plantinga and Vardy hold it out as a possibility).[63] One original human pair created at the beginning of the universe does not fit the views of those convinced by archaeology and Darwin. This picture of a Fall has also been attacked on ethical grounds, in that it has led to some undesirable effects, for example in attitudes to women[64] (though the Islamic account of the Fall holds Adam and Eve equally responsible). Many modern theologians deal with some of these questions by not taking the Fall story as literal history. But then they need to find other answers for how evil gets into the world of a good God.

Karma

For all of the Indian religions that accept the concept of karma, human agency and responsibility accounts for good or ill.

What is karma?

Obeyesekere sets out the 'karmic eschatology' shared by Hinduism, Jainism and Buddhism in this fashion:

> *A theory of rebirth that postulates a cyclical theory of continuity, so that death is merely a temporary state in a continuing process of births and rebirths.*
>
> *A theory of karma that postulates that one's present existence is determined for the most part by the ethical nature of one's past actions.*
>
> *A theory of the nature of existence known as saṃsāra, which includes all living things in the cycle of endless continuity.*
>
> *A theory of salvation (nirvana), the salient characteristic of which is the view that salvation must involve the cessation of rebirth, and must therefore occur outside of the whole cycle of continuity, or saṃsāra.*[65]

Obeyesekere thinks this eschatology evolved out of a simpler belief in rebirth, which was later 'ethicized' into the karmic eschatology.[66]

Jaina theory differs. While all action, whether good or bad, causes karmic matter to attach to the soul, which weighs it down into rebirth, the only way to cease the cycle of death and rebirth is to avoid all action, in total ascetic renunciation.

How far is God bound by the structures of the moral universe? This question was explored in greater depth in the East than in the West. Does the notion of karma and *saṃsāra* require the idea of a God, or not? The Nyāya, Yoga and Vedāntin traditions all maintained that the divine existed and is the controller of karma. But Sāṃkhya and Purva Mīmāṃsā philosophies both disputed the existence of God. The Purva Mīmāṃsā thinkers, pre-eminently Jaimini and Kumārila, argued that if there is something like karma or apūrva administering justice on the basis of merit or demerit, there is no need for a god to do so. Or, if God also is subject to the universal law of karma, God is not omnipotent. It is better to understand karma as operating by its own necessity. Every act carries the potency of producing its own effect. As Sinari observes, a self-subsistent principle like this has no need of a God; but even if a deity exists, the principle need not come under God's influence but can enjoy a kind of independence or even transcendence.[67]

Non-theistic traditions of Buddhism clearly understand the cycle of *saṃsāra* and the workings of karma to operate without any form of divine assistance, as does Jainism, which also rejects the need of a deity.

Von Glasenapp examines the place of 'gods' in Buddhism, which he likens to Christian or Muslim saints in many respects. Where they differ from the gods of other religions is that they too are subject to birth and death, karma and *samsāra*. This, he suggests, is not an exclusively Buddhist idea but a 'general Indian view'.[68] (I suppose it does depend on what you consider a 'god'.)

Like all other beings, the Buddhist gods are subject to the karmic law of cause and effect, and natural law sets a beginning and an end for their status as gods. They are neither almighty nor omniscient, nor can they grant liberation. In all this they take second place to the Buddha, and even after the more advanced of his disciples.[69]

Dependent origination

Buddhism has as its foundation the explanation of the origin of evil and suffering, which is laid out against the backdrop of Indian philosophy and religion. The origin of the suffering of human existence is set forth in the Buddha's doctrine of Dependent Origination,[70] the lack of understanding of which gives rise to our misery. Each phenomenon of human experience is dependent on, connected to, another; they arise inseparably in a chain, but can also cease as each link is broken.

Dependent origination in Buddhism

Karma depends on ignorance;
Consciousness depends on karma;

Name and form depend on consciousness;
The six organs of sense depend on name and form;
Contact depends on the six organs of sense;
Sensation depends on contact;
Desire depends on sensation;
Attachment depends on desire;
Existence depends on attachment;
Birth depends on existence;
On birth depend old age and death, sorrow, lamentation, misery, grief, and despair. Thus does this entire aggregation of misery arise.[71]

When there is a 'complete fading out and cessation of ignorance', karma ceases; when karma ceases consciousness ceases, and so on through the chain; and thus the knitting of misery can unravel once that first stitch is severed. Ignorance, then, is the root cause of all suffering and evil in the Buddhist tradition.

In contrast, the Hindu scriptures all recognize a diversity of possible causes. The problems of the world could arise from immediate or past human action, from divine action, from hereditary traits, from natural causes, from sorcery, or simply 'fate'.[72]

Does evil grow out of ignorance?

The Vedāntin tradition of India faces a particular problem in accounting for the source of evil and suffering. The whole universe itself, good and bad, in their view, arises from ignorance. But Advaitins also maintain that we are not ultimately differentiated from one another but are all, at our most real, identical with Brahman. If this is so, how can Brahman give rise to what is delusory?[73]

Three styles of solution are offered, but not necessarily as alternatives, for they can be found in a single thinker. One form of justification is to emphasize human responsibility and thus separate Brahman from ignorance; another is to distinguish 'Brahman' from 'Īśvāra' and give responsibility for ignorance to Īśvāra; and a third straightforwardly sees Brahman itself in support of ignorance.

The distinction of Brahman and Īśvāra

Śaṇkara distinguished 'Brahman', from 'Īśvāra', or nirguna Brahman *from* saguna Brahman; *the two terms indicate the divine with and without attributes. The ultimate reality is Brahman without attributes: nirguna Brahman. It is unconditioned, indescribable, and cannot be separated into itself and its properties (for example, it doesn't 'have consciousness'). Beyond any name or form, it assumes different forms because it is its nature to express itself. Brahman as saguna, on the other hand, for whom Śaṇkara uses the name Īśvāra ('God', 'Lord'), possesses all qualities. Īśvāra is a relational reality, a mode of Brahman's expression which makes the empirical world possible. The separation of Īśvāra makes it possible to know Brahman by many names and forms; these in themselves are ultimately unreal but mediated to us through Īśvāra. Īśvāra is phenomenal appearance, and unlike Brahman is conditioned by māyā. It is Īśvāra who is the material and efficient cause of the world, is immanent in it, as its inner self, its 'inner controller', as the Upaniṣads so often put it. Īśvāra is not, however, the highest, most ultimate reality. Thus Śaṇkara can maintain the absolute purity and transcendence of the divine, while incidentally accounting for the origin of the world,[74] the misunderstood realm of appearance, and with it evil and suffering.*

Nevertheless, Śaṇkara will not be drawn on the question: Whose ignorance is it that causes the sufferings of existence; ours or Brahman's? Where does it come from? These are philosophically irrelevant; to ask them betrays misunderstanding; he sets them aside with 'frivolity'.[75] Ignorance does not have a positive existence; insofar as it is not a thing you can have, no-one has it. What is important, in Śaṇkara's view, is to recognize the widespread misrecognition on which all our perception and action is based – better still, to get rid of it.

Followers of Śaṇkara did not stick to these distinctions.[76] Maṇḍana attributes ignorance to individual souls; thus Brahman would not be subject to *samsāra*, the cycle of births and deaths. Śaṇkara's pupil Sureśvara stresses that ignorance is not a 'property', and therefore neither a property of Brahman, nor distinct from it. He associates it with individual souls, who in their ignorance generate the perceptions of the material world and its conditions. Under the power of imagination, these souls are responsible for the māyā of the world. Both the souls and the ignorance he suggests are eternal, which by-passes the question of how they arise: simply, they don't *arise*. Since they are internally self-contradictory, inconsistencies in the account can be placed at the door of māyā itself, not the philosopher. If we could give a rational and consistent account of it, it wouldn't be māyā; it would be a reality. Nayak finds that Sureśvara's claims just won't do; he says, 'it is difficult to understand how a concept or a principle, which is inconsistent and is not itself explainable, can satisfactorily work as an explanatory theory of the origin of the world'.[77]

Sureśvara, however, does get a grasp on issues arising from the underlying identity of Brahman with individual beings, which gives rise to the very problem.[78] He asserts that ignorance, as the failure to perceive the ultimate oneness of the Self, *does* affect Brahman. There are different ways to take Sureśvara; one can take him as thinking this may be no serious matter, because ignorance is unreal and Brahman remains. Sinari reads him as saying that Brahman 'has transformed itself into the subject–object relation and has generated the entire domain of world distinctions. To account for ignorance, therefore, one must say that the pure Self is ignorant in regard to itself, and eventually produces the illusion of individual persons and empirical phenomena.'[79] Padmapāda and Prakāśātman develop this idea into the view that Brahman is both the object of ignorance, in that it is the absolute unity of Brahman that is misconceived, and also the support of ignorance. Despite variations, all the Vedāntin thinkers are united in believing Brahman remains pure and undefiled by the superimposition of this ignorance. If we return to Śaṇkara's own writing, there is the reminder that it is only important to know the source of suffering if one intends to remedy it.

What is the role of free will in understanding evil in the world?

One of the dominant explanations in the West for the existence of evil is by attributing it not so much to human ignorance as to human wickedness: specifically, to our free will. This has arguably been the most-used theodicy in philosophy of religion in the twentieth century.

Based on the observation that much of the evil in our world arises out of human action, the Free Will Defence (hereafter FWD) argues that for God to have prevented all these evils, human beings would have had to be created without free will. The freedom to choose between good and evil is itself a 'good' – so good, in fact, that it justifies God in allowing us the scope to go wrong.

Why free will is linked to evil

God's omnipotence is construed by most free will defenders within the framework that God cannot act in ways that are logically impossible, or even self-contradictory. This implies that God cannot create a being, such as a human person, if that creation would involve a logical contradiction. Free will defenders claim that it would involve a logical contradiction to create free beings who lacked the moral freedom to make mistakes. That is, it would be logically impossible to create beings who were free to choose rightly but not free to choose wrongly. Therefore, the argument is that God could not have created free moral creatures who lacked the possibility of sin. There is a necessary connection, it is said, between human personality and moral freedom to go wrong; to make us as we are but without this freedom, that is, not free to choose wrongly as well as rightly, would be self-contradictory. Therefore, God could not create free moral creatures without the possibility of sin.

The idea that humans have a free will is contested in Western philosophy, and not only by philosophers but also by scientists. Some theologians also dispute the freedom of humanity; for some Protestant Christians and some Ash'arite Muslims, for example, God's omnipotence and God's omniscience imply a doctrine of predestination: that God knows in advance and wills in advance who is to be saved; and there is nothing we can do about it.[80] The Ash'arite position affirmed God's omnipotence so strongly that it denied human free will.

Other Muslims, with as much support from the Qur'ān as their opponents,[81] ascribed the responsibility for evil to human action. Al-Hasan al-Basrī asserted that we have free will, above all to prevent any accusation that God was unjust, in willing someone's sin then punishing him for it. 'Our God is too just and too fair to blind a man and then say to him, "See! or else I shall punish you", or to deafen him and then say, "Hear! or I shall punish you", or to strike him dumb and then say, "Speak! or else I shall punish you."'[82] Indeed, the Qadarīya school who defended free will were also known as 'the party of justice', since an insistence on divine justice was one of their main concerns in asserting free will. God 'does no wrong nor does He choose it, nor does He fail to fulfill what is obligatory upon Him, and all His acts are good'.[83]

So those monotheists who espouse the notion of free will view it as a necessary ingredient in humanity, personhood and moral agency. Human freedom, then, is a sign of God's goodness – and as the Islamic debate suggests, God's justice.

The East also had its debates on free will; one such debate lies at the beginnings of Buddhism. A contemporary of the Buddha, Gosalā Maskariputra, advocated a kind of extreme determinism, the absence of any free will or moral responsibility. Against this, the Buddha asserted the reality of free action and, with it, moral responsibility. On the other hand, the second Buddha, Vasubandhu, believed that all actions of the body or speech depend on the mind, and the mind wholly depends on causes and conditions. (We will discuss this apparent contradiction below).[84]

The doctrines of *samsāra* and karma are used to explain the origin of evil as we noted above, but also come up in asking if human beings are basically bound or basically free. Paradoxically, a 'bound' condition results from a freedom of action. '. . . Karma is the intellectual statement of the attitude of a bound man.'[85] But these circumstances 'thrust upon us' are in fact the consequences of our own action; we are 'bound' insofar as we cannot escape the consequences of our own *free* action. The doctrine of Dependent Origination asserts that all the miseries of existence ultimately depend on ignorance – and ignorance is something partly under our control. So although human agency alone cannot arrange karmas and their consequences according to our wishes, there is a dialectic of freedom and bondage.

> The pride and confidence borne by the West in its will, resoluteness and power were alien to the Indian spirit, inasmuch as it never discriminated right actions from the wrong ones on any ground other than the ledger of everyone's foregone lives. The general Western attitude towards the universe is one of challenge to the given order of events; it is heavily charged with industriousness, by which it wants to harness everything for the welfare of man. For Indians, on the contrary, until the karmas are paid off, the individual has to surrender to whatever he is destined to get and has to stay bound to the world.[86]

There is a difference from Western philosophy, however, in the way 'freedom' is primarily discussed in Indian philosophy: not as an aspect of will, but primarily as 'freedom from suffering'. That makes it not a starting-point so much as a desired end. Whether in the world or beyond it, this liberty (or liberation) is a goal, for which we must strive. Both freedom and suffering are not understood in purely moral terms; both in fact are more often viewed as the fruits of knowledge and ignorance, as we have seen, than as wickedness and goodness.

We can distinguish a Western view of freedom as an entitlement, and an Eastern notion of freedom as an achievement. Whereas the West either maintains or disputes that 'freedom' is what we are born with, in the 'Upaniṣadic world view' we are born into a state of bondage to the world and to existence. 'Freedom' is not something given, but a goal we must work towards ourselves – and work arduously. As Sinari puts it, we 'live *unto* freedom'.

The dialectic of freedom and bondage in Indian religion demonstrates, however, that 'freedom' is a complex notion, not simply a question of the timing of our freedom or how it is acquired. The fundamental difference between the views is in what really counts as 'freedom', and what needs to be taken into account when considering the scope or restriction of human action.

Why can't God make us free but sinless?

The sceptic Antony Flew challenged the central claim of the FWD: that God could not have made people free without the risk of their making wrongful choices.[87] He insists that God *could* have created human beings who, while still free, always freely chose to do good. But God did not do this, therefore the FWD fails: either God is not good, or God does not exist.

Flew's challenge was subsequently taken up and expounded by J. L. Mackie:

> If God has made men such that in their free choices they sometimes

> prefer what is good and sometimes what is evil, why could he not have made men such that they always freely choose the good? If there is no logical impossibility in a man's freely choosing the good on one, or on several, occasions, there cannot be a logical impossibility in his freely choosing the good on every occasion. God was not, then, faced with a choice between making innocent automata and making beings who, in acting freely, would sometimes go wrong: there was open to him the obviously better possibility of making beings who would act freely but always go right. Clearly, his failure to avail himself of this possibility is inconsistent with his being both omnipotent and wholly good.[88]

I have named this view the 'Freely Impeccable People' objection, fip for short; while for purposes of discussion, a freely impeccable person I call a fip.[89]

Transworld depravity

Alvin Plantinga almost playfully deals with the fip objection with the conjecture that someone might suffer from 'transworld depravity'.[90] In any possible world in which a person was significantly free, they would always go wrong in some respect. If there is just one person suffering from this condition, then any possible world with that person in it which God might create, would include that person's tendency to go wrong. It would in fact be logically impossible for God to create a world in which that person did not go wrong, because to do so would involve a contradiction.[91] If it is at least possible that one person suffers from transworld depravity, Plantinga claims, then, necessarily God could not have created a world with free beings and no moral failings. 'What is important about the idea of transworld depravity is that if a person suffers from it, then it wasn't within God's power to actualise any world in which that person is significantly free but does no wrong – that is, a world in which he produces moral good but no moral evil.'[92]

If we take Plantinga's argument out of its modal language,[93] what it means is that it is possible that human beings are such that it is inevitable that they will go wrong in at least one respect so long as they are free. If so, then by definition God could not have created a world in which they existed, were free, and never went wrong. Plantinga's transworld depravity rebuttal holds only within the narrow limits he has set himself: to demonstrate that it is possible to imagine a state of affairs that makes beliefs in God's good attributes consistent with the existence of evil. He maintains that this minimal defence is all that is required to acquit the theist of contradiction.

Fip objectors could reply to Plantinga that an omnipotent God could in theory actualize any world that we can imagine and therefore could create the freely impeccable or the trans-universally depraved.

Does freedom require an alternative?

In recent years, there has been discussion of whether one can be described as 'free' when one is not 'able to do otherwise', which is precisely the fips' situation.[94]

It is usually supposed that, in order to describe someone as 'free' and to ascribe to them moral responsibility for an action, there must be some alternative to that action. If someone has no choice but to do what they do, then they are not really free in that situation and therefore do not bear (full) moral responsibility for their act. This has been called the 'Principle of Alternate Possibilities'.

Let us imagine that, after my husband goes to work, I look outside and see it is a cold, windy, miserable day. I am tired and I feel a sore throat coming on, and I do not want to go out in the London rain to the college. I decide that to stay home and read in bed is the wiser thing to do. So inclement is the weather that I do not leave the house all day, not to post a letter, buy a newspaper, or walk the dog. Having looked at the alternatives as I see them, I consider that I have chosen to do this freely.

What I do not know until my husband returns with profuse apologies, is that he absent-mindedly took my keys and double-locked the front door. So if I had wanted to leave the house, I could not have done so. Although I couldn't have done otherwise, did I freely choose to do what I did?

It may have been cases like this imaginary one that led Harry Frankfurt to challenge the 'Principle of Alternate Possibilities'.[95] Frankfurt proposed that we abandon the traditional view that moral responsibility requires 'freedom to do otherwise'. In some situations, an agent lacks the possibility of doing other than she does, and yet still bears moral responsibility for what she does. Frankfurt suggested counterexamples designed to illustrate situations where someone freely chose something to which there was no alternative.[96] Whatever the apparent choice, the person will be held morally responsible for the act of choosing.

The mark of freedom, on this view, is doing something *because one really wants to*, not because there are a variety of options. The fact that one couldn't do otherwise in Frankfurt situations plays no role in the decision and action taken. For Frankfurt, 'acting freely' in this sense is all that is required for moral responsibility; not even 'freedom of will' (being undetermined in one's choice) or 'freedom of action' (being able to actualize a different situation).[97]

Can a Frankfurt scenario be used to assert the coherence of the fip concept? Fips 'act freely', but possess no 'freedom of action' to do evil. However, insofar as they do act freely, they bear moral responsibility for their actions. If so, the FWD fails.

Yet the Frankfurt situations help the fip proposer less than it might seem at first, even though the fip 'acts freely' while enjoying neither freedom of choice nor freedom of action. This is because there are two different ways in which one can have no alternative but to do what one does. Either one can be forced to do something, by compulsion or by a lack of choice, or the alternative (which could seem to be a choice) can have some intrinsic obstacle that prevents its realization. All the Frankfurt examples which succeed in showing that an agent *is* morally responsible fall into the latter category. They don't force choice, they just pre-determine the end result, they prevent the alternative from being realized should one choose it. It is fair to say that in Frankfurt counterexamples, one couldn't have *done* otherwise, but one could have *chosen* otherwise (and been prevented from acting upon it). This is not an argument or even an example for how the act of choice itself can be compelled and yet remain free, which the fip's condition requires. Frankfurt examples allow for the possibility of what we might call cips (comparatively impotent people) who could choose evil but not enact it; but not fips: people who *must* always choose the good and yet deserve full credit for so doing.

In addition, it has been questioned that Frankfurt's attempt to dissociate moral responsibility from freedom and control have worked. Peter van Inwagen, for example, claims that in all Frankfurt-style situations one can more precisely distinguish aspects of the state of affairs for which one is responsible from aspects for which one is not. Aspects for which one can be held responsible in Frankfurt situations, he claims, are always those aspects for which one does have an alternative. If we look at the example I gave above in my locked house scenario, we might say that I was not morally responsible for staying at home; for there was no alternative. However, I do bear moral responsibility for not trying to leave, even if unsuccessfully.[98] So, one could say: fips deserve credit for 'choosing good', if they freely embrace their only possibility; however, they do not deserve credit for 'not choosing to do evil'. The two are not always the same, and this may have some bearing on the question of morality. 'Choosing to be pregnant' and 'choosing not to have an abortion' may both refer to an ongoing pregnancy, but do not necessarily describe the same emotional or moral state of affairs.

I see one truth in the fip objection: that freedom and 'being able to do whatever one wants' or 'abundant choice' are not the same. As some Frankfurt examples show, one can be 'free' in the sense that one can do what one wants without having any choice in the matter if the only route available to you happens to be the route you desire. Similarly, one can have a choice and yet be unfree in ways that may matter a great deal – as in 'Sophie's choice'. A woman who decides not to struggle against the rapist who threatens to kill her if she does, possesses a choice between two courses of action but is hardly 'free to do what she wants'.

Mackie writes: 'one would not be directly aware of any antecedent causes of one's choosing, and equally, therefore, one could not be directly aware of the absence of antecedent causes. Contra-causal freedom, or the lack of it, simply is not the sort of thing of which we could have any "sense", any immediate introspective evidence.'[99] So in cases where no fully determining causes can be found or experienced, the determinist must assert the existence of determining forces of which we are completely unaware and for which we have no evidence. If there is no evidence of such forces, however, what justification can there be for overriding the testimony of experience – the experience of the absence of any such forces or compulsion? It may indeed be the case that we are often caused or determined by unconscious or physiological forces of which we are unaware. But in such cases our experience of our behaviour is most often not so much one of total liberty, as of total inexplicability: 'I don't know why, I just couldn't help myself.' The person suffering from a compulsion to wash her hands repeatedly may be unaware of what compels her. What this means, however, is not that she is unaware of being compelled, but rather that she is unaware of the cause. What she certainly does not say is that she has freely chosen to wash her hands thirty times today.

Could God prevent the evil results of free choice?

Could one adapt the structure of Frankfurt's examples as another way to defeat the FWD? Rather than the notion of fips, which focuses on choice, one could imagine God preventing the actualization of any evil choices that were made. Steven Boër has argued that the FWD does not justify the existence of moral evil, since God could always act to prevent any undesirable *results* of the evil action from actually occurring. This argument seeks to give all the benefits of free choice while suffering none of the consequences. 'In short, freedom of the will is freedom of opportunity: it is a licence to choose and try, not a warranty of success.'[100] Wanting to ward off the objection that this would make the world a chaotic place and might create cognitive difficulties, he suggests that God's intervention could be in the form of 'coincidence miracles'. If God does so, these miracles would appear to us as coincidences: 'far from being chaotic, [the world in question] would be exactly like our own except that evil machinations would never result in harm to any innocent party'.[101] What more could we ask?

But Frank Dilley has not been satisfied that this is possible, claiming that it destroys any real process of trying to do good or evil. Never to accomplish evil, to have good always result from one's acts or intentions, whether virtuous or vicious, indeed, to cut intentions loose from their consequences makes a nonsense not only of moral responsibility but also 'cuts the heart out of the notion of the creation of a community of interacting beings'.[102] This is a parallel argument to the one we have already given in the previous chapter in relation to the integrity of the natural world and our epistemic need for consistency.

But can we be free if our actions are caused – not just our choices constricted?

The focus of the debate over the feasibility of fips has centred on the question of whether one can be 'caused' and still 'free'.[103] Flew's argument for a determinism runs in this way: 'acting freely', 'being free to choose', and so on do not require that acts be unpredictable or uncaused. There is no contradiction involved in saying that a particular decision or act was '*both* free, and could have been helped, and so on; *and* predictable, or even foreknown, and explicable in terms of caused causes.'[104] From this, he suggests that 'it really is logically possible for an action to be both freely chosen and yet fully determined by caused causes.'[105] For Flew and Mackie, to be compelled by one's nature does not constitute an absence of freedom,[106] and indeed they claim that something like this is already the case for human beings. Therefore, God should be able to cause us to act freely, and the FWD is vanquished by the fip objection.

Many free will defenders, however, are 'incompatibilists' – that is, they say that freedom and determinism (being caused to act) are incompatible. They will argue that being *constructed*, like fips, to always freely choose good, amounts to being *caused* to always freely choose good; and thus is incompatible with freedom, even if always *opting* to freely choose good is not. Therefore, greater goodness attends on the possession of the freedom to do wrong.

Reflecting on our existence, do we have to choose between the two extremes that *all* our action is *totally* determined, or that *none* is? It is particularly unsatisfactory to abstract the philosophical question from our situation of being in the world, as if it were an issue to be decided in the context of 'human nature' and 'the will' alone.

The Indian picture of intertwined determinism and freedom is more complex and equivocal than most contributions to the Western free will debate. The 'bound' element in the theory of *saṃsāra* and karma, unlike the fip or the Frankfurt notions, is not *compulsion of action*. The lack of freedom is located first and foremost in the inescapability of the *consequences* of our action. Thus in Indian systems even *lack of freedom* is made to support notions of human responsibility. But, more subtly, lack of freedom also arises in the habits and compulsions that *result from our own free choices*. Even our own success can be a source of bondage and unfreedom, because it leads us to habitually restrict our habits and options to what worked last time.

In Indian metaphysics, the problem of freedom and determinism is located within the depiction of causality in the universe as a whole. The urge to understand causality, and with it both 'freedom-from' and 'freedom-to', characterizes all the great Indian philosophical systems; so that, as Karl Potter suggests, the problem of causation is the fundamental philosophical problem in Indian thought, and ontology and epistemology are only introduced to support these causal accounts.[107] Sinari claims:

> [T]he Indian mind exhibits a twofold approach to reality. On the rational plane it asserts the supremacy of a universal and necessary order, a kind of cosmic norma; yet on the transcendental plane it trusts that absolute freedom (*mokṣa*) is realizable. The gap between these two planes has always remained unbridged.[108]

Indian philosophers maintained that a causal order existed, while denying that the spiritual and transcendental aspects of human life were wholly contained within it. For the possibility of breaking out of the deterministic causal chain, of attaining *mokṣa,* always exists.

> The urge for absolute freedom can act against the whole domain of moral causation and bondage, and throw the exit to *mokṣa* open. Man's being in the bound world is conceived as a causally explicable phenomenon, an event in accordance with a universal order; but it is not denied that considering the prospective free choice he is capable of making, the bound existence will some day be annulled.[109]

This solves the apparent Buddhist 'contradiction'. The Buddha repudiates determinism and asserts the reality of free will and responsibility. He also, like his follower Vasubandhu, asserts the inescapability, the necessity of causal laws. This is found above all in the chain of 'Dependent Origination'. But for the Buddhist, necessity is not something fixed – for everything is transient. All is in constant change; so are we. Buddhist epistemology and ontology, which insist on the transience of everything, support a notion of causality as inescapable yet always moving toward a particular end. With insight, we can break the chain of Dependent Origination to achieve release.

This is a complexity that reflects human existence in all its contradiction. We *are* compelled; above all, we are compelled when we do not consider the possibility that we might be otherwise. When we do – when we gain insight into our lack of freedom and the causes of it, a new space does open up for wider possibilities of action. The compulsion was not false; nor is the freedom we can realize.

What does it mean 'to do good'?

Although it is the notion of freedom that has attracted all the attention in the FWD debate, perhaps that is the least of the problems associated with the fip objection. The fip objection speaks, in a blithe sort of way, about always 'doing good'; but this means that the fip must be able to identify the good in order to do it. This is not always as easy as it sounds.

What is it that makes an action good or bad, so that the fip (and we, for that matter) can tell which it is? Underlying the fip proposal is the assumption that goodness is intrinsic to actions, that acts are intrinsically good or bad; thus the fip can impeccably choose good. But is goodness really intrinsic and inseparable from the act itself? Quite often, actions are neutral in themselves and it is only the context, purpose or the result of the action that creates a moral status. In everyday life, people may also find that an act which is a good candidate to be considered intrinsically good does, however, sometimes yield a harmful result, and become potentially a bad moral choice, depending on your theory of ethics. If the same action can be either good or bad, depending on the circumstances, more is required of the fip than making a choice.

The Islamic Basrīan school had a different view of what goodness or badness comes from. As we have seen earlier, the Basrīan view was that an agent's ability has as its object not individual actions but classes of actions. The power to do something refers to an indefinite number of actions, not a single unique action. If one has the power to use a knife to slice, one can use a knife to slice cabbages or throats. One cannot have 'the ability to cut cabbages but not throats', or 'to slice tomatoes but not my finger'. All the moral attributes an action may have come from its performance by a certain agent with certain intentions, how it is done, why, when, in what context – but not from the mere kind of activity it is. My ability to slice is neither good nor bad. A slicing-event which I enact derives its goodness or badness from my intentions, what I slice, the context, and so on. But the ability to perform such acts is not restricted to its performance under certain conditions. One who can do something can do it in circumstances that are ethically good or ethically bad. A recent commentator writes:

> There is no moral quality good 'in itself' attached to 'the soul in the body' (*al-nafs*), the heart, or the spirit, and there is no moral quality bad 'in itself' attached to the body, the senses, or the emotions. It is the human ability to control, to combine, and to guide that determines the ethical quality of individuals, their *nafs*, their hearts, their bodies, feelings, each of their emotions, as well as each of their actions. This perception is the basis of the relationship that Muslims are invited to have with the world, which is not evil in itself (as opposed to the next world, which is presumed to be absolute good).[110]

In Indian philosophy, good is likewise not an intrinsic quality of the act, inseparable from the human's action. On this view of good action, wherever the constraints on the fip lie, it cannot be in the area of the ability to perform actions.

If the Basrīans are on the right track about the many conditions that determine the goodness of an act, more is required to do good than the ability to recognize some moral markers intrinsic to acts. First it needs an accurate reading of *situations* to know whether in these circumstances it is good or bad to do something. Moreover, it requires foreknowledge of the consequences; whether it is a good thing to intervene in a certain way depends in a large part on the results of one's intervention. These are the unacknowledged epistemological problems with fips. For the fip objection to succeed in depicting a world without evil that God should have created, it is not enough for the humans always reliably to *do their best given their state of knowledge at the time*. It is necessary that they must be *correct and infallible* in their moral choices. They do not simply need always to choose what they *think* is best; they must *know* what *is* absolutely the best. Otherwise there would still be evil in the world as the result of well-meaning but misguided choices. And they wouldn't always freely be choosing to do good; they would just be doing their best, like the rest of us.

So the fip proposal, to be functional and therefore successful as a theodicial challenge, requires that human beings are created with perfect moral judgement in assessing situations and contexts, and from birth; and furthermore, that we are able always to foresee with perfect accuracy what the result of a number of different actions would be, in order to accurately choose the best. It requires the ability to know what would be the actual outcome of all future conditionals in any situation – a form of foreknowledge, in short, that some do not even ascribe to an omniscient God, as we have seen in an earlier chapter.

Is freedom worth the disadvantages?

Can the goodness that free will adds to the world compensate for the evil that results from the ability to choose bad which is the painful side-effect of free will? If not, we are likely to think it would be a better world if we gave up freedom. Mesle, for one, is not convinced of its value:

> We do not really value the 'freedom' to become drug addicts and child molesters, murderers or concentration camp guards. . . . Freedom can be meaningful even when it is 'limited' to choices which are good, loving, creative, and enriching. . . . It is the choice between goods that we value, not the temptation to abuse our children in the night.[111]

Mesle may be right that freedom to be evil is not something that moral people treasure. However, freedom in choosing only between good choices is commonly referred to as 'taste', which indeed 'can be meaningful' but has little *moral* import. His mistake is to think that the FWD has to argue that the possibility of doing evil is a value in itself. Instead, it claims that the freedom to choose good is a value in itself, but that this is the same freedom as choosing *not* to. Mesle seems to assume that the freedom to be a child molester is a different item from the freedom not to be; but this hypostasizing language is misleading. We do not possess two different and separated freedoms, as *things*, one for good and a different one for evil. We are able to choose a number of different responses or actions. 'Freedom' refers to a way of being, not to a thing we can possess.

What is the point of freedom?

Mackie claims that any objection to his and Flew's determinist conception of fips implies that in that case, freedom must mean 'complete randomness or indeterminacy, including randomness with regard to the alternatives good and evil, in other words that men's choices and consequent actions can be "free" only if they are not determined by their characters'. But he wonders: 'What value or merit would there be in free choices if these were random actions which were not determined by the nature of the agent?'[112]

He may be right in claiming that moral freedom, if it is considered to be so precious, must consist in something more than sheer randomness. But 'sheer randomness' has not been the libertarian view of freedom or free will. They do not maintain that we can only be free if we have no preference whatsoever between two options or how we carry out our choices. Rather, the FWD assumes that there is a difference in significance – moral significance above all – between situations in which we choose between two options, and situations in which we go along with our only possibility.

It is this kind of freedom the FWD hangs its argument upon, in claiming that there is a virtue to be found in choosing what is good. That virtue does not just derive from the goodness of the result, but also from the chooser being able to make a choice; not just to choose a particular good state of affairs, but to choose to choose goodness itself. Only then does it possess maximal moral value. It seems to me that the fip objection hypothesizes that our natures could be so constructed that moral choices have the same sort of pattern of liberty and constraint that breathing does for us now: something we can control, but not fully choose not to do. But it is not insignificant that breathing, for us, is *not* an ethical issue.

Is there a better framework for discussing freedom?

'Free will' is far too narrow a focus for the question of human moral freedom. It reifies both 'freedom' and 'will', treating them as if they were objects or possessions that we have. Such language suggests a characteristically 'First World' attitude – rather than seeing freedom as a way of being. In some people this free-will emphasis may grow out of a desire for self-sufficiency and independence from God (or whatever is more ultimate than we are), an attempt to gain control over the events in our lives, to justify – or dignify – our bad behaviour as 'a legitimate exercise of freedom'. But either allocating blame for evil or justifying ourselves in the face of our moral hideousness is not really useful for reflecting on freedom.

The doctrines of karma and *samsāra* have several strengths, compared to the notion of free will. They are not focused exclusively on 'the will' as our free spot in our nature, nor on our own abilities or constraints. Instead, they insist that doing good has *agency* and *power*, first and foremost in its impact on one's own life. Good and bad actions are efficacious and are not mere tokens of good or evil intent. Liberation has epistemological overtones, as we see above all in Śaṇkara, for whom freedom *is* illumination or knowledge.[113] One of the greatest constraints on our moral action is not so much a problem of will but of limited epistemological horizons: is the problem *doing* good or having the foresight to *know* what is good?

Although 'free will' in the Western monotheisms and 'freedom from suffering' in the Indian religions appear to be quite different, do they have to be separated? Bondage to suffering and the tribulations of existence restrict our ability to discern, to choose, to act. All that we undergo affects our ability to be good and compassionate, as can be witnessed in the cycles of abuse we see as tragically handed down from one human generation to another. 'Suffering' and 'morality' are not separate issues for one who looks on humanity with a compassionate eye. What is required for more light and less heat in theodicy debates is a broader, but more dynamic notion of freedom: something that embraces both the joy and the tragedy of our participation in the world and something that pertains to both our actions and our being acted upon. Above all, we need a notion of freedom as a starting-point insofar as we realize it, and a goal only insofar as we actualize it.

Hamann wrote: 'Without the freedom to be evil there is no merit and without the freedom to be good no ascription of any guilt, yes, no recognition of good and evil itself.'[114] He was aware that the issue is not so much a 'free will' that can choose between good and evil options, but that the very ability to discern the good from the bad presupposes freedom in a deeper sense.

Freedom, he tells us, 'is the maximum and minimum of all our natural powers and the fundamental drive as well as the final purpose of their entire direction, development and return'. Without freedom we are not fully human; it is the indispensable starting-point for all our activity. And yet it is also the end, the purpose of all our drives and powers, a final accomplishment. Thus he unites both of the perspectives we have contrasted: the view of freedom as a given, and the perception of freedom as an achievement, the goal of fulfilment.

Freedom is also the ground and context for all our activities; all our mental powers, like consciousness, attention, or reflection, he describes as 'energies of our freedom'. In this he echoes Aristotle; and thereby suggests that all that we are and can do is united in the entelechy[115] of freedom. But freedom entails an essential moral responsibility. 'Freedom' is not merely a question of our own inner being nor of only our 'undetermined powers' which belong to freedom. For Hamann, freedom is not an entitlement but a privilege: the privilege of 'being able to contribute to our destiny'.

In this passage Hamann implicitly suggests that one danger in being obsessed with 'freedom' as an inner state, not some faculty we have, is that the wider, social, indeed, political dimensions of freedom are ignored. Political freedom and autonomy cannot be separated from 'inner freedom'; rather these are in a reciprocal relationship. The privilege of contributing to our destiny carries with it the obligation to contribute to others' future in a way that is good, not evil.

Finally, Hamann grounds freedom in a relationship to God, by alluding to a passage from the New Testament Letter of James: those that look to the 'perfect law of freedom' will be blessed in their doing.[116] The 'perfect law' of religious liberation he contrasts with the unjust political regime under which he lived. Although a 'law', it is not a system of oppressive regulations, but is that order and harmony of our being that makes action ('doing') possible and fruitful.

What is fundamentally at issue in the question of freedom and evil is moral responsibility; and what best fosters our awareness of it. It seems to me that theists should no longer think in terms of a 'Free Will Defence' but rather of a 'Moral Responsibility Understanding': greatest goodness exists in relationships between God and human beings, and between human beings themselves, who bear a maximal degree of moral responsibility. Perhaps we should also cease to think of an entity called 'free will' operating in situations in the world, and replace it with an understanding of desire working in harmony with freedom. Desire is what sets us in motion, to realize our 'maximum' from our 'minimum' of freedom; desire is what guides us to our ultimate fulfilment. With the twin ideas of desire and responsibility our reflection on human freedom in action might take a different direction.

The question for theodicy then becomes what relationship we bear to

God. This is the proper context in which to examine questions like free will. In the model of a relationship, acts are *gifts*, not pieces of evidence. If we are in a relationship, what we do has meaning and significance for one another. So instead of blaming and justifying, we ask such questions as, 'When and how do my acts have the most meaning and value for the other? What is the best, the most moral, act in this moment of relationship?' If we consider the question of the freedom to do evil, we can see that in such a situation our decisions have *more significance* and also bring with them *more responsibility*. The freedom offered by alternatives allows scope for our self-expression, self-revelation, as well as self-realization. It allows our desire to reveal who we are and decide what we become.

One can therefore maintain that evil can only be understood in the context of our relationship to God. In this framework, the existence of evil paradoxically signifies God's respect for us. It is based not only on our desire, but *God's* desire, for our action to have as much meaning and significance as possible. It is misleading to brandish the Free Will Defence and maintain that evil is a side-effect which somehow escapes an omnipotent God's control. Rather, the Moral Responsibility Understanding maintains that God desires to be in a relationship with creatures who are morally responsible rather than not. Such creatures possess power and scope for discernment, decision and action; their decisions and actions therefore are meaningful and significant. They are beings who create and reveal themselves in their decision and action; beings who possess autonomy, authority and agency; beings who, apparently, are being treated with more respect than they sometimes want.

At the end of Chapter 10, we explored a picture of divine and human action inspired by Thomist and Shi'a thinkers. On that view the difference between divine and human action, though distinct in that the action of the one is in creation and the other in acts in the world, is in a sense invisible. What we see is human action and natural events; what the believer *understands* is the empowering act of God in sustaining and creating the universe and ourselves. On that view responsibility for evil lies with all of us; but 'responsibility' means 'blame' less than it means 'freedom and power to act on it'.

> First man: Sometimes I'd like to ask God why he allows poverty, famine and injustice to continue when he could do something about it.
>
> Second man: What's stopping you?
>
> First man: I'm afraid he might ask me the same question.[117]

Draw your own conclusions

If you believe in God, do you believe God will make sure that all evil is redeemed and outweighed, or will he just draw a line under it and make sure everyone's OK in the end?

Is everything that happens God's will? Including evil things? If not, how is it that they can happen, given the omnipotence of God?

Does God *will* that I suffer or *allow* me to suffer? Does it make a difference?

Do you believe in meticulous providence – does God maintain complete control of events?

Do free will defences work for really horrific events?

If you cannot see good coming out of an evil act or event, is that evidence that God does not exist?

Are we free in situations where we have no choice, but we want what we've got?

Should we rethink our belief in God's power – or God's goodness – given the fact of evil?

Do philosophical arguments about the problem of evil have any impact on 'the real world'?

Does philosophy have to explain the existence of evil, or justify the fact that it exists?

Further reading

Davies, B. (1985) *Thinking about God*, London, Geoffrey Chapman

Flew, A. (1955) 'Theology and Falsification', in A. Flew and A. MacIntyre (eds), *New Essays in Philosophical Theology*, London, SCM Press

Griffith-Dickson, G. (2000) *Human and Divine: An Introduction to the Philosophy of Religious Experience*, London, Duckworth

Le Poidevin, R. (1997) *Arguing for Atheism: An Introduction to the Philosophy of Religion*, London, Routledge

Mackie, J. L. (1990) 'Evil and Omnipotence', in M. M. Adams and R. M. Adams (eds), *The Problem of Evil*, Oxford, Oxford University Press

O'Flaherty, W. D. (ed.) (1980) *Karma and Rebirth in Classical Indian Traditions*, Berkeley, Calif., University of California Press

Ormsby, E. L. (1984) *Theodicy in Islamic Thought: The Dispute over al-Ghazālī's 'Best of All Possible Worlds'*, Princeton, NJ, Princeton University Press

Peterson, M. (ed.) (1992) *The Problem of Evil: Selected Readings*, Notre Dame, Ind., University of Notre Dame Press
Plantinga, A. (1975) *God, Freedom and Evil*, London, Allen & Unwin
Stewart, M. (1992) *The Greater Good Defence: Essay on the Rationality of Faith*, London, Macmillan
Swinburne, R. (2004 (1979)) *The Existence of God*, Oxford, Clarendon Press

Notes

1 R. Le Poidevin (1997) *Arguing for Atheism: An Introduction to the Philosophy of Religion*, London, Routledge, p. 88.

2 A. Flew (1955) 'Theology and Falsification', in A. Flew and A. MacIntyre (eds), *New Essays in Philosophical Theology*, London, SCM Press, p. 97.

3 E. L. Ormsby (1984) *Theodicy in Islamic Thought: The Dispute over al-Ghazālī's 'Best of All Possible Worlds'*, Princeton, Princeton University Press, p. 264.

4 Ormsby, *Theodicy in Islamic Thought*, p. 264.

5 Job 38.4.

6 Job 42.7–9.

7 M. Maimonides (1963) *The Guide of the Perplexed*, trans. S. Pines, Chicago and London, University of Chicago Press, III.23, p. 496.

8 Maimonides, *Guide of the Perplexed*, p. 497.

9 B. Davies (1985) *Thinking about God*, London, Geoffrey Chapman, p. 212.

10 Davies, *Thinking about God*; and (1998) *Philosophy of Religion: A Guide to the Subject*, London, Cassell.

11 Davies, *Philosophy of Religion*, p. 185.

12 Aquinas, *Summa Theologica*, I.4.1; cited in Davies, *Philosophy of Religion*, p. 186.

13 Davies, *Philosophy of Religion*, p. 187.

14 Davies, *Philosophy of Religion*, p. 189.

15 Davies, *Philosophy of Religion*, p. 186.

16 See A. Plantinga (1975) *God, Freedom and Evil*, London, Allen & Unwin, pp. 12–24.

17 K. E. Yandell (1993) *The Epistemology of Religious Experience*, Cambridge, Cambridge University Press, pp. 322–8.

18 Plantinga, *God, Freedom and Evil*, pp. 23f.

19 Plantinga, *God, Freedom and Evil*, pp. 24–9.

20 The first literature on Bayes' Theorem and the problem of evil included J. L. Mackie (1982) in *The Miracle of Theism*, Oxford, Clarendon Press, and R. Swinburne (2004 (1979)) in *The Existence of God*, Oxford, Clarendon Press. William Rowe has developed Bayesian arguments in his work on the 'evidential problem of evil'; see W. Rowe (1979) *The Problem of Evil and Some Varieties of Atheism*, Oxford, Oxford University Press; (1986) 'Rationality, Religious Belief and Moral Commitment', in *The Empirical Argument from Evil*, Ithaca, NY, Cornell University Press; (1984) 'Evil and the Theistic Hypothesis: A Response to Wykstra', *International Journal for Philosophy of*

Religion 16; and (1996) 'The Evidential Argument from Evil: A Second Look', in *The Evidential Argument from Evil*, Bloomington, Ind., Indiana University Press.

21 O. Bayer (1999) 'Poetological Theology', *International Journal of Systematic Theology* 1, p. 165.

22 Cited in Ormsby, *Theodicy in Islamic Thought*, p. 24.

23 See B. Reichenbach (1982) *Evil and a Good God*, New York, Fordham University Press; and (1988) 'Evil and a Reformed View of God', *International Journal for Philosophy of Religion* 24, pp. 67–85.

24 Swinburne, *The Existence of God*, pp. 210f.

25 D. Basinger (1992) 'Evil as Evidence against God's Existence', in M. Peterson (ed.), *The Problem of Evil: Selected Readings*, Notre Dame, Ind., University of Notre Dame Press, pp. 146–8.

26 D. Birnbaum (1989) *God and Evil: A Unified Theodicy/Theology/Philosophy*, Hoboken, Ktav, p. 97 and p. 144.

27 Basinger, 'Evil as Evidence against God's Existence', p. 147.

28 Basinger, 'Evil as Evidence against God's Existence', p. 147.

29 Basinger, 'Evil as Evidence against God's Existence', p. 147.

30 R. McKim (1984) 'Worlds Without Evil', *International Journal for Philosophy of Religion* 15, pp. 161–70, p. 164. He is supporting the line of argument put forward by S. E. Boër (1978) 'The Irrelevance of the Free Will Defence', *Analysis* 38/2, pp. 110–12.

31 Swinburne, *The Existence of God*, p. 219.

32 F. Dilley (1990) 'The Free-Will Defence and Worlds without Moral Evil', *International Journal for Philosophy of Religion* 27, p. 6. His parodistic citation is of McKim, 'Worlds Without Evil', p. 164 (see above).

33 C. R. Mesle (1991) *John Hick's Theodicy: A Process Humanist Critique*, London, Macmillan, p. 64.

34 Ormsby, *Theodicy in Islamic Thought*, p. 21.

35 Al-Ash'ari (1929–33) *Maqālāt al-islāmīyīn*, ed. H. Ritter, Istanbul, I.246. Cited in Ormsby, *Theodicy in Islamic Thought*, p. 22.

36 Plantinga, *God, Freedom and Evil*, p. 34. Aquinas implicitly rejects the idea, thinking it an important affirmation of God's omnipotence that for every world God creates, he could create a better one. See Thomas Aquinas, *The 'Summa Theologica' of St. Thomas Aquinas*, London, Burns Oates & Washbourne, I.25.6; cf. M. Stewart (1992) *The Greater Good Defence: Essay on the Rationality of Faith*, London, Macmillan, pp. 57f.

37 Mesle, *John Hick's Theodicy*, p. 43.

38 Hans Küng (1992) *Judaism Between Yesterday and Tomorrow*, New York, Crossroad, pp. 593f.

39 See D. R. Griffin (1981) 'Creation out of Chaos and the Problem of Evil', in S. T. Davis (ed.), *Encountering Evil: Live Options in Theodicy*, Edinburgh, T & T Clark.

40 L. Ford (1992) 'Divine Persuasion and the Triumph of Good', in M. Peterson (ed.), *The Problem of Evil: Selected Readings*, Notre Dame, Ind., University of Notre Dame Press, p. 249.

41 Ford, 'Divine Persuasion and the Triumph of Good', p. 257.

42 E. Madden and P. Hare (1992) 'Evil and Persuasive Power', in M. Peterson

(ed.), *The Problem of Evil: Selected Readings*, Notre Dame, Ind., University of Notre Dame Press, p. 267.

43 R. Rubenstein (1966) *After Auschwitz: Radical Theology and Contemporary Judaism*, Indianapolis, Bobbs-Merrill, p. 153.

44 Rubenstein, *After Auschwitz*, p. 46.

45 J. K. Roth (1981) 'A Theodicy of Protest', in S. T. Davis (ed.), *Encountering Evil: Live Options in Theodicy*, Edinburgh, T & T Clark, p. 11.

46 Roth, 'A Theodicy of Protest', p. 14.

47 Roth, 'A Theodicy of Protest', p. 16.

48 Roth, 'A Theodicy of Protest', p. 15.

49 E. Wiesel (1973) *The Oath*, trans. M. Wiesel, New York, Random House, p. 78.

50 E. Wiesel (1976) *Messengers of God*, trans. M. Wiesel, New York, Random House, p. 235.

51 Roth, 'A Theodicy of Protest', p. 18.

52 F. Sontag (1981) 'Anthropodicy and the Return of God', in S. T. Davis (ed.), *Encountering Evil: Live Options in Theodicy*, Edinburgh, T & T Clark, pp. 148f.

53 'The religious drive to be in harmony with Roth's God, rather than countering our own evil tendencies, will actually give support to them. This is the most unfortunate aspect of Roth's position: directly counter to his intentions, his position *does* legitimate evil, since it says that deity itself, the Holy One, the one with an all-inclusive perspective, fosters it unnecessarily.' David R. Griffin (1981) 'Critique of Roth', in S. T. Davis (ed.), *Encountering Evil: Live Options in Theodicy*, Edinburgh, T & T Clark, p. 28.

54 Birnbaum in relating a tale of the early Hasidic master Levi Yitzhak of Berdiczez. See Birnbaum, *God and Evil*, p. 31.

55 Cited in Küng, *Judaism Between Yesterday and Tomorrow*, p. 605.

56 O. Leaman (1995) *Evil and Suffering in Jewish Philosophy*, Cambridge, Cambridge University Press, p. 190.

57 T. W. Tilley (1991) *The Evils of Theodicy*, Washington, D.C., Georgetown University Press, p. 3.

58 Flew, 'Theology and Falsification', pp. 98f.

59 G. Moore (1996) *Believing in God: A Philosophical Essay*, Edinburgh, T & T Clark.

60 Moore, *Believing in God*, p. 127.

61 Moore, *Believing in God*, pp. 128f.

62 *Mahābhārata* 3.179–221; see the discussion in J. B. Long (1980) 'Karma and Rebirth in the Mahābhārata', in W. D. O'Flaherty (ed.), *Karma and Rebirth in Classical Indian Traditions*, Berkeley, Calif., University of California Press, pp. 49–52.

63 See Plantinga, *God, Freedom and Evil*, pp. 57–9, and P. Vardy (1992) *The Puzzle of Evil*, London, HarperCollins, pp. 56–60, respectively.

64 Cf. E. Pagels (1988) *Adam, Eve and the Serpent*, London, Weidenfeld & Nicolson.

65 G. Obeyesekere (1980) 'Rebirth Eschatology and Its Transformations: A Contribution to the Sociology of Early Buddhism', in W. D. O'Flaherty (ed.), *Karma and Rebirth in Classical Indian Traditions*, Berkeley, Calif., University of California Press, pp. 137–64; this list is on pp. 139f.

66 Obeyesekere, 'Rebirth Eschatology and Its Transformations', p. 146.

67 R. A. Sinari (1970) *The Structure of Indian Thought*, Springfield, Ill., Charles C. Thomas, p. 50.

68 See H. von Glasenapp (1970) *Buddhism: A Non-theistic Religion*, trans. I. Schloegl, London, Allen & Unwin, p. 23.

69 Von Glasenapp, *Buddhism: A Non-theistic Religion*, p. 30.

70 Principal sources for this doctrine of *paticca-samuppāda* are the *Samyutta Nikāya* 2.1–133, and the *Dīgha Nikāya* 2.55–71.

71 *Samyutta Nikāya*, 22.90. This version is my arrangement of the text.

72 'The fact that various spokesmen in the *Mahābhārata* designate first one then another factor as the cause of events would seem to indicate that they did not feel that the total complexity of forces at work in the world could be accounted for by reference to a single principle or agent.' Long, 'Karma and Rebirth in the Mahābhārata', p. 47. Both Long and O'Flaherty provide numerous textual examples.

73 For two illuminating discussions of this problem, see R. A. Sinari (1970) *The Structure of Indian Thought*, Springfield, Ill., Charles C. Thomas, pp. 140ff., and K. Potter (ed.) (1981) *Encyclopedia of Indian Philosophies*, vol. 1: *Advaita Vedānta up to Śaṇkara and His Pupils*, Princeton, Princeton University Press, pp. 78ff.

74 Although, according to Nayak, explaining the origin of the universe was not Śaṇkara's interest or intention; he thought this was not the business of philosophy. See G. C. Nayak (1987) *Philosophical Reflections*, Delhi, Varanasi, Patna, Bangalore, Madras, Motilal Banarsidass, p. 50.

75 Nayak, *Philosophical Reflections*, p. 53.

76 Nayak sighs, 'The entire programme of Śaṇkara, to my mind, has been seriously misunderstood by and misrepresented at the hands of his own followers, not to speak of his opponents.' Nayak, *Philosophical Reflections*, p. 50.

77 Nayak, *Philosophical Reflections*, p. 49.

78 In the Naiṣkarmyasiddhi, presuming Sureśvara is its author (authorship of the work is uncertain and disputed).

79 Sinari, *The Structure of Indian Thought*, p. 141.

80 See H. A. Wolfson (1976) *The Philosophy of the Kalam*, Cambridge, Mass., and London, Harvard University Press.

81 Qur'ān 3:165; 4:79.

82 Cited in Ormsby, *Theodicy in Islamic Thought*, p. 19.

83 Cited in Ormsby, *Theodicy in Islamic Thought*, p. 21.

84 For a discussion of Buddhist conceptions of causality and free will, see the interesting discussion in F. T. Stcherbatsky (1962) *Buddhist Logic*, 2 vols, Mineola, NY, Dover Publications, vol. 1, pp. 131–4.

85 Sinari, *The Structure of Indian Thought*, p. 17.

86 Sinari, *The Structure of Indian Thought*, p. 19.

87 A. Flew (1955) 'Divine Omnipotence and Human Freedom', in A. Flew and A. MacIntyre (eds), *New Essays in Philosophical Theology*, London, SCM Press, pp. 144–69; cf. on this point pp. 149ff.

88 J. L. Mackie, 1990, 'Evil and Omnipotence', in M. M. Adams and R. M. Adams (eds), *The Problem of Evil*, Oxford, Oxford University Press, p. 33.

89 See G. Griffith-Dickson (2000) *Human and Divine: An Introduction to the*

Philosophy of Religious Experience, London, Duckworth, ch. 11.

90 See A. Plantinga (1974) *The Nature of Necessity*, Oxford, Clarendon Press; and *God, Freedom and Evil*.

91 To create her in such a way that she didn't correspond to her nature is a logical contradiction; so it would be as impossible as making a square circle.

92 Plantinga, *God, Freedom and Evil*, p. 48.

93 Some have rejected the possible-worlds-ontology that Plantinga deploys. Kenny raises several critical questions, such as that of what God needs to know in advance in creating an allegedly best possible world. (See, for example, A. Kenny (1979) *The God of the Philosophers*, Oxford, Clarendon Press, pp. 65ff.) For God to create the best possible world, he needs to know in advance which possible world this is; and in order to do this he must know all the counterfactuals: he must, so to speak, know the truth about what isn't true, but what could have been. Stewart suggests that if possible worlds talk is disallowed, Plantinga's defence collapses. However, Plantinga himself gives clear indications that he sits lightly to any 'ontology' of possible worlds; far from claiming as his defence that God has made the best of all possible worlds, he makes it clear that he repudiates such a notion. Plantinga, *God, Freedom and Evil*, p. 34. In this case, Kenny's objections that God could not know in advance which is the best possible world in order to create it is entirely misplaced as a refutation of Plantinga. Plantinga also makes it clear that God does not create *any* possible world: '. . . God does not, strictly speaking, *create* any possible worlds or states of affairs at all. What He creates are the heavens and the earth and all that they contain. But He has not created states of affairs.' Plantinga, *God, Freedom and Evil*, p. 38. In Plantinga's conception, God creates the theatre but does not write the script; so problems concerning God's foreknowledge of which play ought to be produced therefore are quite irrelevant.

94 This discussion has taken place in the context of the debates about causal determinism and moral responsibility, but is clearly relevant here – even if, curiously, these debates from 'mainstream' philosophy have not been raised in the context of theodicy.

95 H. Frankfurt (1969) 'Alternative Possibilities and Moral Responsibility', *Journal of Philosophy* 66, pp. 828–39. This article and a number of related articles are reprinted in John Fischer (ed.) (1986) *Moral Responsibility*, Ithaca, NY, Cornell University Press. A further collection of articles on the question was published by John Fischer and Mark Ravizza (eds) (1993) *Perspectives on Moral Responsibility*, Ithaca, NY, Cornell University Press. These two volumes should be consulted by anyone who wants to investigate the debate in more detail and depth.

96 The general structure of such Frankfurt situations is that one can choose, as one thinks, between two options – while unbeknownst to one, conditions exist that would actually prevent the alternative from being realized, should one choose it.

97 The theological correlate to the FWD/fip dispute is the question of predestination in Christianity and Islam. Those Christians who believe in predestination may suggest a notion of freedom as 'the liberty of spontaneity' rather than 'the liberty of indifference', as is seen in debates between Luther and Erasmus. The liberty of spontaneity holds that one is free in a choice so long as one wills it,

whether or not one had an alternative choice. To use an example from Duns Scotus, even after jumping off a cliff, one's falling is still 'free' (although causally necessary) as long as one continues to wish to fall while doing so. The liberty of indifference holds that freedom is only real where there is a genuine possibility of realizing either course of action.

98 P. van Inwagen (1986) 'Ability and Responsibility', in John Fischer (ed.), *Moral Responsibility*, Ithaca, NY, Cornell University Press, pp. 153ff.

99 J. L. Mackie (1982) *The Miracle of Theism: Arguments for and Against the Existence of God*, Oxford and New York, Oxford University Press, p. 167.

100 Boër, 'The Irrelevance of the Free Will Defence', p. 111.

101 Boër, 'The Irrelevance of the Free Will Defence', pp. 111f.

102 F. Dilley (1982) 'Is the Free Will Defence Irrelevant?' *Religious Studies* 18, pp. 355–64, p. 357.

103 The philosophical debate may be inextricable from the scientific disputes over freedom and determinism, but there is no clear agreement here either.

104 Flew, 'Divine Omnipotence and Human Freedom', p. 151.

105 Flew, 'Divine Omnipotence and Human Freedom', p. 153. Mackie, in his later attempt to expand on this issue, locates the dispute between the incompatibilist and the determinist in one understanding of what it means that 'A can do X and A can do Y': the incompatibilist accepts and the determinist rejects that it can mean 'that there is nothing at all that excludes either possibility, in particular, no set of antecedent sufficient causes for his doing X rather than Y, or vice versa'. Mackie, *The Miracle of Theism*, p. 167.

106 It is interesting to compare the Flew/Mackie position to the Kantian view of freedom, according to which human beings are only really free when they choose the good; on a Kantian scenario, then, fips would indeed be paragons of 'freedom'. However, this view seems counter-intuitive when contrasted to the ways in which human freedom is usually construed.

107 K. H. Potter (1963) *Presuppositions of India's Philosophies*, Englewood Cliffs, NJ, Prentice-Hall, p. 105.

108 Sinari, *The Structure of Indian Thought*, p. 38.

109 Sinari, *The Structure of Indian Thought*, p. 51.

110 Tariq Ramadan (2004) *Western Muslims and the Future of Islam*, Oxford, Oxford University Press, p. 15.

111 Mesle, *John Hick's Theodicy*, pp. 42f.

112 Mackie, 'Evil and Omnipotence', p. 34.

113 So argues Nayak, *Philosophical Reflections*, p. 73.

114 See G. Griffith-Dickson (1995) *Johann Georg Hamann's Relational Metacritism*, Berlin and New York, de Gruyter, p. 478, and the discussion on pp. 194–8.

115 The realization or actualization of something, as opposed to potential, in Aristotle's system.

116 James 1.25.

117 Taken from the Rowntree trust website: www.jrct-visionaries.org.uk/page.asp?section=000100020003 (accessed 22 December 2004).

13

Interpreting Religious Experience: What Is It Really?

The revealed and mystical literature of mankind bears ample testimony to the fact that religious experience has been too enduring and dominant in the history of mankind to be rejected as mere illusion. There seems to be no reason to accept the normal level of human experience as fact and reject its other levels as mystical and emotional. The facts of religious experience are facts among other facts of human experience and, in the capacity of yielding knowledge by interpretation, one fact is as good as another. (Mohammad Iqbal)[1]

If the experience of evil is one 'fact' of human existence, then religious experience is another. Many believers take their own experience as the strongest evidence for the God/s they believe in. On the other hand, sceptics or atheists label such accounts as unreliably subjective, or as illusions. They also note that a variety of experiences have been described from within many different traditions and claim this shows that such accounts give us no good reason for thinking that there is a God.

Can experience give us any dependable knowledge of God? Many branches of philosophy as well as science claim experience as a basis of knowing; therefore can we consider religious experience a primary source of religious knowledge? It depends on what you interpret it to mean. So that is the question we will consider in this chapter. In the next chapter we will look at how religious experience has been used as part of an argument for God's existence, and whether or not it is considered to give us knowledge of God.

Prevalence of reported religious experiences

In a secular culture, it may seem that religious experiences are rare, maybe confined to either 'saints' or 'madmen', but that is not the case. Carefully balanced studies find that between one-third and one-half of the population in the English-speaking world have had religious or spiritual experiences of some kind. This suggests a phenomenon that requires some investigation. It is striking how many people have these experiences. When the British psychologists David Hay and Ann Morisy first investigated a balanced sample of the population of the United Kingdom, they found that a little more than a third reported having had an experience of a 'presence or power, whether referred to as God or not, which was different from their everyday selves'.[2] *Researchers in North America and Australia obtain broadly similar results with positive responses of between 20 and 50 per cent.*[3] *The variation seems partly due to the exact question asked; and is also dependent on the method of investigation. These results were obtained with the more impersonal method of a poll, but when you interview people and spend some time gaining their trust, and perhaps allow them more time to run through their memory accessing such events, the positive response rate rises dramatically to 62–67 per cent.*[4]

Ways of categorizing experience

Different writers tend to present their own typology or taxonomy of religious experience. Glock and Stark distinguish confirming experience, responsive experience, ecstatic experience and revelational experience (in ascending order of rarity and intensity).[5] *Caroline Franks Davis categorizes according to nature or content, and makes the following distinctions: religious experiences can be* 'interpretive', *in which a believer interprets experience in a certain religious way (like seeing an event as an answer to prayer);* 'quasi-sensory', *in which the experience is primarily of a sensory nature, something is 'seen' or 'heard' (visions, dreams, etc.);* 'revelatory', *which includes sudden convictions, revelations, enlightenment, flashes of insight;* 'regenerative' *– these renew the subject's faith and improve his well-being;* 'numinous', *in which the divine is revealed in its awesome, even terrifying majesty; and* 'mystical' *experiences.*[6] *Yet another scheme is provided by Keith Yandell, who divides experiences by their 'object' rather than by their distinctive style, and distinguishes between experiences that are monotheistic, nirvanic (Buddhist), kevalic (Jain, which involves seeing oneself as the indestructible subject of experience), mokṣa (Hinduism, of Brahman, as Yandell describes it, although this is not what mokṣa means) and nature mysticism.*[7]

Is there a 'common core' to religious experiences? Or is each experience utterly different and incommensurable with another?

Almond notes five different attitudes on the question ranging from the assertion that all mystical experience is the same to claiming that there are as many different types of mystical experience as there are interpretations of them.[8] *In between these extremes are claims that all mystical experience is the same, but that the interpretations differ according to the mystic's religious framework; or that there are a few different types of experience which cross religious or cultural divides; or that there is only one form of interior mystical experience, even if one can subdivide it into types.*[9] *Stace suggests that there is a basic unity involved in religious experience: what we have is a case of a fundamentally identical experience being interpreted in different ways by different mystics. 'The language of the Hindus on the one hand and the Christians on the other is so astonishingly similar that they give every appearance of describing exactly the same experience.'*[10]

Steven Katz, on the other hand, allows for no such common core, and maintains instead a radical particularity of religious experiences.[11]

Are psychological explanations exhaustive?

Sceptics suggest many alternatives to the supernatural as the source of reported events. Anyone with a smattering of psychology or sociology, plus ingenuity, can come up with purely human explanations for any alleged 'experience of the supernatural'. Obvious candidates are: social pressures ranging from brainwashing and mass hysteria to overbearing parents, repressed sexuality, a parent's role projected onto divinity, effects of emotional stress or a life crisis. Certain personal characteristics, like an overwhelming sense of guilt, hyper-suggestibility in responding to hypnotic suggestion or sheer auto-suggestion; psychological disorders, physiological factors, or effects of hallucinogenic substances are other possibilities. Culture and social structures such as education and upbringing affect the way people understand and report their experience. Sceptics looking at religious experience have offered all of these as 'explanations', but what they often want to imply is that these (and not any spiritual being or power) is the 'real' cause. Does that necessarily follow? It is hard to think of any moments in life in which one or more of the above factors was not present. Does a believer have to say that an experience can only be 'religious' if it could not be explained in any other way?

Looking at the way we may regard any of the many possibilities, we can distinguish a 'naturalistic' from a 'reductionist' explanation. Naturalistic explanations operate purely in terms of the natural world and describe experiences claimed to be spiritual in terms from psychology, sociology, anthropology, or physiology. They do leave out any theological reference, but this means the religious or theological import can still be considered, for it is open to the believer to see the event having *both* a natural aspect and still something that they feel is beyond nature. 'Reductionism' more strictly seeks to 'reduce' a phenomenon to a single explanatory context and by insisting that only natural conditions are present, rejects any possible religious meaning or value.

Proudfoot tries to solve the issue by distinguishing 'descriptive reductionism' from 'explanatory reductionism'.[12] *Descriptive reductionism, he holds, describes a phenomenon by using the wrong category: 'To describe an experience in non-religious terms when the subject himself describes it in religious terms is to misidentify the experience.' Explanatory reduction explains an experience in terms that the person who had the experience might not agree with; but in a manner that Proudfoot argues is justifiable. The experience is set into a new context and this will stand or fall on how well it accounts for the evidence. What Proudfoot calls 'explanatory reductionism' is not always 'reductionist' in the sense of the previous paragraph. His 'explanatory reduction' may 'relocate' an experience into a new framework but, he feels, this is not 'reducing' it. While we may appreciate his effort to be sensitive to those who describe their own experiences, Proudfoot's distinction between a wrongly reductive 'description' and a rightly reductive 'explanation' is not so easy to make in practice. Where does explaining stop and describing begin? If we respectfully describe an experience as religious but maintain that one cannot explain it in those terms, what are we saying?*[13]

Scientists and philosophers often suppose that simplicity, even reductionism, is a desirable goal. But what if this parsimony is mistaken, and richness and diversity will give us a more complete understanding of phenomena? Consider the fact that reported religious experience itself is diverse. What might we be missing if we do not allow for that, and for a variety of explanations? Most 'explanations' of religious experience tend to focus on a single type of experience. Some researchers equate religious experience with psychotic or pathological conditions and therefore discuss dramatic, quasi-sensory reports such as visions and voices, experiencing demons or other entities – which are precisely the kinds of religious experience that most resemble psychotic episodes. But in fact, the majority of reported experiences are not at all like that. Investigators who attribute religious experiences to suggestion or hysteria tend to focus on spectacular emotional experiences such as those that happen at such intense events as revivalist meetings with their strong call to 'being saved', or on public demonstrations of instant healing. These too are in the minority.

What emerges from this unintended bias on the part of the researchers is that a single psychological explanation does not fit every believer's psyche. Can a single cause even cover all the aspects even of one particular case? In the sciences, for example, researchers do not insist that *only* genetic factors account for cancer, or *only* family relations explain schizophrenia.

As scientists look at both genetic predisposition and environment, so too we can consider a complex interrelation (even of purely natural factors) while looking for a plausible account of religious experience.[14] We can take as an example, a guru who may suggest to his novice that a religious experience will take place, but without spelling out any content for the experience. We might say that 'suggestion' adequately explains *that* the experience happened, but that does not account for *what* happened. Here we might look for a number of other naturalistic accounts (past experiences of the subject, personal mood, and written accounts, are among many possibilities) which may all help to give a full *psychological* picture of the event, even without thinking of the purely religious possibilities.

No single psychological theory has shown itself to be exhaustive. A variety of reductionist explanations must supplement the limitations or deficiencies of each one, but many of these theories are 'natural enemies': Freudianism and behaviourism, for example, operate from different frameworks and 'reduce' in different directions. If a single reductionist account is not adequate for all cases, it subverts a reductionist claim to be the sole explanation for the phenomenon.

What I find misguided about 'reductionist' explanations is that they often give a *narrower* frame of reference than the person having the experience provides, when what is often required is a larger context of explanation than the person herself sees. This means that it cannot provide any more adequate or profound understanding of the phenomenon than the original claimed meaning. When we find the subject's account seems insufficient or 'misunderstood', what is more helpful is suggesting a *wider* frame of reference, something that opens up much more than was present in the original account. When we feel someone has misinterpreted their own experience, it is often because their range of possible explanations seems too narrow: like the reductionist, they only consider one possible meaning or interpretation. Someone who is depressed and lonely may have a dramatic emotional experience while in a welcoming religious meeting and think this must mean that all the religious claims made are true; they may feel they must comply with instructions, even reluctantly breaking off contact with family and friends. If we want to help those who see only one possible interpretation, we would do better to widen their interpretative horizons, rather than reduce them to a different explanatory context even narrower than the one they see. The same is true if we want to have a deeper philosophic understanding of the event.

Naturalist explanations are often helpful in deepening or expanding understanding of religious experience; this is true for the believer as well as for the philosopher. It is simplistic, however, to take them as 'explaining it away', for any one explanation leaves too much unaccounted for. No single theory has been shown to be adequate for the *whole* of reported religious experiences, nor often as a complete explanation for one individual experience.

Is there significance or meaning beyond an 'explanation'?

Even if it might appear that all possible natural explanations have been applied, does this framework exclude the possibility of any remaining religious truth or meaning? Two questions still hang in the air: Do explanations say anything about whether the experience really happened or not? (This will be dealt with later.) Second, do all such explanations tell us anything about the meaning of the experience?

The meaning that subjects give to their experience, even when they acknowledge the effects of natural factors, may not be something that is identical to what they would see as 'explanation', 'cause' or 'origin'. Meaning requires its *own* different interpretative framework. Karl Jaspers introduced a distinction between 'understanding', which is proper to the humanities, and 'explaining', which belongs to the natural sciences.[15] But in recent years this sort of neat distinction has been doubted. Recent critique from the philosophy of science rejects a simple ascription of 'facts' to science and 'values' to the humanities; nor does it see factual explanation as belonging to scientific method while a different sort of 'understanding' applies to the arts.[16] While scientific enquiry is also value-laden, it can also contribute to reflection on values. We can in addition raise the question of whether scientific methods are well equipped to deal with existential questions of meaning that other hermeneutical (interpretative) disciplines have been designed to do.

Even when an experience is provided with a hermeneutic that fits its *psychological* aspects, the question of its specifically *theological* meaning remains. Every interpretative discipline is designed for particular clients and is not necessarily well equipped to deal with other methods of enquiry in areas for which it has not evolved. Optimally, every aspect of a phenomenon should be examined and accounted for within an appropriate interpretative framework. But in dealing with religious experience, we face the problem that both the experience and the human being having it are complex while most explanatory frameworks are narrowly specialized. Such interpretative methods, designed for a very specific job, lose credibility when they are overextended outside their intended boundaries. Shoppers have learned that garments labelled 'one size fits all' do have their limits, and won't fit both a small child and a 15-stone man.

Are religious experiences self-authenticating?

Is a religious experience 'self-authenticating'; that is, its own justification and validation? The idea that an experience might be 'self-authenticating' is usually scornfully rejected, but as Alston observes, it is in fact hard to find someone that actually asserts it in the form that its critics attack. Yandell holds that any acceptable proposition that is deemed to be self-authenticating must be radically restricted in what it claims, so much so, he says, that 'one could not base a religion or a philosophy or even plans for a picnic on what it epistemically contains'.[17] A person might say that, 'I have felt something', and that is self-authenticating; but a religion cannot be based on such a minimal claim. The more you increase the scope of what the experience covers, the less plausible it becomes to assert that it is entirely self-authenticating. Alston charges that self-authentication for 'propositions of the wealth of ramifications possessed by basic religious claims' 'is just out of the question'.

I suspect that issues about self-authentication rest on a misunderstanding about the nature and scope of the claim. Few mystics make a real claim for self-authentication of the experiences they report; and when they do, it is for the validity of *their* own particular experience. They do not state that a single experience in meditation authenticates the entirety of their belief system, whether Christianity or Islam or Advaita Vedānta.

It hangs then on a question of how much is 'authenticated'. I suspect that many of us feel uneasy with the idea of refusing to grant that someone's experience has a particular meaning for them, but are even more uneasy that someone else's 'meaning for them' must be accepted as a meaning for me. People surely have the right to take their own experience seriously, and it can be as difficult to assess the veridicality of someone's reported experience as it is to assess the level of pain they claim to feel. At the same time, a single person's experience has no universal validity, unless there are powerful arguments to say why it should offer evidence for general knowledge and truth-claims that might be generally valid.

Interpreting experience

On the other hand, few are inclined to deny that many features of our experience *are* 'contributed' to some degree by us – or even if we want to feel some ultimate certainty about our own experiences, we often find it easy to point out how others have been affected by their predispositions. We might ask if there is any experience which we do not in some way interpret.

My boss once said to me, 'Your figures er looking good.' I was proud. My female colleague was indignant on my behalf. I heard 'figures are', and took this as praise for the increase in student enrolment figures in my School. She heard 'your figure's, errr, looking good!', and took 'figure' to refer to my feminine shape. She did tend to take things that way.

Even with such a simple event, factors like past experiences, cultural conditioning, psychological expectations come into play. How to interpret data is a vital question that lies behind many issues of trying to understand people's religious experiences (or even everyday, interpersonal ones). In some cases, we can distinguish different aspects or 'moments' within the whole 'phenomenon'. There was my boss's utterance; his facial expression; my interpretation of his words. What relationship do these different 'moments' have to one another?

One view is that experience and the interpretation of it are something like a *kernel in a husk*, or a nut in its shell. There is a fundamental, immediate core experience – as of hearing words spoken and seeing the speaker – which is then covered by a shell of interpretation to give some sense of understanding what the experience is and what it means – 'being praised for my performance' (or 'being leered at'?) Finally this understanding can be fleshed out in the concepts, images, terminology and world view belonging to the individual, perhaps of my place in the universe – successful academic leader or object of sexual harassment. The interpretation, in this view, is in some sense separable from the experience; as can be seen in the different interpretations my female colleague and I made of the utterance.

What is the impact of holding that experience is separable from interpretation when considering religious experience? Even if one can distinguish reality from what we make of it only in theory and not in practice, it makes it much easier to cope with the fact that people's religious experiences are so diverse. If you claim to experience Kuan-Yin, I say I experience Laka (a Hawaiian goddess of hula), a Catholic says she experiences Mary and a Hindu claims he experiences Lakshmi, a philosopher may see this as a conflict that refutes the veridicality of all these claimed experiences. However, if we can say that each one first experiences a female figure which only then they *interpret* as a figure from our own religious tradition, using the language and beliefs of our own religion, it does not follow that we are all deluded about our experience. It can be argued that all witness to the same underlying truth but in individual ways influenced by such things as differing cultures. This would be a Hickean way to deal with the differences of religious experience and the challenge of conflicting truth claims.

'Experiencing-as'

One way this can work is to take this one step further and suggest that religious experience is 'nothing but' interpretation, an ordinary experience cloaked in religious language or imagery. John Hick has suggested that all experience is an '*experiencing-as*'. His paradigm is the kind of ambiguous figures which can be seen – 'experienced-as' – with equal plausibility as two different things. Some common ones are two mirror-image wavy lines that can be seen as a goblet or alternatively as two faces in profile. Another is Jastrow's figure that can either be seen as a duck or as a rabbit looking upwards (the duck's beak being the rabbit's ears). For Hick, experience is inherently ambiguous; like such figures it needs to be 'experienced-as' something before it has any meaning. An event is constituted as an experience by the interpretation which is embedded in the very act of perception. Thus a religious believer might validly experience the sunrise as having a religious significance in showing the magnificence of God's creation, while the atheist alongside equally validly sees it as a natural event with no added meaning. This allows Hick to deal with questions raised by religious pluralism, and to explain how diverse religious traditions can all be said to witness to religious truth; we experience the same Ultimate Reality as it is in Itself 'as' a figure from our own tradition.

While this kind of view may help in considering other faiths, it can also be useful in discussing atheism. If *all* experience is 'experiencing-as', this is true for the atheist's as well. Both the atheist and the religious believer might agree on the experience they shared, which they interpreted 'as' a natural or supernatural moment. This parity between claims about religious experience and other kinds of experience some find desirable, as it seems to allow real agreement about 'the facts' and finds the difference in interpreting the experience 'as'.

Caroline Franks Davis, however, thinks that too much has to be left out in claiming that the atheist and the believer agree on the facts. For her, the atheist and the believer do *not* have the same experience.[18] Davis makes the further point that the paradigm cases of 'experiencing-as', such as the duck-rabbit, are cases of genuine ambiguity, in which there *isn't* one 'right' perception. Donovan in agreement with Davis wants to keep the category of 'experiencing-as' for unusual ambiguous cases like the duck-rabbit. This will preserve the difference between 'taking something to be the case that really isn't the case, and taking something to be the case and being right in doing so'.[19]

Hick's choice of figures like the duck-rabbit is misleading as a paradigm case, for not all visual perceptions are genuinely ambiguous. In fact, it is their rarity that gives optical illusions the moment of surprise that makes them enjoyable puzzles. Would most religious believers really want to say that their experience is just one way of interpreting an ambiguous event? Nor can we squeeze all religious experience into this model; arguably, there are religious experiences which, rather than ordinary experiences interpreted in a religious way, arise only as a result of first having a religious world view. Donovan notes that 'only under the religious interpretations do they have the profound personal significance and the subtle interconnections with an overall world-view and understanding of life which they have when experienced by the believer'.[20]

Moreover, the gain in making peace between traditions and conflicting claims comes at the cost of losing any evidential value for religious experiences. If the religious content comes down to personal interpretation or 'experiencing as', spiritual experiences are not independent evidence for religious truths.[21] If all religious experience comes ready-shaped, interpreted or even created by religious beliefs, any attempt to justify belief on the existence of religious experience is circular.[22] Since the interpretation could be infected by bias or prejudice, it must be justified by some evidence which is independent of the personal experience itself. Flew, for one, demands prior evidence for the truth of religious doctrines before someone is warranted in placing a 'religious interpretation' on an 'experience'.[23]

No experience without interpretation?

Experience and interpretation may in this way be seen as separate, either conceptually or in practice. But actually: *can* you divide experience and interpretation, leaving such a thing as pure, unmediated, uninterpreted experience? You may feel that the experience, what it is of, and what it means, all happen in an instant, rather than a spaced out process. Does one say that the humiliation a rape victim feels in the attack is just 'her interpretation' of the event, distinct from the physical sensations, or is it an integral part of it?

Try to imagine a 'pure' experience that came to you through your senses: think how it looked, sounded, tasted, felt, smelled, and how you identified it – imagine 'an old-fashioned rose'. Strip away the categories you bring from past experience to identify it – flowers, structure, plant growth, what others call it, where you see it, all the learned and acquired ways you distinguished it from a modern hybrid rose or a plastic imitation. What is left? Now further slowly strip off all the phenomenal sense perceptions: red, soft to touch, scented, silent, sweet-tasting. What is left now? Is there anything 'pure' that can be called 'an experience'?

Yandell says not. 'In the case of tasting a lemon drop, remove the sense of smooth round hard object on my tongue and a lemon taste, and nothing whatever is left. In the case of sensing the presence of a holy God while partaking of the Eucharist . . ., remove the sense of a holy presence, and your religious experience is gone.'[24] How does an experience with no content differ from 'no experience'? If you try to remove all concepts from experience to leave the pure experience, Yandell points out that the idea of a 'pure experience' is itself a concept.[25]

Alston claims perceptual experience is 'essentially independent' of interpretation, conceptualization or the application of concepts, beliefs or judgement. The contrary idea, that no experience comes to us unmediated by general concepts and judgements, he calls a 'baseless prejudice'.[26] Donovan notes that all experiences are *someone's* experience, so it is contrived to speak of there being neutral, uninterpreted experience. Experiences can't be compared at an 'uninterpreted' level. The fact that we can be undecided or change our interpretation doesn't demonstrate that experience is just there prior to interpretation; rather experiences are interpreted from the first moment.[27] Katz observes that an experience reported by a mystic is shaped by the beliefs and concepts of the mystic's particular religion. The ideas even model the experience that the mystic expects to have, shaping the experience as it were even before the believer has it. He can see no 'core' experience that is religiously neutral, which is only interpreted afterwards.[28]

Proudfoot writes:

> *There is no uninterpreted experience. Our experience is already informed and constituted by our conceptions and tacit theories about ourselves and our world. All observation is theory-laden. We can design procedures in which certain hypotheses can be tested, but any perception or experience is already shaped by the concepts and implicit judgments we bring to it. In this sense, we are constantly engaged in interpretation and reinterpretation.*[29]

Proudfoot considers that this position allows for 'optimism' in understanding people from very different cultures: if we study their concepts and beliefs and the rules that govern them, we can in principle have 'access to the variety of experiences available to persons in that culture'.[30]

This optimism, however, may be misleading. If all observation is conditioned by theory, so too is this observation, this hopeful concept. If you claim that your view escapes the shaping conditions under which all others suffer, you must provide reasons why your belief is not questionable while the religious believer's is.

Does interpretation compromise evidential value?

In either case, the question can be asked about the effects of interpretation: does the presence of prior conditions, beliefs and concepts weigh against the use of experience as evidence for the reliability of a belief?

The approaches considered so far stress the *disjunction* between experience and interpretation. By emphasizing the role that prior concepts or ways of conceptualizing play in the way we regard our experience, they can be taken as showing how much comes from us and not from any divine reality itself. The implication can be that interpretation is a distortion. Making a division between the divine or ultimate reality *as it is in itself* on the one hand, and *as it appears to us* on the other, all the phenomenal features of the experience (that is, the qualities we experience) are treated as coming only from the human side. My feelings, my sense that this was a particular God or Goddess, are interpretations which I made of some original pure experience.

But interpretation may also play a positive role; it certainly seems to in everyday life. Simply for survival, we have to learn a variety of interpretative techniques, such as when it is safe to cross a busy street or whether we can trust advice about health care or financial investments.

Donovan has questioned the assumption of other philosophers that the less interpretation, the better. It is not necessarily the case that by reducing the amount of interpretation we will allow, we get closer to the genuine meaning of the experience. 'It is, after all, just as possible to miss the genuine significance of an experience through under-interpretation as it is through over-interpretation.'[31] An 'uninterpreted, neutral' experience is not a source of information in science or any other form of knowledge; experience only becomes 'knowledge' or 'understanding' when our basic experiences of the world are transformed by 'quite elaborate theoretical interpretations'. Might this be true of mystical experiences as well? As a 'pure core' they may tell us virtually nothing. 'If so, then trying to strip off interpretations in search of a neutral, core experience could be quite the wrong approach to take.'[32] If we accept making such rich use of interpretative techniques in science, art and everyday life, are we justified in refusing the same toleration to religious experience?

Here too people articulate their experience as they have been culturally taught to do. The commonsense *physical objects dispersed in space* conceptual scheme is inculcated in a thousand subtle and not so subtle ways in the course of socialization. Does this imply that we are not proceeding rationally in forming perceptual beliefs in the standard way? If not, how can we condemn [religious experience] for this reason?[33]

Davis thinks that even unconscious interpretations should be acceptable until proved otherwise, for 'if they were not generally reliable, the human race would not have survived so long'. She concludes that 'it is reasonable to believe that in ordinary, real-life situations these rules of inference generally lead to veridical perceptions'.[34]

The many facets of 'interpretation'

Is there a comprehensive model of interpretation of religious experience that allows us all the benefits of these various points of view? I suggest that rather than using a single model, like a kernel and a husk, for experience and interpretation, we create as broad and varied a picture as possible. 'Interpretation' can have the meaning of 'bringing something to expression'. Often an original, inexpressible, or at least wordless, phenomenon is brought into speech and available for communication. A paradigm for this is performing a piece of music. We speak of the performer's 'interpretation', but we do not mean the piece can be heard 'objectively' outside someone's performance. The music only exists in its being performed; 'interpretation', while not creating the piece, nevertheless is the only manner in which it can exist. In the same way, we can say that the language used to describe experience – even if it is 'added on later' – is not there to conceal but to reveal. We see one aspect of this when someone says, 'I didn't really see the meaning of that until I started talking to you about it.'

Another meaning of the word 'interpret' is 'to translate' – as in 'an interpreter' between two languages. The point of translation is to make something more intelligible than it was before, in fact it may mean that only with translation can I make any sense of the original message at all. This model also gives us useful possibilities for understanding accuracy, truth or falsity in a situation of diversity. Many translations of a poem can exist, and all of them might be 'correct' in that they offer meanings that are possible for the original word, but the variants may bring out subtle variations in tone. One might be more literal, and useful for study; another might rhyme and scan like the original, and give us more sense of how it was designed to sound. For someone to insist that, because they are different, one must be right and the other wrong is to fail to understand the complexity of languages and the business of translation. However, this does not mean that *every* translation is correct. While there may be no single *right* translation, there nevertheless is such a thing as a *wrong* one. There is variety in language, but there are also rules.

Interpretation can also name what happens when we try to understand another in conversation. 'You misinterpreted what I said,' can be used as an objection, but also as a way of improving understanding. All of these variant meanings of 'interpretation' bring out the important insight that what is going on is a linguistic event; acts of language. They also suggest further that interpretation is *relational*, that is, if interpretation is a question of language, it is most like that language that takes place between at least two people. We expect dialogue to move back and forth between one and another and in this way to get closer to understanding and, in fact, to 'truth'.

Interpretation as disclosure and manifestation?

We need to take responsibility for the ways in which we see things, to be able to say that 'it seems that way to me, this is how I interpret it now, but I could be wrong'. If my boss only meant to compliment my recruitment numbers in complimenting my 'figure', I cannot impute to him an offensive remark. But what if he *was* propositioning me? The fact that I take responsibility for my interpretations does not relieve anyone of responsibility for their actions. Both parties in communication, or an event, remain responsible for their actions and interpretation. Translated into religious experience, it suggests that my acknowledgement that I have interpreted an experience as religiously significant does not obliterate the role of some spiritual entity who was also the partner of the experience.

Meanwhile, many of the ways we perceive things *are* genuinely perceptive, and the fact that I am responsible for my interpretation does not mean that that interpretation discloses an insight that is more than merely 'interesting'. It is possible that genuine discovery exists not only in 'passive' experience but also in the more 'active' moment of when we bring it into language and interpretation. An interpretation may well be accurate, and may reveal more profound insights than a presumed 'recording', especially any effort to recount it as a 'pure experience'.

Imagine if experience came to us with its meaning obvious, stuck on it like the label on a tin of soup. What would life be like? Not to interpret an experience may not deprive us of all capacity to learn from an experience – if learning can sometimes be largely passive. But it does deprive us of intellectual agency. It means we do not ever have to exercise our cognitive faculties, develop our judgement, our powers of discrimination. The need to interpret experience is part of the adventure of being human and forging our path. It enables us to manifest ourselves.

It is not just religious experiences that are 'interpreted' and derive their meaning largely from our reception and understanding of them. Love and courtship experiences, sexual experiences (even the hostile or violent ones), and even some experiences at the start of more scientific enquiry, all share this feature. Some are more ambiguous than others, and we can distinguish between situations where I know I am doing a lot of work to make sense of what I experience and those where identifying or understanding is immediate and straightforward. It is not the case that I am an 'interpreter' in the first instance and a video camera in the second. The difference between them is not the difference between 'subjective' and 'objective', nor is it between 'biased' and 'accurate'; for either case could be unduly swayed by prejudice or be accurate. But they do have different implications for what I can claim on the basis of these experiences.

We have stayed largely within contemporary Western philosophical debates in this chapter for a particular reason. The challenges of interpreting religious experience, seen through the lens of contemporary Anglo-American analytical philosophy, are all ultimately turned to a particular direction: the ultimate utility of these experiences as evidence or fodder for a proof. Even if – so far – religious experience is not being used as a stage in a proof, it soon will be. The underlying purpose of the debated issues is whether religious experience is veridical or reliable, not for the sake of spiritual progress or personal enlightenment and discipline, but because there is a question about the value these experiences have for convincing someone else. It is not so easy to get a cross-cultural perspective on this narrow debate.

But that is not because other traditions aren't interested in the problem of interpreting religious experience. It is that they want to see it in a different light.

For one thing, this discussion has had a somewhat obsessive focus on the idea of An Experience. 'Experience' in this chapter has not meant the whole of existence, or the wisdom one has gained in the course of one's life. It means a single event. In another context, say a spiritual one, this would actually be seen as unhealthy and undesirable. It is the philosophical counterpart to the 'sensation seeking' that can beset the novice and which is usually discouraged by the master.

To unpack this chapter's ambiguous title: what is interpreting religious experience really? It is not about amassing proof. It is not about focusing on specific, dramatic, colourful, out-of-the-ordinary experiences, just as religious experience is not just about either moments of drama or stress-relief and personal self-realization. It is about a whole way of life, probed for its meaning and its messages and lessons, the epistemological end of personal self-discipline.

Tariq Ramadan writes:

Developed societies seem to offer us only two choices by which to overcome unease: either to dive into the most intense feelings and emotions, which, even if they are not always real or deep, do give us the sense that we exist, or to go into a sort of exile, which, whether for an hour or a lifetime, takes us away from the world to live inwardly, in psychological or mystical introspection and meditation, listening for one's self, one's being, and/or one's feelings. Though many have become expert at the first option, people who speak of a 'spirituality' as distinct from religion often today turn toward the second. It consists of a kind of retreat and distancing from the rhythm of daily life, taking time and giving meaning to things. The secularization of societies has caused a rise in this phenomenon, and people find a great need to be grounded at the private and intimate levels, far from the hubbub of public life.

This retreat-spirituality is today felt to be a great necessity, a need, and it sometimes takes the form of not very well considered types of 'consumption.' Some people practice exotic forms of yoga without really studying or understanding it, others get involved in sugar-coated varieties of Buddhism adapted to their 'need for a break,' yet others choose undemanding types of Sufism that help them to escape from themselves without hindrance, rather than helping them find themselves by exertion. Some essentially psychological techniques . . . are also suggested to help people live 'more inwardly,' develop 'emotional intelligence,' or achieve more self-control. The 'spiritual' life is often confused with techniques that enable one to find a balance between living out one's emotions and desires to the full and developing in oneself the means to control them.

In fact, these practices often are only superficially associated with long-established and authentic spiritual teachings such as Buddhism, which are, by contrast, built on rigorous disciplined work, control of desires, and denunciation of the 'I,' which is the object of this spiritual project. Muslim mysticism shares the demanding nature and in-depth work on the 'I' of these Far Eastern traditions. . . . Muslim spirituality has nothing in common with . . . trends and fashions, and neither is it a simple exercise in managing the emotions. It requires awareness, discipline, and constant effort . . ., because it is the expression of a returning to one's self, which should be a liberation. Today, at the very heart of Western societies, this exercise is a test.[35]

To take these reflections further would lead us into the practical, into the concrete how-to of how disciplined philosophical reflection and disciplined spiritual practice interact in one's life and how to manage them. So I will excuse myself from writing any more about it now. But I encourage you to seek out such writing elsewhere, even if only for curiosity's sake.

Draw your own conclusions

What would lead you to describe an experience as 'religious'? If it could not be explained in any other way? If it seemed to have 'religious content' to it? If the person said it was? What are the consequences for other kinds of experiences of taking the view that you do?

Could *every* experience be described or interpreted as 'religious'? Or are religious experiences one kind of experience alongside others?

Are all spiritual experiences ultimately of *one* divine or ultimate reality? How can you tell?

How do you explain the fact that some people's religious experiences seem deluded, or even dangerous?

What factors do you feel affect people's interpretative tendencies?

If someone with psychological problems has a powerful religious experience, does it mean that that experience was not veridical?

Does interpretation distort or reveal?

Further reading

Alston, W. P. (1991) *Perceiving God: The Epistemology of Religious Experience*, Ithaca, NY, Cornell University Press

Davis, C. F. (1989) *The Evidential Force of Religious Experience*, Oxford Clarendon Press

Donovan, P. (1979) *Interpreting Religious Experience*, London, Sheldon Press

Flew, A. (1974) *God and Philosophy*, London, Hutchinson

Gellman, J. (1997) *Experience of God and the Rationality of Theistic Belief*, Cornell Studies in the Philosophy of Religion, Ithaca and London, Cornell University Press

Griffith-Dickson, G. (2000) *Human and Divine: An Introduction to the Philosophy of Religious Experience*, London, Duckworth

Hay, D. (1982) *Exploring Inner Space*, London, Penguin

Hood, R. W., Jr (1994) *Handbook of Religious Experience*, Birmingham, Ala., Religious Education Press

Katz, S. T. (1978) *Mysticism and Philosophical Analysis*, London, Sheldon Press

Martin, M. (1990) *Atheism: A Philosophical Justification*, Philadelphia, Temple University Press

Mitchell, B. (1981) *The Justification of Religious Belief*, New York, Oxford University Press

Proudfoot, W. (1985) *Religious Experience*, Berkeley, University of California Press

Swinburne, R. (1979) *The Existence of God*, Oxford, Clarendon Press

Yandell, K. (1993) *The Epistemology of Religious Experience*, Cambridge, Cambridge University Press

Notes

1 Mohammad Iqbal (1988) *The Reconstruction of Religious Thought in Islam*, Lahore, Ashraf, p. 16.

2 This question posed to the experimental subjects is known as 'Hardy's question'. Cf. D. Hay (1982) *Exploring Inner Space*, London, Penguin; cf. D. Hay and A. Morisy (1978) 'Reports of Ecstatic, Paranormal, or Religious Experience in Great Britian and the United States: A Comparison of Trends', *Journal for the Scientific Study of Religion* 17/3, p. 259.

3 Other studies include: Andrew Greeley, asking about the experience of a 'powerful spiritual force', with a total positive response of 35 per cent; Glock and Stark (1965) 'Have you ever as an adult had the feeling that you were somehow in the presence of God?'; Back and Bourque (1970) 'Would you say that you ever had a "religious or mystical experience;" that is, a moment of sudden religious insight or awakening?' receiving 20.5 per cent the first time and 41.2 per cent the second time; Wuthnow (1976) 'Have you ever felt you were in close contact with something sacred?' with a positive response of 50 per cent. For further discussion of these studies, see Hay and Morisy, 'Reports of Ecstatic, Paranormal, or Religious Experience', or J.-P. Valla and R. H. Prince, in Coleen A. Ward (ed.) (1989) *Altered States of Consciousness and Mental Health: A Cross-Cultural Perspective*, London, Sage, pp. 149f.

4 When Hay and Morisy first encountered this surprisingly large positive response, they checked to see if perhaps they had over-represented groups that were likely to respond positively, whether groups of age, sex, education or class. Finding that the sample was indeed balanced, they finally concluded that that was the true response rate; theorizing that the difference was the style of investigation, which encouraged more confidence and trust in the people than does a poll. The subsequent experience of other researchers confirms this idea.

5 C. Glock and R. Stark (1965) *Religion and Society in Tension*, Chicago, Rand McNally.

6 C. F. Davis (1989) *The Evidential Force of Religious Experience*, Oxford, Clarendon Press, pp. 33–65.

7 K. Yandell (1993) *The Epistemology of Religious Experience*, Cambridge, Cambridge University Press, pp. 25–30.

8 See P. C. Almond (1982) *Mystical Experience and Religious Doctrine: An Investigation of the Study of Mysticism in World Religions*, Berlin, Mouton.

9 Otto divides experiences into theistic and mystical (subdivided into 'inward' and 'outward'), R. Otto (1987) *Mysticism East and West: A Comparative Analysis of the Nature of Mysticism*, trans. R. C. Payne, London, Theosophical; Stace divides experiences into extravertive and introvertive, W. T. Stace (1961) *Mysticism and Philosophy*, London, Macmillan; Smart divides experiences into numinous and mystical, N. Smart (1965) 'Interpretation and Mystical Experience', *Religious Studies* 1, pp. 75–87; Zaehner divides experiences into panenhenic, monistic, theistic, Zaehner (1961) *Mysticism, Sacred and Profane*, Oxford, Oxford University Press. See also the discussion in M. Poloma (1995) 'The Sociological Context of Religious Experience', in R. W. Hood Jr (ed.), *Handbook of Religious Experience*, Birmingham, Ala., Religious Education Press, pp. 167f.

10 Stace, *Mysticism and Philosophy*, p. 36, cited in P. Donovan (1979) *Interpreting Religious Experience*, London, Sheldon Press, p. 27. Cf. also 'There is reason to suppose that what are basically the same experiences have been differently interpreted by different mystics'. Stace, *Mysticism and Philosophy*, p. 18.

11 See S. T. Katz (1978) *Mysticism and Philosophical Analysis*, London, Sheldon Press.

12 W. Proudfoot (1985) *Religious Experience*, Berkeley, University of California Press, pp. 196f.

13 Proudfoot argues that while beliefs can normally be assessed without attention to their origin or cause, beliefs that include a claim about the cause must be an exception: perceptual beliefs and judgements. For someone to identify an experience as religious 'assumes an embedded causal claim; consequently the experience has an epistemic quality, as in the case of sense perception' (Proudfoot, *Religious Experience*, p. 178). *Certain* religious experiences do make causal claims or have causal implications; however, others do not. The causal implications of experiences are more varied for religious experiences than Proudfoot allows for.

14 As Bruno Bettelheim observes, 'most important psychological phenomena are overdetermined', i.e. have more than one cause or explanation. B. Bettelheim (1988) *A Good Enough Parent*, London, Pan Books, p. 192.

15 See K. Jaspers (1963) *General Psychopathology*, trans. J. Hoenig and M. W. Hamilton, Manchester, Manchester University Press.

16 Among other examples, Michel Foucault has suggested that not merely the arts but also the sciences are culturally constructed. They are not simple objective accounts of the way things are but are affected by cultural values. See in particular M. Foucault (1989) *Madness and Civilization: A History of Insanity in the Age of Reason*, London, Routledge. Paul Feyerabend has subjected the 'persistent fog of objectivism' in science to repeated critique: P. Feyerabend (1988) *Against Method*, London, Verso; (1996) *Farewell to Reason*, London and New York, Verso; (1981) *Realism, Rationalism and Scientific Method*, Cambridge, Cambridge University Press. Littlewood advocates an 'ironic simultaneity' of 'understanding' and 'explanation'. Neither understanding nor explaining is completely true, nor completely false. See note 3 in R. Littlewood (1996) 'Psychopathology, Embodiment and Religious Innovation: An Historical Instance', in D. Bhugra (ed.), *Psychiatry and Religion: Context, Consensus and Controversies*, London, Routledge. See also R. Littlewood (1993) *Pathology and Identity: The Work of Mother Earth in Trinidad*, Cambridge, Cambridge University Press.

17 Yandell, *Epistemology of Religious Experience*, p. 182.

18 Davis, *The Evidential Force of Religious Experience*, p. 85.

19 Donovan, *Interpreting Religious Experience*, p. 80.

20 Donovan, *Interpreting Religious Experience*, p. 82.

21 Proudfoot, *Religious Experience*, p. 108.

22 Davis calls it the 'vicious circle challenge', and observes: 'Such a narrowly empiricist and foundationalist position is rarely found now outside discussions of religious experience.' Davis, *The Evidential Force of Religious Experience*, p. 143.

23 A. Flew (1974) *God and Philosophy*, London, Hutchinson, p. 139.

24 Yandell, *Epistemology of Religious Experience*, p. 186.

25 Yandell, *Epistemology of Religious Experience*, p. 188.

26 W. P. Alston (1991) *Perceiving God: The Epistemology of Religious Experience*, Ithaca, NY, Cornell University Press, pp. 37f.

27 Donovan, *Interpreting Religious Experience*, pp. 28–30.

28 Katz, *Mysticism and Philosophical Analysis*.

29 Proudfoot, *Religious Experience*, p. 43.

30 Proudfoot, *Religious Experience*, p. 219.

31 Donovan, *Interpreting Religious Experience*, p. 28.

32 Donovan, *Interpreting Religious Experience*, p. 28.

33 W. P. Alston (1991) 'Is Religious Belief Rational?' in A. Loades and L. D. Rue (eds), *Contemporary Classics in Philosophy of Religion*, La Salle, Ill., Open Court, p. 150. Yandell lodges a similar complaint, using an analogy with sense perception: 'Why should it not be true of a scientist who has been trained to run a certain sort of experiment, is devoted to a theory that says that a certain event will occur under certain experimental conditions, and knows that her theory is false if that event does not occur, that she will have an experience in which that event at least seems to occur once she has created the relevant experiential conditions?' Yandell, *Epistemology of Religious Experience*, p. 203.

34 Davis, *The Evidential Force of Religious Experience*, p. 144.

35 T. Ramadan (2004) *Western Muslims and the Future of Islam*, Oxford, Oxford University Press, pp. 118–19.

14

Religious Experience, Argument and Knowledge

A certain Shaykh was asked: 'What is the proof of God?' He replied: 'His proof is that He is God.' The most learned scholar Fakhr al-Dīn Rāzī asked the Gnostic Shaykh Najm al-Dīn: 'By what did you know thy Lord?' He answered: 'By the inrushes irrupting in the hearts which make the souls incapable of falsifying them.'

So beyond reason is knowledge, which is subtler than what could be perceived by even the utmost limits of the sound reasons. (Mullā Ṣadrā)[1]

The previous chapter considered the issues surrounding the interpretation of religious experience. In this chapter we will see if religious experiences can be used as part of an argument to prove that there is an object (or divine cause) of such experiences.

William Alston suggests there is a 'doxastic practice analogous to sensory perception'.[2] By 'doxastic practice', he means a process of forming beliefs based on experience.[3] When we experience something through our senses, we then 'form a belief' that gives meaning to what we perceive and allows us to act – although this is not the usual way we would describe this constant activity we practise hundreds of times every day. By analogy with sense perception, taken as a paradigm of cognitive types of experience, he claims that mystical experience is probably cognitive as well, for it too gives us information. We form a belief in God based on an experience of God's presence. Both are noetic; they have an intentional object (that is, an object of the experience), both give rise to states of affairs that can be checked independently, and checking procedures for both kind of experience already exist. There are dissimilarities as well, which mostly focus on the procedures for checking whether the experience was veridical or not.

Alston's main strategy is to examine arguments for the reliability and rationality of sense perception as a doxastic practice, and to argue that Christian mystical practice has the same epistemic status because it enjoys essentially the same conditions as sense perception. He is chiefly concerned with rebutting the charge that we have sufficient reason to trust sensory doxastic practice but not enough for mystical doxastic practice.[4] There are no arguments for the reliability of sense perception that are not circular, he argues, and any doxastic practice exhibits this kind of non-vicious circularity: one cannot test or prove the reliability of a way of forming beliefs without using (and trusting) the very things in question. How can we test our memories without somehow using memory to check the results? Or test sense perception without using our sensory input or someone else's? Rationality does *not* depend on proving the reliability of the ways we have of forming beliefs; instead, we act rationally when we form and evaluate beliefs in the ways that are accepted and established in our society. If there are no 'overrides' to the belief, our rationality cannot be faulted for reaching it, and this doxastic practice and its results can be taken as reliable. Christian mystical practice, for Alston, satisfies all the conditions for rational acceptance, and therefore 'can be rationally engaged in, and rationally taken to be reliable and a source of justification, provided it is not disqualified by reasons to the contrary'.[5]

If the theist can successfully maintain that religious doxastic practice is on a par with other ways we have of forming beliefs, such as sense perception or memory, a significant battle has been won in the campaign to justify religious experience as a source of knowledge.

There are also alternative suggestions. One is the 'cumulative case'.

A 'cumulative case' from religious experience?

Basil Mitchell, followed in different ways by Swinburne, Donovan and Davis, suggests that religious experience can be evidence for the existence of God as part of a 'cumulative case'. It is reasonable to believe that religious experiences are genuine only if the religious system within which they are understood is itself found to be plausible. 'The correctness of any particular interpretation cannot be guaranteed simply by the experience itself, but relies on a conceptual framework which draws support from other, independent evidence.'[6] Mitchell argues that, although religious experience itself is not a theoretical matter, showing that the beliefs based on it are able to be rationally justified is. One needs to employ experience and reasoning. Knowledge only comes through the systematic relation of experiences to what we already know and the integration of them into the belief-system as a whole.

Swinburne, in his version of a cumulative case, sets out several principles which he believes will give rationality to believing the evidence from religious experiences. His theory of perception states that someone can have an experience of God 'if and only if its seeming to him that God is present is in fact caused by God being present'.[7] But his conditional 'is in fact caused by God being present' is precisely what is at issue in any debate; and the argument could risk looking like a dog chasing his own tail. To deal with this problem, Swinburne brings in his Principle of Credulity (PC): 'It is a principle of rationality that (in the absence of special considerations) if it seems (epistemically) to a subject that *x* is present, then probably *x* is present; what one seems to perceive is probably so.'[8] If we accept this as a fundamental 'principle of rationality', we do not need other justifications to accept the experience as evidential. The alternative to accepting the PC in general is a 'sceptical bog', according to Swinburne, in which one must doubt everything that is not capable of deductive proof.[9]

With Swinburne's PC the sceptic is challenged to show why the experience should be rejected. 'In the absence of special considerations, all religious experiences are to be taken by their subjects as genuine, and hence as substantial grounds for belief in the existence of their apparent object.'[10]

We may see why those who have had the religious experience can on this basis accept it as rational, but still question why those who did not have the same experience should be convinced. Swinburne answers this with a second ground, the Principle of Testimony (PT). He assumes that 'other people normally tell the truth'; in which case 'the experiences of others are (probably) as they report them'.[11] By combining both principles, we find that it is rational that 'other things being equal, we think that what others tell us that they perceived, probably happened'.[12] If you think this is a little too straightforward, perhaps that illustrates the difference between those more of an analytic orientation than a hermeneutical orientation (recalling the distinction between 'APA' and 'AAR' styles illustrated in Chapter 2). What about someone who is honest but tends to get the wrong end of the stick? I'm sure you know someone like that. Take my female colleague and the 'figure' (see last chapter). If she, in all honesty, reported my boss for making an inappropriate comment about my body, should we apply the PC and PT? I think we can see here what happens when the emphasis is on experience as what is *perceived* – and people do rarely hallucinate, and don't lie too often. When the emphasis is on experience as what is interpreted, the PC and the PT become a little more complex to apply. Too much has to be shovelled in under 'other things being equal'.

Swinburne's principles have had a mixed reception. Among those who do not accept the PC and PT is Rowe, but for non-hermeneutical reasons. Rowe objects that God seems not to be experienced in any predictable way, and therefore the PC is not a rational foundation for belief. Gutting agrees that the PC is prima facie evidence for claims about existence, but that Swinburne misrepresents the strength of that case.[13] Davis argues that some basic principle of rationality like the PC must underpin any successful argument from religious experience.[14] There cannot be inductive justification for trusting our reasoning or memories or other people's reports, but we could not cope without trusting all of these.[15]

Others have taken up Swinburne's PC, and set out to improve or modify it. Yandell has a more elaborate form for his foundational principle and concludes that there are experiences which meet his criteria, and that therefore there is evidence that God exists.

Yandell's procedure for judging religious experiences as evidence

For any subject S and experience E, if S's having E is a matter of its (phenomenologically) seeming to S that S experiences a numinous being N, then if S non-culpably has no reason to think that:

(i) S would seem to experience N whether or not there is an N that S experiences, or

(ii) if E is non-veridical, S could not discover that it was, or

(iii) if E is of a type T of experience such that every member of T is non-veridical, S could not discover this fact,

then E provides S evidence that there is an N, provided that

(iv) 'O exists' (where O is an omniscient, omnipotent, omnibenevolent God) falls within the scope of both collegial and lateral disconfirmation.[16]

If a religious experience clears these hurdles, it must also meet the following demands. There must be no good reason for doubting that the person is capable of distinguishing a veridical experience from a non-veridical one, and there must be some possibility of ruling out the existence of the apparent object of experience, should it not exist. If people have numinous experiences under conditions that satisfy all of Yandell's conditions, then there is experiential evidence that God exists.

Gellman has his own modification of Swinburne's PC with an argument which he titles with the busy acronym BEE: for Best Explanation of Experience, but which also comes with a STING in its tail: Strength in Number Greatness.[17]

> If a person, S, has an experience, E, which seems (phenomenally) to be of a particular object, O (or of an object of kind, K), then *everything else being equal* the best explanation of S's having E is that S has experienced O (or object of kind, K), rather than something else or nothing at all.[18]

Gellman, like Swinburne, claims that BEE is a principle of rationality which people use continually and cannot do without, and as such does not require proof. Gellman's 'STING' is used to support the argument that the more people have such experiences, the stronger the case for its veridicality.[19] Together BEE and STING, Gellman claims, can ground specific claims about God. For example, if many people experience God as loving, it is rational to believe that this is a true description of God.[20]

These arguments are clever and well thought-out, with their reasoned accounts of how we operate in other areas where independent proof is not possible, pointing out that other kinds of experience which are generally considered reliable (sense experience, memory and the like) also rely on their own selves to provide grounds and justification for their claims. This is a very valuable critique. But not everyone is persuaded that something that we find works in everyday life in this world can be equally applied to an allegedly transcendent God, which cannot be universally perceived. An atheist faced with Gellman's Best Explanation of an Experience is not going to accept that a religious explanation will be the best; they would prefer any other account, no matter however improbable or indeed implausible. Not so much a BEE as a WEE, sad to say.

Even from a comparatively neutral point of view there are many reasons why accepting religious experience is more problematic and controversial than sight, smell or memory.

Even if Yandell's argument were accepted by sceptics, they would assert that all experiences of purported numinous beings are either a type of experience that is always non-veridical (iii), or an experience such that if it were non-veridical, one could not know it (ii), and indeed that the person would have that experience whether or not the being existed (i) – since the being doesn't. Yandell could retort that the critic must provide evidence for their assertion that all religious experience comes under (i), (ii) or (iii); following Yandell's account above.

When the sceptic insists that religious experiences are by their nature non-veridical, proving this results in the same sort of circularity: ultimately the decision to accept or not is based on their respective basic beliefs. We are at the very impasse the argument from religious experience has been trying to evade, that is, having nothing to ground an argument on but belief. The dog is chasing his tail again.

Weaknesses of the argument

There remains a body of objections to taking religious experience seriously as a source of knowledge, despite the cases put forward by Swinburne, Davis, Yandell and Gellman.

How reliable a witness is necessary?

We looked at the question of naturalistic explanations for religious experience, which many cite as the reason for rejecting claims using it as evidence. Now we need to consider defences against this objection.

One challenge arises from the claim that religious experiences are not distinguished from psychotic experiences. Davis observes, however, that religious communities themselves usually make a distinction between healthy and unhealthy mystical or other religious experiences. Although there may be no 'intrinsic' differences, if that means that there is a background knowledge that can be consulted to be sure that the way things seem to them is not the way things really are, the same will be true of vivid sensory hallucinations. We cannot step outside, as it were, of a hallucination in order to verify or falsify the perception, but that does not show that all sense experiences are to be understood as hallucinatory. To insist that the experiences themselves must carry some mark of their veridicality would be to impose far harsher conditions on religious experience than on non-religious perceptual experiences.[21]

Second, it appears that many people who have religious experiences cannot be considered pathological by the usual psychiatric categories. We may assume, however, that when dealing with a case which can be certified as pathological, the experience may discounted. Gellman surprisingly disagrees that such experiences must be dismissed out of hand. He adds that although the weight given to such the pathological experiences is weak, it nevertheless still might have some evidential value. Indeed, he argues it is not only that a pathological condition may make someone more likely to *think* they experience God, but may also make it more likely for this to actually happen. Such people may actually have a heightened sensitivity with an increased openness to extraordinary experiences and they may also feel a greater need to experience God.[22]

What weight do reports of 'absence' have?

While there is a good percentage of people reporting religious experiences, there are others who report an absence of any religious feeling or experience. Indeed, some say they have actively tried to have an experience of God but have not succeeded. Is this evidence against the existence of a God? Among those who think it is, Michael Martin has argued that the absence of a chair is good evidence for there being no chair in the room.[23] Bertrand Russell objects that not only do some fail to experience God even when they try; but that even to suggest the attempt makes questionable demands on the observer:

> The man of science, when he wishes others to see what he has seen,

> arranges his microscope or telescope; that is to say, he makes changes in the external world, but demands of the observer only normal eyesight. The mystic, on the other hand, demands changes in the observer, by fasting, by breathing exercises, and by a careful abstention from external observation.[24]

The arguments based on absence as proof have been countered in various ways. An analogy can be made with aesthetic experiences. I may experience rapture while listening to Wagner's *Parsifal*, but if you are tone-deaf and musically ill-educated, you will not. Does that mean I am hallucinating the aural perceptions, or my delight is illusory? Even sense-experiences which are in principle in the public domain and should be available to all may not be experienced by others, or reported as producing the same kind of experience. Many differences can be attributed to different abilities, capacities or education in the person concerned. It does not necessarily follow that all of the features of the experience (or absence of experience) can be ascribed to the 'object' failing to convey them. Since this is the case with ordinary experience, the variation for religious especially can be seen as no more problematic.

It can also be argued that reports of presence and reports of absence cannot be given the same weight, nor do they have the same implications for the existence of what is in question. As an illustration, take an imaginary incident in Hawaii. Kia'i reports that he did not see a dolphin on Tuesday afternoon when he was surfing at the North Shore of the island of O'ahu, although Hoku claimed he had seen dolphins there the day before. Do we know for certain that there were no dolphins in the ocean off Waimea Beach when Kia'i was there? (They are not always easy to spot.) Furthermore, if we did feel certain of their absence on Tuesday, would we be justified in claiming that this should be taken as evidence that dolphins are as mythical as unicorns?

When we are dealing with what is elusive in nature or hard for us to perceive, we would tend to give different weight to reports of absence than to those of presence. Gellman sees a difference between observing the absence of something and trying but failing to observe the presence of something; sometimes these two are effectively the same, but not always.[25] To know for certain that something is absent, we need enough information and past experience to know what constitutes 'thoroughly searching' for that particular kind of entity. In Gellman's view, we do not have enough knowledge to say when or whether someone has failed to experience God, or someone has experienced God's absence.[26]

We cannot always extend the claim of absence of something to a claim of non-existence; moreover, we cannot always extend the claim of its non-existence here and now to the claim that no such thing exists anywhere. Martin claims that not experiencing a chair in the room justifies him claiming that there is no chair. He does not I presume mean to claim that evidence for there being no chair in a given room at a given time is reason to believe that chairs do not exist anywhere, at any time. The more appropriate analogy would be this: we could say that there was evidence for the absence of God to a certain person at a certain time. This is not grounds for a sweeping negative conclusion that therefore God does not exist or cannot be experienced by another person at another time.[27]

Sceptics like Martin can, however, retaliate by saying that because God is held to be 'omnipresent' according to the believer, God must always be 'there', wherever and whenever, to be experienced. But few believers would hold this view of omnipresence; rather they may feel that there may be a number of reasons why someone does not have an experience of God. God's freedom or sovereignty might be mentioned on the one side, and problems to do with the individual in question, such as the degree of openness to the experience, on the other.

It also could be argued that there is no more problem in claiming that God is present but not experienced, than saying that there is a wireless internet connection available in the room, but I cannot download my email without the right card in my laptop. Not everyone who has an experience of God's absence concludes from this that God does not exist. Believers themselves report the experience of God as absent or hidden, and this is a theme found in Christian mystical literature where God's felt absence may be seen as a crucial phase in the mystic's journey to God.[28]

When reports conflict, are they ruled out as evidence?

Flew, among others, has maintained that religious experience can provide no support or evidence for religious belief on the grounds that what or who is allegedly experienced varies so much that the testimony is in conflict and therefore unreliable.[29] Believers who want to claim some evidential value must, it would seem, rule out all experiences of conflicting theologies, on some such basis as their being misguided or fallacious. A second challenge to them is to say how such fallacious experiences can arise. If this is done, the same form of negative analysis could equally be applied to experiences in their own tradition, which Flew presumes they would want to avoid. If believers want to stick to the possibility of different religions having equally valid experiences, they must show some way of reconciling the diverse religious experiences without weakening their evidential value.

Various arguments have been deployed against his challenge. One is to point out that differences in testimony do not necessitate that some must be right and others wrong; still less that *all* must be wrong. There are conflicts in scientific testimony, as when there is agreement about the existence of something but not as to what its nature is. Alston draws on this kind of analogy with scientific discovery. It is not clear that the different revelations are incompatible, he suggests; for one thing, it is not clear what degree of diversity can be included in the divine nature. The fact that there are conflicts in beliefs does not mean that both believers cannot be rational, even if one is wrong. It can be rational to believe something incorrect, if the limited evidence one has points in that direction. Sceptics often point to an unfavourable contrast between the diversity of religious opinions and scientific unanimity. However, Alston observes, there was no such unanimity in science 300 years ago and religion is in a position comparable to that of science several centuries ago. Perhaps now with increased communication, and awareness of and dialogue between religions, we are working towards a common understanding in religion too.[30] These reflections, though they may help extend the debate, seem insufficient to deal with the issues involved. It may be only Anglo-Saxon analytic philosophers who would be consoled by the suggestion that, although wrong, they are 'rational' in their error. Another way to cope with this challenge is the Hickean, interpretation-oriented explanation considered in the previous chapter.

Swinburne advocates an 'ascent to generality'. Specific conflicts between religious claims are just that: conflicts between *specific* descriptions of the religious object which do not support a scepticism about all claims based on religious experience.[31] The conflicts can be avoided by avoiding the detail, he suggests, reducing the claim, and rising to a sufficiently general level of discussion so that conflicts do not appear. This may be a useful process for avoiding disputes in personal interfaith dialogues, but it does not resolve the philosophical problem of whether the contrasting claims from different religious traditions can all be accepted as true.

Davis says that while different types of numinous and mystical experience cannot all be reduced to 'the same type of experience with differing interpretations', a complex reconciliation of mystical and numinous experiences is still possible. She argues that most alleged conflict among mystical experience is superficial, and a less superficial reading indicates that mystics essentially have the sort of experience which she describes as 'freedom from all sense of time, space, personal identity, and multiplicity, which leaves them with a blissful, "naked awareness" of perfect unity and a sense that "this is it", the ultimate level of reality'.[32] She points out that religious traditions within themselves allow for diversity of experience, and that the major religions have theories which reconcile the apparently incompatible experiences within one system. Therefore it is possible to distil a 'common core' to these experiences.[33] One imagines therefore that the defence is: the core, most important parts of the different testimonies agree, and they differ on the trivial details.

(Are the core parts of the experience necessarily the most important though?)

Gellman provides several arguments on diversity. He denies that most experiences amount to propositions about God which conflict with other people's propositions; instead most experiences of God pertain to that person alone, rather than being generalized 'truths'. Even where the content of the experience is propositional and in conflict with another experience which also contains a proposition, this does not necessarily rule out that it was God who was experienced by both. The incompatibility could be put down to 'local differences' in the two perceptions.[34] Other possibilities are that one person may have misunderstood, or truly experienced God's presence but only imagined what the revelation was. This type of event can happen often enough between human beings without reducing our sense that our reports of encounters with others are generally reliable.[35] He would also allow the incompatibility to originate from God, who may wish one person to believe one thing and another person something else. Further, all conflicts are not between religions; differences in experience and testimony arise principally within the religious traditions. He thinks it is harder to make the incompatibility argument work than we might think. Experiencing God as 'loving' or as 'just' might not be the same claim, but they are not logically incompatible, and it is not necessary to conclude that both cannot be true. Experiences are only incompatible if the claims are that God's nature is *exclusively* one kind, and a claim of something different is logically incompatible with the first.[36]

Gellman's answer to the dilemma posed by 'multiple theisms' is to see 'networks' of experiential knowledge about God, which build up over time and gradually diverge.[37] There will of course be differences between one network or set and another, but these differences exist in a larger context of similar experiences of God. 'The situation here no more bars the identification of God from one member of a network set to another than it does with respect to varied richly endowed ways of identifying a single human person.'[38]

A number of these responses attempt to unify religions as all ultimately worshipping the same God though variously perceived. But this overlooks the important fact that some religions do not believe in a God, or do not conceive of Ultimate Reality as being personal. Gellman gets around this by asserting that God exists in inexhaustible fullness, a plenitude which can never be encompassed in a single experience or aspect. For him, even being 'personal' is limiting. Accepting Buber's idea that God is personal and enters into a personal relationship with us, but that the concept of personhood is utterly incapable of describing the nature of God, Gellman suggests that God could be experienced either as personal or impersonal without entailing a real contradiction.[39]

Are confirmation and falsification possible?

One objection made to taking religious experiences for evidence is seeing insurmountable difficulties in confirming or falsifying them and what they are meant to prove. Based on the idea that seeming to have an experience which has the nature of 'being of something' does not entail that that thing exists, Flew rejects drawing inferences from religious experience, 'considered as a purely psychological phenomenon, to conclusions about the supposed objective religious truths'.[40] If Flew means a dramatic conversion experience would not justify me in trying to change your behaviour, he has a point. But if he means I cannot draw inferences from my own experience, that's another matter. It is not difficult to counter this if a 'purely psychological phenomenon' means one's perceptual experience. By his standard, I wouldn't be able to draw any inferences about objects in the world from the fact that I perceive them. And yet I make this sort of assumption continually, and could hardly write this book without doing so.

But the questions of the sceptic cannot be so easily dispatched. If challenged on my sense perceptions, I can call in another witness. Or if the evidence of my eyes is in question, I can test other modes of sense perception. These allow for a degree of 'checking' and confirmation that are difficult, if not impossible, to obtain in spiritual experiences. Neither of these options is generally thought to be possible with God. Russell complains:

> When a man of science tells us the result of an experiment, he also tells us how the experiment was performed; others can repeat it, and if the result is not confirmed it is not accepted as true; but many men might put themselves into the situation in which the mystic's vision occurred without obtaining the same revelation. . . . Science depends upon perception and inference; its credibility is due to the fact that the perceptions are such as any observer can test. The mystic himself may be certain that he knows, and has no need of scientific tests; but those who are asked to accept his testimony will subject it to the same kind of scientific tests as those applied to men who say they have been to the North Pole.[41]

A wider look at science shows, however, that not all empirical data that is held to be reliable results from experiments under the control of scientists. Vulcanologists cannot call up a second eruption to double-check results, and many aspects of the climate and the natural world are also one-off, as might be the Big Bang. In many scientific situations, data are more likely to be built up analogous to a 'cumulative case'.

Sensory perceptions are often confirmed or falsified in a second manner: if no-one is available to corroborate my perception, I can check again on a later occasion to see if the experience recurs. When I become familiar with the situation, I can even make predictions as to future recurrences. Religious believers are generally reluctant, however, to make predictions about how and why God will or must appear, and the few who do are usually embarrassed by the failure of God to live up to their predictions. On the other hand, many people after having a religious experience for the first time, go on to have more. They tend to form their own purely personal 'cumulative case' for the believer.

There are in various disciplines, like a particular science, accepted standards of what counts as confirmation or falsification of a theory. Religious believers are often charged by sceptics with refusing to let anything falsify or count against their religious beliefs. So for example, the sceptic complains, if someone predicts that God will appear on a certain date, and this does not happen, most would-be prophets claim that they had just miscalculated the date and they start over again, rather than concluding that God doesn't exist after all. If there is no agreed basis for evaluating evidence as true (confirmed) or false, there can then be no basis for adjudicating experiences in the case of God. If we don't know what makes religious experiences delusory, Rowe argues that no experiences can count as evidence.[42]

Some attempts at showing that falsification is possible

Supporters of the evidential value of religious experience have responded with providing lists of criteria or conditions which could challenge the veridicality of a given religious experience. These do not claim global falsification of the validity or veridicality of all religious experience; but aim at means that will identify spurious or deluded experiences. This is done precisely to safeguard the evidential value of other experiences.

Davis, developing Swinburne's 'special considerations', lists numerous 'challenges' that can be made with respect to the description, the subject or the object of the experience.[43]

'Description-related challenges' include obvious logical inconsistencies or incoherence, conflicts with background knowledge, or faults in beliefs taken to be background knowledge, such as claims to see an animal now extinct, or conflicts between the subject's actual and expected behaviour if they had had the experience, evidence that the subject is a habitual liar or prone to exaggeration, or has a poor memory, or is not competent in terminology used,[44] *or is retrospectively interpreting the experience in an inappropriate way.*

Subject-related challenges include a past unreliability of the subject, or that the subject was in a certain state such that experiences under those conditions usually are unveridical, or that the subject was likely to have had that experience whether the percept was there or not, or the subject hasn't had the training necessary for that type of experience.

Object-related challenges include conflicts with the background evidence: that against the background evidence, it is probable that the alleged object of the experience was not present, or if present was not the cause of the experience, or that it is highly unlikely the percept was there as described.

Yandell also allows that there are situations which could disqualify a given religious experience as worthy of being taken as evidence; but he disputes that this fact disqualifies religious experience as a whole. (In fact, by throwing a scrap of falsifiability to the ravening sceptic, he is probably safeguarding the evidential value of religious experience.) First, if there are conditions that make it possible to have delusory experiences of a numinous being, if one were in such a condition, one could know it, then one could know that it would call into question the veridicality of that experience.[45] One can know that an experience is non-veridical, he maintains against the sceptic's complaint, if an anti-theistic argument succeeds, or if the 'putative information content' of an experience conflicted 'with the information content of most others in a context in which there was no good reason to overturn the majority testimony'.[46] Specifically, numinous monotheistic religious experience could be shown to be non-veridical if any of the following were true: if an appeal to evil disproves theism; if there is a contradiction in the concept of a numinous being; if some other contradicting variety of religious experience shows that numinous monotheistic experience is non-veridical; or if some purely secular explanation is shown to be sufficient in a way that rules out causation by anything numinous.[47]

Yandell distinguishes between 'polar', 'collegial' and 'lateral' forms of confirmation or falsification. 'Polar' disconfirmation is a situation in which not experiencing God could be counted as evidence against God's existence.[48] Yandell argues that this kind of disconfirmation is nonsensical in relation to an omnipotent, omniscient God, who presumably has the choice of being experienced or not.[49] 'Lateral' disconfirmation occurs if something very like the Object has a quality which contradicts qualities the Object ought to have.

Thus, if one had an experience of an omniscient, omnipotent, awesome being who was horrid and evil, this could count as experiential evidence against the proposition that an omniscient, omnipotent, awesome and all-good and holy being exists.[50] 'Collegial' disconfirmation occurs if it is logically possible for an experience to take place which would provide evidence of O lacks A, e.g. God exists but is not holy. Where it is logically necessary that O has A, and an experience takes place that contradicts that notion, one has collegial disconfirmation. (Where, for example, one experiences something very like O but lacking A, like an evil omnipotent being that one cannot call God.)

Yandell claims that, while the theist must surrender polar disconfirmation in the case of God, one can conjoin the other two. One could then construct possible disconfirming experiences, such as: 'What I thought was God turned out not to be holy. This putative-God is omnipotent, and if so then there cannot be a real omnipotent God that is holy. (This assumes, as monotheists mostly assert, that there cannot be two omnipotent beings.) Putative-God has some of the properties of God, but lacks a property God must have, and it is not likely that there be two beings with the properties that God has.'[51] If Yandell is right, then the believer in religious experience could allow for the possibility of disconfirmation in a manner that is not self-contradictory or absurd.

Are there other criteria for validation?

Attempts have also been made to supply criteria for confirming the validity or veridicality of religious experiences, which is a more challenging effort. Gutting argues that we would expect, if there was 'a very good and very powerful being concerned about us', that those who have had those experiences would have them again; further that others would have similar experiences; and that those who have them would be empowered to lead better lives. All three of these conditions he sees fulfilled; so religious experiences of God's presence can be taken to establish God's existence. 'The experiences themselves give prima facie warrant to the claim that he exists, and the fulfilment of the expectations induced by the assumption that the experiences are veridical provides the further support needed for ultimate warrant.'[52]

A Sufi story

One danger is that the seeker may unknowingly perform [prayer] with the intention of gaining prestige, visions, or other experiences. There is also a risk of misinterpreting one's experiences and imagining oneself to have attained to some advanced degree of sanctity or gnosis. Najm al-Dīn Rāzī . . . tells of a disciple who fancied that he had been blessed with some tremendous vision of light. When he told his spiritual instructor, the latter told him: 'You immature man, that was the light of your ritual ablution!'[53]

Davis notes that four criteria for genuine versus delusive mystical experiences exist in several different religious traditions: internal and external consistency; the moral and spiritual 'fruits' or consequences of the experience; consistency with orthodox doctrine of the religious tradition in question; and the evaluation of the subject's general psychological and mental condition. In addition, she points out that there are many criteria other than sense perception which we use to assess things of undisputed reality and importance: among these are 'other people's emotions and character, causality, the passage of time, and the meaning of words and signs'.[54] Foreshadowing Alston's later work, Davis calls for an argument which does not treat religious experience as analogous to some other kind of experience less controversial, but rather 'as one type of perceptual experience among others'.[55]

Yandell claims that a degree of corroboration is possible with religious experience by comparing descriptions of experiences in different times and places, cultures and religious traditions. This is similar to the useful comparisons made, for example when testing an astronomical theory against past records of astronomical events in different historical cultures.[56] Allowing for different metaphors and symbols, Yandell still finds 'considerable agreement' between those from different cultures, places and times. This diversity of confirming evidence, in his view, supports the claims of religious experience against the charges that it cannot be corroborated by other persons or the other senses of the subject in the way that seeing a visible object can.[57]

Alston argues that it is rational to engage in Christian doxastic practice not because it is analogous to sensory doxastic practice, but because it is socially established, and there is insufficient reason to think it unreliable. Alston would also argue that the exponent of the rationality of religious doxastic practice, however, could provide other modes of religious 'input' to test the 'output' of a religious experience; indeed, the traditions of discernment in the long-established religions are teeming with ways of testing one's outputs against other people's, and the tradition. Thus the doxastic practice based on religious experience could be confirmed by other kinds of religious doxastic practice, in the way that visual doxastic practice can be confirmed by auditory doxastic practice.

If we accept Alston's view that his argument is not really an analogy, his argument is not demolished by finding ways that the two doxastic practices differ any more than finding important differences between swimming and rugby undermine the claim of both to be classified as a sport. I am not convinced however that his argument doesn't, in the end, appeal intuitively (if not explicitly) to our natural affinities for analogical reasoning. To describe religious doxastic practice as 'socially established' is a little euphemistic given how controversial it is, and how potentially dangerous, for that matter. Whose religious experience are we going to consider reliable and socially established? Men of war as well as women of peace?

But this raises the question of what differences would make a difference in accepting the analogy or claim to parity. It is the nature of analogy to break down at some point; how do we tell which differences are crucial to making the analogy applicable? When we are dealing with questions of 'parity' or 'analogy' as evidence, we need agreed conditions on how much similarity is required, how much dissimilarity tolerated. Analogical language, however, is not capable of such stringency, nor can 'parity' be supported by a list of conclusive criteria. Both of these rely on their power to convince when used in argument, and therefore properly belong not to logic but to rhetoric. This means that with a determined sceptic an argument based on an analogy or parity will fail, whatever its merits or insights. But when this happens, it follows also that the sceptic's rejection of the analogy and parity is not based on rational grounds and alleged failures of logic.

In other words, whether we are talking about the sceptic's case or the arguments themselves, we are not really talking about solidly logical procedures and arguments. Whatever the sleek structure that proponents have tried to create, we are really talking about persuasion, urging people to see experience in a certain light. In other words, we are talking about a process that has two moments often overlooked: interpretation and rhetoric.

Religious knowledge as disclosure and manifestation

There is something a little bit ironic about all this, because throughout human history religious experience has often been seen as *opposed* to logic and proof. Here it has been captured by the philosophers and pressed into service – some would say against its nature.

Another striking feature about this kind of discussion is the way that knowledge of God through religious experience is treated as if it is inferential; a conclusion one draws from experience by deductive or inductive moves, and which require the usual sorts of justification and warrant. Meanwhile, knowledge of God by experience has most often been treated by the religious traditions as direct, not indirect or inferred.

The Sufi Rūmī maintained that in addition to scholastic or scientific knowledge, there is also another kind of knowledge, which he called variously knowledge gained through spiritual realization, knowledge of the real and Eternal existence, or knowledge of real religion. For Rūmī it was not necessarily completely different in content from what one could learn from reading philosophical theology or studying ontology. But he called people who did the latter 'imitators', because they imitated the words without a real awareness of their profound meanings.[58]

Before you dismiss this with the assumption that it is just mysticism that has nothing to do with what this book should be about, stop and reflect that in some traditions, such as many schools of Hinduism and Buddhism or the Islamic school of *'irfān*, the two are not necessarily opposed.

The relation of philosophy to mysticism: theoretical *'irfān*

Muṭahharī explains:

> *Theoretical* 'irfān *. . . is concerned with ontology and discusses God, the world and the human being. This aspect of* 'irfān *resembles theological philosophy, which also seeks to describe being. Like theological philosophy,* 'irfān *defines its subject, essential principles and problems, but whereas philosophy relies solely on rational principles of its arguments,* 'irfān *bases its deductions of principles discovered through mystic experience and then reverts to the language of reason to explain them.*
>
> *The rationalistic deductions of philosophy can be likened to studying a passage written originally in the same language; the arguments of* 'irfān*, on the other hand, are like studying something that has been translated from some other language. To be more precise, the* 'ārif *[practitioner of* 'irfān*] wishes to explain those things that he claims to have witnessed with his heart and his entire being by using the language of reason.*[59]

As I wrote in an earlier work, Muṭahharī's account of theoretical *'irfān*, as my account above also intended, suggests that in one's reflection on religious issues, one can move back and forth between a 'philosophical' moment of analysis and an existential moment of one's experience and action,[60] or between the 'language of reason' and 'mystic experience' as Muṭahharī calls them.

Al-Ghazālī, whom you have met many times in these pages, moved from a life of scholastic reflection to a life of spirituality and prayer. In his book of guidance on meditation, he wrote:

> The fruits of meditation, then, consist of varieties of knowledge, states and actions. The fruit specific to each, however, is nothing other than a form of knowledge. When knowledge is acquired within the heart, the state of the heart is altered. When the heart's state changes, the actions of the bodily members change. Thus action follows spiritual state, states follow knowledge, and knowledge follows meditation. Meditation is therefore the beginning of and the key to all action.[61]

In other words, even when he is talking about the mystical practice of meditation, al-Ghazālī is in no doubt that what he is engaged with is *knowledge*, not mere 'faith'. (And, moreover, it should lead to *action*.) Clearly a particular understanding of knowledge is required in order to make sense of this. Much of the discussion of religious experience in Western analytic philosophy seems to see religious experience as analogous to sensory perception. We perceive a tree in a sensory experience; we perceive God in a religious experience. But perhaps the picture of knowledge as deriving from perception, especially sensory perception, is not the best for our purposes. It raises in a heightened form the particular problems we have seen in this chapter.

Allāma As-Ṣadr's theory of knowledge is that it has the quality of 'disclosure'.[62] Knowledge 'is revelatory of what lies beyond its specific mental limits'. We do not construct what we see and know; it is shown to us, given to us. Realism essentially rests on the acceptance of 'essential disclosure' – that the world is real, exists outside our minds and perceptions, and that it is given to us in knowledge.[63] '. . . Knowledge of the assent type is that which discloses to us the objectivity of our conception and the existence of an objective reality of the concept present in our minds.'[64] Ṣadr is speaking here of ordinary knowledge, knowledge given by the senses of the material world. However, the model of 'disclosure', rather than sensory perception, can be adapted for knowledge of what is not empirical, which arguably displays even more the quality of 'disclosure'.

Ṭabāṭabā'ī's image of immediate, intuitive knowledge he calls 'knowledge by presence'; it is the way God and we know ourselves. (Both Ṣadr and Ṭabāṭabā'ī, interestingly, are rather dismissive of Kantian epistemologies that overstate the element of human construction of knowledge, and the idea that we can't really know things as they are in themselves.) Again, this can suggest a model of knowledge which might be fruitful for our purposes. The emphasis is not on sensory organs or the reliability and credibility of the perceiver, but the power of reality or the Other to disclose.

This view claims that reality, material or personal, does truly disclose itself to us in knowledge. Our reception is the hermeneutical moment, the act of interpretation that receives knowledge – as an active reception and appropriation that neither distorts what is disclosed, nor receives it passively and uncritically like data being written onto a CD. It involves judgement and assent, along with the many aspects of interpretation discussed in the previous chapter. Our reception is neither unquestionably reliable, nor inescapably subjectivist.

This may be well and good, but how can you put forward your own personal experience as a source for someone else's knowledge? This is really the nugget of the problem for arguments from religious experience, whatever their individual strengths or weaknesses. For all the care they take over their propositions and inferential moves, the real question is: what does someone else's experience have to do with me?

Here perhaps we can take a leaf from Johann Georg Hamann's book. In writing about the role of the senses in the face of Cartesian scepticism, he gives this verdict: 'We cannot dispense with these witnesses for ourselves, but can refute no one with their agreement.'[65] In other words, our own experiences (sensory or spiritual) have a testimony for us that we cannot do without. At the same time, what they cannot do is to convince someone else – unless that someone trusts us and our judgement. *Pace* Swinburne, perhaps an understanding 'testimony', even as a source of knowledge, is not most at home in the context of 'proof'. Is there an important distinction then to be made between what we might call 'testimony' and 'proof' or 'argument'?

Testimony vs. proof?

Al-Ghazālī, who was critical of the 'proofs' of the existence of God, nevertheless put forward something apparently similar in his book on meditation. He exhorts us to regard the spider – who could have made something so wondrous? Is it not testimony to its Omniscient Maker?[66] *It is not proof, but testimony.*

For the gentle of spirit, 'argument' and 'proof' can be epistemically coercive. It compels agreement; only a stubborn irrationalist would hold out against it. That, of course, is traditionally seen as its strength in philosophy. Testimony, on the other hand, leaves the door open, and allows the listener to construct their own interpretation of your experience, and to form their own judgement. Testimony invites that response of assent present in Ṣadr's epistemology. Philosophically speaking, it allows people that epistemic freedom and scope. Religiously, why would you want your own experiences to be the ground of someone else's knowledge or faith? Isn't it better to leave them the space to have their own experiences and reach their own subsequent conclusions than to consent to your verdicts?

In the chapter on language we saw that some of the Indian traditions insist on the importance of testimony as a pramāṇa, a source of knowledge, as part of their epistemology. Different schools took different stances on whether or not testimony was a valid source of knowledge. Conditions were laid down for the reliability of the witness (which could include scripture). But although there have been centuries of discussion of this dimension of epistemology in India, it has only just begun in the West, and those who are interested in Swinburne's Principles should look East and see what can be learned by those who have investigated the lures and traps of interpersonal epistemologies. For while Swinburne's principles of credulity and testimony are an attempt to abstract and generalize, testimony as it is used here is an individual, case-by-case judgement based on a relationship of trust in another.

In the chapter on religious language, we considered the claim that relationships and the idea of a community and its traditions are supportive of understanding religious language and its meaning. The same could be said of religious experience, even though mystical experience seems to be a highly 'individualized' part of life. Yet those traditions in which it is inculcated have always maintained the need for an expert soul friend to assist in interpretation. Looking through the other end of the telescope, the difficulty of convincing someone else is not so much an epistemic problem, as the indispensable antidote to the excessive ease of convincing oneself. It is a good thing, in short, a necessary corrective, that we cannot always easily convince someone else of the veridicality of our experience and our interpretation of it. For that task, relationships and being rooted in a community and its traditions are the solution for our own lacks. Hamann tells us that our very lack make us all the more able to enjoy nature through experiences and to enjoy community with our people through traditions. Our reason arises from this twofold lesson of sensuous revelations and human testimonies, he claims.[67] So this approach is not opposed to philosophy and reason, but claims that they are best understood for what they are, and viewed in a particular matrix: the web of relationships that make up a community and its traditions of faith and philosophy.

From Tariq Ramadan:

> A man once exclaimed to the mystic Rabia al-Adawiyya, 'I have discovered a thousand proofs of the existence of God!' She closed the conversation by saying that she had only one proof and that was enough for her. 'Which?' he asked. 'If you are alone in the desert and you fall down a well, to whom will you turn?' 'To God,' he said. 'That proof is enough for me!' A strange reply, seemingly simple, even simplistic, that a rationalist or atheist would without hesitation take as confirmation of what he had always believed: 'God is the refuge of the destitute, the hope of the hopeless, a consolation, a reassuring invention!'
>
> *On the surface, on the surface only* . . . suffering and the unknown seem to press the mind to look for a refuge, a consolation. This is the logic our reason proposes when it looks on the human being on the outside of its nature. The Islamic tradition says exactly the opposite: the ordeals of life, sadness, encountering the death of those we love, for example, take the human being back to its most natural state, to its most essential longing. Consciousness of limitation brings it back to the need for the Transcendent, to the need for meaning. To call on God

is not to console oneself – it is to rediscover the condition God originally wanted for us – the spark of humility, the awareness of fragility.

Before your eyes is a child . . . life, dependence, fragility, innocence. To be with God is to know how to keep this state: a humble acceptance of your fragility, a comprehension of your dependence – going back to the beginning. In fact, the temptation to pride consists in thinking that man can cut himself off from his nature and attain total intellectual autonomy to the point where he can take on his own suffering, deliberately and alone. Pride is to affirm outward independence by maintaining the illusion of liberty at the heart of one's being. Humility is to rediscover the breath of the primordial need of Him at the heart of our being, in order to live in total outward independence.[68]

Draw your own conclusions

Does your own religious experience or lack of any religious experiences predispose you to accept/reject them as evidence?

Is believing someone's transcendental experience more difficult than believing a physical experience someone has had? Why?

Think of a highly questionable experience someone has reported to you (or you have had) and think of one you are inclined to believe. What are the differences between them? Which features inclined you to doubt one and trust the other?

Take the example of some highly personal kind of experience – falling in love, or having an orgasm are two powerful examples. Reflect on the objections that have been made to crediting religious experience made by critics such as Russell and Flew. How does your example fare under the same criteria?

Are there plausible ways to either verify or falsify a religious experience? What is it exactly that you are verifying or falsifying?

Does what you get from an experience count as *knowledge*? Why or why not? What are the criteria for *knowledge* that you are using?

Is such experience essentially private and incommunicable – or does it become easier to understand when you have communicated it to someone who is knowledgeable and experienced?

Further reading

Alston, W. P. (1991) *Perceiving God: The Epistemology of Religious Experience*, Ithaca, NY, Cornell University Press

Davis, C. F. (1989) *The Evidential Force of Religious Experience*, Oxford, Clarendon Press

Flew, A. (1974) *God and Philosophy*, London, Hutchinson

Gellman, J. (1997) *Experience of God and the Rationality of Theistic Belief*, Cornell Studies in the Philosophy of Religion, Ithaca and London, Cornell University Press

Griffith-Dickson, G. (2000) *Human and Divine: An Introduction to the Philosophy of Religious Experience*, London, Duckworth

Martin, M. (1990) *Atheism: A Philosophical Justification*, Philadelphia, Temple University Press

Mitchell, B. (1981) *The Justification of Religious Belief*, New York, Oxford University Press

Swinburne, R. (1979) *The Existence of God*, Oxford, Clarendon Press

Yandell, K. (1993) *The Epistemology of Religious Experience*, Cambridge, Cambridge University Press

Notes

1 M. S. Ṣadrā (2004) *On the Hermeneutics of the Light Verse of the Qu'ran*, trans. L.-P. Peerwani, London, ICAS Press, p. 93.

2 W. P. Alston (1991) *Perceiving God: The Epistemology of Religious Experience*, Ithaca, NY, Cornell University Press. Alston is building on an idea from Wainwright: see ch. 3 of W. J. Wainwright (1981) *Mysticism*, Madison, Wis., University of Wisconsin Press.

3 'Doxa' means belief or opinion in Greek.

4 Alston, *Perceiving God*. Cf. pp. 42–50 for his rebuttal of reasons for rejecting mystical experience as a mode of perception, and ch. 5 for his refutation of objections to religious doxastic practice.

5 Alston, *Perceiving God*, p. 183.

6 B. Mitchell (1981) *The Justification of Religious Belief*, New York, Oxford University Press, p. 112.

7 R. Swinburne (1979) *The Existence of God*, Oxford, Clarendon Press, pp. 247f.

8 Swinburne, *The Existence of God*, p. 254.

9 Burhenn argues that Swinburne's position is only possible because of the more general critique of empiricism as theory of knowledge that has taken place since the mid-twentieth century. 'But if we reject that sort of foundationalism, then we are led to recognize that our whole picture of our world depends on our trusting many kinds of experience and also on our trusting the reports of others. Religious experience and reports about such experiences are among the items to which we must grant initial credibility since there are no valid general reasons for

rejecting the evidential value of this kind of experience'. H. Burhenn (1995) 'Philosophy and Religious Experience', in R. W. Hood Jr (ed.), *Handbook of Religious Experience*, Birmingham, AL, Religious Education Press, p. 154.

10 Swinburne, *The Existence of God*, p. 254.

11 Swinburne, *The Existence of God*, p. 272.

12 Swinburne, *The Existence of God*, p. 271.

13 G. Gutting (1982) *Religious Belief and Religious Skepticism*, Notre Dame, Ind., University of Notre Dame Press, p. 148. He provides a counterexample in supposing that he walks into his study and seems to see his recently deceased aunt. He seems to me to be right in judging that the PC should not warrant the acceptance of this experience as veridical; but wrong I think in using this to rebut Swinburne; it would seem to be overridden by Swinburne's third 'special consideration', 'that on background evidence it is probable that X was not present' (Swinburne, *The Existence of God*, p. 261). Gutting rules out the applicability of this third consideration, claiming that he knows 'nothing at all about the habits or powers of the dead, so I have no reason to think that my aunt could not now be in my study or, if present, could not be seen by me.' (Swinburne, *The Existence of God*, p. 148). I think Gutting claims too much ignorance of the habits of the dead.

14 C. F. Davis (1989) *The Evidential Force of Religious Experience*, Oxford, Clarendon Press, p. 93.

15 Davis, *The Evidential Force of Religious Experience*, p. 100.

16 K. Yandell (1993) *The Epistemology of Religious Experience*, Cambridge, Cambridge University Press, p. 274.

17 J. Gellman (1997) *Experience of God and the Rationality of Theistic Belief*, Cornell Studies in the Philosophy of Religion, Ithaca and London, Cornell University Press.

18 His version allows for another person more experienced than the subject of the event to interpret it authoritatively; he speaks of a 'best explanation' of an experience rather than speaking about what is 'probable' (which avoids the problems of calculating the 'probability' of God as a hypothesis). BEE only applies to what is phenomenally present, not to hunches or inner conviction. It creates a presumption for O's existence, thus is evidence; but it can be defeated by countervailing factors, so it does not speciously claim to be self-validating. Finally, the effect of saying 'everything else being equal' is to place the burden of proof on one who argues everything else is *not* equal. Gellman, *Experience of God and the Rationality of Theistic Belief*, p. 46.

19 Verbatim: 'If a person, S, has an experience, E, which seems (phenomenally) to be of a particular object, O (or of an object of kind, K), then our belief that S's having experienced O (or an object of kind K) is the best explanation (everything else being equal) of E, is strengthened in proportion to the number of purported experiences of O there are and in proportion to the variability of circumstances in which such experiences occur.' Gellman, *Experience of God and the Rationality of Theistic Belief*, pp. 52f.

20 'If a person, S, has an experience, E, in which it seems (phenomenally) that a particular object, O (or of an object of kind, K), has a property, P, then *everything else being equal*, the best explanation of S's having E is that S has (truly) experienced O (or an object of kind, K) possessing P.' Gellman, *Experience of God and the Rationality of Theistic Belief*, p. 54.

21 Davis, *The Evidential Force of Religious Experience*, p. 218.

22 Gellman, *Experience of God and the Rationality of Theistic Belief*, pp. 128–36; cf. also p. 133: 'We therefore conclude that in the various forms of it that we have considered, we have been given no reason to think that a person who is in a pathological condition and who seems to perceive God is not really perceiving God.'

23 M. Martin (1990) *Atheism: A Philosophical Justification*, Philadelphia, Temple University Press, p. 170, 'the negative principle of credulity'.

24 B. Russell (1935) *Religion and Science*, Oxford, Oxford University Press, p. 187.

25 Gellman, *Experience of God and the Rationality of Theistic Belief*, p. 59; on this point generally, see ch. 3, 'On Not Experiencing God', pp. 57–89.

26 Gellman, *Experience of God and the Rationality of Theistic Belief*, p. 63.

27 Davis argues similarly: 'Where the very existence of an entity is at issue, then, a failure to perceive it is not by itself *prima facie* evidence for its non-existence, whereas an experience of its *presence* is itself *prima facie* evidence for the entity's existence.' Davis, *The Evidential Force of Religious Experience*, p. 98.

28 For an interesting hands-on discussion of this experience, see the work of Ruth Burrows, e.g. R. Burrows (1976) *Guidelines for Mystical Prayer*, London, Sheed & Ward; or (1978) *To Believe in Jesus*, London, Sheed & Ward.

29 A. Flew (1974) *God and Philosophy*, London, Hutchinson.

30 W. P. Alston (1991) 'Is Religious Belief Rational?', in A. Loades and L. D. Rue (eds), *Contemporary Classics in Philosophy of Religion*, La Salle, Ill., Open Court, pp. 151f.; cf. also Alston, *Perceiving God*, p. 278.

31 Swinburne, *The Existence of God*, p. 266.

32 Davis, *The Evidential Force of Religious Experience*, p. 178.

33 Davis, *The Evidential Force of Religious Experience*, pp. 174f. The common core, in my summary of her description, is: mystics generally agree that the ordinary world is not the ultimate reality, nor the everyday self the deepest self. Ultimate reality is holy, and however it is described, all descriptions are inadequate. Some form of union with ultimate reality is our highest good. See pp. 190f.

34 Gellman, *Experience of God and the Rationality of Theistic Belief*, p. 95.

35 Gellman, *Experience of God and the Rationality of Theistic Belief*, p. 96.

36 Gellman, *Experience of God and the Rationality of Theistic Belief*, p. 102.

37 Gellman, *Experience of God and the Rationality of Theistic Belief*, pp. 103f.

38 Gellman, *Experience of God and the Rationality of Theistic Belief*, p. 105.

39 Gellman, *Experience of God and the Rationality of Theistic Belief*, p. 118.

40 Flew, *God and Philosophy*, p. 129.

41 Russell, *Religion and Science*, p. 178.

42 W. Rowe (1982) 'Religious Experience and the Principle of Credulity', *International Journal of the Philosophy of Religion* 13, pp. 90f.

43 Davis, *The Evidential Force of Religious Experience*, pp. 116ff.

44 As in the case of the small school-boy who complained to my brother-in-law, a headmaster, that he had been 'kicked in the testaments'. There are rational grounds for doubting this proposition, while allowing the injured party a degree of incorrigibility about his experience.

45 Yandell, *The Epistemology of Religious Experience*, p. 266.

46 Yandell, *The Epistemology of Religious Experience*, p. 268.

47 Yandell, *The Epistemology of Religious Experience*, p. 269.

48 'The proposition *O has A* comes within the scope of *polar disconfirmation* if and only if there is some condition C such that O's not being experienced in C is evidence in favor of *O does not exist*.' Yandell, *The Epistemology of Religious Experience*, p. 245.

49 Yandell, *The Epistemology of Religious Experience*, pp. 250ff.

50 Or, in Yandell's formulation, 'The proposition *O has A* comes within the scope of *lateral disconfirmation* if and only if it is logically possible that there be an experience that provides evidence for *O* has B* (where, of course, O* is different from O) and the truth of *O* has B* is evidence against the truth of *O has A*.' Yandell, *The Epistemology of Religious Experience*, p. 246.

51 Yandell's version is:

> 'What I took to be O turns out to lack A;
> O* has B, and if so then there cannot be an O that has A;
> O* has some of the properties of O, but lacks a property O must have, and it is not likely that there be two things with the properties that O has.'

See the discussion in Yandell, *The Epistemology of Religious Experience*, pp. 250–55.

52 Gutting, *Religious Belief and Religious Skepticism*, p. 152.

53 M. I. Waley (1990) 'Contemplative Disciplines in Early Persian Sufism', in L. Lewisohn (ed.), *The Heritage of Sufism*, Oxford, Oneworld, vol. 1, p. 527.

54 Davis, *The Evidential Force of Religious Experience*, pp. 76f.

55 Davis, *The Evidential Force of Religious Experience*, p. 77.

56 Yandell, *The Epistemology of Religious Experience*, p. 267.

57 Yandell, *The Epistemology of Religious Experience*, pp. 267f. Gellman's 'STING' argument (see above) is also an attempt to harness the question of confirmation in religious experience to the advantage of the religious believer. Gellman, *Experience of God and the Rationality of Theistic Belief*, pp. 52f.

58 See the discussion of M. Este'lani (1999) 'The Concept of Knowlege in Rumi's Mathnawi', in L. Lewisohn (ed.), *The Heritage of Sufism*, Oxford, Oneworld, vol. 1, p. 404.

59 M. Muṭahharī (2002) *Understanding Islamic Sciences: Philosophy; Theology; Mysticism; Morality; Jurisprudence*, London, ICAS Press, p. 92.

60 See also G. Griffith-Dickson (2000) *Human and Divine: An Introduction to the Philosophy of Religious Experience*, London, Duckworth, pp. 241–2: 'It is not a question of opposing understanding, reason and rationality to desire, longing and passion. Responsible reflection on religion is a question of bringing *all* one's powers to bear in analysis and critique. Attempts to separate a non-thing called reason from emotions, passions, longings and desires is not only disabling, it is self-deceiving. It obscures the truth. Such a "quest for the truth" ironically becomes a "defence of the faith" – the faith in "rationality". Why not instead have faith in the legitimacy of being as we *really* are, when we reflect?'

61 Waley, 'Contemplative Disciplines in Early Persian Sufism', p. 544.

62 As-Ṣadr, Allāma Muhammad Bāqir (1989) *Our Philosophy*, trans. S. C. Inati, London, Muhammadi Trust, pp. 90–1 *et passim*.

63 As-Ṣadr, *Our Philosophy*, pp. 92, 113 *et passim*.

64 As-Ṣadr, *Our Philosophy*, p. 115.

65 See G. Griffith-Dickson (1995) *Johann Georg Hamann's Relational Metacritism*, Berlin and New York, de Gruyter.

66 Waley, 'Contemplative Disciplines in Early Persian Sufism', p. 543.

67 See Griffith-Dickson, *Johann Georg Hamann's Relational Metacritism.*

68 T. Ramadan (2004) *Western Muslims and the Future of Islam*, Oxford, Oxford University Press, p. viii.

Index of Names and Subjects